American Literary Scholarship

1983

American Literary Scholarship

An Annual / 1983

Edited by Warren French

Essays by Roger Lips and Wendell Glick, Rita K. Gollin, Kent P. Ljungquist, Robert Milder, Robert Weisbuch, Louis J. Budd, Robert L. Gale, Hugh Witemeyer, Linda W. Wagner, Jackson R. Bryer, William J. Scheick, David J. Nordloh, John J. Murphy, Louis Owens, Jerome Klinkowitz, James K. Guimond, Lee Bartlett, Walter J. Meserve, John M. Reilly, Michael J. Hoffman, Marc Chénetier, Rolf Meyn, Keiko Beppu, Mona Pers

Duke University Press, Durham North Carolina, 1985

PS
3
.A47
1983

Foreword

This is the twentieth-anniversary volume of this ambitious project to provide a continuing review of American literary scholarship, launched by James Woodress while he was at San Fernando State College (now California State University at Northridge). Remarkably, through two decades, the series had only two editors. J. Albert Robbins of Indiana University at Bloomington replaced Woodress after the first five years and edited the volumes from 1968 to 1973. Woodress, by then at the University of California at Davis, returned as editor from 1973 to 1975. Between 1976 and 1982, Robbins returned to alternate with the founding editor in even years, and he will return again in 1984. Although he speaks of being retired, Jim Woodress keeps a constant eye on this major contribution to systematizing our knowledge of research in American literature.

It was an unexpected honor to be asked to accept responsibility for this twentieth volume, after having contributed 11 essays between 1966 and 1976 as the volumes grew from 284 pages to nearly 500. The series now seems to be stabilizing, having reached a peak of 625 pages in 1980. Over the years the original 17 chapters have grown to 22, with several correspondents involved in the valuable overview of foreign contributions added after the first decade in 1973.

Although a comparatively slim book of 240 pages, the inaugural volume listed contributors who are recalled today as among the most eminent American literary scholars of our time, although some of them, like Frederick J. Hoffman, Richard Beale Davis, and Charles T. Davis, are no longer with us. One of this original group remains active, however; Louis Budd of Duke University, after writing the first four essays on 19th-century literature, returned in 1976 to launch an even longer series on Mark Twain, an example of incredible devotion to this effort.

The roll, however, constantly changes. To this twentieth-anniversary volume we welcome six new contributors, as well as welcome back two veterans. Roger Lips joins his colleague Wendell

Glick as collaborator on Professor Glick's final chapter in his series
on the transcendentalists. Kent P. Ljungquist of Worcester Polytechnic Institute has taken over the Poe chapter from Donald B. Stauffer;
and Robert Weisbuch of the University of Michigan is substituting
this year on the Whitman and Dickinson chapter for Jerome M.
Loving, who returns next year. David J. Nordloh of Indiana University at Bloomington assumes responsibility for the chapter on
19th-century literature that George Hendrick prepared last year; and,
after 13 years of faithful service, Richard Crowder, Professor Emeri-
tus at Purdue, has turned over the chapter on early 20th-century
poetry to James K. Guimond of Rider College. Among our foreign
correspondents, Keiko Beppu of Kobe College has relieved Hiroko
Sato for this year. Linda W. Wagner, who wrote the chapter on
poetry since the 1930s from 1972 to 1976, has returned for two years
to evaluate Faulkner scholarship, while Jackson R. Bryer, who also
wrote the Fitzgerald and Hemingway chapters from 1971 to 1978,
agreed to accept the assignment again this year.

Three new contributors are expected to join next year's staff.
Philip F. Gura of the University of Colorado at Boulder will take
over the chapter on the transcendentalists from Wendell Glick; and
Brian Higgins of the University of Illinois at Chicago will assume
responsibility for the Melville essay from Robert Milder, whom we
wish to thank for his services for the last edition and this one. We
are also particularly grateful to Professor Glick for eight years' service since 1976. Michael S. Reynolds of North Carolina State University will contribute the next chapter on Hemingway and Fitzgerald.
Authors and publishers are urgently requested to see that appropriate material reaches these new contributors, as well as continuing
staff members and Professor Robbins, who will prepare next year's
chapter on general reference works.

We regret the absence this year of reports from Eastern Europe
and Italy, but we hope that Professor Lyra will be able to resume
his valuable survey next year and that Professor Maria Vittoria
D'Amico of the University of Catania will bring us up to date on
scholarship in Italy. Meanwhile, our deepest thanks to those other
contributors whose willingness to continue to assume this heavy annual duty assures a continuity especially essential to a project of this
kind as it moves into its third decade.

Warren French
Indiana University–Purdue University at Indianapolis

Table of Contents

Key to Abbreviations

Festschriften, Essay Collections, and Books
Discussed in More Than One Chapter

American Autobiography / Albert E. Stone, ed., *American Autobiography: A Collection of Essays* (Prentice-Hall)

American Fiction / Richard Gray, ed., *American Fiction: New Readings* (Barnes and Noble)

American Fictions, 1940–1980 / Frederick Karl, *American Fictions, 1940–1980: A Comprehensive History and Critical Evaluation* (Harper and Row)

American Gothic / Donald A. Ringe, *American Gothic: Imagination and Reason in Nineteenth-Century Fiction* (Kentucky)

American Novelists Revisited / Fritz Fleischmann, ed., *American Novelists Revisited: Essays in Feminist Criticism* (Hall, 1982)

American Renaissance: New Dimensions / Peter Carafiol, ed., *The American Renaissance: New Dimensions* (Bucknell)

American Women Writers / Maurice Duke, Jackson R. Bryer, and M. Thomas Inge, eds., *American Women Writers: Bibliographical Essays* (Greenwood)

Anglo-American Landscapes / Christopher Mulvey, *Anglo-American Landscapes: A Study of Nineteenth-Century Anglo-American Travel Literature* (Cambridge)

Animals in American Literature / Mary Allen, *Animals in American Literature* (Illinois)

The Art of Slave Narrative / John Sekora and Darwin T. Turner, eds., *The Art of Slave Narrative: Original Essays in Criticism and Theory* (Western Illinois, 1982)

Distant Obligations / David C. Duke, *Distant Obligations: Modern American Writers and Foreign Causes* (Oxford)

Faulkner and Idealism / Michel Cresset and Patrick Samway, S.J., eds., *Faulkner and Idealism: Perspectives from Paris* (Mississippi)

The Haunted Dusk / Howard Kerr, John W. Crowley, and Charles L. Crow, eds., *The Haunted Dusk: American Supernatural Fiction, 1870–1920* (Georgia)

Home Girls / Barbara Smith, ed., *Home Girls: A Black Feminist Anthology* (Kitchen Table)

Inviolable Voice / Stan Smith, *Inviolable Voice: History and Twentieth-Century Poetry* (Humanities, 1982)

The Journey Narrative in American Literature / Janis P. Stout, *The Journey Narrative in American Literature: Patterns and Departures* (Greenwood)

Law and American Literature / Carl S. Smith, John P. McWilliams, Jr., and Maxwell Bloomfield, *Law and American Literature: A Collection of Essays* (Knopf)

Literature at the Barricades / Ralph F. Bogardus and Fred Hobson, eds., *Literature at the Barricades:*

The American Writer in the 1930s
(Alabama, 1982)
The Modern American Novel /
Malcolm Bradbury, *The Modern
American Novel* (Oxford)
The Modern Poetic Sequence / M. L.
Rosenthal and Sally Gall, *The
Modern Poetic Sequence: The
Genius of Modern Poetry* (Oxford)
Modernism Reconsidered / Robert
Kiely and John Hildebidle, eds.,
Modernism Reconsidered
(Harvard)
Of Huck and Alice / Neil Schmitz,
*Of Huck and Alice: Humorous
Writing in American Literature*
(Minnesota)
*Revolution and Convention in
Modern Poetry /* Donald E.
Stanford, *Revolution and Con-
vention in Modern Poetry:
Studies in Ezra Pound, T. S. Eliot,
Wallace Stevens, Edwin Arling-*

ton Robinson and Yvor Winters
(Delaware)
Southern Literature in Transition /
Philip Castille and William
Osborne, eds., *Southern Literature
in Transition: Heritage and
Promise* (Memphis State)
Studies in Black American Literature I
/ Joe Weixlmann and Chester J.
Fontenot, eds., *Studies in Black
American Literature, Volume I:
Black American Prose Theory*
(Penkevill)
Through the Custom-House / John
Carlos Rowe, *Through the
Custom-House: Nineteenth-
Century American Fiction and
Modern Theory* (Hopkins, 1982)
Yeats and American Poetry / Terence
Diggory, *Yeats and American
Poetry: The Tradition of the Self*
(Princeton)

Periodicals, Annuals, Series

ABBW / AB Bookman's Weekly
ABC / American Book Collector
*AI / American Imago: A Psycho-
analytic Journal for Culture,
Science, and the Arts*
AL / American Literature
*ALR / American Literary Realism,
1870–1910*
AmBR / American Book Review
AmerP / American Poetry
*AmerSS / American Studies in
Scandinavia*
*AmSI / American Studies
International*
Amst / Amerikastudien
*AN&Q / American Notes and
Queries*
APR / American Poetry Review
*APSAUT / Scholarly Journal of the
Faculty of Philosophy of the
Aristotelian University of
Thessaloniki*
AR / Antioch Review
*ArAA / Arbeiten aus Anglistik und
Amerikanistik*
L'Arc (Aix-en-Provence, France)

*ArielE / Ariel: A Review of
International English Literature*
ArQ / Arizona Quarterly
ASch / American Scholar
*ATQ / American Transcendental
Quarterly*
*BALF / Black American Literature
Forum*
BB / Bulletin of Bibliography
BBr / Books at Brown
BLM / Bonniers Litterära Magasin
BuR / Bucknell Review
*BWVACET / The Bulletin of the
West Virginia Association of
College English Teachers*
Café Existens (France)
*Calamus: Walt Whitman Quarterly:
International*
Caliban (Toulouse, France)
*Callaloo: A Black South Journal of
Arts and Letters*
*CCrit / Comparative Criticism:
A Yearbook*
CE / College English
CentR / The Centennial Review
ChiR / Chicago Review

CL / Comparative Literature

CLAJ / College Language Association Journal

ClioI / Clio: A Journal of Literature, History, and the Philosophy of History

CLQ / Colby Library Quarterly

CLS / Comparative Literature Studies

Clues: A Journal of Detection

CollL: College Literature

CompD: Comparative Drama

Conditions

ConL / Contemporary Literature

ConP / Contemporary Poetry: A Journal of Criticism

Corps Ecrit (France)

CP / Concerning Poetry

CRCL / Canadian Review of Comparative Literature

CRevAS / Canadian Review of American Studies

Crit / Critique: Studies in Modern Fiction

CritI / Critical Inquiry

Criticism: A Quarterly for Literature and the Arts

CritQ / Critical Quarterly

DeltaES / Delta: Revue du Centre d'Etudes et de Recherche sur les Ecrivains du Sud aux Etats-Unis (Montpellier, France)

DHS / Dix-Huitième Siècle

DicS / Dickinson Studies

Dires (Montpellier, France)

DQ / Denver Quarterly

DQR / Dutch Quarterly Review of Anglo-American Letters

DramaR / The Drama Review (formerly Tulane Drama Review)

DrN / Dreiser Newsletter

EAL / Early American Literature

EAS / Essays in Arts and Science

EIC / Essays in Criticism

EigoS / Eigo Seinen: The Rising Generation (Tokyo)

ELH / English Literary History

ELN / English Language Notes

ELT / English Literature in Transition (1880–1920)

ELWIU / Essays in Literature (Western Ill. Univ.)

English: The Journal of the English Association (London)

EON / The Eugene O'Neill Newsletter

ES / English Studies

ESA / English Studies in Africa: A Journal of the Humanities (Johannesburg)

ESQ: A Journal of the American Renaissance

Etudes de Lettres (France)

EWN / Eudora Welty Newsletter

ExEs / Explorations in Ethnic Studies

Expl / Explicator

Extrapolation

Fabula (Lille, France)

GaR / The Georgia Review

GPQ / Great Plains Quarterly

GR / Germanic Review

HC / The Hollins Critic

Helix (Melbourne, Australia)

HJR / Henry James Review

HK / Heritage of the Great Plains

HudR / Hudson Review

HUSL / Hebrew University Studies in Literature and the Arts

IJPP / Interpretation: A Journal of Political Philosophy

Interpretations: A Journal of Ideas, Analysis, and Criticism (Memphis)

IowaR / Iowa Review

JAC / Journal of American Culture

JAH / Journal of American History

JAmS / Journal of American Studies

JEGP / Journal of English and German Philology

JEthS / The Journal of Ethnic Studies

JHI / Journal of the History of Ideas

JLC / Journal of the Library of Congress

JLN / Jack London Newsletter

JML / Journal of Modern Literature

JNT / Journal of Narrative Technique

JOHJ / John O'Hara Journal

JPC / Journal of Popular Culture

KR / Kenyon Review

Lang&S / Language and Style

Line: A Journal of the Contemporary Literature Collection (Simon Fraser University)

LitR / Literary Review

Maledicta: The International Journal of Verbal Aggression
Manuscripts
MarkhamR / Markham Review
MD / Modern Drama
MELUS: Journal for the Society for the Study of the Multi-Ethnic Literature of the United States
Menckeniana
Métaphore (Nice, France)
MFS / Modern Fiction Studies
MidAmerica: The Yearbook of the Society for the Study of Mid-.western Literature
MissR / Missouri Review
MLN / Modern Language Notes
MLS / Modern Language Studies
Mosaic: A Journal for the Interdisciplinary Study of Literature
MP / Modern Philology
MPS / Modern Poetry Studies
MQ / Midwest Quarterly
MQR / Michigan Quarterly Review
MSE / Massachusetts Studies in English
MSEx / Melville Society Extracts
MTJ / Mark Twain Journal
MTSB / Mark Twain Society Bulletin
N&Q / Notes and Queries
NCF / Nineteenth-Century Fiction
NConL / Notes on Contemporary Literature
NDEJ / Notre Dame English Journal
NDQ / North Dakota Quarterly
NEQ / New England Quarterly
NHS Newsletter / Nathaniel Hawthorne Society Newsletter
NMAL / Notes on Modern American Literature
NMW / Notes on Mississippi Writers
NOR / New Orleans Review
Novel: A Forum on Fiction
Obsidian: Black Literature in Review
OL / Orbis Litterarum: International Review of Literary Studies
Paideuma: A Journal Devoted to Ezra Pound Scholarship
PAPS / Proceedings of the American Philosophical Society
ParisR / Paris Review
PCL / Perspectives on Contemporary Literature

PerfAJ / Performing Arts Journal
Phylon: The Atlanta University Review of Race and Culture
PLL / Papers on Language and Literature
PMHB / Pennsylvania Magazine of History and Biography
PMHS / Proceedings of the Massachusetts Historical Society
PMLA / Publications of the Modern Language Association
PNotes / Pynchon Notes
PoeS / Poe Studies
Poétiques
PoetryR / Poetry Review (London)
PQ / Philological Quarterly
PR / Partisan Review
Prévue (Montpellier, France)
Prospects: An Annual Journal of American Cultural Studies
RALS / Resources for American Literary Study
Ranam / Recherches Anglaises et Américaines (Strasbourg, France)
RCF / Review of Contemporary Fiction
REH / Revista de Estudios Hispanicos
Renascence: Essays on Value in Literature
RES / Review of English Studies
RFEA / Revue Francaise d'Etudes Americaines (Paris)
RLC / Revue de Littérature Comparée
RMR / Rocky Mountain Review
RMS / Renaissance & Modern Studies
Roman (France)
RSAA / Rivista di Studi Anglo Americani
SAF / Studies in American Fiction
Sagetrieb (Orono, Maine)
SALit / Studies in American Literature (Japan)
Salmagundi
SAQ / South Atlantic Quarterly
SAR / Studies in the American Renaissance
SB / Studies in Bibliography
SBHC / Studies in Browning and His Circle
SCR / South Carolina Review

SELit / *Studies in English Literature* (Tokyo)

Sémiosis: Internationale Zeitschrift für Semiotik und Ästhetik

SHR / *Southern Humanities Review*

Signs: Journal of Women in Culture and Society

SIR / *Studies in Romanticism*

SLitI / *Studies in the Literary Imagination*

SLJ / *Southern Literary Journal*

SMy / *Studia Mystica*

SN / *Studia Neophilologica*

SNNTS / *Studies in the Novel* (North Texas University)

SoQ / *Southern Quarterly*

SoR / *Southern Review*

SR / *Sewanee Review*

SSF / *Studies in Short Fiction*

StQ / *Steinbeck Quarterly*

Style

SubStance: A Review of Theory and Literary Criticism

SWR / *Southwest Review*

TCL / *Twentieth-Century Literature*

Thalia: Studies in Literary Humor

TheatreHS / *Theatre History Studies*

TheatreRI / *Theatre Research International*

ThQ / *Thoreau Quarterly*

TJ / *Theatre Journal*

Topic: A Journal of the Liberal Arts

TriQ / *TriQuarterly* (Evanston, Ill.)

Trivium (Dyfed, Wales)

TSL / *Tennessee Studies in Literature*

TUSAS / *Twayne United States Authors Series*

TWN / *Thomas Wolfe Review*

UTQ / *University of Toronto Quarterly*

VQR / *Virginia Quarterly Review*

WAL / *Western American Literature*

WE / *The Winesburg Eagle: The Official Publication of the Sherwood Anderson Society*

WiF / *William Faulkner: Materials, Studies, and Criticism* (Tokyo)

WMQ / *William and Mary Quarterly*

WSJour / *Wallace Stevens Journal*

WWS / *Western Writers Series* (Boise State Univ., Idaho)

YULG / *Yale University Library Gazette*

Publishers

Alabama / University: Univ. of Alabama Press

Allen and Unwin / Winchester, Mass.: Allen and Unwin

AMS Press / New York: AMS Press

Ananse / Seattle: Ananse Press

Archon / Hamden, Conn.: Archon Books

Arizona / Tucson: Univ. of Arizona Press

Associated Faculty Press / Port Washington, N.Y.: Associated Faculty Press

Barnes and Noble / Totowa, N.J.: Barnes and Noble

Belknap / Cambridge, Mass.: Belknap Press of Harvard Univ. Press

Black Sparrow / Santa Barbara, Calif.: Black Sparrow Press

Bowker / New York: R. R. Bowker Co.

Bowling Green / Bowling Green,

Ohio: Bowling Green State Univ. Popular Press

Bucknell / Lewisburg, Pa.: Bucknell University Press

Calif. / Berkeley: Univ. of California Press

Cambridge / Cambridge, England, and New York: Cambridge University Press

Carcanet / New York: Carcanet Press

Cherry Valley Editions / Silver Spring, Md.: Cherry Valley Editions

Chicago / Chicago: Univ. of Chicago Press

Columbia / New York: Columbia Univ. Press

Congdon & Weed / New York: Congdon & Weed

Continuum / New York: Continuum

Cornell / Ithaca, N.Y.: Cornell Univ. Press

Creative Arts / Berkeley, Calif.:
Creative Arts Book Co.

Croom Helm / Dover, N.H.: Croom
Helm, Ltd.

Crown / New York: Crown
Publishers

Croissant & Co. / Athens, Ohio:
Croissant & Co.

Da Capo / New York: Da Capo
Press, Inc.

Delaware / Newark: Univ. of
Delaware Press

Dodd, Mead / New York: Dodd,
Mead and Co.

Doubleday / New York: Doubleday
and Co.

Dover / New York: Dover Books

Drama Books / New York: Drama
Book Specialists

Duke / Durham, N.C.: Duke Univ.
Press

Eerdmans / Grand Rapids, Mich.:
William B. Eerdmans Publishing
Co.

Fairleigh Dickinson / Madison, N.J.:
Fairleigh Dickinson Univ. Press

Farrar, Straus and Giroux / New
York: Farrar, Straus and Giroux

Fisher Publications / Statesville,
N.C.: Fisher Publications

Florida / Gainesville: Univ. Presses of
Florida

Florida State / Tallahassee: Florida
State Univ. Press

Fordham / Bronx, N.Y.: Fordham
Univ. Press

Fortress Press / Philadelphia: Fortress
Press

Gale / Detroit: Gale Research Co.

Garland / New York: Garland
Publishing Co.

Georgia / Athens: Univ. of Georgia
Press

Gothic Press / Baton Rouge, La.:
Gothic Press

Greenwood / Westport, Conn.:
Greenwood Press

Grey Fox / San Francisco: Grey Fox
Press

Grosset and Dunlap / New York:
Grosset and Dunlap

Grove / New York: Grove Press

Hall / Boston: G. K. Hall & Co.

Harcourt / New York: Harcourt Brace
Jovanovich, Inc.

Harper / New York: Harper and Row

Harvard / Cambridge, Mass.: Harvard
Univ. Press

Haworth / New York: Haworth Press

Holmes and Meier / New York:
Holmes and Meier Publishers

Hopkins / Baltimore: Johns Hopkins
Univ. Press

Houghton Mifflin / Boston: Houghton
Mifflin Co.

Humanities / Atlantic Highlands,
N.J.: Humanities Press

Illinois / Urbana: Univ. of Illinois
Press

Indiana / Bloomington: Indiana Univ.
Press

Kansas / Lawrence: Regents Press of
Kansas

Kent State / Kent, Ohio: Kent State
Univ. Press

Kentucky / Lexington: Univ. Press
of Kentucky

Kitchen Table / New York: Kitchen
Table, Women of Color Press

Lawrence Hill / Westport, Conn.:
Lawrence & Co., Inc.

Library of America / New York:
Library of America (Viking/
Penguin)

LSU / Baton Rouge: Louisiana State
Univ. Press

Macmillan / New York: Macmillan

Maine / Orono: Univ. of Maine Press

McFarland / Jefferson, N.C.:
McFarland & Co.

McGraw-Hill / New York: McGraw-
Hill

Mellen / New York and Toronto:
Edwin Mellen Press

Memphis State / Memphis, Tenn.:
Memphis State Univ. Press

Methuen / London: Methuen

Michigan / Ann Arbor: Univ. of
Michigan Press

Minnesota / Minneapolis: Univ. of
Minnesota Press

Miss. / Jackson: Univ. Press of Mississippi

Missouri / Columbia: Univ. of Missouri Press

Morrow / New York: William Morrow & Co.

N.C. / Chapel Hill: Univ. of North Carolina Press

Nebraska / Lincoln: Univ. of Nebraska Press

New Directions / New York: New Directions Publishing Corp.

New England / Hanover, N.H.: Univ. Press of New England

NIUP / DeKalb: Northern Illinois Univ. Press

N. Mex / Albuquerque: Univ. of New Mexico Press

North Point / San Francisco: North Point Press

Norton / New York: W. W. Norton & Co.

Norwood / Norwood, Pa.: Norwood Editions

Ohio / Athens: Ohio Univ. Press

Ohio State / Columbus: Ohio State Univ. Press

Oklahoma / Norman: Univ. of Oklahoma Press

Oxford / New York: Oxford Univ. Press

Penguin / New York: Penguin

Penkevill / Greenwood, Fla.: Penkevill

Penn. / Philadelphia: Univ. of Pennsylvania Press

PerfAJ / Beverly Hills, Calif.: Performing Arts Network

Peter Lang / New York: Peter Lang Publishing

Phoenix Bookshop / New York: Phoenix Book Shop

Prentice-Hall / Englewood Cliffs, N.J.: Prentice-Hall

Princeton / Princeton, N.J.: Princeton Univ. Press

Prometheus / Buffalo, N.Y.: Prometheus Press

Purdue / West Lafayette, Ind.: Purdue Univ. Press

Random House / New York: Random House

Rodopi / Amsterdam: Rodopi N.V.

Routledge / London: Routledge and Kegan Paul

Running Press / Philadelphia: Running Press Book Publishers

St. Joseph's / Philadelphia: St. Joseph's Univ. Press

St. Martin's / New York: St. Martin's Press

Salem Press / Pasadena, Calif.: Salem Press

Scarecrow / Metuchen, N.J.: Scarecrow Press

Scholar's Facsimiles / Delmar, N.Y.: Scholar's Facsimiles & Reprints

Sherwood Sugden / Baton Rouge, La.: Sherwood Sugden

Simon and Schuster / New York: Simon and Schuster

So. Ill. / Carbondale: Southern Illinois Univ. Press

Stein and Day / Briarcliff Manor, N.Y.: Stein and Day

Swallow / Athens, Ohio: Swallow Press

Syracuse / Syracuse, N.Y.: Syracuse Univ. Press

Temple / Philadelphia: Temple Univ. Press

Tenn. / Knoxville: Univ. of Tennessee Press

Texas / Austin: Univ. of Texas Press

Texas Monthly / Austin: Texas Monthly Press

Ticknor and Fields / Boston: Ticknor and Fields

Transaction / New Brunswick, N.J.: Transaction Books

Twayne / Boston: Twayne Publishers (G. K. Hall & Co.)

UMI / Ann Arbor, Mich.: University Microfilms International

UMI Research Press / Ann Arbor, Mich.: UMI Research Press

Ungar / New York: Frederick Ungar Publishing Co.

Union College Press / Schenectady, N.Y.: Union College Press

Univ. Microfilms / Ann Arbor, Mich.:
    University Microfilms International
Univ. Press / Washington, D.C.:
    Univ. Press of America
Viking / New York: Viking Press
Vintage / New York: Vintage Books
    (Random House)
Virginia / Charlottesville: Univ.
    Press of Virginia
Vision / London: Vision Press
Wayne State / Detroit: Wayne State
    Univ. Press

Western Ill. / Macomb: Western
    Illinois Univ. Press
Whitston / Troy, N.Y.: Whitston
    Publishing Co.
Wis. / Madison: Univ. of Wisconsin
    Press
Wolf House Books / Grand Rapids,
    Mich.: Wolf House Books
Yale / New Haven, Conn.: Yale
    University Press

Part I

1 Emerson, Thoreau, and Transcendentalism

Roger Lips and Wendell Glick

1983 brought a lull in research on Emerson, following the burst of activity in celebration of the Emerson centennial in 1982. The volume of Thoreau scholarship increased somewhat, as did interest in the large group of minor New England figures, chiefly clergymen, who occupied the fringes of the Transcendental movement. Progress was made in establishing reliable texts of Emerson's writings, and publication of the first two volumes of Margaret Fuller's letters will prove a boon to the growing number of scholars who are discovering in Fuller a foreshadowing of much contemporary thought.

i. General Studies

Sterling F. Delano's *The Harbinger and New England Transcendentalism* (Fairleigh Dickinson) is the first book-length study of the weekly journal launched at Brook Farm in the summer of 1845 to disseminate the dreams of George Ripley and his associates for a new social order. Though they disclaimed fealty to Fourier and the "Associationists," the founders of *The Harbinger*, as Delano makes clear, were but a hairsbreadth away from Fourier's and Brisbane's socialistic doctrines; unlike Emerson and Thoreau, they rested their faith in reform less upon the inherent sanctity of the individual than upon cooperative community effort. The interests of the Brook Farm participants and *The Harbinger*'s other distinguished contributors were predominately social, political, and economic, but included the works of contemporary American, French, and English authors. Some original poetry was published and much music criticism, which

The section of this chapter on Emerson was written by Roger Lips, the remainder of the chapter by Wendell Glick. We acknowledge the aid of Mara Hart in locating the periodical criticism.

Delano labels "the most noteworthy of the time" (p. 149). *The Harbinger* was to the Ripley branch of Transcendentalism what *The Dial* was to the individualistic Concord group surrounding Emerson. In an appendix, Delano compiles a listing, by author, of all contributions to the journal in its four years of life. Among the best known were Albert Brisbane, William Henry Channing, Christopher Cranch, George W. Curtis, Charles A. Dana, John S. Dwight, Parke Godwin, Horace Greeley, Henry James, Sr., J. R. Lowell, George Ripley, and William W. Story. The Concord Transcendentalists are conspicuous by their absence.

Michael Kramer in "Critical Myths and Historical Realities; or, How American Was the American Renaissance?" (*Review* 5 [Virginia], pp. 31–39) raises the old issue of the "American-ness" of the "nation's literary heritage" (p. 31) in commenting upon two recent books, *The Unsounded Centre: Jungian Studies in American Romanticism* by Martin Bickman, which views both romanticism and Jungian psychology as arising from a broad matrix of thought spanning many centuries; and *The Development of American Romance* by Michael Bell, which attempted to isolate "the distinctive features of the American literary tradition" (p. 35). Kramer finds a satisfactory answer to his question in neither book; "to get at the American-ness of the American Renaissance, we must first understand American culture," he argues, and he finds that to be "a formidable venture" (p. 38). Roland Hagenbüchle in "Spontaneity and Form: Unresolved Tensions in American Transcendentalism" (*Amst* 28:11–33) sees at the heart of American Transcendentalism "a profound tension between experience and form" (p. 12), in other words, a fear in both Emerson and Thoreau that form in language inhibited spontaneous experience, the latter being the greater good. Form signified limitation, and limitation to Emerson signified the fall of man. "Since experience cannot forego the element of form," Hagenbüchle argues, the strategy of the Transcendentalists was "to deconstruct traditional culture, using it as a rich quarry from which they can quote *ad libitum*" (p. 21). What held the elements of Transcendentalism together is alleged to have been "the all-controlling generative metaphor of the Over-Soul" (p. 11).

Dennis Berthold's "A Transcendentalist Aesthetics of Imperfection" (*ATQ* 50:138–48) addresses also the romantic's problem of form: since the ideal conception in the writer's mind is unrealizable, and the conception is more valuable than the execution, perfection "ceases to be a positive value" (p. 141), and imperfection, as Browning and Ruskin believed, becomes the quality of art most admired. "The American romantic realized," Berthold asserts, "as Ruskin did in 1853, that 'All things are literally better, lovelier, and more beloved for the imperfections which have been divinely appointed, that the law of human life may be Effort, and the law of human judgment, Mercy'" (p. 147).

ii. Emerson

a. **Editions.** Published this year as volume 3 of *The Collected Work of Ralph Waldo Emerson* was *Essays: Second Series* (Harvard), a CSE-approved text, ed. Alfred R. Ferguson and Jean Ferguson Carr with assistance from Joseph Slater. Ferguson and Carr also established the text for volume 2, *Essays: First Series* (Harvard, 1979). They were working on both volume 2 and 3 prior to Ferguson's death in 1974. Text for volume 3 was completed by Carr. Slater provided historical introductions and informational notes for both. The valuable introductions lend perspective on Emerson's slow, meticulous struggles to create the volumes that would solidify his fame, and the excellent notes identify and quote sources, clarify obscurities, and provide historical, biographical, and geographical contexts. These exciting volumes offer newly established texts based on and correcting first printed American editions of the *Essays*. Textual apparatus includes a record of all emendations by the editors within the copy texts and collation of all rejected variants found in significant later editions. Extremely useful also are citations pointing to parallel passages found in *The Journals and Miscellaneous Notebooks*, the Centenary *Works*, *The Early Lectures*, and Rusk's *Letters*. The volumes contain useful indexes. A useful list of other major Emerson projects currently under way may be found in Joel Myerson's "An Emerson Celebration" (*NEQ* 56:275–83), where he identifies four stages in the history of Emerson criticism.

Other newly edited Emerson material includes the poems of his youth printed in Albert J. von Frank's "Emerson's Boyhood and Collegiate Verse: Unpublished and New Texts Edited from Manuscript" (*SAR*, pp. 1–56). Von Frank gives us a discussion of Emerson's poetry written 1812–21, mostly unpublished, followed by 35 pages of poems. He thoroughly explains the influences, starting with Sabbath day hymn writing, that led young Emerson to write poetry. Von Frank believes these poems to be quite different from Emerson's mature poetry, except that they reveal enduring attitudes and themes formed by young Emerson, and influences seen to bear better fruit later in his life. Along with each poem or fragment, von Frank supplies information about manuscripts. *SAR* also includes one of the year's best essays, a major contribution to Emerson biography and textual study, Nancy Craig Simmons's "Arranging the Sibylline Leaves: James Elliot Cabot's Work as Emerson's Literary Executor" (pp. 335–89). This meticulous and fascinating essay makes clear the weaknesses of volumes 7, 9, 10, 11, 12 of the Centenary edition, and reveals much about the last years of Emerson as lecturer, the condition in which he left his unpublished manuscripts, and the three parties heavily involved in publishing his work after his death: Ellen and Edward Emerson, and Cabot. The long-time labors of the remarkably astute and self-effacing Cabot are carefully detailed, as well as his patient struggles with the Emerson children. He did not want to publish additional second-rate essays or artificially constructed volumes that might tarnish Emerson's reputation. This article gives a precise account of Cabot's extensive editorial role, including even the creation, under family pressure, of numerous "synthetic" essays, such as "The Sovereignty of Ethics," that make up "probably fifteen of the fifty-four pieces" (p. 337) of volumes 10, 11, 12 in the Centenary edition.

b. **Life and Thought.** The only new full-length biography is *Emerson's Optic:* by Richard A. Hutch (Univ. Press), a meager contribution to the growing body of unreliable psychological biographies of American authors. Its weaknesses include inadequate use of major biographies, numerous inaccurate quotes from Emerson texts, much jargon (derived, for example, from Erik H. Erikson, a major influence on the author), an undergraduate writing style, and scant discussion of Emerson's writing. The author professes to follow the spirit of Wagenknecht's "psychographic" approach; his argument is that "a single, architectonic pattern, which is called 'expansion within diminishment,' is identified as undergirding Emerson's essential character, or personality." The book's title relates to Hutch's belief that the "architectonic pattern" is "visual in quality" (pp. iv–v). Hutch offers new perspectives but no new facts. In its best parts, the book offers connections between Emerson's many health problems as a young man and his prolonged periods of vocational indecision, and revisionist perspectives on Emerson's marriages.

This year's only collection, *Critical Essays on Ralph Waldo Emerson* (Hall), ed. Robert E. Burkholder and Joel Myerson, includes selections of criticism on Emerson dating from his beginnings as a published author to the present. Many familiar names are missing because the editors try to avoid reprinting authors readily available (e.g., O. W. Firkins, Jonathan Bishop, Stephen Whicher). Half the volume contains 19th-Century essays and reviews "with the intention of providing a greater sense of the texture of Emerson's reception by contemporaries than has previously been available" (p. 3), revealing that in addition to the published puffs and jibes of friends and enemies, many reviewers were judicious and perceptive. These selections provide well-chosen, pleasant reading for novice scholars without time to search out important old volumes and periodicals. For the most part familiar names have been selected (e.g., Orestes Brownson, Andrews Norton, Thomas Carlyle), but lesser known and forgotten reviewers are presented also. The negative responses illustrate that many of Emerson's 19th-Century detractors were sectarian believers who feared that Emerson would reduce Bible study and church attendance. Selections from the 20th Century, starting with Alexander Kern's 1940 "Emerson and Economics," include essays focusing on "specific periods in Emerson's life," "general topics of interest to Emerson," and essays placing him "in the broad context of American literature and thought" (p. 8). Essays focusing on one or two works have been excluded. Professor Myerson's 19 selections are uniformly excellent. Included are many of the best Emerson scholars at work today, such as Merton Sealts, Jr., Leonard Neufeldt, David Robinson, and R. A. Yoder. Topics covered relate Emerson to economics, democracy, history, science, natural theology, and mythology. Emerson is seen in such perspectives as materialist, homiletic lyceum lecturer, mystic visionary, dialectical thinker, poet, and prose craftsman. With regard to overall balance, the volume might have been improved with inclusion of more 20th-Century essays on Emerson's poetry to add to the fine ones by Carl Strauch and Norman Miller. The whole assemblage is made more useful by an index.

Each year's Emerson essays reveal anew that many old questions

remain, such as whether his philosophy lacks system, whether he was
mystic or materialist, whether he was a New England-style religious
idealist or an European romantic, and whether he was blind to the
world's evil. Herwig Friedl in "Mysticism and Thinking in Ralph
Waldo Emerson" (*Amst* 28:33–46) uses old and new arguments to
insist that Emerson had genuine mystical experiences, spoke with an
authority similar to that of other mystics, and can best be understood
"once the mystical center of his writing is seen as an 'experiential'
reality" (p. 33). Friedl places Emerson in the company of visionaries
such as Eckhart, Kierkegaard, and Nietzsche. Such thinkers, he says,
do not write out satisfactory systems of philosophy because "Thinking
as the articulate account of our becoming is thus necessarily open-
ended and never to be totally resolved into a system" (p. 42). To
R. A. Yoder, Emerson is a visionary of a different sort, in middle age
less interested in the individual's potential for mystical transcendence
and more in the progress of the bourgeoisie. In his complex and
stimulating essay, "An Engineer for the Age" (*CentR* 27:156–85),
he describes Emerson in 1847 and after as developing the perspective
of "a poetical scientist and a moral engineer" (p. 173). Returning
from his second trip to England, Emerson looks to "physical science"
as "apparently the only way . . . we come to knowledge of the mental
and moral sphere" (p. 160). He thinks less about *the* individual and
more about society and culture and the way individuals function
within larger groups. Emerson becomes, says Yoder, a "literary
systems-analyst, and 'system' is the reiterated, central concept in *The
Conduct of Life*, his major and culminating work of this era" (p. 162).
Yoder's Emerson has an engineer's faith in melioration through technology and inventions reducing human problems, and through an
evolution of human culture expected to effect reconciliation between
peoples. Yoder believes Emerson imagined and predicted a "world-
machine . . . astonishingly moral" (p. 168), functioning harmoniously
by beneficent necessity. Consequently, "one thing dramatically lost
in these later Emersonian essays is the quality of transcendence" (p.
167). In holding up the machine as a perfect model for society,
Emerson seems to Yoder to have been moving with the current of
his times, "for by the 1850s this analogy between society and the
machine had already become an American commonplace" (p. 173).
Yoder concludes that Giametti in his 1981 attack on Emerson failed
to realize that Emerson the social engineer fostered "connectedness

rather than disconnectedness, to further 'the weaving of the web of state'" (p. 177).

In "'The Age of the First Person Singular': Emerson and Antinomianism" (*ESQ* 29:171–83), Amy Schrager Lang joins with Yoder and others who would make Emerson a supporter of bourgeoisie values and methods rather than leave him in the dangerous company of mystics and antinomians. Lang's excellent essay suggests that, despite some similarities between Anne Hutchinson and Emerson, evidence shows him to be no antinomian, no advocate of "individualism so extreme that it defies any relationship between self and society." Such a perspective, Lang says, "obscures the essential usefulness of his philosophy" (p. 177). Unlike Hutchinson who threatened to undermine social norms since her "belief was that the visible and invisible, the public and private, bear no necessary resemblance to one another," Emerson "posited a universe in which the visible and the invisible mirror one another" (p. 172). Hutchinson's antinomianism "released her from all the obligations of social membership" (p. 172), but Emerson taught "passive cooperation with a world changing always for the better" (p. 176). Lang says his perfectionism "accords with the secular notions of progress which surrounded him. . . . Rather than challenging the dominant ideology, then, Emersonian philosophy mimics it" (p. 176). Emerson's faith in the control of divine law enabled him to conceive that the genuinely self-reliant man would "inevitably prove to be the perfect member" of society (p. 178). This year's only vicious attack on Emerson comes from Ulrich Horstmann, "The Whispering Sceptic: Anti-Metaphysical Enclaves in American Transcendentalism" (*Amst* 28:47–57). Horstmann believes "the Emersonian dream of human omnipotence has turned into a suicidal nightmare" (p. 47). Horstmann sees Emerson as a naive visionary whose words were turned into a "categorical imperative for the industrial usurpation of nature . . . a metaphysical sanction for the ruthless exploitation of resources" (p. 49). Despite his expressed love of nature, Horstmann says, Emerson had a deep and unacknowledged fear of nature and a sense of alienation from it seen in his "escapist" faith in the Over-Soul (p. 53). In contrast Thoreau is applauded by Horstmann for attempting to discover the "factual behind the screen of human projections." He avoided "facile metaphysical formulae" such as the Over-Soul. "His scepticism and empiricism" caused him to shift his focus from "man to nature," a nature realistically seen in that he "never repressed his primordial awareness of the otherness of nature and the exposed position of man" (p. 55). Because Thoreau "had a deep aversion to the glorification of culture and intellect" (p. 57), he should be disassociated from the absurd and nightmarish aspects of modern American culture. In one of the year's best essays, "Self-Reliance and Corporate Destiny: Emerson's Dialectic of Culture" (*ESQ* 29:59–72), John Peacock examines Emerson's conception of the relationship between self-reliant individuals and society, and Emerson's dialectical discussion of causes both for affiliation and disaffiliation. Peacock provides an excellent discussion of *English Traits*, showing how it preserves "the paradox that all society devolves on the individual, and yet the individual is a mutilated product of society" (p. 62). Peacock concludes that Emerson's second trip to England caused him to deprecate the English as much as to praise them: "Emerson attributes positive traits to . . . laissez-faire individualism and negative traits to too much institutional interference" (p. 63), believing that "social institutions fatally alienate individuals, while culture, which is something altogether different, profoundly affiliates them" (p. 64). He saw in England a small "perceptive class" tutoring twenty million of "the practical finality class," the materialist masses subject to the humanizing influence of culture. "Polarizing society and culture enabled Emerson and other 19th-Century writers to make sense of the paradoxical responses of both estrangement and affiliation that individuals were beginning to feel toward their communities" (p. 67). Peacock believes Emerson doubted the likelihood of England's twenty million responding adequately to her cultured "dozen," but he expected unconquered Nature in America to raise up increasing numbers of individuals active in opposing the growth of mechanization, dehumanization, and institutionalization. Floyce Alexander in "Emerson and the Cherokee Removal" (*ESQ* 29:127–37) discusses the ejection of the Cherokees from Georgia in 1838. Emerson spoke at a Concord protest meeting where townspeople insisted that he write a protest letter to President Van Buren. Rusk and others have briefly discussed this incident, but Alexander explains more fully the circumstances surrounding the composition of the forceful protest letter. The essay shows Emerson "caught in the net of his own feelings of impotence and of duty" (p. 135), revealing the reasons why one might expect him to have been eager to help the Cherokees but also the causes of personal agony which made the letter a difficult task. Emerson's aversion to participating in political reform is given context by Manfred Pütz in "Emerson and Andrew Jackson: An Antagonism and its Alleged Reasons" (*Amst* 28:75–85). Without much originality, Pütz discusses Emerson's "negative view of almost all political dealings and personalities" (p. 75). Emerson praised democracy and its processes in the abstract, yet wrote: "There is nothing of the true democratic element in what is called Democracy," strongly disapproving of Andrew Jackson and the Democratic Party. Gertrude R. Hughes focuses on another of the rare moments when Emerson publicly took a political stand, his 1854 Address on the Fugitive Slave Law. In " 'How came he there?': Self-Reliance, Misalliance, and Emerson's Second Fugitive Slave Law Address" (*ATQ* 52:273–86) Hughes proposes that the 1854 "Address" is "Self-Reliance" written anew "as an occasional piece" (p. 280). Emerson's castigation of Webster and others who failed their social and moral obligation to American slaves is related, says Hughes, to Emerson's sense of their refusal to obey the moral voice of the God-Self, for Emerson believed obedience to the divine inner voice creates affinities between people. To Hughes self-reliance is Emerson's "principle of social order" (p. 276). Oddly this prolix essay fulsomely praises Emerson's morality but avoids directly addressing the matter of Emerson's reluctant response to the immorality of slavery.

Julie Ellison, in "Emerson's Sublime Analysis" (*The American Renaissance: New Dimensions*, ed. Peter C. Carafiol [Bucknell], pp. 42–62), discusses young Emerson's liberation from "emotional and stylistic prostration" before the splendor of great authors (p. 45) through discovery that his "accumulated knowledge about the past gives him the opportunity to determine its meaning" (p. 48), and that his own soul offers inspiration equal to that of the masters. The essay's originality consists partly in its attribution of Emerson's development as a "creative" reader to the influence of his study of the methods of "deconstructive" Biblical scholars. Moreover, Ellison detects a dramatic pattern in "The Lord's Supper" and the Divinity School "Address." Emerson begins by presenting subjects in the context of historic disagreements, next portrays himself painfully caught up in conflict and uncertainty, and then, after comparative analysis of competing views, he establishes the necessity of final arbitration by the autonomous, thinking self. He "adduces history" but "devalues its historicity" (p. 55), thus making essential the interpretive role of the God-conscious individual. Ellison arrives at conclusions remarkably like those of Andrews Norton. Emerson's concept of the autonomous self is also the theme of Olaf Hansen's "Truth—The Irresistible Metaphor: Emerson's Concepts of History, Nature and Language" (*Amst* 28:59–74). Hansen suggests stages in which Emerson developed his method of expressing philosophical truth metaphorically. After reducing the importance of printed scripture and elevating the book of Nature, Emerson realized that man's vision is never coincident with the axis of things ("I please myself rather with contemplating the penumbra of the thing than the thing itself") and that he needed to insist on the autonomy of self. Thus, Emerson's mature use of organic metaphors replaces "the text of nature with his own text *about* her" (p. 71). Hansen provides valuable insights into Emerson's philosophy: "Theodicy and history became his central themes and the invention of a language that would enable man to understand his place in a world where the meaning of words like history, nature and God was dramatically changing" (p. 61). Unfortunately, Hansen fails to relate Emerson's attempted reconciliation of theodicy and history to the millenial cast of New England theology, and to relate his use of emblematic images to New England tradition.

H. Melli Steele also examines links between Emerson's philosophy and style in "Romantic Epistemology and Romantic Style: Emerson's Development from *Nature* to the *Essays*" (*SAR*, pp. 187–202). Methodical and clear, this essay should have more evidence from *Essays* to support its sweeping generalizations. *Nature* is said to illustrate Emerson's "shift from an Enlightenment to a Romantic epistemology" (p. 187), with retention of the Enlightenment assumption that "the structure of the mind is identical to the structure of the world" (p. 187). Steele believes its style and structure reflect Emerson's felt obligation to create "a philosophical system founded on ultimate truth" (p. 193). However, *Essays* reflect a romantic epistemology in that "he no longer maintains that the structure of the phenomenal world is accessible to man; rather the mind projects itself onto the world, it interposes a screen which both conceals and reveals" (p. 195). Free of his obligation to demonstrate a system, Emerson changed his style, for the romantic's identity comes from "his unique expressive capacity" (p. 191). In *Essays* hierarchical arrangements disappear, paragraphs are less often controlled by topic sentences, connectives decrease, and even the sentence arrangements reflect less cohesion. "As a Romantic, Emerson discovered the importance of . . . experimentation that does not have to answer to the demands of logical coherence and linear development" (p. 200). In contrast, Dieter Schulz's excellent "Emerson's Visionary Moments: The Disintegration of the Sublime" (*Amst* 28:23–32) suggests how Emerson fails significant tests of romanticism. Examining Emerson's metaphors of light and vision, and comparing Emerson to romantic writers, Schulz demonstrates "the collapse of the organic metaphor . . . the disintegration of the High Romantic synthesis" (p. 25), signs of which can be traced from early journal entries to later essays. Schulz argues that, since Emerson could not sustain the romantic sense of the relation between nature and the soul, his later essays reflect increasing frustration about the possibilities of man's quest for transcendence. Charles W. Mignon in " 'Classic Art': Emerson's Pragmatic Criticism" (*SAR*, pp. 203–21) discusses cogently Emerson's evaluations of Jones Very, Ellery Channing, Bronson Alcott, Milton, Shakespeare, Goethe, and A. D. Woodbridge, and thoroughly examines Emerson's theories of art and criticism. Emerson's responses to specific authors demonstrated that he established "moral norms for moral art" (p. 220). However, though his moralist side expected art to reflect divine revelation and moral purpose, his pragmatic side demanded highly skilled craft as evidenced in "compression, omission, and revision" (p. 209). Especially worthwhile in this essay is Mignon's argument for Emerson as both moral critic and "Equilibrist" conceiving "an organic unity of universe, artist, work, and audience" (p. 205).

c. Studies of Individual Works. Two articles this year focus primarily on individual works, one of them being "The Language of Identity in Emerson's 'The Sphinx' " (*ESQ* 29:138–43) by Gayle L. Smith. A worthwhile contribution to the long critical dialogue about "The Sphinx," the essay examines "linguistic patterns" that reinforce "Reece's interpretation" (see *ESQ* 24:12–19). "Both Sphinx and poet use rhetorical figures, syntactic patterns, and phonological patterns that illustrate the 'perception of identity,' which Reece sees as the crux of the proper answer to the riddle" (p. 140). "Self-Reliance" is discussed in a slipshod essay that escaped close inspection by editors, "The Conversion Drama of 'Self-Reliance': A Logological Study"

(*AL* 55:507–24). The exemplary editing of *Collected Works* is wasted on Thomas Joswick who makes about thirty small alterations of words and punctuation in his quoted texts. Using several ideas derived from Kenneth Burke concerning the relationship between language and theology, Joswick creates a tortured analysis of "Self-Reliance" showing how Emerson may have linked the "spontaneous power" of original language to an "immediate relation to God." His essay aims to show the primacy of language over Emerson's religious thought, "how rhetorical strategies already gave form to what Emerson called 'the religious sentiments' and to what he took to be the dynamics of conversion about which theology reasoned" (p. 508).

d. **Emerson and Other Writers.**   Finally, the year's work on Emerson includes three short items linking him to other 19th-Century authors. Gary Scharnhorst's "Longfellow and Emerson's Divinity School 'Address': An Unpublished Letter" (*AN&Q* 21:44–45) presents a letter establishing that Longfellow heard with pleasure Emerson's delivery of the 1838 "Address." In "Speaking of Emerson: Two Unpublished Letters Exchanged Between John Jay Chapman and James Elliot Cabot" (*HLB* 31:181–87), Nancy Craig Simmons presents an interesting exchange between the 75-year-old Cabot and Chapman, aged 34, who had just published the first part of his now-famous essay on Emerson. Simmons's excellent discussion brings out how these authors "in many ways represent the extremes of Emerson criticism in the nineteenth century" (p. 184), Cabot viewing Emerson as a conservative at heart and Chapman viewing him as a radical. In "Whitman on Emerson: New Light on the 1856 Open Letter" (*AL* 56: 83–87), Kenneth M. Price uses three newly discovered manuscript fragments to clarify Whitman's perspective on Emerson. Though Whitman admired Emerson's achievement, he disparaged Emerson's aristocratic good manners and dependence on the authority of books. Two fragments of the 1870s show Whitman's desire "to distance himself from the mentor he both used and loved" (p. 83), perhaps to avoid being perceived as a disciple of a man who "had become the quintessential insider" (p. 87).

iii. Thoreau

a. **Life and Thought.**   In October of 1982, the long and eagerly awaited volume 1 of the *Journal* (1837–44) joined the other volumes of the definitive (Princeton) edition of *The Writings of Henry D. Thoreau*, under the general editorship of Elizabeth Hall Witherell, the *Journal* editorship of John C. Broderick, with Witherell, William L. Howarth, Robert Sattelmeyer, and Thomas Blanding serving as editors of this initial volume. More than a dozen other scholars cooperated in various phases of this massive enterprise. The volume bears the CEAA seal. Nothing else that I mention in this essay compares in its significance to Thoreau scholarship with this event. As new volumes of the *Journal* appear, the 1906 edition which we have used for so long will, volume by volume, become obsolete.

The reasons are clear. Francis H. Allen and Bradford Torrey, the 1906 editors, did not attempt to preserve the journal as Thoreau originally wrote it. The Princeton editors have done so, though the effort expended to achieve this end has been immense. As those who have consulted the original holograph volumes in the Morgan Library know, Thoreau scissored, interlined, and marked up these ms. volumes for later purposes, transposing, canceling, and revising. He created in so doing a monumental task for the Princeton editors. Though much of the material that Thoreau excised was lost, much also has now been located in private and public repositories, and the present editors have gone to great lengths to fill wherever possible the hiatuses Thoreau created. The CEAA seal speaks to the volume's textual authority. This edition of the *Journal* is probably as complete and authoritative as we are ever likely to have.

To the probes into Thoreau's psyche that were noted last year (*ALS 1982*, pp. 17–18), this year's scholarship adds several more. An epidemic may be upon us. *Thoreau's Psychology: Eight Essays*, ed. Raymond D. Gozzi (Univ. Press), prints the lectures delivered by eight participants in a conference organized by Walter Harding, held in Geneseo, New York in April 1978, along with digests of the question and answer periods that followed five of the lectures. Gozzi's "A Freudian View of Thoreau" (pp. 1–19) is a summary of his well-known unpublished doctoral dissertation of 1957; Richard Lebeaux's "Identity Crisis and Beyond: Eriksonian Perspectives on the Pre–Walden and Post–Walden Thoreau" (pp. 19–77) is an Eriksonian postscript to Lebeaux's *Young Henry Thoreau* and a precursor of a forthcoming book delineating Thoreau's post–1845 "crises"; "A Personality Profile of Henry David Thoreau: A New Method in Psycho-History" by Everett and Laraine Fergenson (pp. 79–107) reports the

results of administering to twenty Thoreau scholars the Minnesota
Multiphasic Personality Inventory, the scholars serving as surrogates
of Thoreau in 1854; Paul Hourihan discovers "inordinate love" to be
the chief cause of the much celebrated rift between Thoreau and
Emerson ("Crisis in the Thoreau–Emerson Friendship: The Symbolic Function of 'Civil Disobedience'" [pp. 109–22]); James Armstrong explores once again the problem of Thoreau's sexual asceti-
cism in "Thoreau, Chastity, and the Reformers" (pp. 123–45); and
Walter Harding in "Thoreau and Eros" (pp. 145–65) comments on
Thoreau's supposed homosexuality. Norman N. Holland reflected on
the conference as a whole in "A Summing-Up" (pp. 165–87). Whether
the product of this psychological delving is hagiographical or icono-
clastic or neither I cannot decide. But I come away from reading it
with no better understanding of Thoreau's genius than I started with.

John Hildebidle's *Thoreau: A Naturalist's Liberty* (Harvard) is a
scholarly study of Thoreau's puzzling attitudes toward science and
toward history. Relying principally on the late natural history essays,
Walden, and *Cape Cod*, Hildebidle shows that to Thoreau, "the only
history of real importance is that history which the self can somehow
re-experience, by walking . . . over the ground personally" (p. 149).
As to science, Hildebidle believes, Thoreau adopted its methodology,
but with an awareness of its limitations, an "awareness of those states
of being where science is simply of no interest" (p. 151). Thoreau
thus combined "the habits of the naturalist" with "the frame of mind
of the mystic" (p. 108). Since facts flower into truths, Thoreau seems
to have sought "to teach mankind enough science so that they could,
in the end, move beyond science into . . . Transcendental elevation or
sainthood" (p. 97). Hildebidle's well-written book demonstrates how
Thoreau could question both science and history and yet make his
own use of them.

Joan Burbick in "Henry David Thoreau: The Uncivil Historian"
(*The American Renaissance: New Dimensions*, ed. Peter Carafiol
[Bucknell], pp. 81–99) sees less ambiguity than does Hildebidle in
Thoreau's attitude toward history: *A Week*, for example, she views
as "a knot of accusations against historians and an attempt to seize
their power to tell the story of America" (p. 82). But like Hildebidle,
she emphasizes Thoreau's insistence upon "the centrality of the observer" in defining what history is, and his rejection of the tendency
of such historians as Bancroft and Motley "to view the past as a se-

quence of *pictures* in which a *theater* of events was witnessed" (p. 84). Instead, history to Thoreau was an interpreting of "vestiges"—a vestige being "any object bearing the marks of cultural or natural time" (p. 91). Rather than reading the Declaration of Independence, Thoreau read Indian arrowheads. Read in juxtaposition, Hildebidle's carefully reasoned book and Burbick's well-argued essay add considerably to our knowledge of Thoreau's view of history and the past.

Thoreau Amongst Friends and Philistines and Other Thoreauviana by Dr. Samuel Arthur Jones, ed. George Hendrick (Ohio), is a valuable book that brings together in one volume the remains of Thoreau's most active and enthusiastic 19th-Century partisan and defender. Busy as he was in his medical practice, Jones in his many rejoinders to Thoreau's detractors contributed significantly to the making of Thoreau's modern reputation. Much of the material included by Hendrick in this volume has not previously been published, having been spectacularly and serendipitously exhumed by Hendrick in 1974 from an Urbana attic. Hendrick has organized these materials into three sections: following an interesting biographical sketch of Jones, Section I comprises six essays by Jones on Thoreau's life; Section II follows with six essays by Jones on Thoreau's early biographers, editors, and critics, many of whom Jones attacks; and a final section gathers contemporary articles on Thoreau collected by Jones with the intention of using them in a book. Death thwarted Jones in this intention.

Lauriat Lane, Jr., in "Many More Thoreaus" (*CRevAS* 13:199–211) summarizes a spate of recent books, making the point that scholarly interpretations of Thoreau are still widely divergent, and as a rule lacking in depth. The essay is a sequel to his earlier "Three Thoreaus (in One?)" (*CRevAS* 9:201–8) in which Lane made the same point, that in spite of the perceptiveness of such critics as Cavell, the "baffling intricacy" of Thoreau's works and the contradictions of his life have not yet been sounded (p. 208). In "Henry David Thoreau as Amerindianist" (*Studies in Language and Culture* [Osaka] 9:225–36), Richard Fleck deplores what he deems to be a lack of interest in, or an ignorance of, Thoreau's knowledge and use of Indian culture. Quoting effusely from the *Journal* and the Indian Notebooks, he overstates his point in an essay that I find highly subjective and diffuse. Robert Sayre remains our best authority on Thoreau and Indian life and thought. Joel Myerson (as editor) and

Walter Harding (as compiler) have rendered Thoreau scholarship a
signal service by publishing "A New Checklist of the Books in Henry
David Thoreau's Library" (*SAR*, pp. 171–86), the sort of monograph
this is too long for most scholarly journals but most appropriate to the
permanent format of *Studies in the American Renaissance* (Virginia).
Harding's listing updates his compilation in *Thoreau's Library* (Virginia, 1957), adding items that he has discovered since that compilation and such additional information about separate items as
"how the book is inscribed and/or annotated; from whom or why
Thoreau obtained the copy; to whom he gave it, and its present location, where known" (p. 151). The list is comprised of about 400
items. They are widely scattered, quite a number having been given
away by Thoreau himself or taken to Bangor and distributed by
Sophia Thoreau following Thoreau's death.

b. **Studies of Individual Works.**   Research on *Walden* this year ac-
centuates a growing concern in Thoreau criticism, Thoreau's view of
the relation of the self to language. Not without reason had Thoreau
so much to say about language in the *Journal,* in *Walden,* and elsewhere, though not until philosophers and linguists began to probe
the relation have interpreters become tardily aware that consideration of Thoreau's subtle insights into human expression is essential
to understanding his view of the self. Janet Varner Gunn, in "*Walden*
and the Temporal Mode of Autobiographical Narrative" (*The American Autobiography: A Collection of Critical Essays,* ed. Albert E.
Stone [Prentice-Hall], pp. 80–94), represents Thoreau as a "faithful
reader" who saw language as deriving its power, "Antaeuslike, from
its rootedness in the earth" (p. 86). Thoreau's autobiographical goal
in *Walden,* to use his own words, was "to lay the foundation of a true
expression," and he believed language to be the "very atmosphere
and medium through which we look" (p. 88).

But the fullest philosophical analysis of the language of *Walden*
is Stanley Cavell's *The Senses of Walden,* and *The Thoreau Quarterly*
during the year devoted a double issue to a symposium on *Walden*
by philosophers and Thoreau scholars using Cavell's thesis as their
point of departure. Karen Hansen in "Sounding the Philosophic
Voice" (*ThQ* 14:103–10) accepts Cavell's contention that *Walden* is
a book of such intellectual depth and scope that it established a new
tradition in American thinking. While Thoreau was using the Father

Tongue, the written word, to compose his book, he was examining perceptively and consciously the act in which he was engaged, delineating the conditions that the writer must obtain (the writer must be born again to utter heroic thoughts) if he/she is to consummate the relationship with the reader. Frederick Garber draws the title of his essay, "Thoreau's Ladder of Alertness" (*ThQ* 14:111–24) from the Thoreau dictum, "no method nor discipline can supersede the necessity of being forever on the alert" (p. 118). To Cavell's interpretation Garber offers a caveat. Cavell's Thoreau, Garber believes, "comes through primarily as a man of written words; but that is to offer an understanding of Thoreau which Thoreau's own words cannot sustain" (p. 122). What Cavell's book lacks, Garber believes, "is a sense of context, an awareness that Thoreau sees all words in terms of a larger design of life" (p. 122). Thoreau's alertness to catch some tint of the rainbow, some trace of the Wordsworthian Ineffable, subsumed his use of the Father Tongue; the study of language was but one Thoreau activity among many. "What Thoreau finally speaks of is wholeness as a way of being in the world, a making-ready to meet futurity" (p. 124). Stanley Bates, in "Self and World in *Walden*" (*ThQ* 14:125–32), laments the failure of fellow philosophers to respond to Cavell's attempt to use the "philosophy" of *Walden* to heal the rift between the English and German traditions of philosophy. Cavell sees *Walden*, Bates believes, as a "sustained reflection on the self and the world . . . on subjectivity and objectivity" (p. 126), a traditional task of philosophy. "The quest of this book," as Cavell put it, "is for the recovery of the self" (p. 127). Bates accepts Cavell's view that Thoreau in *Walden* was pondering " 'self' and 'world' in a context largely created by Kant," that Thoreau "understood Kant in a way that Emerson didn't," and that Thoreau, moreover, "corrects Kant in an important way (p. 130)." It surprises students of literature to find philosophers settling Thoreau into a tradition of philosophy that begins with Descartes and includes Kant, Kierkegaard, and Nietzsche.

William Howarth, in "On Reading *Walden*" (*ThQ* 14:133–40), is skeptical of Cavell's interpretation. Cavell's problem, Howarth believes, is that he "sees *Walden* as a treatise, one that announces principles in the early chapters and applies them consistently thereafter" (p. 135). Howarth argues that the theme of the book is "the inevitability of human growth" (p. 136), and declines to accept the centrality of "Reading" as Thoreau's guide to his central meaning. He sees the book as a stage in Thoreau's evolution (Thoreau wrote it over a period of seven years), the final chapters prefiguring his expanded interests in *Cape Cod*, *The Maine Woods*, and the late pieces written just before his death. Howarth praises Cavell's style, however, as highly accomplished and thus appropriate to commentary on Emerson and Thoreau.

Stanley J. Scott's "Neighboring Reality: Stanley Cavell and the Experience of *Walden*" (*ThQ* 14:141–50) is, of all the essays in this symposium, the most lucid and sympathetic critique of Cavell's thesis. Rather than viewing *Walden* from a critical distance, as traditional criticism prescribes, Cavell "implicitly invites *us* not into conceptual knowledge about *Walden*, but into experiential understanding and creative responses of our own" (p. 141). Cavell's book becomes a personal record of his experience in reading *Walden*, using Thoreau's guidance as to how *Walden* is to be read; for "the meaning of *Walden*, like that of the Bible [and of all great books, Scott suggests] is its ability to awaken in the reader a native ability to understand the laws governing experience" (p. 145). Scott is patently impressed also by Cavell's claim for the epistemological contribution of the book: Thoreau's "recovery of the object" from the impasse left by Kant, "a recovery of the thing-in-itself, in particular, of the relation between the subject of knowledge and its object," Scott views as the "germ of a more complete study of Thoreau's metaphysics of relationship" (p. 145).

Sacvan Bercovitch in "The Ritual of American Autobiography: Edwards, Franklin, Thoreau" (*RFEA* 13:139–50) posits a ritual function for the autobiographies of these three authors, viewing American autobiography as a vehicle of social revitalization. Thoreau would certainly squirm to discover that inadvertently, subconsciously, he had put Walden, his pond, to the task of instructing Americans in "the ideological premises of Jacksonian America, consecrated by Nature's God and justified in a life of exemplary self-reliance" (p. 141). But "conscious or not," Bercovitch argues with his customary cogency, "these autobiographies have served to perpetuate the culture. To understand their ritual function is to recognize the astonishing vitality of rhetoric and myth in shaping the American Way" (p. 149). Edward C. Jacobs in "The Bible in *Walden*: Further Additions" (*SAR*, pp. 297–302) strains hard to add a dozen or so echoes

of the Bible in *Walden* to the list compiled by Larry R. Long in 1979
(*ALS 1979*, p. 13). That allusions to the Bible reverberate through
Walden is clear enough, but some of Jacobs's parallels are tenuous.
I question, for example, Jacobs's tying Thoreau's "to drive life into a
corner . . . and be able to give a true account of it in my next excursion" to Romans 14:12: "So then every one of us shall give account of
himself to God" (p. 298). Weak evidence weakens the thesis it is
cited to support.

A *Week on the Concord and Merrimack Rivers* was reissued
during the year by Princeton, embellished by the photographs of
Herbert Gleason, the accomplished photographer and Thoreau student who between 1899 and 1937 revisited the locales described by
Thoreau in his books and took pictures of them. Gleason's sensitive
understanding of Thoreau's words, combined with his remarkable
photographic eye, make his pictures complement the text and enhance the reader's appreciation of Thoreau's skill in rendering a sense
of place through words. From the Amoskeag Falls in Manchester,
N. H., to the cattle under the oaks in Hosmer's pasture in Concord,
the tone and feeling of these photographs harmonize with the poetry
of Thoreau's prose. Gordon V. Boudreau in " 'Here Lies . . . Rear
Admiral Van': Thoreau's Crowded Grave" (*NEQ* 56:523–37) converts, by a skillful analysis of Thoreau's word play, a seemingly
innocuous poetic epitaph submerged in *A Week* into a meaningful
comment upon Thoreau's early view of faith and death. Boudreau's
argument develops force from his analysis of five early forms of the
epitaph that appear in Journal I; taking issue with Perry Miller,
Boudreau argues that Faith for Thoreau was "more than a stratagem
of consciousness" (p. 533). This essay, which begins with the explication of a seeming bit of nonsense verse, ends with the conclusion
that "In *A Week* Thoreau had fabled of the fall of man; in *Walden*,
he would fable of his resurrection" (p. 535). Clearly, those err who
assume *A Week* to be a potpourri of fragments rather than a carefully
conceived whole. Donald M. Murray's "Thoreau's Uncivil Man Rice"
(*NEQ* 56:103–9) also expands upon a segment of *A Week*, Thoreau's
portrait of the rude farmer, Rice. The portrait is so graphic that it is
easy to accept it as unvarnished reporting. But in a careful job of
sleuthing, retracing Thoreau's steps up the Deerfield Valley and examining old deeds and records, Murray shows that "the whole episode, including both the journey and the portrait, is not so much a

realistic report as it is a work of art" (p. 109). Again Thoreau shaped external facts to his aesthetic purposes.

In "Contexts of Bravery: Thoreau's Revisions of 'The Service' for *A Week*" (*SAR*, pp. 281–96), Linck C. Johnson proposes to trace the evolution in Thoreau's conception of personal heroism from the time of the composition of "The Service" in 1840, to 1847 and 1848, when Thoreau was accumulating material from his previous writings for *A Week*. Johnson's claim is that the martial imagery of "The Service" seemed discordant to Thoreau in 1848, who was then much more cynical toward soldiering (as "Resistance to Civil Government," written in 1849, attests), and consequently he abandoned his attempt to fit into *A Week* more than a few sentences from "The Service." To me, the military imagery of "The Service" seems inappropriate even in 1840 to the expression of the impulse to action that Emerson had preached in "The American Scholar" and that Thoreau had imbibed, as Margaret Fuller may have realized in rejecting "The Service" for *The Dial*. As Perry Miller observed, Thoreau's thinking in this period is sophomoric and confused, and Johnson in his essay may have treated it too seriously as representing a well-thought out position on bravery in 1840.

Thoreau scholars are becoming increasingly attentive to *Cape Cod*, and the once-accepted opinion that it is an expression of Thoreau at his most lighthearted has undergone an eclipse. The most illuminating (for me) of the three essays published during the year on *Cape Cod* is Sam S. Baskett's "Fronting the Atlantic: *Cape Cod* and "The Dry Salvages'" (*NEQ* 56:200–19), a carefully documented study showing that the "commonality" between Thoreau's book and Eliot's poem "is extensive and radical, at once apparent in the geographic setting of each and in the poetic strategy the writers employ in dealing with the New England coastal landscape" (p. 202). The underlying strategy of the two is the same: "Sensory apprehension verges into the symbolic as landscape and seascape, through the grace of language, become metaphors of an inward vision of salvation" (p. 203). No extravagant claims mar this paper: Baskett marks dissimilarities in the perceptions of the two authors as well as similarities. But clearly, the point that they shared the New England vision of the world is well-taken. In a less rigorously argued case, Naomi J. Miller in "Aspects of Vision in Thoreau's *Cape Cod*" (*ESQ*

29:185–95) views Thoreau's book as a statement of the old 19th-Century problem of the discrepancy between appearance and reality —the "distortions of vision," as she puts it, that come from both "within" and "without" (p. 190). Miller's essay is only a slight advance over Richard J. Schneider's *"Cape Cod*: Thoreau's Wilderness of Illusion" (*ALS 1980*, p. 16); the key question is whether Thoreau found it possible to read Transcendental significance in the natural landscape of the Cape. David Robinson argues, in "Thoreau's Human Landscape" (*Sweet Reason: Oregon Essays*, Issue 2, pp. 33–36), that Thoreau's exposure to human death on the Cape led him to the paradox that "nature must be inhuman to have human value" (p. 34). Robinson's essay is much too brief to support such a claim.

Stephen Adams and Donald Ross, Jr., in "Thoreau's 'Ktaadn': 'The Main Astonishment at Last' " (*ELN* 20:39–47), undertake to correct the position of Frederick Garber and James McIntosh that the descent from the mountain in the Ktaadn essay describes Thoreau's recovery from the shock of alien hostility he experienced on the inhospitable mountaintop. The descent into civilization again, they argue, did not assuage the shock. Before the ascent, Thoreau emphasized the encroachment of civilization upon nature; after it, the eventual swallowing up of civilization by the wilderness. Steven Fink, in "Thoreau and His Audience in 'Natural History of Massachusetts' " (*The American Renaissance: New Dimensions*, ed. Peter C. Carafiol [Bucknell], pp. 65–80), views this Thoreau essay as marking an important shift in Thoreau's writing career. Though the aim of the Transcendentalists was to bring about moral reform, Fink explains, their language with its dedication to the expression of intuited truths was impenetrable to the audience they sought to reach. "Natural History of Massachusetts" was Thoreau's first success in tying facts to his Transcendental insights to make them accessible to general readers. His "attention to tangible facts allowed him to work on both a literal and a metaphorical, or spiritual, level. The reader could appreciate his work in either way, or both" (p. 79). Thoreau would later, Fink believes, use the same approach in *Walden*.

Though we do not ordinarily mention reviews in *ALS* essays, Quentin Anderson's "Making it Alone," (*Review* 5 [Virginia]: 17–30) is considerably more than a comment upon volume I of the *Journal* in the Princeton edition. Anderson examines *why* Thoreau (and so many other Americans of his century, including Emerson) kept journals, and he views the keeping of a journal as a response to the unique impersonal conditions of American life. "We will get some instruction about our culture," he suggests, "if we admit that they [the keepers of journals] tried to make it alone because they were faced by a society they could find no other way of dealing with" (p. 30). The writing of journals was thus a "desperate device" to escape enclosure by a materialistic society, and the "device," Anderson believes, albeit "noble," was "unsuccessful" (p. 30). This essay can profitably be read in conjunction with the essays on American autobiography by Janet Varner Gunn and Sacvan Bercovitch (above).

Restrictions of space prevent my mention of the many short comments and studies that appear quarterly in *The Concord Saunterer*, published in Concord, Mass., by the newly merged Thoreau Society and Thoreau Lyceum; in *The Thoreau Society Bulletin*, edited by Walter Harding at Geneseo; and by *The Thoreau Quarterly*, published from the Philosophy Department of the University of Minnesota, Minneapolis. Thomas Blanding, editor of *The Saunterer*, continues to unearth new and original information on Thoreau, the Thoreau family, and Thoreau's neighbors and friends, and is attracting important contributions from other scholars. Walter Harding in *TSB* continues to publish the most up-to-date and complete bibliographical record of activity in the community of people interested in Thoreau. *ThQ*, late in its publishing schedule, will be issuing under a 1983 imprint the most complete and thoroughly annotated botanical index to Thoreau yet undertaken, compiled by Ray Angelo; but it is unavailable to me as I write this essay.

iv. Minor Transcendentalists

This year's most auspicious addition to the critical literature on the minor Transcendentalists is Robert N. Hudspeth's *The Letters of Margaret Fuller* (Cornell), two impressively edited volumes to be followed shortly by a third. Volume I covers the period from 1817 to 1838—from Fuller's seventh year to her 28th—and volume II continues the correspondence to 1841. Hudspeth's claim in his "Introduction" that "these letters give what we need—a full account of the writer's interior life" is fully supported by the letters themselves;

"They amply document the personality that made her both loved and feared" (p. 27). No more tragically gifted person struggled to find a role in the turbulent life of the first half of the American 19th Century; reading these letters chronologically arranged, with Hudspeth's ample annotations, one sees behind the protective facade Fuller presented to the public and into her tempestuous personality. Precocious and gifted, with no peers among her women friends, and held at arm's length by Emerson and other intellectual equals, she traveled a lonely road in the van of the new currents of European and American thought, generally unappreciated, often scorned, her potential never realized. Yet I find no self-pity, little maundering. This edition, as biography, is a great advance upon the *Memoirs*, warped as they were by the well-intentioned desire of Emerson, Clarke, and Channing to soften and repress the more extreme elements of the Fuller personality. Helpful as biographies of Fuller have been, particularly those by Higginson, Wade, and more recently Chevigny and Blanchard, Fuller's autobiography in her letters supersedes them all for me in yielding a sense of her life.

David M. Robinson's "Margaret Fuller and the Transcendental Ethos: *Woman in the Nineteenth Century*" (*PMLA* 97:83–98) is an apparent spin-off of Robinson's *Apostle of Culture: Emerson as Preacher and Lecturer* (*ALS 1982*, p. 12) in which he identifies "self-culture," having its origin allegedly in Unitarianism, as a central tenet of Emerson's thought. In *Woman in the Nineteenth Century* Robinson also discovers this "central intellectual commitment of the transcendental movement, the belief in the possibility of 'self-culture,' or the continual spiritual growth of the soul" (p. 84), and he consequently reads Fuller's book as a seminal Transcendental document as well as a major feminist one. By carefully examining Fuller's studies of Goethe's "cold intellectualism" (p. 89), Robinson is able to clarify Fuller's ambivalence toward Emerson's "chastened moralism" (p. 90), and he moves on to argue that though Fuller was attracted to the intuitive element in Transcendentalism (its "feminine" component), she believed that women, in order to achieve equality with men, had need to stress the intellectual (masculine) element, the achievement of "self-culture" requiring a kind of balanced androgyny. Robinson finds a justification for Fuller's social and political activism in the claim that Fuller "discovered that self-

culture as an end required social reform as a means, that the fulfillment of woman necessitated the concerted action of women" (p. 96).
The sudden terminal leap to this conclusion is uncharacteristic of
the careful sequiturs of the remainder of the essay. Marie Olesen
Urbanski in the *PMLA* "Forum" (97:873-74) questions the validity
of Robinson's argument on the grounds that Robinson derived his
evidence from the *Memoirs*, tainted by Emerson's personal ambivalence toward Fuller. She suggests that critics of Fuller should go
back to her original papers for their texts. But the authoritative editions of Fuller by Hudspeth and Joel Myerson will relieve scholars
of this necessity.

"Theodore Parker and the Orient" (*ATQ* 52:263-73) by Carl T.
Jackson is an attempt to set Parker's view of Eastern religions against
that of the major Transcendentalists. A good portion of this essay has
to do with Parker's interest in comparative religion rather than in
Indian religion per se; Jackson attempts to show by citing scattered
comments from Parker letters and other remnants that Parker was
more critical, more systematic, and more skeptical of Oriental religion than were Emerson and Thoreau, and that in his late thinking
he "viewed the Asian religions as a lower stage in the evolution of
what he usually called absolute religion" (p. 271). I find the scaffold-
ing of this essay too weak to support its conclusions. A more closely
reasoned and hence a more convincing essay is R. Joseph Hoffman's
"William Henry Furness: The Transcendentalist Defense of the Gospels" (*NEQ* 56:238-60), which places Furness at about the theological midpoint between Andrews Norton and Emerson. Furness
sidestepped the Unitarian dilemma over miracles: to him "the presiding spirit of Christianity . . . harmonizes fully with nature; its truth
depends not on the attestation of supernatural events" (p. 242). The
truth of the Gospels had to be grasped intuitively, Furness believed;
it could not be proved by science, by genetic studies of the scriptures,
or by the methods of German Biblical criticism or of Renan. For
him, in other words, "transcendentalism was the . . . way around
biblical authorities, pulpit formalism, and the social traditionalism
of the churches" (p. 259). But Furness's romantic approach had the
unintended effect, Hoffman points out, of raising "questions as to
what basic Christian affirmations should be" (p. 259).

Francis B. Dedmond's "Sylvester Judd on *Margaret*—An Unpub-

lished Letter" (*ATQ* 53:42–49) reflects Judd's fear, expressed to his
fellow minister Frederic Henry Hedge, that his novel might be misunderstood: it is a "New-England book," he tells Hedge, that "seeks
especially for the reproduction of a pure Christianity" (p. 46). As an
American minister, Judd was staying clear of French fiction. Dedmond prefaces his publication of "Christopher Pearse Cranch's
'Journal. 1839.'" (*SAR*, pp. 129–49) with a brief sketch of Cranch's
life to 1839, a year when he and James Freeman Clarke "amused ourselves making illustrations of Emerson's writings" (p. 140), two of
which Dedmond reproduces. The prose in Cranch's journal, covering
the short period from Jan. 8, 1839, to Apr. 23, 1839, is pedestrian and
anecdotal; Cranch's genius lay in his satirical drawings. Very clearly,
Cranch wrote to Clarke, they would "descend to posterity as the
immortal illustrators of the great Transcendentalist" (p. 148). Dedmond's annotations to the Cranch text are extensive and helpful.

Charles Wesley Grady in "A Conservative Transcendentalist: The
Early Years (1805–35) of Frederic Henry Hedge" (*SAR*, pp. 57–87)
has written an absorbing narrative of the pastoral trials of this brilliant youthful friend of Emerson and Margaret Fuller, caught up in
the stimulating intellectual ferment in Cambridge in the early 1830s.
Or, one might more aptly put it, "trapped" as a Unitarian between
an expiring Calvinistic theology and a rising Universalist movement
that was depleting Unitarian parishes of the financial support of their
constituents. Hedge's removal from Cambridge to Bangor was not
wholly voluntary, Grady points out, but necessitated by the rancor
of some of these intercine disputes, and the dilemma of Hedge is
offered as a microcosm of what was going on generally throughout
the region. In his articles on German thought and on Coleridge,
Hedge did much, in the early 1830s, to strike "the first blows in behalf
of the transcendental philosophy" (p. 73).

Kevin P. Van Anglen's "'That Sainted Spirit'—William Ellery
Channing and the Unitarian Milton" (*SAR*, pp. 101–27) uses Channing's response to Milton to typify the "more general attitude towards
the poet during the American Renaissance" (p. 101). Van Anglen
develops his article through an analysis of Channing's review in the
Christian Examiner of Milton's Latin treatise, *De Doctrina Christiana*.
Channing attributed to Milton "*Moral* greatness, or magnanimity,"
"largeness of soul," "intellectual energy," "strength of character"—

qualities that move Channing as close as he ever came, Van Anglen believes, "to the inspired bard of Emerson's 'The Poet'" (p. 105, passim). In Channing's review of the Milton piece in 1826 Van Anglen discovers "generically and thematically a precursor of the Transcendental biographies and autobiographies of Emerson and Thoreau" (p. 123).

University of Minnesota, Duluth

2. Hawthorne

Rita K. Gollin

Although 1983 was not a banner year for Hawthorne scholarship, a few useful volumes appeared—a few good editions of the novels, and three books about Hawthorne. A number of essays, taking discrete methodological approaches, intelligently explore the ways Hawthorne's narratives at once reveal and conceal his problems as a writer and as a member of the human community. This year's total number of essays is far less than last year's, but largely because no separate collection of essays appeared. (The final issue of the *Nathaniel Hawthorne Journal* is promised for next year.) One "new" letter to Hawthorne and one from him appeared in print (while the Centenary edition of the letters continues to move toward completion). And the *Nathaniel Hawthorne Newsletter* continues to publish short notes, abstracts of program papers, and Buford Jones's annotated bibliography.

i. Editions, Biography, General Studies, Primary Materials

All of this year's new Hawthorne editions are of novels, and all are appropriate for both the general reader and the student. All five of Hawthorne's completed novels are included in the second of the Hawthorne volumes in the nicely printed and nicely bound Library of America series. As with last year's *Tales and Sketches*, this volume follows the Centenary Edition (correcting a few typographical errors); it includes the identical chronology; and editor Millicent Bell provides clear textual notes.

The two paperback Hawthorne novels published this year in the Penguin American Library series also follow Centenary texts, and they include reading lists, textual notes, and well-balanced introductions which discuss social as well as biographical and aesthetic issues. (This is also true of *The House of the Seven Gables*, published in 1981 with an introduction by Milton Stern.) Nina Baym's introduction to *The Scarlet Letter* responds to and enlarges the average reader's experience of the novel as a tightly structured fiction about the reality of inner experience. Defining Hawthorne's situation as a 19th-Century American writer, Baym examines conflicts of individual and social constraint in his first long fiction and discusses the ways both the novel and "The Custom-House" are "intricately tied" to Hawthorne's private experience. Annette Kolodny begins her introduction to *The Blithedale Romance* by assessing its reception in the context of 19th-Century attitudes toward utopian communes. Then, after examining Hawthorne's motives for joining and then leaving Brook Farm, she discusses the novel, its narrator, and its author and their essential preoccupation with the stratagems of inner experience rather than with social issues.

Three books about Hawthorne appeared this year, including a revision of the 1965 Twayne volume. As its title suggests, James O'Donald Mays's *Mr. Hawthorne Goes to England* (Burley, England: New Forest Leaves) is an enthusiastic study. Drawing on materials from English periodicals and American archives, Mays displays the Liverpool Hawthorne knew (including photographs and engravings of streets, buildings, and people) and his consular activities (including his relations with Buchanan and his efforts on behalf of abused American seamen). The topical chapter organization sometimes results in overlap, and there is some disproportion (e.g., Mays at once blows up and limits the English response to *Our Old Home* to furor over Hawthorne's remarks about beefy English women). But Mays has put together a generously illustrated narrative of Hawthorne's "adventures" as Consul.

Rita K. Gollin's *Portraits of Nathaniel Hawthorne: An Iconography* (NIUP) presents the dozens of life portraits of Hawthorne (some new to the canon) and their most important progeny, together with information about their occasion and reception, developments in 19th-Century portraiture, Hawthorne's comments about their truthfulness, and his use of portraits in fiction. We not only come to see Hawthorne more clearly (particularly in the photographs of his last years) but also understand him better as a practical man of letters who accepted the consequences of fame with an admixture of vanity, humility, shrewdness, and rueful resignation. The book includes a descriptive catalog, an introduction, a discussion of apocryphal portraits, a glossary, and a bibliography.

The text of Terence Martin's revised version of his *Nathaniel Hawthorne* (Twayne) differs little from the judicious 1965 volume, but all the changes are enrichments—for example, new discussions of Goodman Brown's dilemma and Dimmesdale's "doubleness" and an expanded treatment of the Hawthorne legacy. And Martin has thoroughly revised his notes and the "Critical and Biographical Studies" section of his annotated bibliography (under the letter B, for example, adding nine entries and deleting four). Thus, he simultaneously presents and contributes to the work of the past two decades, giving an example of, as well as a report on, the state of the art of Hawthorne studies.

A chapter of Donald Ringe's *American Gothic: Imagination and Reason in Nineteenth-Century Fiction* (Kentucky) is devoted to Hawthorne, and *The Marble Faun* serves as springboard for the final chapter. After identifying the Gothic fiction Hawthorne read and borrowed from, Ringe concentrates on techniques he used for "Gothic ends"—the uncertain light that provided license to introduce the marvelous, as in *The House of the Seven Gables*; demonism, which as in "Young Goodman Brown" often draws on Puritanism (here Ringe draws parallels to the fiction of Dana and Allston); and enclosed spaces used as symbols of the mind or heart, where demonic encounters occur (as in *The Marble Faun*). Ringe's synopses of Hawthorne's fiction are reliable, if not probing; and he is informative about contemporaries who used similar Gothic devices. But Hawthorne did not limit the "neutral territory" of intermingled perception and imagination to the Gothic; and he appropriated Gothic devices for many more purposes than Ringe considers—using nightmares and spectres of guilt to dramatize individual anguish, for example, or (as in the abortive romances) to speculate about what might lie beyond the dark veils of mortality. Certainly Hawthorne drew on his Gothic heritage to proffer dark insights, and Ringe argues well that the "major phase of American Gothicism" ended with *The Marble Faun*, because post–Civil War America embraced literary realism (though his judgments of such works as "The Turn of the Screw" can be disputed). In the end, when he says that for Hawthorne, as for

Brown and Poe, "the Gothic mode was the primary means of expression," Ringe claims at once too little and too much.

The only primary materials published in 1983 are two letters once owned by Elizabeth Hawthorne and recently given to the Essex Institute—"Two Lost Letters: Hawthorne at College; Longfellow and Hawthorne: The Beginning of a Friendship," edited by Peter Balakian (*NEQ* 16:425–32). Hawthorne's lively letter to his "Dear Sister" a month after arriving at Bowdoin College shows him already objecting to compulsory prayer and enjoying such unlawful occupations as card playing. The letter from Longfellow of Mar. 9, 1837, fills in the gap between Hawthorne's respectful note soliciting his former classmate's attention to *Twice-told Tales* and his expansive second letter. It is clear from this gracious first letter that Longfellow had already identified Hawthorne as the author of some of the anonymous tales in the *Token* and the *New England Magazine*, and his praise of their "simple" realism indicates he was predisposed to review the collection favorably (even though he would find it included only one of the tales his letter mentions, and we cannot determine whether he then knew that such complex tales as "My Kinsman, Major Molineux" and "Young Goodman Brown" were also Hawthorne's).

ii. Novels

Again this year, more attention was paid to *The Scarlet Letter* than to any other novel: seven studies of it (eight, including Baym's introduction), as compared to three of *The Blithedale Romance* (four, including Kolodny's introduction); two of *The Marble Faun*; and none of *The House of the Seven Gables*. Most of the essays depend on sophisticated critical terminology, though some trip on it.

Three of the *Scarlet Letter* essays theorize about the relation of author, narrator, and narrative, especially the narrator's evasiveness. Gordon Hutner focuses on Hawthorne's personal situation in "Secrets and Sympathy in *The Scarlet Letter*" (*Mosaic* 16:114–24); he studies the "strategies for simultaneously concealing and revealing secrets" in both the novel and "The Custom-House," where Hawthorne vents his anguish about losing his job yet diverts attention from analogues between Hester's humiliation and his own. Hawthorne's concealment of his secret from the reader whose sympathy he nevertheless courts is likened to Dimmesdale's riddling revelations of guilt: for both, self-mockery serves as a defense mechanism, and self-punishments avoid worse pain. Hawthorne's technique of alternative possibilities frustrates "our desire to know something completely" but implicates the reader in the problem of discovery. Though Hutner sometimes equivocates about the sympathy Hawthorne sought, he firmly concludes that "by making the revelation into a riddle, Hawthorne transforms the minister's ambiguous act of self-disclosure into the narrative's closure."

Dennis Foster, in "The Embroidered Sin: Confessional Evasion in *The Scarlet Letter*" (*Criticism* 25:141–63), also energetically examines Dimmesdale's tactics of concealing while revealing his sin, and likens Dimmesdale's deviousness to the narrator's, though he sometimes overstates his case or distorts motive and response. (For example, Chillingworth turns his desire for Hester "into a relentless attempt to possess Dimmesdale by appropriating his language," while the minister's desire for her fuses "with the desire for grace that Chillingworth's words explicitly address. Consequently he constantly feels his desire as sin.") It is nonetheless easy to agree that the narrator's duplicity is comparable to the minister's and that both entangle the reader in complicity. Foster is most forceful, if not completely persuasive, in arguing for the novel's use of "rhetoric as repression, as the displacement of the dangerous element into acceptable forms" whose veils are raised only briefly, because narcissism and the will for power can "destroy both personal and communal relations" within the narrative and in the writer's transactions with his reader.

In "Mrs. Hawthorne's Headache: Reading *The Scarlet Letter*" (*NCF* 37:552–75), David Leverenz also treats Hawthorne's narrative stance as a subversion of communal values, though with a different focus—on "Hawthorne's profoundly contradictory affinities with a rebellious, autonomous female psyche and an intrusive male accuser." As Leverenz says, *The Scarlet Letter* troubles the reader because of its double-twisting attitudes toward Hester, a sympathetic and admirable heroine who is put in her place—"pacified"—by Chillingworth, Dimmesdale, and the narrator. She is complicitous in her "patriarchal punishment," and the novel is energized by her constrained passion as well as Chillingworth's rage. But a few readings in which Leverenz ignores the narrator's careful "mights" and "maybes" are open to question. It distorts Hester's hope of spending eternity with Dimmesdale to say she hopes to spend it in hell, and there is no warrant for saying that "Dimmesdale's revelation leads to eternal separation" nor that he "gains his final reward of celestial approval." It is not true that Hester's advice to Dimmesdale, "Do anything but lie down and die!" applies "only to men, not to herself": she would never "lie down and die." And when the narrator speculates about whether the hatred between Chillingworth and Dimmesdale might be "transmuted into golden love" in the afterlife, that does not mean that "the cuckold and the lover rise together to an all-male paradise," the narrator momentarily escaping with them.

Each of the next three *Scarlet Letter* essays is governed by its own sustained methodology. (A fourth is discussed in part iv.) Louise K. Barnett draws on the insights of semiology and speech act theory in "Speech and Society in *The Scarlet Letter*" (*ESQ* 29:16–24). Insisting on the structured clarity of Hawthorne's first novel, she argues persuasively that it "demonstrates a confidence in the resources of language to communicate meaning," even when speech is inhibited or deformed by social restraints. "To an unusual extent the poles of speech and silence define public and private worlds and create the dynamic of *The Scarlet Letter*," she says. Private speech reveals character and emotion; public speech reinforces shared values and masks what is socially unacceptable (though it is going too far to say that Dimmesdale's "struggle between public and private is played out solely in terms of speech"). In "*The Scarlet Letter* and a New Ethic" (*CollL* 10:50–59), Carmine Sarracino applies the distinction made by Eric Neumann in *Depth Psychology and a New Ethic* (1973) between "old-ethic" and "new-ethic." Puritanism is old ethic: its ideals of perfection require the repression or suppression of whatever is incompatible. This is an appropriate construct for Dimmesdale, though calling Chillingworth his "shadow" (or repressed "other") seems of limited validity. Occasionally Sarracino overreads (Hester's statements to Dimmesdale about the "consecration" of their love do not prove that she has become a new-ethic individual who is "the source and justification" of her own values) or misreads (Hester did not come "to the new world in pursuit of a utopian dream," nor is there a "progression from Hester to Pearl" that suggests "an evolution of human consciousness is possible"). It is true that *The Scarlet Letter* pits Puritan ethical absolutes against a relativistic quest for values, but Hawthorne did not claim that ethical consciousness evolves "in slow, generational steps." The last article in this group uses *The*

Scarlet Letter to prove Hawthorne was "a great psychologist." In "Pathography, Hawthorne, and the History of Psychological Ideas" (*ESQ* 29:113–26), Michael Vannoy Adams begins by applauding Frederick Crews's "reversal" in 1980 of his psychobiographical or "pathographical" argument in *The Sins of the Fathers* that characters' symptoms reveal their author's neuroses; but he flogs the dead horse while rejecting Crews's rejection of psychoanalytic criticism. Praising Hawthorne as a precursor of Freud, Adams reads *The Scarlet Letter* as evidence not of the writer's incestuous desires but of his insights into character, and offers in support ten psychoanalytic propositions that can be documented by Hawthorne's novel (for example, the etiology of psychosomatic symptoms). The argument is sound, though Adams seems unaware that other critics have preceded him in observing that many of Hawthorne's insights into human behavior coincide with Freud's.

Two novels published this year—one purportedly serious and the other comic—give a different kind of testimony to the currency of *The Scarlet Letter* by taking it as their point of departure. Charles R. Larsen's *Arthur Dimmesdale* (A&W) claims to "retell" the novel from Dimmesdale's point of view, but it is a travesty that does violence to Hawthorne's moral conceptions, his characters, plot, themes, language, and images. In the forest scene, for example, Larsen says some woodsman had "forged" a path, he describes the lovers' "elfin grot," and Hester addresses Dimmesdale by saying, "It has been so long, Arthur, how are you?" Larsen is wrong about the Puritans (he says Dimmesdale wonders why he had failed Hester at every station of the cross), and his inventions are (at best) curious: Dimmesdale fantasizes himself in childbirth; Hester is half-Jewish and "really" named Miriam; she deliberately trapped Hawthorne by bathing naked in a forest pool she knew he would pass; Chillingworth had earned his living in Europe as a music hall conjurer; the election sermon ends with a Rappaccini-like parable that no one can understand; in the governor's hall, Dimmesdale sees his own reflection in the armor bearing Hester's A on his breast. I cannot understand why the novel was issued in paperback, though it might give dull readers a few prurient thrills and the delusion of "really" understanding Hawthorne and his novel. By contrast, Peter De Vries's *Slouching Towards Kalamazoo*, which its jacket calls a "modernization" of Hawthorne's novel, essentially uses it as a subtextual trampoline

permitting comical leaps. The anxious young narrator impregnates
the high school teacher who had taught him *The Scarlet Letter*; after
she is fired, she stands on a balcony and displays on her blouse a
scarlet A+; then she achieves commercial success by selling T-shirts
bearing that insignia.

Each of two *Blithedale* essays asks similar questions but reaches
divergent conclusions. The first is a chapter in John Carlos Rowe's
Through the Custom-House (Hopkins), in which one "anomalous"
work by each of six major 19th-Century American writers is read in
the context of a 20th-Century theory which elucidates their "modern"
reflexivity about "the literary function of language." In "The Metaphysics of Imagination: Narrative Consciousness in *The Blithedale
Romance*," Rowe reads *Blithedale* in the context of Sartrean phenomenology, arguing that questions about the nature and value of the
imagination are here more problematic than in the preceding romances, since characters' conceptions of reality are more fanciful and
egotistical. Only Coverdale transcends "the personae that trap and
imprison the other characters," because his imagination gives him
the freedom "to negate the stubborn sense of the world." He learns
to use his imagination for self-discovery, which nevertheless remains
incomplete; thus the reader must enter the text as interpreter, instructed by Coverdale himself "that neither our choices nor our wishes
are free." Focusing on the variant parables of the Veiled Lady, Rowe
reads the veil as symbolic of the imagination, of consciousness constructing meaning. Thus, for Theodore, lifting the veil brings only
loss. While this does not take account of the fact that in both the
legend and Priscilla's performance someone is "really" under the
veil, Rowe rightly insists on the paradoxical nature of the imagination, which permits sympathetic self-transcendence yet depends on
estrangement. Readers may question whether all the detail about
Husserl and Sartre is essential for Rowe's explication of the fiction;
and on the other hand, they might want more precise detail about
Hawthorne's conceptions of inner experience (for Hawthorne, the
imagination could not become "uncontrolled passion," and Clifford
Pyncheon does not represent an extreme of "spiritualism"). But
Rowe's analyses force us to rethink *Blithedale* and Hawthorne's entire
achievement.

In "Behind the White Veil: Self-Awareness in Hawthorne's *The
Blithedale Romance*" (*MLS* 12:81–92), Bill Christopherson takes a

darker approach to the problem of masked reality in the novel, which he considers "modern" in its pessimism and cynicism, its author "tracking evil and confusion to its fundamental source, discovering humanity 'mesmerized,' as it were, rendered deaf to reality, blind to its own unconscious determinants, and . . . dumb to the truth." Christopherson is aware of Hawthorne's strategies of evasion, but sometimes ignores them. He takes Coverdale's avowal of love for Priscilla at face value, though Hawthorne knew truth is never that simple. And to say that the characters' limited knowledge of each other and of their own amoral and depraved "undersouls" argues against Transcendentalism ("It becomes presumptuous to scrutinize the external world for veiled correspondences while this preemptive inner world remains unsounded") oversimplifies the novel, the characters, and Transcendentalism. In two related misreadings, Christopherson says that Coverdale's disgust at Westervelt's mesmeric power suggests Hawthorne's "resentment against God himself," and that Westervelt "imbibes the aura of a hostile Deity of seemingly infinite power." Certainly Priscilla is isolated behind her veil, but that does not mean she was self-deceived; nor does removing her veil suggest "the dropping of all facades . . ., the confrontation of self and reality." Hawthorne's sorrowful awareness of the veils we all adopt and adapt precluded his staging such an ultimate confrontation; and never did he present "the veil as the very source—and anagram—of evil."

The last item in this group is a brief note. In "Hawthorne's *Blithedale Romance* (*Expl* 41:28–29) Dorena Allen Wright provides the source of the "unearthly groan" Coverdale thinks of sounding from his hermitage to warn Zenobia and Westervelt of his presence "as if this were one of the trees of Dante's ghostly forest." In the *Inferno* 13:33–37, in the Second Round of the Seventh Circle, Dante hears the voices of sinners punished for suicide by imprisonment in the Wailing Wood. Thus, Wright suggests, the groan serves to foreshadow Zenobia's death.

Both articles on *The Marble Faun* take fresh approaches to familiar topics. In "Artistic Communication and the Heroines' Art in Hawthorne's *The Marble Faun*" (*ESQ* 29:81–90), Robert Brooke concentrates on the heroines' studios and the different ways the characters and the narrator describe and thus interpret what they see. It is true that such interpretation is crucial to the novel yet necessarily remains incomplete and provisional, dependent on characters' "interpretive needs," and Brooke is right to insist that these needs include assumptions about proper roles for women. But sometimes he oversimplifies by fastening on a single strand from the alternative possibilities the novel proposes. Hilda's copy of the Beatrice Cenci painting "may be taken as a kind of self-portrait," he says, but then question-begs by referring to it as "her self-portrait." And although he says the narrator believes an artist's intention is "recoverable," in fact the narrator and his characters acknowledge that an artist does not always understand his own intentions or even his own creation. Brooke is right in stating that works of art in the novel are heuristic, requiring "artist and viewer to re-examine, not to reaffirm, their previously held ideas"; but that does not mean "art cannot function communicatively." The romance proves on many levels that art does communicate, though the communications is not exactly the same for every viewer, nor even for a single viewer every time.

In the last essay in this group, "The 'Grim Identity' in Hawthorne's *Marble Faun*" (*SNNTS* 15:108–21), James G. Janssen cogently argues that Hawthorne's last romance is characterized by "fused images" that show the " 'grim identity' between gay things and sorrowful ones." Images on sarcophagi conjoin merriment and death and skeletons in the Capuchin burial chambers seem to grin; Kenyon's best works of art and (even more) Miriam's conjoin such "seemingly discordant elements"; and the carnival scene shows the wisdom of seizing opportunities for joy even in time of grief. Although most of these points have been made before, Janssen amplifies the usual reading of the *felix culpa* theme by stressing Hawthorne's fusion of enjoyment with wisdom, based on his assessment of "a human race that has fallen—but not very far—from grace; and which, paradoxically, has gained in the process!" Janssen rightly observes that the ability to move " 'between jest and earnest' " is a measure of the novel's characters, its philosophic vision, and Hawthorne himself.

Brook Thomas's far-reaching essay, "*The House of the Seven Gables*: Reading the Romance of America" (*PMLA* 97:195–211), inadvertently omitted from last year's discussion, relates contradictions inherent in Hawthorne's romance form to those inherent in "the romance of America." Since both are based on possibility and on conventions and documents provisionally accepted as authoritative, Thomas poses a "social" reading of *The House of the Seven Gables* against a "rhetorical" reading of America as a "product of the same imaginative freedom that produces romances." Hawthorne was a self-conscious romancer who raised questions about the relationship of the imagination to social and historical fact and the authority of texts —the Pyncheons' deeds of ownership, the laws governing American society, and the book Hawthorne wrote. Thomas takes a fresh and essentially optimistic approach to its happy ending: readers play a crucial role as interpreters of what is possible in a romance and may be provoked to criticize and perhaps reshape American society. Thus, human effort—of the writer and the reader—can effect social change; and Hawthorne "locates hope in human history."

iii. Short Works

There are even fewer essays on the short stories than on the novels this year. Most of them discuss philosophical ideas and historical backgrounds; and the only story addressed by two authors is "My Kinsman, Major Molineux." Taking the epistemological issue known as the "Molyneux problem" as his point of origin, John Franzosa in "Locke's Kinsman, William Molyneux: The Philosophical Context of Hawthorne's Early Tales" (*ESQ* 29:1–15) learnedly explains Robin's puzzlement about his experiences in terms of Lockean and Common Sense assumptions about perception and knowledge. Lockeans believed the mind passively receives discontinuous sensations; Common Sense philosophers assumed a continuous identity and considered perception an act of interpretation dependent on such laws as cause and effect. Franzosa argues somewhat overingeniously that in this tale Hawthorne was enacting the ambivalence he located at the heart of Common Sense philosophy, which combined a theory of perception with a belief in reason. Since Franzosa believes the story depends upon but deliberately undermines both Robin's and the reader's faith in the perceiving mind's ability to make sense of the world, he criticizes Hawthorne's clear explanations of what puzzles Robin; but that is to deny Hawthorne credit for the complexity of his story's statements. The second study takes a different kind of ingenious historical approach to the story. In "Robins and Robinarchs in 'My Kinsman, Major Molineux'" (*NCF* 38:271–88), James Duban connects Hawthorne's protagonist to Robert Walpole, whose critics attacked the nepotism and political corruption which characterized his "Robinocracy." Drawing on this context of political animosity, Duban read Hawthorne's story as his deliberate challenge to "the American concept of democratic self-origination." Walpole's England is linked to Boston both by Robin's hope for preferment from his kinsman and by the democratic mob, which mimics the authority it deposes and so practices its own inverse "Robinocracy" or corrupt favoritism. Although Duban cannot prove that Hawthorne had Walpole in mind, his wide-ranging speculations about the story's historical ramifications are lively and well-supported.

In one of the most useful essays in this group, "Transcending the Myth of the Fall in Hawthorne's 'The May-Pole of Merry Mount'" (*ESQ* 29:73–80), Gayle L. Smith argues that Hawthorne's tale is his humanistic and optimistic version of *Paradise Lost*, based on a historical event but "epitomizing the psychic, archetypal nature of the myth of the fall." Smith analyzes how selectively Hawthorne draws on historical sources and Milton's poem, as in his portrait of Endicott (which incorporates traits of Satan, Michael, and Christ). But the essay also discusses important divergences from the sources, such as the mutual devotion of Edith and Edgar, whose passion is a condition of wisdom and vital proof of the fortunate fall.

Two of the year's essays include somewhat startling propositions. Bill Christopherson in "Hawthorne's 'The Wives of the Dead': Bereavement and the 'Better Part'" (*SSF* 20:1–6) argues that the two "sisters" of the tale have begun a lesbian marriage each of them regrets losing, and also that the tale challenges Christian morality and does not answer the question of whether news about the husbands' survival is dream, hearsay, or reality. I think he is mistaken on all three counts, but particularly on the first. The women draw closer for mutual consolation; they do not regret the loss of that bond but only (in each case) the other's presumed solitary sorrow. The tale does have New Testament echoes that avoid simple Christian norms, but it is not "an ironic parable of self-salvation." It is a tenderly ironic tale of compassionate affection with an essentially secular sensibility, whose symmetrical structure relies heavily on coincidence, and which blurs but does not obliterate the borders between dream and reality. Nevertheless, Christopherson is provocative and energetic. So is Jules Zanger in "Speaking of the Unspeakable: Hawthorne's 'The Birthmark'" (*MP* 80:364–71); he seeks fuller understanding of Hawthorne's story by connecting the "fictive particulars" of the marriage relationship and the red stain on Georgiana's cheek to "quotidian concerns of the common culture" including sexual taboos. All his propositions are closely reasoned and interesting—for example, about the vampire-like relationship between experimenter and subject, the lab as a kind of male Coketown with dominion over the lady's boudoir, and resemblances between Alymer's idealism and Ralph Waldo Emerson's. But the suggestion that Georgiana's crimson birthmark emerged from some level of the new groom's "response to the menstrual aspects of woman's biological life" seems hypostatic. Certainly, marriage brought Hawthorne into a new level of intimacy with female sexuality, and perhaps some of it repelled him; but limiting the birthmark to the menstrual cycle is at once reductive and distorting. Nevertheless, Zanger reads the story well as a reflection of Hawthorne's "complete involvement with his world," which led him to warn about the excesses of America's expanding technology and its obsessive idealism, while warning himself about "the dangers of traditional male domination in marriage."

Tony Siebers, in "Hawthorne's Appeal and Romanticism" (*BuR* 28:100–17), firmly places Hawthorne in the historical context of "the Romantic's appropriation of the victim's position" in his Gothic inventions (the "Romantic fantastic") as in his Puritan narratives ("moral Romance"). Siebers concentrates on "Alice Doane's Appeal," in which both Gothic and historical narratives decry the immorality of accusation. To an extent his discussion of this tale and others exaggerates the issue of supernaturalism: for Hawthorne, all long-held communal beliefs convey truths about the heart, and he was repelled by all destructive malignity whatever its embodiment. And there is occasional misreading: Ethan Brand did not wish "to be possessed by a devil," though his obsession led him to the dead end of despair. But Siebers makes strong points about the boomeranging dynamic of accusation in "Ethan Brand" as in "Young Goodman Brown" and "Egotism; or, The Bosom Serpent" (and he might have included the example of Chillingworth) in which the Puritan spirit of persecution rebounds against the persecutor, and about the synthesis of historical fact with moral perspective that constitutes "Hawthorne's appeal."

The only essay this year that does not directly address Hawthorne's fiction is James Walter's " 'The Old Manse': The Pastoral Precinct of Hawthorne's Fiction" (*ATQ* 51:195–209), an original but unconvincing reading of Hawthorne's introductory essay as allegorizing his Concord years "into a pattern of what I shall call sincere pastoral in a realistic mode." It is true that Hawthorne's essay shares with pastoral works a concern for the harmonious relationship of external nature with human needs, but it is a stretch to fit it to a "pastoral topography" with a pure "supernatural" inner circle surrounded by two concentric outer circles, the outermost of which could include artificial urban society or primitive wilderness. The "golden-tinted paper-hangings" of Hawthorne's study do not really suggest "a golden realm with transforming powers," nor does he find the garret sacred (the newspapers that retain "sap" interest him more than dead sermons). The construct of the outer perimeter is even more problematic: Concord is not seen as excessively artificial nor the gentle Assabeth as primitive wilderness, and it overweights the bewildered visionaries attracted by Emerson's magnetism to call them the "source of outer disorder." Yet Walter is right about Hawthorne's view of "The Old Manse" period as a relaxed time of regeneration.

In "Hawthorne and Melancholy: A New Source for 'Rappaccini's Daughter'" (*ATQ* 52:255–58), Diane Elizabeth Dreher suggests that Hawthorne might have read Timothy Bright's *Treatise of Melancholy* (1586), where he would have found an expanded version of Thomas Browne's account of the poisonous woman sent to kill Alexander. Bright explains how individuals could be "nourished" on poison and how the Indian woman could have been immunized to a poison her nature had "embraced." Although Dreher cannot establish that Hawthorne read Bright, she argues that his interest in melancholy might have led him to it and that perhaps other Renaissance studies of melancholy might "cast further light on the dark shadows of human motivation" in his writing.

The last item in this group is a note by Leonard C. Butts, "Diorama, Spectroscope, or Peepshow: the Question of the Old German's Showbox in Nathaniel Hawthorne's 'Ethan Brand'" (*SSF* 20:320–22). Butts finds it strange that no one has questioned Hawthorne's use of the word "diorama" for the tale's showbox, since the term was coined by Daguerre to describe the large three-dimensional translucent paintings first exhibited in Europe in 1821 and in America twenty years later. It is true that the German's showbox with removable pictures is the kind commonly known as a peepshow. But since (according to the *OED*) the word "diorama" was used as early as 1823 for "a mode of scenic representation in which a picture, some portions of which are translucent, is viewed through an aperture," it is really no surprise that Hawthorne used the word in that generalized sense.

iv. Hawthorne and Others

As in the past few years, there is vitality and variety in analyses of Hawthorne's literary relationships, particularly in discussions of his legacy. But there was some discussion of indebtedness (for Wright's note on *Blithedale* and the *Inferno*, see part *ii*, and for Smith's comments on *Paradise Lost* as a source for "The May-Pole of Merry Mount" and Dreher's suggestion of a possible source for "Rappaccini's Daughter", see part *iii*). And one of the year's most immediately useful studies compares Hawthorne to a contemporary.

Lawrence Buell in "Rival Romantic Interpretations of New England Puritanism: Hawthorne versus Stowe" (*TSLL* 25:77–99) judiciously compares the two authors' attitudes toward their New England past by examining two texts—*The Scarlet Letter* and *The Minister's Wooing*. Each is set in an "age of establishment" with discrete social rituals and consequent challenges to individuals. The central characters reflect their authors' ambivalence about Puritanism: each novel has a minister at the center who represents "the Puritan ethos in extreme form" and a more practical and more emotionally developed heroine who is pitted against the traditional male world in ways that modify romance stereotypes. Buell also analyzes the ways the novels reflect their authors' different experiences of the Puritan past: Stowe, daughter of a Calvinist minister, could create intimate scenes of domestic experience while couching discussion in theological terms; Hawthorne, more removed from his ancestors, presented the Puritan community more abstractly yet probed more deeply into such anguishing issues as personal salvation, presented as essentially psychological and moral problems. Emplacing Stowe in the conservative orthodox tradition and Hawthorne in the "Unitarian–Transcendental mainstream," while showing how both modified those traditions, Buell discusses the "limitations in range" of both authors and—more emphatically—their "distinctive strengths." Hawthorne is linked to two of his contemporaries by Sylvie L. F. Richards in "The Eye and the Portrait: the Fantastic in Poe, Hawthorne and Gogol" (*SSF* 20:307–15). Starting from Todorov's definition of the fantastic as a genre that requires the reader to hesitate between natural and supernatural interpretations of puzzling visual perceptions, she discusses three tales that raise questions about the kinds of truth that portraits can capture—Poe's "The Oval Portrait" and Gogol's "The Portrait" as well as Hawthorne's "The Prophetic Pictures." Although the readings and comparisons are lucid, Richards ends where she began, simply showing that all three conform to Todorov's definition of the fantastic through their similar use of portraits. John Idol, Jr., contributes to our knowledge of Hawthorne's contemporary reputation in England in "Mary Russell Mitford: Champion of American Literature" (*SAR*, pp. 313–34). The English novelist's letters, anthologies, and *Recollections of a Literary Life* establish her as an enthusiastic promoter of 19th-Century American authors, Hawthorne in particular. After reading *The Scarlet Letter* she praised him as a major American writer. She corresponded with him and hoped to meet him, but first his consular obligations and then her failing health prevented it.

Two good articles assess Henry James's relationship to Hawthorne. In "The Idea of 'Too Late' in James's 'The Beast in the Jungle'" (*HJR* 4:128–39), Michael Coulson Berthold assesses James's indebtedness to Hawthorne for that theme. He analyzes passages from the *American Notebooks* that probably influenced James, suggests that Hester and Dimmesdale resemble May Bartram and Marcher, and argues that comments in *Hawthorne* "cement the connection." He also considers how and why James's fiction differs from Hawthorne's, notably in its greater concern with character. Berthold's most provocative section discusses James's transformation of his borrowed theme into a structural device compatible with his own theories of fiction, particularly the relation of fictive form to untidy experience: thus, the theme of "too late" determines the narrative line and climax of "The Beast in the Jungle," though its ending has the indeterminacy of real life. As its title and its length suggest, John Carlos Rowe's "What the Thunder Said: James's *Hawthorne* and the American Anxiety of Influence: A *Centennial Essay*" (*HJR* 4:81–119) is a much more ambitious essay. Rowe begins with the problem of American writers' relations to their cultural heritage, particularly their problem of what to reject and what to incorporate. Then, as both critic and historian, he takes on James's relation to Hawthorne and subsequent critics' treatments of it. *Hawthorne* is read as James's effort to "transume" his predecessor and *Portrait of a Lady* as a successful "translation" of his fiction. (Rowe cites parallels of characters, the treatment of sin, and the international theme.) He concludes with a Bloom-based discussion of James's creative misreading of his formidable predecessor. The result is fine criticism of James, of James's criticism of Hawthorne, and the past hundred years' criticisms of both.

In a brief note on another Hawthorne heir, "Miles Coverdale and Basil March: The 'Philosophical Observers' of Hawthorne and Howells" (*NHS Newsletter* 9:11–14), Elsa Nettels compares the two detached observers of their flawed societies and other peoples' lives who are ironically aware of their own "superior endowments" and "inner deficiency." Both criticize the social system but do not expect it to change; both distrust fanaticism yet mock philosophical detachment. Clearly, Coverdale was one of Howells' models for the self-denigrating ironist of *A Hazard of New Fortunes, An Open-Eyed Conspiracy,* and *Their Wedding Journey.*

The only study of Hawthorne's influence on a contemporary is Susan V. Donaldson's " 'Let that Anvil Ring': Robert Penn Warren's *The Cave* and Hawthorne's Legacy" (*SLJ* 51:59–73) which draws on Warren's criticism as well as his novel to analyze his intellectual and artistic debt. Donaldson discusses the "startling similarities" of *The Cave* to "The Man of Adamant," "Ethan Brand," and other Hawthorne writings under three headings, with the "religious framework" the most important. She notes that both writers present individuals who seek redemption despite their feelings of alienation and uncertainty and their need for a change of heart; and quoting Warren on "My Kinsman, Major Molineux," she points to his parallel insistence in fiction that we must each recognize our own dark selves. In her discussion of formal similarities, Donaldson points out that both writers develop pervasive symbols whose meanings proliferate, and she suggests that for both, the gap between abstract idea and real embodiment is an index of human imperfection. Her third section concentrates on particular parallels of text and theme—Warren's cave description, for example, compared to descriptions in Hawthorne's notebooks and "The Man of Adamant." She concludes that Warren's vision is not as dark as Hawthorne's and that he is more

interested in commitment and change, in part because he was not
bound by 19th-Century "tentative belief" in transcendent absolutes.
He invested his heritage and made it his own.

Hawthorne's heirs remain in his debt. Although occasionally a
novelist distorts his work, most of them—like James and Warren—
assimilate him into their own substance. What they have in common
with the critics, particularly astute critics such as Rowe and Buell, is
that they provoke us to read Hawthorne in new ways.

State University College of New York, Geneseo

3. Poe

Kent P. Ljungquist

Impelled by French critical theory and its focus on the text itself
(*l'écriture*), the notion that the subject of Poe's works is writing itself
has become somewhat of a commonplace. The idea that the craft of
fiction can be reduced to mere craftsmanship is advanced this year
sometimes without even token recourse to Poe's letters or to his biography. Nevertheless, theoretical approaches continue to result in interesting assessments of Poe's attitudes toward language and author-
ship. With fewer dissertations devoted exclusively to Poe, we can
expect more studies that relate Poe to other authors or to specialized
genres. Source study, influence study, and other forms of traditional
interpretation continue to result in good work, and two collections
of essays by diverse hands also appeared in 1983, one on supernatural
fiction and the other on satiric hoaxing.

i. Sources, Influences, Editions, Bibliography

Scholars continue to mine traditional sources for their possible influence on Poe. In "'The Masque of the Red Death': Yet Another Source"
(*PoeS* 16:13–14), Michael Tritt notes verbal parallels and similar settings in Poe's tale and Byron's *Childe Harold's Pilgrimage*, Canto III,
in which gay revelry at a ball in Brussels precedes the intervention of
sinister fate. In "Poe's Use of *The Tempest* and the Bible in 'The
Masque of the Red Death'" (*ELN* 20:31–39), Patrick Cheney discusses tragic and ironic reversals of mythic patterns in Shakespeare
and the Bible. Suggesting that abuse of the human will can result in
a kind of masquerade, Cheney claims that the Biblical associations
of the number seven receive ironic treatment in Poe's hands. In "William Wilson: A Possible Source for the Name" (*PoeS* 16:13), David
K. Jackson calls our attention to a Richmond schoolteacher named
Wilson who was active just before Poe attended Clarke's Academy.

Two explicatory notes unmentioned in previous surveys deserve brief citation. Burton R. Pollin detects echoes of *Measure for Measure* and *Macbeth* in "The Conqueror Worm" (*Expl* 40[1982]:25–28), while Nicholas Canady compares "William Wilson" and the "Sonnet —Silence" as studies of twin entity, corporate and incorporate silence (*Expl* 40[1982]:28–29).

In "Edgar Allan Poe and John G. Chapman: Their Treatment of the Dismal Swamp and the Wissahiccon" (*SAR*, pp. 245–75), Pollin turns what probably should have been a note into a laboriously detailed survey of Poe's allusions to the American painter John Gadsby Chapman. An engraving of Chapman's "The Lake of the Dismal Swamp" appeared in the 1839 *Knickerbocker* and could have inspired several minor details in Poe's fiction. Poe may have also derived his "Morning on the Wissahiccon" from Benjamin Matthias's "The Wissahiccon" (*Southern Literary Messenger*, 1835), though the "wild, romantic, and imposing" scenery in the earlier tale may not comport with that in Poe's sketch, the vista possessing, he says, "aught of the sublime." Poe's impact on the visual arts is exemplified by a gift-book edition of *The James Carling Illustrations of Edgar Allan Poe's The Raven*, ed. Roscoe Brown Fisher (Fisher Publications, [1982]), a volume that also presents brief essays by various contributors. George F. Scheer surveys the life of James Carling, Bruce K. B. Laughton provides notes on the handsome illustrations, and the late Thomas Ollive Mabbott recounts the poem's composition. Floyd Stovall adds a concluding note to this attractive book for collectors. In "Poe, Mrs. Osgood, and 'Annabel Lee'" (*SAR*, pp. 275–80), Buford Jones and Kent Ljungquist advance as a probable source of Poe's poem Frances Sargent Osgood's "The Life Voyage. A Ballad," a poem appearing in *Graham's Magazine* (1842) and in a volume (1846) reviewed by Poe. The two poems share the phrase "sounding sea," a fair maiden of "bright eyes," the presence of angels and demons, and fairy-tale settings by the sea.

In "'A Great and Original Genius': Hayne Champions Poe" (*SLJ* 16:105–12), Rayburn S. Moore explores Poe's impact on the late 19th-century poet Paul Hamilton Hayne. Insisting that literature be judged on its own merits rather than on allegations of misconduct, Hayne began his defense of Poe in magazine columns that took issue with harsh British criticism. Hayne also reviewed the fourth volume of Rufus Griswold's edition of Poe and made an interesting comparison between *Arthur Gordon Pym* and *Robinson Crusoe* (See *ALS 1976*, p. 33). His championship of Poe continued in the pages of *Russell's Magazine, Appleton's Journal,* and in correspondence with Elizabeth Oakes Smith. At the end of his informative essay, Moore reprints Hayne's memorial poem occasioned by a series of tributes to Poe in the 1870s.

Several essays investigate Poe's affinities with 20th-century authors. Catherine Rainwater's "Encounters with the 'White Sphinx': Poe's Influence in Some Early Works of H. G. Wells" (*ELT* 26:31–51) suggests that the "white sphinx" in Wells's *The Time Machine* was inspired by the "shrouded human figure" in *Pym*. She also notes Wells's use of Poe-esque settings and disoriented narrators in "The Red Room," *The Island of Dr. Moreau,* and *The First Men in the Moon*. Starting with a paper on Poe delivered at the University of Nebraska literary society in 1895, Merrill Maguire Skaggs's "Poe's Shadow on *Alexander's Bridge*" (*MissQ* 35[1982]:365–74) shows convincingly how Poe's presence haunted the career of Willa Cather. The central theme of "Usher"—a house divided—influences imagery and characterization in Cather's first novel. In "Shadows Striking Eldorado: Poe's Presence in Abbey's *The Brave Cowboy*" (*SwAL* 7 [1982]:24–27), Kent Ljungquist notes Edward Abbey's allusions to "Mountains of the Moon" and his adaption of other motifs from the Western quest exemplified in Poe's 1849 ballad. Burton R. Pollin notes the repetition of the phrase "dream within a dream" in James Clavell's best seller ("Poe in Clavell's *Shogun: A Novel of Japan,*" *PoeS* 6:13).

Other essays do not focus so much on explicit influence as on affinities with Poe. In "The Eye and the Portrait: The Fantastic in Poe, Hawthorne, and Gogol" (*SSF* 20:307–15), Sylvie L. F. Richards, using Todorov's theories as a departure, suggests that the eye is the prime organ of the fantastic in "The Oval Portrait." She also discusses Hawthorne's "The Prophetic Pictures" and Gogol's "The Portrait." In a gracefully written essay, "The Detective Fiction of Poe and Borges" (*CL* 35:262–75), Maurice J. Bennett sees Jorge Luis Borges's "Death and the Compass" as both a parody and serious rewriting of Poe's tales of ratiocination. Both writers, insisting on the intelligibility of the universe, use the detective genre as a formal antithesis to the chaos of human experience. Although Borges is receiving increasing attention as a prime literary heir of Poe's methods, he is not the only author of mystery stories to be so influenced, as Peter Wolfe's survey of over 30 scholarly or popular books on the detective genre attests ("The Critics Did It: An Essay-Review," *MFS* 29:389–433).

Two commercial editions of Poe's works appeared this year. *The Other Poe: Comedies and Satires*, ed. David Galloway (Penguin), is a medium-priced paperback containing 19 comic and satirical tales. Except for "The Man That Was Used Up," singled out by Galloway for its satire of military technology, the texts are identified as "the Scribner edition of the works," actually a reprint of the Stedman-Woodberry edition. Galloway provides informative explanatory notes and an introduction tracing anticipations of serious themes in Poe's satires, the "savage comedy" of early tales, for example, foreshadowing murderous elements in "The Tell-Tale Heart" and "The Black Cat." Furthermore, the grotesque devices and characters in Poe's tales anticipate developments in the fiction of Crane, Anderson, West, Faulkner, and Heller. In sum, Galloway's edition presents Poe as a writer sensitive to the political, literary, and scientific fashions of his day, a figure who found in humor a convenient cleansing and distancing technique. *The Unabridged Edgar Allan Poe* (Running Press) purports to provide first printings of the full range of the tales and poems, though a cursory check of the contents reveals that this policy is not followed for "Usher," "Ligeia," and "The Island of the Fay." Included are seldom reprinted pieces, such as "Lines on Ale," "Instinct vs. Reason," "Desultory Notes on Cats," "Morning on the Wissahiccon," and "Some Secrets of the Magazine Prison House." Full texts of *Politian, The Journal of Julius Rodman*, and *Arthur Gordon Pym* also appear. The editor Tam Mossman offers the dubious assertion that "the first version of a poem or story had a fresh, direct, vivid approach that was obscured in later changes."

A critic who would certainly disagree is Benjamin Franklin Fisher IV. Continuing his study of Poe's revisions (see *ALS 1976*, pp. 36–38) in "How to Write a Blackwood Article: Revise, Revise, Revise" (*Interpretations*, 12[1980]:22–30), Fisher notes tightened structure, reduced comedy, and less reliance on sources in several tales. Poe's improved sound effects in prose reflect his growing preference for poetic suggestiveness over concrete detail. Fisher also notes textual irregularities in the Harrison edition, as Kent Ljungquist does for the Mabbott and Pollin editions in a review-essay, "The Growth of

Poe Texts," *Review* 5 (Virginia), pp. 49–57. (See also David B. Kesterson, "New Resources for Poe Studies," *SLJ* 15:102–6.)

The Poe scholar now has at his disposal a wealth of textual and bibliographical material, sometimes perplexing in its diversity and range of quality. In addition to "Current Poe Bibliography" (*PoeS* 16:34–38), compiled by J. Lasley Dameron, Thomas C. Carlson, John E. Reilly, and Fisher, *The Annual Bibliography of Gothic Studies* (Gothic Press) now appears in chapbook form. Compiled by Frederick S. Frank, Gary Crawford, Ljungquist, and Fisher, it picks up out-of-the-way items in secondary literature on the supernatural. "Fugitive Poe References" (*PoeS* 16:7–13) continues in the hands of Fisher, who helpfully records items that have not appeared in the Hynemann or Dameron-Cauthen volumes. Fisher has also provided "The Residual Gothic Impulse," in *Horror Literature: A Core Collection and Reference Guide* (Bowker, [1981], pp. 177–220), a primary bibliographical tool that finds Poe "residual" because his Gothic touches seemed incongruous during an age of prevailing optimism. Poe also receives mention from other contributors to this volume, most notably in Steve Eng's pioneering survey of "Supernatural Verse in English" (pp. 401–52), which notes Poe's influence on major figures and on minor poets, such as Charles Gardette, Stanley Coblentz, and Clark Ashton Smith.

ii. Books and General Studies

Dennis Eddings has edited a collection of essays by various contributors, *The Naiad Voice: Essays on Poe's Satiric Hoaxing* (Associated Faculty Press). All but one of the pieces have been previously published, though the editor adds an introductory note that sets forth the problem of reconciling Poe's comic and serious tonalities. Eddings returns to the same crux in the concluding essay, "A Suggestion on the Unity of Poe's Fiction" (pp. 155–65). The heart of his argument is the notion of duplicity, a characteristic of the physical universe mirrored in the psyche of man. With a clever reading of "The Devil in the Belfry," he shows how an imbalance between imagination and reason heightens this sense of duplicity. It is finally up to the reader to observe how comic and serious elements merge in Poe's artistic rendering of the unity of God's universe. In sum, Eddings makes a valiant, intelligent attempt to find common ground in the ironic and visionary approaches to Poe. Several essays in this volume touch upon general matters of irony and point of view; those by Bruce I. Weiner, J. Gerald Kennedy, and Kent Ljungquist have been revised for their reappearance.

The title of the other critical book to appear this year, *Why Poe Drank Liquor* (Sherwood Sugden), suggests Marion Montgomery's condescension toward Poe. In one sense, this flippant title, taken from a speech by Flannery O'Connor, is a misnomer, since Montgomery exploits Poe as a convenient foil in his campaign to ascertain the validity of a Christian vision. This fascinating and infuriating book raises many important philosophical and political issues, but Poe generally plays the role of a false prophet, a harbinger of modern maladies in direct contrast to O'Connor, the proponent of forgotten but essential truths. One has the uneasy sense that Poe's ox is being gored via an assault from the intellectual Right, since numerous gratuitous digressions and opinions smack of the author's righteous conservatism. Montgomery's comments on failed romanticism deserve an airing, but one wishes that he had pursued his task in a less tendentious manner, that is, with less zeal in endorsing O'Connor's artistry at Poe's expense.

Either the primary or secondary focus of several essays in *The Haunted Dusk*, Poe receives fullest treatment from J. Gerald Kennedy in "Phantasms of Death in Poe's Fiction" (pp. 37–63). Arguing that the Gothic tradition afforded a means of articulating man's fear of mortality, Kennedy identifies four conceptions of death: (1) annihilation, or terror of man's creaturely condition; (2) compulsion, or longing for the abyss; (3) separation, or estrangement from the Beautiful Other; and (4) transformation, or depiction of spiritual reunion. Kennedy's penchant for categories owes something to the large-scale, encyclopedic survey of attitudes toward mortality in Philippe Aries's *The Hour of Our Death* and also draws from Ernest Becker's *The Denial of Death*. While Kennedy will invite skepticism with his claim that Poe's visionary works reflect a material system that leads inevitably to universal dissolution, he does succeed in placing Poe's attitudes in an identifiable cultural context.

Designating Poe as an important literary forebear, other studies in this collection treat him in a more orthodox manner. Howard Kerr aligns two of Henry James's supernatural tales with the Gothic tradition, although his suggestion that "The Ghostly Rental" marks a conscious demystification of "Usher" turns up little firm evidence ("James's Last Early Supernatural Tales: Hawthorne Demagnetized, Poe Depoeticized," pp. 133–48). With appropriate nods toward "Ligeia" and "Masque," Barton Levi St. Armand shows how Harriet Prescott Spofford transformed features of the Gothic romance (pp. 99–119). Alan Gribben's survey of Mark Twain's occult interests contains useful queries about Poe's influence (pp. 169–89), and G. R. Thompson, by mentioning Poe's ventures into the supernatural, clearly outlines Washington Irving's pioneering achievements in the tradition of ghostly literature (pp. 11–36).

In contrast to Thompson's acknowledgement of psychological ambiguities in Gothic fiction, Donald Ringe's chapter on Poe in *American Gothic* (pp. 128–51) appears simplistic and unresolved. Discounting psychological readings, Ringe allows that Ligeia's return, taken as a literal event, reflects opposition to rational explanations of supernaturalism that prevailed in 19th-century literary circles. When he turns his attention to "Usher," "A Descent into the Maelström," and "The Pit and the Pendulum," however, the rational observer plays such an important role in his analysis that one comes to doubt that Poe's commitment to the unexplained supernatural remained ironclad. Ringe's conclusion is that Poe neither explained away nor insisted on the reality of horrific experience.

Poe's contribution to the genre of fantasy is the subject of two essays, both appearing in the multi-volume *The Survey of Modern Fantasy Literature* (Salem Press). Kent Ljungquist's survey of "Poe's Short Fiction" (IV, 1665–78) addresses Poe's critical comments on Fantasy in which he defines its essential constituents as novelty, unexpectedness, disproportion, and incoherence. He also implies that a conscious attempt to accentuate "antagonistical elements" or "novel combinations" could heighten fantastic effects. These notions are then applied to over a dozen tales in Poe's fictional canon. In an essay on *Arthur Gordon Pym* in the same series, Richard Kopley (III, 1092–94) provides a compendium of critical approaches to Poe's narrative. Given the brief space allowed in a reference work, he marshals a surprisingly detailed survey of *Pym*'s influence on writers and illustrators.

iii. Individual Works and Special Concerns

Studies of individual tales produce the usual mixed results. In "Victim and Victimizer: Poe's 'The Cask of Amontillado'" (*Interpretations* 15:26–30), Leonard W. Engel advances the unsurprising assertion that enclosure is a source of both terror and delight to Montresor. Engel also covers the same motif in two studies unmentioned in previous annual surveys, "Obsession, Madness, and Enclosure in Poe's 'Ligeia' and 'Morella,'" (*CollL* 9[1982]:140–46) and "Truth and Detection: Poe's Tales of Ratiocination and his Use of Enclosure," (*Clues* 3[1982]:83–86).

A more complex analysis of enclosure distinguishes Geoffrey G. Harpham's "Permeability and the Grotesque: 'The Masque of the Red Death,'" chapter 5 in his learned and witty study, *On the Grotesque: Strategies of Contradiction in Art and Literature* (Princeton, [1982] pp. 106–21). Harpham defines the grotesque as an aesthetic of unnatural partition and the arabesque as a form of organic recombination. In addition to attending to play on the word "disconcert" in "Masque," he sees the tale as a kind of "inside narrative," in which the knowing storyteller recounts a "read death." Although Harpham may strain credulity when he suggests that words become a kind of plague in Poe's works, he does give a fascinating reading of the structure and theme of "Masque." (See also the discussion of Garber's "Centers of Nostalgia" below.) The rest of Harpham's book will be especially useful to subsequent students of the grotesque and arabesque.

In "Kinesthetic Imagery and Helplessness in Three Poe Tales" (*SSF* 20:73–77), Lawrence J. Oliver asserts, somewhat inexplicably, that "The Pit and the Pendulum" and "A Descent into the Maelström" lack strong pictorial qualities. On more solid ground, Rochie Lawes, in "The Dimensions of Terror: Mathematical Imagery in 'The Pit and the Pendulum'" (*PoeS* 16:5–7), claims that Poe's narrator has the manner and training of a mathematician. His vocabulary deriving from the calculus and numerology, he is also concerned with the periodicity and dimensions of the pendulum. Mathematics thus becomes an appropriate skill, a sufficient foundation for dealing with extreme terror.

Daryl E. Jones, in "Poe's Siren: Character and Meaning in 'Ligeia'" (*SSF* 20:33–37), suggests that the story's theme is the duality of the individual will, alternately submissive and aggressive. He provides evidence from Greek mythology to support the notion that Ligeia is a siren. In "Sailing into the Self: Jung, Poe, and 'MS. Found in a Bottle' " (*TSL* [1981]:66–74), Steven K. Hoffman claims that "MS. found in a Bottle" enacts a process of Jungian individuation intensified by contact with the tides and whirlpools of the unconscious mind. His sharply written essay traces the narrator's metamorphosis from sterile rationalism to artistic awakening, though previous scholarship on the "Jungian Poe" by Martin Bickman, Barton Levi St. Armand, Eric Carlson and David Saliba is not cited. (See *ALS 1975*, pp. 46–47; *ALS 1976*, pp. 40, 44; *ALS 1978*, pp. 38–39; and *ALS 1980*, pp. 51–52.)

Other studies seek to establish firmer relationships between Poe and his culture. In "Poe and the Tory Tradition: The Fear of Jacquerie in 'A Tale of the Ragged Mountains' " (*ESQ* 29:25–30), Andrew Horn shows that Poe derived only cursory descriptions from Macaulay's essays. (See the essay by Muktar A. Isani mentioned in *ALS 1973*, p. 36.) By rejecting the political tenor of Macaulay's record of events, Poe displayed a characteristic fear of mobocracy. While J. Lasley Dameron's contention that C. Auguste Dupin is a hero, a self-sacrificing agent of justice, may not sound novel, his further development of this notion does indeed make a convincing case for Poe's detective as a cultural prototype deriving from Plato's Socrates and the rational values of the Renaissance ("Poe's C. Auguste Dupin," *Tennessee Phililogical Bulletin* 17 [1980]:5–15). Continuing the series of pamphlets produced by the Baltimore Poe Society and the Enoch Pratt Free Library, *The Grand and the Fair: Poe in the American Landscape* by Kent Ljungquist looks at the short shrift given to Poe by students of American scenery, analyzes *The Journal of Julius Rodman* as an example of Poe's inability to integrate beauty and grandeur, and investigates "Ligeia" as a more successful fictional reconciliation of these aesthetic categories. In 1982, Alexander G. Rose also published *A History of the Edgar Allan Poe Society of Baltimore: A Footnote to a Cultural History of Baltimore* (Baltimore Poe Society), a clear record of the organization's role in stimulating Poe scholarship.

Frederick Garber's "Centers of Nostalgia," chapter 9 in *The Autonomy of the Self from Richardson to Huysmans* (Princeton [1982], pp. 220–25), also investigates selected landscapes, especially those tales that present an oscillation between the values of aloofness and association, autonomy and engagement, separateness and participation. In the fictional landscapes, Poe is not interested in nature per se but in the individual self's ability to work out its own autonomy. Garber makes the added point that walls and partitions in Poe's fiction are all self-enclosures. (See the discussion of essays by Engel and Harpham above.) In addition to the landscape tales, he discusses "Masque," "Cask," and "Ligeia." This penetrating, subtly argued essay fails, however, to cite much relevant Poe scholarship.

In "That 'Daughter of Old Time': Science in the Writings of Edgar Allan Poe" (*PAPA* 9:36–41), B. F. Fisher acknowledges that Poe could endorse the claims of science when they did not result in the pitfall of sterile rationalism. Fisher devotes most of his analysis to the "Sonnet—To Science." When he turns his attention to "The System of Dr. Tarr and Professor Fether," he makes the original point that this tale represents a comic treatment of the imbalance between reason and intuition.

Two critical studies that deal more exclusively with Poe's poems appeared in 1983. Christian Kock's "The Poetics of Poe's Last Poems," published in *The Romantic Heritage,* ed. Karsten Engleberg (Pubs. of the Dept. of English, Univ. of Copenhagen, pp. 105–22), is a rather unfocused study of musical elements in "The Bells" and "Annabel Lee." Kent Ljungquist's reading of "The Coliseum" connects Poe to a poetic tradition dealing with ruins, often exemplified in the form of a dialogue that embraces complex feelings and unresolved cultural tensions; " 'The Coliseum': A Dialogue on Ruins" (*PoeS* 16:32–33) locates a prose analogue in C. F. Volney's *The Ruins* and detects elements of serious wordplay in Poe's poem. While approaches such as the one advanced by Steve Eng (mentioned at the end of section 1 above) lay a firm foundation for intelligent study of Poe's verse, the poetry remains the most neglected part of his literary output.

iv. Poe's Attitudes Toward Writing, Language, and Authorship

In one of the more stimulating essays of the year, "Edgar Allan Poe and the Life of Literature" (*EdL*, pp. 3–12), Bruce Robbins suggests that for Poe writing is synonymous with salvation, that the author who has found an audience has achieved something on the order of a miracle. A problematic effort to overcome individual iso-lation, writing is comparable to sending messages into a void, an act of faith implicit in "MS. Found in a Bottle." Robbins notes that Poe's satires, like "The Literary Life of Thingum Bob," reduce writ-ing to a minimal set of appliances, the raw materials of the periodical press. A form of literary survival can, however, be achieved by using extraordinary materials: a symbolic stylus of iron, a special parch-ment in "The Gold Bug," blood instead of ink in *Pym*. Robbins shows how a sophisticated approach, informed by modern theory, can make us look at neglected tales in fresh ways.

Michael T. Gilmore attempts to put Poe's attitudes toward lan-guage in a cultural context by claiming that material reality emerged as a victor in the 19th-century contest between words and things. Poe, however, both affirmed and challenged the national skepticism about the artistic vocation in "Usher." By allowing Usher's domain to collapse, Poe acknowledges that the palace of art lacks a firm con-nection to practical reality, but "The Mad Trist," nevertheless, over-turns commonly held assumptions about literary powerlessness. At the conclusion of "Usher," a form of writing anticipates and engen-ders real events. Reading a book in "Usher," rather than showing lit-erature's impotence, actually opens one to the compelling forces of irrationality. The topic of Gilmore's tentative, provisional, and thoughtful discussion, which also deals with Hawthorne and Mel-ville, will no doubt repay his further attention ("Words and Things in Antebellum American Literature," *Brandeis Essays in Literature*, ed. John Hazel Smith, pp. 85–99).

In " 'The Voice in the Text': Poe's 'Some Words with a Mummy' " (*PoeS* 16:1–4), Michael Williams claims that Poe's satire posits a skepticism about recovering the past through language. As history becomes explicated, annotated, and increasingly refined by layers of verbiage, any derivation of an authentic "voice" from the past becomes problematic. Rather than helping to satirize topical con-cerns of Poe's era, the tale's narrative frame and punning texture disclose that history may ultimately be an ambiguous fable colored by a succession of interpretive confusions.

In a rather abstract essay that touches upon "Berenice," "Mo-rella," and "Usher" ("Poe: Writing and the Unconscious," *BuR* 28: 144–69), Gregory S. Jay discusses the conjunction of sexuality, phi-losophy, and textuality in Poe's tales. In his discussion of the role of the unconscious, the purported "truth" of writing suffers twin assaults. First, since Poe freely repeats material from other texts, the notion of originality is undercut. Moreover, his doublings of character call into question the notion of unique personal identity as well as the ability to communicate the characteristics of discrete personality. These concerns are reflected in his obsession with plagiarism and family inheritance.

John Carlos Rowe strikes a more polemical tone in his chapter on *Pym* in *Through the Custom House* (pp. 91–110), an attempt to recover "eccentric" texts from obscurity. Like Williams and Jay, Rowe finds that the doubling of reading and writing processes in Poe's works creates epistemological uncertainty. The numerous exemplars of textuality in *Pym*—the preface, fabricated stories, forged notes, books, writing implements, paper and ink—indicate that the narrative marks an adventure of the writing and written self. (For comments on the chapter's original appearance in article form, see *ALS 1977*, p. 44.)

The topic of Poe's interest in language raises the issue of his own unique contributions to 19th-century idiom. Burton R. Pollin, in "Poe's Word Coinages: A Supplement" (*PoeS* 16:39–40), supplements the coverage in his own *Poe, Creator of Words* (see *ALS 1974*, p. 32) with a survey of 24 entries in the uncollected writings. Alerting us to some amusing verbal sleight of hand, Pollin may value Poe's originality over soundness in language, especially in view of his idiosyncratic compound forms.

This is perhaps the best place to mention Nancy Harrowitz's "The Body of the Detective Model: Charles Sanders Peirce and Edgar Allan Poe," chapter 9 in *Dupin, Holmes, Peirce: The Sign of Three*, eds. Thomas A. Sebeok and Umberto Eco (Indiana, pp. 179–97). While those not well-versed in semiotics will find this essay heavy going, Harrowitz does offer the interesting tidbit that the American philosopher Peirce was a devotee of the detective genre. She also finds in Poe's tales of ratiocination the first fictional use of the method of *abduction*. A term roughly synonymous with "hypothesis" or "presumption," "abduction" is a largely unrecognized epistemological mode that was defined by Peirce. Despite the volume's title, other essays in this collection treat Poe with less amplitude.

Finally, two review-essays appeared in 1983 that survey the impact of French critical theory. Donald Pease provides an overview of the Lacan-Derrida–Barbara Johnson debate in "Marginal Politics and 'The Purloined Letter': A Review-Essay" (*PoeS* 16:18–23). Surveying more recent analyses in "The Fold is the Thing: Poe Criticism in France in the Last Five Years" (*PoeS* 16:25–31), Henri Justin notes how French critics have fixed their attention on the verbal motifs of "letter," "text," and "double" to the point of using these and other words as stimuli for capricious puns. Despite the best efforts of the French critics, the topic of Poe's comic and serious word play has yet to find its authoritative interpreter.

Worcester Polytechnic Institute

4. Melville

Robert Milder

The event of the year was the discovery of an extraordinary trove of Melville family letters and other materials (including twenty manuscript pages labeled "First draught of Typee. . . .") in the corner of a barn in upstate New York. The repercussions of so large and unexpected a find will not be known for some time, but already scholars are looking ahead to significant revisions in the biographical portrait of Melville. Apart from the find, the most that can be said for Melville studies in 1983, save for a handful of contributions, is that they are probably in transition. Scholarship was sparse but will certainly revive under the stimulus of the new papers. The prospects for criticism seem more uncertain. Considering the general ferment in literary theory, critical work this year was surprisingly conventional, especially after last year's experimentation. Hardly anyone came forward with a New Critical "reading," but neither did many writers know how else to approach a work with wholeness and method. The result was a criticism of fragments and footnotes that may persist until literary theory becomes more widespread and engages traditional criticism in a renovating debate about practice. Amid the year's collective uncertainties no pronounced trends were evident, though the drift toward Melville's later works continued. And by chance or not, nearly all of the year's longer writings dealt in one way or another with Melville and politics.

i. Editions, Bibliography, Biography, Scholarship

The Library of America's *Redburn, White-Jacket, Moby-Dick*, ed. G. Thomas Tanselle, is a convenient reader's edition that reprints the standard texts of *Redburn* and *White-Jacket* and previews the forthcoming Northwestern-Newberry *Moby-Dick*, supplementing these with a "Chronology" of Melville's career, a brief section of explanatory notes, and a seven-page "Note on the Texts" devoted largely to the editorial problems involved in establishing an authoritative *Moby-Dick*. Commentary on the new text will have to await the Northwestern-Newberry historical and textual appendices, but students of Melville can be thankful for Tanselle's decision to forego "modernization" in this popular volume and remain "as faithful to Melville's usage as surviving evidence permits." One editorial revision with important critical consequences is the reassignment of the "Oh, grassy glades!" passage in "The Gilder" from Ishmael to Ahab, a change considered by Hayford and Parker in the Norton edition of 1967 but never before adopted.

John Bryant's *Melville Dissertations, 1924–1980: An Annotated Bibliography and Subject Index* (Greenwood/The Melville Society) updates and expands the Myerson/Miller compilation of 1971 and describes (without evaluation) 531 dissertations wholly or in part about Melville; an introduction by Bryant enlarges upon his interim report of last year, "Trends in Melville Scholarship: Dissertations in the 1970s" (*MSEx* 50:12–14; see *ALS 1982*, p. 58), and surveys the development and character of Melville studies from the beginnings to the present. Another bibliography, *Herman Melville's Foreign Reputation: A Research Guide* (Hall), prepared by Leland R. Phelps with the assistance of Kathleen McCullough, lists all discoverable editions, translations, and adaptations of Melville's work published in 47 languages from Afrikaans to Vietnamese, plus a secondary literature on Melville published in non-English-speaking countries, including over 280 items in English. Entries are arranged chronologically within each language to allow scholars to trace the course of Melville studies in that language, and all materials contained in The Newberry Library's substantial collection of foreign Melville publications are so indicated. Supplementing the Phelps-McCullough guide, Emily Tall's "Herman Melville in the Soviet Union" (*MSEx* 54: 1–8) follows Melville's reputation in Czarist and post-Revolutionary Russia, sketches some of the general principles of Soviet literary criticism, and describes a few of the better Russian-language studies. According to Tall, Melville, though more respected than read, "has been integrated into the Soviet canon as a critic of religion, idealistic philosophy, and bourgeois society, a writer who, though disillusioned with America and apprehensive for its future, still believed in mankind, brotherhood, and humanistic ideals"—not so different a Melville from the one native critics have been finding. Daniel A. Wells adds a bit of evidence about Melville's American reputation in his latest compilation of magazine references, "Melville Allusions in the *Atlantic Monthly,* 1857–1900" (*MSEx* 55:14–15), which reminds us once again that "when Melville was remembered at all in these decades," it was as a man who had lived among the cannibals.

Publications from *The New York Times* to *Connoisseur* carried news of the Melville discovery, but a firsthand account, "Finding the New Melville Papers" (*MSEx* 56:1–3), is offered by John and Carolyn DeMarco of the Lyrical Ballad Bookstore in Saratoga Springs, New York, who describe acquiring and exploring the materials and arranging for their transfer to the New York Public Library. The prolonged sifting we can expect for the new biographical information is anticipated in Carl L. Anderson's "The Minister's Advice to Elizabeth Melville" (*MSEx* 54:10–12), a footnote to Walter D. Kring and Jonathan S. Carey's "Two Discoveries Concerning Herman Melville" (*PMHS* 87:137–41; see *ALS 1976,* p. 47). Reconsidering Dr. Henry Whitney Bellows's suggestion of 1867 that Elizabeth leave Melville by submitting to a feigned kidnapping, Anderson finds Bellows's recommendation "extreme" yet not wholly unwarranted given "the law regarding separation and divorce which then prevailed." Biographers and local historians may have some use for John P. Runden's "Old School Ties: Melville, the Columbia Grammar School, and the New Yorkers" (*MSEx* 55:1–5), which reprints without comment the Columbia Grammar School Register of 1828–30 on the grounds that it "reveals the childhood origin of social and professional relationships which Melville scholars most often have judged to have had their beginnings in adult life." Also marginal but not without interest is Hennig Cohen's "The Real Israel Potter" (*MSEx* 53:7–11), a transcription of documents from the National Archives and the Rhode Island State Archives that show the failure of the historical Potter's attempt to secure a Revolutionary veteran's pension; Henry Trumbull's *Life and Remarkable Adventures of Israel R. Potter,* Melville's major source, had left this point ambiguous.

ii. General Studies

While only passingly about Melville, J. J. Healy's "Structuralism Applied: American Literature and its Subordination to Structure"

(*ArielE* 14:35–51) is an absorbing essay about cultural identity that renovates 1950s theories of American literary exceptionalism by arguing that the preoccupation with myth and symbol described by Chase, Feidelson, and others can be understood as a sign of the American's "innate predilection for the paradigmatic," or his "submission to" and "heightened consciousness of" the underlying "*forms* and *structures* of experience and history" addressed on a more abstract level by Lévi-Strauss and Lacan. Another theoretical essay, "Archetypal Depth Criticism and Melville" (*CE* 45:695–704) by Ralph Maud, uses Melville illustratively to introduce literary critics to the work of "post-Jungian" psychologist James Hillman, whose writings on " 'soul-making' " are not well served by Maud's fragments.

After a fine introduction in which he promises to show how the story of Cain and Abel exemplified for Melville "the close and hidden relationship between fraternity as a personal and social ideal, and fratricide as a fact of human history," Wyn Kelley in "Melville's Cain" (*AL* 55:24–40) settles down into a competent but unexceptional survey of the two traditional interpretations of Cain as they appear in Melville's work, the Romantic (Cain as tormented rebel) and the Augustinian (Cain as criminal). Curiously, Kelley's well-informed article neglects one of the most interesting and important sources for Melville's Cain—Pierre Bayle's discussion of the Gnostic sect of Cainites, whose vision of the Old Testament Jehovah as a usurper led them to invert the Decalogue and combine rebel and criminal in a way that prefigures Ahab's position in "The Candles." Another promising essay, "Melville's Comic Debate: Geniality and the Aesthetics of Repose" (*AL* 55:151–70) by John Bryant, labors under its terminology as it tries to argue that Melville's fiction after *Pierre* is characterized by an opposition "between integrative (genialist) and subversive (confidence man) sensibilities," which Melville ultimately resolves in the "wary confidence" of the " 'genial misanthrope.' "

Among the year's political approaches, Kristin Herzog's "Women and Savages in Melville" (*Women, Ethnics, and Exotics* [Tenn.], pp. 55–101) explores *Typee, Omoo, Mardi, Pierre,* and a few of the tales in light of Herzog's thesis that 19th-Century American writers saw women and nonwhites as having "an innate power," redemptive or demonic, "which the white civilized male has lost or repressed." Herzog's Noble Savage and middle-class "True Woman" make an odd pair, but the deeper objection to Herzog's book is that it combines an unexamined 1980s ideology about cultural repression with an old-fashioned generalist's methodology untouched by the pertinent insights of feminists, Marxists, structuralists, or poststructuralists. Handsomely printed and illustrated and more scholarly than Herzog's book, *Melville's Major Fiction: Politics, Theology, and Imagination* (Northern Illinois) by James Duban "seeks to meet . . . the challenge of 'a new historicism'" by locating Melville's work within contemporary debates on messianic nationalism, democratic individualism, slavery, the Mexican War, the miracles controversy, and Transcendentalism, among others. Duban is knowledgeable about his issues and manages his argument fairly well, but in practice his version of the new historicism consists of the discovery of analogies between a text and a context, the contexts themselves varying widely through Duban's seven chapters and represented with disproportionate frequency by an article from the *American Whig Review* (which Melville never subscribed to and may not have read). Missing from Duban's series of discrete readings—Duban touches on all of Melville's full-length works save *Israel Potter*—is a coherent sense of the nature and roots of Melville's political and religious commitments and of their evolution from book to book within a lived career.

In contrast, the originality of Michael Paul Rogin's *Subversive Genealogy: The Politics and Art of Herman Melville* (Knopf) is its effort to understand Melville's writings as they grew out of the experienced political microcosm of the Melvill[e], Gansevoort, and Shaw families, whose members assumed a spectrum of roles and ideological postures as they responded to the legacy of the Revolutionary fathers. Ambitious in its coverage of nearly all of Melville's work, Rogin's book is most exciting in its early chapters, when it stays closest to the family. Even here, however, Rogin's "family" is a gallery of tableaux vivants, not a milieu, and readers may question whether the symbolic poses Rogin assigns his figures impinged on a developing consciousness in anything like the manner he implies. In place of a subtle work of psychobiography that would portray Melville internalizing and reshaping the politicized world of the family, Rogin fashions his argument from outside in, juxtaposing biographical, literary, and historical evidence in elliptical, staccato sentences that leave the receptive and creative "Melville" untouched. Impressive but unsatisfying, and prone like Duban's book to a reductive allegorical criticism, *Subversive Genealogy* is a work of energy and ingenuity that makes one admire the skill of the performer without necessarily benefiting from the performance. For a different estimate of Rogin's achievement, readers should consult Richard H. Brodhead's fine untitled review (*NCF* 38:214–19), which also comments perceptively on books by Bainard Cowan, David Simpson, and Merton M. Sealts, Jr., all from 1982.

iii. *Typee* through *White-Jacket*

Aside from Herzog's chapter and sections in Duban's and Rogin's books—both authors are near their best on *Redburn* and *White-Jacket*—scarcely anything appeared on Melville's early writing, a marked contrast to the *Typee* boomlet of 1982. The development of and prospects for *Typee* criticism are among Robert Milder's subjects in "Melville in the South Seas, Again" (*ESQ* 29:99–111), a review-essay that discusses the Library of America's *Typee, Omoo, Mardi,* Milton R. Stern's *Critical Essays on Herman Melville's "Typee,"* and Thomas F. Heffernan's *Stove by a Whale*; Milder also remarks at length on T. Walter Herbert, Jr.'s effort to combine literary criticism with history and anthropology in *Marquesan Encounters: Melville and the Meaning of Civilization* (1980). Consistent with this year's political readings, Kenneth Alan Hovey's "*White-Jacket* vs. *Mr. Midshipman Easy*" (*MSEx* 56:13–15) presents Melville's fifth book as "a many-side critique" of Captain Frederick Marryat's romanticized portrait of life at sea and defense of authoritarianism and class privilege. The only other contribution on Melville's early work is Kris Lackey's "Charting Chartless *Mardi*" (*MSEx* 56:7–9), a picturesque map of the voyages of Taji, Hautia, and Aleema's avengers.

iv. *Moby-Dick*

Moby-Dick is one of several texts Lawrence Buell discusses in "Literature and Scripture in New England Between the Revolution and the Civil War" (*NDEJ* 15:1–28), an excellent piece of scholarly criticism that traces the literary use of Biblical narrative from Timothy Dwight's Scripture-based *The Conquest of Canaan* (1785) to the efforts of Emerson, Melville, and Emily Dickinson to revitalize

Biblical stories by reconceiving them as myths and even to create a new scripture themselves. Illustrative of this move toward allegory is Melville's treatment of the Jonah story in Father Mapple's sermon and "Jonah Historically Regarded," which subvert the literal authority of the Biblical narrative in order to salvage its core of spiritual truth. Bainard Cowan had argued similarly in *Exiled Waters: "Moby-Dick" and the Crisis of Allegory* (see *ALS 1982*, pp. 68–69), but Buell's solid historicism sharpens and confirms Cowan's theoretical presentation of Romantic allegory, just as Cowan's new-fashioned reading of the Mapple chapters vastly enriches Buell's example.

In Michael Paul Rogin's *"Moby-Dick* and the American 1848" (*Subversive Genealogy*, pp. 102–51) and James Duban's "Nationalism and Providence in Ishmael's White World" (*Melville's Major Fiction*, pp. 82–148), *Moby-Dick* is an allegory of the impending disaster of the American ship of state brought about by the betrayal of Revolutionary ideals during the Mexican War and the crisis over slavery. To this dark picture Duban adds another cloud by arguing (unconvincingly) that Ishmael is a flawed Jeremiah whose millennialist "outlook and historiography make him an unwitting post facto accomplice to his captain's worst nationalistic transgressions."

Among the general essays on *Moby-Dick*, Christopher S. Durer's "Mocking the 'Grand Programme': Irony and After in *Moby-Dick*" (*RMR* 36[1982]:249–58) traces four stages in an "ironic education" by which Ishmael moves from a half-belief in Providential order to a "'creative isolation'" that realizes Melville's "search for a new 'natural man.'" Persuasive in his general thesis, Durer is careless about point of view and writes as if the early chapters of *Moby-Dick* could be read as an unrefracted expression of the young Ishmael's state of mind. Ambitious but prolix, "Melville's New Witness: Cannibalism and the Microcosm-Macrocosm Cosmology in *Moby-Dick*" (*SIR* 22: 65–91) by Randall Bohrer invokes the analogical tradition from Pythagoras to Emerson in the course of describing a Melvillean world "made up of living mirrors" and sharkishly devouring itself in a "horrifying" pageant of cannibalism. At the other extreme, Mary Allen's bland and ingenuous "The Incredible Whale: Herman Melville" (*Animals in American Literature* [Illinois], pp. 18–35) is a cetological *Wild Kingdom* that appreciatively recounts the wonders of the flesh-and-blood whale. More useful for critical purposes are Robert M. Greenberg's remarks on the whale in "The Three-Day

Chase: Multiplicity and Coherence in *Moby-Dick*" (*ESQ* 29:91–98),
which shows how the descriptions of the whale in the chase scenes
extend "the epistemological and theological themes" of the middle
chapters, preserve the balance between a naturalistic and a supernatural Moby Dick, and help maintain the book's "ambivalence of
attitude" toward Ahab.

Critical theory pressed lightly on this year's readings of *Moby-
Dick*, but in at least one case its absence was missed. Arguing a
provocative thesis about Ishmael's "defensive" art, Daniel Cottom's
"Parody as Originality in *Moby-Dick*" (*ATQ* 51[1981]:165–81)
moves through half a dozen of last year's theory-tinged subjects (e.g.,
figuration, the search for origins, bodily identity, and wholeness and
mutilation) and gropingly regenerates perceptions of Derrida on
decentering, Bate and Bloom on the burden of the past, and de Man
on writing and originality. Though Cottom is partly a victim of the
critical lag to which all contributors to *ATQ* are vulnerable, the time
is past when inventive writers can mount a philosophical argument
hand-to-mouth in ignorance of contemporary theory. By contrast,
Louise K. Barnett's "Speech in *Moby-Dick*" (*SAF* 11:139–51) is
theoretical without being new. Applying the speech act vocabulary
of Austin and Searle to *Moby-Dick*, Barnett analyzes the speech
situations of Ahab and Ishmael symptomatically for what they reveal
about character and vision, which turns out to be a variation on the
tragic isolation vs. human community theme that critics have been
discovering for forty years.

Several of the year's articles addressed motifs or specific sections
of *Moby-Dick*. In " 'Warmest Climes but Nurse the Cruellest Fangs':
The Metaphysics of Beauty and Terror in *Moby-Dick*" (*SNNTS* 15:
332–43), Frank G. Novak, Jr., deals observantly with the recurrent
dualism in Melville's presentation of nature and the whale; the major
difference between Novak's reading of this pattern and Robert Zoellner's more philosophical one in *The Salt-Sea Mastodon* is that Novak
sees a "binary opposition" of rival perspectives that need to be held
in balance, Zoellner a vertical juxtaposition of surface and depth.
Edward Stone's "The Function of the Gams in *Moby-Dick*" (*CollL*
10:268–78) is a graceful essay that also treads a worn path, Stone's
most original point being that the gams allowed Melville to create
"the illusion of a real-life voyage" punctuated by contact with the

outside world without requiring him to have the *Pequod* do what "every other real-life whaler [would have] done: put into port." In a revisionist essay, "The Other Side of Steelkilt: The *Town-Ho's* Satire" (*ATQ* 52[1981]:237–53), Allen C. Austin inverts the "prevailing interpretation" that Steelkilt is "a noble, Christ-like character" and Radney a fiend by proposing that the *Town-Ho's* story is a "concealed allegory" in which "Heaven kills Christ (in the person of Radney) and permits Satan (attractively rendered in the figure of Steelkilt) to go free"—yet another example, Austin says, of the anti-Christian satire that runs through *Moby-Dick* and dramatizes Melville's belief that "man lives in an impersonal and inhumane universe from which he can expect only death." Another allegorical reading, Frank Shuffelton's "Going Through the Long Vaticans: Melville's 'Extracts' in *Moby-Dick*" (*TSLL* 25:528–40), recalls Viola Sachs's *The Game of Creation* in its effort to uncover a secret meaning that Melville encoded "in his book for eventual discovery by eagle-eyed, contemplative readers" who also have a knack for numerology. The key to *Moby-Dick's* depths, according to Shuffelton, is hidden prefiguratively in its eighty Extracts, which "form an implicit history of human consciousness" from the "revelations of the biblical scribes" down to "the self-conscious fictions and personal myths" of a mid-19th-Century "Romantic novelist."

Among the scholarly notes on *Moby-Dick*, John M. J. Gretchko's "New Evidence for Melville's Use of John Harris in *Moby-Dick*" (*SAR*, pp. 303–11) is a no-frills source study that documents Melville's debt to the 1705 edition of Harris's *Navigantium atque Itinerantium Bibliotheca; or, a Compleat Collection of Voyages and Travels*, not (as previously thought) to the edition of 1744–48, a much altered work. A second note by Gretchko, "Herman Melville's Soiled Sailors" (*Maledicta* 6[1982]:189–92), points out a pattern of scatalogical puns and anagrams that Gretchko claims (without elaboration) "fit into much greater underlying structures in *Moby-Dick*." Finally, in a note on "Ahab's Leg" (*MSEx* 54:14–16) David Ketterer suggests that Melville was deliberately obscure about which leg Ahab lost in order to force the reader to construct his own Ahab (thus "underlining the philosophical point that all human knowledge depends upon some form of projection") and to emphasize the hint of emasculation. Which leg did Ahab lose? The right, Ketterer speculates, as did three commentators before him, two of whom Ketterer acknowledges while supplementing his note in "Addendum to 'Ahab's Leg'" (*MSEx* 58[1984]:12).

v. Pierre

Once again critics turned profitably to *Pierre* and asked essential questions about what Melville was doing in his book. Unlike Milton R. Stern's G. K. Hall collection on *Typee*, which was weighted toward contemporary readings, *Critical Essays on Herman Melville's "Pierre; or, The Ambiguities"* (Hall), ed. Brian Higgins and Hershel Parker, is a scholar's volume which makes available most of the "known commentary" from 1852 through the Melville revival and reprints only a limited number of modern critical interpretations. Although these include many of the best responses to *Pierre*, from E. L. Grant Watson's pathfinding essay of 1930 to Higgins and Parker's own work, let the reader beware. From its Introduction, which draws on Parker's previous work and speculates broadly about the composition of *Pierre*, to its concluding "Prospects for Criticism on *Pierre*," which proselytizes for the "New Scholarship" (see *ALS 1981*, pp. 60–61), the Higgins-Parker volume is an exercise in critical canon-formation that institutionalizes the editors' preferred literary method and claims unwarranted authority for critical conclusions drawn from an arguable reading of the external evidence. Moreover, anyone seeking an alternative to the Higgins-Parker hegemony is left to discover it for himself, since unlike Stern's volume, which contained a comprehensive bibliography of *Typee* criticism, Higgins and Parker's contains no bibliography at all.

A fresh and vigorous essay, Michael S. Kearns's "Interpreting Intentional Incoherence: Towards a Disambiguation of Melville's *Pierre; or, The Ambiguities*" (*MMLA* 16:34–54) sets aside compositional hypotheses and tries to discover the book's "constructive intent" by investigating the nature of its sentences and the demands they make upon the reader. Assuming that the "errors and gross infelicities" of style in the early chapters "were crafted by Melville to achieve a certain end," Kearns analyzes them in detail and demonstrates how they violate the "normally preconscious processing strategies" of the reader. The purpose Kearns infers from Melville's rhetoric ("to stimulate not just a philological reform but a perceptual revolution") is too narrow to account for the totality of *Pierre*'s form, but Kearns leaves one point abundantly clear: no one who began a book in the style Melville did could have imagined he was addressing a popular audience unless he had entirely lost his senses.

For Paul Lewis in "Melville's *Pierre* and the Psychology of Incongruity" (*SNNTS* 15:183–201), the book's pattern of crisis and overreaction suggests a unifying intent to render "the incongruous moment," by which Lewis means an experience of disjunction that can stimulate "problem solving and creativity" provided one can respond to it (as Ishmael does in "The Hyena") with "the relaxation of humor" and "the concentration of fear." *Pierre* does turn upon moments of crisis, but in focusing on Pierre's failures of response without regard to the issues involved, Lewis transforms Melville's *bildungsroman* into a cautionary tale whose episodes have no point other than to dramatize fixation. Invoking the miracles controversy of 1836–45 and contemporary reactions to Bailey's *Festus* and Feuerbach's *Essence of Christianity*, James Duban in "Subjective Transcendentalism: *Pierre*" (*Melville's Major Fiction*, pp. 149–91) identifies the book's constant as a critique of "Transcendental intuition," which Melville presents "as arising from the mind's fabrication of mandates that it projects onto the outside world" and mistakes for the imperatives of duty. Though the articles Duban relies on for his context may well have been unknown to Melville, Duban's thesis does bring forward an important theme in *Pierre* and suggests an internal rationale for the "Young America in Literature" sections to complement biographical explanations.

The only writings on *Pierre* not to focus upon its unifying intention are Michael Paul Rogin's chapter "Herman Melville's *Eighteenth Brumaire*" (*Subversive Genealogy*, pp. 155–86), which discusses *Pierre* as a retreat from politics to the suffocating institution of the family, and Leon Chai's "Melville and Shelley: Speculations on Metaphysics, Morals, and Poetics in *Pierre* and 'Shelley's Vision'" (*ESQ* 29:31–45). The latter, which resists summary, is either too long or too short, depending on whether one reads it as a discussion of the ethics and psychology of the Beatrice Cenci story, of the cosmology implied by *Pierre*'s "magnetism," or of Melville's general debt (or likeness) to Shelley. In either event, Chai's is a fertile essay that holds its reader and offers a rewarding alternative to the standard journal piece.

vi. Stories

"Benito Cereno" claimed most attention among Melville's stories, as critics continued to interest themselves in Melville and slavery. Originally delivered as a paper before the Southern Political Science Association, "Melville's 'Benito Cereno': Civilization, Barbarism, and Race" (*IJPP* 11:43–72) by William D. Richardson repeats the commonplaces of criticism as it distinguishes between the "citizen perspective" in which most of Melville's Delano-like contemporaries would have understood the story and the "statesman perspective" which grasps Melville's covert attempt to instruct the nation's leaders on the explosive subject of race. That new things *can* be said about Melville and race is illustrated by Allan Moore Emery's "The Topicality of Depravity in 'Benito Cereno'" (*AL* 55:316–31), which tries to heal the division between those who read the story as "a powerful portrait of human depravity" and those who read it as an attack on American slavery. Citing the contemporary debate about the nature of both races—on one side, eulogies of black affectionateness and docility, as in *Uncle Tom's Cabin* and popular treatments of the minstrels; on the other, Southern polemics for white supremacy—Emery contends that Melville's emphasis on depravity belonged to the historical moment, encompassing black and white alike in a "firmly integrationist tale" too skeptical of all humanity to be racist. Although Emery overlooks one important strain of counterevidence—Melville's muting of the white atrocities described in Amasa Delano's *Narrative of Voyages and Travels*—his article joins Rogin's and Duban's work as a worthy effort to rehistoricize Melville's fiction by embedding it within a specific contemporary discourse.

Gloria Horsley–Meacham suggests a less immediate historical context in "The Monastic Slaver: Images and Meaning in 'Benito Cereno'" (*NEQ* 56:261–66), which explains "the references to monks and monasteries so recurrent in the novella" as attempts on Melville's part to "link the nascent American slave tradition with the church and the crusade for Christian dominion." Central to this pattern, Horsley-Meacham says, is the figure of the early 16th-Century Dominican priest Bartholomew de Las Casas of Santo Domingo, whom Melville may have known from Washington Irving's *The Life and Voyages of Christopher Columbus*, and whose name and career seem associated with events in "Benito Cereno" through particular monastic images. Reexploring Melville's primary source, Audrey Roberts in "Another Chapter for 'Benito Cereno'" (*MSEx* 55:10–11) speculates that the characterization of the Spanish captain (so different from that in Delano's account) may have been inspired by an earlier section of Delano's *Narrative* that deals with the death of his friend Captain George Howe, a noble but broken man whose final circumstances included fainting fits and a shaving scene.

Writing on "Bartleby, the Scrivener" took a much-needed sabbatical in 1983. The only exceptions were Michael Paul Rogin's remarks in "Class Struggles in America," an omnibus chapter on the stories (*Subversive Genealogy*, pp. 187–220), and "Bartleby or, The Ambiguities" (*SSF* 20:132–36) by Donald H. Craver and Patricia R. Plante. Applying Plinlimmon's chronometricals and horologicals to "Bartleby" (should one be a relativist like the narrator or an absolutist like Bartleby?), Craver and Plante seem unaware of Harold Schechter's *SSF* article of 1982, "Bartleby the Chronometer," just as Schechter seemed unaware of Walter E. Anderson's related *SSF* article of 1981. The authors themselves may not be at fault, but editors at *SSF* ought to know what is in the works and make sure that contributors don't repeat one another.

Allan Moore Emery's "Melville on Science: 'The Lightning-Rod Man'" (*NEQ* 56:555–68) is an accomplished scholarly reading that demonstrates Melville's probable debt to Benjamin Franklin's *Letters and Papers on Electricity* and Lucius Lyon's *Treatise on Lightning Conductors* (1853), and argues that science, not religion, was Melville's satiric target in "The Lightning-Rod Man," the scientist having substituted his desacralizing and unreliable technology for faith in Providence. Thorough and enriching, Emery's article is weakened only by its easy identification of Melville with his God-reliant narrator and by its stance of divisiveness that casts other readings as misreadings and seems to say "*Mine* is the only true rod." Lastly, in "Four Old Smokers: Melville, Thoreau, and Their Chimneys" (*ATQ* 51[1981]:151–64), Pamela R. Matthews supplements biographical sources for "I and My Chimney" by calling attention to parallels between Melville's story and Thoreau's "Housewarming" chapter in *Walden*. Matthews's evidence is fairly persuasive; less so is her critical conclusion that Melville dramatizes his ambivalence toward

Transcendentalism by presenting his narrator as a "Solomonic" figure
overly given to blackness and in need of correction by his Transcendental wife.

vii. The Confidence-Man, Poetry

Carolyn L. Karcher's "Philanthropy and the Occult in the Fiction of
Hawthorne, Brownson, and Melville" (*The Haunted Dusk*, pp. 67–
97), a revised and expanded version of Karcher's 1979 article "Spiritualism and Philanthropy in Brownson's *The Spirit-Rapper* and
Melville's *The Confidence-Man*" (*ESQ* 25:26–36; see *ALS 1979*, p.
56), contends that while Hawthorne and Brownson used spiritualism
to debunk the reformist impulse of the day, Melville turned the
conventions of "antireform satire" to "a two-pronged attack on the
watered-down Christianity and hollow philanthropy that conservative satirists lamented, and on the ossified orthodoxy and callous
social creed they promulgated in its place." I will leave it to Hawthorne readers to rescue their author from Karcher's drastic over-
simplifications; enough to say that Karcher wants nothing of ambivalence and expects her authors consistently to tow the line, which
means that a 19th-century "radical deeply committed to humanitarian values" (as Karcher assumes Melville was and Hawthorne
ought to have been) should share the same basic convictions on the
same cluster of issues as any right-minded modern. Thus Karcher
reshapes the story of Goneril into a satire on "antifeminism," reads
the Tom Fry chapter as a plea for prison reform, and in general
misuses Melville's book in her effort to portray its author as a cru-
sading humanitarian whom 1980s progressives can claim as their own.

Drawing loosely upon Wolfgang Kayser's and Frances K. Ba-
rasch's theories of the grotesque, Dale Jones in "The Grotesque in
Melville's *The Confidence-Man*" (*CLQ* 19:194–205) attributes the
form and content of Melville's book to his "increasing recognition of
a terrifying, although sometimes ludicrous, ambiguity at the heart of
experience." Perhaps, but Jones is obscure about the relationship
between the grotesque as a vision, a genre, and a literary technique
and fails to explain why, if the grotesque was a late development, it
should have been so prominent in *Mardi*. Better focused but in the
footnote category, "Melville's Most Fascinating Confidence Man"
(*ATQ* 52[1981]:229–36) by Melody Graulich elaborates upon the

rattlesnake passage from the Cosmopolitan's encounter with Mark Winsome by likening Winsome's appeal to the proverbial power of the snake to charm its victims—in Winsome's case, to "bewitch man into giving way" to the alluring but deceptive "dream of unity."

Two scholarly contributions cast light on the backgrounds of *The Confidence-Man*. In "A Shrewd 'Confidence Man'" (*MSEx* 56:3–4) George Monteiro reprints the *New-York Daily Tribune*'s accounts from January 1856 of the arrest and confession of a local confidence man named Benjamin Greer, a cool, gentlemanly swindler who formerly plied his trade in the South and West. The *Tribune* stories may have interested Melville, but they appeared too late to influence his first conception of his character, or so it appears from Alma A. Mac-Dougall's "The Chronology of *The Confidence-Man* and 'Benito Cereno': Redating Two 1855 Curtis and Melville Letters" (*MSEx* 53: 3–6). Carefully sifting the evidence, MacDougall finds support for Watson G. Branch's conjecture that Melville began thinking about *The Confidence-Man* by the summer of 1855 and for Leon Howard's that he initially hoped to serialize the book in *Putnam's*. The reservations of *Putnam's* adviser George William Curtis about a proposed Melville work (formerly thought to be "Benito Cereno") appear to have squelched the project, leaving it "unclear," MacDougall says, why Melville proceeded with so unprofitable a book. (How much money did Satan make gulling Eve?) In any case, one consequence of MacDougall's findings is to lend a motive to Melville's pillorying of Curtis in *The Confidence-Man*, if indeed Hans-Joachim Lang and Benjamin Lease are right in seeing Curtis in Mark Winsome's disciple Egbert (Lang and Lease, "Melville and 'The Practical Disciple': George William Curtis in *The Confidence-Man*," *Amst* 26:181–91; see *ALS 1981*, p. 68).

Among the contributions on the poetry, Michael Paul Rogin's chapter "The Iron Dome" (*Subversive Genealogy*, pp. 259–87) relates *Battle-Pieces* to the "filial sacrifice" of the Civil War as it was mythologized by Northern intellectuals anxious to purge the nation of the sin of slavery and resanctify the Union. As a contextual study, "The Iron Dome" is a major contribution to our understanding of Melville's themes in *Battle-Pieces*; the difficulty comes when Rogin links vision to form and tries to explain the supposed lifelessness of the poems by reference to Melville's shift of allegiance from "outcasts" to the institutional state. As if to document Rogin's theme of filial sacrifice, David McAuley in "A Source for Melville's 'The March into Virginia'" (*MSEx* 55:12–13) finds a suggestion for Melville's poem in a *New York Times* editorial of July 22, 1861, entitled "Slaughter of the Innocents," which condemns the alleged Confederate practice of sending "'extremely youthful persons—in some cases boys, or mere children'"—into battle.

Intended for a mixed audience that may not have read the poem, Janis P. Stout's "The Profound Remove: Melville's *Clarel*" (*The Journey Narrative in American Literature: Patterns and Departures*, Greenwood, pp. 123–57) is sensible and fluent but burdened by summary as it presents *Clarel* as developing "from the pilgrimage tradition with which it begins to an idiosyncratic blending of symbolic narrative, character sketch, and verse essay, all strung on the linear structure of the journey." A more valuable introduction to a little-read work, "*Weeds and Wildings*: Herman Melville's Use of the Pastoral Voice" (*EAS* 12:61–85) by Lucy M. Freibert, shows the late Melville, freed from Timonism, availing himself of pastoral conventions to comment playfully and "with ironic joy" on "the ambiguities of life," including those of his marriage and literary career. Informed and gracefully written, Freibert's essay is particularly sensitive in its comments on "The Rose Farmer" as an allegory of Melville's reflections on the creative possibilities of his final years. Also addressing several of Melville's later poems (as well as his lecture "Statues in Rome"), Ekaterini Georgoudaki's "Ancient Greek and Roman Pieces of Art in Herman Melville's Iconography" (*APSAUT* 21:85–95) offers a more disillusioned Melville who found his artistic and intellectual hopes for America betrayed by "the materialism and utilitarianism of his time" and "finally turned to the classical Golden Age in an effort to place and assess his contemporary American experience within the historical context of Western civilization as a whole."

viii. *Billy Budd, Sailor*

The most thoughtful essay on *Billy Budd*, Brook Thomas's "*Billy Budd* and the Judgment of Silence" (*BuR* 27:51–78), is a response to Barbara Johnson's deconstructionist reading of 1979 ("Melville's Fist: The Execution of *Billy Budd*," *SIR* 18:567–99; see *ALS 1979*, p. 58) and an augury of the debate between deconstructionists and Marxists that seems likely to dominate the critical frontier for some time.

While acknowledging *Billy Budd's* ambiguity, Thomas attacks Johnson's "refusal to judge." Vere as acquiescent in the status quo that
reveals "a conservative ideology." Thomas's answer to the conflicting
evidence in the text is to invoke "a basis for judgment beyond textuality"—Marxism—as if the knot of indeterminateness could be cut
by appealing to an extra-literary system that itself depends upon a
"text" (i.e., an ordering frame of reference with no ultimate ground
of authority). Provocative on *Billy Budd*, Thomas's essay is most interesting for the questions it raises about the criticism of politics and
the politics of criticism, and for the struggle it dramatizes between the
interpreter's skeptical self-awareness and his political commitment.

Like his 1982 pamphlet on "Bartleby, the Scrivener" (see *ALS
1982*, p. 74), Merton M. Sealts, Jr.'s *Innocence and Infamy: Resources
for Discussing Herman Melville's "Billy Budd, Sailor"* (Madison:
Wisconsin Humanities Committee) was prepared for an all-day
seminar of lawyers and offers a particularly thorough and judicious
introduction to Melville's text. By contrast, the remaining articles on
Billy Budd seem labored or windy. In John H. Timmerman's "Typology and Biblical Consistency in *Billy Budd*" (*NDEJ* 15:23–38),
typology means virtually any grouping of Biblical allusions that can
be arranged to form a pattern and related in some way to the containing narrative. Timmerman's reading of Billy-as-Adam/Billy-as-
Christ makes sense, but "myth" or "archetype" would serve Timmerman just as well, particularly since Lawrence Buell in the *NDEJ*
article preceding Timmerman's argues convincingly that typology
became a branch of comparative mythology in the 19th Century and
entered "the artist's repertoire of metaphor" "stripped of the assumption of coherence" it had for the Puritans. Inquiring "why 'Billy
Budd' is written in the way it is," Brian Lee in " 'Billy Budd': The
American 'Hard Times' " (*English* 32:35–54) attributes the work's
"pedantic, pretentious, tortuous" style to Melville's effort to address
his audience in the language of the times. Where Dickens could
transcend his utilitarian age through imagination and poetry, Melville (according to Lee) "has to twist and turn in indirection and
ingenuity" out of a mistaken impulse to "persuade"—hardly the first
word that comes to mind for Melville's Chinese boxes of irony. In
W. D. Redfern's "Between the Lines of *Billy Budd*" (*JAmS* 17:
357–65), Lee's encumbered Melville becomes a "punster-artist" who
"pleads for a participating audience" that "will register and decode

his tangle-talk" and meet him in an "enriched consensus." Rounding off the year's work on *Billy Budd* are political readings by James Duban (*Melville's Major Fiction*, pp. 221–48) and Michael Paul Rogin (*Subversive Genealogy*, pp. 288–306), the latter of which, "The *Somers* Mutiny and *Billy Budd*: Melville in the Penal Colony," originally appeared in 1980 (*Criminal Justice History* 1:186–224). (In *ALS 1982* [p. 78], Richard Weisberg, author of an article on *Billy Budd* was incorrectly identified as Robert Weisberg. This writer wishes to apologize for the error.)

Washington University, St. Louis

5. Whitman and Dickinson

Robert Weisbuch

Two kinds of readers always exist for Dickinson, those who wish to appropriate this poet who wrote "Subjects hinder talk" to a special interest and those who keep their minds open to her multidimensional power, viewing the poet as exactly that. Both groups are much in evidence this year, the first in a large number of feminist interpretations that too often enlist Dickinson as a soul-sister in the reductive terms of a myth of resentment. Margaret Homans alone brings an appreciation for Dickinson's intricacies to bear on the difficult, important questions of gender and imagination. The second, more disinterested group is well-represented in fresh discoveries concerning the poet's idea of symbols, her poetic fashioning of self and nature, and her employment of etymology. The year's work in Whitman, slighter in bulk, features important articles on influences and a precise, wonderfully suggestive treatment of the poet's rhetorical strategies, C. Carroll Hollis's *Language and Style in Leaves of Grass*.

i. Whitman

a. **Bibliography, Editing.** In the "Introduction" to his anthology *Critical Essays on Walt Whitman* (Hall), James Woodress soundly reviews the history of responses to Whitman. His emphasis on early British commentaries is especially welcome; and the selection of essays from Whitman's lifetime forward is sensible, though it is a bit thin on recent criticism.

Worth noting under this heading is the consensus among many of the year's published readers—Hollis, Loving, French, Parkinson, Diggory—that Whitman's early poetry and first versions of poems subsequently revised are superior to his later work. Publishers of

Preparation of this chapter was facilitated by the research assistance of Anna Battigelli and Susan Roberson.

popular editions should take note. This consensus has been developing for some time and is now a majority view.

b. **Biography.** James Doyle usefully recounts the poet's 1880 summer in Canada and his view of the north in "Whitman's Canadian
Diary" (*UTQ* 52:277–87). Doyle contrasts Whitman's generous appreciations of Canada to Thoreau's sense of the nation "as an inex-
plicable, fragmented anomaly." Whitman could accept French
Canada as "part of the unity-plurality paradox" and espouses a continental unity that will lead to a larger, cosmic merge that yet retains
diversity.

More speculative and too sensational is Karl Keller's "The Puritan Perverse" (*TSLL* 25:139–64), which opens with a section titled
"Emerson Seduces Whitman on Boston Common." By this, Keller
means that Emerson, in warning Whitman that his sexual emphasis
would limit the popularity of *Leaves of Grass* and then in his gracious
giving-way when Whitman insisted on the importance of this theme,
secretly directed Whitman to extend Emersonian ideas into an aspect
of life that made Emerson skittish. Keller recreates the meeting with
accuracy and verve; but when he relates Emerson's sexual reticence
to Puritan prudery he ignores the many frank celebrations of physical
love in marriage that distinguish Puritan literature, and he carica-
tures Emerson unfairly. For all its pyrotechnics, the article merely
reinforces the dull cliché that Whitman adds body to Emerson's soul
and mind.

c. **Criticism: General.** Whitman became a poet almost by accident,
C. Carroll Hollis contends in *Language and Style in Leaves of Grass*
(LSU). He determined not to be a specific sort of poet but a specific
kind of man and eventually discovered poetry as his most apt expression. A frustrated orator, he brought oratorical conventions into
the poetry and journalistic habits as well. But these most-distinctive
features decrease after 1860 and with them decreases Whitman's
unique value: "Up to 1860, the persona is a speaker, from 1865 he
is a poet."

Hollis employs various language theories unpretentiously, clearly,
and cannily to objectify his view. From J. L. Austin he takes the idea
of certain speech acts that are elocutionary or performative—statements like "I bet you a dollar" that enact what they are saying in the

saying—and shows that Whitman employs them far more often than any of his British or American contemporaries. This is a stylistic means of making his book less a record than an action, less a book than a man. And the fifty-to-one ratio of speech acts in Whitman's early poetry as compared to his post–1865 work is startling evidence of a change. Or again, Hollis adapts Jakobson's distinction between metonymy and metaphor to describe Whitman as unique in his reliance on metonymy. This implies a "concern with sensation and surface" that is "fascinated with and glorying in the realistic details of American life." The employment of the negative as a means of imitating verbal debate, the preponderance of present-tense statements, and the employment of an oratorical system of metrics called cursus all contribute to the oratorical status of the poetry to 1860. From journalism derives Whitman's coining of new terms and his new uses of idiomatic expressions. In each instance, Hollis brings statistical evidence to bear tellingly in comparisons with other poets; and each cited feature is absent from the later poetry as Whitman "tries to invade the high formality of English traditional poetry."

Hollis's method leads him too much to discount literary models for Whitman's 1855 emergence; the book tends to wander; the discussion of cursus is muddy and unpersuasive; and one often wishes that Hollis would draw conclusions at once more bold and intricate from his idea of Whitman's decline. Had Whitman merely become fainthearted and conventional? Was he attempting something interesting if failed, perhaps a cultural maturity for Walt and Walt's America? But others can extend Hollis's work to these questions, and the work itself is finally most impressive. Whitman's style is considered with more precision than heretofore; extremely difficult concepts of language are rendered with a cheerful explanatory wit that can serve as a model for linguistic literary study; and the features that Hollis isolates elicit shocks of recognition out of one's gut-impressions of Whitman.

In unrewarding contrast, a chapter on Whitman in M. L. Rosenthal and Sally Gall's *The Modern Poetic Sequence: The Genius of Modern Poetry* (Oxford) is fatuous to a laughable extreme. Rosenthal, who has done far better work, and Gall begin their book promisingly by considering sequences of individual lyrics as "*the* modern poetic form," but they fail to say why this phenomenon occurs or to define the form with any rigor or historical awareness. If this is "Po-

etic Criticism in a New Key," as the authors boast, the key is a most
minor one. Their work, they claim, "forbids translation into abstractions" and yet we get descriptions of "Song of Myself" like this one:
" 'Song of Myself' projects the interaction among its major fields of
affect (affirmation, confrontation with the negative, ecstatic experience) in a series of dynamically related states, in the context of a
recurring struggle for transcendence." Elsewhere, the language becomes sentimental to provide a Hollywood version of Whitman with
his "courageous facing-up, at once generous and bitter, to the degradations of existence." Rosenthal and Gall simply don't know enough
about Whitman, don't know, for instance, that the Deathbed edition
they are employing for "Song of Myself" constitutes a decisively
different structuring of the poem than earlier versions. Nor do they
anywhere show that this work is better considered as a sequence
of individual lyrics than as a single poem divided into sections. Perhaps they should be dealing with *Leaves of Grass* as a whole, but it
is with a certain gratitude that we are denied that.

Lewis Hyde does say something new about Whitman in his chapter on the poet in *The Gift: Imagination and the Erotic Life of Property* (Random House), though he takes too long to do so. For Hyde,
a work of art is properly a gift even though it is commercially distributed; indeed, gifts and thus art oppose commercialism and modern isolation as well, for gift-exchange is the product of families and
tribes, an erotic bonding. Ethnography and literature are the poles
of the book's wide, sometimes scattered, range. In the Whitman
chapter, which can wander badly, Hyde is nonetheless persuasive in
seeing Whitman's twin emphases on generosity and receptivity as a
contentious claim on values. Gifting for Hyde underlies and combines all of Whitman's major attitudes: gifts oppose the analytical
bent of the cash-oriented to create "erotic commerce, joining self
and others"; gift-exchange, made internal, informs Whitman's stress
on simple breathing and, made eternal, gift-exchange relates life
and death as a double generosity; and the equality of gifts (as talents) "puts hierarchy to sleep." At times Hyde may extend his idea
of gift to the point where one is unsure whether the trope is truly
Whitman's or Hyde's alone; Hyde's Whitman is too consistent, un-
changing, and simple in his attitudes; and he ignores the more
troubling aspects of giving that, as Emerson wrote in "Gifts," may
place an intolerable burden on the receiver. But Hyde's spirited writ-

ing expresses a fresh idea of some real power, as when he describes
the cure to Walt's crises of identification with suffering in "Song of
Myself" as the substitution of an outbreathing of faith for the infusion
of grief. We knew that, but by Hyde's lexicon the crisis and its resolution are integrated newly into the poem's patterns of concern.

Far less original and no better focused is R. W. French's essay
with the ambitious title "Reading Whitman" (*ELWIU* 10:71–80).
French argues that Whitman sought to be the American laureate
but found that the nation would not absorb a poet "too quirky, too
experimental and eccentric, too unsettled and unsettling." To achieve
his goal, he sunk to accommodation, beginning with the Civil War
poems. The discussion is too vaguely adjectival to illuminate the
glories claimed for Whitman's early works or the blame charged
against the later ones; and the conflict between an official Walt and
a self-doubting, more furtive aspect of the poet is described much
more tellingly in Kerry Charles Larson's twisty, superb 1982 article,
"Voices in the Free Grass: Whitman and the Conception of 'Free
Growth'" (*CentR* 26:199–220) because Larson can see Whitman's
opposing impulses in concurrent contest within "Song of Myself."

Roger Asselineau treats another self-division in "Nationalism Vs.
Internationalism in *Leaves of Grass*," the final essay in the aforementioned Woodress anthology. Asselineau chronicles Whitman's
wavering between a purer ideal of nationalism as leading to world
union, displayed variously in such features as his delighted employment of foreign phrases and his welcomings to immigrants, and the
low, conventional ambition of American annexation. Assilineau
points to an intriguing contradiction in charging that expansionist
bravado taints Whitman's fellow feeling until, late in his career, he
disowns political nationalism to emphasize the solidarity of workers
everywhere. But Assilineau fails to see that, beyond Whitman, New
World myths encourage both responses, and he seems unaware that
Whitman knowingly plays upon the contradiction. He organizes a
topic that deserves more intricate thought.

d. **Criticism: Individual Works.** Four articles helpfully complicate
the prevalent idea of Whitman's post–1860 decline. In "Retrievements
Out of the Night: Prophetic and Private Voices in Whitman's 'Drum
Taps'" (*ATQ* 51:211–23), Denise T. Askin distinguishes between a
prophetic voice that idealizes the Civil War into "the historical sign

of divine election" and a private voice that confesses anguishing details. The public voice, which Askin never quite calls fatuous, proclaims a resolution that the second voice alone can earn "by the silent kiss for the fallen enemy." Robin Riley Fast affirms Whitman's skill if not his genius at a still later stage by arguing for the canny reordering of his 1860 lyrics in the 1881 edition of *Leaves*. In "Structure and Meaning in Whitman's 'Sea Drift'" (*ATQ* 53:49–66) Fast convincingly describes the sequence as one in which the narrator is continually beset by fears that nonetheless culminate in "reaffirming the coexistence of natural and human power, and material and spiritual power." Fast's rich article nonetheless fails to engage the issue of whether such a narrative does not rob the lyrics of a more emotionally real, less scheduled alternation of moods.

More ambitiously, Thomas Parkinson praises the post–war Whitman at the expense of the 1881 rearranger in " 'When Lilacs Last in the Door-Yard Bloom'd' and the American Civil Religion" (*SoR* 19: 1–16). He shows in persuasive detail how the elegy constitutes "the most egregious example of a great poem tampered with to its detriment" by a blending of originally discrete sections that deprives the poem of its structural clarity. Parkinson sees the poem as a bridge between the democratic individualism to which Whitman devoted his earlier work and the democratic nationalism to which he claimed to devote the last half of his career. Parkinson too readily accepts this division, which many commentators now view as a rationalization, even as he deplores the failure of the nationalist poet: surely both modes mingle throughout Whitman's works and the poetic decline is more the result of a failure in the merging force rather than in a simple change of purpose. Further, Parkinson badly needs the ideas of Sacvan Bercovitch to fill out the idea of an American civil religion, "which has its own heroes and martyrs, holy places and rituals of sacrifice." Still, the reading of the elegy's major symbols of lilac, star, and bird is expressive and illuminating.

Finally, while one longs for a strong rebuttal to C. Carroll Hollis's too-easy disparaging of Whitman's prose, Robert J. Scholnick's "Toward a 'Wider Democratizing of Institutions': Whitman's *Democratic Vistas*" (*ATQ* 52:287–302) is not it. Scholnick emphasizes Whitman's revisions of the essay from its form as a series of essays in *Galaxy* to its book publication as evidence of Whitman's new refusal of American social realities in favor of his own insight. But Whitman

never depended on the simpleminded national consensus that Scholnick attributes to him for his early optimism; and the more valid assertion that Whitman wished for a democracy that would educate
the individual to his self-realization and then would form its institutions out of such realized selves is hardly news.

e. Affinities and Influences. Kenneth M. Price explores the mystery
of Whitman's development toward the 1855 *Leaves* by considering
Whitman's early readings of the English romantics and his notations
on them in his valuable article "The Margin of Confidence: Young
Walt Whitman on English Poets and Poetry" (*TSLL* 25:541–57).
Price notes Whitman's Emersonian disrespect for predecessors and
his growing emphasis on a poetic structure informed subtly by a
democratic aesthetic. For instance, Whitman applauds the empathic
aspect of Keats's negative capability while insisting on the retention
of a strongly individuated poetic self; or he will enthuse over the
meditative ecstasies of Wordsworth and Coleridge but demand the
active involvement of the senses rather than their cancellation in any
such ecstacy. Romantic and early Victorian nostalgias are consistently
despised; so too any evidence of aristocratic tendencies. Price intriguingly challenges Harold Bloom's generalizations concerning influence by demonstrating Whitman's unanxious, evenhanded dealings with past masters.

Two fine articles adapted by Jerome Loving from his 1982 book
Emerson, Whitman, and the American Muse nicely if tragically complement Price's work by dramatizing Whitman's fall from this height
of confidence. An essay in the Woodress anthology, "Emerson, Whitman, and the Paradox of Self-Reliance" (pp. 306–19), proves by textual echoes that, despite his disclaimers, Whitman had read Emerson's "The Poet" before 1856. The essay "emboldened Whitman to
set up independently," though the poet was well on his way to doing
so without Emerson's aid. But "The Poet" also marks Emerson's beginning movement from Vision to Wisdom or, as Loving puts it pun-
ningly, "good advice under the circumstances"; and by the 1860
Leaves, Whitman is already following the Emersonian pattern as he
"bids farewell to the power of poetry to lull the Understanding into
the illusion that the self-lover is invulnerable to the anxieties produced by death-in-life." Such 1860 lyrics as "Out of the Cradle" and
"As I Ebb'd" imply that "personal love makes death ominous"; like

the Emerson of "Experience," this Whitman is out of the rocked
cradle, "out of the youthful illusions of personal love"; and while
they are powerful crisis works, they lead ultimately to a dreary God-
reliance—"the hoax, therefore, that led Whitman up Emerson's spiral
staircase to nowhere" or, I would add, to Wordsworth, the poet of
memory against whom the 1855 Walt of the present and forward-
looking moment implicitly argues.

The bogus Whitman who evolves from this crisis as a kind of
second Christ or even a Santa Claus is all-too-easily appropriated by
such reductive enthusiasts as William Douglas O'Connor. In "From
Brooklyn Bard to Maryland Myth: Emerson's Poet and Whitman's
Christ" (*Calamus* 23:4–18), Loving shows that the mystic carpenter
who solves the problems of a Maryland family decimated by the war
in O'Connor's tale "The Carpenter" is meant to be identified as
Whitman. Loving goes on to argue that the poet himself, in his
secretly despairing turn outward that recapitulates Emerson's "movement toward exhaustion," is responsible for such reductive mytholo-
gizers as O'Connor, author of *The Good Grey Poet*.

Loving's work extends Whicher's vision of Emerson's career as a
sequence of freedom and fate to Whitman, and it is powerful and
necessary, especially in its intricate readings of individual poems.
Loving particularizes tellingly the notion put forth by Harold Bloom
and R. A. Yoder that American poetic careers retreat to convention
and compromise almost immediately. But we stand in balancing need
of a consideration of Whitman's later stages which might perceive
more generously what he was, however inadequately, attempting as
the pre–Jamesian representative of a national maturing.

Price's article on Whitman's responses to British poets is comple-
mented differently, in a transatlantic context, by the first thirty pages
of Terrence Diggory's *Yeats and American Poetry*. "Yeats wanted
the Irish to follow the American lead," Diggory argues, in declaring
aesthetic independence from England. Whitman served as a particularly powerful example, for he did not, like the English romantics, employ poetry to express a self already formed but to create a
self in the poetry. Yeats was attracted all the more to Whitman
because the personal and national aspects were made inextricable in
the Walt speaker. Those who find Yeats less manipulative and stagey
or Whitman more so than this writer will be fascinated by Diggory's
research and conjectures; and I, too, am won over by his work's

freshness and importance in forging a link at once surprising and inevitable. Diggory grants a questionable dignity to Yeats's subsequent repudiation of Whitman as "one of the errors of our youth" and his demeaning categorization of Whitman's Walt as representative of a primitive stage not yet personality. But one reads Yeats newly and better by Diggory's work, and his distinction between romantic self-expression and American self-creation performs something of the same service for Whitman.

In general, Whitman criticism is rapidly improving, and we can know that by being able to dismiss without passion such anachronistic, fuzzy work as Rajnath's "Whitman, Eliot, and the *Bhagavadita*" (*CLS* 20:94–101). In this essay the comparisons are too general and partial—Whitman's mysticism is determined to be Eastern rather than Western because the *Bhagavad Gita* stresses active involvement while St. John advocates a contemplative retreat from the world (as if a Christian Positive Way does not exist)—to mean anything at all.

ii. Dickinson

a. **Bibliography, Editing.**   Aside from two brief and quixotic offerings from Frederick L. Morey, there is nothing to report here. Morey offers a slapdash, unrationalized critical history in "Great, Deep, or Interesting? Emily Dickinson and Her Importance" (*DicS* 46:29–38) and lists the scant Dickinson holdings at major British libraries in "England 1980 Research" (*DicS* 46:42–47). This may be the appropriate place to express thanks to Morey, as editor of *Dickinson Studies* and the *Higginson Journal,* for serving as a clearinghouse of Dickinson criticism while urging on him a more rigorous editorial policy that would eliminate the publishing of dissertation prospecti and hobbyhorse work.

Perhaps the real bibliographic news concerns the growing influence of R. W. Franklin's edition of *The Manuscript Books of Emily Dickinson* (*ALS, 1981,* 84–85). Two critical studies this year attempt to make the fascicle-orderings signify, though, as we will note, these attempts ignore Franklin's careful admonitions against forcing upon the sequences an undue, definitive import.

b. **Biography.**   It is difficult to decide whether to place William H. Shurr's *The Marriage of Emily Dickinson: A Study of the Fascicles*

(Kentucky) in this category or in "criticism." It perhaps deserves a place in neither, for the study lives down to its title by proffering a sensational discovery based on no real evidence other than an insultingly literal misreading of some poems. The Reverend Charles Wadsworth was the secret hubby, "pregnancy or the deep fear of pregnancy" was the poem-powering result, and the sequence of poems in some of the fascicles are made to signify something akin to a Harlequin Romance. Shurr knows that Dickinson insisted her poems concerned "a supposed person" but he doesn't care: "just the opposite is true." And we shouldn't care about Shurr's sexist and sophomoric work except to wonder why a major university press would wish to devalue the rest of its catalogue by such an inclusion.

In comparison, merely amateurish articles serve as delightful reliefs. Dorothy Huff Oberhaus focuses on Susan Dickinson's obituary notice of her sister-in-law to argue for her personal and literary understanding in "In Defense of Sue" (*DicS* 48:1–25). The article recounts for the umpteenth time the Martha Dickinson Bianchi–Millicent Todd Bingham war for the claiming of the poet's affection on behalf of Austen's wife or mistress. Oberhaus states the obvious in arguing that Mrs. Todd was not objective in her view of her lover's wife, and she quotes from Dickinson's letters to Sue as proof of a continuing depth of feeling when they convey—and just barely—Dickinson's usual warmth toward all. It is difficult to see such a final comment as "The tie between us is very fine, but a Hair never dissolves" as an expression of continuing intensity. More bizarre but more enjoyable and relevant is Winthrop S. Dakin's "Lawyers Around Emily Dickinson" (*DicS* 47:36–40). Here we learn that Dickinson's maternal grandfather lost two-thirds of his cases while Edward Dickinson nearly split even. But one is delighted by quotations from the jurists' frank obituaries of Dickinson's only verifiable beloved, Otis P. Lord: "a good hater," "his temperament was always too impatient for research," "forcible." If Judge Lord finally lost his case with Dickinson, one understands better her consideration of him hereby.

Of a different order entirely is Sandra M. Gilbert's serious and challenging essay "The Wayward Nun Beneath the Hill: Emily Dickinson and the Mysteries of Womanhood" in *Feminist Critics Read Emily Dickinson*, ed. Suzanne Juhasz (Indiana). Gilbert puts forward the inviting hypothesis that Dickinson knowingly con-

structed the biographical mysteries that now engage us. The poet
employed the materials of a distinctly female daily reality as metaphors to construct "the ironic hagiography, say, of a New England
Nun" and created a series of enigmas, such as the wearing of white,
to transform and transcend a feminine mystique. Thus "the 'real'
Emily Dickinson was as much a 'supposed person' as the so-called
'Representative of the Verse.'" At times Gilbert ignores her own insight, as when she reads some love poems as literally autobiographical; but her view of the known person as a cunning fiction holds a
promise of taking us beyond impossible guesses to capitalize on the
very unknowable quality of much of Dickinson's life.

c. Criticism: General. There are a few other searching essays in
Feminist Critics Read Emily Dickinson but much lax work is represented in it as well. Suzanne Juhasz sets an unfortunate tone in an
introductory essay which reviews the critical history. Juhasz correctly criticizes those interpreters, from Whicher to Cody, who
imagine that the poetry is Dickinson's compensation for her sadness
as a woman or who discuss Dickinson's life with no regard for the
real fact of womanhood. But for Juhasz, to get Dickinson whole is
equally facile: it is to admit that she was both a woman and a poet.
What of her relation to New England or to European and American
romanticisms or to Calvinism or to scripture or. . .? Juhasz's totality is slender indeed. And a witch-hunt mentality prevails to
wreck the critical review by measuring each text against Juhasz's
rigid standard. Thus one disdains the flattery of such a comment
as this: "Weisbuch's book is not feminist, but neither is it sexist,
either implicitly or explicitly. That is something." Whew! Sharon
Cameron's superb *Lyric Time* is dismissed for daring to think of
Dickinson first as a lyric poet and for attributing philosophical sophistication to her. Juhasz prefers Karl Keller's description of Dickinson as "antiphilosophical" without seeming to comprehend that
such a view, aside from being provably wrong, reinforces a particularly nasty female stereotype. And one is reduced to staring by
Juhasz's inclusion of Karl Keller's "Notes on Sleeping with Emily
Dickinson" in this volume. This essay begins, "Sleeping with Emily
Dickinson, you discover a woman who loves words more than she
loves *you*," proceeds to speak of his need for "imaginative penetra-
tion," and encourages any number of scurrilous replies by conclud-

ing, "But I notice she has not noticed me here in bed with her at all. What should I do now?" Keller is no Barthes and an article that speaks of what aspects of Dickinson's work "men can get off on" examples an ugly, puerile sexism that would be evil were it not merely pubescent.

Some of the other articles in the anthology are less nasty but equally simple. Barbara A. C. Mossberg calls Dickinson "a career child" and "a Mother Goose" in "Emily Dickinson's Nursery Rhymes," wherein Mossberg inexplicably neglects to define at all the genre to which she so quixotically assigns Dickinson's work. Amateur Hour continues in Adalaide Morris' "'The Love of Thee—a Prism Be': Men and Women in the Love Poetry of Emily Dickinson," wherein all poems sent to Sue are wrongly assumed to be about her and thereby to constitute an alternative feminine world. By such an interpretative error, Dickinson's symbolic reach is amputated. Jo-anne A. Dobson begins more promisingly in "'Oh, Susie, it is dangerous': Emily Dickinson and the Archetype" by emphasizing that in many poems "assigning a referent to the masculine pronoun is intriguingly impossible." Dobson is importantly right too in describing Dickinson's idea of the masculine as "simultaneously omnipotent, fascinating, and deadly." But then she cheats by making all indeterminate "He's" into the Masculine Idea and reduces the Idea to rapacious power. By the end of the article, Dobson is finding the destructive male threat in a poem like "I know that He exists," where the real threat is that "He" does not exist at all.

Nowhere in the volume is there an essay representative of that advanced feminist criticism that engages in really intensive sociological and historical research. Too often here, being a woman in 19th-century America is seen as simply bad, and this impoverishing of women's lives is ultimately self-humiliating. Dickinson's individual power is diminished as well by an insistence on her typicality as a victim. Dickinson is neither typical nor a victim. The best essays in the volume, including Sandra Gilbert's contribution previously discussed, keep their thoughts on poetry to show how Dickinson transformed potentially victimizing aspects of her literary-social status into triumph.

Cristanne Miller argues effectively that Dickinson violates linguistic expectations to gain power over a world of words in "How Low Feet Stagger: Disruptions of Language in Dickinson's Poetry."

It is not clear why language norms are considered male, but Miller is more locally convincing in showing how male and female roles are reversed in "Wild Nights—Wild Nights" so that the speaking "she" wishes to moor herself in a male "thee." Joanne Felt Diehl fills in the blanks of Miller's argument by actively and precisely defining the male-dominated poetic conventions that Dickinson overturns. In "'Ransom in a Voice': Language as Defense in Dickinson's Poetry," Diehl further complicates Miller's argument by showing that, while Dickinson's reversals of expectation constitute assertions, they often go to revealing conflicts within the self. Dickinson finally becomes a recognizably complex poet in Diehl's argument, which includes a fine discussion of the poems of naming as examples of poising new word-meanings against a preformed world.

But the only brilliant essay here is Margaret Homans's "'Oh Vision of Language!' Dickinson's Poems of Love and Death." In subject-object dualities, Homans says, woman is traditionally aligned with the object, and the male's subjectivizing power is particularly emphasized in an Emersonian aesthetic. Dickinson attempts to correct this opposition that is really a hierarchy by pushing language to the far borders of meaning where the terms of the dualities become more nearly equal. But only in the death poems does the duality utterly close, as if to imply that a world beyond the sexes must remain a post–mortal goal. The essay includes the first serious readings of Dickinson's two earliest poems, a superb interpretation of "The Daisy follows soft the Sun—," and, more largely, what should be—but surely will not be—a devastating, once-and-for-all argument against viewing Dickinson's poems as centrally homoerotic. For Dickinson, Homans implies, only difference is enabling, however terrifying difference may be.

Several of these articles usefully condense the arguments of previously published book-length studies: Gilbert's influential *Madwoman in the Attic* (with Susan Gubar, Yale, 1979), Mossberg's self-indulgent *Emily Dickinson: When a Writer is a Daughter* (Indiana, 1982), and Homans's consistently sophisticated *Women Writers and Poetic Identity: Dorothy Wordsworth, Emily Brontë, and Emily Dickinson* (Princeton, 1980). Suzanne Juhasz has published her own study as well this year, *The Undiscovered Continent: Emily Dickinson and the Space of the Mind* (Indiana), which begins with a continuation of the witch-hunt tone of her bibliographical essay in her anthology. Samples: "Nothing in fact tends to happen to most women, because, as we know, patriarchal history has a propensity for cataloguing battles, not dinner parties"; and again, this startling qualification, "I am not claiming that men—in particular, male poets—have not also taken mental experience seriously." This is the language of bigotry. Yet the main body of her book has nothing to do with her feminist views, and this makes for a different disappointment. Juhasz asserts that Dickinson lived in the mind to escape a male world out there, and then proceeds to provide pedestrian readings of internalizing poems: sensible, usually accurate paraphrases with occasional, helpful notes on the workings of Dickinson's language. There is little new in claiming that Dickinson valorizes the internal; and Juhasz's feminist and formalist perspectives bear scant relation. The book has phenomenological pretensions, but to state "I take literally Dickinson's assessment of the mind as tangible space" is to proclaim an error.

Julia M. Walker needs only five pages to refute Juhasz and the psychobiographers in "Emily Dickinson's Poetic of Private Liberation" (*DicS* 45:17–22). She stresses that it is impossible and vulgar to assign meanings to a person's privacy and warns that ideals of narrowly feminist liberation cheapen Dickinson's ideal of a personal liberation of spirit. This may be to substitute a transcendentalist bias for a feminist one, but it has the virtue of crediting Dickinson's rage and love without confining their direction.

The real corrective to special-interest readings is in the doing, and it is difficult to recall articles that present a truly whole Dickinson better than L. C. Knights's "Defining the Self: Poems of Emily Dickinson" (*SR* 91:357–75). Knights centers on the problem of self-definition "through some responsive relationship to what is there, in the world of nature." Dickinson's intimate facticity in writing of nature and death expresses "on the one hand an uncommonly heightened enjoyment of the mere experience of being alive, on the other a constant awareness of mortality." In splendid readings of poems like "A Narrow Fellow in the Grass," "I watched the Moon around the House," and "The Moon upon her Fluent Route," Knights displays Dickinson finding something of her own mind in nature or nature even evoking qualities in the mind "that it did not know it had." The article serves as a fine general introduction to Dickinson. But while Knights places nature precisely in Dickinson's scheme of importances, readers might wish to contrast his view with Homans's, for she views as nigh-impossible the subject-object convergence that he sees, with equally convincing logic, as easy and frequent.

E. Miller Budick also provides a refutation of Knights's view in an article that impressively fulfills its weighty title, "The Dangers of the Living Word: Aspects of Dickinson's Epistemology, Cosmology and Symbolism" (*ESQ* 29:208–24). Budick emphasizes Dickinson's "denial of the capacity of language and art to bridge in any way the gap between the universe of God and that of human thought and discourse." Dickinson challenges the philosophical idealism of American romantic symbol-making to dramatize "cosmic disparity, perceptual confusion, and linguistic autonomy." A gloriously abundant, all-fusing idealism fixes and limits meaning; Dickinson's syntax of self-sufficient fragments implies an alternative worldview "characterized by gaps not bridges, by disruption not harmony." Budick's interpretation of "Blazing in Gold—and Quenching in Purple" as "a veritable parody of meaningful action" seems to me forced: what Budick calls disorder might be seen as a vitalizing dynamism. But her reading of "A Bird came down the Walk," in which the bird flies away from an alien trap of Christian idealist understanding, provides startling evidence for her case. The challenge now is to figure a sufficiently large and flexible idea of Dickinson's symbology to accommodate the partial truths of Knights and Budick alike.

Richard Benvenuto inaugurates a different mode of inquiry into Dickinson's language in "Words Within Words: Dickinson's Use of the Dictionary" (*ESQ* 29:46–55). By following Willis J. Buskingham's identification of Dickinson's dictionary as the 1844 reprint of the 1841 Webster's American rather than the 1847 revision that had been wrongly cited previously, Benvenuto, for instance, can buttress Knights's reading of "A Narrow Fellow in the Grass" by noting the meaning of fellow as "counterpart." But the dictionary also defines "fellow" as "an appelation of contempt" and "narrow" can mean both "nearby" and "barely sufficient to escape evil." Thus Benvenuto can complicate Knights's reading to argue that the speaker is learning from the snake a world of experience that is already an innate part of himself. Benvenuto's etymological readings are boldly creative, for he includes the dictionary's examplings of words as metaphors and often brings together variant meanings where other readers might find some of the meanings irrelevant. But this is only to say that etymology is another interpretative tool rather than an inarguable authority, and Benvenuto's deft hand at it encourages others to try theirs.

This is not to imply either that an interest in Dickinson's language guarantees acumen. Andrew Gibson claims that Dickinson's poems emphasize a speculative mode in a tone of hypothesis, as if no one has comprehended that before, in "Emily Dickinson and the Poetry of Hypothesis" (*EIC* 33:220–37). Gibson then turns on himself inexplicably to criticize the poet for her idea of sumptuous destitution, which he (wrongly) sees as her single, unchallenged doctrine. This is a strangely peevish article that liberally insults earlier commentators while nearly paraphrasing their ideas; but between snits Gibson does specify helpfully various means by which Dickinson expresses uncertainty.

One wishes for Gibson's lexicon of scorn to describe the chapter Rosenthal and Gall devote to Dickinson in *The Modern Poetry Sequence*, which outranks their Whitman chapter for vagaries and misinformation. They claim for Dickinson and Whitman "kindred sensibilities" without citing a single likeness. "Stranger things have happened than that Dickinson should have read Whitman secretly," they continue in a particularly silly sentence. Next, they misapply R. W. Franklin's pioneering work with the fascicles and ignore his warning against overconfidently arguing for a sequential meaning in the poems to consider fascicle fifteen as "the poetry of psychic trauma." Nearly every poem they treat is misread. More importantly their fascicle narrative shows not a jot more coherence than one could derive from any random grouping of any of Dickinson's poems.

d. **Criticism: Individual Works.** The most intriguing new readings of individual poems occur in the more rigorous studies mentioned in the foregoing section. Still, Martin Bickman is right to insist in "'The Snow that Never Drifts': Dickinson's Slant of Language" (*CollL*:139–46) that the poem is more about the nature of similarity, difference, and the mind that designates each than it is about a snowstorm or a petal falling. And in "Dickinson's 'Our Journey Had Advanced'" (*Expl* 41:29–31), Douglas Lovich Leonard sensibly eschews absolutist readings to emphasize the poem's thorough ambivalence, "the complex response of consciousness to its inchoate movement out of finity," though Leonard takes too literally the finite and noumenal realms in the poem. The year's craziest moment in Dickinson criticism is produced by Travis Du Priest, who claims in "Emily Dickinson's 'Pink—small—and punctual'" (*DicS* 46:20) that the object of the poem's title is "the female nipple ready for nursing."

e. **Affinities and Influences.** The lowest circle of feminist criticism is inhabited by critics like Wendy Martin who posit a ridiculously simple historical progression of women's poetic utterances that travels from frightened obfuscation to frank directness. Natalie Harris forwards this view in "The Naked and the Veiled: Sylvia Plath and Emily Dickinson" (*DicS* 45:23–34). She contrasts Plath's "A Birthday Present" and Dickinson's "There Came a Day at Summer's Full" for no reason more compelling than that suggested by her B-movie title. On the other hand, one wishes that George A. Tackes could provide better logic to support a likably surprising connection between Dickinson and Swift in "Dickinson's 'He put the Belt around my Life'" (*Expl* 42:26–27), but the cloud in the poem cannot allude to Swift's Laputa for it has nothing to do with a dehumanizing scientism.

Real discovery occurs in the course of an incisive polemic against the deconstructive refusal of meaning in literary chronology by Jonathan Morse, "History in the Text" (*TSLL* 24:329–46). Morse convincingly establishes a connection between "The Soul selects her own Society—" and a passage in Emerson's essay "Friendship" where Emerson argues for silence in contemplating "the select souls" until "thy heart shall speak." This is for Morse an example of how meaning is altered by every new historical discovery as we annex Emerson's complex of meanings to the poem.

Differently speculative is George Monteiro's "'A Way *Out* of Something': Robert Frost's Emily Dickinson" (*CentR* 27:192–203). Monteiro documents Frost's admiration—"the best of all women poets who ever wrote"—records Frost's annotations of his Dickinson volumes, and lists the critical works on the poet in Frost's library. Most interestingly, Frost understood the poetry well enough to dismiss all hidden-lover theories: "There was no man at all" or rather "a composite image." Monteiro concludes by imagining the speech Frost might have spoken had he been invited to address the Amherst Bicentennial on Dickinson, from which he resentfully noted his exclusion. Monteiro has Frost decrying Dickinson's irregularities of verse and meter but admiring greatly specific phrases and images. Monteiro's tour de force is enjoyable and convincing, though one longs for a more ambitious and systematic comparison of the poets.

Finally, two interesting articles consider Dickinson in the light of contemporary women writers. In "The Compensations of Solitude in the Work of Emily Dickinson and Sarah Orne Jewett" (*CLQ* 19:206–14), Lynn M. Patnode does not claim direct influence but forges a telling comparison. Both writers are shown to rebel against going notions of sentimental altruism by constructing dramas in which heroines "transform . . . loss and the melancholy of their spirits into a seclusion that is noble in itself." Their pain leads not to the formulaic do-gooding of sentimentalism but to self-discovery.

In a year during which Dickinson's poetry has attracted the usual number of quacks along with a sadly lesser number of attuned and bold readers, it is a particular pleasure to conclude by mentioning one more of the latter: Barton Levi St. Armand, whose essay " 'I Must Have Died at Ten Minutes Past One': Posthumous Reverie in Harriet Prescott Spofford's 'The Amber Gods' " appears in *The Haunted Dusk* (pp. 101–19). Prescott Spofford was another of Thomas Wentworth Higginson's protegies, and Dickinson praised an early Spofford story as "the only thing I ever saw in my life that I did not think I could have written myself." St. Armand is persuasive in suggesting that Spofford's description of the moment of death from the dying one's point of view in "The Amber Gods" encourages Dickinson to try for the same perspective. This may seem a small point, but as Spofford herself adopts Poe in this, a Dickinson-Poe connection, one which long has seemed inviting, is established; and, far more importantly, St. Armand is beginning to show that Dickinson was not as lonely a woman writer as we have imagined, but that she could draw knowingly upon female literary traditions. St. Armand possesses what too many of the Dickinson newcomers lack: knowledge and an historical sensibility that knows how to make that knowledge mean.

University of Michigan

6. Mark Twain

Louis J. Budd

Like one of Faulkner's favorite tableaux, I feel a sense of tautly suspended animation. Scholars and printers are switching to technologies that will do lightning miracles for us. Meanwhile, the *Mississippi Quarterly* and *PMLA* bibliographies for 1983 are late. I do take some reassurance from the thorough work of *America: History and Life* and from growing familiarity with the complicated *Arts and Humanities Citation Index*. Of course Thomas A. Tenney steams ahead with his *Seventh Annual Supplement* (*ALR* 16:163–222) for his *Mark Twain: A Reference Guide*, though because of deadlines he has more entries for 1982 than 1983. Most impressive perhaps are the older items—back to 1874 this time—that he continues to dig out and annotate expertly.

The biggest news was the resuscitation of the *Mark Twain Journal* under Tenney's editorship. Scholars should observe that his "Salutatory" invites "factual" articles and even informational notes (such as one about Twain on Japanese television). A curious effect of his clearing out the backlog accumulated by Cyril Clemens is to see that some essays obviously submitted five or ten years ago have been scooped since then. Happily, that effect supports the hope that scholarship advances toward ideas embedded in some kind of reality. The year also brought the news (*MTSB*) that Quarry Farm has become the Center for Mark Twain Studies, administered through Elmira College.

i. Editions

In the fascinating *Mark Twain's Rubáiyát* (Jenkins: Austin, Texas) Alan Gribben recovers forty-five quatrains and explicates them for the amateur poet's mood in 1898 as he worked out of his gloom but stayed aware of old age and family troubles. A printing of only 600 makes this handsome volume at least as good as gold for collectors. Limited to 1,015 copies, in *Adventures of Huckleberry Finn (Tom Sawyer's Comrade): A Facsimile of the Manuscript* (Gale) the 696 leaves of the holograph—three-fifths of the completed novel—get a high quality reproduction (at a matching price). Louis J. Budd sums up the known history of their composition, and an afterword by William H. Loos reveals that the director of the Buffalo Library had hoped in 1885 for *Life on the Mississippi* instead. Now the facsimile itself will often go into the rare-book room. Rarer still, judging by my failure to get it, is an edition announced in September 1983 by a new firm, John H. Wallace and Sons. Wallace, previously an administrator at a secondary school who opposed assigning *Huckleberry Finn*, has substituted "slave" for every use of "nigger."

From the annual trickle of anthologies only *Mark Twain: Selected Writings of an American Skeptic* (Prometheus) deserves mention. Mixing short pieces, excerpts from the major books, and a few manuscript passages, Victor Doyno has scaled it generously to show that Twain's naysaying raged throughout his life, not just during his final fifteen years. Since Doyno's thesis is sound, any debate would concern how much psychic space this side of Twain took over.

ii. Biography

Richard Gray's "Kingdom and Exile: Mark Twain's Hannibal Books," pp. 80–99 in *American Fiction: New Readings* (Barnes and Noble), includes *A Connecticut Yankee in King Arthur's Court* for the sake of his argument that Twain's novels constitute "one long imaginative autobiography," oscillating between nostalgia and a rejection of values instilled during childhood. Gray himself strikes a fine balance between identifying Twain's failures of purpose and his achievements. Louis J. Budd's *Our Mark Twain: The Making of His Public Personality* (Penn.) tries for such balance in analyzing how he functioned as a celebrity from 1870 until his death and in highlighting his own shrewd moves toward shaping that popularity, especially through his insider's knowledge of journalism. More broadly, Budd emphasizes Twain as a platform figure instead of an author visualized fuzzily by readers. In "How Mark Twain Survived Sam Clemens' Reformation" (*AL* 55:299–315) Jeffrey Steinbrink sensitively probes a period when, engaged to a sedate maiden, the slambang humorist faced his worst temptation to tame his public self. Fortunately, the "most telling effect" was a "greater stability and even maturity" in his split identity. Though Budd's "Moods and Tenses in Interviews with Mark Twain" (*SAQ* 83:79–92) essentially supplies a chapter of his book, "Deconstructing Mark Twain's White Suit" (*PAPA* 9:1–16) amplifies some details and also claims Twain mostly for the party of change rather than nostalgia.

As more conventional biography Coleman O. Parsons's "Mark Twain in Adelaide, South Australia" (*MTJ* 21,iii:51–54) was worth publishing though finished about twenty-five years ago. Another of his articles that combs local newspapers during the lecture tour in 1895–96, it recovers glimpses of Twain on his best behavior, anxious to help ease British-American relations. Still less accessible materials underlie Anna Katona's "Mark Twain's Reception in Hungary" (*ALR* 16:107–20), which traces his readership and critical standing since the 1890s. James Glen Stovall's "Samuel Langhorne Clemens," pp. 31–46 in *American Newspaper Journalists, 1873–1900* (*DLB* 23), marshals dependably the appropriate facts. Unfortunately, he assumes that once Twain had risen to the status of publishing marketable books, he sloughed off his experience as a reporter and columnist.

iii. General Interpretations

Building on massive research Edgar M. Branch's "Mark Twain: Newspaper Reading and the Writer's Creativity" (*NCF* 37:576–603) proves the importance of his enthusiasm, as just a consumer, for "run-of-the-mill journalism." After showing that Twain drew more on its "ordinary stuff" than we have suspected while searching for the door to his private memories, Branch expands to two yet larger issues: the interplay of Twain's unplanned recall and his conscious scrounging for material; and his mediation of a belief in full determinism and a need to allow for individualistic coloring of ideas. Branch's careful theorizing, banded with steely fact, makes "Lowbrow Animals: Mark Twain," a chapter of Mary Allen's *Animals in American Literature*, seem a pleasant ramble that will soon grow vague.

Suiting the format and audience of a series, Robert Keith Miller's *Mark Twain* (Ungar) depends mostly on familiar sources and often accepts the autobiographical dictations as trustworthy. Interestingly, he makes *Life on the Mississippi*—Twain's "first great work"—his point of entry for proceeding judiciously through the novels: while *The Adventures of Tom Sawyer* maintains a loose unity, it keeps sliding into genteelist, condescending diction; *Huckleberry Finn*, which centers on a boy clearly short of adulthood, has greater profundity than to believe in a lasting escape from society but deserves to be enjoyed more and expounded less; on the other hand *A Connecticut Yankee* gets deadly serious about a "supreme egotist" and "hypocrite" who "sets out to remake the world in his own image" and never learns that "neither the past nor the present is any more ideal than human nature itself"; despite its gaping seams, *Pudd'nhead Wilson* mounts a coherent, probing case against racism. Miller closes with an even-handed chapter on the "representative short fiction," a bin that can hold *The Mysterious Stranger*. Twainians will enjoy his survey, take few notes, and recommend it to undergraduates.

For a scarce new periodical Raymond Sousa's " 'Be It What It Will, I'll Go To It Laughing': Mark Twain's Humorous Sense of Life" (*Thalia* 2, i–ii[1979]:17–24) keys on a late essay by Freud and makes a test case of *Roughing It* before extolling the healthy effects of Twain's comedy. Two chapters in *The Haunted Dusk* examine Twain's obvious fascination with eerie phenomena. Jay Martin briefly argues that he "tended to think of the unconscious as an ever-present source of instantaneous revelation." With customary preciseness Alan Gribben in " 'When Other Amusements Fail': Mark Twain and the Occult" (pp. 171–89) itemizes his startling range of interests from hypnotism to palmistry. Gribben's thesis, always kept in sight, is that Twain wanted to impress posterity by discovering arcane, unorthodox truths yet the faith healers or spiritualists aroused his ingrained skepticism.

Searching for a fresh perspective Jules Chametzky's "Realism, Cultural Politics, and Language as Mediation in Twain and Others" (*Prospects* 8:183–95) presents him as showing Stephen Crane and Theodore Dreiser how to make language bring the worlds of high and vernacular culture together. In *Critical Essays on Mark Twain, 1910–1980* (Hall) Louis J. Budd avoids the formalists' preference for *Huckleberry Finn* in order to feature both his midbrow audience and his appeal for other writers, whether W. D. Howells or Herman Wouk. David Ketterer, moving with a trend he helped start, grows enthusiastic in "The 'Science Fiction' of Mark Twain" (*Mosaic* 16, iv:59–82). Above all he claims precedence for Twain as "The Halley's Comet" of a subgenre, though to insist that *A Connecticut Yankee* is the "first genuine time-travel story" may blur its intentions.

While John J. Pullen's *Comic Relief: The Life and Laughter of Artemus Ward, 1834–1867* (Archon) will be discussed in *ALS* for its main subject, I point out that besides a chapter directly about "Mark Ward and Artemus Twain" the younger (by a year) humorist lurks behind or, rather, just ahead of this entire study, which is maturely dependable.

iv. Individual Writings through 1884

Too few critics care about the hundreds of short pieces published before *The Innocents Abroad*. It's comforting to encounter Trygve Thoreson's "'Virtuous According to Their Lights': Women in Mark Twain's Early Work" (*MTJ* 21,iv:52–56), which points out that his sketches during the 1860s not only made fun of genteel matrons but also showed objectivity and even kindness toward some down-and-out females. Thoreson could find more traces of sexual ease in the first two volumes of *Early Tales & Sketches* (*ALS 1979*, p. 87; *1981*, pp. 98–99).

After a relaxed yet magisterial preface, Walter Blair creates a new work in *Mark Twain's West: The author's memoirs about his boyhood, riverboats and western adventures* (Lakeside Press). Borrowing most heavily from the travel books, it has Twain embroider his career up until the excursion on the *Quaker City*. With "'The Blue Hotel': A Source in *Roughing It*" (*SSF* 20:39–44), Brenda Murphy reasonably compares Twain's bully "Arkansas" and Crane's Swede. As for that excursion, Jeffrey Steinbrink's "Why the Innocents Went Abroad: Mark Twain and American Tourism in the Late Nineteenth Century" (*ALR* 16:278–86) argues that Twain basically typified his countrymen while sensitive enough to feel troubled for doing so. Backed up by the rest of *Anglo-American Landscapes*, Christopher Mulvey superbly explains why Twain stood awed a few years later by Westminster Abbey but not the Tower.

Having urged the "continuing need" to treat his sketches with "greater seriousness," W. Gerald Marshall in "Twain's 'A Curious Dream' and *The Inferno*" (*MTJ* 21,iii:41–43) claims anagogical scope for one that ridiculed the neglect of a Buffalo cemetery. With " 'Everybody Chases Butterflies': The Theme of False Hope in *The Gilded Age*" (*JAC* 6:69–75), Jerry O'Brien contends just as doggedly that Clemens and Warner managed to attain unity on their major theme, the tension between the benefits of optimism and the "inevitable danger of disillusionment." Still harder but more cheeringly Richard A. Sax's "Living in the Realm of Possibility: Beriah Sellers in *The Gilded Age*" (*MTJ* 21,iv:38–41) promotes the Colonel to a quasi-hero for his warm loyalty to family and his restless ambition. "His decision to study law completes and epitomizes" his "personification" of striving to forge ahead.

More cautiously and persuasively, Bernard Macaigne, "From *Tom Sawyer* to *Penrod*: The Child in American Popular Literature, 1870–1910" (*RFEA* 8:319–31) ties Twain's first novel into a tradition of narrative about boys who remain firmly juvenile. But Charles A. Norton's *Writing Tom Sawyer: The Adventures of a Classic* (McFarland) is puzzling in several ways. While much too scholarly for a general audience, it has overlooked some relevant articles. It discusses "The Growth of Criticism" yet omits obvious landmarks. Its best chapter traces the later attempts to adapt the novel into a play, and "*Tom Sawyer* on Film" is helpful for teachers, who will keep wary of Norton while grateful for his speculations and regrouping of details.

More than I would, Macaigne distinguishes sharply between the intended audiences of *Tom Sawyer* and *Huckleberry Finn*. The majority agrees with him, of course. Ten of the twenty-two articles in the Fall issue of the *Mark Twain Journal* are devoted primarily to the later novel. Neil Schmitz's *Of Huck and Alice* makes it the centerpiece in a subtle and ambitious theory, which brings up *Tom Sawyer* only in order to fault it for lacking the magic ingredient of "Huck-speech." Because Schmitz thinks with Twainlike energy, he thrusts in many directions beyond his enthusiasm for the vernacular style; with so much to choose from, reviewers will diverge in their paths of discovery (or disagreement). For me, he contributes most on the relationship of Huck with Jim, whom we see only through a white boy's mind and may visualize far too superficially.

Aside from Schmitz, who binds *Huckleberry Finn* to Krazy Kat and Gertrude Stein, the novel got an unusual spread of tributes. An Australian, Greg Matthews, spun out five hundred pages for *The*

Further Adventures of Huckleberry Finn (Crown), which quickly abandons Tom but keeps Jim all the way to California. A Japanese critic marvels (*Shonan English Lang and Lit* 13:1–14) at how Twain not only creates all varieties of humor but also blends them. In "Huckleberry Finn, Modernist Poet" (*MQ* 24:261–73), Sanford Pinsker admires Huck's "terrible honesty," equal to Hemingway or Plath in "darkness of vision." For the *Texas Speech Communication Journal* (7[1982]:37–41), W. F. Strong cares to study how Twain adjusted sections of his text for live audiences. Huck himself would now hardly presume to read so classic a work.

Four brief articles directly confront him as the teller of the tale. Richard H. Passon's "Twain and Eighteenth-Century Satire: The Ingenu Narrator in *Huckleberry Finn*" (*MTJ* 21,iv:33–36) argues that traveler-outsider Huck is modeled on preceding classics; the point would gain from citing "Goldsmith's Friend Abroad Again," satirical letters that Twain wrote in 1870–71. For "The Overt, Unreliable, Naive Narrator in the Tall Tale and *Huckleberry Finn*" (*MTJ* 21,iii:39), Mary K. Lee gets surprisingly much said with one page—a lesson to us all—as she explores the dynamics of reflexivity for both the humorist, pretending naiveté, and the audience, knowingly accepting that pose to enjoy it. John F. Desmond's "*Huckleberry Finn* and the Failure of Anamnesis" (*MTJ* 21,iv:8–10) refines the problem that Huck, who had functioned as a self-evaluating mind, flattens toward a narrative device during the Evasion. Backing off to the scale of literary history Patrick W. Shaw in "Huck's Children: the Contemporary American Picaro" (*MTJ* 21,iv:42–43) erects him as a "Janus, looking backward" toward the European rogues while anticipating our modern antisocial hero.

Concentrating on theme, Carol Coclough Strickland's "Of Love and Loneliness, Society and Self in *Huckleberry Finn*" (*MTJ* 21, iv:50–52) shows that "something amounting to a debate has for nearly two decades been developing" on the "passages relating to loneliness." In "*Huckleberry Finn*: The Sacred and the Profane" (*MTJ* 21,iii:27–28), Randy K. Cross points out instead the relative silence about the treatment and, in fact, lively ridicule of organized religion. Not contradicting Cross in practice, "Huck's Great Escape: Magic and Ritual" (*MTJ* 21,iii:17–18) by Earl F. Briden suggests that the fake murder mixes Biblical "dimensions" and black lore, especially witchcraft. On another general theme Marden J. Clark's "No

Time to be Sentimentering" (*MTJ* 21,iii:21–23), ignoring Twain's own weakness for the overwrought, finds a running contrast of sentimentality to earned or deserved emotion. More narrowly John D. Reardon's "'Shakespearean Revival!!!': A Satire of American Elizabethans" (*MTJ* 21,iv:36–38) with a perhaps obvious point that's new to me applies the Duke's version of *Hamlet* against the 19th-Century reverence for and lame imitation of imported drama. Finally, George Anastaplo's broad yet brief chapter in his *The Artist as Thinker* (Chicago: Swallow Press) does best in arguing that the man who shoots down Boggs should not have been granted the dignity of repelling the lynch mob.

The major article by far was Victor Fischer's "Huck Finn Reviewed: The Reception of *Huckleberry Finn* in the United States, 1885–1897" (*ALR* 16:1–57). Mobilizing the resources of the Mark Twain Project he combed newspapers from coast to coast to prove that the novel was widely reviewed after all, with an inevitable spread of response that tipped well toward praise. He also enriches the primary materials about the second round of commentary that followed its banning by the Concord Public Library. Helpfully, he goes on to the rise of its reputation by the time when the first collected edition of Twain's works was organized. Clear and meticulous, Fischer's article is definitive, a rare effect in Twain studies.

v. Individual Writings after 1884

Ignoring the famous boys, Paul Delaney's "The Genteel Savage: A Western Link in the Development of Mark Twain's Transcendent Figure" (*MTJ* 21,iii:29–31) searches "Tom and Huck Among the Indians" to support his thesis that the awesome heroes Twain also enjoyed creating—Brace Johnson in this story—have mastered another realm of experience besides that they grew up in. Such a pattern doesn't quite fit Hank Morgan though nobody denies him aggressiveness. Indeed, Nancy S. Oliver's "New Manifest Destiny in *A Connecticut Yankee in King Arthur's Court*" (*MTJ* 21,iv:28–32) makes him the exemplar of the rising American drive to establish "superiority" in world affairs. Likewise drawing on history with "A Connecticut Yankee in Merlin's Cave: The Role of Contradiction in Mark Twain's Novel" (*ALR* 16:58–72) Richard S. Pressman suggestively if sweepingly accounts for the paradoxes often perceived in Hank's ideas and actions: Hank-Twain is a "petit-bourgeois" entrepreneur who cannot realize that monopoly capitalism has outmoded his world, a romantic who crumbles before the imperatives of socio-political reality. After such solemnity it's a shock to read Karen Nolle–Fischer's more mundanely oriented "Selling Mark Twain's *Connecticut Yankee* in America: Marketing and Illustrations" (*RFEA* 8:265–81), which proves that he privately distinguished between Hank's neo-populist drive and his appeal as entertainment. Through new illustrations the reprints would stress the adventure story and a quaintly comic return into the past. More than any other Twain book, she leads me to conclude, *A Connecticut Yankee* should appear with all of its original drawings by Dan Beard.

I don't mean to denigrate bold perspectives, however, if only because Stanley Brodwin has brought off an outstanding essay with "Wandering Between Two Gods: Theological Realism in Mark Twain's *A Connecticut Yankee*" (*SLitI* 16,ii:57–82). Too finely co-ordinated for a quick précis, it gains depth from his old interest in Twain's "counter-theology" (*ALS 1976*, p. 83), a sophisticated mixture of a Calvinist heritage, Deism, and Darwinian principles that poises between reaction and hope. Convincingly, Brodwin adds a social dimension here—Twain's doubt that humankind can progress without renouncing a punitive God for a beneficent Deity. He also shows that the humor in *A Connecticut Yankee* moves from entertainment into functional satire before receding as the main issues head toward the climax. The genuine climax is the dream-ending (for a Hank now lost in the 1880s), which accepts tense contradictions as part of the collective struggle through history. If Twain himself thought at so high a level of abstraction, then Brodwin has glimpsed the foot on the treadle of the loom. Frank Ancone with his packed "Kurt Vonnegut and the Great Twain Robbery" (*NCL* 13,vi:6–7) interprets the Yankee's narrative as the artistic source for that modern classic, *Slaughterhouse Five*.

Pudd'nhead Wilson has convinced more critics that claims for Twain's profundity are sound. For instance, the new *Cambridge Guide to English Literature* calls it a "striking novel, his best work apart from" *Huckleberry Finn*. Robert H. O'Connor's "Some Allegorical Elements in *Pudd'nhead Wilson*" (*BWVACET* NS8:10–16) finds that the "tyranny" of Dawson's Landing represents not simply "social injustice" but "the more universal injustice of cosmic determinism." Specifically the master-slave relationship stands for subjection to a God who always lets the strivings for temporal justice turn self-defeating. In "The Other Half: A Study of *Pudd'nhead Wilson*" (*MTJ* 21,iii:14–16), John M. Brand develops the religious theme more familiarly as abhorrence of that "pernicious form of Calvinism," the bifurcation of humankind into the elect and the damned. Adding Luigi and Angelo to the damned in "Brothers under the Skin? The Use of Twins in *Pudd'nhead Wilson* and *Those Extraordinary Twins*" (*MTJ* 21,iv:10–11), Jo Ella Powell Exley concludes that their cruelties toward each other emphasize the lack of human solidarity even where nature tried to insist on it.

I suspect that the tide toward profundity will sweep over Hershel Parker's polemic yet densely substantiated "The Lowdown on *Pudd'nhead Wilson*: Jack-Leg Novelist, Unreadable Text, Sense-Making Critics, and Basic Issues in Aesthetics" (*RALS* 11[1981]:215–40). Yet he convinces me that Twain's cavalier attitude in all stages of composition left a tangle of manuscripts that never can be edited definitively. Because he did so little to harmonize his existing manuscript with the revisions or, still worse, with new chapters, Parker denies that the various patterns of unity found by some critics can be intentional or even actual. Raising the banner of Derrida, however, Allan Gardner Smith's "*Pudd'nhead Wilson*: Neurotic Text" (*DQR* 11,i:22–33) welcomes the "distortions" of the "surface" since they "betray a complex disturbance beneath," revealing "with startling clarity both the traces of erasure" and the "suppression of unacknowledgable material." Rather than working carelessly Twain could not control the childhood traumas his narrative had reawakened.

In all modesty John Carlos Rowe may think he already rebuts Parker with "Trumping the Trick of Truth: The Extra-Moral Sense of Twain's *Pudd'nhead Wilson*" in *Through the Custom-House* (pp. 139–67), which also operates under Derradaist principles (see *ALS 1982*, pp. 62–63): "The repeated critical complaint that *Pudd'nhead Wilson* suffers from undeveloped or contradictory characters seems absurdly at odds with the themes of the work itself; certainly, every member of a slave-holding society is affected by those contradictions and hypocrisies that constitute the infrastructure of the culture." As a "literary monstrosity" the "grotesque form" carries the "metacommentary" on social politics. However, Rowe cannot be formulized even while applying to each character his approach that *Pudd'nhead*

Wilson "achieves its greatness by virtue of its strategic dissonance."
He launches more warheads than *ALS* is scaled to handle.

Disapprovingly, Fordyce Richard Bennett's "The Moral Obliquity
of 'The Man That Corrupted Hadleyburg'" (*MTJ* 21,iii:10–11) finds
thematic dissonance in one of Twain's best praised stories. If "im-
pulsive generosity or vengefulness generates equally ruinous effects,
what moral values can possibly establish" a "norm for its satire?" But
in "'Hadleyburg': Mark Twain's Dual Attack on Banal Theology and
Banal Literature" (*ALR* 16:240–52), Susan K. Harris insists—too
flatly—that the Richardses are made the most "corrupt" persons in
the community, which otherwise accepts a moral drubbing with good
humor. Its redemption is nevertheless a "cover story," a sop to popular taste so that Twain could exemplify innate depravity through the
old couple. Along with other points of strength Harris gives force to
the problem of why he treats them harshly while letting (most of)
the town off the hook.

The "Mysterious Stranger" manuscripts got the attention only of
Carroll R. Schoenewolf's "Possible Sources of Twain's 'No. 44'" (*MTJ*
21,iii:50), which undercuts other theories more convincingly than it
supplies its own. Twain does inspire keener questions than answers.
Still 1983 brought Gribben's edition of his own *Rubáiyát*, the facsimile
of the *Huckleberry Finn* holograph, and major articles by Branch,
Brodwin, Fischer, and Parker (published late). Many critics would
doubtless add Rowe for the most vigorously speculative essay on
Twain that I can recall. But the centennial of *Huckleberry Finn* will
stir up many ideas. (Typically for Twain, it will be observed in competing years, both 1984 and 1985.) As Henrietta Stackpole says,
"Look here, just you wait!"

Duke University

7. Henry James

Robert L. Gale

A new Henry James boom may be starting. The year 1983 saw four excellent books, more than 60 fine articles, and much valuable editorial work on the Master. Comparative, source, and ultramodern critical concentration is much in evidence. Especially well treated this year were *What Maisie Knew, The Ambassadors, The Golden Bowl*, "The Turn of the Screw," and "The Beast in the Jungle." James's nonfictional work came in for good discussion. And two journals, *Modern Language Studies* and *Topic*, devoted a special issue each to James.

i. Editions, Letters, Bibliographies, Biographical Studies

A sumptuous republication of James is now under way, as part of the Library of America. The first volume, now available, contains James's first five novels, with texts as follows: *Watch and Ward*, 1871 *Atlantic Monthly* serial version; *Roderick Hudson*, first American edition, 1875; *The American*, first American edition, 1877; *The Europeans*, first American edition, 1878; and *Confidence*, first American edition, 1880. William T. Stafford, who selected the texts and provides detailed notes in justification, also includes some explanatory textual endnotes (and several quoted revisions) for each novel. He makes great use of Herbert Ruhm's excellent edition of *Confidence* (Grosset & Dunlap, 1962), the first to be based on the manuscript. The finest non-Jamesian feature of this magnificent example of bookmaking is a 15-page "Chronology," which is nothing less than a mini-biography of James. The Library promises nine more volumes of James's writings.

In "An Unpublished Letter of William James" (*Manuscripts* 35: 145–48), Adeline R. Tintner prints a 1904 letter from William James to a woman who wanted to engage Henry James for a lecture in Wisconsin. Tintner uses the letter to discuss the sibling rivalry of the two strange brothers. John R. Byers, Jr.'s "Half a Henry James Letter" (*ALR* 16:129–31) makes available the last two pages of a 1902 or 1903 letter by James, apparently to George Gissing, encouraging him, and evaluating H. G. Wells, who is "launched in . . . pother," and Joseph Conrad, whose matter is so different from his manner as to "threaten . . . trouble ahead."

Welcome is the reprinting in paperback by Princeton of James's *Autobiography* from the plates of the 1956 Criterion Books edition. It includes Frederick W. Dupee's autumnal introduction and his notes.

We have many bibliographies listing criticism of James. Beatrice Ricks (see *ALS 1979*, pp. 93–94) and more recently Linda J. Taylor, *Henry James, 1866–1916: A Reference Guide* (Hall, 1982) together list scholarship to 1975. Taylor's guide differs from earlier volumes in the Hall bibliography series under the general editorship of Jack Salzman, through its chronological limits, and through being limited to reviews, essays, books on James, mention of him in other books, and reviews in forty-three newspapers arbitrarily chosen if representative. (See review of Taylor by Robert L. Gale, *ALR* 16:151–54.) Now comes John Budd's *Henry James: A Bibliography of Criticism, 1975–1981* (Greenwood) with a startling 909 entries, divided into dissertations and theses, books, chapters and material in books, and articles. An introduction attempts to account "for the longevity of interest in James." Most of the bibliographical entries are descriptively annotated. Book reviews are noted, where pertinent. The overall arrangement is alphabetical by authors. Included is a useful subject index. Richard A. Hocks's "James Studies 1981: An Analytic Bibliographical Essay" (*HJR* 5:29–59) is an informative survey of books, general articles, articles on specific novels, and miscellaneous articles concerning James published in 1981. More thorough than the pertinent *ALS 1981* essay, partly because it can avail itself of the 1981 *MLA Bibliography* but mostly because it is more than four times as long, this essay is a model of tact; Hocks does, however, bridle at "high-tech methodology, algebraic formulas, and jargon that . . . is *à la mode*" nowadays. Bruce Whiteman in "The Henry James Collection at McMaster University" (*HJR* 5:66–67) describes the growing James collection at that Canadian university in Hamilton, Ontario, which was doubled in 1977 by the acquisition of Simon Nowell-Smith's James holdings. Whiteman notes certain rarities and calls "the collection an excellent one for detailed textual and bibliographical study."

The title of Michael W. Anesko's "'Friction with the Market': The Publication of Henry James's New York Edition" (*NEQ* 66:354–81) springs from James's stated belief that "solitary artists . . . steeped in . . . mere personal dreams" may benefit from "*friction with the market.*'" Disproving Leon Edel's long-accepted contention that James's plan for his selected edition was firm from the start, Anesko uses much evidence (including unpublished letters) to show that "James was prepared to frame his artistic goals in distinctly marketable forms" by offering "'intimate, personal'" prefaces, stressing stories in the popular early manner of "Daisy Miller," and "'quietly disown[ing]'" items that would swell the edition to a risky bulk. Anesko summarizes how Scribner's dealt with James's competing publishers; selections for the edition depended in part on their generosity or protectionism. Almost until deadline time, James "remained open to outside suggestions" and at the end "collapsed into the arms of his editor," surrendering to marketplace exigencies. In a fascinating collaboration entitled "The Library of Henry James, From Inventory, Catalogues, and Library Lists" (*HJR* 4:158–90) Leon Edel narrates events concerning the disposition, scattering, and partial reassemblings (now in seven main places) of James's huge personal library; then A. R. Tintner discusses problems connected with listing and describing the items, and finally lists them all (about 1,300 in number) in alphabetical order by authors. The dedicated compilers invite additions to the list and promise a "forthcoming book publication of this inventory." Tardy mention should be made of Robert L. Gale's efficient, well-illustrated essay "Henry James" (*DLB* 1982, pp. 297–326), which reviews its subject's life and summarizes salient features of his oeuvre.

ii. Sources, Parallels, Influences

This category was statistically the most popular in 1983, as it has often been in the recent past.

In "The Museum World of Henry James: The Classical Sculpture Wing" (*Trivium* 18:87–101) A. R. Tintner shows that James's references and allusions to classical and neoclassical statues and intaglios are "to be regarded by the cultivated and informed reader as clarifying analogies." Tintner finds evidence in James's "The Last of the Valerii," "The Solution," "Adiña," "Longstaff's Marriage," *Roderick Hudson,* and "The Tree of Knowledge." Tintner's *"Paradise Lost* and *Paradise Regained* in James's *The Wings of the Dove* and *The Golden Bowl"* (*MiltonQ* 17:125–31) details James's "life-long" admiration for John Milton and theorizes that *The Wings of the Dove* and *The Golden Bowl* are a pair of works that "involve . . . the expulsion from Paradise [*Wings*] and the regaining of a true paradise which Adam and Maggie [*Bowl*] must earn." In "Henry James, Orientalist" (*MLS* 13:121–53) Tintner proves that James "responded to the romantic cult of Orientalism," which in general had standards unlike those of 19th-century Western civilization. Orientalism gave vent to often suppressed emotions, ritualistically worshipped strange gods, accepted slavery, subjugated women, condoned cruelty, and seemed deliciously inscrutable to outsiders. Tintner details James's steady interest in Orientalist writers and painters (too numerous to list here); then she surveys his intermittent iconographic references and allusions to them in his fiction, especially including "The Impressions of a Cousin" and *The Golden Bowl.* Tintner also shows in "Henry James and the Sleeping Beauty: A Victorian Fantasy on a Fairy-Tale Theme" (*Topic* 37:10–22) that three stories by James "not only contain . . . explicit references" to the Sleeping-Beauty fairy tale but also "admit . . . to being . . . retelling[s] of the legend . . . based in part on the illustrations of the tale by . . . Gustave Doré and Edward Burne-Jones." In each story, love of the dormant one is tragic or unconsummated, with Doré ruins or Burne-Jones medievalisms in the background.

Elizabeth Schultz and Fumiko Yamamoto begin their "Egos vs. Relationships in James's *The Golden Bowl* and Soseki's *Light and Darkness"* (*CLS* 20:48–65) by detailing parallels in the careers of James and "his great contemporary, the Japanese novelist Natsume Soseki" (1867–1916). James was unfamiliar with Soseki's fiction; but the Japanese writer owned several of James's works, including *The Golden Bowl,* which may have influenced Soseki's *Light and Darkness.* The critics specify several close parallels but admit that they may be a "coincidence of . . . shared vision." More probing is Peter Barry, who in "Citizens of a Lost Country: Kawabata's *The Master of Go* and James's 'The Lesson of the Master' " (*CLS* 20:77–93) shows that both James's story and Kawabata's novel, which narrates events in a 1938 Go match, query "the relationship between life and art," have "areas of reticence," and challenge the reader to participate in the structuring of the narrative. Other parallels are pointed out.

William W. Stowe's "Intelligibility and Entertainment: Balzac and James" (*CL* 35:55–69) concerns both great 19th-Century writers, their processes of knowing reality, and their requirements as to reader response. Both perceived reality with an eye to using it, asked their readers to learn as their fictive characters do, and offer texts explicable only "by processes similar to the ones their plots describe." But whereas Balzac's works call for "structural analysis," James's call for "rhetorical analysis," because while Balzac probes society James "explore[s] the processes of perception and narration." A. R. Tintner in "Henry James's 'The Pension Beaurepas': 'A Translation into American Terms' of Balzac's *Le Père Goriot*" (*RLC* 57:369–76) shows that in "The Pension Beaurepas" James "refashioned" his favorite Balzac novel, since "[i]ts plot has been partly appropriated, its setting is actually imitated and some of its characters, names and relationships are clearly referred to."

Tintner offers five more influence studies. In "Henry James and Miss Braddon: 'Georgina's Reasons' and the Victorian Sensation Novel" (*EIC* 10:119–24) she shows that James followed the example of Mary Elizabeth Braddon, authoress of the sensational *Aurora Floyd* (which James had admiringly reviewed) and *Lady Audley's Secret*, and used some of her wild plot ingredients in his "Georgina's Reasons," commissioned by the sensational New York *Sunday Sun*. In "Rudyard Kipling and Wolcott Balestier's Literary Collaboration: A Possible Source for James's 'Collaboration'" (*HJR* 4:140–43) Tintner sees the joint-authorship by Kipling (British) and Balestier (American) of their East-West novel *The Naulahka*—as well as "the conjunction of their talents and personal histories"—as possibly "reflected" in James's story "Collaboration." She also contends in "A Source for James's 'Maud-Evelyn' in Henry Harland's 'The House of Eulalie'" (*NMAL* 7: item 13) that James derived the idea of dramatizing in "Maud-Evelyn" the morbid parental delusion that a "dead daughter still lives" from Harland's story "The House of Eulalie," appearing in his *Comedies and Errors*, which James "appreciatively reviewed." Tintner's "W. Somerset Maugham vs. Henry James" (*ABBW* 72:3092–3120 passim) "bring[s] together the curiously ambivalent criticism that Maugham made of James' work and character, the persona of James as he appears in Maugham's fiction, and the use Maugham made of James' stories in his own creation." Tintner concludes that "it seems to be a question of [Maugham's] biting the hand that fed him." And Tintner in "Mothers vs. Daughters in the Fiction of Edith Wharton and Henry James" (*ABBW* 71:4324–28 passim) shows that Wharton presents only "bad" mothers in her seven short stories dealing with mothers and daughters, thus following the lead of James, who has nine bad mothers in his ten novels with mother-daughter themes and five "silly" to "savage" mothers in his five mother-daughter short stories. (It should be noted, by the way, that Tintner in "A Jamesian as a Collector" [*Professional Rare Bookseller*, No. 6, pp. 3–8] ecstatically describes the fun she has had as a collector-scholar.)

Kenneth Graham's "Stevenson and Henry James: A Crossing" in *Robert Louis Stevenson*, ed. Andrew Noble (Vision/Barnes and Noble), pp. 23–46 discusses the "dialectic between form and life, which Stevenson and James as critics each recorded and revealed in their different ways." To James, art should struggle to render solicitous life complexly; to Stevenson, art should not correspond to life but neatly abstract from it.

In *The Collected Letters of Joseph Conrad: Volume I 1861–1897* (Cambridge), editors Frederick R. Karl and Laurence Davies present early evidence, some not published before, to show how Conrad timidly started a notable literary friendship with James. Daniel Mark Fogel's essay " 'The Last Cab' in James's 'The Papers' and in *The Secret Agent*: Conrad's Cues from the Master" (*MFS* 29:227–33) suggests that Conrad used bits from James's "unjustly neglected long tale 'The Papers' as inspiration for the last cab ride of Winnie Verloe's mother in *The Secret Agent*" and for certain cannibal imagery as well. Conrad admired James's delicacy of touch, in "The Papers" and elsewhere; but, sadly, *The Secret Agent* displeased James because of its morbidity. In "The Hermeneutics of Literary Impressionism: Interpretation and Reality in James, Conrad, and [Ford Madox] Ford" (*CentR* 27:244–69), Paul B. Armstrong takes off from concerns expressed in the "Epilogue" of his *The Phenomenology of Henry James* (see below) to show how the three authors challenge their readers to think about "consciousness in representation and interpretation." Adam Gillon's "Conrad and James: A World of Things Beyond the

Range of Commonplace Definitions" (*Conradiana* 15:53–64) is concerned with how "both James and Conrad endow *thing* (or *things*) with a symbolic meaning which determines its value, *real* or *imagined*." Both are "more concerned with symbolic vision than with seeing," so as "to present the artist's *real thing*"—something authentic rather than merely factual or documentary.

In "Another Model for Christina Light" (*HJR* 5:60–65), B. Richards says that the notorious Eleanor Strong, estranged wife of Charles Edward Strong, may be partly the model of Christina Light of *Roderick Hudson* and especially *The Princess Casamassima*. Revisions in both novels hint at James's increasing disapproval of her irksome histrionics.

iii. Criticism: General

Into this group fall four splendid books and many great articles.

The best book of the year on James is Paul B. Armstrong's interdisciplinary study *The Phenomenology of Henry James* (N.C.), which, building on two previous essays (*ALS 1978*, pp. 98–99, 106), suggests that James's understanding of the method of learning, the process of writing fiction, and indeed all of experience "coincides" with phenomenological and existential theories as they elucidate "the interdependence of the epistemological and moral explorations that James's art undertakes." This startling young critic then discusses "five major aspects of experience that . . . map James's understanding of being human." They are "the 'impression' as a way of knowing, the imagination, freedom, personal relations, and the politics of the social world." These aspects both preoccupy "James's consciousness as a [literary] creator" and also "demarc[ate] . . . man's being." Armstrong opens with a "global reading" of *What Maisie Knew*, to show how "James the epistemological novelist and James the moral dramatist complement and complete each other [since] . . . dilemmas with knowing and existential trials are inseparable." Armstrong uses "The Art of Fiction" to "ask . . . the impression about the way it knows the world"; *Roderick Hudson* to "explore . . . James's awareness of . . . imaginative extravagance"; *The Portrait of a Lady* to analyze "the relation between possibility and limitation"; *The Golden Bowl* to consider "the epistemological dilemma of intersubjectivity and the existential crisis of care"; and *The Spoils of Poynton* to demonstrate "[p]ower, mediation, and the relation of individual experience to its social context."

Edward Wagenknecht's august survey called *The Novels of Henry James* (Ungar) is the best introduction to its subject ever written. This sage old critic (born 1900) treats the twenty–two long fictions of the writer he calls "the greatest of American novelists" in chronological order through to the major-phase trio—"a high tableland flooded with light unmatched in the whole terrain of American fiction." The nine meaty chapters between the introductory and concluding ones are vintage Wagenknecht. His formula is simple and telling: composition and publication data, inspiration for the work, possible sources and influences, discussion of plot (usually brief, sometimes featuring structure), and evaluation of characters (central and otherwise). As does James, Wagenknecht essentially begins and ends with characters and their interpersonal relationships. He relishes blasting imperceptive critics and praising the proper-minded. Conservative in orientation, he has a point when he rebukes "these critics [who] seem . . . too much at home with modern realistic literature to be able to understand anything . . . older, more idealistic." Perhaps thin on *Watch and Ward, Roderick Hudson, The Europeans*, and even *The Golden Bowl*, he is spellbinding on *Washington Square, The Portrait of a Lady, The Tragic Muse* (which he rescues), and especially *The Spoils of Poynton* and *The Ambassadors*. He is adept with endings, though perhaps too sure of the goodness of Milly Theale (*The Wings of the Dove*) and the defection of Chad Newsome (*The Ambassadors*). He rightly downgrades *Confidence, The Reverberator, The Awkward Age*, and *The Outcry*; and he lavishes ingenuity on *The Sense of the Past*. The two main values of this wonderful book, which has insights on every page, are these: Wagenknecht interprets James's best characters as models of the decent, freedom-loving spirit; and he surveys previous scholarship, often in long, bracing, educative footnotes.

Robert Emmet Long in *Henry James: The Early Novels* (TUSAS 440; Twayne) discusses *Watch and Ward, Roderick Hudson, The American, The Europeans, Confidence, Washington Square, The Portrait of a Lady*, and *The Bostonians*. His format is simple and effective: circumstances of James's life at time of composition, details of publication, royalties, revisions, possible sources and influences, and critical interpretation—intertwining of realism and romance, fairy-tale elements, inner plots, doubling of opposing characters, and the Hawthornean sin of pride in self vs. Emersonian transcendence. Previous scholarship on the eight novels is cited in big footnotes. Long does what he can with *Watch and Ward*, spending too much time on sources, writing well on Mrs. Keith, suggesting that the novel prefigures later works. He is excellent on minor characters in *Roderick Hudson*, sees Roderick and Rowland Mallet as "paired protagonists," may be too hard on the latter. He seems thin on *The American*, is too sure that critics prefer the unrevised version, discusses theater and art imagery well, pairs Christopher Newman and Noémie Nioche neatly. Long likes *The Europeans* awfully well, sees it as satirical of New England, condones Eugenia Münster more than seems proper. *Confidence* wastes Long's immense talents. He presents Austin Sloper and Morris Townsend in *Washington Square*— "proprietor and pretender to the house"—as two more doubles, is wonderful in analyzing tenacious Catherine Sloper. *The Portrait of a Lady*, with literary impressionism and stream of consciousness, features house, garden, art, eye, and water imagery, certain deficiencies in characterization, and a controversial ending. In treating cruxes in *The Bostonians*, Long really shines: the characters' homelessness and blighted landscapes, the assertiveness of some women and the effeminizing of some men, unconsciously lesbian Olive Chancellor and harshly seen Basil Ransom (they, too, are linked opposites). Long electrifyingly concludes that James, like pairs of his characters, is in truth "two Jameses, one of whom embraces the finitude of experience and is skeptical of the transcendence the other at times urges."

The thesis of Marcia Jacobson's *Henry James and the Mass Market* (Alabama) is simple and brilliant: James flirted with French naturalism and the British theater (1885–99) to please the capricious popular market, to write bestsellers, and to make money; but "he could not foresee that his refusal to play the role of entertainer and moralizer would cut him off from a wide spectrum of readers." In *The Bostonians* he combined current interest in feminism, mesmerism, and spiritualism with the popular post–Civil War romance; but his females here are awesome, and his hero is not acceptable as local color. In *The Princess Casamassima* "a similar resistance to popular thinking is at work in his rejection of meliorative patterns of the working-class novel," i.e., rich heroine cannot go slumming successfully, while poor hero's aspirations to "leisure time, money, and beauty" are tragic. James designed the heroine of *The Tragic Muse* to capitalize on the mass-market delight in fiction concerned with professional actress vs. lure to marriage, but again he went against public taste by making that heroine anti-Victorian in devotion to profession. Further, in limning Gabriel Nash (*The Tragic Muse*) James tried to make points with the popular stereotype of aesthete as poseur, manipulator, and decadent. Next James turned to the stage, failed, then wrote some "self-indulgent" short stories about unpopular but brilliant writers. His abiding problem lay, says Jacobson, in his simultaneously "working within and against popular conventions." Ergo: *What Maisie Knew*, for which he "read up" on harassed children and also on sentimentalized ones in Victorian fiction for adults to read as escape. But in Maisie's story he confrontationally offers a critique of upper-class British society where "male and female sexuality are essentially the same." Adopting the popular juvenile point of view, he makes the girl "go from a storybook world to one in which authentic emotion and compassion operate." Last: *The Awkward Age*, in which James combines two popular elements, putting New Woman in dialogue novel. Here again he varied, making his New Woman not young girl but mother, whose daughter therefore "takes on the abdicated maternal role" and permits James to show up hypocritical, manipulative British society. Jacobson opposes received critical opinions refreshingly, accuses the Master himself of prefatory evasiveness, and provides fine footnotes.

Next, three shorter works of general criticism. Veronica A. Makowsky edits and provides an introduction for R. P. Blackmur's *Studies in Henry James* (New Directions), which reprints Blackmur's thirteen published essays on James plus one left in fragmentary form at his death entitled "The Spoils of Henry James: A Special Case of the Normal." Makowsky reports that Blackmur read James and Henry Adams in an effort to understand the relationship of life and art, concluding, however, that for him "James's novels were not liberating dramas of awakening consciousness but claustrophobic morality plays of imperious conscience." The previously unpublished piece reasons that James was so addicted to art that his life and works interacted to make him normal in a modern way: he faces chaos with sensibility. Thomas H. Getz in "Henry James: The Novel as Act" (*HJR* 4:207–18) defines James the novelist as one who creates "dialectical interaction" with the reader by letting us watch him watch his characters "watch each other watch each other," and listen to them too—often as James and they fill a loving silence. Positive evidence comes mainly from *The Portrait of a Lady* and *The Golden Bowl*; negative, from *What Maisie Knew*. And Robert Gregory in "Henry James and the Art of Execution" (*Topic* 37:43–48) theorizes with playful deadliness that inspiration scares as it entices. Therefore in following it by executing sentences the writer passes sentence on and executes it.

The Haunted Dusk is a beautifully printed book, containing ten splendid essays by eleven critics (one essay being coauthored). Editors Howard Kerr, John W. Crowley, and Charles L. Crow, in a tersely informative introduction place James among others in the tradition of the American ghost story as it moves from "Gothicism to its merger with psychologism early in this century." James figures partly in one essay, Jay Martin's "Ghostly Rentals, Ghostly Purchases: Haunted Imaginations in James, [Mark] Twain, and [Edward] Bellamy," and exclusively in another, Kerr's "James's Last Early Supernatural Tales." Martin suggests that James, as did others, "shared [Elizabeth Stuart] Phelps's belief that the unconscious was spatial, a 'great good place,'" with continuous activities, superior truths, and operations swifter than reason, and therefore "the conscious mind must . . . maintain a connection with its superficially dark—but really brighter, more angelic—side." Kerr theorizes that James, in "Professor Fargo" and "The Ghostly Rental," respectively, repudiates Hawthorne's use of "the 'magnetic miracles' of mesmerism" and—by parodic paralleling—Poe's too marvelously melodramatic story "The Fall of the House of Usher."

Next, four short works on James's fiction in general. Dorothea Krook in "Prefigurings in Two Early Stories of Henry James" (*MLS* 13:5–21) ramblingly develops the thesis that James's first short stories contain "prefigurings of the great things to come," as to character, action, scene, and theme. She shows that "Master Eustace" partly overtures "The Turn of the Screw" and *The Golden Bowl*; "Osborne's Revenge," *The American* and *The Princess Casamassima*. David H. Hirsch's "Henry James and the Seal of Love" (*MLN* 13:39–60) is a major essay. It reverses two truisms in Jamesian criticism, that the international theme is of primary importance to James, and that he is not "an incisive anatomist of sexual or romantic love." Hirsch argues that the main motif in *The Portrait of a Lady* is "love against death," dramatized by Isabel Archer's and Ralph Touchett's love for each other, but finds counter-analogies in *The Song of Songs*. Hirsch rebukes downgraders of sick Ralph and those who defend healthy Caspar Goodwood, suggesting instead that "eroticism is, for Isabel (and probably for James), a destructive force," since "*eros* is [often] not only divorced from *agape*, it is wed to *thanatos*" in novels during James's time. More terrifying is the story of Milly Theale (*The Wings of the Dove*), the model for whom may be, not James's cousin Minny Temple, but his dying sister Alice James, whose diary James read shortly before recording in his *Notebooks* the germ of Milly's love story. "If Alice is the life model, the Shulamite is the literary-mythic model," says Hirsch, who also discusses dove imagery in *The Song of Songs*. Robert K. Martin's "James and the 'Ecstatic Vision'" (*MLS* 13:32–38) discusses James as halfway between impressionist and realist because of his ability to convert a revelatory moment into something truth-yieldingly significant. And Eben Bass's "Henry James and the Venetian Voice" (*CLQ* 19:98–108) parallels Morgan Moreen of "The Pupil" and Milly Theale as "victims of verbal deceit": in both narratives, "language and voice allusions" are used "as means of persecution." Psalm 55 contains pertinent thematic imagery of voice and tongues of the enemy, terror of death, storm, deceit of friend. Bass brilliantly traces these four patterns in "The Pupil" and *The Wings of the Dove*.

A pair of essays discuss recent film adaptations of fiction by James. John C. Shields's "*Daisy Miller*: Bogdanovich's Film and James's *Nouvelle*" (*LFQ* 11:105–111) castigates most of the "condemnatory" reviews of Peter Bogdanovich's work. Allen Hirsch's "*The Europeans*: Henry James, James Ivory, and 'That Nice Mr. Emerson'" (*LFQ* 11:112–19) interprets Ivory's *The Europeans* as a defense of the "expatriate sophistication" of Eugenia Münster and Felix Young.

iv. Criticism: Individual Novels

This year, treatment of specific novels outdid discussion of specific short stories.

K. G. Probert in "Christopher Newman and the Artistic American View of Life" (*SAF* 11:203–15) says that James's *The American* alludes to "traditional romance types" to shed light on the international theme and also to condemn "American Gilded Age acquisitiveness." Daniel J. Schneider applies the thesis of his book *The Crystal Cage* (*ALS 1978*, p. 98) to James's *Confidence* in "The Figure in the Carpet of James's *Confidence*" (*HJR* 4:120–27); that is, the thin novel "was interesting and worthwhile to James because it was part of his life-long effort to dramatize the problem of the free spirit in conflict with the worldly aggressors who would use their victims, forcing them into submission to worldly ends and thus denying the spontaneity and the possibilities of the soul."

Linda A. Westervelt demonstrates in " 'The Growing Complexity of Things': Narrative Technique in *The Portrait of a Lady*" (*JNT* 13:74–85) that James helped shape the modern novel, not alone with his major-phase masterpieces, but as early as *The Portrait of a Lady*, in which he partly avoids being an author-guide and instead presents character directly.

Janet Holmgren McKay in *Narrative and Discourse in American Realistic Fiction* (Penn., 1982) uses James's *The Bostonians*, William Dean Howells's *The Rise of Silas Lapham*, and Mark Twain's *Adventures of Huckleberry Finn* to show that their mingling of narration with characters' discourse led to the meeting of narrative voice, the "foregrounding [of] the voices of the characters," and varied perspectives—i.e., to nothing less than the modern American novel. Using current narratological theories, McKay begins with *The Bostonians*, in which "narrative techniques and methods of discourse presentation, ranging . . . from traditional narrator commentary to complex free indirect discourse," make for "unresolved ambiguity." McKay analyzes narrator voice, and also directly and indirectly reported discourse of minor and then major characters. Problems arise since here we see around characters as in Balzac and "see through their perspective" as in the usual James.

In "Misogynist Stereotypes in *The Princess Casamassima*" (*Topic* 37:35–42), Virginia C. Fowler shows that in *The Princess Casamassima* "sexual identity can be as oppressive as class identity, and even more inescapable." James does not treat gender differences so satisfactorily as he does class differences, implying instead that resolution of class problems must preserve "civilization's treasures," that "women, like the lower classes, are powerless," and that "given their nature, this powerlessness is probably for the best." Fowler sees the Princess as stereotypical Eve-Mary and Millicent Henning as stereotypical Whore-Goddess.

Judith E. Funston argues in "'All Art Is One': Narrative Techniques in Henry James's *Tragic Muse*" (*SNNTS* 15:344–55) that in *The Tragic Muse* James tries to prove that big novels can "duplicate life's complexity and multiplicity while subjecting those qualities to the discipline of form." James's narrator is "painterly," thus "reduc[ing] narratorial omniscience," but also "goes behind" his gallery-like subjects to define their feelings, tidy loose ends, and show awareness that novel is not life. Funston schematizes the novel thus: Peter Sherringham sees Miriam Rooth in dramatic terms; Nick Dormer sees her in painterly terms.

A. R. Tintner in "A Textual Error in *The Spoils of Poynton*" (*HJR* 5:65) notes a hitherto undetected mistake in the New York Edition of *The Spoils of Poynton* and quotes the correct 1897 version.

Three fine essays treat *What Maisie Knew* this year. Merla Wolk's "Narration and Nurture in *What Maisie Knew*" (*HJR* 4:196–206) discusses "maternal failure" in behavior toward little Maisie by her mother, her stepmother, her guardian, and even Sir Claude, from whom, however, she does get her "best mothering." Wolk posits that the world of the poor child is given by the narrator "a coherence . . . [which] imitates the action of mother to child"; further, the narrator's relationship with Maisie "approximates a symbiotic one." Geoffrey D. Smith in "How Maisie Knows: The Behavioral Path to Knowledge" (*SNNTS* 15:224–36) concentrates not on what Maisie comes to know but on how she learns. She does so by making mistakes, by rejection, by distinguishing "between professed intention and active motive" in others, by finding patterns in "individual gestures and mannerisms," and especially by developing her own way of choosing companions. And Laurence E. Oelschlegel in "Henry James and Meta-metaperspective" (*Topic* 37:49–50) quotes and explicates a long passage from *What Maisie Knew* (opening of chapter 19; New York Edition, 11:182–83, beginning "When he had lighted . . ." and ending ". . . directed to diplomacy"), which he sees as "an example of meta-metaperspective perhaps the first, perhaps the only explicit example in Anglo-American literature." "Meta-metaperspective" is defined as "W's view of H's view of W's view of (X)."

Now for the major-phase novels. In "Structure and Process in *The*

Wings of the Dove" (*Topic* 37:23–34) Clarence A. Brown discusses "[t]he employment of the 'successive centres [of consciousness]' . . . at the heart of James's process in the presentation of the two sides of the 'medal' [Milly Theale mortally stricken and Milly adventurously struggling] and of the movement from the circumference to the center and back to the circumference, which forms the structure of the work of art." We move from the social edge of the European world to which Milly is introduced, toward the foreshadowed center, Milly herself; her adventure now is both to live and to "sacrifice . . . her 'selfhood' by offering "love and compassion for others." Mary Cross in " 'To Fnd the Names'; *The Ambassadors*" (*PLL* 19:402–18) argues that "the quest for language, the search 'to find the names,' provide the basic narrative movement of *The Ambassadors*, the thrust of a plot which will . . . be resolved when [the hero Lambert] Strether's understanding—and his vocabulary—match his experience." K. P. S. Jochum in "Henry James's Ambassadors in Paris" (*MLS* 13:109–20) defends James from F. W. Bateson's ridiculous 1973 charge that serious novels, including *The Ambassadors*, unpardonably "mix . . . verifiable and fictitious elements." Jochum maps James's putting his imaginary hero into real Parisian gardens and other places, selectively and with "moral and aesthetic intentions." Bernard Richards in "Henry James's 'Fawns' " (*MLS* 13:154–68) nominates Surrenden Dering as the model for the estate called Fawns in *The Golden Bowl*. He presents much evidence that Surrenden Dering, which "[i]n the summer of 1898 . . . had a moment of social and diplomatic glory when it became the American Embassy in the country," also "provided some of the architectural and landscape influence on Fawns, some of the patterns of social intercourse, and some of the models of statecraft and diplomacy." And Eileen H. Watts's heady theory in "*The Golden Bowl*, a Theory of Metaphor" (*MLS* 13:169–76) is that "knowledge comes to James' characters through metaphor"; therefore "language, knowledge, reality, and the self . . . become coterminous." Watts adduces supporting evidence from *The Golden Bowl*, in no little part from the over-explicated pagoda trope.

v. Criticism: Individual Tales

The finest essay I have ever read on "Daisy Miller" is Motley Deakin's "Two Studies of *Daisy Miller*" (*HJR* 5:2–28). It tour guides us

through several interpretations of Daisy—spoiled, flirtatious, innocent, rebellious—as each impinges on James's backdrops of Vevey
and then Rome. They are Baedeker's Vevey, with its Castle of Chil-
lon, Trois Couronnes Hotel, Geneva nearby, and half-forgotten 19th-
Century literary memorializings; and Baedeker's Rome, with its
Monte Pincio, St. Peter's, Palazzo Doria, Palatine, Protestant Cemetery, and especially Colosseum—which is all sentiment, melodrama,
moonlight, and fever. Next Deakin analyzes "the devices James used
to establish his authorial relationship with the characters": point of
view plus authorial comment, with James as tourist, observer of
tourists, and moralist; James interprets by epithets, use of words in
quotation marks, and repetition of key words, to encourage the interpretation of Daisy as modest, naive, and innocent. One virtue among
many that this essay displays is its valuably countering much of the
prevailing nonsense now being written on James.

George Monteiro in " 'He Do the Police in Different Voices':
James's 'The Point of View' " (*Topic* 37:3–9) discusses the unpopu-
larity in America of "the combination of James's expatriation and his
talent for acute satire," especially when James followed his 1881
visit home with oblique criticism of America in his 1882 story "The
Point of View," in which seven people of three nationalities write
eight letters about the United States. Monteiro notes that "no one
totally speaks for James" and yet "[s]omething of James appears in
every letter." Monteiro's "Geography in 'The Siege of London' "
(*HJR* 4:144–45) points out that an *Overland Monthly* columnist
twitted James, who in "The Siege of London" placed San Diego in
the Southwest within easy riding distance from New Mexico a couple
of times a week. James renamed the town San Pablo for the New
York Edition.

"The Deadly Figure in James's Carpet" (*MLS* 13:79–85) is, according to Gerald M. Sweeney, that "artistic questers, like other
questers, can become so monomaniacally obsessed with the objects
of their pursuit, that they can easily lose contact with their essential
humanity." Since "The Figure in the Carpet" features two marriages,
two births, one sickness, and five deaths, the cold search in the story
for a figure may be for a figure grown "irrelevant."

Sharon Dean in "The Myopic Narrator in Henry James's 'Glasses' "
(*HJR* 4:191–95) explicates the title of the tale: Flora Saunt wears
glasses and is finally kept flower-like "under the protective glass of

Geoffrey Dawling"; the narrator tries to examine Flora by a magnifying glass. Dean evaluates the narrator as tactless, able to see only surfaces, and hence "incapable of transferring his few moments of insight into profound art." James challenges the reader "to see the depths" of the tragedy that his narrator cannot.

"The Turn of the Screw" generated four essays of varying worth this year. "Hesitation, History, and Reading: Henry James's *The Turn of the Screw*" (*TSLL* 25:558–73) by Tobin Siebers applies Tzvetan Todorov's "concept of hesitation"—"the fantastic . . . [is] a literature in which reader and characters hesitate between natural and supernatural explanations of events" (*The Fantastic*, 1970)—to James's celebrated ghost story. Thus, the governess hesitates on first seeing Peter (and again later). Better, we as readers periodically hesitate through being "unable to decide whether the governess is insane or clairvoyant." Best, the governess's pauses are "superstitious" and radiate dead air about her "fantastic visitants," who act in it to unfold the story. Howard Faulkner in "Text as Pretext in *The Turn of the Screw*" (*SSF* 20:87–94) argues that the psychic governess creates and imposes on the "equivocal and confused" events about her a meaningful pattern, as though "they were already a coherent text." She must create an artistic "written document," in which silence speaks, faces are legible, words are ambivalent and translatable, and actions become elements in a sometimes curtained "drama of salvation." In "Jamesian Parody, *Jane Eyre*, and 'The Turn of the Screw'" (*MLS* 13:61–78), Alice Hall Petry tries to prove that James's ghost story is narrated by a deluded governess, "a basically normal albeit sensitive and impressionistic young lady . . . unduly influenced by her reading of . . . *Jane Eyre*." In having the governess "emulate Charlotte Brontë's heroine, James not only exploits but also both undermines "the literary tradition of the plucky heroine" and parodies *Jane Eyre*. James read that book, yes; both Jane and James's governess are similar, yes; but parody? James had more important things to do. Best here is Petry's suggestion that James's governess, when she sees Peter Quint, blurs his image with those of her Harley Street employer and Brontë's Rochester. (For a healthy corrective, see E. A. Sheppard [*ALS* 1975, p. 126].) Applying elements of recent speech act theory, Marcia M. Eaton in "James's Turn of the Speech-Act" (*BJA* 23:333–45) elucidates James's "two-layer ambiguity" in "The Turn of the Screw." James warns us in its prologue that he pities single-minded theorists, then consistently "us[es] sentences that could be construed as one action by one reader and as another action by a different reader"; he also invites plural interpreting both by adding phrases "used to back off . . . from a claim" and by avoiding "clarifying devices," which if used would render the governess's narration less subject to contrary explications. Eaton concludes this provocative essay by advising us to direct our attention to possible interpretations but not to accept any as definitive.

"The Beast in the Jungle" seems perennially to challenge the critics. David Smit in "The Leap of the Beast: The Dramatic Style of Henry James's 'The Beast in the Jungle'" (*HJR* 4:219–30) faults earlier critics of James's "use [of] syntax to create . . . suspense and expectation" in "The Beast in the Jungle" because they insufficiently comment on "the way in which this sense of expectation is satisfied stylistically throughout the story." George Monteiro in "Henry James, Great White Hunter" (*MLS* 13:96–108) argues that in "The Beast in the Jungle" James "metaphorically crossed Hawthorne and Stockton's jungle tigers with the beast in the labyrinth," that is, used both Nathaniel Hawthorne's image of Hollingsworth (from *The Blithedale Romance*) as glaring like a jungle tiger and the ending of Frank Stockton's famous conundrum yarn "The Lady, or the Tiger?" James's John Marcher think that he opts for tiger not lady; but May Bartram becomes sphinx, beast, Minotaur for James's non-hero, who is perhaps patterned also in part on Arthur Evans, discoverer in 1900 of Minoan relics. As labyrinth guide, Monteiro holds his critical torch before riches labeled Walter Pater, Constance Fenimore Woolson, and John Howells (son of William Dean Howells). After tracing the "too-late" theme in earlier works by James, Michael Coulson Berthold in "The Idea of 'Too Late' in James's 'The Beast in the Jungle'" (*HJR* 4:128–39) discusses the uniqueness of the theme as presented in "The Beast in the Jungle," where it is "explore[d] . . . without the distraction of other themes." Berthold shows "the unlived life" to be Hawthornean; better, he analyzes lifelike elements in the artistically wrought "quest manqué," which we watch to its end—the revelation to Marcher of his May-defined failure.

Deborah Esch in "A Jamesian About-Face: Notes on 'The Jolly Corner'" (*ELH* 50:587–605) mainly suggests that conventional interpretations of "The Jolly Corner" as concerning "a character's becoming reconciled to . . . hard-won self-consciousness" disregard a

more *au courant* explication: that "finding the 'terms' [of psychological and epistemological reconciliation] ... will turn its experience
into a writable, readable narrative."

In "'Superior to Oak': The Part of Mora Montravers in James's
The Finer Grain" (*ALR* 16:121–28), W. R. Martin and Warren U.
Ober show that, though ironically discredited in the first part of
"Mora Montravers," the titular heroine of the tale is, in general, "the
model of behavior in James's [entire] last volume of stories [*The
Finer Grain*]," while she is, in particular, the source of the real hero
"Sidney Traffle's gradual realization of the power of the imagination
—the artistic consciousness." The real life-denier is his wife Jane
Traffle, who is all convention, cliché, stupidity, and vulgarity.

vi. Criticism: Specific Nonfictional Work

After a little undeserved neglect, is James's nonfictional writing
making a comeback?

John Carlos Rowe begins his essay "What the Thunder Said:
James's *Hawthorne* and the American Anxiety of Influence: A Cen-
tennial Essay" (*HJR* 4:81–119) by combining Melville's saying that
Hawthorne said "No! in thunder" to European tradition with T. S.
Eliot's three-*Da* summoning back of Western tradition. That done,
Rowe sees James's *Hawthorne* as preface to *The Portrait of a Lady*,
which started as a serial a year later and "translat[es] ... Hawthorne's
romantic themes into James's realism." Rowe reviews critics of James's
Hawthorne, from Eliot and Ezra Pound through F. O. Matthiessen
and R. W. B. Lewis to Richard Chase, Peter Buitenhuis, and Richard
Poirier, and hence to post–1966 criticism, which seems stagnant to
Rowe, who concludes by explicating his view that "James mythologized Hawthorne as the last American innocent, alienated by the
provinciality of young America, precisely to establish a local and
native American tradition that James would hazard to take up ...
to denationalize."

In "James's Later Plays, a Reconsideration" (*MLS* 13:86–95)
Brenda Murphy begins by granting the commonly held opinion that
James often wrongly patterned his dramas on outmoded French
models, tried to be too sophisticated, and employed novelistic dialogue. But then she praises some of his later dramas. The revision of
his *Summersoft* into *The High Bid* gives his characters more human

traits. *The Outcry* integrates a current topic, dramatic discussion of it, and comic form. *The Other House*, though antithetical to some Henrik Ibsen works, evolves from other Ibsen works. And in both *Owen Wingrave* and *The Saloon* "James combined elements of the Shavian discussion with elements drawn from Ibsen and . . . Jamesian tone and structure."

Rosalie Hewitt in "Henry James's 'Autumn Impression': The History, the Manuscript, the Howells Relation" (*YULG* 57[1982]:39–51) analyzes the typescripts and holograph manuscript of the three parts of James's *The American Scene* chapter on New England for the light they shed on his major-phase "composing process," and on his personal and professional friendship with William Dean Howells.

Carol Holly's "A Drama of Intention in Henry James's Autobiography" (*MLS* 13:22–31) discusses the "unfolding interplay between the rhetorical and psychological motives which lie behind an individual's public recollection of personal history." In his *Autobiography* James intended to use selections from his brother William's letters and his own memories to create a family book. Soon, however, he found William's part less engaging, and the subject became James himself, including the history of his "imaginative faculty." Holly stresses the tension in James here between his aim to make suffering a memory and his expression of anxieties carrying into the present.

University of Pittsburgh

8. Pound and Eliot

Hugh Witemeyer

i. Pound

Are the executors, publishers, and archives of Pound and Eliot meeting their responsibilities well? Ten years after the deposit of the Pound Archive at Yale, it has no published catalogue, and Michael J. King's *Collected Early Poems* (1976) remains the only gathering of Pound's original poems edited from it according to acceptable modern scholarly standards. New Directions remains firmly committed to the existing editions of *Personae*, *Selected Poems*, and *The Cantos*—all of them seriously inadequate. The condition of Pound's texts, as George Bornstein has observed in these pages, leaves much to be desired.

a. **Text, Biography, and Bibliography.** The most important textual work of the year is *Pound's Cavalcanti: An Edition of the Translations, Notes, and Essays*, ed. David Anderson (Princeton). One appendix of the book also appears as "Cavalcanti: Canzone to Fortune" (*Paideuma* 12:41–46). Anderson prints all of Pound's known translations, with variants and facing Italian texts. He reproduces Pound's critical writings on Cavalcanti and other related materials. Two of Anderson's texts differ significantly from the more casually edited versions given by Charlotte Ward in "Translations" by Ezra Pound (*IowaR* 12[1981]:37–49). Ward includes nine previously unpublished renderings of medieval poems by Cavalcanti, Arnaut Daniel, Bertran de Born, Walter von der Vogelweide, Gianni Alfani, and an Anglo-Saxon poet. Coincidentally, Pound's opera, *Cavalcanti*, received its world premier in San Francisco on March 28 under the direction of Robert Hughes. In "Ezra Pound: Composer" (*Paideuma* 12:499–509), Archie Henderson describes the occasion, tells how Hughes reconstructed Pound's score, and lists the major public performances of Pound's musical works since 1962.

Meanwhile, Pound's correspondence continues to appear piece-meal. Mary FitzGerald's "Ezra Pound and Irish Politics: An Unpub-lished Correspondence" (*Paideuma* 12:377–417) presents twelve missives exchanged by Pound and the Irish poet and politician, Des-mond FitzGerald, between 1918 and 1928. Daniel Pearlman's "Fight-ing the World: The Letters of Ezra Pound to Senator William E. Borah of Idaho" (*Paideuma* 12:419–26) prints letters written be-tween 1933 and 1939 as part of Pound's futile effort to influence American public policy.

A special Pound issue of *Helix* 13–14 (Melbourne, Australia) contains various texts of interest. "Three Letters on Imagism" by Pound and F. S. Flint, ed. Wallace Martin (pp. 25–29), document the poets' disagreements about the history of the Imagist movement. Two letters from Pound to William Fleming were written in 1955 (pp. 178, 186–87). Tim Redman translates three examples of "Pound's Italian Journalism" into English (pp. 117–123); their titles are "Crawfish?" (1933), "Joyce, Historically" (1930), and "Poisoned Pipelines" (1939). Several U.S. government documents concerning Pound's indictment and arrest for treason are reproduced in "Ad-ministration Interest in Pound" and "Pound's Interrogation at Genoa" (pp. 124–32).

The appearance of Noel Stock's *The Life of Ezra Pound: An Ex-panded Edition* (North Point, 1982) underlines the need for good new biographical studies of Pound. Stock has "expanded" his 1970 text by only four brief passages and a caustic "Afterword, 1982." This year's work, which ranges from the superb to the superficial, suggests some of the information that a comprehensive new biography might include.

Superb research informs two important articles on Pound's early life by James J. Wilhelm: "Ezra Pound's New York, 1887–1908: A Recreation" and "The Wadsworths, the Westons, and the Farewell of 1911" (*Paideuma* 12:55–75,305–47). Wilhelm discovers a rich cache of documented information about the New York environment of Pound's youth and about the history and activities of his mother's family, the Westons. Elsewhere, the father's side of the family is the subject of "T. C. P.'s Heritage" by Mary de Rachewiltz (*Helix* 13–14:1–9).

The London and Paris periods of Pound's career are the focus of several studies. Robert Schultz presents "A Detailed Chronology of Ezra Pound's London Years, 1908–1920: Part Two: 1915–1920" (*Paideuma* 12:357–73). Part Two has the same weaknesses as Part One (see *ALS 1982*). Pound's contacts with expatriate American artists in Paris around 1911 are recalled by Martha Ullman West in "Lady with Poet: Margaret Cravens and Ezra Pound" (*Helix* 13–14: 15–22). Thomas Dilworth records the Paris reminiscences of "Virgil Thomson on George Antheil and Ezra Pound: A Conversation" (*Paideuma* 12:349–56). Thomson was underwhelmed by Pound's musical acumen around 1925–26: "Those red-heads always talk a lot." Finally, four brush-and-ink portraits and one wooden totem sculpture of Pound are listed in *Henri Gaudier-Brzeska, sculptor 1891–1915*, ed. Jeremy Lewison (Kettle's Yard Gallery).

Pound's attitudes toward Social Credit, Fascism, and America during the 1930s interest David C. Duke in a competent but derivative chapter of *Distant Obligations: Modern American Writers and Foreign Causes* (Oxford). Elsewhere, the late Ben D. Kimpel and T. C. Duncan Eaves survey the views of "Ezra Pound on Hitler's Economic Policies" (*AL* 55:48–54), taking both published and unpublished evidence into account. Pound's incarceration at Pisa in 1945 is recalled by John L. Steele, then commander of the Disciplinary Training Center, in "Ez at the DTC: A Correspondence between Carroll F. Terrell and John L. Steele," ed. Michael Fournier (*Paideuma* 12:293–303). Steele offers evidence that Pound's treatment at Pisa was less inhumane than many narrators have supposed.

Pound's treatment at St. Elizabeths Hospital is the subject of two controversial articles. E. Fuller Torrey's "Party in a Madhouse" (*Esquire*, August: 86–92) and Stanley L. Kutler's " 'This Notorious Patient' " (*Helix* 13–14:133–49) both contend that Pound "was not insane in any accepted clinical or legal sense" (Kutler), that Dr. Overholser, the head of St. Elizabeths, lied about his condition to protect him from prosecution, and that Pound led a pampered and privileged life in the hospital. Neither of these essays documents its assertions; both depend more upon innuendo than upon reasoning supported by clear evidence.

In "St. Elizabeths Diary" (*Helix* 13–14:151–52) Jerome Kavka, who was a resident in psychiatry during 1946, responds to Charles Olson's memoir of his visits to the hospital. Looking back to the same

period of Pound's life, William French offers a sincere, effusive, and
badly written tribute to Mrs. Pound in "For 'Gentle Graceful Dorothy,' a Tardy Obit" (*Paideuma* 12:89–113).

The Bollingen controversy of 1948–49 is recalled by William
McGuire in "The Bollingen Foundation: Ezra Pound and the Prize
in Poetry" (*JLC,* 40:16–25) and by Eileen Simpson in *Poets in Their
Youth: A Memoir* (Vintage). According to Simpson, who was then
his wife, John Berryman planned to write an introduction to Pound's
Selected Poems. Pound's eventual release from St. Elizabeths is a
recurrent theme in the *Letters of Archibald MacLeish, 1907 to 1982,*
ed. R. H. Winnick (Houghton Mifflin), which includes twenty-four
letters from MacLeish to Pound written between 1926 and 1959.

Last and certainly least among this year's biographical studies is
Alan Levy's *Ezra Pound: The Voice of Silence* (Sag Harbor, New
York: Permanent Press). Levy expands his 1972 *New York Times
Magazine* interview with Pound into a superficial, Arthur-Frommer
guide to the poet and his work ("If *The Pisan Cantos* were your meat
and left you hungry for more, then you should . . ."). The book
contains many factual and typographical errors and unsupported
assertions.

Among bibliographical studies, we may welcome Donald Gallup's
Ezra Pound: A Bibliography (Virginia), a revised and updated edition of the author's distinguished 1963 work. Expanded from 454 to
548 pages, Gallup's listings now include material published through
the end of 1981. Users will also want to consult Donald Gallup and
Archie Henderson, "Additions and Corrections to the Revised Edition
of the Pound Bibliography" (*Paideuma* 12:117–30), which contains
seventy-one supplementary items.

Partial descriptions of research holdings in six major libraries are
also of interest to Pound scholars. *A Catalogue of the Poetry Notebooks of Ezra Pound,* ed. Mary de Rachewiltz (Yale University Library, 1980) lists the bound notebooks in the Pound Archive of the
Beinecke Library. This "preliminary edition" is by no means a complete catalogue of the Archive. More than 12,500 items recently
acquired by Indiana University are surveyed in E. R. Hagemann's
"Incoming Correspondence to Dorothy and Ezra Pound at the Lilly
Library" (*Paideuma* 12:131–56). More than 600 items from Pound's
personal library purchased by the Humanities Research Center at
Austin are the subject of Michael J. King's "An ABC of E. P.'s Li-

brary" (*LCUT* 17[1981]:30–45). In "Pound's *Personae*: From Manuscript to Print" (*SB* 35[1982]:111–32), C. G. Petter describes the
drafts and proofs of the 1909 *Personae*, now held by the McPherson
Library of the University of Victoria. Simon Fraser University has
acquired more than 200 pieces of correspondence exchanged between
1946 and 1959 by the Pounds, James Laughlin, and Willis Hawley, an
expert on the Chinese written character. In "The Ezra Pound/Willis
Hawley Correspondence" (*Line* 1:3–25) Tom Grieve reproduces
eleven letters and explains "how much time this correspondence
could save one trying to identify and understand" the ideograms in
the later *Cantos* and Pound's translations of Confucius. Finally, Neda
M. Westlake and Francis James Dallett itemize the Pound manuscripts at the University of Pennsylvania in an article described below.

b. **General Studies.** Pound's work is central to the argument of the
important genre study, *The Modern Poetic Sequence*. Two chapters
discuss *Homage to Sextus Propertius, Hugh Selwyn Mauberley*, and
The Cantos as examples of the sequence—"a grouping of mainly lyric
poems or passages" that embody no logical, narrative, dramatic, or
thematic order but present instead "an affective progression" of "in-
teracting tonal centers." This book crowns M. L. Rosenthal's earlier
expositions of a concept that has already proven its value in discussions of modern poetry.

What Cairns Craig calls "The Ghost of the Modern" (*Helix* 13–
14:85–95) haunts several other general studies of Pound this year.
Craig's suggestive essay argues that the high modernist works of
Pound and Eliot incorporate "versions of Yeats's cosmology . . . in
which the mind is the repository of the totality of human history" and
ghosts haunt the present to connect it with the past. For Donald E.
Stanford in *Revolution and Convention* the modernist movement
itself is the specter to be exorcised, "a deviation from the main line of
poetry in English." Stanford's critique of Pound is a stale rehash of
Winters's.

The Lacanian deconstruction of Pound (see *ALS 1981*) continues
in Paul Smith's *Pound Revised* (Croom Helm) and Robert Casillo's
"Anti-Semitism, Castration, and Usury in Ezra Pound" (*Criticism*
25:239–65). According to Smith, Pound's "writing and language are
intrinsically totalitarian" because they mistakenly seek "to rectify the
absence of the signified" through their assertion of the representa-

tional power of signifiers, "the unified power of the subject," and the factive power of the phallus. Casillo applies a similar analysis to Pound's statements about Judaism and usury, concluding that his hatred of usury "has less to do with economics than with castration" and that his Fascism "is continuous with his phallocentrism." Meanwhile, Donald Davie argues in "Adrian Stokes Revisited" (*Paideuma* 12:189–97) that Lacanian readings of Pound are "reductionist."

Pound's quest for religious presence "as shaman-visionary, traveler between worlds, self-healed healer, guide of souls" interests Scott Eastham in *Paradise and Ezra Pound: The Poet as Shaman* (Univ. Press). Despite some promising insights this study is spotty in its research and jumpy in its argumentation. The main trouble with the argument of James J. Wilhelm's *Il Miglior Fabbro: The Cult of the Difficult in Daniel, Dante, and Pound* (Orono, Maine: National Poetry Foundation, 1982) is that the author never articulates his theory of hermeticism clearly enough to unify his detailed discussion of the three poets. An appendix contains lively commentaries on Pound's translations of Arnaut Daniel.

Pound's translations also figure in Charles Tomlinson's *Poetry and Metamorphosis* (Cambridge), which traces a pattern of "literary metempsychoses" in the translations, personae, and mythopoetic writings, praising *Cathay* especially. It was in *Cathay* and *Propertius*, according to William Fleming, that "Ezra Pound's Famous Ear" (*Helix* 13–14:81–85) perfected a "flexible line—racy, abrupt, unpredictable"—that depends more upon pitch than upon stress.

Pound's literary criticism receives a hearing in five recent studies. Marianne Korn's *Ezra Pound: Purpose/Form/Meaning* (London: Middlesex Polytechnic Press) is a lucid and well-grounded primer of Pound's aesthetic theory, particularly illuminating as a study of his critical prose. Martin A. Kayman provides "A Context for Hart's 'Complex': A Contribution to a Study of Pound and Science" (*Paideuma* 12: 223–35). Kayman places the psychological writings of Bernard Hart, to whom Pound alludes in his definition of the Image, into a context of Georgian attitudes toward the concept of the unconscious. In Pound's transition from Imagism to Vorticism, "Marinetti's manifestoes and his London performances" were "the key experience" according to Giovanni Cianci in "Futurism and the English Avant-Garde: The Early Pound between Imagism and Vorticism" (*ArAA* 6[1981]: 3–40). What unites the sister arts in Pound's Vorticist theory, John J.

Tucker argues in "Pound, Vorticism, and the New Esthetic" (*Mosaic* 16,iv:83–96), is that in each of them "the conjunction of two minimal units of form" creates "a minimal unit of meaning." Finally, in "A Map of Ezra Pound's Literary Criticism" (*SoR* 19:548–72) Natalie Harris covers no new ground.

We still need "maps" of Pound's work, apparently, but do we need duplicates of them? Christine Froula's *A Guide to Ezra Pound's "Selected Poems"* (New Directions) is a competent and useful companion to the New Directions edition of 1949. Inevitably, though, it challenges comparison with Peter Brooker's *Student's Guide* (1979) to the Faber edition of *Selected Poems* (1975). Both English books are more inclusive than their American counterparts, and Brooker's commentary is slightly shrewder and more informative than Froula's. New Directions would have done better to take over the Faber texts.

Three lively new essays appear in *Ezra Pound and William Carlos Williams: The University of Pennsylvania Conference Papers*, ed. Daniel Hoffman (Penn.). In "Gathering the Limbs of Orpheus: The Subject of Pound's *Homage to Sextus Propertius*" Ronald Bush offers a frankly romantic reading of the sequence, contending that it "proclaims the power of imagination rooted in desire to marry self and world, to redeem the self from a fragmented and ghostly existence." In his discussion of "The Revolution of the Word" Michael F. Harper, like other recent critics who approach Pound from the viewpoint of structural linguistics, relates the flaws in Pound's poetry and politics to his belief "that language did originally and can again capture" reality. For Wendy Stallard Flory in "The Pound Problem," on the other hand, the poet's racial politics are a result of his naive and self-deluding personality. Flory's view of Pound, itself not a little naive, ignores his statements about minorities and eugenics during the mid-1950s. In "Ezra Pound and William Carlos Williams Collections at the University of Pennsylvania" Neda M. Westlake and Francis James Dallett present a useful checklist of letters, manuscripts, typescripts, and academic records. This book also contains previously published papers by Hugh Kenner, James Laughlin, and Emily Mitchell Wallace.

c. **Relation to Other Writers.** Pound's dealings with Virgil, Catullus, Propertius, Ovid, and Horace are the subject of Ron Thomas's *The Latin Masks of Ezra Pound* (UMI Research Press). Part of one chapter also appears as "Pound and Horace's 'Odes' 3.30" (*Helix* 13–14:57–59). Thomas often digresses from the actual textures and interactions of poems to a simplistic thesis about Hellenism *versus* Hebraism, eros *versus* agape in Pound's work.

Pound's relation to Dante and Cavalcanti merits a chapter in Steve Ellis's *Dante and English Poetry: Shelley to T. S. Eliot* (Cambridge). Ellis concludes that Pound did not understand either author very well. The same three poets figure in Richard Reid's "Determined Cones of Shadow" (*Helix* 13–14:109–16). Reid notes that in both "Inferno X" and "Canto 73" the speaker encounters the spirit of Cavalcanti in the underworld.

The same issue of *Helix* contains additional studies of Pound's relationships to other writers. Jay P. Corrin discusses "Ezra Pound and G. K. Chesterton" (pp. 49–56), emphasizing the many points of agreement between their political, social, and economic views. Jonathan Marwil describes the biographical and literary links between "Ezra Pound and Frederic Manning" (pp. 9–15), while Warren Roberts recalls "London 1908: Lawrence and Pound" (pp. 45–49) and K. E. Csengeri offers a sketchy review of Pound's relationship with T. E. Hulme in "This Pound Business" (pp. 23–25). Three other essays recall Pound's connections with the so-called "Melbourne Vortex" during the 1950s: Les Harrop, "The Cabbala of Ezra Pound" (v–xiv); Noel Stock, "Ezra Pound in Melbourne, 1953–57" (pp. 159–78); and Earl Philrose, "Melbourne Papers" (pp. 179–91). Sheila L. Roper psychoanalyzes A. D. Hope's antipathy to Pound's poetics in "An Exhumation: A. D. Hope's Short Pathology of Imagism" (pp. 191–94). Finally, Timothy Materer, in "Ez to WynDAMN: Pound at St. Elizabeths" (pp. 153–57), surveys the relationship of Pound and Lewis between 1946 and 1957, printing excerpts from their correspondence.

The Pound-Lewis connection also concerns Sue Ellen Campbell in "The Enemy Attacks: Wyndham Lewis Versus Ezra Pound" (*JML* 10:247–56). Campbell tries to account for the distortions and suppressions of Lewis's attack on Pound in *The Enemy* and *Time and Western Man*. Another friendship that survived differences of opinion is the subject of Christina Stough's "The Skirmish of Pound and Eliot in *The New English Weekly*: A Glimpse of Their Later Literary Relationship" (*JML* 10:231–46). Surveying a quarrel-by-correspondence that the poets conducted in 1934, Stough quotes abundantly from material that has never been republished.

Two studies this year examine Pound's relationship with W. B. Yeats. In the third chapter of *Yeats and American Poetry: The Tradition of the Self* (Princeton), Terence Diggory surveys a subject upon which more has been written than he acknowledges. He points out some previously unnoticed echoes of Yeats in Pound's early poems. In a note on "Yeats's 'Those Dancing Days Are Gone' and Pound's 'Canto 23'" (*Yeats Annual No. 2*: 93–95), George Bornstein contends persuasively that a translation of Stesichorus incorporated into Canto 23 is the source of a Yeatsian refrain.

Pound's impact upon subsequent poets remains an attractive area of investigation. In "Pound: A Divergent Influence" (*CritQ* 25:29–34), Donald Monk argues that Pound has done better things for Basil Bunting's poetry than for Charles Olson's. Bernard Bergonzi's "Davie and Pound" in *Donald Davie and the Responsibilities of Literature*, ed. George Dekker (Carcanet), suggests that the "deeply personal subtext" of Davie's changing assessments of Pound probably has more to do with Davie's own poetry than with his other literary criticism. And Lewis Turco notes Pound's influence upon the contemporary American poet, Wesli Court, in "The Age of Pound" (*ConP* 4[1982]:33–46).

d. **The Shorter Poems and the Cantos.**   This year's studies of Pound's shorter poems are fit though few. Several important discoveries highlight Jo Brantley Berryman's *Circe's Craft: Ezra Pound's "Hugh Selwyn Mauberley"* (UMI). Berryman identifies the singer in "Envoi" and "Medallion" as Raymonde Collignon, locates the probable original of the "Luini in porcelain," and suggests several plausible models for Mauberley himself. These finds are embedded in a questionable argument about the structure of the sequence.

In a valuable study of *Ezra Pound and Japanese Noh Plays* (Univ. Press) Nobuko Tsukui sets the fifteen plays translated by Pound against their Japanese originals, pointing out Pound's accuracies and felicities, his errors and misunderstandings, and his omissions and additions. Tsukui might have related Pound's deviations more closely to his other poetic interests and to the Fenollosa manuscripts.

Meanwhile, K. K. Ruthven's helpful 1969 *A Guide to Ezra Pound's*

"Personae" (1926) is reissued in a paperback edition (Calif.). And in a note on "'Red-Bloods': Pound's 'The Condolence' and William James" (*N&Q* 30:333–34) Ian F. A. Bell argues unconvincingly that Pound's phrase "We are 'Red-Bloods'!" derives from a 1911 lecture by James.

Turning to *The Cantos*, we find a wealth of specific studies but relatively few general discussions. The genre of the poem (modern verse epic or Menippean satire?) continues to be debated by Michael André Bernstein and Max Nänny, the latest word being Bernstein's "Distinguendum Est Inter et Inter: A Defense of Calliope" (*Paideuma* 12:269–74). Pound's use of history evokes three different responses from James McDonald in "Inexact Definition: Pound and History" (*Helix* 13–14:75–80), Ben D. Kimpel and T. C. Duncan Eaves in "Some Curious 'Facts' in Ezra Pound's *Cantos*" (*ELH* 50: 627–35), and Stan Smith in *Inviolable Voice*. McDonald criticizes Pound's historiography; Kimpel and Eaves defend it, though acknowledging that he sometimes invents or distorts facts; and Smith ignores it completely, preferring to pass judgment on Pound's politics.

The earlier cantos attract the finest criticism this year. Guy Davenport's 1961 Harvard dissertation appears as *Cities on Hills: A Study of I–XXX of Ezra Pound's Cantos* (UMI), with evergreen readings of individual passages and a stimulating emphasis upon Pound's affinities with Blake and Ruskin. An important new study of the sources, composition, themes, and style of Cantos 8–11 is Peter D'Epiro's *A Touch of Rhetoric: Ezra Pound's Malatesta Cantos* (UMI). In "The Architecture of Memory: Pound and the Tempio Malatestiano" (*AL* 55:367–87) Michael North explores Pound's conception of architecture as "the model for a poem of memory" and expounds the formal analogy between the Tempio at Rimini and the Malatesta cantos. Michael Culver sensitively analyzes "The Art of Henry Strater: An Examination of the Illustrations for Pound's *A Draft of XVI Cantos*" (*Paideuma* 12:447–78). And Ben D. Kimpel and T. C. Duncan Eaves, in "The Birth of a Nation: A Note on Pound's 'Canto XIX'" (*PQ* 62:417–18), identify a book by Henry Wickham Steed as the probable source of an anecdote about Czechslovakian soldiers in 1914.

The middle cantos draw a mixed group of studies this year. That Avicenna influenced Pound's use in Cantos 30, 35, and 77 of the Greek term *hyle*, or matter, is the contention of Matthew Little's "Pound and 'YΛH: Bishop Carame's Translation of Avicenna as Background" (*Paideuma* 12:33–40). Frances E. Neidhardt discusses the importance of Botticelli and Duccio di Buoninsegna to Canto 45 in "From Apelles to Pound's 'Usury' Canto: Botticelli's *La Calumnia* Goes Modern" (*Paideuma* 12:427–45). According to Woon-Ping Holaday in "Making Poetry out of History" (*Helix* 13–14:61–73), Pound's Chinese history cantos fail to make "a living, contemporary reality" out of their source materials. Those materials are made available to future scholars by John J. Nolde, who prints and translates the relevant passages of De Mailla's *Histoire Générale de la Chine* and Pound's other sources in *Blossoms from the East: The China Cantos of Ezra Pound* (Maine). Nolde's book is a worthy companion to Frederick Sanders's *John Adams Speaking: Pound's Sources for the Adams Cantos* (1975). John Cayley's " 'New Mountains': Some Light on the Chinese in Pound's *Cantos*" (*Agenda* 20,iii-iv:122–58) is a diffuse and impressionistic appreciation of Pound's ideograms. William Cookson's more succinct "Notes on Pound's Confucian Odes" (*Agenda* 20,iii-iv:61–64) finds the poems "strangely English in their beauty."

The Pisan Cantos remain a favorite subject of investigation. "Pound's Lucifer: A Study in the Imagery of Flight and Light" by Angela Elliott (*Paideuma* 12:236–66) is a bizarre and obsessive study of "veiled" allusions in Canto 74 and elsewhere to the "satanic" flight of the Wright Brothers at Kitty Hawk. Carroll F. Terrell offers "A Couple of Glosses" of other lines in Canto 74 (*Paideuma* 12:51–52). Colin McDowell traces Pound's references to " 'The Toys . . . at Auxerre': Canto 77" (*Paideuma* 12:21–30) to its probable source in three essays by G. R. S. Mead. Ben D. Kimpel and T. C. Duncan Eaves suggest that "the milk-white doe" in "Pound's Canto LXXX" (*Expl* 41:43–44) comes from Tennyson's "Lady Clare." Carol H. Cantrell points out parallels of theme, image, and allusion in "Quotidian to Divine: Some Notes on Canto 81" (*Paideuma* 12:11–20). And Mohammed Y. Shaheen, in "Pound and Blunt: Homage for Apathy" (*Paideuma* 12:281–87), notes that the "live tradition" that W. S. Blunt gathers from the air in Canto 81 is not a European but an Arabic literary tradition, fostered by Blunt's translations during the 1890s.

Four explications of post-Pisan cantos appear this year. Michael Fournier identifies the "Chauncey Alcot" (*Paideuma* 12:289–90) mentioned in Canto 104 as the author of "My Wild Irish Rose." Peter Stoicheff in "CX/778 Revisited" (*Paideuma* 12:47–50) somewhat inconclusively discusses five Chinese words that appear without ideograms in Canto 110. Timothy Materer explores the biographical dimensions of "H. D., Serenitas, and Canto CXIII" (*Paideuma* 12: 275–80), using an unpublished 1959 letter from Pound to H. D. Finally, Walter Baumann offers a characteristically intelligent, informed, and detailed reading of a late canto in "But to Affirm the Gold Thread in the Pattern: An Examination of Canto 116" (*Paideuma* 12:199–221).

ii. Eliot

Are the executors, publishers, and archives of Pound and Eliot meeting their responsibilities well? The heated *TLS* correspondence aroused by *Tom and Viv* (January 27–March 16, 1984) suggests that some researchers feel thwarted by restrictions upon Eliot's letters and other archival material. Eliot's estate seems neither to be expediting the publication of such material nor to be permitting its free use by others. These restrictions pinch all the harder as more and more scholars take biographical and psychoanalytical approaches to Eliot's work.

a. Text and Biography.   Michael Hastings's new play, *Tom and Viv*, which opened at the Royal Court Theatre, February 3, 1984, draws upon Mrs. Eliot's personal papers at Oxford and upon the reminiscences of her brother to present a more sympathetic view of Vivienne Haigh-Wood and her family than is common in most accounts of Eliot's first marriage. Act One is especially well-balanced in its treatment of the main characters. But Hastings plays down the relationship between "Bertrand Russell and the Eliots" that interests Robert H. Bell (*ASch* 52:309–26). Bell puts forward an undocumented claim that Russell and Vivienne slept together briefly in October 1917, "only after an intense and protracted (if ambiguous) friendship." In *Stuff of Sleep and Dreams: Experiments in Literary Psychology* (Harper, 1982) Leon Edel speculates upon the psychic "sources of Eliot's profound and unending depression and his life's struggle to overcome his inertia of the will."

The Tempering of T. S. Eliot (UMI), a critical biography by

John J. Soldo, focuses upon "the first twenty-one years of his life," making excellent use of unpublished material such as school records and an autobiography by Eliot's father. Elsewhere, Soldo relates Eliot's "interest in the mystic way" to "The Mysticism of the Heart: The Poetry of T. S. Eliot's Mother" (*SMy* 6:24–36). Unlike Soldo, Caroline Behr relies exclusively upon published material in *T. S. Eliot: A Chronology of His Life and Works* (St. Martin's). Behr's year-by-year summary of Eliot's activities is judiciously selected but marred by factual and typographical errors.

Several other studies and memoirs concentrate upon Eliot's later career. In "T. S. Eliot and Ralph Hodgson, Esqre." (*JML* 10:342–46), Stanford S. Apseloff tells of Eliot's friendship with the man to whom one of the "Five-Finger Exercises" is dedicated. Eliot's work in the house of Faber is described by a former secretary and junior editor, Anne Ridler, in "Working for T. S. Eliot: A Personal Reminiscence" (*PoetryR* 73,iii:46–49). The *Letters of Archibald MacLeish, 1907 to 1982*, ed. R. H. Winnick (Houghton-Mifflin), include four letters and many references to Eliot. And Eileen Simpson's *Poets in Their Youth: A Memoir* (Vintage) recalls Eliot's presence at Princeton in 1948 and his importance to Delmore Schwartz and John Berryman.

Using an account in the Scripps College newspaper, William Baker reconstructs the main points of Eliot's 1933 California lecture on Edward Lear and modern poetry in "T. S. Eliot on Edward Lear: An Unnoted Attribution" (*ES* 64:564–66).

b. General Studies.   Ronald Bush's *T. S. Eliot: A Study in Character and Style* (Oxford) is one of the best books ever written on the poet. Bush reads Eliot's published and unpublished writings in terms of "the powerful and fundamental split in his psyche between thought and feeling," between acquired and buried selves. Eliot's later poetry seeks "to escape from the self" toward impersonal music and symbolist incantation, as Bush also emphasizes in "Modern/Postmodern: Eliot, Perse, Mallarmé, and the Future of the Barbarians" in *Modernism Reconsidered*, ed. Robert Kiely and John Hildebidle (Harvard). Bush's own prose style avoids cliché and mirrors the "rigorous emotional honesty" he attributes to Eliot.

Like Bush, Gregory S. Jay stresses "the silenced logic" of emotion "behind the manifest content" of Eliot's poetry and criticism. However, Jay's *T. S. Eliot and the Poetics of Literary History* (LSU) con-

veys little sense of Eliot's character or style, because its Lacanian/
Bloomian methodology reduces all considerations of individuality to
a single paradigm: "An understanding of castration topoi as indicators
of a certain crisis in textual or psychological economy will, I believe,
explain much about Eliot's choice of precursors in his criticism and
redirect our readings of the sexual signifiers in his poetry." Jay's reading of *Four Quartets* is less clotted by jargon than most of the study.

Whereas Bush sees a rapprochement with Mallarmé in Eliot's
later work, A. V. C. Schmidt in "Eliot and the Dialect of the Tribe"
(*EIC* 33:36–48) detects "a clear movement away from Mallarméan
esotericism towards the notion of a social, even civic role for the
poet." In "T. S. Eliot and the English Language" (*ESA* 25[1982]:
117–43) Schmidt applies the stylistic principles announced in the
fifth section of "Little Gidding" to a close examination of passages
selected from Eliot's poetry and prose.

The critical wars over Eliot's modernism seem revived this year
in two studies untouched by what Jay calls "modern speculative
criticism." In *Revolution and Convention* Donald E. Stanford offers
a stale rehash of Winters's critique of Eliot's "irrationalism," cen-
suring *The Waste Land* because it is "impossible to paraphrase successfully" and *Four Quartets* because it "has no formulable meter or
prosody." Stanford is answered effectively in *The Modern Poetic
Sequence*, in which M. L. Rosenthal and Sally M. Gall show how to
read Eliot's major poems as "almost instinctual balancings of affects
and tonal streams," with no "externally imposed narrative, dramatic,
or logical structuring" and a "glorious independence of surface con-
tinuities." The concept of the sequence, first articulated in earlier
genre studies by Rosenthal, again demonstrates its value here.

To view Eliot "from an Indian angle" is the aim of A. N. Dwivedi's
T. S. Eliot's Major Poems: An Indian Interpretation (Humanities,
1982). The author summarizes Eliot's study of Sanskrit and Hindu
literature, traces "echoes of Indian thought and tradition" throughout
his writings, and offers a useful exposition of Hindu and Buddhist
concepts. But Dwivedi ignores the manuscripts of *The Waste Land*
and Craig Raine's exposition of Buddhist elements in the poem (see
ALS 1973, pp. 314–15). In a related study of "Whitman, Eliot, and
the *Bhagavadgita*" (*CLS* 20:94–101), Rajnath concludes that "it is
Whitman who has got the spirit of the *Gita* right," whereas "Eliot
seems incapable of imagining a healthy worldly action that liberates

the human soul from worldly fetters." Elsewhere, Eliot's struggles with "the sordid, polluting world of history" are discussed superficially by Stan Smith in *Inviolable Voice.*

c. Relation to Other Writers. Eliot's relation to Dante is the subject of two new studies. The stronger of the two is Eloise Knapp Hay's "T. S. Eliot's Vergil: Dante" (*JEGP* 82:50–65). From Dante, according to Hay, Eliot learned the use of the "Vergil-figure—the figure of a mediator between two worlds" who appears in various guises throughout his poetry and criticism. In *Dante and English Poetry: Shelley to T. S. Eliot* (Cambridge) Steve Ellis argues that Eliot romanticizes Dante's conception of evil and neglects the political dimensions of his work.

Like Ellis, the authors of three recent essays on Eliot and 19th-century French writers ignore most of the existing scholarship on their subjects. In the first chapter of *Eliot, Auden, Lowell: Aspects of the Baudelairean Inheritance* (Macmillan), Lachlan Mackinnon discusses Eliot's perpetuation of Baudelairean "dandyism," which Mackinnon defines in religious terms. Celso de Oliveira's "A Note on Eliot and Baudelaire" (*AL* 55:81–82) argues none too persuasively that Baudelaire's "Le Jeu" is the source of several lines in "The Hollow Men." Finally, John J. Soldo's "T. S. Eliot and Jules LaForgue" (*AL* 55:137–50) stresses that LaForgue taught Eliot "to speak in *his* own voice" and to make his poetry "the *recreation of his own life.*"

Looking across the English Channel, David Ned Tobin focuses upon *The Presence of the Past: T. S. Eliot's Victorian Inheritance* (UMI). No single study can do justice to this huge topic. Tobin writes well about Eliot's debts to Arnold, Tennyson, Newman, Swinburne, and Kipling, but scants his connections with Carlyle, Ruskin, Browning, Rossetti, Pater, and Hardy. Elsewhere, Cory Bieman Davies examines "'Another Pattern': T. S. Eliot's Shifting Relationship to Robert Browning" (*SBHC* 10[1982]:35–48). Davies pays more attention to explicit critical statements than to unacknowledged poetic debts. In "Edward Carpenter and *The Waste Land*" (*RES* 34:312–15) Tony Brown points out some striking parallels of imagery and voice between Eliot's poem and Carpenter's *Towards Democracy* (1881–82). Back across the pond, Eliot's affinities with Thoreau interest Sam S. Baskett in "Fronting the Atlantic: *Cape Cod* and 'The Dry Salvages'" (*NEQ* 56:200–19). Baskett finds "kindred perceptions and strategies" in "the precise recording of the New England coastal landscape" by the two Americans.

Eliot's relationship to his fellow modernists is the subject of several recent studies. In *Yeats and American Poetry* Terence Diggory discusses Yeats's influence upon several aspects of Eliot's work and contrasts their conceptions of personality and religious tradition. Cairns Craig in "The Ghost of the Modern" (*Helix* 13–14:85–95) suggests, on the other hand, that the cosmologies of Yeats and Eliot have important similarities. Ronald Bush discusses "The 'Rhythm of Metaphor': Yeats, Pound, Eliot, and the Unity of Image in Postsymbolist Poetry" in *Allegory, Myth, and Symbol*, ed. Morton J. Bloomfield (Harvard, 1981). Bush argues that *The Waste Land* is indebted to discussions among the three poets of unifying images in the lyrical Noh drama of Japan. Elsewhere, Christina C. Stough describes "The Skirmish of Pound and Eliot in *The New English Weekly*: A Glimpse of Their Later Literary Relationship" (*JML* 10: 231–46), quoting abundantly from a 1934 quarrel-by-correspondence that has never been republished. Erwin R. Steinberg investigates the connections between "*Mrs. Dalloway* and T. S. Eliot's Personal Waste Land" (*JML* 10:3–25), arguing that Virginia Woolf used elements of Eliot's life and poetry in her presentation of Septimus Smith. In "T. E. Hulme and Eliot's *Four Quartets*" (*ELWIU* 10:25–31), Michael Gillum argues unconvincingly that a cluster of metaphors from Hulme's essays on "Humanism and the Religious Attitude" influenced the imagery of Eliot's suite. Finally, in "The Community of Interpretation: T. S. Eliot and Josiah Royce" (*CCrit* 5:21–46) Piers Gray amplifies his analysis (see *ALS 1982*) of the philosophical connections between the poet and his Harvard mentor.

Three studies concern Eliot's impact upon poets whose native language is not English. Howard T. Young's "Juan Ramón Jiménez and the Poetry of T. S. Eliot" (*RMS* 25[1981]:155–65) narrates "the history of Eliot's reception by his Spanish contemporary." C. G. Bellver examines another Spanish connection in "Luis Cernuda and T. S. Eliot: A Kinship of Message and Motifs" (*REH* 17:107–24). Finally, Tetsuya Taguchi explains "What T. S. Eliot Meant to Ayukawa Nobuo" (*CLS* 20:34–43), a modern Japanese writer.

d. **The Poems and Plays.** Once again *The Waste Land* and *Four Quartets* hold the spotlight, leaving the early poems and the plays in comparative obscurity. Two slender pieces are devoted to "Prufrock." Marcia Levenson's " 'The Love Song of J. Alfred Prufrock' as a Cubist Poem" (*ESA* 26:129–40) treats "those structural and stylistic aspects of the poem which are analogous to Cubist art," but the critic's analogies are too loose and general to be illuminating. Max Nänny's "Michelangelo and T. S. Eliot's 'The Love Song of J. Alfred Prufrock' " (*NMAL* 7:#4) argues cleverly that the women who come and go are talking not of Michelangelo's sculpture or painting but of his *Rime*, love-poems with often-ironic thematic and formal parallels to Prufrock's song.

Two other studies trace "the theme of the inarticulate" from Eliot's early poems to *The Waste Land*. The phrase comes from Charles Sanders's lively though overwritten essay, " 'Beyond the Language of the Living': The Voice of T. S. Eliot" (*TCL* 27[1981]:376–98). Also concerned with the alternations of speech, song, and silence in Eliot's "soundscape" is Charles Tomlinson in *Poetry and Metamorphosis* (Cambridge).

Seven other studies concentrate upon *The Waste Land* alone. Grover Smith's *The Waste Land* (Allen and Unwin) is a highly learned, occasionally testy monograph by a scholar who has written with distinction about Eliot since 1946. Once again Smith argues that a knowledge of Eliot's sources and his transformations of them is essential to "an in-depth experience" of the poem and its drafts. "All through the poem," according to Smith, "a ritual level and a personal level make counterpoint" in a "music of allusions" indebted to Mallarmé.

Smith accepts Tiresias as the "spectator-unifier" of the sequence, as does Eiko Araki in "The Tiresias Consciousness" (*SELit*, English No.: 33–48). Araki compares Tiresias's vision "to that of a dying man" such as Conrad's Kurtz, who experiences a "Bergsonian recapture of time through consciousness." In "*The Waste Land* as Dramatic Monologue" (*ES* 64:330–44), Anthony Easthope agrees with Araki that the presiding consciousness of the poem is "at the edge of oblivion, either dying or in madness imagining itself so." According to Easthope, however, the speaker is not Tiresias but an unnamed subject who has much in common with the speakers of Tennyson's "Maud" and Browning's madman monologues.

Max Nänny sees the poem not as a dramatic monologue but as a Menippean satire in "*The Waste Land* and Michail Bakhtin's Defini-

tion of the Menippea" in *Deutscher Anglistentag 1981: Vorträge*, ed.
Jörg Hasler (Frankfurt: Trierer Studien zur Literatur). Nänny offers
a lengthy taxonomy of formal generic characteristics that Eliot's
poem shares with such satires as Petronius's *Satyricon*. In " 'Cards
Are Queer': A New Reading of the Tarot in *The Waste Land*" (*ES*
62[1981]:335–47), the same critic interprets the Madame Sosostris
passage in terms of the "emotionally crucial experiences" in Eliot's
personal life.

Wolfgang E. H. Rudat examines the satiric aspect of "T. S. Eliot's
Allusive Technique: Chaucer, Virgil, Pope" (*Renascence* 35:167–82),
concentrating upon *The Waste Land* but acknowledging few earlier
discussions of his subject. And Jonathan A. Bate suggests in "Berlioz
in *The Waste Land* (and *Tristan* beside It?)" (*N&Q* 30:331) that a
passage of Hector Berlioz's *Mémoires* (1870) may be a source of the
closing lines of Eliot's poem.

A quartet of uninspired studies rehearse Eliot's last major poem.
Julia Maniates Reibetanz's *A Reading of Eliot's Four Quartets* (UMI)
makes some perceptive observations about the accentual meter of
the poem but contains far too much tedious and uncritical paraphrase. Frank Burch Brown's " 'The Progress of the Intellectual Soul':
Eliot, Pascal, and *Four Quartets*" (*JML* 10:26–39) finds a reductive
key to the poem in Eliot's 1931 essay on "The Pensées of Pascal."
David Bernstein's "Dance in *Four Quartets*" (*HUSL* 9[1981]230–61)
dutifully surveys Eliot's dance imagery as a "symbol of order and
harmony." And Konstantin Kolenda's reading of the poem in *Philosophy in Literature* (Barnes and Noble, 1982) offers a feeble restate-
ment of abstract ideas.

In contrast to these sleepers is Joan Fillmore Hooker's alert examination of *T. S. Eliot's Poems in French Translation: Pierre Leyris
and Others* (UMI). Hooker identifies 25 translators who tackled
Eliot between 1922 and 1976, including St. John Perse, Georges
Cattaui, Sylvia Beach, Adrienne Monnier, and André Gide. Hooker
awards the laurel to Pierre Leyris, whose correspondence with Eliot
and John Hayward forms the backbone of her sophisticated analysis
of translation as interpretive criticism.

Two in One (Cambridge, 1981) is the professional autobiography
of E. Martin Browne, who directed all of Eliot's plays from *Murder
in the Cathedral* (1935) to *The Elder Statesman* (1958). This memoir supplements Browne's *The Making of T. S. Eliot's Plays* (1969)

by documenting the director's passionate involvement with modern verse drama in general.

e. The Criticism. The characteristic strategy of Eliot's criticism is "the rediscovery of a marginal elite standing in an apocryphal relation to the established canon," John Guillory argues in a probing essay on "The Ideology of Canon-Formation: T. S. Eliot and Cleanth Brooks" (*CritI* 10:173–98). Eliot opens the oppressively closed canon of English literature by his "high valuation of the minor stance," aspiring through such revision to gain for himself the status of a minor classic.

Three other recent studies view Eliot's critical thought in different historical contexts. In "Eliot and Pater: Criticism in Transition" (*ELT* 25[1982]:169–77), John J. Conlon argues that Eliot's theory of impersonality, concept of the objective correlative, and image of the platinum catalyst all owe more to Pater's writings than Eliot acknowledged. According to Timothy Steele in "The Dissociation of Sensibility: Mannered Muses, Ancient and Modern" (*SoR* 19:57–72) "the disjunction of thought and feeling" is not a uniquely modern problem but one recognized by classical, medieval, and Renaissance rhetoricians as well. Finally, William H. Quillian discusses *Hamlet and the New Poetic: James Joyce and T. S. Eliot* (UMI). Relating Eliot's essay on "Hamlet and His Problems" (1919) to the writings of J. M. Robertson, E. E. Stoll, and many 19th-century Shakespeare critics, Quillian concludes rather lamely that the Hamlets of Eliot and Joyce "are now no more than curiosities for the literary historian."

The *Yeats Eliot Review* did not appear in 1983.

University of New Mexico

9. Faulkner

Linda W. Wagner

The relative dearth of criticism on Faulkner's work, commented on in the essays of the past several years, ended abruptly in 1983. Nineteen books appeared, as well as several collections and chapters in other studies, along with many expert and far-reaching individual essays. Critics both established and new provided a range of commentary, especially valuable for study of the later novels. Some of that commentary reflected healthy trends in linguistic and reader-response approaches.

i. Bibliography, Editions, and Manuscripts

John Earl Bassett published the thorough and meticulous *Faulkner: An Annotated Checklist of Recent Criticism* in The Serif Series (Kent State). This bibliography of secondary criticism and reviews extends through 1982, and mentions 1983 publications; it continues from his 1972 (David Lewis) listing. Although Bassett says that he has been chary with inclusion of reviews, particularly those from newspapers, his listings of books, essays, reviews, dissertations, and less specific sources is impressive. He divides his compilation into topical studies and those of individual novels, stories, poetry, and miscellaneous writings, with helpful cross-references. He corrects errata in his 1972 listing and includes an index of authors. While the quantity of material published on Faulkner already seems overwhelming, Bassett lists over 330 dissertations completed since 1968 in the United States alone. One assumes that many of these scholars will also become active publishers.

The Faulkner Concordance Series (Univ. Microfilms) continued in 1983 with two publications, *The Wild Palms* (edited and with an introduction by Kenneth L. Privratsky) and *Intruder in the Dust*, ed. Noel Polk, with an introduction by Patrick Samway, S.J.

Louis Daniel Brodsky and Robert W. Hamblin published two exhibition guides. *Brodsky: A Faulkner Collector/Scholar at Work* accompanied a University of Mississippi exhibition, which included materials related to Faulkner and Joan Williams, Phil Mullen, and Brodsky, while *Brodsky: The Evolution of a Faulkner Collector/Scholar*, accompanied a University of Tulsa exhibition. The year also saw the publication of Petra M. Gallert's "Italian Translations of Faulkner" (*MissQ* 36:329–36) and two installments of "William Faulkner: An Annotated Checklist of Research and Criticism in Japan": VIII (*WiF* 5,i:111–26) and IX (*WiF* 5,ii:82–97). The twentieth annual Faulkner issue of *Mississippi Quarterly* (Summer ed. by James B. Meriwether) continues to publish a survey of scholarship similar to *ALS*, that survey now edited by Diane L. Cox (pp. 483–505). *The Faulkner Newsletter & Yoknapatawpha Review* continues to offer information for collectors as well as reviews and notes. This year it lists the magazines Maud Faulkner saved that included work by her son, as well as recent publications on Faulkner.

The most important publication of Faulkner's previously unpublished work is the text of his second novel, the unfinished *Elmer* (*MissQ* 36:337–460). Written in August and September, 1925, while he was in Europe, Faulkner attempts in this evocative fiction to link the themes of romantic love and art as vocation. According to James B. Meriwether, who edited the manuscript from the University of Virginia and the University of Mississippi holdings, Faulkner used the unfinished novel as the source "for a major episode in *Mosquitoes* and for the short story 'Divorce in Naples.' He also drew on it for *Wild Palms*, and shortened and changed it for 'A Portrait of Elmer.' " Its affinities with *The Sound and the Fury* (particularly Elmer and his sister Jo Addie's parallels with Quentin and Caddy) are remarkable, but Elmer's love affair is presented much more directly than any other romance in Faulkner's early fictions. Meriwether includes a table of emendations from the manuscripts as well as a helpful foreword.

Gail Moore Morrison has edited Faulkner's unpublished story, "Never Done No Weeping When You Wanted to Laugh" (*MissQ* 36:461–74). Housed in the Beinecke Collection at Yale, this story was probably written in 1928 or 1929 and differs from "That Evening Sun Go Down" and "That Evening Sun," although closely related to both. In the same issue, Meriwether has edited "The Manuscript of

Faulkner's Introduction to *Sanctuary*" (pp. 475–81), reprinting the original first paragraph and compiling a table of variants for the remainder. Louis Daniel Brodsky has compiled versions of the poem "The Lilacs" to reveal a compositional sequence very close to the later published version ("The Autograph Manuscripts of Faulkner's 'The Lilacs,'" *SB* 36:240–52).

Arthur Kinney and Doreen Fowler have catalogued the four boxes of papers found at Rowan Oak in 1971 (now available at the University of Mississippi) and report their findings in "Faulkner's Rowan Oak Papers: A Census" (*JML* 10:327–34).

Of related interest are two essays, "The Copyright of Faulkner's First Book" (*MissQ* 36:263–87) in which Rebecca Meriwether claims that *Marionettes* was Faulkner's first book because he sold his copies (six or more) for $5 each in 1921; and Joan St. C. Crane's "Faulkner's *The Marble Faun* Redivivus" (*ABC* 4:11–22), which suggests that 1000 rather than 500 sets of sheets of the text were printed in 1924.

ii. Biography

Ben Wasson's *Count No'Count, Flashbacks to Faulkner* (Miss.) provides a succinctly informative account of Faulkner as a friend. Written shortly before Wasson's death in 1982, the text is prefaced with Carvel Collins's reminiscence of Wasson's involvement in the whole texture of Faulkner's life, even years after the novelist's death. Wasson befriended Faulkner in Oxford and Greenville, Mississippi, as well as in New York and Hollywood. In both the latter places, Wasson acted as agent for Faulkner (even though he was himself a novelist when he assumed the role of agent for *Flags in the Dust*). Wasson's memoir gives authenticity to the apochrypha of Faulkner's life—his bad puns with the *Algonquin* crowd, his ruse to introduce Meta Carpenter to Estelle, his hatred of the Hollywood scene, his drinking bouts. But it also provides a recounting of Faulkner's grief over family deaths (those of his brother Dean and his first child Alabama), his protective love for his daughter Jill, and his seemingly complete absorption in his writing. The memoir ends with the mysterious "falling out," and Wasson's explanation that he did not know what led to Faulkner's anger and permanent estrangement from him in 1953. Filled with previously unpublished photographs, Wasson's book is an important account of nearly forty years of Faulkner's life.

Joseph Blotner attempts some correlation of Faulkner's later life and writing in "Continuity and Change in Faulkner's Life and Art" (*Faulkner and Idealism*, pp. 15–26). Once Faulkner was rid of his despair over what Blotner calls his "Hollywood servitude," he evinces a greater sense of affirmation in his fiction. Some of this is fairly simple biography: his fondness for his grandchildren gave him theme and structure for *The Reivers*, his relationship with Joan Williams provided impetus for Gavin Stevens's love for Linda Snopes in *The Town*. But more generally, Blotner contends, Faulkner's "sense of amelioration in the work and the process of mellowing in the life" were closely related.

Susan Snell describes the importance of Faulkner's friendship with Katrina Carter, the woman who introduced him to Phil Stone as well as being Estelle's bridesmaid when she—hesitantly—married Cornell Franklin ("William Faulkner, Phil Stone, and Katrina Carter: A Biographical Footnote to the Summer of 1914," *SLJ* 15,ii:76–86).

iii. Criticism: General

a. **Books.**   Many of the books considered in this section are fine contributions to understanding Faulkner's work; most present convincing arguments in support of reasonable theses. Perhaps the consistency of quality scholarship is the most impressive trait about these studies.

Martin Kreiswirth has written a modest but central book in *William Faulkner, The Making of a Novelist* (Georgia). Beginning with Faulkner's poetry and early prose sketches, Kreiswirth suggests the processes by which Faulkner wrote his major novels. This book ends with *The Sound and the Fury* as a product of all these starts, imitations and transformations. It traces the importance of Willard Huntington Wright's *The Creative Will: Studies in the Philosophy and the Syntax of Aesthetics* with its insistence that "true style . . . is an ability to change one's manner at random so as to harmonise the expression with the thing expressed." Kreiswirth writes clearly and directly, and maintains his focus on the way Faulkner incorporated all the elements traceable to earlier works into his later writing. His condensed study is rich with interesting illustrations of his points, and is fascinating reading.

Thomas Nordanberg's *Cataclysm as Catalyst, The Theme of War in William Faulkner's Fiction* (ACTA Universitatis Upsaliensis #49) is more comprehensive than its title indicates. In order to discuss the "war" fiction, which Nordanberg defines as whatever work was prompted by considerations about the effects of war (including *Absalom, Absalom!*), he draws on the work entire. He views "war," too, as an image for man's inhumanity to man, "something of a touchstone for the testing of other problems."

The three-part organization of the book derives from the fact that Faulkner's use of war changes during his career. Part I includes the fiction written about World War I, written from 1925 to 1932; Part II, fiction about the Civil War, written chiefly from 1930 to 1942; and Part III, fiction about World War II (except for *A Fable*, which is ostensibly about the First World War), written from 1941 through 1959. Within each segment, Nordanberg describes relevant fiction and then discusses Faulkner's pervasive attitudes during the appropriate years. His focus throughout is on character, because he views Faulkner as a writer interested less in abstract ideas than in characterization. But he protects himself by including all key figures— Linda Snopes in *The Mansion*, for example—rather than just those more obviously connected with the theme of war. His remarks about *A Fable*, especially David Levine, are as good as any published in the past decade (see also chapter 21, "Scandinavian Contributions").

Character is the chief focus of Gail L. Mortimer in *Faulkner's Rhetoric of Loss, A Study in Perception and Meaning* (Texas). Using Emily Grierson as a prototype, Mortimer sees much of Faulkner's works as a re-creation of his characters' and narrators' need to cling, to deny loss. Mortimer then divides her study into three sections, based on what she calls "perceptual style." Strongly psychoanalytic, the work relies on Minter (but not on Wittenberg), and seems less rhetorical than biographical.

One of Mortimer's interests is Faulkner's treatment of women characters. She claims that most of the male characters are nervous about women and experience "a dis-ease with women, a basic conviction of their threatening otherness, their ineluctable alienation." Aside from the terminology of object relations theory, Mortimer's approach is less innovative than her title and introduction would suggest. But she does draw good distinctions about male and female uses of myth and ritual that lends credibility to her reading of, particularly, *Light in August.*

One of the most comprehensive, and most convincing, of these studies is Cathy Waegner's *Recollection and Discovery, The Rhetoric of Character in William Faulkner's Novels* (Peter Lang). Systematically using reader-response theory that is loosely based on Wolfgang Iser, Waegner divides her chapters into two parts—one theoretical, the other practical—so that readers can choose their approach. She discusses *Absalom* (and *Knight's Gambit* in relation to it) as an archetypal fiction, its "incessant" narrative focused on tableau images; *Light in August* as a narrative of negation, marked by inversions, contrasts, exclusions, non-actions, and oppositions; *The Hamlet* as a narrative of displacement; and *Go Down, Moses* as a fiction of disparity. She is at her best here, or perhaps her terminology has come together as she works with this novel, which she describes as a "narrated monologue," a technique that "effaces the borderline between linguistic and narrative concerns." Here, the reader "is misled, cornered, conned, shocked, and left in the lurch, yet these tactics are always finally constructive, guiding the reader in the process of making meaning." In all of Faulkner's best work, the reader must constantly revise notions of happening and character—a process that leads to complete, active involvement.

Elizabeth M. Kerr continues her production of wide-ranging Faulkner studies with *William Faulkner's Yoknapatawpha, "A Kind of Keystone in the Universe"* (Fordham). Her title does not indicate how comprehensive this study is, and in that comprehensiveness lies what weakness it has. Any one of its three sections might have made a single book. In her first section, Kerr discusses theme through what she calls thematic symbols. In her second, she builds the mythology of Yoknapatawpha, going into a study of myth as preamble, as well as the mythology of the South. This section includes new readings of many of Faulkner's heroines and heroes (Narcissa, for example, and Lena). Part III, entitled "The Quest for Freedom," presents her major argument, that Faulkner is motivated by "individualistic Christian humanism." She then studies many aspects of that terminology— humanism and its history, existentialism and its relation to humanism. Then she concludes with an Afterword about the twentieth anniversary of James Meredith's enrolling at the University of Mississippi in 1962, the Ku Klux Klan, and politics in the South.

For the general reader, less information would have proved easier to handle. The mythology section could have been a separate study, whereas the first section is repetitious of much recent work (Kerr comments that she began this book during the 1960s), and the third is more redundant than Kerr's writing usually is. Luckily, her compressed bibliographical system obviates the need for separate notes.

Cleanth Brooks's new study, *William Faulkner: First Encounters* (Yale) is what it says, an introduction for students. Very pedagogical in tone, with much explication, introduction, and description of characters and plots, the book does less well what Brooks has done superbly through the years. His discussions are of the short stories, *The Sound and the Fury, As I Lay Dying, Hamlet, Go Down, Moses, Light in August,* and *Absalom, Absalom!,* an order that reflects his movement from "local color" to tragedy in his introductory comments. Because the book is written as though he were talking to an undergraduate class, Brooks's discussions are often over-simplified (Dewey Dell, for example, is "simply instinctual womanhood"; Joe Christmas, "allowed the full dignity of his defiant attempt to assert and maintain his lonely identity").

Three books in this section are a part of the new UMI Research Press series of reprinted dissertations, with Joseph Blotner as series editor. The best of these is Joan M. Serafin's *Faulkner's Uses of the Classics,* which is a model of information-giving. The introductory essay discusses the classical tradition and the Southern classical tradition, touching on influences, quotations, rhetoric, imagery and symbols, mythology, structure, and values. Index I lists allusions and quotations; Index II, names; and Index III provides a general catalog of Faulkner's uses. The only reservation I have about this series, and this book in particular, is that the bibliography is reprinted from the date of the dissertation, 1969, rather than being updated. To publish a book in 1983 that students will use and have it include only works from before 1969 seems needlessly misleading.

Jessie McGuire Coffee's study, *Faulkner's Un-Christlike Christians, Biblical Allusions in the Novels,* also includes valuable information in its second section, "Concordance and Commentary." It is worth publishing for this part, but the introductory essay presents readings of the fiction that are much too narrow. Even though this bibliography has been made current, the discussions of the novels have not benefited from the good criticism of the past decade. Part of the problem is probably her need to divide characters into rigid patterns—to find Mink Snopes, Benjy, Nancy Mannigoe, and Joe Christmas "scapegoats," for example.

Much the same comment can be made about Doreen Fowler's *Faulkner's Changing Vision, From Outrage to Affirmation.* As her title indicates, she sees the progression in Faulkner's fiction as somewhat simple, from negative to positive, pessimistic to idealistic. Faulkner's fictions seldom yield such neat patterns, and characters like Mink Snopes and Nancy Mannigoe are hardly paragons.

For the first time in several years, this chapter must omit the review of the Faulkner Conference proceedings because of delayed publication. The 1982 conference papers will appear next year as *Faulkner: International Perspectives,* ed. Ann J. Abadie and Doreen Fowler. Another collection, *Faulkner & Idealism,* includes papers from the 1980 Paris First International Colloquium on Faulkner. In the editors' "Introduction," Cresset and Samway stress the generic use of "idealism," naming Faulkner's lack of satisfaction with his accomplishment as characteristic of idealists. Each contributor defines the term according to the focus of his or her essay; some essays will be discussed elsewhere, but several are appropriate here.

André Bleikasten in "For/Against an Ideological Reading of Faulkner's Novels" (pp. 27–50) sees Faulkner's assertion of his individuality against society and "even reality itself" in his fiction. In *Light in August,* ideology is an exorcism of the real through myth; in *Absalom, Absalom!* Faulkner allowed destructive forces to serve as positive ones for the birth of a new kind of novel. Bleikasten comments on the fact that much criticism of Faulkner is dated in its attitudes and contends that Faulkner wrote about the South to bring the past to the light of consciousness so that he could break its hold over the present.

Michel Gresset sees the fiction as divided into two movements, with *Pylon* coming at the center. After realizing that he could not achieve the effect he wanted with characters as observers, he moved to the "recapitulative" tactics of *Absalom, Absalom!* The early Faulkner is "abrupt and visual"; the later, "sinuous and verbal" ("The 'God' of Faulkner's Fiction," pp. 51–70). Gresset's title refers to the fact that Faulkner changes a subject into a "Subject," which becomes the god of his writing; and his motivation in writing is idealistic.

Thomas L. McHaney's "The Development of Faulkner's Idealism: Hands, Horses, Whores" (pp. 71–85) traces the writer's philosophy through his imagery, seeing Faulkner as being both faun and
eagle, with the tension between the personae helping him to create
his best work. *The Reivers* represents the culmination of fragmented
patterns of unhandiness in his male characters, of horses, and of
whores in earlier writing.

François L. Pitavy claims that in *The Sound and the Fury* Faulkner
learns how both to indict and escape from the South. But because
Faulkner was so dubious about the possibility of escape, he creates
very few innocent characters and those that are innocent, are often
idiots ("Idiocy and Idealism: A Reflection on the Faulknerian Idiot,"
pp. 97–111). He discusses "The Kingdom of God" and Benjy in *The
Sound and the Fury*, progressing to Ike Snopes in *The Hamlet*. Because the latter novel is comic, Pitavy claims that Faulkner's *angst*
was ameliorated.

Monique Pruvot's "Faulkner and the Voices of Orphism" (pp.
127–43) sees much of the fiction as an image of loss and search. From
Faulkner's early poem "Orpheus," he often used the frustrated lover,
the poet who may disclose the origin of the world, the color white,
doubles, the act of mourning, and other evidence of his knowledge
of the Orpheus-Eurydice myth.

b. Essays.   Michel Gresset writes of Faulkner's concept of "home"
in "Home and Homelessness in Faulkner's World and Life" (*WiF* 5,
i:26–42) as a means of showing the alienation/separation of his characters. Only men are alienated, however; most of Faulkner's women
characters are either home, or they do not care where they are. He
lists the Compsons, Horace Benbow, Darl and Vardaman, Joe Christmas, Henry Sutpen, the Reporter, and Harry Wilbourne as the home-
less characters, and draws the parallel with Faulkner himself, isolated
at Rowan Oak, writing essays about privacy: the poet of homelessness, at home.

Joyce Carol Oates discusses the problem of modern writers who
maintain reactionary views of women ("'At Least I Have Made a
Woman of Her': Images of Women in Yeats, Lawrence, and Faulkner," *GaR* 37:7–30). She describes Faulkner's "crude portraits of
mammalian beauties or castrating 'neuters' who deserve death," an

assessment that makes one wonder whether or not she has read much recent Faulkner criticism. Concentrating on Joanna Burden (whose name she spells Johanna), she terms her "not really a woman" but rather "Joe's Nightmare Double" that must be exorcised. A parallel to Temple Drake, Joanna represents Faulkner's "deep-buried terror" and "mesmerized repugnance," and the novel is therefore a "cautionary tale."

The most important essay in this year's coverage is Michael Millgate's "William Faulkner: The Two Voices" in *Southern Literature in Transition*, pp. 73–85. Millgate defines the "two voices" as those of despair and hope, negative and positive thinking, resolved in favor of the latter but in terms that leave the reader wondering whether the defeated, nay-saying voice might not after all have had the better of the argument. He justifies Faulkner's pervasive use of dialogue, debate, and opposition in his fiction as the apt means of conveying this polarity: "the debate becomes a standard element in almost all of Faulkner's novels."

With his usual wide-ranging command of the *oeuvre*, Millgate proves that Faulkner achieves his open, fluid texts through characterization (multiplicity, lack of hero or heroine) and structure (things always in process). His novels are "town meetings of the imagination, loud with the rhetoric of advocacy, complaint, and self-justification." In culmination, *The Reivers* becomes not Faulkner's deliberately final word, "but as one work among many, expressive of truths, but not of THE truth."

Malcolm Bradbury finds Faulkner "the most crucial and exemplary figure" in modern American literature, writing fiction of "extraordinary complexity" (*The Modern American Novel*, pp. 87–94ff). He praises in particular his language that worked through "imagistic distillation," and his creation of a modern form that could cope with temporal and psychic disturbances. So, too, does Frederick R. Karl, whose *American Fictions, 1940–1980* calls Faulkner the only one of America's modernists to rank with Joyce and Kafka and to maintain pervasive world influence. Karl sees *A Fable* as a testimony to the writer's attempt to "grasp it all," and not lapse into the expected, as Hemingway did in his later work. Richard Ford echoes the primacy of Faulkner among American modernists in "The Three Kings: Hemingway, Faulkner, and Fitzgerald," *Esquire* 100:577–87. And Mark Allister traces the development of Faulkner's use of the "grand design" in the plantation house in "Faulkner's Aristocratic Families: The Grand Design and the Plantation Family," *MQ* 25:90–101.

iv. Criticism: Special Studies

a. **Ideas, Influences, Intellectual Background.** Walter F. Taylor, Jr., in *Faulkner's Search for a South* (Illinois) sees Faulkner's progression through levels of texts, later works questioning the process and methods of early ones, as one means of his questioning attitudes about the South. This well-argued book touches on issues of race relations that are more fully developed in section c's coverage, but provides important insights into Faulkner's themes. Taylor sets a paradigm of Cavalier and Puritan philosophies in motion and ties many of Faulkner's characters to those two life-styles. Quentin, for instance, was a Cavalier (elitist, High Church, conservative, protective of women and values). By the time of *Absalom* (*A Dark House*, its title in draft), Faulkner had realized that the values he thought had existed in the old South were fantasy; and so the novel is full of disillusion. Ike McCaslin was intended "to fuse Bayard's paternalist outlook with Quentin's tragic revulsion at the curse of inherited guilt; fully steeped in the Cavalier tradition, Isaac would yet be capable of identifying the curse." But the fiction proved that Ike was not capable of coming to the knowledge that for Faulkner was invaluable. Taylor's study continues through *The Reivers* and is convincing.

Other commentaries on Faulkner as a Southern writer occur in separate essays. Louis D. Rubin, Jr., comments in "Trouble on the Land: Southern Literature and the Great Depression" (*Literature at the Barricades*, pp. 96–113) that Faulkner was particularly relevant to the poverty during the 1930s because his fiction focused on change, the facing up to the impact of new demands and ways. Two of Rubin's essays have been reprinted in his *A Gallery of Southerners* (LSU, 1982), and his most recent discussion of Faulkner occurs in "The Mockingbird in the Gum Tree: Notes on the Language of American Literature" (*SoR* 19:785–801). Here Rubin stresses that Faulkner brought to American literary English "the full rhetorical intensification of the high style," and uses *The Hamlet* as a showcase for the comic vernacular mixed with the high style. His choice of language showed his fear of oversimplification; he had to hang on to his language resources.

Other discussions of Faulkner and his Southern milieu occur in
Cleanth Brooks's *William Faulkner: First Encounters*, pp. 3–16, and
Lewis P. Simpson ("Home by Way of California: The Southerner
as the Last European," *Southern Literature in Transition*, pp. 55–70,
with an opposing view by Noel Polk ("The Southern Literary Pie-
ties," pp. 29–41). Simpson aligns Faulkner with the Agrarians, stressing that his themes really depended on the "economy of leisure" in
"The State of Letters: The Southern Writer and the Economy of
Leisure" (*SR* 91:512–18). And Gerald W. Johnson's influential essays
on Southern literature as "The Congo of the Bozart" and Faulkner,
Wolfe, Stribling and Caldwell as "the horror-mongers-in-chief" are reprinted in *South-Watching, Selected Essays*, ed. Fred Hobson (N.C.).

Several shorter essays comment on influences on Faulkner's work:
Steve Glassman traces "The Influence of Conrad's *Chance* on *Absa-
lom, Absalom!*" (*NMW* 15:1–3); Robert W. Hamblin comments on
"James Street's *Look Away!* Source (and Non-Source) for William
Faulkner," (*AN&Q* 21:141–43); Marta Powell Harley writes about
"Faulkner's Medievalism and *Sir Gawain and the Green Knight*,"
(*AN&Q* 21:111–14), describing the episodes in *The Town* and *The
Bear* as resembling those of *Sir Gawain*–the chastity test, the courage
test, and the bear hunt.

Lance Olsen comments on Faulkner's influence in "Faulkner's
Echo in Robbe-Grillet: Narrative Constructions and Destructions"
(*MFS* 29:609–22), but his remarks are suggestive rather than con-
clusive. And yet again, more explication of Faulkner's Nobel Prize
remarks in David Rife ("Rex Stout and William Faulkner's Nobel
Prize Speech," *JML* 10:151–52), listing eleven sources in addition to
the Nero Wolfe mystery, *The League of Frightened Men*.

b. **Style and Structure.**   Hugh M. Ruppersburg's *Voice and Eye in
Faulkner's Fiction* (Georgia) is a point of view study that concentrates on four novels (*Light in August, Pylon, Absalom, Absalom!*
and *Requiem for a Nun*, with focus as well on *The Reivers* and other
works). He traces the "contrasting internal and external views of
characters," and creates such terms as "directed narrative" and "retrospective character narrative"; his readings of the novels, however, are
standard ones. One might have included the books by Gail L. Mortimer and Cathy Waegner here, but I have chosen where possible to

place materials with their subject, as in the case of several essays to appear later.

Betty Jean Craige's inclusion of Faulkner, particularly *The Sound and the Fury*, in her discussion of "the writerly text," one characterized by juxtaposition and lack of authorial judgment, places the writing in the context of graphic art (*Literary Relativity*, Bucknell, 1982). Louis G. Ceci's "The Case for Syntactic Imagery" (*CE* 45: 431–49) analyzes *Light in August* as illustration of his thesis, that "there are certain inherent properties of syntax, that writers can and often do take advantage of these properties, and that the foregrounding or subversion of these properties produces effects in the mind of the reader which can be called syntactic imagery." A different stylistic concept forms the basis of Sallie McFague's "The Parabolic in Faulkner, O'Connor, and Percy," (*NDEJ* 15:49–66), a comparative study of the way these writers draw parables in their fiction, not unlike the parables in the Bible.

c. Race. Some of the richest criticism to be included in this essay falls in this category. Books by Thadious M. Davis, Erskine Peters, and Eric J. Sundquist all trace Faulkner's treatment of racial relations, from different perspectives; all three yield much information and insight. Davis's *Faulkner's "Negro": Art and the Southern Context* (LSU) provides new readings of *The Sound and the Fury*, *Light in August*, and *Absalom, Absalom!* by showing the clear centrality of many of the black characters. Davis emphasizes the way Faulkner uses the Gibson family to contrast the Compsons, for example, and in each reading, convinces us that he sees black religious and social roles as positive. Her distinction between his use of "black" and "Negro" is also helpful. She makes no false claims for Faulkner's somewhat dated understanding of racial matters, but neither does she criticize him for being what he was, a Southern writer caught in a somewhat obsolete time.

By the time of *Light in August*, Davis contends, Faulkner's concern with racial matters gave him structure as well as character; and that tendency matured in *Absalom, Absalom!* Faulkner saw his way clear to picture society's use of the racial situation, rather than the situation itself, as the real evil; and by so doing, wrote a self-critical fiction with ramifications far beyond the 1930s.

Erskine Peters's study ranges further into Afro-American literature than does Davis's treatment, but the two readings are not in
conflict. *William Faulkner: The Yoknapatawpha World and Black
Being* (Norwood) begins with more cultural history, the legacy of
the black world that modern fictions attempt to reflect. Working
from the concept of stereotype, Peters shows the ways Faulkner's
early writing made use of them, but also the ways he moved—
quickly—away from their use. Quite often in the fiction, Faulkner
uses pairs of blacks and whites, male and male or female and female;
and part of his comment about race relations lies in what happens to
those relationships in the course of time. As he reads the fiction,
Peters stresses the themes of miscegenation and the mulatto crisis,
with major sections on Dilsey, Lucas, and Nancy. Although he mentions Faulkner's late racial activity, he does not emphasize it, being
content to close with this statement: "The best that one can say is
that the man who had wanted to be a moderate was, even more than
the label itself denotes, caught rather disturbingly in the middle."
Peters's impressive study is even more helpful because it includes
a glossary of the black characters in all of Faulkner's work, a listing
that corrects and adds to all previous such information.

In contrast to these two informative works, Eric J. Sundquist's
Faulkner: The House Divided (Hopkins) provides a less satisfactory
view of Faulkner's involvement in racial themes. Strangely mixed,
this study at times takes on the elite critical establishment, except for
John T. Irwin; again, it provides a cultural history of the 1960s and
1970s, sometimes with little reference to Faulkner's works. In theory,
the book is brilliant. Sundquist divides his study into two parts, the
first dealing with the fiction written before Faulkner came to racial
consciousness (*The Sound and the Fury*, *As I Lay Dying*, and *Sanctuary*); the second, after the recognition (*Light in August*, *Absalom,
Absalom!* and *Go Down, Moses*). He uses *Sartoris* and *Intruder in the
Dust* as frame novels, but refuses to credit any non-Yoknapatawpha
novel, or any work beyond *Intruder*, in his reasoning. The whole
thrust of Faulkner's writing was to identify, and then to deal with,
racial issues, Sundquist claims, and he further sees all sexual themes
as being images for the racial. Quentin's major concern was race
equality; Caddy's body was only an image for that consideration.

While most of us agree that Sundquist's choices in Part II are
among Faulkner's best novels, his contention that they *are* the best

because of his involvement in racial themes discounts too much of the rest of Faulkner's life, too much of his attention as writer—which pointed consistently toward technical and structural interests. For Sundquist to "write off" *The Sound and the Fury* as an accidental explosion makes us glad the Krieswirth book is now in print. In short, *The House Divided* is provocative, not definitive.

Craig Werner's "Tell Old Pharaoh: The Afro-American Response to Faulkner," (*SoR* 19:711–35) distinguishes between Faulkner's importance to black writers and the respect with which they read him. Because Faulkner never drew on black traditions or folklore and always placed his black characters in the Euro-American community, black writers could not really learn from him. He writes a "narrative of endurance," and keeps his focus firmly on the past. Black writers, are more interested in narratives of "ascent" or "immersion," and look toward the future. There are also scattered references to Faulkner's work in Charles T. Davis's *Black Is the Color of the Cosmos, Essays on Afro-American Literature and Culture, 1942–1981*, ed. Henry Louis Gates, Jr., (Garland, 1982).

v. Individual Works to 1929

Most of the attention on single novels fell on works from *Light in August* through *Go Down, Moses*, with some interest in *A Fable*. Increasingly, *The Reivers* and *The Sound and the Fury* become touchstone novels, mentioned frequently to anchor points, but less often in this year's publications treated separately. (Many of the essays on *Absalom, Absalom!* include the Quentin Compson of the earlier novel, of course.) A plethora of brief essays can be mentioned quickly: Emily Dalgarno's "Faulkner's Notes to *Soldiers' Pay*" (*JML* 10:257–67) describes his attempt to integrate history with domestic satire, as Gilligan reads Gibbon. The notes (found in the Berg Collection of the New York Public Library and the Virginia Collection) sketch most fully the chapters in which Mahon, Jones, Cecily and Mrs. Powers play important roles. In the same journal, Julie M. Johnson relates the clock imagery in *The Sound and the Fury* to Faulkner's interest in Einstein and relativity ("The Theory of Relativity in Modern Literature: An Overview and *The Sound and the Fury*," 10:217–30). Two essays treat the family composition in that novel: Carol A. Kolmerten and Stephen M. Ross, "The Empty Locus of

Desire: Woman as Familial Center in Modern American Fiction,"
DQ 17:109–20, and Sandra D. Milloy, "Dilsey: Faulkner's Black
Mammy in *The Sound and the Fury*," *NHB* 46:70–71. Floyd C. Wat-
kins comments on "Benjy Compson and His Jimson Weed" in *NConL*
13:10–11.

André Bleikasten writes an interesting comparison of Flaubert's
Madame Bovary and *Sanctuary*, tracing parallels between Emma and
Temple, in "'Cet Affreux Gout D'Encre,' Emma Bovary's Ghost in
Sanctuary" (*WiF* 5:1–25). And Hershel Parker uses *Sanctuary*, as
well as *Sartoris*, to illustrate the importance of revision by the author
rather than an editor ("The Determinacy of the Creative Process and
the 'Authority' of the Author's Textual Decisions," *CollL* 10:99–125).
One very important essay on *Sanctuary* explains Temple's perjury as
an index to the terrible fear she has been scarred by during the night
before her rape (Joseph R. Urgo, "Temple Drake's Truthful Perjury:
Rethinking Faulkner's *Sanctuary*," *AL* 55:435–44). It was Goodwin
who put her in the position to be raped: "He was the leader of the
pack . . . and abused that responsibility by giving Temple a room to
sleep in and then not granting the security such an offer implies, by
telling Tommy how to have sex with Temple, and by terrorizing her
back into the rat-infested barn." Urgo reads *Sanctuary* as "a novel
concerned with the forms of human interaction and the limits of
responsibility," and sees Temple as the victim of "inaction and neglect" as well as rape.

J. Douglas Canfield edited *Twentieth Century Interpretations of
"Sanctuary"* (Prentice-Hall, 1982), drawing from studies by Vickery,
McHale, Kinney, and Philip M. Weinstein, as well as George Toles,
David Williams, Lawrence S. Kubie, T. H. Adamowski, David L.
Frazier, Aubrey Williams and William Rossky. Canfield's Introduc-
tion emphasizes Faulkner's skill as seen through the revision of the
manuscript.

vi. Individual Works, 1930–1939

Many important essays were published this year on *Pylon, The Wild
Palms, Light in August, As I Lay Dying*, and—still leading critical
production—*Absalom, Absalom!* Dieter Meindl chose to write about
"Romantic Idealism and *The Wild Palms*" in *Faulkner & Idealism*
(pp. 86–96), stressing that *Wild Palms* is the dominant story, with

Old Man a background effect piece. The whole point of the novel is that romance is false, that life must be bigger than the kind of love Charlotte and Harry create. Meindl sees Faulkner as a romantic, not because of his belief system but because of his synthesizing imagination. One of the best essays of 1983 is Marta Paul Johnson's "'I Have Decided Now': Laverne's Transformation in *Pylon*" (*MissQ* 36:289–300). Reading Laverne as a developing character, prompted to mature through the death of Roger, Johnson proves that the Reporter, Jack, and Jiggs are all untrustworthy narrators. Because Laverne Shuman exists only in others' words (and imaginations), the reader receives only distorted images of her, images that reflect the depravity of the surrounding world. George Monteiro has translated a 1935 review of *Pylon*, which shows that the novel was appreciated in Europe ("'Il Tono del grande Faulkner di *Pylon*': Mario Soldati's Review of *Pylon* and *Doctor Martino and Other Stories*," NMW 15: 11–18).

Dixie M. Turner's *A Jungian Psychoanalytic Interpretation of William Faulkner's As I Lay Dying* (Univ. Press, 1981) is a descriptive monograph focusing on each character of the novel. Kathleen L. Komar has adapted her essay about the novel (*ALS 1980*, pp. 160–61) into a chapter in *Pattern and Chaos: Multilinear Novels by Dos Passos, Döblin, Faulkner and Koepeen* (Camden House, Studies in German Literature, Linguistics and Culture, Vol. 14). Here she discusses "the coherent structures which underlie the fragmented surfaces," finding that this novel supports two symmetrical arrangements, one yielding a mythic plot pattern, the other, a range of individual consciousnesses. Faulkner's novel works with more discrete narrators than any work preceding it, but the central consciousness of Addie gives the book its focus. Michiko Yoshida describes Faulkner's imagery of eyes and looks ("The Act of Looking in *As I Lay Dying*," WiF 5:64–92), claiming that that imagery is the structuring device of the book. He points out that Faulkner uses little dialogue (more interior monologue); most of the action is conveyed visually. He praises the creation of Addie, a typical woman living in "a closed society." Paul Meleback also finds image patterns in "'Just a Shape to Fill a Lack': Receptacles in Faulkner's *As I Lay Dying*" (*ES* 64: 447–51), and John T. Matthews, in comparing this novel with an Updike work, makes the point that *Addie* as a name derives from the influence of *The Scarlet Letter*, in which—were it not for Hawthorne's

license—an adulteress would have been branded with *AD*, not *A*
("The Word as Scandal: Updike's *A Month of Sundays*," *ArQ* 39:
351–80).

One important essay on *Light in August* emphasizes Faulkner's
accurate, innovative chronology, which illuminates the psychology of
the characters (Harold Hungerford, "Past and Present in *Light in
August*," *AL* 55:183–98). Joanna Burden, for example, is most tied to
actual dates; Lena Grove is oblivious to chronology. He also excuses
Faulkner's lack of integration of early dates, seeing that the novel is
"a kind of private war among strangers." The larger theme of the
book is that "freedom and serenity lie in the eternal present. Thus
the time-scheme, and the characters' perception of their relation to
and responsibility for the past, *are* the moral structure." Other essays
treat Christmas from various perspectives: Maria Gillan, "Joe Christmas as Symbol of Southern Protestant Christianity," *NDQ* 51:137–43;
Joan Peternel, "The Double in *Light in August*: Narcissus or Janus?"
NMW 15:19–37 (which treats imagery as well as character, as does
Stanley R. Gillespie, "Light in Faulkner's *Light in August*," *Interpretations* 14:39–47).

Several major essays appeared this year on *Absalom, Absalom!*
David Krause sees Chapter 8 of the novel as the key to Shreve's involvement with the narrative ("Reading Shreve's Letters and Faulkner's *Absalom, Absalom!*" *SAF* 11:153–69). His invention of the letters shows his capacity for empathy, and provide Faulkner "with
unusually interesting and sophisticated occasions to provoke the
kinds of radically self-reflexive questions about writing and reading
and authority that trouble him and his text on a multiplicity of
levels." As a result, both writer and reader are free to rewrite and
reread.

Magdalene Redekop also views the text from Shreve's perspective,
but hers is more character oriented ("*Absalom, Absalom!*: Through
the Spectacles of Shreve McCannon," *WiF* 5:17–45). Since the major
conflict is recognition between father and son, though the recognition
scene never occurs, attention is turned to the white male narrators.
Shreve, in his position as outsider, speaks as often for the unrepre-
sented—the women and blacks—as for the white males. This perspective is crucial because the story is that of black experience. She
also points to the way Shreve changes appearance as his role in the
narrative develops.

Linda Kauffman studies Rosa's narrative as examples of kinds of lovers' discourses in "Devious Channels of Decorous Ordering: A Lover's Discourse in *Absalom, Absalom!* (*MFS* 29:183–200), while Philip J. Egan tries to convey the accomplishment of the whole in "Embedded Story Structures in *Absalom, Absalom!*" (*AL* 55:199–214). Egan finds 9 "spoken narratives" and 4 narrators, and is most interested in the patterns of juxtaposition. Each story addresses a specific audience on a specific occasion for a specific purpose; there are stories of biography, frames, and those that connect the two. "In every case the framing material—the popular legend, the faded letter, the weathered gravestone—has endured to the novel's fictional present, whereas the world of the enclosed narrative has passed away." All segments are, however, tragic, so the individual stories only amplify the tragic vision.

Other essays that concern this novel are J. Hillis Miller, "The Two Relativisms: Point of View and Indeterminacy in the Novel *Absalom, Absalom!*" (*Relativism in the Arts,* ed. Betty Jean Craige, [Georgia] pp. 148–70); Jeremy Hawthorne, the chapter "Race, Relationship and Identity: William Faulkner and Jean Rhys" from his *Multiple Personality and the Disintegration of Literary Character, From Oliver Goldsmith to Sylvia Plath* (St. Martin's), in which Quentin's "double-bind" situation is articulated; and Loren Schmidtberger, "Names in *Absalom, Absalom!*" (*AL* 55:83–88).

vii. Individual Works, 1940–1949

Most critical attention falls this year on *Go Down, Moses*—the entire novel, with little mention of "The Bear" as separate. Readers have finally begun to understand Faulkner's structuring, and several essays and the book-length study, *Threads Cable-Strong: William Faulkner's "Go Down, Moses"* by Dirk Kuyk, Jr. (Bucknell), attest to its importance within the canon. Kuyk's book, intended for the general reader, works through close analysis (in the first chapter, of the first four paragraphs of the text) and the presentation of "fabula" for each chapter, an order of events, with appropriate page numbers. Kuyk anticipates other readings of this novel with his emphasis on the women's roles, his ambivalence toward Ike, and his contention that Roth is somewhat better than Ike thinks him to be.

Meredith Smith's "A Chronology of *Go Down, Moses*" (*MissQ*

36:319–28) also orders the novel, giving several possible dates for one event when Faulkner seems in error. Dorothy L. Denniston speaks to the evolution of Faulkner's racial views in "Faulkner's Image of the Black Man in *Go Down, Moses*" (*Phylon* 44:33–43), and Michael Toolan presents a masterful linguistic analysis of Faulkner's language in "The Functioning of Progressive Verbal Forms in the Narrative of *Go Down, Moses*" (*Lang&S* 16:211–30). This study shows the way Faulkner changed verb forms for specific effects: the progressive forms all occur "in contexts where the reader is strongly aware of the mental processing activities of Ike and Sam."

Laura P. Claridge's "Isaac McCaslin's Failed Bid for Adulthood" (*AL* 55:241–57) views the character as immature because a more positive solution to his dilemma would have been repudiating, not relinquishing. Claridge sees his weaknesses as stemming from too little parental relationship, from too few fathers, not too many. His prolonged identity confusion leads to his lifelong pattern of retreat and narcissistic withdrawal. See also Section ix, for studies of individual stories within the novel.

Patrick Samway, S. J., studies "Gavin Stevens as Uncle-Creator in *Knight's Gambit*" (*Faulkner & Idealism*, pp. 144–63) to conclude that the strongest family relationship lies between Stevens and his nephew Chick Mallison. This provides Faulkner with a variation on his familiar father-son pattern, and it also allows the characters to grow in the novels of the later years. Samway sees Stevens as very positive in this work, revealing his wisdom in fragments as his role of detective allows him freedom from the Southern establishment.

A brief note by Elaine D. Johnson suggests that the spotted horses represent the effect of the Snopeses on Frenchman's Bend ("Faulkner's *The Hamlet*," *Expl* 41:48–51). Johnson also points to the unreconciled tension between men and women throughout the novel.

viii. Individual Works, 1950–1962

Keen Butterworth's model study, *A Critical and Textual Study of Faulkner's "A Fable"* (UMI), sees the novel as "an optimistic book for it trusts in redemption: the possibility of confronting man's fate with dignity and honor." Butterworth uses Lukacs and other contemporary critics to define the work as modernist and gives ample instruction in ways to read *A Fable*. He sees the marshal rather than the corporal as the moral center of the book, but contends that all characters deserve sympathy. Appendix A lists criticism of the work (and it is up-to-date); B collates versions of the novel and adds a table of suggested emendations. Kanzaburo Ohashi uses this text (as a fabula) to prove Faulkner's contemporary standing in "William Faulkner and Contemporary American Literature," (*WiF* 5:43–63). He sees the later trilogy as Faulkner's burlesque of the American Dream, working through parody, farce, and paradox.

Noel Polk's essay on *The Mansion* appears twice, in *Faulkner & Idealism* (pp. 112–26) and *WiF* 5:1–16. He sees this text as a culmination of more than just the trilogy, a means by which Faulkner brings in history external to his County. Flem parallels Sutpen; Mink remains a murderer: the Snopes's stories are a part of the human stream, not separate because of their Snopesism.

Gary Lindberg presents a somewhat different view of the Snopes family in *The Confidence Man in American Literature* (Oxford, 1982). The Snopes take on the character of the Robber Barons, whereas Gavin Stevens, Chick Mallison, and V. K. Ratliff emerge as muckrakers. But as Faulkner enjoys this world of trading, talking, and conning (or so the tone of his later novels suggests), the "evil" of the Snopes becomes more ridicule than outrage; and the palm for survival goes to Ratliff, the best Snopes watcher of all. The society as a whole becomes Faulkner's subject in these later novels, and Lindberg sees the existence of the Snopeses as necessary: without them, Ratliff would never become the "trickster, trader, tale-teller par excellence" that he is at the end of the trilogy. Lindberg also describes the evolution of Ratliff as a mature character and ends by placing him in a long tradition of American literary characters: "The art of survival, then, is not to keep clear of the games but to restore the balance and complexity and communal pleasure to them. Ratliff's virtue is not that he feels more deeply than other people but that he preserves a range of feelings and enough balance among them so that he can play on them."

David Laird discusses *The Reivers* and the meaning cars have for the characters of that novel in "Versions of Eden: The Automobile in the American Novel" (*MQR* 19–20 Fall 1980–Winter 1981:639–51), and David Paul Ragan discusses Ike once again in " 'Belonging to the Business of Mankind': The Achievement of Faulkner's *Big*

Woods," MissQ 36:301–17. Ike's lack of responsibility, and his imperviousness to that lack, dominates the revised stories. Ragan concludes, "The destruction of the woods is terrible, but the inability of man to deal with the loss is even more so."

ix. The Stories

M. E. Bradford's "The Anomaly of Faulkner's World War I Stories" (*MissQ* 36:243–62) is a substantial account of both the short fiction and the relevant novels, showing that Faulkner's consistent condemnation of the war as a waste of life and a nightmare was "extremely fashionable." Bradford relates the fiction to the culture, but also shows major patterns of motive, emphasizing that for Faulkner, men involved in war were "the living dead." Max Putzel's "Faulkner's Memphis Stories" (*VQR* 59:254–70) treats these stories as they relate to *Sanctuary*.

Three articles relate to "Barn Burning." Joseph Comprone uses the story to illustrate pedagogical practices, especially writing exercises ("Literature and the Writing Process: A Pedagogical Reading of William Faulkner's 'Barn Burning,'" *CollL*[1982]:1–21); Brenda Eve Sartoris describes "Cornbote: A Feudal Custom and Faulkner's 'Barn Burning,'" *SAF* 11:91–94; and Merrill Maguire Skaggs writes a fascinating account of making the film of the story on location in "Story and Film of 'Barn Burning': The Difference a Camera Makes," *SoQ* 21:5–15. In the process of making the "American Short Story" film, the narrative became Ab's tale.

Several others discuss "Was," particularly the poker game. Robert L. Yarup comments on the game's structural importance ("Faulkner's 'Was,'" *Expl* 41:43–45); Ezra Greenspan sees the game as revealing the importance of women, here, Tennie Beauchamp and Sophonsiba ("Faulkner's 'Was,'" *Expl* 41:42–43); and Helen M. Poindexter provides a detailed exegesis of the fine points of the poker game in "Faulkner, the Mississippi Gambler," *JML* 10:334–38. Joel I. Barstad looks at still another chapter from *Go Down, Moses* in "Faulkner's 'Pantaloon in Black'" (*Expl* 41:51–53), suggesting that the respiratory problems Rider has are the struggle between life and death within him. Janice Townley Moore traces imagery of dust and snakes, connecting them with a line from *Isaiah*, "And dust shall be the serpent's food." Dust signifies racial prejudice in "Faulkner's 'Dry September,'" *Expl* 41:47–48.

Alma A. Ilacqua uses "That Evening Sun," "Delta Autumn," and "The Bear" to illustrate Faulkner's view of cosmic order ("The Place of the Elect in Three Faulkner Narratives," *Christian Scholar's Review* 12:126–38). Ilacqua sees strong similarities between Faulkner's philosophy and that of Jonathan Edwards. She is particularly effective in her discussion of Ike, who exhibits many of the signs of graciousness but does not, finally, possess "excellency." Rather, he "remains untouched by the 'Irresistible Grace' which alone is capable of restoring the special grace lost at the fall."

The Faulkner Journal announces publication, with the premier issue scheduled for September 15, 1985. Coeditors of the new journal are James B. Carothers and John T. Matthews, with Charles M. Oliver as managing editor.

Michigan State University

10. Fitzgerald and Hemingway

Jackson R. Bryer

It is comforting to find, after a four-year sabbatical from doing this survey, that two axioms still apply to the year's output of scholarship and criticism on Fitzgerald and Hemingway. The first is that, as soon as you are certain that the last imaginable word has been said on a particular topic, along comes a book or essay that is a distinct contribution in that very area. It is just as predictable that several pieces will appear annually that are totally ignorant of their redundancy. Thus, 1983 saw two worthwhile full-length biographies of Fitzgerald and a fascinating book on the women in Hemingway's life, when it would seem that previous scholarship should surely have exhausted those fields of inquiry, as well as the usual quota of useless foolishness. Further evidence of this "good news/bad news" dichotomy can be found in the positive sign that scholars are continuing to make intelligent and profitable use of the Hemingway manuscripts at the Kennedy Library and in the negative statistic that the disproportion of Fitzgerald articles and book chapters compared with those on Hemingway was even more striking than in recent years (of 111 items mentioned in this survey, 21 are on Fitzgerald). After some encouraging indications during the last decade that critics were finally giving some attention to Fitzgerald's style and to his short stories, there were almost no pieces on these topics in 1983. There was only one critical study on either writer; and it was unenlightening. Finally, the total number of books surveyed—seven—is misleading in that two of them are not, strictly speaking, new; one is a translation and the other is essentially a reprinting in a more accessible form of an earlier volume.

i. Bibliographical Work and Texts

James L. W. West, III's *The Making of "This Side of Paradise"* (Penn.), as he notes in his Acknowledgements, did exist in an earlier

version in 1977 (see *ALS 1977*, p. 164). Although he claims that the
present text represents "a complete revision" and that copies were not
distributed in 1977, most of the changes appear to be stylistic refine-
ments and updating of the scholarship and do not substantially add
to the information presented previously by West. There is a new
section in the Appendixes that describes the physical characteristics
of the fragments of the first version of the novel ("The Romantic
Egotist") that survive. Of course, the evaluation of this important
book remains the same as it was in 1977: despite the unfortunate fact
that West was prohibited from quoting directly from Fitzgerald's
fragments and manuscripts and thus cannot provide a very heavily
documented story of the novel's composition, he does contribute valuable evidence to account for its unevenness and for its disregard for
consistency of point of view in Book 1. The story he tells of how
Fitzgerald literally pieced together his first book is a fascinating one
and it is good to have it more easily available and taking its rightful
place alongside Matthew J. Bruccoli's composition studies of *Tender
Is the Night* (1963) and *The Last Tycoon* (1977). Surely a similar
study of the composition of *The Great Gatsby* is now long overdue.

In *Hemingway & "The Sun Also Rises": The Crafting of a Style*
(Kansas), Frederic Joseph Svoboda does not provide a straight
chronological account, as West does; but because of the availability
of the Hemingway manuscripts at the Kennedy Library, he not only
quotes extensively and effectively from the various drafts of the novel
he also has convinced his publishers to reproduce in facsimile form a
number of pages from Hemingway's holographs and typescripts.
Svoboda's technique is to focus on four scenes—the love scene between Jake and Brett in chapter 7, the discussion between Jake and
the waiter of the death of Vincente Girones, the description of Romero's performance in the bullring before Jake and Brett on the day
after he is beaten by Cohn, and the final chapter—and to show in
great detail how and why Hemingway reworked them. His conclusions—that Hemingway, in general, tried to substitute direct recreation in description for interpretation, that he eliminated a great
deal in an effort to emphasize what was left unsaid, that he moved
in the composition of the book from an essentially journalistic account of his experiences in Pamplona in which he used the names of
real people toward "a completely realized fictional whole," and that

his decision to delete the first chapter and a half at Fitzgerald's suggestion was a wise one—are not very surprising or original. But never before have they been so carefully documented; and never before has the amount of work Hemingway actually did in transforming his first draft (written in six weeks) into a novel been so fully and convincingly demonstrated. And, as Svoboda's title implies, this process of revision helped Hemingway shape "a set of principles that he was to follow and elucidate for the rest of his life." The useful appendices to Svoboda's study include descriptions of the manuscript and typescript versions of *Sun* at the Kennedy Library, the text of the beginning of the novel that Hemingway cut, and Fitzgerald's letter recommending the change.

Like Svoboda, Paul Smith has used the materials at the Kennedy Library extensively and wisely. His "Hemingway's Early Manuscripts: The Theory and Practice of Omission" (*JML* 10:268–88) is the most substantial shorter textual study of the year. Smith first traces Hemingway's "Theory of Omission" through his published pronouncements on it, concluding that "a rather commonplace idea was used on various occasions to serve various ends, until it became for him *the* theory of his fiction." Then, in the second and more important half of his essay, he explores the "Practice of Omission" in Hemingway's writing of "The Killers," "Big Two-Hearted River," and "Up in Michigan." Of particular value is his use of the contrast between the revision processes used in the latter two stories to show Hemingway's progress as an artist. Kathryn Zabelle Derounian, in "An Examination of the Drafts of Hemingway's Chapter 'Nick sat against the wall of the church . . .'" (*PBSA* 77:54–65), is also interested in showing Hemingway's "successful blend of theory and practice." By examining the three drafts of the 200-word chapter (all three are helpfully reproduced as illustrations), she shows in convincing detail how he "gradually omitted irrelevant details and succeeded in expressing an exact sequence of events in simple yet forceful style" and how he "accurately showed Nick's view of his situation; and through restricted style and sentence structure, he conveyed Nick's shocked reaction to it."

Two shorter textual pieces, Robert E. Fleming's "An Early Manuscript of Hemingway's 'Hills Like White Elephants'" (*NMAL* 7: Item 3) and Paul J. Lindholdt's "Hemingway's 'Summer People': More

Textual Errors and a Reply" (*SSF* 20:319–20), are less ambitious but still worthy of mention. Fleming discovers, in the earliest manuscript version of "Hills," a false start which, written in the first person, tells of a train trip Hemingway and his first wife Hadley took from Pamplona to Madrid during which she "spots the white mountains that would provide the title of the later story" and offers this as an additional source. Lindholdt helpfully points out a number of substantive errors in the text of "Summer People" in *The Nick Adams Stories* (1972) by comparing it to the manuscript in the Kennedy Library, asserting that we "deserve a more accurate edition."

Although there was a paperback reprinting of Hemingway's 88 *Poems* (see *ALS 1979*, p. 156) entitled *Complete Poems* (Nebraska), no new Fitzgerald or Hemingway texts appeared during the year. As in the past, however, there was a certain amount of updating, correcting, and supplementing of the available bibliographical resources; all items surveyed here concern Hemingway. George Monteiro's "Grover Cleveland Alexander in 1918: A New Kansas City Piece by Ernest Hemingway" (*AL* 54[1982]: 116–18) identifies and reprints an unsigned Kansas City *Star* piece, attributing it to Hemingway on the basis of a letter the author wrote to his father. James B. Meriwether, in "Addendum to Hanneman: Hemingway in *The Albatross Book of American Short Stories*" (*PBSA* 77:65–66), adds to Hanneman's section of anthologies a 1935 collection published in Hamburg that reprinted "The Undefeated."

In "'Manner' and 'Fact', Attributed to 'E. Hemingway'" (*PBSA* 76[1982]:350), William White supplies full titles for two items incompletely cited in Michael S. Reynolds's *Hemingway's Reading* (1981). Reynolds himself reprints, in "Hemingway's Stein: Another Misplaced Review" (*AL* 55:431–34), Hemingway's March 5, 1923, *Chicago Tribune* review of Stein's *Geography and Plays* and uses it to clarify Stein's review of *Three Stories and Ten Poems* and also to give us some "clues" to Hemingway's literary tastes in 1922 (he was reading Lawrence and Wells, had lost interest in Mencken, and was learning from Stein herself).

Jackson J. Benson's "Hemingway Criticism: Getting at the Hard Questions" in Donald R. Noble's *Hemingway: A Revaluation* (Whitston, pp. 17–47) is a gracefully written, good-humored yet pointed and perceptive survey that divides the books on Hemingway into categories and selects the most worthwhile in each. Although his account is already almost a decade out-of-date (it was originally prepared for the University of Alabama Symposium on Hemingway in 1975), the pervasive areas of weakness Benson cites—fatuous influence studies, redundancy without acknowledgement, and the persistence of the biographical fallacy—are still applicable, as are some of the needs he mentions—studies of style, work on Pound and Stein as influences and on time in the fiction.

Another survey in the Noble collection, Robert O. Stephens's "Hemingway's British and American Reception: A Study in Values (pp. 83–97), is confined to the responses of reviewers, using examples effectively to support its contention that, during his lifetime, American reviewers tended "to concentrate on the writer rather than the subject"; while, for British commentators, once they "accepted Hemingway as a writer of full stature, his work became part of a mature literary tradition, and the emphasis . . . was on the subject matter as a contribution to literary knowledge." Stephens acknowledges that, after Hemingway's death, his life and work "finally became inseparable" for all reviewers.

As a partial updating of Stephens's essay (also originally prepared for the Alabama Symposium), Delbert E. Wylder looks at "The Critical Reception of Ernest Hemingway's *Selected Letters, 1917–1961*" (*HemR* 3,i:54–60) and provides both his own informed assessment of the collection and how it expands our knowledge of and insight into Hemingway and also a brief overview of the earliest American reviews it received. Scott Donaldson's "Woolf vs. Hemingway" (*JML* 10:338–42) deals with one very important English reviewer's response to Hemingway, focusing on Virginia Woolf's not very complimentary comments about *The Sun Also Rises* and *Men Without Women* and on Hemingway's equally unflattering response in a letter to Maxwell Perkins.

Each issue of *The Hemingway Review* carries two very helpful features by William White—"For the Collector" (2,ii:56–61; 3,i:71–72), which tends to deal with Hemingway editions available abroad, and "Hemingway: A Current Bibliography" (2,ii:63–65; 3,i:73–76), which goes well beyond the MLA Bibliography and other listings by including reviews of books by and about Hemingway, new editions and translations, and books that contain significant mention of him.

Since the suspension of the *Fitzgerald/Hemingway Annual* in 1979, there have been no comparable annual compilations for Fitzgerald and this represents a serious gap for scholars.

ii. Letters and Biography

No new Hemingway or Fitzgerald letters surfaced in 1983; but two of the three biographies published relied for much of the new information they contributed on letters written to Hemingway and Fitzgerald and on letters about them written to earlier biographers. Scott Donaldson, in *Fool for Love: F. Scott Fitzgerald* (Congdon & Weed), finds much original material in letters to Fitzgerald and in notes Arthur Mizener and Henry Dan Piper kept of the interviews they conducted with Fitzgerald's friends and associates. Donaldson tries to find "the special set of mind that made Fitzgerald the kind of man and writer he was"; his thesis is that he "was driven to please other people, especially rich and prominent people," a propensity he derived principally from his mother (who was "also largely responsible for his social insecurity"), and one that he accomplished far more successfully with women than with men. Donaldson traces this in a technique reminiscent of that in his earlier book on Hemingway (see *ALS 1977*, pp. 166–67): although arranged around a chronological account, he provides a mosaic of chapters that combine sensitive literary analysis with informed biographical information in looking at various facets of Fitzgerald's life and career—his childhood and relationship with his mother, his years at Princeton, his drinking, his womanizing, his attitudes toward Jews and blacks, his crack-up. The overall psychological portrait provided is valuable and much of the criticism (the chapters on *Tender Is the Night* and on the short stories are particularly strong) is suggestive and worthwhile. And, as always, reading Donaldson's prose is a pleasure.

Bernice Kert also does her scholarly homework well in *The Hemingway Women* (Norton). She has interviewed three of Hemingway's wives, as well as many others; she makes good use of unpublished letters written to Hemingway by the women in his life, as well as of correspondence exchanged between members of Hemingway's family; she has mined the interviews, correspondence, and other materials Carlos Baker assembled in preparing his biography; and she has consulted the relevant scholarship. The result is a well-written straightforward chronological account of Hemingway's relationships with his wives and with the "other" women in his life (principally his mother, Lady Duff Twysden, Agnes von Kurowsky, Jane Gingrich, and Adriana Ivancich). Her narrative occasionally uses the fiction as biographical data, and she tends to shy away from analyzing the relationships she describes; but she has brought Hemingway's women out from the large shadow he cast over them by giving us their view of him in their own words and by telling us about them before they met him and after he ceased to dominate their lives. Grace Hall Hemingway and Martha Gellhorn, in particular, benefit from this more objective treatment; and Kert's statement that Hemingway's "yearning to be looked after and his craving for excitement was never resolved" is convincingly supported by the compelling narrative she provides.

The 1979 publication of André Le Vot's *Scott Fitzgerald* (Paris: Julliard) in French has not been previously noted in these pages. The book is now available in English as *F. Scott Fitzgerald: A Biography* (Doubleday), in a translation by William Byron. As previous reviewers have pointed out, Le Vot's vantage as a European enables him to view Fitzgerald and his times in a fresh way—his sections on Fitzgerald at Princeton, on America in 1920, on the corruptness of the Jazz Age, on Prohibition, and on Paris in the 1920s are especially good —but his book also has major flaws. Le Vot seems remarkably ignorant of or unwilling to mention previous scholarship. His long analysis of the *The Great Gatsby* deals with such matters as parallels with the Fuller-McGee case, color symbolism, and Dr. T. J. Eckleburg's eyes without citing any earlier studies. He has not updated his footnote references to Fitzgerald's and Hemingway's letters that he read at Princeton to cite their inclusion in Baker's or Bruccoli's recent editions. A twenty-five page critical analysis of *Gatsby* suddenly interrupts the biographical account, when the rest of Fitzgerald's fiction receives very little attention throughout the rest of the book. Finally, there is the matter of Le Vot's—or his translator's—obtrusive overwritten style. Despite its flaws, the book is necessary reading for all serious students of Fitzgerald, especially for its foreign perspective.

In an intriguing shorter piece with an unfortunately hysterical title, "Wanted By the FBI!" (*NYRB*, March 31, pp. 17–20), Jeffrey Meyers uses material from the F.B.I.'s file on Hemingway to supplement what is already known about his intelligence work in Cuba during World War II. The seriousness with which the Bureau treated Hemingway's "Crook Factory" (his name for the group of under-cover agents he had assembled) is as pathetic as it is ludicrous and supports Meyers's claim that they "feared his personal prestige and political power" and, as a consequence, "made unsuccessful attempts to control, mock, and vilify him," attempts that continued until just before his death when they even tracked him to the Mayo Clinic.

John L. Idol, Jr., in "Ernest Hemingway and Thomas Wolfe" (*SCR* 15,i:24–31), does a good job of assembling Wolfe's and Hem-ingway's published and, in one important instance, unpublished (a Wolfe review of *Farewell to Arms*) assessments of each other's work and examining their respective relationships with Maxwell Perkins. He finds, not very surprisingly, that both valued Perkins's friendship and expertise highly and that each "hungered mightily for fame and . . . came to defend his own style as essentially right for himself." Eva B. Mills's "Ernest Hemingway and Nathan Asch: An Ambivalent Relationship" (*HemR* 2,ii:48–51) uses unpublished Asch letters to document a less publicized and less important relationship than the one with Wolfe.

iii. Criticism

a. **Collections.**   Three new collections of criticism, all on Heming-way, appeared in 1983. Michael S. Reynolds's *Critical Essays on Ernest Hemingway's "In Our Time"* (Hall) contains a section of reprinted reviews, several of which are not included in Stephens's *Critical Reception* (1977) volume, and an "Articles and Essays" sec-tion that is divided into three parts—reprinted pieces on the 1924 *in our time*, reprinted articles on the 1925 *In Our Time*, and a large number of essays and notes, (most reprinted) on the individual stories. Reynold's choices are good ones; many leading Hemingway critics (Linda W. Wagner, E. R. Hagemann, Jackson J. Benson, Robert W. Lewis, and George Monteiro, among others) are repre-sented; and the volume also includes a solid Introduction by Reyn-olds that traces—using much new manuscript material—the genesis of *In Our Time* and three original essays that will be discussed below.

The other two collections, A. Robert Lee's *Ernest Hemingway: New Critical Essays* (Vision and Barnes and Noble) and Donald R. Noble's *Hemingway: A Revaluation* (Whitston), contain a preponderance of original essays (Noble's volume includes previously published pieces by Alfred Kazin, Michael S. Reynolds, and Richard B. Hovey, and ten new essays), which are discussed elsewhere in this survey.

b. **Full-Length Studies.** The Donaldson and Le Vot Fitzgerald biographies, as noted above, both contain some literary analysis. J. Bakker's *Fiction as Survival Strategy: A Comparative Study of the Major Works of Ernest Hemingway and Saul Bellow* (Rodopi) is of negligible value as Hemingway criticism. Each of Bakker's chapters links a Bellow work with one by Hemingway; but there is a heavy emphasis on plot summary and on stressing great differences between the two writers. Bakker's central point about Hemingway seems to be the familiar one that, towards the middle of his career, he underwent an "irreversible change of sensibility, which made it extremely difficult . . . to go on treating some of his favorite subjects as artistic material." His final chapter does include some interesting remarks on why Bellow's heroes were appropriate for the post-World War II era and Hemingway's were the same for the 1920s and 1930s; but it is not worth wading through the rest of Bakker's book to get to them. A far more concise and balanced look at the Hemingway-Bellow links is offered by Allan Chavkin in "Fathers and Sons: 'Papa' Hemingway and Saul Bellow" (*PLL* 19:499–60). Unlike Bakker, who suggests few similarities and never mentions influence, Chavkin sees Hemingway as "an oppressive influence" that Bellow "had to repudiate in order to forge his own art." His examinations of Hemingway's "negative influence" on *Seize the Day* and of the common elements in the two writers' work are convincing.

c. **General Essays.** The four general essays on Fitzgerald this year all make contributions. Michael Spindler's "The Rich Are Different: Scott Fitzgerald and the Leisure Class" suffers some from the fact that it is a chapter in a book, *American Literature and Social Change: William Dean Howells to Arthur Miller* (Indiana), whose thesis is so applicable to Fitzgerald that it has become a cliché of Fitzgerald criticism. Spindler is concerned with a shift in American capitalism from a "production-oriented phase" (1880–1920) to a "consumption-oriented phase" (1920–1950) bringing with it the rise of a new leisure class that rejected Puritan and work-ethic ideals. He examines

Fitzgerald's four completed novels as reflections of their author's—
and middle class America's—ambivalent attitudes toward this leisure
class, an approach that proves most fruitful in his remarks about
Tender Is the Night.

Donald Monk's "Fitzgerald: The Tissue of Style" (*JAmS* 17:77–
94) is the year's only essay that deals with the still by no means totally
explored topic of Fitzgerald's style. His piece is especially good because it traces changes in the style from *Gatsby* through *The Last
Tycoon* rather than restricting itself to one work or even part of a
work as so many of the earlier studies of style have done. Mary A.
McCay's "Fitzgerald's Women: Beyond Winter Dreams" *American
Novelists Revisited* [Hall, 1982]) also takes a broader view, looking
at women characters in the full range of Fitzgerald's fiction. She contends that he was "truly contemptuous" of "useless women" who
used beauty as masks for their weakness, drawing "brave young men
to wreck like sirens," and depicted these feelings in early heroines
like Isabelle and Rosalind (*This Side of Paradise*), Gloria (*The Beautiful and Damned*), and Judy Jones ("Winter Dreams"). Later in his
career, influenced by his pride in his daughter and by Sheilah Graham, McCay sees him creating far more positive heroines like Rose-
mary (*Tender Is the Night*) and Cecilia and Kathleen (*The Last
Tycoon*). Her essay is a convincing blend of biography and criticism.

In "F. Scott Fitzgerald and Charles G. Norris" (*JML* 10:40–54),
Richard Allen Davison blends scholarship and criticism in the definitive exploration of a relationship that other critics have alluded to
superficially. Davison carefully examines the correspondence between the two men and the echoes of Norris's work in Fitzgerald's
(particularly the similarities between *Brass* and *Gatsby* and between
Salt and "May Day"); and his essay is as modestly argued as it is
suggestive.

There is an abundance of general essays on Hemingway and
the best of them are either from *The Hemingway Review* or from the
Noble and Lee collections. This implies that good original work is
more likely to be produced when it is screened, commissioned, or
written by scholars familiar with Hemingway studies.

All three *Hemingway Review* general essays deliberately attempt
to suggest new directions. Allen Josephs's "Hemingway's Out of Body
Experience" (2,ii:11–17) takes as his point of departure Hemingway's statements about his "soul or something" leaving his body on

the night he was wounded in Italy in July 1918 and sees that as an Out of Body Experience that he depicted in "Now I Lay Me" and "A Way You'll Never Be" and that may well have affected him more than the famous wounding itself. Wayne G. Holcombe also questions a commonly held assumption in "The Motive of the Motif: Some Thoughts on Hemingway's Existentialism" (3,i:18–27), where he argues that Killinger's 1960 labeling of Hemingway as an existentialist is "simplistic." Acknowledging that there are similarities between Hemingway's thought and that of the existentialists, Holcombe focuses on his heroes' refusal to think about "metaphysical or extraexperiential topics" and points out that this puts them at odds with such leading existential thinkers as Sartre and Camus.

The third *Hemingway Review* general essay, John Leland's " 'The Happiness of the Garden': Hemingway's Edenic Quest" (3,i:44–53), while it contains some provocative ideas, is haphazardly organized and doesn't cohere around a clear central point. Leland seems to be setting up a worthwhile contrast between wasteland and Edenic refuge settings in Hemingway's fiction; but this gets submerged in an overabundance of other examples. A far clearer motif study is Leo Gurko's "Hemingway and the Magical Journey" (Noble, pp. 67–82). Gurko finds several common factors in the various journeys in Hemingway's fiction and further sees the protagonists of the first three novels (excluding *Torrents of Spring*) as not changed by their journeys while the heroes of the last three novels "advance toward new ground" and are noticeably altered.

This effort by Gurko to see differences between Hemingway's early and late major fiction echoes another recurrent theme of the year's general essays—an attempt to explain and/or defend Hemingway's artistic decline at the end of his career. Philip Young's entertaining and self-effacing "Hemingway: The Writer in Decline" (Noble, pp. 225–39) begins with marvelous excerpts from letters Hemingway wrote to Young (some were never mailed) objecting to the critic's insistence on identifying the author with his protagonists. Young observes that Hemingway often "wish-fulfilled" reality, especially with respect to his heroes' relationships with women; and he attributes his artistic decline after *For Whom the Bell Tolls* to the fact that "the author became increasingly his own undisguised subject." Like Gurko, Young makes his points simply and clearly.

Brian Way, in "Hemingway the Intellectual: A Version of Mod-

ernism" (Lee, pp. 151–71), also tries to grapple with Hemingway's
decline. After 1930, Way contends, Hemingway began "to reason
about his writing from the outside, instead of following his instinct,"
feeling he ought "to force himself to write about tragic situations and
exalted emotions." Way's essay is complex; but it rewards a careful
reading. So too does Faith Pullin's "Hemingway and the Secret Language of Hate" (Lee, pp. 172–92), which posits the thesis that
"Hemingway's sense of the relationships between people, and particularly between men and women, is that they are invariably destructive"; therefore he had "no genuine comprehension of, or expertise
in, the fictive treatment of human relationships." His protagonist
becomes, for Pullin, "the archetypal loner fighting against a hostile
world" and his hostility is "to the relationship itself as much as to
women."

Eric Mottram's "Essential History: Suicide and Nostalgia in Hemingway's Fictions" (Lee, pp. 122–50) begins where Pullin ends, with
the lone male, "released from work and family," searching for "ideal
self-definition" in a century when male domination has begun to
erode. Hemingway's fiction then explores, Mottram claims, "how to
make a life and a work out of the decaying body of the history of
male prerogatives"; and, viewed against this background, *Islands in
the Stream* becomes the "voice of a mid-twentieth-century man who
above all has had enough of the futile politics and wars of his time
and who knows that the creativity of the arts and the practice of the
skills are primary."

As usual, there were a number of influence studies, some dealing
with influences on Hemingway and others (including the Hemingway and Bellow piece discussed above) dealing with Hemingway's
influence on other writers. Frank McConnell's "Stalking Papa's Ghost:
Hemingway's Presence in Contemporary American Writing" (Lee,
pp. 193–211) also begins with Bellow's "refutation of the entire
Hemingway mystique" in *Dangling Man*; but he goes on to suggest
that the "Frederick Henry vision of the separate peace, the code-
aesthetics of the dropout and the deserter, the . . . solution of style as
a counterpoint to the horror of history . . . have been . . . the shape of
the best American fiction" of the 1960s and 1970s. McConnell's
tracings of Hemingway's presence in the work of Vonnegut and
Pynchon are brief but suggestive of worthwhile further study.

The most substantial work currently being done on influences on Hemingway is by Mark Spilka. Two products of his ongoing project on "Victorian Keys to the Early Hemingway" appear in the *Journal of Modern Literature*. The first (10:125–50) conjectures that Dinah Craik's 1856 novel, *John Halifax, Gentleman*, which was greatly admired by Hemingway's parents, had a profound effect on their lives and on their son. Spilka's second essay (10:289–310) focuses on Frances Hodgson Burnett's famous 1886 novel, *Little Lord Fauntleroy*, and on *Huckleberry Finn*, as representing two contrasting phases of Hemingway's childhood, one dominated by his mother (*Fauntleroy*) and the other by his father (*Finn*). Throughout both pieces, Spilka shows his command of Hemingway biography as well as his talents in reading the fiction carefully and sensitively.

The other general essays are weaker than those surveyed above. James T. McCartin's "Ernest Hemingway: The Life and the Works" (*ArQ* 39:122–34) is filled with clichés about Hemingway's negative view of women and about his tendency to mythologize his own life. Similarly, in "The Quest for Happiness in Hemingway" (*IJAS* 13,i: 119–25), E. Nageswara Rao centers his analysis of several Hemingway texts on the discovery that, for his heroes, a "healthy catharsis is possible through fishing, hunting, killing, sexual intercourse, and creative writing." Herbie Butterfield's "Ernest Hemingway" (*American Fiction: New Readings*) is a discursive and rapid journey through numerous Hemingway works that touches on his kinship with Thoreau, his depiction of loneliness, his obsession with death, his politics, his depiction of courage, and his poetic qualities. Mary Allen's Hemingway chapter in her *Animals in American Literature* (also ranges widely, with predictable close attention paid to bulls, African animals, fish, and horses, along with some more interesting remarks on the neurotic relationship of women with animals in "Cat in the Rain" and "A Canary for One." Richard Godden's " 'You've Got to See It, Feel It, Smell It, Hear It,' Buy It: Hemingway's Commercial Forms" (*Essays in Poetics* 8,i:1–29) assembles a multitude of examples of Hemingway's "commodification" of life but does so in a desultory and floundering fashion.

d. Essays on Specific Works: Fitzgerald. In keeping with the general trend this year, there are only 13 items covered under this heading; further, 4 are 1982 pieces inadvertently omitted last year and 2 others deal with Zelda Fitzgerald. Even *The Great Gatsby* was the subject of only three full-length essays and two notes. The most original of these is Ruth E. Roberts's "Nonverbal Communication in *The Great Gatsby*" (*Language and Literature* 7[1982]:107–29), which analyzes such nonverbal components of Daisy and Gatsby's interaction as body language, tone of voice, and "interactional synchrony" in order to draw a "clearer picture of Daisy's allure for Gatsby." Roberts also glances briefly at similar elements in the depictions of Tom, Jordan, and George Wilson. In "The Unfinished American Epic: Fitzgerald's *The Great Gatsby*" (*The Twenties*), Marcella Taylor takes on a promising (albeit not terribly original) topic—the epic qualities in the novel—but proceeds so woodenly and disjointedly that her many examples of epic characteristics are ineffectively presented. Ann Massa's section on *Gatsby* in her *American Literature in Context, IV* (Methuen, 1982), centers rather simplistically on Jay Gatsby as "a quintessential American dreamer" whose idealism "led to his death."

Edward J. Piacentino speculates intriguingly, in "Dan Cody-Ella Kaye and Gatsby-Daisy: Speculations on a Cyclical Pattern in *The Great Gatsby*" (*NMAL* 7:Item 18), that "Nick seems to perceive what Gatsby, enraptured by his obsessive idealism, may only partially comprehend but fails to acknowledge: namely, that the Dan Cody-Ella Kaye adventure foreshadows his own disillusioning and eventually fatal experience with Daisy Buchanan." In "Acts of Madness or Despair: A Note on *The Secret Agent* and *The Great Gatsby*" (*SAF* 11:101–06), Ted Billy usefully extends the Fitzgerald-Conrad echoes through similarities in plot, in use of the lunacy motif, in emphasis on blindness and faulty perception, in ironic kitchen scenes following deaths, and in theme—"the attempt to alter (or obliterate) the passage of time."

Both of the year's essays on *Tender Is the Night* are provocative. Jacqueline Tavernier–Courbin suggests, in "Sensuality as Key to Characterization in *Tender Is the Night*" (*ESC* 9:452–67), that "sensual desire and consciousness are . . . the most important elements which motivate the characters, further the action, and give the novel its life force" and that the "more basic desire is, the more positive it appears to be" and the "more complex and indefinite it is, the more destructive it becomes." She applies this to Dick Diver and Tommy

Barban, contending that Nicole and Tommy prevail "because they have accepted one of the basic instincts of life as a natural thing and are satisfying it with cheerful simplicity."

In "*Tender Is the Night* as a Tragic Action" (*TSLL* 25:597–615), Robert Merrill sees the 1951 revised version as superior to the 1934 edition because it establishes the "gradual, 'progressive' character of Dick's alteration" more clearly. He claims that viewing the novel as a tragedy "allows us to gauge the structural logic of Fitzgerald's revisions" and supports this well; he is best when suggesting that looking at Fitzgerald's other novels as tragedies different in assumptions from *Tender* would give us new insights into Fitzgerald as a literary artist.

Reversing an encouraging trend of recent years that has seen increased attention paid to Fitzgerald's short stories, there were only two essays and one note on them this year. Both essays were by Alice Hall Petry; happily, both dealt with largely neglected stories. In "Love Story: Mock Courtship in F. Scott Fitzgerald's 'The Jelly-Bean'" (*ArQ* 39:251–60), Petry asserts that the story's excellence lies in its juxtaposition of "double protagonists," Jim Powell and Nancy Lamar, who represent, respectively, the best and worst of the Old South and the best and worst of the New South. In their "mock courtship," she sees Fitzgerald depicting "a couple, a town, a region undergoing a serious identity crisis." Petry's "F. Scott Fitzgerald's 'A Change of Class' and Frank Norris" (*MarkhamR* 12:49–52) seems unaware of some of the earlier studies of the Norris-Fitzgerald connections but does enlarge these slightly by citing parallels in characterization, plot, values, and structure between *The Pit* and Fitzgerald's story.

William Harmon and Susan W. Smock, in "How T. S. Eliot Probably Borrowed a Sentence From F. Scott Fitzgerald" (*AN&Q* 21:110), offer the highly dubious conjecture that a phrase in "Animula" (1929) has its origins in a similar phrase in "The Love Boat" (1927), a Fitzgerald story. In a far more legitimate note, "Fitzgerald's 'Euganean Hills' Allusion in 'The Crack-Up'" (*AN&Q* 21:139–41), Ronald J. Gervais corrects the footnote in the *Norton Anthology of American Literature* that cites Catullus's "Farewell to my Brother" as the source for Fitzgerald's reference and substitutes Shelley's "Lines Written Among the Euganean Hills."

The figure of Zelda Fitzgerald continues to fascinate and intrigue.

In "Zelda Fitzgerald: An Unromantic Revision" (*DR* 62:196–211),
Anna Valdine Clemens examines Mizener's and Turnbull's portraits
of Zelda in their Fitzgerald biographies and the two Zelda biographies by Milford and Mayfield, finding some fault with each and
calling for a new appraisal that would "involve a closer examination
of Zelda's breakdowns and years of confinement, a reassessment of
her skills as a writer, and more pointed emphasis on the nature of the
forces that curtailed her freedom." Lane Yorke's "Zelda: A Work-
sheet" (*ParisR* 89:210–63) consists of a chronologically arranged
gathering of excerpts from Zelda's writings (largely her letters to
Scott but a few to others and some fiction) that Yorke used in helping playwright Bill Luce put together a one-woman show about
Zelda. Because some of the excerpts are previously unpublished and
because many are excellent samples of Zelda's unique and evocative
writing style, this unusual piece merits attention.

e. Essays on Specific Works: Hemingway.   Essays on Hemingway's
novels were quite evenly distributed this year. *The Sun Also Rises*
and *A Farewell to Arms*, as usual, got the most attention, with five
and four, respectively; but three other novels were the subjects of
more than one piece. Two of the articles on *Sun* are by H. R. Stoneback and both deal with Chapter 12 (the fishing trip to Burguete).
In " 'For Bryan's Sake': The Tribute to the Great Commoner in Hemingway's *The Sun Also Rises*" (*C&L* 32,ii:29–36), Stoneback focuses
on the three-page discussion of Bryan that is the "very center" and
"the pivot" of the chapter. He sees the fact that Jake is more in sympathy with Bryan than with Mencken regarding the Scopes Trial as
reflecting his seriousness about "matters of faith and belief" and
points out that "belief, not disbelief—faith, not mockery—is the
norm, the center of this scene as of the entire novel." Stoneback's
"Hemingway and Faulkner on the Road to Roncevaux" (Noble, pp.
135–63) sets out to look at the use made of Roncevaux by Hemingway in *Sun* and by Faulkner in *Flags in the Dust*. He stresses how
the religious associations of Roncevaux and its monastery emphasize
the motif of the quest in *Sun*, "the pilgrimage undertaken in order to
grow in grace," and the depiction of Jake as a good Catholic whose
pilgrimage has religious overtones in a novel whose "deepest thrust
. . . is radically spiritual."
     The two other full-length articles on *Sun*, Andrew Hook's "Art and

Life in *The Sun Also Rises*" (Lee, pp. 49–63) and Jesse Bier's "Jake
Barnes, Cockroaches, and Trout in *The Sun Also Rises*" (*ArQ* 39:
164–71), are both helpful in exploring aspects of the novel that,
although previously studied, are not exhausted as topics. Bier is concerned with Jake's "psychological and moral" impotence as revealed
in his "repeated and powerless reversions to adolescent and even in-
fantile feeling" and in his "moral laxness." Through pointed and
effective use of the text, Bier shows him to be the perfect "central
consciousness though not hero" for a book in which "nothing will
decisively happen though there is excitation enough." Hook begins
sensibly by discounting the autobiographical elements of *Sun*, calling "place" the controlling factor. He then examines in detail the
symbolic functions of Paris, Burguete, Pamplona, San Sebastian, and
Madrid.

The one note on *Sun*, Dale Edmonds's "How Now Bocanegra?:
Jake's Bull in the Afternoon" (*NMAL* 7:Item 10), establishes that,
because Bocanegra is referred to as Romero's second bull, he must
therefore be the afternoon's sixth, as the text clearly establishes that
Romero was to fight the third and sixth bulls; but his contention that
the error is Hemingway's as well as Jake's seems spurious.

Two of the four essays on *A Farewell to Arms*, Scott Donaldson's
"Frederic Henry's Escape and the Pose of Passivity" (Noble, pp.
165–85) and Peter Balbert's "From Hemingway to Lawrence to
Mailer: Survival and Sexual Identity in *A Farewell to Arms*" (*HemR*
3,i:30–43), come to somewhat different conclusions about Frederic.
Balbert defends the polarized male and female roles in the novel in
asserting, rather simplistically, that "Frederic Henry's practical, sol-
dierly, but delimiting brand of merely 'survivalist' ideology is broadened and enriched, under the influence of Catherine Barkley, to
become a courageous commitment to love, life, and family responsibility." Donaldson is more aware of the novel's complexities in his
perception of the deliberateness and calculation with which Frederic
plans his escape from the war and in his explication of scenes in
which Frederic clearly acts more passive and dumber than he really
is. Donaldson is particularly good in showing, through passages Hemingway excised from the text, how he made Frederic less sympathetic,
how he distanced him from his creator, and how he emphasized his
guilt for his actions and his inability to forget the war he has deserted.

Robert E. Fleming, in "Hemingway and Peele: Chapter I of *A*

Farewell to Arms" (*SAF* 11:95–100), has also made good use of the manuscript in his exploration of the ironic contrasts between the novel's opening chapter (which the manuscript suggests either may have been added late in the composition process or "split off from what followed during the revision process") and George Peele's poem, "A Farewell to Arms." Fleming shows convincingly how several of Hemingway's specific revisions to the chapter strengthened this contrast. While he does not deal with the manuscript, William Wasserstrom, in "*A Farewell to Arms*: Radiance at the Vanishing Point" (Lee, pp. 64–78), is also intent on finding the greatness of *Farewell* in its "fabled style," its uniting of "avant-garde experiments of language with a presiding mode of American demotic speech." His essay, unfortunately, substitutes the elegance of Wasserstrom's own flowery allusive style for the close textual analysis that his subject demands.

In what is certainly the most convincingly damning essay of the year, "Hemingway's Poor Spanish: Chauvinism and Loss of Credibility in *For Whom the Bell Tolls*" (Noble, pp. 205–23), F. Allen Josephs marshals an impressive array of misspellings, errors in accents, and errors in capitalization to support his claim that the novel is "marred by over sixty [separate] errors [in the Spanish] . . . which seriously undermine [its] credibility." The worst of these is Hemingway's choice of Robert Jordan's nickname for María, "rabbit," the Spanish word for which (*conejo*) is a common vulgar euphemism for the female sexual organ. While less sensational, A. Robert Lee's " 'Everything Completely Knit Up': Seeing *For Whom the Bell Tolls* Whole" (Lee, pp. 79–102) is as valuable as Josephs's article. Lee is correct in his premise that "Hemingway has by no means won his due as the conscious pattern-maker in his larger fiction." He does his part to rectify this by showing how the structure of *Bell* "reflects with extraordinary precision its theme, subject and means blended into one another." The bridge and the camp are the "thematic" and "structural" center, with flashbacks, insets, and interior monologues working around the circumference, all "knit together" by a "dialectical play" that contributes to the whole.

Wayne Kvam's "Ernest Hemingway and Hans Kahle" (*HemR* 2,ii:18–22) makes effective use of a newly discovered Hemingway letter to Kahle in giving biographical information on the former Prussian officer who fought for the Loyalists and in supplying background for his appearance in *Bell*.

Perhaps because of the trend noted earlier in this survey that has sought to defend or at least explain Hemingway's later fiction, there are two essays and a textual note on *Islands in the Stream* this year. James H. Justus, in "The Later Fiction: Hemingway and the Aesthetics of Failure" (Lee, pp. 103–21), views *Islands* in the context of its author's career-long concern with "the fact of failure" that Hemingway saw as "the one clear-eyed and undeviating purchase on reality in the midst of falsifying stratagems, masks, and those defensive bursts of justification that weave together author and authored, life and art." Justus draws interesting parallels between *Islands* and *The Old Man and the Sea* and argues cogently for the structural coherence of the former as well as for its thematic complexity. In "Art and Ardor in *Island in the Stream*" (Noble, pp. 263–80), Gregory S. Sojka is also concerned with the novel's "artistic integrity" and with its "narrative progression and thematic continuity" within the body of Hemingway's work. He sees it as a "fictional transition" between the Nick Adams stories and *Old Man*; but his essay does not document his claims very well. Jesse Bier's "Don't Nobody Move— This Is a Stickomythia (Or: An Unfinal Word on Typography in Hemingway)" (*HemR* 3,i:61–63) is, as its overly cute title suggests, one of this year's two entrants in the seemingly endless debate over typographical mislineation of dialogue in Hemingway.

Wolfgang Wittowski's "Crucified in the Ring: Hemingway's *The Old Man and the Sea*" (*HemR* 3,i:2–17) originally appeared in German in 1967 and is here translated for the first time. It suffers considerably for being unfamiliar with close to two decades of Hemingway criticism in its delineation of the juxtaposition in the novel of "the fighter-in-the ring and Christ on the cross" as models for Santiago. In "Santiago's Apprenticeship: A Source for *The Old Man and the Sea*" (*HemR* 2,ii:52–55), Bruce Morton shows in detail how heavily Hemingway relied on his 1935 essay "Marlin Off Cuba" in composing his novel. Morton's placing of paragraphs from each next to one another is particularly striking.

Three other Hemingway books are the subjects of essays. W. Craig Turner's "Hemingway as Artist in *Across the River and Into the Trees*" (Noble, pp. 187–203) helpfully points out the novel's circular structural pattern ("a series of separate circles interconnected at the point of the Colonel's final weekend in Venice"), its motifs of the wind as death, its repeated religious overtones, and its characteriza-

tion of Cantwell as part man of action and part artist. Barbara Lounsberry, in *"Green Hills of Africa*: Hemingway's Celebration of Memory" (*HemR* 2,ii:23–31), views that work not as "an experiment to
see if 'actuality' can compete with the imagination, but an effort to
demonstrate how the *memory* of actuality can extend that actuality
and ultimately serve as the basis for transforming that actuality
into art."

In "Hemingway, Ford Madox Ford and *A Moveable Feast*" (*CritQ*
25,ii:35–42), Jeffrey Meyers draws fruitfully upon biographical data
in comparing Hemingway's treatment of Ford in the book with the
facts of their relationship. His conclusion, that Hemingway's "inability to learn from Ford as well as profit from him, helps to account
for the egoism and arrogance of *A Moveable Feast*," is amply supported. Paul Smith and Jacqueline Tavernier-Courbin, in " 'Terza
Riruce': Hemingway, Dunning, Italian Poetry" (*Thalia* 5,ii:41–42),
present evidence of Hemingway's knowledge of Italian poetics, probably learned from Pound, based on passages in the "An Agent of
Evil" chapter in *A Moveable Feast*.

Study of Hemingway's short stories continues at a brisk pace.
Michael S. Reynolds's collection on *In Our Time* includes three new
essays. The best is Paul Smith's "Some Misconceptions of 'Out of
Season' " (pp. 235–51), which examines the genesis of the story, what
Hemingway said about it in later years, and the versions of it in the
Kennedy Library, and then presents a very careful scene-by-scene
explication that focuses on the patterns of misunderstanding and
misspeaking in it. In "The Two Shortest Stories of Hemingway's *In
Our Time*" (pp. 218–26), Jim Steinke explicates "A Very Short Story"
and "The Revolutionist," devoting more space to the latter and concentrating on the tone of the narrator in the story. In "Nick Adams
on the Road: 'The Battler' as Hemingway's Man on the Hill" (pp.
176–88), Nicholas Gerogiannis compares Hemingway's story to the
Man on the Hill chapters in *Tom Jones* and also draws parallels between Nick and Ad; but a long section dealing with the incest theme
in the drafts and final version of the story seems extraneous.

Lee's *Ernest Hemingway: New Critical Essays* contains two
complementary essays on the stories. Although not highly original, David Seed's " 'The Picture of the Whole': *In Our Time*" (pp.
13–35) is a clearly written and concise presentation of the experiences and influences that shaped Hemingway's early stories, of

the differences between the 1924 and 1925 volumes, and of the unity achieved in the later collection through such devices as common themes, common locations, recurring figures, quasi-poetical links, and verbal details. In "The Short Stories After *In Our Time*: A Profile" (pp. 36–48), Colin E. Nicholson contributes a similarly comprehensive survey of the recurrent features in the post–1925 stories, finding that Hemingway "charts a landscape of failed possibility."

Two other full-length essays deal with more than one story. Charles G. Hoffman and A. C. Hoffman's " 'The Truest Sentence': Words as Equivalents of Time and Place in *IN OUR TIME*" (Noble, pp. 99–113) looks at prevalent motifs in the stories—the road, fire signaling danger, walls, rain—but after a promising start dealing with small linguistic units, the authors drift off into unoriginal discussions of thematic patterns in the collection. In "Imagistic Landscape of a Psyche: Hemingway's Nick Adams" (*HemR* 2,ii:2–10), Frank Scafella notes "remarkable imagistic parallels" between A. R. Ammons's poem "Terrain" and Hemingway's stories, claiming that the latter "dramatize Nick Adams's quest for an achievement of an 'area of poise' in the volatile and boundless region of inner space." Scafella's essay is not always clear; but it does contain some good close readings.

Of the essays on individual Nick Adams stories, Robert E. Fleming's "Hemingway's Dr. Adams: Saint or Sinner?" (*ArQ* 39:101–10) provides through detailed textual analysis some valuable new insights. Fleming finds that two discarded manuscript versions of "Ten Indians" show "Hemingway did not intend to depict Nick's father unfavorably but rather as a man who has suffered a good deal and knows that the boy Nickie, who has been living in a child's world where romanticized betrayed lovers suffer from 'broken hearts,' is about to enter adolescence." In a shorter piece, " 'Big Two-Hearted River:' The Artist and the Art" (*SSF* 20:129–32), B. J. Smith also makes good use of manuscript materials by observing that the ending that Hemingway cut from the published story and that Philip Young published as "On Writing" in *The Nick Adams Stories* (1973) provides clues to "another metaphoric level in the story," one in which the burned down devastation of Seney represents "the loss of Hemingway's work, either the actual physical loss or, possibly, the break with youthful forms that artists suffer." James Hinkle's note, "Where the Indian's Razor Came From in 'Indian Camp'" (*HemR* 2,ii:17),

attributes the razor's presence in the husband's upper bunk to early
midwives' superstitious belief that "'a knife under the pillow would
help cut the pain.'"

"The Short Happy Life of Francis Macomber" is the subject of
four pieces this year, more than any other Hemingway story; but all
are notes. The most substantial is K. G. Johnston's "In Defense of the
Unhappy Margot Macomber (*HemR* 2,ii:44–47), which is a systematic attempt to show that Margot tries to save her husband's life by
firing at the buffalo. Robert F. Fleissner (*Expl* 41,iv:45–47) finds
echoes of *Othello* and *2 Henry IV* in the story; Jeffrey Meyers
(*AN&Q* 21[1982]:47–49) suggests Hemingway's notorious February
1936 fight with Wallace Stevens as an influence on its composition;
and Michael S. Reynolds (*HemR* 3,i:28–29) finds allusions to two
Oak Park families in characters' names.

George H. Thomson's "'A Clean, Well-Lighted Place': Interpreting the Original Text" (*HemR* 2,ii:32–43) is a surprisingly worthwhile summary of the wearying topic of the story's textual problems,
along with some quite sensible conclusions. It would be a good place
to send someone lacking information on this topic rather than to all
the notes and articles that have preceded it. William E. Meyer, Jr.'s
thesis, in "The Artist's America: Hemingway's 'A Clean, Well-Lighted
Place'" (*ArQ* 39:156–63), is that the story "holds striking parallels to
the mythic America of the visually biased and to the artist's dilemma
in such a realm"; but he fails to present enough specific evidence
from the text to support this ornately stated position.

Two notes on "The Light of the World" supply background details that add to our understanding of the story. Randall Scott Davis
(*HemR* 2,ii:65–66) points out that in an article Hemingway published five and a half years after the story he verified that he knew
the true circumstances of Ketchel's death, thus signaling to readers
of "Light" that he deliberately had the blonde whore lie and more
subtly pushing critics "toward the real meaning of the story." Michael
S. Reynolds (*SSF* 20:317–19) discovers that Hemingway's mother in
1905 gave to her church a copy of Holman Hunt's religious painting
"The Light of the World" in memory of her father and contends that
Hemingway's choice of title for his "brutal short story" reflects his
anger and ironic resentment of his mother and her gesture.

Larry Edgerton's "'Nobody Ever Dies': Hemingway's *Fifth* Story
of the Spanish Civil War" (*ArQ* 39:135–47) is the first article on this

story. Edgerton provides a good close reading that is sensitive to its weaknesses. James Leo Spenko's "A Long Look at Hemingway's 'Up in Michigan'" (*ArQ* 39:111–21) centers on the portrayal of Liz Coates whom he sees as "finely etched." Bruce Morton, in "Music and Distorted View in Hemingway's 'The Gambler, the Nun, and the Radio'" (*SSF* 20:79–85), shows how Hemingway "has used music as a device to reveal the failure of stoical realism, religion, and the assorted worldly fare of the radio to provide a solution for Frazer's spiritual and emotional dilemma." David R. Gilmour's note on "Hills Like White Elephants" (*Expl* 41,iv:47–49) looks at the symbolic function of the bamboo bead curtain across the doorway of the barroom.

University of Maryland

This essay could not have been completed without the research assistance of Ruth M. Alvarez.

Part II

Part II

11. Literature to 1800

William J. Scheick

This year the most outstanding studies of colonial American literature concern a subject that up to now we have hardly suspected to bear importantly on the development of American writing. In two remarkable books the Puritan conversion narrative emerges as an embryonic stage of American expression, as a seminal work (paradigmatic of subsequent developments in American letters) in which a narrator tries to discover his saintly identity by understanding where he is, whether in the disappointing literal wilderness of New England or in a disheartening figurative or cultural desert. At the heart of these narratives and of the American writing in their tradition is the narrator's quest for sainthood—i.e., to be born again—through language.

i. Puritan Poetry

In "Taylor's 'Upon Wedlock, and Death of Children'" (*Expl* 42:17–18), Jes Simmons notes that the flowers making up the garden knot in the poem are uncultivated and cultivated perennials, a fact suggesting Taylor's cultural and personal consolation expressed in the image of the plant that lives on even though its flowers die. Plants also figure in "Edward Taylor's Herbalism in *Preparatory Meditations*" (*AP* 1:64–71), in which William J. Scheick argues that Taylor's references to herbs are not gratuitous or random, but contribute to an underlying pattern of meaning; in "Meditation 2.26," for example, this pattern is a thrice reiterated tripartite progression from purgation, through improving health, to regeneration. Taylor's scientific knowledge is also the concern of Scheick's "Edward Taylor's Optics" (*AL* 55:234–40). For Taylor, Scheick explains, the Aristotelian optical theory of light's reflection in the eye pertains to the postlapsarian condition of the otherwise blind eye of the soul; the Platonic optical theory of light's emission from the eye pertains to the fully regen-

erated state of the soul, a condition recalling Adam's and Christ's
capacity for spiritual sight and a condition to be restored to the soul
through the alchemy of sunlike grace. Taylor's alchemical notions
are traced to a 17th-Century source in "John Webster's *Metallo-
graphia*: A Source for Alchemical Imagery in the *Preparatory Meditations*" (*EAL* 18:233–41), in which Joan Del Fattore concludes:
Taylor's alchemical images imply that grace vitalizes the soul just as
liquid gold infuses the passages of the earth and that grace is like a
tincture that transforms the soul into goldenness by relating it to the
origin of grace.

Taylor's paraphrases of the Psalms follow the metrical patterns
of the Sternhold-Hopkins psalter, which was popular with the Puritans before their emigration from England. In the New World they
created *The Whole Booke of Psalms*, which Margaret P. Hannay
believes (on the basis of contextual and textual evidence) was consulted by Milton when he composed his translation of the Psalms
(" 'Psalms done into metre': The Common Psalms of John Milton and
of the Bay Colony" [*C&L* 32:19–29]).

That the authors of the Bay Psalm Book were all male is significant, Cheryl Walker would argue. In *The Nightingale's Burden:
Women Poets and American Culture* (Indiana 1982), Walker identifies Anne Bradstreet's ambivalence about her role as Philomel, the
female bird of poetry, and about her related desire for the authoritative stance, or male power, associated with poetry. In *Critical Essays
on Anne Bradstreet* (Hall), which I have not seen, editors Pattie
Cowell and Ann Stanford reprint a number of early and recent responses to Bradstreets's poetry as well as publish for the first time
" 'Contemplations': Anne Bradstreet's Spiritual Autobiography" by
Helen Saltman, "Anne Bradstreet's Emblematic Garden" by Ann
Stanford, "Anne Bradstreet and the *Arbella*" by Donald P. Wharton,
and "The Early Distribution of Anne Bradstreet's Poems" by Pattie
Cowell.

ii. Puritan Prose

Puritan conversion narratives receive attention in John Owen King's
important *The Iron of Melancholy: Structures of Spiritual Conversion
in America from the Puritan Conscience to Victorian Neurosis* (Wes-
leyan). King focuses on the distance between the author himself and

the first-person narrator of these conversion narratives, which comprise a genre of self-examination in which the prospective saint is beset mentally by doubt and melancholy in accord with (the saint believes) divine design. The story of this trouble, the spiritual narrative, signifies the narrator's membership in the New England community of saints. Both this confessional mode of literature and the vocational crises it expresses become, for 17th-century American Puritan and 19th-century American scholar alike, a way of defining oneself by disclosing a waste in which to work; in this desert one's outcast status makes the strange/estranged self a saint capable of creating art. King has given us a keenly intelligent, well-documented major work elevating the conversion narrative to the status of a central originator of American literature, a conclusion supported in an equally important study of the genre, Patricia Caldwell's *The Puritan Conversion Narrative: The Beginnings of American Expression* (Cambridge). Cogently Caldwell details the differences between English and American conversion narratives; whereas the English examples of the genre emphasize reassuring conclusions with dreams of heavenly hope, a sense of England as a place of adamant identity and reality, clear similes based on Scripture, and a direct, somewhat conventional and unmysterious morphology of conversion, the American examples of the genre emphasize irresolute or perfunctory limp conclusions with eddies of discontent, a sense of New England as a disappointing and meagre place without identity, similes with blurred biblical boundaries often evincing an emotional urgency, and a pattern of asymmetry concerning an uncertain and mysterious morphology of conversion that leaves the narrator in a limbo of semi-conversion. In the course of her discussion Caldwell proves that Elizabeth White was not a colonial resident, a fact that certainly requires us to revise those previous discussions of American autobiography that have included her.

The man who was partly responsible for the establishment of the conversion narrative in Massachusetts is the subject of Jeffrey A. Hammond's helpful "The Bride in Redemptive Time: John Cotton and the Canticles Controversy" (*NEQ* 56:78–102). Whereas some exegetes denied that Canticles contained any historical dimension, Cotton stressed an historical-prophetic reading that, in the second edition of his book on the subject, broadened the sense of the Bride (church, state, time) to include the individual experience of faith in the mystical chronology of redemption. The writings of Cotton and others inform " 'God's Well-Trodden Foot-Paths': Puritan Preaching and Sermon Form" (*TSLL* 25:503–27), in which Edward H. Davidson argues that Puritan sermons evinced two modes: a communal subjective mode comprised of unified and consistent preparation sequences and fulfillments collectively shared by the community; and a temporal mode comprised of a vertical axis (the vision of God's word and plan) and a horizontal axis (God's immediate purpose and the practical meaning of the sermonic words). The point where the sacred and the ordinary axes meet in the sermon allowed for variety, individuality and psychological tension.

The sacred and the ordinary intersect as well in John Eliot's *The Christian Commonwealth*, which is the subject of "John Eliot's Empirical Millenarianism" (*Representations* 1,iv:128–53) by James Holstum. Eliot, Holstum explains, converts his practical organization of Native American praying towns into a model for the theoretical reformation of civil government in England, which then would progress toward the millennium. Government is also an issue in Eldon R. Turner's "Peasants and Parsons: Readers and the Intellectual Location of John Wise's *Churches Quarrel Espoused*" (*EAL* 18:146–70). Turner thoughtfully indicates that Wise intended his book as an antireform (antidemocratic) defense of the Cambridge Platform, a defense designed to appeal to New England peasants and their country parsons—people who worshipped their ancestors, feared change, suspected outsiders and were proud of their small towns.

Fear, suspicion and pride of a different kind were experienced by New England settlers nearly a hundred years before the publication of Wise's book. For example, Bradford's history, according to Janis P. Stout in *The Journey Narrative in American Literature: Patterns and Departures* (Greenwood), initiates the American literary tendency to transform the fulfillment of the home-seeking journey to the new world into an impulse to retreat from this new-found homeland. The ways in which, for the home-seeking pilgrim, Christ fulfills biblical prophesies, as well as the ways in which the four gospels interrelate, are discussed in four volumes of Edward Taylor's *The Harmony of the Gospels*, ed. Thomas M. and Virginia L. Davis with Betty L. Parks (Scholar's Facsimiles).

A mode of narrative harmony based on dialectic informs three essays on Puritan prose this year. In "The Spectral Identity of Sir

William Phips" (*EAL* 18:219–32), David H. Watters argues that the design of Cotton Mather's biography of Phips borrows from *The Wonders of the Invisible World* a contrapuntal structure, in terms of which Phips's divinely directed rise in the world through service to New England and the Mather family is opposed by his demonically influenced adversaries. A similar use of unambiguous moral antitheses, in lieu of a narrative structure based on temporal/causal sequences, is remarked in "Purpose and Design in Joshua Scottow's *Narrative*" (*EAL* 18:275–90) by Dennis Powers. Finally, in "'Syllabical Idolatry': Benjamin Colman and the Rhetoric of Balance" (*EAL* 18:257–74), Teresa Toulouse examines Colman's notion of the needs of his audience and how these perceived needs resulted in rhetorical strategies in his sermons: specifically, Colman carefully frames affective passages appealing to emotion with passages attractive to reason when, for example, he uses repetition to build tension while initially and finally containing this repetition within a balanced structure.

iii. The South

A poem by a North Carolinian Quaker is printed in Thomas E. Terrell, Jr.'s "'Some Holsom Exhortations' Henry White's Seventeenth-Century Southern Religious Narrative in Verse" (*EAL* 18:31–44), which suggests that religious diversity existed in the southern colonies. Religious sentiment as well as the nature of servitude in the southern colonies are apparent in *The Vain Prodigal Life, and Tragical Penitent Death of Thomas Hellier*, which is reprinted in "Motive for Murder: A Servant's Life in Virginia, 1678" (*WMQ* 40:106–20) edited by T. H. Breen, James H. Lewis, and Keith Schlesinger.

Religion contributes a tragic dimension to Robert Beverly's *The History and Present State of Virginia*. According to Judy Jo Small in "Robert Beverley and the New World Garden" (*AL* 55:525–40), the power of this early 18th-Century record derives from an arrangement of realistic details in a subtly suggested structure derived from the Christian myth of the loss of paradise; the two central books suggest (albeit with some disturbing details) a prelapsarian state of nature and the two framing books present postlapsarian life in time. Whereas Beverley uses a religious context to heighten the effect of his work, Dr. Alexander Hamilton managed the typical

18th-century southern jeremiad to impress upon his readers the
importance of luxury to one's mental well-being; the history behind
Hamilton's mock-jeremiad and its contents are described by Robert Micklus in "'The History of the Tuesday Club': A Mock-
Jeremiad of the Colonial South" (*WMQ* 40:42–61).

iv. Edwards and the Great Awakening

In *Studies in Religion in Early American Literature* (Univ. Press)
David Lyttle explains that Jonathan Edwards stressed inherited
genetic moral worth as more important than the uniqueness of the
individual soul and that Edwards considered Supernatural Light to
be an innate, non-cognitive principle of perception, different from
the senses, albeit united with the senses in the non-mystical experience of the saint. That Edwards distinguished between a "sense
of the heart" (the willful or emotional experience of both saints
and sinners) and a "new spiritual sense" (the saint's holy predisposition to be pleased by goodness) is argued by James Hoopes in
"Jonathan Edwards's Religious Psychology" (*JAH* 69 [1982–83]:849–
65). Emphasizing Edwards's anti-Lockean stance, Hoopes concludes
that Edwards did not make religious experience consistent with
empirical psychology and that the notion of a "new spiritual sense"
is informed by Edwards's idealist metaphysics.

     To celebrate this "new spiritual sense," according to David
Laurence in "Moral Philosophy and New England Literary History:
Reflections on Norman Fiering" (*EAL* 18:187–214), Edwards very
much needed lyrical language; nevertheless, he cut himself off from
the lyrical insofar as Christian truth seemed unable to limit it firmly.
Edwards might have backed away from lyrical language, but for
Thomas J. Stelle and Eugene R. Delay in "Vertigo in History: The
Threatening Tactility of 'Sinners in the Hands'" (*EAL* 18:242–56),
Edwards certainly used language to suggest the sense of touch;
"Sinners in the Hands of an Angry God" uproots the listener from
an embeddedness in tactile space and temporal duration through
abundant references to tactility, very few of which are positive.
Edwards's uprooting of the hearers of this sermon also interests
Ross J. Pudaloff, whose "'Sinners in the Hands of an Angry God':
The Socio-economic and Intellectual Matrices of Edwards' Sermon"

(*Mosaic* 16:45–64) claims that Edwards at times could use a language devoid of an absolute system of meaning; specifically in the Enfield sermon Edwards's words undercut security of the colonial sort associated with land by verbally manipulating its audience's anxiety over Enfield's current experiences of dislocation resulting from its changing social order, and by verbally making this audience confront the meaningless blank of landscape and experience.

Language with social and economic implications figures as well in "James Davenport and the Great Awakening in New London" (*JAH* 70:556–78) by Harry S. Stout and Peter Onuf, who contend that Davenport's theatrical, vulgar delivery of a sermon sacralized everyday language. Davenport also exploited music by composing songs diverging from the Bay Psalm Book, songs serving as an important outlet for communal speech and helping to give birth to a new solidarity at the center of life in New London, which was undergoing a crisis in the ministerial profession, rapid social change, popular rebellion against established authority, lay congregationalism, and economic and social adjustments.

v. Franklin, Jefferson, and the Revolutionary Period

In *Benjamin Franklin: A Biography* (Random House) Ronald W. Clark reviews our current sense of Franklin, without adding to it, and he oddly accepts as unqualifiedly true information Franklin's various personae give concerning his life. Melvin H. Buxbaum has complied a useful, copiously annotated secondary bibliography in *Benjamin Franklin, 1721–1906: A Reference Guide* (Hall).

In 1749 Franklin published the journal of a Quaker, who evidently saw himself quite differently from how he appears in print. By comparing Franklin's edition with the manuscript of the journal George J. Willauer, Jr., demonstrates in "Editorial Practices in Eighteenth-Century Philadelphia: The Journal of Thomas Chalkey in Manuscript and Print" (*PMHB* 107:217–34) that Quaker overseers made the work conform to the framework of their tradition by subordinating the individual to the ideal; this instance, Willauer warns, alerts us to be cautious when relying on Quaker publications. The journals of another Quaker, whom Franklin urged to write a natural history of America, is the subject of "Telling a Wonder:

Dialectic in the Writings of John Bartram" (*PMHB* 107:235–48), in which William J. Scheick remarks Bartram's need to range beyond the scientific language of precise measurement. Between *Observations* (a somewhat didactic work evincing a dialectical interplay between backgrounded nature reportage and foregrounded polemic) and the later Floridian journal (a non-didactic work evincing a dialectical interplay between backgrounded nature reportage and foregrounded narrative silence) Bartram instinctively discovers that a natural wonder is best related by making the reader enter an authorial devotional silence and thereby participate in the text.

The writings of a man whose first almanac predated Franklin's by eight years and whose series of almanacs was the most popular after Franklin's are discussed descriptively and enumeratively in "The Influence of Nathaniel Ames on the Literary Taste of His Time" (*EAL* 18:127–45) by Marion Barber Stowell, who concludes that Ames's essays on astronomy constitute his most important contribution to almanac literature. Preachers were sometimes the target of Ames's satire, and had he been alive at the time he might have had fun with the fact that Peter Whitney, a Massachusetts minister, read the Declaration of Independence as an evangelical tract. Focusing on Whitney in "Reading, and 'Misreading,' the Declaration of Independence" (*EAL* 18:71–83), Barry Bell observes that the protean nature of the elegant language of the Declaration with its wide-ranging metaphors evoked various conflicting traditions in American thought and allowed for diverse and divergent interpretations. The ambiguous images in the Declaration include slavery, involuntary social and historical rupture, and paternal and Christian responsibility. The paternal feature of 18th-Century American culture especially interests Jay Fliegelman, whose *Prodigals and Pilgrims: The American Revolution Against Patriarchal Authority, 1750–1800* (Cambridge, 1982) notes that during this time works with sentimental heroes and heroines reflect a social and political movement in the colonies away from paternal and deific authority to the independence of prodigals and pilgrims.

Another literary shift during this period is remarked in "Happiness in Society: The Development of an Eighteenth-Century American Poetic Ideal" (*AL* 55:541–59), in which David S. Shields suggests that poetry, which had defined contentment in terms of an historical private (individual) country retreat during the early decades of the century, increasingly as the century progressed depicted happiness in terms of an historical social (communal) American village. Something of this optimism about society can be found as well in notes John Adams made while reading Greek philosophers. According to Constance B. Schulz in "John Adams on 'The Best of All Possible Worlds'" (*JHI* 44:561–77), Adams's notes evidence a strain of optimism and liberality concerning human possibilities.

The darker side of life that informed Adams's more apparent reservations about human nature is also evident in "'Liberty Further Extended': A 1776 Antislavery Manuscript by Lemuel Haynes" (*WMQ* 40:85–105), in which Ruth Bogin publishes a work by a mulatto New England minister. While Haynes was urging a further extension of liberty, Loyalist Jonathan Odell was upholding political order against the threats of anarchistic freedom. Several of his poems, with an account of the political and personal factors behind them, are presented in Cynthia Dubin Edelberg's "The Shaping of a Political Poet: Five Newfound Verses by Johathan Odell" (*EAL* 18:45–70).

vi. The Early National Period

In "Foundations of Liberty: The Christian Republicanism of Timothy Dwight and Jedidiah Morse" (*NEQ* 56:382–97), K. Alan Snyder concludes that the Christian republicanism of Dwight and Morse was not a reaction against the American Revolution but was based on a notion of liberty that required human virtue, absolute truth and Christian morality. Concern with ethics and such human foibles as vanity and avarice also characterizes the writings of William Hill Brown, whose *Selected Poems and Verse Fables* (Delaware, 1982) is edited by Richard Walser.

In "Mercy Otis Warren versus Lord Chesterfield" (*WMQ* 40:616–21), Edmund M. Hayes edits a letter by Warren warning her son against the ideas about comportment and women found in the letters of Lord Chesterfield. The published versions of Warren's writings are reprinted in *The Plays and Poems of Mercy Otis Warren* (Scholars Facsimiles, 1980), ed. Benjamin Franklin V. Whereas Warren's satiric works were widely read, the work of her fellow

playwright William Charles White suffered from neglect. His three
attempts to gain public approval are documented in Lewis Leary's
"William Charles White: 'The American Garrick' A Footnote to the
History of Early American Drama" (*EAL* 18:84–94).

vii. Brown and Contemporaries

We now have a new and valuable edition of Charles Brockden
Brown's *Ormond* (Kent State, 1982), which features 90 pages of
wonderfully copious glosses concerning Brown's interests and cross-
references to his other works. In the introductory essay to this
edition, Russel B. Nye reviews current opinions about *Ormond*
and emphasizes such thematic elements as sincerity and secrecy,
benevolence and selfishness, reason and impulse, experience and
innocence. These tensions and more are remarked by Alan Axelrod,
whose well written and engaging *Charles Brockden Brown: An
American Tale* (Texas) especially emphasizes Brown's emotional
and intellectual ambivalence toward the New World (wilderness)
and toward the Old World (civilization). This "ambivalent frontier
consciousness," Axelrod contends, results in an epistemological fiction evincing a dialectic between fact and self, intellect and emotion, eastern confidence and western doubt, restrictive civilization
and seductive wilderness, social consciousness and the demands of
the imagination—an epistemological fiction that attains no truth save
the fact itself of no revelation and that achieves no balance in its
contesting parts. This irresolution, even against Brown's goals,
characterizes what is most American in his work: the author's lack
of control over both Old and New World sources, the "frontier"
intersection of goal (order) and execution (chaos) in his work. For
Donald A. Ringe in *American Gothic* what is most American in
Brown's work is the fact that, unlike British and German romances,
narrative material does not serve trivial purposes (e.g., the problems of perception) but becomes an intellectual center highly
charged with symbolic significance touching the deepest philosophical issues concerning the basis of human knowledge.

The concern that Ringe identifies as Brown's probe into the nature of human knowledge and that Axelrod describes as an irresolution of the contest between intellect and emotion finds support in
"Charles Brockden Brown's Ambivalence toward Art and Imagina-

tion" (*ELWIU* 10:55–69), in which Maurice J. Bennett surveys Brown's miscellaneous magazine sketches that help diagnose how Brown's attraction to, but distrust of imagination led to his eventual rejection of the novelist's trade and to his movement toward reason and convention. A similar concern interests Edwin Sill Fussell, whose "*Wieland*: A Literary and Historical Reading" (*EAL* 18:171–86) interprets Carwin as a representative of the American writer (including Brown) producing social disruption in the early years of the Republic (represented by the Wieland family).

Interest in Brown's sources has yielded mixed results. Ringe offers some interesting comparisons between Brown's romances and European Gothic fiction, and Axelrod tries harder than anyone previously to identify influences (some too speculative, others worth considering) and to pinpoint similarities or contrasts between Brown and his American contemporaries. In "The Sleepwalker and the Great Awakening: Brown's *Edgar Huntly* and Jonathan Edwards" (*PLL* 19:199–217), John F. Slator unconvincingly tries to prove by circumstantial and speculative evidence that Edwards was in the back of Brown's mind while he wrote his romance. I do not doubt that Calvinistic undertones occur in Brown's fiction, but the images noted by Slator are too commonplace in religious writings and often too apparent in their biblical origin to be attributed specifically to Edwards's influence on Brown.

viii. Miscellaneous Studies

In "The Nationalistic Criticism of Early American Literature" (*EAL* 18:17–30), Carl R. Kropf argues that the search for what is uniquely American about our early writings implies a nationalistic approach that tacitly overlooks the fact that early Americans thought of themselves as British subjects; this problem of perspective has resulted in the neglect of a large body of literature because these works seem to have little to do with the American identity that emerged after they were written. We ought, Knopf urges, to accept these works, too, and both appreciate them as worthy imitations of English models and note in them whatever modifications they make of the familiar literary formulae they express. William C. Spengemann is also interested in broadening the definition of early American literature and in "Discovering the Literature of British America"

(*EAL* 18:3–16) he encourages the compilation of a complete list of extant documents composed in England before 1765 by persons who had been to the New World.

Editors William L. Joyce, David D. Hall, Richard D. Brown, and John B. Hench have collected ten essays in *Printing and Society in Early America* (AAS) that will be of interest to literary historians. A list of American children's literature printed before 1800 appears in Jerome Griswold's "Early American Children's Literature: A Bibliographic Primer" (*EAL* 18:119–26). A more ambitious, even bold undertaking is the three volumes of *American Writers Before 1800: A Biographical and Critical Dictionary* (Greenwood), eds. James A. Levernier and Douglas R. Wilmes. Their work is not free of error (e.g., the identification of William Stork as the coauthor of Bartram's Floridian journals; the misidentification of a journal in the bibliography appended to the Brackenridge entry) and the essays on the authors are sometimes too brief; but the books are handy and, if used cautiously, they make a fine resource tool. Levernier and Wilmes undertook a difficult project; they have done more than reasonably well with it, and we should appreciate their effort.

A man hardly appreciated by the New England establishment or even by Roger Williams, is the subject of Philip F. Gura's "Samuel Gorton and Religious Radicalism in England, 1644–48" (*WMQ* 40:121–24). And, finally, there appeared a special issue of *TSLL* (25:5–178) devoted to "The Puritan Imagination in Nineteenth-Century America," which treats such matters as Puritanism and photography, William James and Puritan confession, and Frederic Church's *Niagara* and the fortunate fall.

University of Texas at Austin

12. 19th-Century Literature

David J. Nordloh

It was a year like other recent years, filled with enough quantity to tire the reviewer and a wide enough sampling of quality to warn him from sleeping. Still, the good word was solidly good: nothing startlingly redefining or school-creating, but some very skillful critical thinking and writing in several books, useful gatherings of work in anthology volumes and special issues of journals, and a few really fine essays. The old-line "major writers" shared attention with the New England and southern women writers, though the feminist criticism attracted to the latter still hasn't adequately matched vivid pronouncement with historical accuracy. Two of the long-standing editions of American authors issued volumes, and a more recent one—*The Letters of Henry Adams*, handsomely packaged by the Belknap Press—released an impressive three-volume set.

i. General Studies

Fred C. Hobson's *Tell about the South: The Southern Rage to Explain* (LSU), distinguished by a wide range of reference and by fine writing, is another preliminary foray into the mystery of what Southerners are, intellectually and imaginatively. But rather than looking at novelists and historians and scholars, Hobson cites "certain individual Southerners—some journalists, some teachers, some belletrists, some writers of no precise description—who have approached the South with a purpose that went beyond professional interest or intellectual curiosity, who have responded to it emotionally, even viscerally, and have written books, usually of a highly personal nature, in which they have set forth their feelings." Two major sections, Ante Bellum and After Appomattox, not only divide the material chronologically but articulate his strategy. The first sets out the possible versions of the Southerner's relationship to his world by examining three books published in 1860 and the three men who wrote them: *The Impending Crisis of the South* by Hinton Rowan Helper, *Social Relations in Our Southern States* by Daniel R. Hundley, and the novel *Anticipations of the Future* by Edmund Ruffin, often identified as the man who fired the first shot at Fort Sumter and who committed suicide at the war's end. The second section then draws upon the terms of the disputes set out by those three works and lives to identify variations played on them by later 19th- and 20th-century writers, including Thomas Nelson Page and George Washington Cable. Hobson's perspective is traditional but his synthesis is refreshing, and may prove productive for other scholars of the South and its literature.

Two new books about women writers and women's questions don't advance that frontier very far. Linda Huf, *A Portrait of the Artist as a Young Woman: The Writer as Heroine in American Literature* (Ungar), begins by objecting to Maurice Beebe's *Ivory Towers and Sacred Founts* (1964) as not recognizing that artist novels by women are so different from those by men and so like each other "that they must be supposed to have their own tradition and development." Huf then offers chapters on six women's novels, including Fanny Fern's *Ruth Hall*, Elizabeth Stuart Phelps's *The Story of Avis*, and Kate Chopin's *The Awakening*, identifying conflicts and crucial images (monsters, entrapment, and flight are everywhere). The book is strongest in its introduction; the chapters are mostly plot summary interrupted by objection to past critical work, and except for the reading of *Ruth Hall* reach fairly standard conclusions. In Mary P. Ryan's *The Empire of the Mother: American Writing about Domesticity, 1830 to 1860* (Haworth), social rather than literary difference is the issue. Ryan takes evidence from such writers as Louisa May Alcott, Lydia Maria Child, the Careys, Mrs. Sigourney, and Harriet Beecher Stowe to demonstrate how the move toward industrialism in America increased maternal responsibility, so that "patriarchal rankings according to age and sex" slowly gave way to emphasis on "the emotional and domestic bonds between women and children." Description of that transformation introduces a useful distinction into the welter of domestic fiction.

David E. E. Sloane's *The Literary Humor of the Urban Northeast, 1830–1890* (LSU) is more anthology than analysis, offering 39 selections from a variety of writers, including James Kirke Paulding, William Cox, Joseph C. Neal, P. T. Barnum, Seba Smith, Charles G.

Leland, Artemus Ward, and Josh Billings. The items are well chosen, and supported by an intelligent apparatus of headnotes and bibliography. Sloane's introduction defines the humor of the Urban Northeast, in contrast to that of the Southwest, as the humor not of the horse swap but of "mercantile agreement on credit and service," a humor in which "negotiation and verbal cleverness replace violent action," nonetheless reflecting "a persistent concern with human values in changing settings." Others may argue the facility of Sloane's distinctions, but they are at least clearly stated, and attached to engaging evidence.

Another book about humor takes the same potential for interest and ruins it. Neil Schmitz's *Of Huck and Alice: Humorous Writing in American Literature* (Minnesota) explores "the stylistic character of humorous writing in American literature," with particular interest in Mark Twain, Krazy Kat, the Marx Brothers, and Gertrude Stein. Background material includes James Russell Lowell's *Biglow Papers* and George Washington Harris's *Sut Lovingood's Yarns*, Schmitz arguing that Lowell was ambivalent about the value of writing that didn't take itself seriously as writing and that Harris escaped that dilemma by identifying his prose with speech rather than with writing. Outside the context of the book these perceptions seem fairly ordinary; within it they are clothed in stylistic pretension, facile allusiveness, and offhand paradox.

Real and imagined journeys fill two books. The theme of *Anglo-American Landscapes* is that Britons came to America "to look at the Europe of the future" while Americans went to England "to look at a world of the past." Those perspectives frame a popularizing treatment arranged by country and place visited, with evidence from Irving, Cooper, Hawthorne, Twain, and James, as well as Frederick Law Olmsted (on Chester), A. Cleveland Coxe (*Impressions of England*, 1851), Henry Ward Beecher, and Harriet Beecher Stowe. Appropriate to its appeal to a wider general audience, the book is lavishly illustrated and just challenging enough. Though much of the commentary is standard, it does add reaction to place to the list of American responses to English culture. Janis P. Stout's *The Journey Narrative in American Literature: Patterns and Departures* (Greenwood) makes passing reference to Howells and to Robert Montgomery Bird, in a refreshing demonstration of the value of even the most time-worn critical commonplace when it is carefully applied.

In another book devoted to a theme, *The Rescue and Romance: Popular Novels Before World War I* (Bowling Green), Diana Reep proposes, without belaboring the feminist implications of the point, that rescue reinforces "accepted, traditional roles and relationships of the sexes." The book devotes chapters to the conventional rescue situations—rescue of child, of woman from physical danger by a man, of woman from a "dilemma" by a man, of man by woman—and proves the truth of the definition by plot summaries of some fifty novels. Since the examples include Cooper's *The Last of the Mohicans*, Simms's *The Yemasee*, and Howells's *Dr. Breen's Practice* and *Indian Summer*, some readers may think of using it as a kind of *omnium gatherum* Cliff's Notes. It is hardly worth considering more seriously than that: it belabors a shallow topic with the barest competence in organization and prose.

The most specific and engaging addition to the critical bookshelf for the year is a collection of ten essays, all but two of them original, entitled *The Haunted Dusk*, which takes its title from W. D. Howell's 1907 anthology *Shapes That Haunt the Dusk*. The editors' introduction argues that supernatural fiction is not simply a matter of supernatural trappings: "as part of the development of modern psychological fiction, these works explored the mysteries of consciousness and the unconscious." Of relevance to this chapter are G. R. Thompson, "Washington Irving and the American Ghost Story" (pp. 11–36); Barton Levi St. Armand, "'I Must Have Died at Ten Minutes Past One': Posthumous Reverie in Harriet Prescott Spofford's 'The Amber Gods'" (pp. 99–119); Jay Martin, "Ghostly Rentals, Ghostly Purchases: Haunted Imaginations in James, Twain, and Bellamy" (pp. 121–48); John W. Crowley and Charles L. Crow (two of the editors), "Psychology and the Psychic in W. D. Howells's 'A Sleep and a Forgetting'" (pp. 149–60), expanding their earlier essay on that topic; and Cruce Stark, "The Color of 'the Damned Thing': The Occult as the Suprasensational" (pp. 209–27), a survey of 19th- and 20th-century positions on spiritualism (particularly those of William James) as they reflect wider attitudes toward the place of humanity in nature. The essays are uniformly strong, and the book is well conceived as scholarship and as physical object.

Among essays on general topics are three analyses of religion in literature. Lawrence Buell's "Literature and Scripture in New England Between the Revolution and the Civil War" (*NDEJ* 15,ii:1–28) concludes that the paradox of proliferation of Scriptural references in an increasingly secularistic age signaled the "literary liberation" of the Bible. The necessarily sketchy coverage of a book-demanding topic (the essay requires eight pages of notes!) includes Nathaniel Parker Willis and Joseph Holt Ingraham among writers relevant to this chapter. Buell also contributes a disappointingly jargony excursion into "Rival Romantic Interpretations of New England Puritanism: Hawthorne versus Stowe" to a special gathering on "The Puritan Imagination in 19th-Century America" (*TSLL* 25:77–99), which arrives at the tired conclusions that Stowe had an orthodox and conventionally informed understanding of Puritanism and Hawthorne a deeper academic enthusiasm and a more liberal imagination. In the same collection Linda K. Kerber, "Can a Woman be an Individual? The Limits of Puritan Tradition in the Early Republic" (*TSLL* 25:165–78), assesses "the continued inability of the Puritan component in a Romantic age," and discovers that women identified in the Puritan tradition "ever repeated images of restraint, resignation, and endurance." As a result, the new myth that arose from the clash of Puritanism and Romanticism offered exclusively *male* liberation.

A very different look at American attitudes is addressed in "Slave Imagery in the Literature of the Early Republic" (*MissQ* 36:53–71). William L. Van Deburg finds a consistency in images about slaves and slavery from the earliest stages of American literature to late in the 19th century and suggests that the survival of such ideas reflects "a deep-seated psychological need in the minds of many Americans" for "'reasonable' explanations for the continued existence of slavery in a God-fearing, liberty-loving, rapidly modernizing country." He perceives that though some works of the early 19th century, like Cooper's *The Spy*, add individualizing traits to the stereotypes of weak will or illness, later ones return almost entirely to those stereotypes, fitting them to pro- or anti-slavery positions. Van Deburg's argument is not convincing: the little specific evidence can't bear the mass of generalization.

There's nothing new in John J. Burke's *The Writer in Pennsylvania 1681–1981* (St. Joseph's), but having the twenty-five brief sketches assembled in one place may encourage a different kind of regional interest. Maxwell Bloomfield, in "Law and Lawyers in American Popular Culture" (*Law and American Literature*, pp. 125–77) supplies an extensive, if necessarily shallow, survey that includes Stowe's *Dred*, Delaney's *Blake*, Brown's *Clotel*, Simms's *Richard Hurdis*, and Baldwin's *The Flush Times of Alabama and Mississippi*. Bloomfield suggests that these works both chronicle professional legal life and suggest popular opinion, and he adds a bibliographical essay. Another contribution to the study of popular culture is Christine Bold's "The Voice of the Fiction Factory in Dime and Pulp Westerns" (*JAmS* 17:29–46). Bold describes the shifting relationship between the writers of pulps (most notably Ned Buntline, Edward Ellis, Prentiss Ingraham, and Edward Wheeler) and their audiences, and the gradual replacement of the writer who talks to his audience about writing by an editor who talks to him about buying books. Lee Steinmetz's "Immortal Youth Astride a Dream: The Cowboy in Western American Poetry" (*BBr* 29–30:129–57), drawing heavily on Brown University's Harris Collection, is more useful as a bibliographical resource than as criticism.

An interesting episode in literary history is provided by Sydney P. Moss, "An American Episode of *Martin Chuzzlewit*: The Culmination of Dickens' Quarrel with the American Press" (*SAR*, pp. 223–43). Moss demonstrates that Dickens introduced anti-American satire into a book whose earlier installments had already been pirated by American publishers so that he could have the satisfaction of watching them "squirm at becoming the unhappy purveyors of his pictures of ugly Americans." The essay sometimes wanders from the point, but its picture of trans-Atlantic literary relations is instructive.

ii. Irving, Cooper, and Their Contemporaries

Volume XIV of the Complete Works of Washington Irving, *The Alhambra*, edited by William T. Lenehan and Andrew B. Myers (Twayne), is one of the shakier contributions to a series that has generally been a tribute to Irving and to the patience of his scholarly editors. The choice of Irving's 1851 revision of the text as basis for the edition on the grounds that it and the first edition of 1832 are "different" works may be right, and the apparatus may be correct, but the historical and textual introductions don't create much confidence, with annoying typographical errors and unintentional puns ("free now to let his imagination run with loose reign") and sloppy prose. That the textual apparatus is reproduced from typescript and not typeset signals harder times for the edition.

There were also two reprints of Irving. The more handsome of them, *History, Tales, and Sketches* (Library of America), contains the entirety of *Letters of Jonathan Oldstyle, Gent.*, *Salmagundi*, *The Sketchbook of Geoffrey Crayon, Gent.*, and *A History of New York*, all but the last taken from the Complete Works. The obligatory chronology, notes on the texts, and annotations are supplied by James W. Tuttleton. *Washington Irving, Hearthside Tales*, selected and introduced by Patrick F. Allen (Signature Series, Union College Press), prints twelve chapters drawn from the *Sketch Book*, *Bracebridge Hall, and Tales of a Traveller*.

In "The Art of Literary Tourism: An Approach to Washington Irving's 'Sketch Book'" (*ArielE* 14,ii:67–82), David Seed combines an explication of Irving's work as the "broad analogy of a tour" with comments on the relationship of writing and the visual arts, narrative presence, and the virtue of avoiding nationalistic extremes. Seed seems to be suggesting that the book says as much about Irving as a personality as it does about England, but the chatty and diffuse quality of the essay frustrates certainty. A more satisfying reading is John D. Hazlett, "Literary Nationalism and Ambivalence in Washington Irving's *The Life and Voyages of Christopher Columbus*" (*AL* 55:560–75). Hazlett offers a strong case for the book as an embodiment of the complexities of Irving's conscious espousal of literary nationalism, his artistic concern to provide "an unmediated version of events and personalities," and his "obtrusive skepticism about America's past and his own role in society."

Three competent essays treating Cooper's uses of history took the place of a new volume from the Cooper Edition, which was quiet after several years of enviable productivity. In "Cooper's Genres and American Problems" (*ELH* 50:711–27), Ross J. Pudaloff, examining all the novels set in America, proposes that the Leatherstocking Tales are not significantly different from the others, and that the similarity is explained by Cooper's greater interest in culture than in nature. If Pudaloff's conclusion is standard—that the mix of genres "stems from Cooper's belief in both an aristocratic social order and a democratic political one"—his comprehensive overview of the larger body of fiction is not.

Cooper's *The Pioneers* and *The Ways of the Hour* are among the works treated by John P. McWilliams, Jr., in "Innocent Criminal or Criminal Innocence: The Trial in American Fiction," another section of *Law and American Literature*, pp. 45–124. McWilliams concludes of a number of major American novels climaxing in a criminal trial that none provides a sense of restoration or enlightenment. His discussion of the Cooper novels explains their relationship to contemporary legal problems. *The Pioneers*, he suggests, enacts a legal position that the controlling property rights asserted by a first developer took precedence over the natural rights of personal use asserted by the first settler. *The Ways of the Hour*, a fictionalized version of the well-known criminal trial of Mary Bodine, demonstrates "the jury's abilities to make law and to distort justice simultaneously," and the novel in turn says both that the system of justice often fails and that there is no satisfactory alternative to it.

In "James Fenimore Cooper: Historical Novelist," one of 13 original essays on individual authors in Richard Gray's *American Fiction* (pp. 15–37), Charles Swann repackages conventional critical wisdom to propose that Cooper's central achievement was to use the materials of American history "in a brilliantly successful attempt to find ways of discovering and defining its special qualities." Swann moves onto new ground briefly in rejecting the notion that by *The Prairie* Cooper's sequence has moved to myth. Adopting Frank Kermode's terms, Swann argues instead that the novel emphasizes the impossibility of reenactment and is closely tied to a specific historical moment that denies mythical possibilities.

Bryant scholarship is solidly served in a collection of 15 original essays edited by Stanley Brodwin and Michael D'Innocenzo, *William Cullen Bryant and His America: Centennial Conference Proceedings 1878–1978* (AMS Press). Especially good in surveying Bryant's literary and political ideas, his poetry and his fiction, are David J. Baxter, "The Dilemma of Progress: Bryant's Continental Vision" (pp. 13–25); Brodwin's "The 'Denial of Death' in William Cullen Bryant and Walt Whitman" (pp. 113–31); Albert F. McLean, "Progress and Dissolution in Bryant's Poetry" (pp. 155–66); and David J. Moriarity, "William Cullen Bryant and the Suggestive Image: Living Impact" (pp. 209–22), identifying Bryant as a "pioneer on the frontiers of modernism." The strongest essay, with the most provocative ideas, is Donald A. Ringe, "Bryant's Fiction: The Problem of Perception" (pp. 167–77).

John L. Idol, Jr., provides a nice perspective on trans-Atlantic literary relations in "Mary Russell Mitford: Champion of American Literature" (*SAR*, pp. 313–34). Idol identifies Mitford (1787–1855) as "an extremely active and successful builder of the bridge linking British and American literature," and traces her conversion from early abhorrence to energetic and "generous" (the description is Hawthorne's) endorsement of "many American writers now regarded as among our best." The essay cites Mitford's letters and autobiographical and critical volumes, as well as her friendships with many of those she championed in print.

iii. Popular Writers of Midcentury

Of the poets, only Lowell (see Schmitz, *Of Huck and Alice*, above) and Longfellow received any attention this year—and very modest attention at that. Harold Aspiz gives a dull explication of "Longfellow's 'Nature'" (*Expl* 42:22–23), and Edward L. Tucker, "Longfellow's Bowdoin Dialogue" (*SAR*, pp. 89–100), prints the manuscript of an 1823 college assignment and comments on Longfellow's uses of sources and ambivalent views of Indians.

It's no particular credit to Harriet Beecher Stowe that the principal study of her to appear recently is Gayle Kimball, *The Religious Ideas of Harriet Beecher Stowe: The Gospel of Womanhood* (Mellen [1982]), a contribution to the series "Studies in Women and Religion." Kimball examines Stowe essentially as a theologian of womanhood, expressing herself partly in literature, who advocated women as the central agents of salvation. Kimball argues that Stowe took a different means to the same feminist end than her contemporaries in believing that "women had more avenues open to them by piously influencing children and husbands." These ideas have already aged quickly, and aren't given enough substance here to justify a whole book. Stowe is even worse served in an incredible indulgence in Freudian analysis, Alexander Grinstein's "*Uncle Tom's Cabin* and Harriet Beecher Stowe: Beating Fantasies and Thoughts of Dying" (*AI* 40:115–44). Would Lincoln have approved a book hiding an oedipal complex and death wishes?

In a more modest essay, Lynn Veach Sadler, "The Samson Figure in Milton's *Samson Agonistes* and Stowe's *Dred*" (*NEQ* 56:440–48), argues not for Miltonic influence but for the continuing appeal of a common source, the Samson figure in the Bible. Despite the other influences identified by Stowe herself (including Nat Turner and Dred Scott), the Biblical Samson seems best to inform Stowe's view of her Dred as "first and foremost the giant would-be deliverer who stands in contrast to Nat Turner, a man of similar intentions but one 'below the ordinary stature.'"

Stowe's *Uncle Tom's Cabin*, William Wells Brown's *Clotel*, and Martin R. Delany's *Blake* are among the works treated in individual chapters of Kristin Herzog's *Women, Ethnics, and Exotics: Images of Power in Mid-nineteenth-century American Fiction* (Tenn.), which devotes longer sections to Hawthorne and Melville. Herzog's interest is in the portrayal of women and nonwhites as harboring "an innate power—however demonic it might sometimes appear—which the civilized white male has lost or suppressed." Her analyses are competent but somehow static, describing characters fixed in place rather than moving or changing, and they rely too heavily on narrow comparisons. What are asserted as innovations seem rather to be alternative conventions.

Elizabeth Stuart Phelps gets TUSAS-style treatment from Lori Duin Kelly in *The Life and Works of Elizabeth Stuart Phelps, Victorian Feminist Writer* (Whitston). Indeed, the faults of the recent Twayne book on Phelps, mentioned here last year, are repeated in this narrowly feminist tract that ignores Phelps's extra-feminist interests. At least Kelly is nicely honest in faulting Phelps for being callously indifferent to the plight of men, humorless, overly serious, and "oblivious to the artistic weakness in her fiction."

iv. Local Color and Literary Regionalism

Josephine Donovan's *New England Local Color Literature: A Women's Tradition* (Ungar) draws upon both literary history and a feminist perspective to urge a view of the New England female local-colorists as constituting virtually a "school," whose crucial accomplishments were to create "a counter-tradition to the sentimental/domestic convention that dominated American women's writing through most of the nineteenth century" and to move beyond "a negative critique of reified male-identified customs and attitudes." Individual chapters set out the theoretical underpinnings of the work of the group, the influence of Annie Adams Fields in creating the "network" among them, and analysis of the works of five major representatives—Harriet Beecher Stowe, Rose Terry Cooke, Elizabeth Stuart Phelps, Sarah Orne Jewett, and Mary Wilkins Freeman. The work is ambitious, and suffers from a regrettable narrowness as a result. The notion of these writers as a coherent group doesn't hold up well, since many of the parallels in form and substance in their works also occur in the work of the male local-colorists, and the importance of Annie Fields is overstated. In sum, Donovan does damage to her readings of the women's perspective in the fiction by insisting on too exclusive a definition of literary influence and social vision.

The enduring skill of Sarah Orne Jewett continues to attract a pleasant variety of critical response. In "Going in Circles: The Female Geography of Jewett's *Country of the Pointed Firs*" (*SLitI* 16,ii:83–92)—one of several strong essays in a special issue on "American Realism: The Problem of Form"—Elizabeth Ammons describes the work as structured around "two essentially female psychic patterns: one of web, the other of descent." Ammons then associates the use of those patterns with an idea advanced by Carol Gilligan (*In a Different Voice: Psychological Theory and Women's Development* [1982]) that women, unlike men, are more concerned to develop to "'a maturity realized through interdependence and taking care.'" Ammons concludes that the essential pattern of the narrative of *Country of the Pointed Firs* is female rather than male: "Patterns of concentricity, net-work, web, and oscillation mold a narrative that does not know how to march and scale."

Laurie Crumpacker's "The Art of the Healer: Women in the Fiction of Sarah Orne Jewett" (*CLQ* 19:155–66) collects Jewett's views of women as uniquely gifted in their roles as doctors, herbalists, ministers, and writers not only to heal physical ailments but to form bridges to spiritual health—notions growing in part from Jewett's Swedenborgianism. But Crumpacker is not quite so convincing in her assertion that these attitudes are eclectic and advanced, and that Jewett is especially modern in holding them. A concern for the patient rather than for science, for example, was already a platitude when Hawthorne implied it as the conclusion of "The Birth-Mark."

Gayle L. Smith sets out a very insistent explication of a Jewett story in "The Language of Transcendence in Sarah Orne Jewett's 'A White Heron'" (*CLQ* 19:37–44). Smith ascribes to Jewett "a truly transcendental vision uniting man not only with green nature but with animal life as well," and she proposes that the story, which ends with Sylvy not revealing the heron's nest to the young man, is enhanced by "linguistic choices" that "argue a great oneness between human and non-human life that powerfully affirms the girl's choice. . . ." The weight of the argument is almost too heavy for the story on which it depends.

In "The Compensations of Solitude in the Work of Emily Dickinson and Sarah Orne Jewett" (*CLQ* 19:206–14), Lynne M. Patnode offers an interesting comparison of two writers who conceive solitude as a woman's opportunity to "explore her own resources." Patnode sees the women in Jewett's *Country of the Pointed Firs* as enacting a range of possible uses of solitude, and Dickinson's poetry as encompassing this same range as well. To this point the essay is nicely informed and interesting. It falters when Patnode goes on, in a section that seems tacked on and vaguely reasoned, to describe the two writers as rebelling against the sentimental tradition even as they supported it, focusing not on the world but on self. Finally, Jewett receives *Eight American Authors* treatment in a new bibliographical survey, *American Women Writers*.

Another of the New England local-colorists, Mary Wilkins Freeman, is represented in two explicatory essays by Marjorie Pryse, "An Uncloistered 'New England Nun'" (*SSF* 20:289–95) and "The Humanity of Women in Freeman's 'A Village Singer'" (*CLQ* 19:69–77). In both Pryse complains that male critics have misunderstood because of insensitivity to women's activities and attitudes. She sees Louisa Ellis in the first story as achieving "visionary stature" as she "defends her power to ward off chaos just as strongly as nineteenth-century men defended their own desires to 'light out for the territories'," and Candace Whitcomb's fate in the latter as tragedy rather than redemption. The readings in themselves are useful enough; the feminist reactionism is unnecessary.

Feminism meets children's literature in Joy A. Marsella's *The Promise of Destiny: Children and Women in the Short Stories of Louisa May Alcott* (Greenwood). Conclusion: "Alcott's girls and women . . . are domestic feminists who believe in preparing themselves for the coming crisis in women's destiny by doing the best they

can with what they have to work with, but in the traditional roles."
Introductory sections on childrearing literature, the moral tale, children's periodicals, and the conventions of domesticity are as elementary as this assertion is ahistorical.

Among studies of southern writers, Michael J. Kreyling's essay on Lafcadio Hearn, Grace King, and G. W. Cable, "After the War: Romance and the Reconstruction of Southern Literature" (*Southern Literature in Transition*, pp. 111–25), concludes that, although all three writers produced literature intended to capitalize on the extraregional popularity of New Orleans, they responded to the challenge of being southern writers in different ways—Hearn leaving the South and the material to answer the needs of a wider imagination, Grace King enamored of the Old South but also willing to accept the New, and Cable, for all his skill, defeated by the pressure to succeed.

In a companion book to David Kirby's TUSAS critical introduction to Grace King (1980), Robert Bush has completed a soundly researched biography, *Grace King: A Southern Destiny* (LSU). Drawing generously on its sources, especially King's correspondence, Bush portrays a serious writer with strong contemporary interests, "a southern woman of letters." Like Kreyling, Bush contrasts King with Cable, whom she thought disloyal to the South in creating a deliberately false picture of New Orleans. The book's flaw is a vagueness about the larger literary context (Howellsian Realism, for example).

Another essay in *Southern Literature in Transition* examines the stories in King's *Monsieur Motte* as well as Caroline Lee Hentz's *Eoline; or, Magnolia Vale* and Chopin's *The Awakening*. Miriam J. Shillingsburg, "The Ascent of Woman, Southern Style: Hentz, King, Chopin" (pp. 127–40), is interested in the ways the female characters in these fictions "bucked convention and their 'place' in society, the reactions of those societies to their rebellion, and the degree of success each heroine (and quite likely each author) felt in being her own self in spite of the circumscriptions of being a female in the South."

Two minor essays focus on George Washington Cable. Robert O. Stephens, "Cable and Turgenev: Learning How to Write a Modern Novel" (*SNNTS* 15:237–48) traces the influence of the Russian, particularly in reducing the rhetorical self-indulgence typical of southern writers. And Alice Hall Petry explicates "A Fable of Love and Death: The Artistry of Cable's 'Jean-ah Poquelin'" (*SLJ* 15:87–99).

Thomas Bangs Thorpe gets a bit more attention. Another explication by Petry, "The Common Doom: Thorpe's 'The Big Bear of
Arkansas'" (SoQ 21,ii:24–31), pushes a pretentious moral. Much
better written—and with a more significant conclusion—is Stanton
Garner's addition to biographical information about Thorpe: "Thomas Bangs Thorpe in the Gilded Age: Shifty in a New Country"
(MissQ 36:35–52). Garner finds proof in New York and United
States government records of Thorpe's "complicity in the fast-dollar
practices of the Gilded Age," which culminated in 1877 in his removal from the New York Custom House for bribery and corruption.
But Thorpe then managed to have his removal redefined as "resignation," and was soon after rehired in a lesser position. As a result of
those maneuvers, "All of the subsequent dictionaries and cyclopedias
of American biography that listed him at all simply noted that, once
in the Custom House, he had remained an employee until his
death...."

Two minor items on southern writers round out the year's work
on regionalism. Rayburn S. Moore, "'A Great Poet and Original
Genius': Hayne Champions Poe" (SLJ 16:105–12), reviews Paul
Hamilton Hayne's comments on and memorialization of the great
poet whom Hayne also considered a bad man. John L. Idol, Jr., and
David B. Kesterson treat local opinions of the rich in "Wealth in
Their Midst: Bill Nye and Thomas Wolfe on the Asheville Vander-
bilts" (TWN 7,ii:27–35).

v. Henry Adams

The premier publishing event of the year was the release of the first
three of six planned volumes of The Letters of Henry Adams, edited
by J. D. Levenson, Ernest Samuels, Charles Vandersee, and Viola H.
Winner (Belknap). The attractively illustrated volumes, covering
the periods 1858–68, 1868–85, and 1886–92, print only letters written
by Adams, not to him, but include both private and public documents—eight essay letters, officially addressed to Charles Francis
Adams, which appeared in the Boston Courier in 1860, for example.
The "Bibliographical Note" in volume I indicates that 1,277 of 1,519
letters extant for the periods represented are published in the volumes, 549 of them for the first time and another 261 in their entirety
for the first time. An "Editorial Note" describes the selection process

and the policy concerning annotation, which is restricted mostly to historical fact and crucial identification, and indicates that the usual textual record of alterations in the letters has been prepared though it is not printed.

This magnificent and meticulous addition to Adams scholarship will no doubt absorb the energies of Adams scholars for many generations. What is immediately impressive is the efficiency of the arrangement of the volumes. One general introduction to the whole series—a nicely thorough and sensitive twenty-three pages by Levenson—appears in volume I, and one-page headnotes consolidate individual sections of letters (seven sections in volumes I and III, six in volume II). Publishing the three volumes together was not simply a publishing strategy but an intellectual one. A single index at the end of volume III serves for all three; that arrangement is more efficient than separate indices, and more immediately useful than one that would not appear until volume VI. The whole is so beautifully conceived and executed that I hesitate to complain. But supplying dates in the running heads on the pages would have helped. And the fact of letters *to* Adams should have been made something of, even if briefly, in the annotation. Whether intentionally or not, the volumes give the impression of a man talking to himself. An interesting review of the edition and a discussion of what Adams material isn't there (missing letters, most of Adams's diary) is offered by Paul C. Nagel, "Searching for Henry Adams" (*VQR* 59:693–702).

On Adams editorial matters of another sort, Philip B. Eppard, "Henry Adams and the Letters and Diaries of John Hay" (*BBr* 29–30:119–28), draws attention to the John Hay Library manuscript of Adams's preface to Clara Hay's *Letters of John Hay and Extract from Diary*. And in a related and equally slight piece, George Monteiro, "The 'Biographising' of John Hay" (*BBr* 29–30:109–17), contributes a grab bag of information about Adams's association with Mrs. Hay's edition.

vi. Realism and the Age of Howells

The principal addition to the study of the Realistic period is as much social and political history as it is literary criticism. Masterfully written by John L. Thomas (winner of a Bancroft Prize for his study of William Lloyd Garrison), *Alternative America: Henry George,*

Edward Bellamy, Henry Demarest Lloyd and the Adversary Tradition (Belknap) examines *Progress and Poverty, Looking Backward,* and *Wealth Against Commonwealth* as responses to rapid modernization and as definitions of redirected social possibilities. The whole is a tightly interlocked analysis of the relationship "between writing and acting, between the text and the program." The book should form a definitive expression of the public issues that so engaged the older Howells and his younger contemporaries.

Publication of *Letters VI: 1912–1920* (Hall) in "A Selected Edition of W. D. Howells," covering the final years of a reformer reduced finally to reflection, marks completion of that segment of a project whose pace has slowed in recent years. The volume is edited and annotated by William M. Gibson and Christoph K. Lohmann, with a very graceful introduction by Gibson, and includes not only letters selected from the period in question but also the text of Howells's essay "Eighty Years and After" (1919) and an appendix of fourteen letters belonging to earlier volumes selected from the Fréchette Collection recently acquired by Alfred University. Annotation of the letters is helpfully factual, and includes references to and even quotations from other letters by Howells and his correspondents. But the index covers only the final volume, not the six-volume set as the editors had earlier indicated.

Edwin H. Cady and Norma W. Cady have edited *Critical Essays on W. D. Howells, 1886–1920* (Hall). The first of two planned volumes (the second will cover 1920 to the present), this one prints 58 items, including two batches of seventy-fifth birthday tributes and several interviews, besides widely known and little-known essays. The arrangement is chronological, with divisions into periods. The period 1908–11 is missing, probably mistakenly, since one of the essays placed in the 1898–1907 section is Van Wyck Brooks's "Mr. Howells at Seventy-Two," originally published in 1909. Professor Cady's introduction is a mostly satisfying mixture of biographical information and evaluation of the swings in Howells's reputation.

Howells is a focal figure in Michael Spindler's predominantly Marxist formulation, *American Literature and Social Change: William Dean Howells to Arthur Miller* (Indiana). Spindler associates social and economic changes from "the production-oriented phase" to "the consumption-oriented phase" with shifts in literature from Romance to Realism to Naturalism. Or, to suggest the thrust as well as the jargonism of the book—"Realism and Naturalism with their positivist emphasis on the primacy of fact and their preoccupation with new social formations articulated in a general way an historically specific capitalist mentality." There are chapters on "The Rise of the Entrepeneur in the Work of Howells, Norris and Dreiser" and "The Condition of the Poor in the Work of Howells, Dreiser and Sinclair," with annoyingly insistent readings of *The Rise of Silas Lapham* and *A Hazard of New Fortunes* and Norris's *The Pit* and *The Octopus.*

A very different kind of essay explores dimensions of Howells's struggle with moral truth. Andrew Delbanco, "Howells and The Suppression of Knowledge" (*SoR*, pp. 765–84), starts from the commonplace, articulated by Henry James, that Howells had a "small . . . perception of evil," and suggests that "Howells' work becomes a record of lifelong modulation, not vacillation, between two sides of the same problem: the problem of sin." He concludes that Howells was not ignorant of evil but rather suppressed his doubt "in order to conserve what he could of his hope that human decency, independent of transcendent guidance, might endure, if not prevail." An interesting reading of the fiction, which would have been more successful if it had drawn on Howells's Swendenborgianism, his autobiographical statements, and his strong sense of family values.

John W. Crowley, author of excellent essays on individual Howells works, attempts too much in "Howellsian Realism: A Psychological Juggle," another contribution to the special issue on "American Realism: The Problem of Form" (*SLitI* 16,ii:45–55). Crowley begins with a question according to Freud—what in Howells's psyche made him choose Realism as a literary mode—and probes Howells's childhood for the answer. He insists that early on Howells borrowed strength from literature as part of his "psychological juggle," a process involving a dramatic method—"to draw a character from the inside but to remain outside as well"—and that later his awareness of that strategy led him to use it as a conscious principle of composition "by daring to experiment with the dramatic method in a frankly therapeutic way." The essay is skillful and provocative, though fuller evidence seems called for. A less clinical approach to related issues is Ellen F. Wright's "William Dean Howells and the Irrational" (*NCF* 38:304–23), which confronts the episodes of irrationality in Howells's "normal, nonmythic, nonpsychologically tortured characters." Wright finds Howells approving these moments, which are characterized by sentiment, impulsiveness, and poetry, as "an essential and desirable part of the human personality." The tone of the essay echoes Howells at his most illuminating.

Four different Howells works receive four different readings, with varying effect. Mario Maffi, "Architecture in the City, Architecture in the Novel: William Dean Howells's *A Hazard of New Fortunes*" (*SLitI* 16,ii:35–42), discusses the novel's innovative use of an urban architectural imagery, including mapmaking, the city as spectacle, the flat as enclave, and the transition from photography to cinema. An ambitious essay, but weakest when it defines the very concepts it applies. George R. Uba isolates Howells's Utopian works, *A Traveller from Altruria* and *Through the Eye of the Needle*, in "Howells and the Practical Utopia: The Allegorical Structure of the Altrurian Romances" (*JNT* 13:118–30). Proposing the books as "literary works containing within them social critiques" rather than as "social critiques made agreeable through the cosmetic of fiction," Uba interprets *Traveller* as a version of a traditional debate among character types and *Through the Eye of the Needle* as an allegorical "progress." The readings are refreshing, but don't completely comprehend the special real-unreal, detailed world Howells creates. Further, Uba assumes that Howells is defining an acceptable Utopian formula, though the author himself tended to remark the opposite. In a second essay, Uba provides a telling legal context for understanding *A Modern Instance*, "*Status* and *Contract*: The Divorce Dispute of the Eighties and Howells' *A Modern Instance*" (*CLQ* 19:78–89). Underlying the novel and discussion of divorce in the period were views of history and marriage associated with the eminent English jurist Sir Henry Sumner Maine, who contrasted Status (legal preeminence of the family) with Contract (legal acknowledgment of the requirements of individuals), and who "also contributed a shorthand for the conception of marriage as a special state and the conception of marriage as an ordinary civil agreement." Applying these distinctions to the dispute between Marcia and Bartley as the principal characters, Uba says something valuable about the issues and emphases of one of Howells's most studied works. Finally, Marcia Jacobson, "William Dean Howells's (Auto)biography: A Reading of *A Boy's Town*" (*ALR* 16:92–101), argues the relegation in the book of causal relationship to detached memory, of autobiography to biography. That thesis is shaky, and the conclusion—that Howells appears to use his childhood to solve his adult problems—has been better developed elsewhere.

The lesser Realists received much less attention. Barbara C. Gannon supplies an odd, incomplete assortment of secondary items and play summaries in "James A. Herne: A Bibliography" (*ALR* 16: 102–6). In *The Tanyard Murder: On the Case with Lafcadio Hearn* (Univ. Press), Jon Christopher Hughes uses Hearn's gruesome newspaper reportage of a crime to create a second-rate popular account of the event, in the process failing to specify which materials are Hearn's and which his own, which are fact and which invention. Alice Hall Petry, " 'Always, Your Attached Friend': The Unpublished Letters of Constance Fenimore Woolson to John and Clara Hay" (*BBr* 29–30:11–107), prints 21 letters from the John Hay Collection at Brown, with a competent introduction and full annotation.

vii. Fin-de-Siècle America: Stephen Crane and the 1890s

Suggestive explications of major as well as minor works are the strongest part of Chester L. Wolford's *The Anger of Stephen Crane: Fiction and the Epic Tradition* (Nebraska). Acknowledging his debt to other scholarship dealing with Crane and the epic, Wolford proposes that Crane attempted to repudiate the "Christian-Miltonic vision" reflected in the formal epic tradition but then drew upon that same source to forge a new fiction with an older "Homeric vision of life as a losing struggle for significance." Wolford's book is short— only four chapters, one of them devoted entirely to *The Red Badge of Courage*—but still becomes repetitious, and weakens badly in the effort to place Crane as a transitional figure in the fuller epic tradition upon which he drew. On a smaller scale, Laura Hapke takes a good look at Nell, "that rare figure in American literature, the thoroughly unrepentant prostitute," in "The Alternate Fallen Woman in *Maggie: A Girl of the Streets*" (*MarkhamR* 12:41–43).

Various essays trace sources and parallels for Crane stories. Edward J. Piacentino overwrites the obvious in a comparison of Mrs. C. E. S. S. Norton's "Bingen on the Rhine" to Crane's use of the poem and its theme in "Kindred Spirits: The Correspondent and the Dying Soldier in Crane's *The Open Boat*" (*MarkhamR* 12:64–67). David H. Jackson, "Textual Questions Raised by Crane's 'Soldier of the Legion' " (*AL* 55:77–80), supposes Crane misremembered rather than misquoted that poem, and faults Fredson Bowers for "correcting" it in the Virginia Edition. Alice Hall Petry, "Stephen Crane's Elephant Man" (*JML* 10:346–52) belabors the coincidental parallels between Henry Johnson in "The Monster" and the celebrated English freak John Merrick. Petry also assays a clever explication—verging on reader-response criticism—of "Crane's 'The Bride Comes to Yellow Sky'" (*Expl* 42:45–47). Elsa Nettels, "'Amy Foster' and Stephen Crane's 'The Monster'" (*Conradiana* 15:181–90) describes Joseph Conrad's debts to Crane's story. Nina Galen suggests intriguingly that Crane himself was Conrad's inspiration in "Stephen Crane as a Source for Conrad's Jim" (*NCF* 38:78–96). Donald Pizer mentions "Stephen Crane's 'The Monster' and Tolstoy's *What to Do?*: A Neglected Allusion" (*SSF* 20:127–29). Brenda Murphy, "'The Blue Hotel': A Source in *Roughing It*" (*SSF* 20:39–44), points to Mark Twain's account of being cooped up in a small inn with a crowd of miners for eight days, and the absolutely different responses of the two artists to the same condition.

Joseph Katz supplies biographical information for "Solving Stephen Crane's *Pike County Puzzle*" (*AL* 55:171–82). And Stanley Wertheim cites documents in the Columbia collections to settle controversies about how Stephen and Cora Crane got to Greece and what Stephen's relations were with his brother William in the matter of Cora, in "Stephen Crane in the Shadow of the Parthenon" (*CLC* 32:3–13).

Besides inclusion in Spindler's book (cited above), Frank Norris is the subject of three barely tolerable essays, and a well-written, wide-ranging, considered one. Michael Davitt Bell, "Frank Norris, Style, and the Problem of American Naturalism" (*SLitI* 16,ii:93–106) gathers Norris's "confusions and fallacies" about Naturalism for a weak, derivative analysis of the effects of those confusions on the fiction. Allusively, intuitively, and unannotatedly, David Wyatt, "Norris and the Vertical" (*SoR* 19:749–64) pronounces of Norris that "the paradox of his work is that while its theme is motion throughout time, its plots appear to measure man within a space. Actions he initiates as dramas of development attempt to convert themselves, through his insistence on making fate visible, into dramas of position." Alice Hall Petry strikes again, launching a preliminary investigation into Norris's influence on Fitzgerald with "F. Scott Fitzgerald's 'A Change of Class' and Frank Norris" (*MarkhamR*

12:49–52). On the positive side, Ron Mottram explores Norris's interest in the techniques of the motion picture in "Impulse Toward the Visible: Frank Norris and Photographic Representation" (*TSLL* 25: 574–96). Citing Norris in his school writing, reviews, and fiction, Mottram suggests that the artist "was not content with merely rendering the visible world; rather, he sought to capture the dynamic of turn-of-the-century America through a creative act of perception that included the relativity of point of view and the transforming power of movement on what is perceived." That effort establishes Norris, then, as a transitional figure in literature, philosophy, and even the film, as Mottram demonstrates from D. W. Griffith and Erich Von Stroheim. A rewarding, idea-stirring essay.

Besides Miriam Shillingsburg's essay in *Southern Literature in Transition*, cited above, the only other critical essay about Chopin in a strangely quiet year appears in the same volume. "Kate Chopin: Tradition and the Moment," by Thomas Bonner, Jr. (pp. 141–49), is a weak effort to assert Chopin's interest in the present rather than the past, the larger world and its issues rather than just the South. And a Chopin bibliography is provided in *American Women Writers*.

"Ambrose Bierce: A Bibliographic Essay and Bibliography," by Philip M. Rubens and Robert Jones (*ALR* 16:73–91) is better than nothing, but oddly user-unfriendly—no annotation, no comment about inclusiveness, no note on sources.

Finally, for those seeking a respite from the tendentiousness of some of the bad work of the year, I recommend the refreshing clarity and humane voice of Jacques Barzun's "William James, Author" (*ASch* 52:41–48). Barzun's discussion of James as stylist begins with a personal observation on the difficulties of both teaching and writing, and returns to that point in noting that "one influence that encouraged James to use imagery and the conversational tone was the lecturing to which he was compelled."

Indiana University

13. Fiction: 1900 to the 1930s

John J. Murphy

The major and minor writers of this period continue to receive significant attention. Wharton, Dreiser, Cather and London emerge as the most considered; Stein remains the subject of some of the most careful work; Anderson holds his own, and a group of lesser voices—including Ludwig Lewisohn and Mary Austin—clamor for attention. Two general works offer competent introductory essays that deserve mention on several of these writers: Frank Magill's eight-volume *Critical Survey of Long Fiction* (Salem) and Anna Massa's more modest *American Literature in Context, IV: 1900–1930* (Methuen, 1982). I have positioned writers according to the quantity of current interest in them and according to their subjects or the quality of current interest.

i. Edith Wharton

Two book-length studies appeared on Wharton, one native feminist and the other a somewhat panoramic perspective from India. In *The Female Intruder in the Novels of Edith Wharton* (Fairleigh Dickinson) Carol Wershoven sets out to prove Wharton's relevancy, that she was hardly a fossilized Old New Yorker with little significance for modern readers. Wershoven's thesis, carefully constructed if not startlingly original, is that Wharton made significant social comments through the fates of various female intruders: victims like *The House of Mirth*'s Lily Bart, too fine to live according to society's values but too weak to strike out in new directions; vulgarians like Undine Spragg in *The Custom of the Country*, who devastated society by taking it at face value; or reformers like Fulvia Vivaldi (*The Valley of Decision*) and Justine Brent (*The Fruit of the Tree*). Wershoven's reading of *The Age of Innocence* is discriminating in seeing intruder Ellen Olenska as abiding by loyalties to which Old New York merely pays lip service and in acknowledging May Welland's potential for growth and rebellion. This book is a worthwhile addition to Wharton scholarship, despite occasional instances where the thesis is somewhat forced, and gives thorough readings of several neglected works, among them *The Children, Twilight Sleep* and *The Buccaneers*. G. S. Rahi's *Edith Wharton: A Study of Her Ethos and Art* (Guru Nanak Dev University Press) disposes the novelist more fondly toward Old New York, at least before its invasion by the new rich. As a post-R. W. B. Lewis consideration, Rahi is surprisingly levelheaded about Wharton's attitudes toward society, money, marriage, divorce and women, around which topics he organizes his work. The initial chapter, drawing heavily on Thorstein Veblen's sociological studies, provides an excellent analysis of the society upon which Wharton based her fictional world and toward which she developed "affection and indulgence" while lamenting its failure to participate in significant pursuits. Wharton's moderation assumes many guises: she was critical of the exploitation and waste of women yet failed to conceive of an independent identity for them; she lamented destructful marriages yet saw marriage as necessary for mature society; she divorced yet feared the chaos resulting from easy divorces. Mere luxury was vulgarity but, combined with aesthetic and moral sensibilities, necessary for meaningful life. Rahi, then, approaches Wharton as a serious if limited social thinker. Despite its imperfect manufacture and convolutions of style, this is a solid contribution, although it might prove difficult to obtain.

Wharton's place as woman and novelist in the larger world of her time concerns the authors of two studies on American literature and foreign wars. Perhaps the great activist of her hesitant society, Theodore Roosevelt, inspired her Great War activities, which are traced by David C. Duke in *Distant Obligations: Modern American Writers and Foreign Causes* (Oxford, pp. 62–100). Wharton's contributions to the French cause included a Parisian workshop for wartime unemployed, sales promotion for its products, refugee centers, a clothing depot, nurseries, sanitariums, and fund-raising—all managed with a surprising degree of Yankee ingenuity. Jeffrey Walsh, in *American War Literature, 1914 to Vietnam* (St. Martin's, 1982; pp. 81–83), notes that Wharton's mature idealism and attitudes toward the wasp-waisted ambulance volunteers from America, evident in *The Marne* and *A Son at the Front*, challenge the "self-evaluation of the lost generation," including Hemingway and Dos Passos: "*A Son at the Front* . . . is an interesting novel to set beside such accepted war classics of its time as *A Farewell to Arms* and provides an illuminating ideological source of comparison. . . ." Wharton's unique contribution to the American novel occupies Ann Massa in *American Literature in Context* (pp. 5–17). Massa attempts to place *The House of Mirth* squarely within the history of our novels by noting that Lily Bart's tragedy "pinpoints the difficult transition in American culture from the frequent restriction and hypocrisy of late nineteenth-century America to the relative freedom and honesty of a less certain and more tolerant society." By creating a heroine of unusual potential trapped by circumstances, Wharton demonstrated the psychological, tragic and muckraking dimensions of the novel of manners realistically and naturalistically conceived. In *Critical Survey of Long Fiction* (vol. 7, pp. 2848–58), W. J. Stuckey sees Wharton's achievement similarly, classifying her a novelist of manners while crediting her with a range of characters and aspects of life "unrivaled in American fiction of her time." Two of several journal articles on Wharton are distinguished by their attention to technique. Orlene Murad contributes a fine survey of narrational inconsistencies in Wharton's most popular novel and attempts to blame them on her identification with the title character in "Edith Wharton and Ethan Frome" (*MLS* 13, iii:90–103). As an invalid's inhibited wife awakened through an affair, Wharton failed to exert her usual control over materials but created a "monumental Ethan Frome. . . . because she identified so closely with his pathos and grief." Michael J. O'Neal's "Point of View and Narrative Technique in the Fiction of Edith Wharton" (*Style* 17: 270–89) is an analysis of a few paragraphs at the beginning and ending of *The House of Mirth* demonstrating how Wharton communicates linguistically her ambivalence toward social and psychological forces. Through idiom she blends consciousness reflectors; through case she judges these reflectors, and through syntax she enables feelings and emotions to victimize her characters.

A group of essays approach Wharton from feminist angles. The least reductive of these, Nancy A. Walker's " 'Seduced and Abandoned': Convention and Reality in Edith Wharton's *Summer*" (*SAF* 11:107–14), examines Wharton's exposure of the truth behind the stereotype and Charity Royall's story as a variation on the classic fable, as that of a "woman of integrity and insight" rather than as "an

embodiment of conventional morality." The consequences of lim-
iting women to married life and thus manipulating their direct per-
ceptions of the world is highlighted in Mary Suzanne Schriber's
"Convention in the Fiction of Edith Wharton" (*SAF* 11:189–201).
After tracing the effects of convention on Lily Bart and Undine
Spragg, Schriber detects the rebel in May Welland in *The Age of
Innocence*, who merely appears conventionally stupid due to her
husband's blindness. In "The Destruction of Lily Bart: Capitalism,
Christianity, And Male Chauvinism" (*DQ* 17,iv:97–108), Nancy Top-
ping Bazin's attempt to blame Christianity for Lily Bart's tragedy
because its antimaterialistic ideas prevent Lily's "success" is somewhat forced. Adeline R. Tintner credits Wharton's series of unsatis-
factory mother-daughter relationships to the consistent series of bad
mothers in Henry James's fiction as well as to Wharton's hatred of
her own mother and incestuous feelings for her father in "Mothers
vs. Daughters in The Fiction of Edith Wharton and Henry James"
(*ABBW* 71:4324–28). Lois A. Cuddy's "Triangles of Defeat and Liberation: The Quest for Power in Edith Wharton's Fiction" (*PCL*
8:18–26) tries to trace Wharton's control over her life as reflected in
The House of Mirth, Ethan Frome and *The Age of Innocence* in tri-
angular relationships inaccurately perceived by the protagonists.
Cuddy's method is perhaps more contrapuntal than clear, but the
conclusion is that women are winning out over men.

ii. Theodore Dreiser

The Dreiser projects of University of Pennsylvania Press continue as
the foremost contributions to Dreiser scholarship. Dreiser's *An Amateur Laborer*, carefully edited by Richard W. Dowell with the assistance of James L. W. West III and Neda M. Westlake, is the latest
Pennsylvania contribution to restoring Dreiser's texts. Written for
publication in 1904 but never published in its original form, this
account of Dreiser's 1903 bouts with neurasthenia in New York after
the *Sister Carrie* trouble with Doubleday and Page was mined constantly—for periodical features and major works. Dowell's excellent
introduction not only supplies the factual structure necessary for an
intelligent reading of Dreiser's twenty-five chapter account but details the author's alterations of circumstances to fit his purposes over
the years and contains an informative section on aspects of the work

surfacing in the struggles of Eugene Witla in *The "Genius."* The completed chapters of *Laborer* are supplemented by what West terms "private" texts, a body of fragments either discarded from the completed chapters or indicative of sections never completed. Intriguing aspects of the 1904 work include Dreiser's distaste for laborers yet embarrassing ineptitude at their work and the depiction of a series of events that makes Hurstwood's degradations in *Sister Carrie* prophetic of Dreiser's own. A good preview to this volume is Dowell's "Will the Real Mike Burke Stand Up, Please!" (*DrN* 14,i:1–9), illustrating the freedom Dreiser took with his sources. The specific focus here is Dreiser's foreman on the New York Central, who underwent repeated and somewhat contradictory transformations "depending on the philosophical interest or narrative demand of the individual work." Another bit of Dreiser lore is offered by Joseph Griffin in "Theodore Dreiser Visits Toronto" (*CRevAS* 14:31–47), in this case the full story of Dreiser being "set-up" in 1942 by the *Toronto Telegram* to make disparaging remarks about the British and then kicked out of Canada before giving the lecture that occasioned the visit.

The significant critical study of the year, also from Pennsylvania, is *Dreiser and His Fiction: A Twentieth-Century Quest* by Lawrence E. Hussman, Jr. Acknowledging Charles Child Walcutt's recognition of Dreiser's development from dark determinism in *Sister Carrie* to reverence for life in *The Stoic*, Hussman emphasizes the conflict between the two in each of the novels. His analysis of Carrie's conversations with Ames [Desire] prepares the reader for his discussion of *The Stoic*, where the guru's words on Divine Love are termed "the most convincing explanation of desire that Dreiser ever offered." Hussman sees Dreiser's stories ("Married," "The Second Choice," "Free," "The Lost Phoebe," "Chains," "Marriage—For One," and "The Shadow") as comparable to Chaucer's "marriage group" and prefatory to *An American Tragedy*, in which "larger questions of responsibility and culpability" are tackled. This career of earnest confusions and questions, usually unanswered and unanswerable, enables Hussman to emphasize the human significance of Dreiser's quest. In "Dreiser's Last Work: *The Bulwark* and *The Stoic*—Conversion or Continuity?" (*DrN* 14,ii:1–15), Barbara Hochman's thesis that the last works develop from the early ones rather than change direction somewhat confirms Hussman's. She sees the portraits of

Etta and Solon in *The Bulwark* (reworkings of those of Jennie Gerhardt and her father) and of Berenice in *The Stoic* "as part and parcel
of Dreiser's life-long interest in all possible modes of seeking and
striving—for material goods, spiritual satisfaction, love, money, nir-
vana." Although Mary G. Land acknowledges Dreiser's flirtations
with divine creative force in his later career in "Three Max Gottliebs:
Lewis's, Dreiser's and Walker Percy's View of the Mechanist-Vitalist
Controversy" (*SNNTS* 15:314–31), she emphasizes that his greatest
work, *An American Tragedy*, is informed by the mechanism of biolo-
gist Jacques Loeb. The crucial conflict in the boat is a matter of
"chemic" response involving Loeb's and Freud's views as well as
Dreiser's socialism. Clarence O. Johnson's able introduction to Dreiser
in *Critical Survey of Long Fiction* (vol. 2, pp. 828–39) contains helpful comparisons involving *Sister Carrie, Jennie Gerhardt, The Finan-
cier* and *An American Tragedy*, and clarifies at the outset that Dreiser
was at his fictional best when combining autobiography with research
and reportage. In "Taking a Part: Actor and Audience in Theodore
Dreiser's *Sister Carrie*" (*ALR* 16:223–39), Deborah M. Garfield gives
a detailed reading of the novel as a combination of audience response, role playing and abdication of will to histrionic illusion.
Garfield notes Dreiser's anticipation of Woolf and Beckett in creating
characters who "obliterate the distinction between the ego and an
external environment." Continuing in the theatrical vein, Bruce
Bawer detects a Shakesperian reference in "Two Jessicas: *Sister
Carrie* and *The Merchant of Venice* (*NMAL* 7: Item 6), which he
believes "to adumbrate a panoply of parallels," including family
division and the felon/victim situation of the fathers.

iii. Jack London and Willa Cather

In a major study of nine London works, *The Novels of Jack London:
A Reappraisal* (Wis.), Charles N. Watson, Jr., mentions that in *The
Valley of the Moon* London bears comparison with Cather. Since
both are Western romantic realists whose works are characterized by
sexual blurring, and both also celebrate humanity's attempts to order
nature (the note on which Watson begins and ends his study), this
insight is a perceptive one. Noting London's attempt to fuse aesthetic
idealism and red-blooded realism, Watson devotes over forty pages
to *Martin Eden* as London's full-length masterpiece. Introducing this

and the other novels with appropriate biographical information, Watson considers character development, imagery and philosophy, citing similarities to Howells, Dreiser, Norris, etc., and in the case of *Martin Eden* to stream-of-consciousness writers. While Watson's delineation of Eden's death according to James Frazer's dying sun god and Nietzsche's Dionysus seems a bit forced, Watson does prove the hero's suicide no sudden whim. Applications to Frazer/Nietzsche continue in the chapter on *Burning Daylight* (here the name is at least appropriate)—the return to civilization equated with rebirth. *The Valley of the Moon* subsequently dramatizes through Saxon Brown the restorative power of a vanishing frontier, and *The Little Lady of the Big House* records the collapse of the dream of a remediable natural world. Watson also devotes chapters to *A Daughter of the Snows*, *The Call of the Wild* (compared to *Huck Finn*), *The Sea-Wolf* (paralleled to *Moby Dick*), *White Fang* and *The Iron Heel* (in the tradition of *The Jungle*, *Looking Backward* and *A Traveler from Altruria*). In each discussion narrative as well as thematic strategies are given attention.

London's strategies are the subject of Donald Pizer's important contribution to the American Realism issue of *Studies in the Literary Imagination* (16,ii:107–15), "Jack London: The Problem of Form," which casts London as a writer of parables and fables in an attempt to determine the source of his strength and appeal despite unevenness and lack of philosophical coherence. *The Call of the Wild* and *White Fang* successfully blend Christian parable love elements within beast fable contexts, and *The Sea-Wolf's* strengths are those of the parable/fable rather than conventional novel. In *Martin Eden*, "London adapts the conventions of the parable/fable to the needs of autobiographical expression." In a similar vein, "Social Philosophy as Best-Seller: Jack London's *The Sea-Wolf*" by Susan Ward (*WAL* 17:321–32) examines the interplay between popular and ideological elements in this novel, the ways London appraised Darwin, Nietzsche and the sorry state of capitalistic society through the popular "education of the young man by the ship's captain" plot and appraised the virtues of the new socialism through the popular love plot. Two other articles concern *The Sea-Wolf*. Martine Elizabeth Ostap, in "Jack London's *The Sea-Wolf*: A Critical Analysis of Wolf Larsen and Humphrey Van Weyden" (*JLN* 15[1982]:109–14), takes to task critics who view Wolf Larsen as simply Nietzsche's superman rather than as the conglomerate of various literary influences and as London's view of capitalism's rugged individualism. Ostap then dismisses those who (like Watson in the above study) view Van Weyden as a manifestation of London's latent homosexuality: Hump is merely fascinated by Larsen "just as a seventh grade boy would be . . . by his fellow-classmates' physiques in a physical education class." In "Character and Perception in *The Sea-Wolf*" (*JLN* 15:119–27), Richard Lessa sees *The Sea-Wolf* as primarily a novel of "characters . . . who see and those who imagine, those who reason and those who feel." Van Weyden fails to see Larsen for the materialist he is and idealizes him accordingly.

In *Critical Essays on Jack London* Jacqueline Tavernier–Courbin has assembled one of the better volumes in G. K. Hall's Critical Essays on American Literature series. In her introduction, "Jack London: A Professional" (pp. 1–21) Tavernier-Courbin laments the neglect of her subject, crediting it mostly to misunderstanding of London's sincere interest in writing as a fine art and to his tendencies to develop conflicting ideologies in different stories and even within individual stories. New essays in this collection include Earl J. Wilcox's "Overtures of Literary Naturalism in *The Son of the Wolf* and *The God of His Fathers*" (pp. 105–13), which carefully establishes London as a serious naturalist. Wilcox documents that selected stories are permeated with qualities now called literary naturalism and indicates evidence of the influence on London of Darwin, Adam Smith, Kant, Benjamin Kidd, Spencer, Nietzsche and Marx. Susan Ward contributes "Ideology for the Masses: Jack London's *The Iron Heel*" (pp. 166–79), noting this socialistic novel's debts to Bellamy's *Looking Backward*, Donnelly's *Caesar's Column* and, in depicting Ernest and Avis Everhard as romantic leads, to popular fiction. London not only managed to criticize capitalistic institutions and pacifistic socialists but popular fiction conventions as well. In "Jack London's Pacific World" (pp. 205–22) Earl Labor discusses the significance of Polynesia as London's Paradise Lost and Melanesia as his Inferno. London's depiction of white exploitation and degeneration in Pacific islands is "in tone and style . . . a remarkable forecast of Ernest Hemingway." London's final "Pacific," Labor claims, is his discovery during his last months of Jung's *Psychology of the Unconscious*, which suddenly brought the Polynesian myths to life. Don Graham sees "The Eternity of Forms" and "Told in the Drooling Ward" as explorations of madness from a comic perspective reminiscent of Poe and anticipating Ken Kesey in "Madness and Comedy: A Neglected Jack London Vein" (pp. 223–28). Tavernier-Courbin's collection is supplemented by a "Notes and Documents" section illustrating London's method of composition.

Several other articles attempt general estimates of London's fiction. Charles N. Watson, Jr., in "Jack London: Up from Spiritualism" (*The Haunted Dusk*, pp. 193–207) maintains that it is misleading to accept London's insistent claims of immunity to the nonrational or implications that he rejected scientific rationalism toward the end of his life. Stories like "Planchette" and "The Eternity of Forms," and especially Darrell Standing's self-hypnosis in *The Star Rover* indicate London's "sense of wonder and mystery that transcends the limits of unimaginative materialism." Mary Allen's "The Wisdom of the Dogs: Jack London" (*Animals in American Literature* [Illinois], pp. 77–96), after a halting attempt to define our elusive brand of naturalism, illustrates London's literal presentation of Darwinism through animal characters in "Diable—A Dog," *The Call of the Wild*, *White Fang*, and "To Build a Fire." In the first and last pieces dogs triumph over environment and humanity, while the others present versions of the classic American frontier hero—rugged, male, celibate, and free. Dale H. Ross, in "Jack London: An American Dilemma" (*JAC* 5[1982],iv: 57–62), sees varying aspects of the conflict between the doomed but glorified rugged individual and the individual-in-society as informing London's major works. In the London essay in *Critical Survey of Long Fiction* (vol. 4, pp. 1691–99) David Mike Hamilton, while explaining the superman-socialism conflicts in *The Sea-Wolf* and *Martin Eden*, points out that London was a better short story writer than novelist.

Finally, there were a few miscellaneous items. Robert H. Woodward's monograph *Jack London and the Amateur Press* (Wolf House Books) documents London's early contributions to the *Amateur Bohemian* and *Dilettante* and prints these in an appendix. "A Problem," a brief piece in the first publication, is an exercise in Socialist argumentation; contributions to the latter journal include a sonnet and "Editorial Crimes: A Protest," a grievance against villainous editors. "Dearest Greek: Jack and Charmian London's Presentation Inscriptions to George Sterling" occupies two numbers of the California Book Club's *Quarterly News-Letter* (48:59–75,87–101), making available London's forty-two inscriptions and Charmian's four. Stanley

Wertheim and Sal Noto edit the entries and provide a record of the friendship with Sterling, including a brief evaluation of his verse. Joe S. Bain, III, in "Interchapter: Jack London's 'The Mexican'" (*JLN* 15:115–18), sees protagonist Felipe Rivera as a breakthrough in the depiction of the Chicano in American literature. In "Jack London's Influence on the Life-Style of Jack Kerouac" (*JLN* 15:158–65), Bob Chessey restricts the influence to Kerouac's public image, as not extending beyond the title of *On the Road* (from London's sociological work *The Road*).

The University of Nebraska Press continues to do for Cather in its *The Troll Garden, A Variorum Edition* what Pennsylvania is doing for Dreiser. James Woodress painstakingly edits the seven stories about art, artists and pseudo-artists that comprise Cather's first book of fiction, incorporating changes made by Cather soon after the 1905 publication of the collection and noting in an emendations section alterations made between magazine and volume publication as well as additional revisions (some substantive) of four stories for subsequent collections. Woodress's helpful introduction considers the influence of Henry James during Cather's early phase and the equilibrium she sought between primitivism and civilization. In clarifying the Kingsley and Rossetti epigraphs Cather selected for her collection Woodress explains the thematic arrangement of the seven stories: the first ("Paul's Case") and last depict characters seduced by art; the second and sixth ("The Sculptor's Funeral" and "A Wagner Matinee") concern environments alien to art; in the third and fifth art and marriage conflict, and the centerpiece ("A Death in the Desert") presents a compendium of artists and careers. The volume as a whole is valuable as a record of Cather's changing attitudes and ability to rework her fiction. The year's other volume on Cather, *Willa: The Life of Willa Cather* by Phyllis C. Robinson (Doubleday), is much the lesser contribution to Cather studies. Robinson entertains the possibility that Cather, a lesbian, sought physical intimacy with college chum Louise Pound, Pittsburgh friend Isabelle McClung, living companion Edith Lewis, and others. The "biography" concentrates primarily on the pre-novel-writing Cather, since this was the period of greatest sexual need, frustration and adjustment. Robinson's method is speculation on inconclusive facts, much like that of scandal sheets, and fails to prove her case. The danger is that suppositions of this kind easily translate into "fact" for many readers. The lesbian issue is much better handled by the Sharon O'Brien essay reviewed in *ALS 1982*, p. 225.

General essays on Cather include Marilyn Arnold's contribution to *Critical Survey of Long Fiction* (vol. 2, pp. 472–84), which focuses on a triple conflict in Cather's novels: tensions between East and West, civilization or art and land are felt throughout; but "the greatest threat to each is an exploitative materialism that has no appreciation for the innate value of the land or of art." Although his thesis seems somewhat inchoate, John Ditsky makes some fascinating observations (e.g., "The habit of making one's personal decisions on the basis of the emblem of another's life was a Cather habit") while surveying the "relationship between character and land and music" in "'Listening With Supersensual Ear': Music in the Novels of Willa Cather" (*JNT* 13:154–63). Latour is said to hear the song of the earth in the stone-lipped cave in *Death Comes for the Archbishop*; a Swedish hymn accompanies Alexandra's communion with the land in *O Pioneers!*; Thea's voice emanates from the land in *The Song of the Lark*, and Ántonia's musicality cannot be separated from her attachment to the land. In "Willa Cather and the Populists" (*GPQ* 3: 206–18), Robert W. Cherny provides an interesting view of Cather's anti-Populist and pro-Republican sentiments as expressed in early magazine pieces and through characterizations in the prairie novels and "Two Friends" and "The Best Years." Cherny argues that the heroine of *My Ántonia* solves as an individual the very problems that drove the Populists to radical party membership.

The several articles on individual Cather novels vary in quality and importance. In the best, "The Lost Brother, The Twin: Women Novelists and The Male-Female Double *Bildungsroman*" (*Novel* 17: 28–43), Charlotte Goodman includes *My Ántonia* in a group of unique novels by women that trace the development of male as well as female protagonists. Cather's novel, concludes Goodman, "laments the fact that a single person cannot experience the female maternal fulfillment of an Ántonia and the male intellectual attainments of a Jim Burden." Mary Kemper Sternshein details how the setting of *My Ántonia* parallels and foreshadows the growth and development of the heroine in "The Land of Nebraska and Ántonia Shimerda" (*HK* 16,ii:34–42). Paul Schach places *My Ántonia*'s wolf tale within the folklore tradition of Germans who immigrated to America from Russia and prints a photograph of the Paul Powis painting believed to have inspired Cather's version in "Russian Wolves in Folktales and Literature of the Plains: A Question of Origins" (*GPQ* 3:67–78). In "The Reliability of Godfrey St. Peter: Self-Knowledge and Isolation in *The Professor's House*" (*SwAL* 8,ii:21–25), Margaret Doane sees the Professor's and Tom Outland's isolation as essential for their self-knowledge and return to the human family. Glen Lick concludes in "Tom Outland: A Central Problem" (*SwAL* 8 [1982],i:42–48) that Cather's young adventurer, like the tower in the ruin, is the ordering principle in *The Professor's House*, that the novel demonstrates the need for a center between the ideal world above and the sustaining world below and dramatizes the Professor like the ancient cliff dwellers "caught down in the plains by marauding Indians." Ann Moseley's "The Pueblo Emergence Myth in Cather's *Death Comes for the Archbishop*" (*SwAL* 8,i:27–35) parallels the Twins, subterranean river, color images, cavern, ceremonial fire, etc. of the Indian myth and Latour's "emergence" toward mystical union—the sacrifice of the ego to the evolving society. Finally, in her Cather chapter in *A Portrait of the Artist as a Young Woman* (Ungar), Linda Huf makes much of Cather's total dedication to art and sees it reflected in Thea Kronborg in *The Song of the Lark*. Seemingly unaware of important criticism of this novel since the early sixties, Huf belabors the obvious while managing to call attention to Cather's admiration for mother-woman as well as career-woman.

iv. Gertrude Stein and Sherwood Anderson

The year's best works on Stein and Anderson focus on technique and language. Marianne De Koven's *A Different Language: Gertrude Stein's Experimental Writing* (Wis.), the most ambitious of these clearly explains Stein's technical complexity and is a must for serious students of Stein and for those in need of an in-depth introduction to to her work. De Koven's first chapter carefully distinguishes between patriarchal or symbolic and matriarchal or presymbolic writing, defining Stein's experimental efforts as "an expression of the pre Oedipal union with the mother's body," as liberating rather than threatening, as "[m]aking conscious the unconscious." Stein's work challenges literary conventions from her abandonment of coherent thematic treatment in *Three Lives* until her re-espousal of themati treatment and other conventions in her "landscape" period (*Lucy Church Amiably* and *Four Saints in Three Acts*). Works between these phases are analyzed to illustrate Stein's progression of styles, a chapter assigned to each of the following: "insistence" (illustrated in the portraits rather than stories and marked by repetition), "lively words" (playful repetition without continuity, as in *Tender Buttons*), "voices and plays" (actors as words moving among word blocks), and "melody" (which reveals the signifier's utter arbitrariness). In the landscape chapter De Koven relates Stein's maleness to her struggle for expression and the greater acceptance of her gender to eventual acceptance of her work, which "may have fostered or enabled the female vision of *Four Saints* and *Lucy Church Amiably.*" In two lengthy chapters in his *Of Huck and Alice* (pp. 160–240) Neil Schmitz examines *Tender Buttons* for its challenge to the logical hierarchy of patriarchal thought and its espousal of self-centered domesticity. Like Whitman in *Leaves of Grass* and Twain through Huck Finn, Stein transfigured forbidden voices (of women, lesbians, Jews) through her humorous writing. Her genius in the *Autobiography of Alice B. Toklas* was to manage an "apology in absentia," to have Gertrude's Alice's Gertrude placed at the forefront of Cubism. In *Ida, A Novel*, the voice of humor becomes the means of "embracing the loony plentitude of meaning in the world." "Gertrude Stein's Dog: 'Personal Identity' and Autobiography" by Shirley Neuman (*CRCL* 10:62–79) introduces a review of recent studies in autobiography as genre with a brief consideration of Stein's autobiographical writings. Stein not only rejected the concept of the unity of the self, claims Neuman, "but . . . she made paradigmatic the failure of belief in that unity."

Introductions of a general nature include Brooks Landon's essay in *Critical Survey of Long Fiction* (vol. 6, pp. 2505–17), which calls attention to Stein's neglected novel for children, *The World Is Round*, and to *Brewsie and Willie,* her pessimistic view of the American economic system. Landon explores each novel for its importance in Stein's development as a technician and thinker: *Q.E.D.* records her identity crisis while hinting at her future style; *Three Lives* "marks the transition from naturalism to modernism"; *The Making of Americans,* "one of modernism's seminal works," illustrates her cinematic movement technique. In *American Literature in Context* (pp. 45–58),

Ann Massa reminds us of the influence of William and Henry James
on Stein's rejection of chronologically ordered history and traditional
narrative and on her making familiar language unfamiliar and exciting. Massa sees Stein as representing "the American dimension of
what was happening elsewhere in the arts and sciences in the early
twentieth century." Among miscellaneous items, Michael S. Reynolds's "Hemingway's Stein: Another Misplaced Review" (*AL* 55:
431–34) sees Stein's review of Hemingway's *Three Stories and Ten
Poems* as a response to his pompous diatribe against Lewis, Mencken
et al. in his review of her *Geography and Plays*. In "H. L. Mencken
Discovers Gertrude Stein" (*NMAL* 7: Item 1) Ray Lewis White reprints Mencken's review of *Tender Buttons*, an expression of outrage
at the woman who made English "easier to write and harder to read."
Joseph Reed's whimsical drawings depict Stein in various attitudes,
alone and with friends and brothers, to illustrate the letters in "A
Gertrude Stein Alphabet" (*CE* 45:589–93). Hilbert H. Campbell in
"Three Unpublished Letters of Alice B. Toklas" (*ELN* 20,iii/iv:
47–51) makes available correspondence with Sherwood Anderson's
widow when Toklas was eighty-four and convalescing from a series
of falls and struggling to complete her memoirs. Toklas comments on
the Stein-Anderson friendship, Hemingway's suicide and the removal
of Stein's valuable paintings from Toklas's apartment.

The year's noteworthy contribution on Anderson, *The Teller's
Tales*, Union College Press's Signature Series edition of twelve Anderson stories, exclusive of those in *Winesburg, Ohio*, contains an
excellent introduction by editor Frank Gado that distinguishes Anderson's method of probing beneath the surface of the text from
Hemingway's method of suggestion. Anderson's method is one of
"*antiguity*" rather than ambiguity, a product of the teller's reaction
rather than of an equivocal author. Helpful commentaries on "In a
Strange Town," "I Want to Know Why," "The Egg," "The Man Who
Became a Woman" and "Death in the Woods" focus on Anderson's
use of form as a function of the teller's psyche. W. J. Stuckey's essay
in *Critical Survey of Long Fiction* (vol. 1, pp. 71–80) surveys the
novels, noting that Anderson's talent was better suited to rendering
moments of "epiphany" than to writing novels, and that all his novels
seem to arise out of his departure from the paint factory and middle-
class life. Ann Massa's consideration in *American Literature in Con-*

text is largely an introduction to *Winesburg*, defining "grotesque" in this context and emphasizing the human need for shared values, inner openness, and instinctive responses. In "Something In The Elders: The Recurrent Imagery In *Winesburg, Ohio*" (*WE* 9,i:1–7) Robert Allen Papinchak, taking a hint from Anderson's preface about truth, concludes: "For the reader who recognizes the recurrent themes—potential and fertility—and the recurrent images—darkness, corn, moon, rain, fields, season—and then connects them with Anderson's concern for fruition, for fulfilled potential, Winesburg becomes a land heavy with truths." David D. Anderson groups *Tar: A Midwest Childhood* with Howells's *A Boy's Town* and Darrow's *Farmington* within a post–Civil War, early 20th-century "sub-movement" of boys' stories exploring the Midwestern past in "From Memory to Meaning: The Boys' Stories of William Dean Howells, Clarence Darrow, and Sherwood Anderson" (*Midamerica* 10:69–84). While describing the innocence and brutality of midwestern farm life, *Tar* also delineates the spirit that sends the youth "into the mainstream of a twentieth century dedicated to hustling, to making money."

Of the essays devoted to individual stories, A. R. Coulthard's "The Failure of Sherwood Anderson's 'Death in the Wood'" (*Interpretations* 14,ii:32–38) is most ambitious. Coulthard takes issue with several critics by dismissing the story due to "shifting perspective," "forced coincidence," "pointless repetition," and "callous use of the woman's pitiable life and death as a symbol of 'completeness' in the story's dénouement." Donald E. Arbuckle and James B. Misenheimer, Jr., in "Personal Failure in 'The Egg' and 'A Hunger Artist'" (*WE* 8,ii:1–3) see both protagonists as defeated by unnatural ambition. Charles E. Modlin's "'In a Field': A Story from *A Story Teller's Story*" (*WE* 8,iii:3–6) makes the short piece available for the first time without its prefatory note and with Anderson's previously unpublished emendations. Finally, Welford Dunaway Taylor tells the story of Julius J. Lankes's woodcut for Anderson's frontispiece in "Sherwood Anderson's *Perhaps Women*: The 'Story in Brief'" (*Midamerica* 10:110–14), and Leland Krauth compares Anderson's *Mid-American Chants* to Wright's *To A Blossoming Pear Tree* for persistent midwestern concerns (destruction of the landscape and regeneration of love through violence) in "'Beauty Breaking Through the Husks of Life': Sherwood Anderson and James Wright" (*Mid-america* 10:124–38).

v. Other Major Writers

Major writers receiving less than usual attention this year include Sinclair, Dos Passos, Lewis and Glasgow. Mencken held his own as the subject of four articles; there were two considerations of Marquand, and the unusual attention given to Cabell earns him at least temporary inclusion in this category.

The most general consideration of Upton Sinclair groups him with David Graham Phillips, London and Norris as a proponent of literary professionalism undermined by American business interests. Christopher P. Wilson claims in "American Naturalism and the Problem of Sincerity" (*AL* 54:511–27) that the "hard sell" diverted the sincerest narrative utterance of these naturalists. In *Critical Survey of Long Fiction* (vol. 6, pp. 2416–27) Hallman B. Bryant reminds us that Sinclair "was a propagandist first and a novelist second," while emphasizing the works that best straddle the two genres: *The Jungle, King Coal, Oil!, Boston* and *Dragon's Teeth*. In a denial that the progressive had softened with age, as Bryant insists, Dieter Herms cites the plays (especially the antinuclear message in *A Giant's Strength*) as indicative of Sinclair's consistency as a thinker and humanist in "The Novelist as Dramatist: A Note on Upton Sinclair's Plays" (*USQ* 7,ii&iii:3–11). Herms also feels the plays reveal a well-developed sense of theater and discusses the dramatic innovations of the early muckraking ones (*John D.: An Adventurer* and *The Indignant Subscriber*) and the streamlining for the stage of the novel *Oil!*. Sinclair the activist is Richard J. Rapaport's concern in "The Plight of the Writer in Politics" (*USQ* 7,i:5–10), a reprinted newspaper article summarizing Sinclair's unsuccessful 1934 campaign for Governor of California and his EPIC plan to decrease unemployment through the tax structure. In "Upton Sinclair and the New Critics of Education" (*USQ* 7,i:11–16), Jack L. Nelson advises current critics to extend their audience beyond academia by rediscovering what Sinclair had to say about capitalist employers dominating American education. Finally, in an excellent article, "Upton Sinclair and the Socialist Response to World War I" (*CRevAS* 14:121–30), Peter Buitenhuis considers *Jimmie Higgins*, a propaganda novel reflecting Sinclair's hoodwinking by British propaganda before the Allies attacked Russia.

John Dos Passos's friendship with Hemingway occupied two critics. In "Swords and Ploughshares: Hemingway and Dos Passos in Spain" (*Distant Obligations*, pp. 165–97), David C. Duke traces the growth and destruction of the relationship between the two men in a painstaking comparison of their different motives for supporting the Spanish Loyalists, their conflicting ideas for the documentary film *The Spanish Earth* and their disagreement over the execution of José Robles. In "Dos Passos' Portrait of Hemingway" (*LGJ* 7,ii:18–22), Dave Sanders traces the development of George Elbert Warner through *Chosen Country, Century's Ebb* and *The Great Days* "as Dos Passos' effort to explain how close friends could differ so drastically as witnesses to the horrors in Spain." Jeffrey Walsh's somewhat unorganized consideration of *Three Soldiers* in *American War Literature* (pp. 69–78) touches upon a variety of subjects, including Dos Passos's debt to Henri Barbusse's *Le Feu*, his "dualistic imagination" and the inadequacy of his characters to support his tragic objectives. Of more significance is Barry Maine's "Representative Men in Dos Passos's *The 42nd Parallel*" (*ClioI* 12[1982]:31–43), a convincing refutation of the prevailing view that historical determinism is the governing thesis of *U.S.A.* After considering the "biographies" of Burbank, Debs, Carnegie, Bryan, La Follette and others, Maine concludes that to Dos Passos "Human nature is the only historical law" and that *U.S.A.* is "more in line with Dos Passos's later work." Finally, in *Critical Survey of Long Fiction* (vol. 2, pp. 789–99), Mary Ellen Stumpf stresses the architectural and visual aspects of Dos Passos's method in *Three Soldiers, Manhattan Transfer* and *U.S.A.*

In the most technical of the three considerations of Sinclair Lewis (*American Literature in Context*, pp. 102–14), Ann Massa attempts to demonstrate his skill as a photographic novelist in describing Gopher Prairie in *Main Street* and emphasizing Carol Kennicott's need to romanticize the place in order to survive and keep faith. The romantic side of Carol and of Babbitt is indicative of Lewis's failure to solve his own personal ambivalence about midwestern life, according to Anna B. Katona in *Critical Survey of Long Fiction* (vol. 4, pp. 1668–81). Katona nicely parallels *Main Street* and *Babbitt* and contrasts the self-serving fanaticism in *Elmer Gantry* and the idealism in *Arrowsmith*. Mary G. Land in "Three Max Gottliebs" (see Section ii above) considers Jacques Loeb as prototype of the mechanist bac-

teriologist idol of Martin Arrowsmith, whose failure to execute Loeb/
Gottlieb theories of scientific experimentation during the plague
blurs disease study with medical art.

John P. Marquand, a novelist of equally broad social concerns, is
the subject of two considerations. The more specific, Kathryn Carlisle
Schwartz's "Cross-Referenced Parallels in *The Late George Apley*"
(*MarkhamR* 12:37–39), uses the affairs of an Apley ancestor and a
cousin to illuminate George's dark affair with Mary Monohan and
explain Marquand's technique of informing certain situations with
others. Marquand is deservedly and adequately represented in *Critical Survey of Long Fiction* (vol. 5, pp. 1811–21) by Charles L.P.
Silet's effort to establish the novelist's ability to provide a comprehensive and unsentimental picture of American society from World
War I to the sixties and, in his best novels (*The Late George Apley*,
So Little Time, Point of No Return, etc.), to portray the American
male with understanding.

H. L. Mencken's method is the subject of Ann Massa's analysis of
"In Memorium, W. J. B." in *American Literature in Context* (pp.
130–43). Massa notes the formal and colloquial vocabulary in Mencken's aggressive iconoclasm and his excessive defensiveness in putting
down the dangerous antiintellectualism he felt Bryan represented.
Mencken's cynicism occupies P. J. Wingate in "The Philosophy of
H. L. Mencken" (*Menckeniana* 87:14–16), which tells how Mencken's unsuccessful attempt to expose his hoax about President Fillmore and the bathtub confirmed his convictions that Americans are
easily duped by quackery and prefer to live in illusion. Mencken
troops forth as progressive in "Mencken and Joyce: Hands Across the
Waters" (*MarkhamR* 12:43–45) by Leo M. J. Manglaviti, who notes
three Joyce letters among the Mencken papers in the New York
Public Library establishing Mencken as the first to publish the Irish
author in America (in the May 1915 *The Smart Set*) and as helping
arrange publication of *Dubliners* by Huebsch (later Viking). In "The
Three Faces of Mencken" (*Menckeniana* 86:1–6), Einer Haugen takes
a comprehensive approach to the man, commenting on the linguist
whose work inspired his own career in linguistics, the writer whose
radicalism turned right wing and disappointing, and the warm-
hearted, earthy talker who in old age was his host at lunch.

Ellen Glasgow received too little attention this year, but her
Richmond contemporary James Branch Cabell got more, compara-

tively speaking, than he deserves. The only journal article on Glasgow, Carol S. Manning's "Little Girls and Sidewalks: Glasgow and Welty on Childhood's Promise" (*SoQ* 21,iii:67–76), examines the prepubescent adventures of Jenny Blair in *The Sheltered Life* and the consequences of having girls conform to inadequate, southern belle models. The most significant Glasgow-related item in *Ellen Glasgow Newsletter* was Mary P. Edwards's "Tea and Metaphysics: Excerpts From Mary Johnston's Diary" (19:2–9), which makes available diary excerpts from 1906–11, when the two novelists were living in Richmond and sharing interest in Darwin, Spinoza, Kant, etc., in current fiction and writing, and in woman's rights. Wilton Eckley's Glasgow essay in *Critical Survey of Long Fiction* (vol. 3, pp. 1117–25) concentrates on *Virginia*, *Barren Ground* and two Queenborough novels, and emphasizes the novelist's moderation, tendency to temper pessimism with optimism, her propriety and honesty, and her "verism."

Foremost among the year's work on Cabell is *James Branch Cabell: Centennial Essays* (LSU), edited by M. Thomas Inge and Edgar E. MacDonald. Besides an interesting photographic essay by MacDonald (pp. 81–107) and Ritchie D. Watson's thorough bibliographical one (pp. 142–79), seven other essays address various aspects of the novelist's life and career. In "A Virginian in Poictesme" (pp. 1–16) Louie D. Rubin, Jr., discusses Cabell's need to distance himself from Richmond to tell the truth about it yet maintain a self-image respectable enough to satisfy its demands. "Cabell In Love" by MacDonald (pp. 17–39) explains the novelist's college relationship with Gabriella Moncure, the "genesis" of all his "fantasy women," details her portrait in *The Cords of Vanity* and surveys the love poems inspired by his separation from her. Cabell's working friendship with his talented McBride editor, Guy Holt, whose impact on the fiction was "inspirational and perhaps psychological rather than material," is Dorothy McInnis Scura's concern in "Cabell and Holt: The Literary Connection" (pp. 40–64), which contains correspondence between the two during the writing of *The Cream of the Jest* and *Beyond Life*. Joseph M. Flora credits Edmund Wilson and other champions of Cabell's later phase with being instrumental in discovering the timely relevancy of the *Heirs and Assigns* trilogy in "After the James Branch Cabell Period" (pp. 65–80). In "James Branch Cabell: The Life of His Design" (pp. 108–21) W. L. Godshalk sees *Figures of Earth* as an ironic, satiric allegory whose disjunctive

narrative intentionally denies its meaning. Mark Allen's "Enchant-
ment and Delusion: Fantasy in the Biography of Manuel" (pp. 122–30)
analyzes Cabell's deft use of language and fantasy devices to sustain
our temporary belief in his world. Leslie A. Fiedler caps the collection with "The Return of James Branch Cabell; or The Cream of the
Cream of the Jest" (pp. 131–41) by entertaining the possibility of a
revival of Cabell as a writer of "juvenile trash" satisfying the needs
of prolonged adolescence. *Kalki*, official organ of the Cabell Society,
reappeared after a delay of two years with "Cabell as Prospero,
Wylie as Miranda, in Richmond-in-Virginia" (8:216–28), Edgar E.
MacDonald's rendering of Elinor Wylie's guarded introduction to
Cabell's literary, social circle after the publication of her novel *Jen-
nifer Lorn*. Finally, Lynne P. Shackelford's contribution to *Critical
Survey of Long Fiction* (vol. 1, pp. 401–10) concentrates on *Figures
of Earth* and manages a clear explanation of Cabell's theory of man's
need for unattainable dreams, "dynamic illusions" rooted in the
libido.

vi. Minor Writers

Among writers currently in this category, the once popular Mary
Hunter Austin attracted most attention. Augusta Fink provided an
emotional biography of the novelist-poet-essayist, *I-Mary*: A Biography of Mary Austin (Arizona), the title referring to Austin's childhood discovery of her deepest self and its relation to all creation, and
also to the central conflict of her life—between the "egoism and insecurity of Mary-by-herself" and the "spiritual strength and solace
of the I-Mary," from whom she periodically was estranged. Fink tells
us little about Austin's work except where it reveals her feelings and
responds to her ongoing crises, many self-created. We relive Austin's
estrangement from her mother, her unsatisfying marriage to Wallace
Austin (whom she abandoned), her anguish over her retarded daughter (whom she put away and never again visited), her infatuation
with George Sterling and her unsuccessful pursuits of Lincoln Stef-
fens and Daniel Trembly MacDougal. The portrait emerging from
Fink's work is of a confused and pushy, self-proclaimed mystic and
exhibitionist of some genius and accomplishment, into many things
at once, who was self-centered, inconsistent, and unreliable. In effect,
the woman is decidedly distasteful, although one wonders if Fink

finds her so. The book contains many interesting photographs of Austin and her circle and deserves its place on the growing shelf of similar studies of literary females. In his *The Santa Fe and Taos Colonies: Age of the Muses, 1900–1942* (Oklahoma) Arrell Morgan Gibson presents a capsule biography of Austin, "Mary Austin: Santa Fe's Literary Dowager" (pp. 199–217), concentrating on her Santa Fe decade, the writing she did during those years (*American Rhythm, The Land of Journey's Ending,* the autobiography *Earth Horizon*) and acknowledging her efforts on behalf of Indian and Hispanic culture and the environment. Gibson calls Austin "environmentally obsessed" about the Southwest, which well describes her spiritual immersion in the landscape. Austin's insights on the impact of landscape on the structure and flow of emotion and idea occupy James Ruppert in "Mary Austin's Landscape Line in Native American Literature" (*SWR* 68:376–90). Ruppert does his best to clarify what Austin meant by "rhythm" in her attempt to explain the geographical determinism linking Amerindian and American poetry. Another writer enamored of the West is the subject of John D. Nesbitt's "Owen Wister's Achievement in Literary Tradition" (*WAL* 18:199–208), which views *The Virginian* as an artful combination of the traditions of historical romance and the novel of manners (even to aping the style of Henry James!).

Three 1982 Twayne U.S. Authors Series volumes overlooked in last year's essay deserve brief mention here. In *Ludwig Lewisohn* (TUSAS 435) Seymour Lainoff attempts with candor to call attention to an almost forgotten author whose Jewish-mindedness and marital embroilments confused and alienated his contemporaries. Lainoff distinguishes two of his fifteen novels as worthy of attention. *The Case of Mr. Crump,* in which the idealistic protagonist is driven by his scheming wife to murder her, is Lewisohn's attempt to liberalize attitudes toward love and marriage in favor of men. *The Island Within* chronicles the conflicts of assimilation through several generations of Jews in Poland, Germany and America, and the tragic consequences of the loss of Jewish identity. Assimilation is also the factor in Carol B. Schoen's *Anzia Yezierska* (TUSAS 424), the subject an immigrant Jew whose writings deal primarily with the lives of Jews on Manhattan's Lower East Side. Schoen selects *Breadgivers,* which focuses on the psychological tensions between an obstinate Old World patriarch and his equally stubborn New World daughter,

and *Red Ribbon on a White Horse,* an intricately structured autobiographical study of a representative immigrant woman, as Yezierska's best. Frank Bergmann presents a very different author in *Robert
Grant* (*TUSAS* 426). Grant, a proper Bostonian, considered the immigrants coming in waves from Southern and Eastern Europe and
Ireland to be of low class and disrupting. His best novel, *Unleavened
Bread,* resembles Wharton's *The Custom of the Country* in treating
the exploits of a female Philistine (in Grant's novel Selma White)
and the disturbing implications of dictatorship of the proletariat.
Bergmann feels that this novel and *The Chippendales,* a balanced
study of how, in the clash between the old and the new in Boston
society, the best of the old contributes to and lives in the new, are
significant contributions to American literature.

Brigham Young University

14. Fiction: The 1930s to the 1950s

Louis Owens

Just as 1982 was a good year for bibliography in this period, 1983 was an outstanding year for biography, with biographies ranging from good to excellent appearing on such writers as Thornton Wilder, Margaret Mitchell, John Steinbeck, Dashiell Hammett, Conrad Aiken, William Saroyan, James Gould Cozzens, and, to mention a late-received 1982 publication, Katherine Anne Porter. Coupled with this biographical industry this year is an outpouring of book-length studies on writers including Edmund Wilson, Porter, Nabokov, H. P. Lovecraft, Allan Seager, S. J. Perelman, John O'Hara, Allen Tate, Robert Penn Warren, and Saroyan along with the publication of Edmund Wilson's *The Forties* and Viking's *The Portable Edmund Wilson*. When we add to this list the special Depression issue of *The Literary Review* and the detective fiction number of *Modern Fiction Studies* and the usual flood of material on Eudora Welty, it becomes obvious that 1983 was a good year for this period in American fiction. One final note worth mentioning by way of introduction is the heritage of New Criticism and the Modernist stress turning up in these studies, a kind of revisionism that raises the question again and again of why individual writers such as O'Hara, Cozzens, Saroyan, Mitchell, Steinbeck and others have not been accepted into the canon of the academy. In one form or another, the answer generated by these critics seems to be that these writers were each, in one way or another, outside the Modernist mainstream and thus have held little appeal for academics.

i. "Art for Humanity's Sake"—Proletarians and Others

Noteworthy this year is the special issue, "The Depression Remembered," of *The Literary Review* (27:1), which set out according to the editors, to "correct misimpressions of the period, especially of its literature, to take a fresh look at familiar works, and to rediscover neglected authors." Much to their surprise, they discovered that most of the writings submitted for this issue "recalled the 1930s as a period of fulfillment and satisfaction." This unexpectedly glowing account of the Depression period becomes very obvious in such pieces as William Saroyan's "Memories of the Uppression" (pp. 9–11), in which Saroyan confesses that "this Depression was the best time of my life in a certain sense," and Karlton Kelm's "Brief Memoirs of the Great Depression" (pp. 12–17), in which Kelm notes paradoxically that "creatively it was a fertile time for writers." Kelm cites the material available for the artist in the human suffering and tests of strength pervasive during the Depression and the sprouting up of innumerable little magazines ready to publish the volume of new material steadily appearing. Kelm takes time out for fulsome praise of a neglected author, declaring, "If I had to pick one writer of that period whose stories impressed me even more than William Saroyan's, it would have to be Meridel Le Sueur." Harry Slochower provides a brief and very personal reminiscence and also finds much to laud about the period, finding it a time of "vibrant militance, which held to a deep humanistic promise." In his essay, "The 1930's: Years of Buoyancy and Promise" (pp. 18–21), Slochower digresses to remind us of 30s novelist Benjamin Appel, whose novels "recreate the thirties as perhaps no other writer does—both its depressive and its daring, radical uplift, its passion and buoyancy." A similar approach to the others here is taken by Walter B. Rideout in "Forgotten Images of the Thirties: Josephine Herbst" (pp. 28–36). Rideout begins by noting a "double sense of the times" in the 30s: the obvious suffering caused by the Depression and culminating in the Second World War, and the "deep, widespread sympathy for others suffering the same disasters, and the hope for a better society." Herbst, he claims, captures this double sense better than any other writer of the time. He singles out for brief summary and special praise Herbst's Trexler trilogy, *Pity Is Not Enough* (1933), *The Executioner Waits* (1934), and *Rope of Gold* (1939). Rideout suggests that one major reason for Herbst's lack of recognition today stems from her radicalism.

a. **Edmund Wilson, James Agee, and Others.** The publication of Edmund Wilson's *The Forties* (Farrar, Straus and Giroux) and *The Portable Wilson* (Viking) makes this a notable year for the premier

American "man of letters." As Leon Edel points out in his foreward to *The Forties*, this fascinating, fragmented compilation of notes, essays, and reactions did not have the benefit of Wilson's own editing as did the earlier *The Twenties* and *The Thirties*. As a result, we get the full sense here of Wilson as hyperenergized and incessant observer and thinker, particularly in such sections as those dealing with Wilson's trips to London, Italy and Greece after the war. We also have an opportunity here to see Wilson, the critic, warming up in "Notes for *The Wound and the Bow*" as well as Wilson the novelist in "Notes for a Novel." Edel's editing is reserved and unobtrusive for this period of incredible productivity on Wilson's part, a period that produced *Memoirs of Hecate County, The Wound and the Bow*, as well as five other books and over one hundred essays, and a period of meagerness in Wilson's journals. Edel's introduction provides a low-key general portrait of Wilson, furnishing a necessary focus before we begin the dislocating experience of threading our way through the fragments of what Lewis Dabney, in his introduction to *The Portable Edmund Wilson*, terms Wilson's "dark period." As Dabney also notes in his introduction to this volume, "Edmund Wilson's reputation continues to grow," and this new portable, first contemplated as early as 1952, will undoubtedly aid in that growth as it brings together more than six-hundred pages of some of Wilson's finest prose, beginning with his reflections upon places and persons such as "The Old Stone House" and Edna St. Vincent Millay and progressing through the decades of Wilson's life. Dabney's selections are well chosen, omitting such Wilsonian provincialisms as *The Boys in the Backroom* and including many masterpieces such as "Philoctetes: The Wound and the Bow," and "Zuñi: Shálako."

The major critical work on Wilson this year is George H. Douglas's *Edmund Wilson's America* (Kentucky), an excellent though somewhat disturbing book. Douglas's announced intention is to "synthesize Wilson's moods and ideas over several generations" and to "locate one major area of Wilson's work within a coherent intellectual framework." The framework is America, and Wilson's response to America is the great subject, and in an eloquent and much-admiring work Douglas accomplishes his goal. He writes very well, a master of paraphrase so adept that it is at times disturbing to find it impossible to tell whether one is reading one of the many digressions that flow from the mind of Douglas in response to the time and thought of

Wilson or a paraphrase of Wilson himself. A lesser study of Wilson as critic this year is Lewis Dabney's essay, "The Critics Who Made Us: Edmund Wilson and *The Wound and the Bow*" (*SR* 91:155–65). In this general, rather diffuse reminder of Wilson's significance and enduring vitality as critic, Dabney focuses on *Wound*, with a major aside regarding Leon Edel's views of Wilson. Wilson's work, Dabney declares, "provides us an opportunity not only to learn from the people whom he writes about but to gain something of his own strength and perspective."

In "Aiken, Agee, and Sandburg: A Memoir" (*VQR* 59:299–315), Bernard C. Schoenfeld offers a tribute and memorial to the three writers, recalling eloquently the "sweat and hurt" of each, while in "Yellow Sky: James Agee and Stephen Crane" (*FLQ* 11,i:46–53), James R. Fultz reviews Agee's contributions to the 1952 film version of "The Bride Comes to Yellow Sky." Fultz notes in particular how much the adaptation was helped along by Crane's cinematic style and points out as a major difference between short story and film-script the way in which Agee openly attacks the "burgeois respectability that has recently come to Yellow Sky." Fultz observes that "All of Agee's scripts . . . are colored by his deep compassion, his essentially tragic view of life. His Scratchy is less sinister, more human, and ultimately more pathetic than Crane's character."

"Others" here comprehends an eclectic swath of American writers this year, beginning with James Gould Cozzens, the subject of a solid biography, *James Gould Cozzens: A Life Apart* (Harcourt), by Matthew J. Bruccoli. Bruccoli has put together a thorough accounting of the life of Cozzens, a writer who chose not to step into the light of literary acclaim. This is a book which should please Cozzens scholars and fans while attracting few new ones as it marches dutifully through Cozzen's life and prodigious literary output, including Cozzens's long youthful preparation for the major novels of his maturity. In spite of Bruccoli's obvious sympathies and generous portrait, the Cozzens who emerges here is for the most part the rather unsympathetic figure the book sets out to deny. Adding value to this work are appendixes dealing with Cozzens's wife and agent Bernice Baumgarten, entries from Cozzens's notebooks, and "The Publications of James Gould Cozzens and Books about Him." Robert Emmet Long's *John O'Hara* (Ungar) focuses on another writer who has drifted to the margins of contemporary criticism. In a work long on summary, Long offers much recapitulation of O'Hara's novels and short fiction but provides little in the way of critical analysis. While he spends significant time examining what he terms "The relation between O'Hara's psychic stresses and compulsive preoccupations and the nature of the fiction he wrote," Long fails to provide sufficient critical examination to support his contention that the disturbingly thorough rejection of O'Hara by the New York and academic "intellectually elitist community" "was based on other than strictly aesthetic grounds." In the end, this study seems to tire under the weight of O'Hara's immense output. A far different work is *The Enthusiast: A Life of Thornton Wilder* (Ticknor & Fields), by Gilbert A. Harrison. In a year of excellent biographies, Harrison's stands out as a beautifully written work that brings Wilder to exuberant life, from the childhood spent in such exotic places as Shanghai, Chefoo, and San Luis Obispo, to the final incredible odysseys across Europe and the American Southwest. Harrison follows Wilder in his development as author and peripatetic genius, one of the most alone and least lonely of authors. *Allan Seager,* by Stephen E. Connelly (TUSAS) is a less scintillating work than Harrison's but a solid contribution—a well-researched, thoughtful, insightful introduction to a writer largely ignored in both popular and academic realms. Beginning with a concise biography that illuminates Seager as a brilliant and self-sustaining intellectual and introduces Seager the writer, Connelly continues with brief introductory synopses and critical commentaries on Seager's short fiction and novels, blending summary and explication adroitly, a rare achievement in this series of studies. Connelly is skillful in showing us Seager the "complex, serious thinker" who "offers no easy answers," and he is deft in his explication of Seager's work, especially in treatment of "This Town and Salamanca," "The Street," and the novels *Amos Berry* and *The Inheritance.* Like other critics this year, Connelly's announced aim is revisionist: the reclamation of Seager's reputation. Also aiming to rectify errors in critical judgment is Robert James Butler, whose "Parks, Parties, and Pragmatism: Time and Setting in James T. Farrell's Major Works" (*ELWIU* 10,ii:241–54) argues for a coherence and structure in Farrell's major fiction that has thus far been largely ignored. Butler founds his argument on two elements in Farrell's novels: "the concept of time which is at the core of his vision, and the use of two symbolic settings which help him to dramatize this central theme." The two settings are the parks and parties of the essay's title. In the Lonigan, O'Neill, and Carr books, according to Butler, "the central character's most successful dealings with time often take place in one of the numerous city parks which occupy such a prominent position in Farrell's writing." Citing the often noted relation between Farrell and American pragmatism, Butler points out that Farrell's characters most often fail to achieve the pragmatist's necessary "temporal poise and self-control," failures that are prominent at parties, the "grotesque occasions for temporal dislocation" in the novels. Butler supports his thesis convincingly, leading persuasively to his conclusion that these books "are quite remarkable not only for their frequently acknowledged power but also for their little-recognized wholeness of vision and formal control."

b. **John Steinbeck.** Steinbeck continues to generate attention this year with the publication of Jackson J. Benson's *The True Adventures of John Steinbeck, Writer* (Viking). Here, at last, Benson's decade-plus labors have produced the authorized Steinbeck biography, a work that follows Steinbeck with microscopic attention and unflagging loyalty from the Salinas, California childhood to the final years as man of the world and advisor to presidents. Though Benson succumbs briefly in the opening pages to the temptation to romanticize Steinbeck's childhood (much as Steinbeck himself liked to do), Benson retains a hard-won objectivity through most of this work with the result that Steinbeck the man and writer comes clear for us in all his dimensions. Stylistically, the book falters at times under the burden of reportage, but Benson has done a masterful job with a difficult subject and is particularly adept at defining Steinbeck's position in relation to the critical/cultural czars of the East during the thirties and following decades. A second book-length study this year is Brian St. Pierre's *John Steinbeck: The California Years* (Chronicle Books), apparently the produce of St. Pierre's labors at the John Steinbeck Library in Salinas as well as at the Stanford University Library and elsewhere. Although nothing new appears here, this brief study should provide an interesting introduction to Steinbeck for those unfamiliar with his life or work. The writer is content to reiterate the familiar thesis that Steinbeck "had drawn his strength as an artist from his native soil and . . . he had lost it when he left."

When St. Pierre ventures more deeply into critical commentary, he is apt to miss the point, as in his claim that Doc Burton as a character in *In Dubious Battle* fails because Steinbeck "tended to sentimentalize Ricketts" (Ed Ricketts, upon whom the character is modeled).

Of considerable value is Tetsumaro Hayashi's *A New Steinbeck Bibliography: 1971–1981* (Scarecrow). As Hayashi points out, this second volume of his Steinbeck bibliography covers only ten years but during those ten years half as much material on Steinbeck appeared as had in the previous forty years. In his introduction to this bibliography, Robert DeMott calls attention to the proliferation of Steinbeck criticism and to a new critical interest in Steinbeck's later works as well as the generally approved early fiction. Still another book-length study of Steinbeck this year is Joseph R. Millichap's *Steinbeck and Film* (Ungar), which provides excellent scene-by-scene analysis of films made from Steinbeck's fiction, from *Of Mice and Men* to the recent spate of television adaptations. Particularly strong is his evaluation of John Ford's revision of the central themes of *The Grapes of Wrath* in the production of that film. In his attempts to provide general critical commentary regarding Steinbeck's fiction, however, Millichap fails notably, displaying a striking lack of comprehension of all but the major works. Millichap's thesis is that Steinbeck's "changing relationship to film" was a major reason for the writer's supposed decline after World War II. With his entry into writing for Hollywood, says Millichap, "Steinbeck had entered the enemy camp"; he then proceeds to flog his thesis that Steinbeck declined as a writer after the thirties and that Hollywood was the gremlin in Steinbeck's career.

The *Steinbeck Quarterly* continues this year to keep Steinbeck readers and critics abreast of developments, but *StQ* has less substantive criticism to offer this year than in the recent past. *StQ* 16,i–ii begins with a brief essay by Tetsumaro Hayashi outlining "Standards for Publishable Writing" (pp. 5–8) and an essay by Richard A. Davison entitled "An Overlooked Musical Version of *Of Mice and Men*" (pp. 9–16). Davison recounts attending a musical version of Steinbeck's play at the Provincetown Playhouse in New York on November 26, 1958, and provides a synopsis of the musical along with evidence o Steinbeck's interest in, approval of, and assistance in the creation of the musical. After a brief summary of the critical reaction to the little-noted play, Davison gives his opinion that the drama "was much better than the relatively limited run might suggest." Davison's essay is immediately followed by a note by John Ditsky suggesting that the musical's failure might have been due to the fact that a very similar musical entitled *The Most Happy Fella* had just previously enjoyed great success on Broadway (p. 17). In the one substantial essay in this number of *StQ*, Patrick W. Shaw's "Tom's Other Trip: Psycho-Physical Questing in *The Grapes of Wrath*" (pp. 17–25), the author declares that Tom's "journey from Oklahoma to California is but the facade for his more important psychic journey from isolato to prophet." Shaw takes the long-familiar transcendental thread of the novel and the long-recognized development of Tom's social conscience and places both in a five-part pattern corresponding to the "five different states of the union" the Joads travel through en route to California. Though well written and reinforced by the catchy phrase "psycho-physical questing," the essay offers little new insight. In this issue of *StQ*, Tetsumaro Hayashi continues his Interview Series with both American and foreign Steinbeck scholars. While interviews with such critics and teachers as John Ditsky, Roy S. Simmonds, Robert M. Benton, and Mimi R. Gladstein will interest anyone reading or teaching Steinbeck, of particular interest here are Hayashi's interviews with outstanding Japanese Steinbeck scholars Kenji Inoue and Shigeharu Yano for the new perspectives they offer on Steinbeck.

StQ 16, iii–iv contains the two most substantial essays this year in John Ditsky's "'Some Sense of Mission': Steinbeck's *The Short Reign of Pippin IV* Reconsidered" (pp. 79–89) and Robert E. Morsberger's "*Cannery Row* Revisited" (pp. 89–95). While careful not to claim too much for *Pippin IV*, Ditsky offers a defense of the novel in the form of an analysis of Pippin's humanity "premised on clear acknowledgement and acceptance of moral flaw"—a characteristic in Pippin prefiguring Ethan Allen Hawley in *The Winter of Our Discontent*. Unlike earlier Steinbeck creations, according to Ditsky, Pippin is not "a Christ-figure in any sacrificial sense; instead, the ability of the prophet to contribute to continuing development is being stressed." Ditsky's ultimate stress in the essay is upon the novel's significance "as a sign of the development of Steinbeck's thinking during his later years." In "*Cannery Row* Revisited," Morsberger provides background information and reviews David Ward's 1982 screen version that merged *Cannery Row* and *Sweet Thursday*. Contrary to most critics and the general public, Morsberger finds this to be "one of the better American films of recent years" and blames the film's critics for a general dislike of Steinbeck. A third essay in this number of *StQ*, "The Facts Behind John Steinbeck's 'The Lonesome Vigilante'" (pp. 70–79) by James Delgado, provides a summary of actual events of a 1933 lynching in San Jose, California that Steinbeck used as material for his story. In "Steinbeck Criticism in Japan: 1980–81" (pp. 96–104), Kiyoshi Nakayama summarizes the most significant of the two books and forty articles to appear on Steinbeck in Japan during the 1980–81 year, evaluating with an impressive critical eye and giving overwhelming evidence of the Japanese affinity for Steinbeck's fiction and the increasing sophistication of their approach to American literature. Along the same lines, Tetsumaro Hayashi continues his interview series here with Yasuo Hashiguchi, President of the Kyushu American Literature Society and of the Steinbeck Society of Japan (pp. 104–7). In a note appearing outside of *StQ* this year, "Steinbeck's *The Grapes of Wrath*" (*Expl* 41,iv:49–51), Joyce Compton Brown argues that "the use of parallels between the turtle and the Okies, particularly Casy, is far more subtle and more crucial to the novel than has been suggested." Other than noting that the eggs Ruthie finds in the novel are probably turtle eggs, Brown offers little new insight into the novel, though her suggestion that Casy's "habit of copulating after each service with one of the girls he has 'saved' might be suggestive of the turtle's custom of preceding copulation with a courtship ritual" might serve well to enliven a Steinbeck seminar.

ii. Expatriates and Emigres

a. **Anaïs Nin and Henry Miller.** Richard R. Centing's *Seahorse: The Anaïs Nin/Henry Miller Journal* continues to provide important bibliographic information and miscellany concerning these two writers, with the strong focus on Nin. *Seahorse* 2:i offers "Autobiography as Seduction," a selection from Nancy Scholar's monograph on Nin (Twayne, 1984). According to Scholar, Nin "invites and excites her readers with intimate suggestions, and then vanishes behind her mask. While offering us 'enticing stories of seductions, abductions and deductions,' she keeps the facts and feelings of her life carefully hidden." In this brief selection, Scholar documents her thesis persuasively with examples from and references to the *Diary* (*Seahorse* 2,i:1–4). Also in this number is another Kenneth Merrill interview, this time with Katy Kadell (pp. 4–9), as much a personal reminiscence on Merrill's part as informative interview. Of more practical value in this number in Centing's "Writings about Anaïs Nin: An Eleventh Supplement to Rose Marie Cutting's *Anaïs Nin: A Reference Guide*" (pp. 10–12). *Seahorse* 2:iii continues Barbara Kraft's *Lux Aeterna Anaïs: A Memoir* (in excerpt form) from *Seahorse* 2:ii, a dramatically written ("the sun sat on the horizon like a blazing temple") remembering of Nin's friendship and influence during the last period of Nin's life (pp. 1–7). Also continued in numbers two and three of the Journal are Centing's twelfth and thirteenth supplements to *Anaïs Nin: A Reference Guide.* Supplementing *Seahorse* in 1983 is a new publication, *Anaïs: An International Journal,* containing a rich miscellany of Nin material, from personal reminiscence to brief critical analysis and bibliography. Finally this year Nin admirers are presented with *The Early Diary of Anaïs Nin (1923–1927)* Volume III, with a preface by Joaquin Nin–Culmell (Harcourt). Nin entitled this segment of her diary *Journal d'une Epouse,* beginning it immediately after her marriage to Hugh Guiler and their move to Paris. In this beautifully produced volume, the reader experiences Nin coming to terms with herself as wife, housewife, blossoming artist and resident of a Paris she at first dislikes and distrusts.

In "Miller on Lawrence" (*ConL* 24:406–10), Charles Rossman offers a review-essay evaluating Henry Miller's *The World of Lawrence: A Passionate Appreciation.* Rossman provides a few paragraphs of background concerning the study and declares it to be "a major document in the education of Henry Miller's tastes and enthusiasms." The book, however, he finds of little significance to Lawrence scholarship, containing "moments of genuine insight" and "passages of searing intensity" but marred by being redundant, poorly organized, and "alternatingly worshipful . . . and vituperative." From the study, Rossman extracts a controlling myth: "The world that Lawrence (and Miller) was born to and matured in was (and remains) deathly, exhausted, and sterile. The artists of the time, particularly Proust, Joyce, and Pound, reek with its decadence. But Lawrence is the *savior*, the *redeemer* . . . who might rescue those who want to live from the world of death." Rossman's analysis does a fine job of explaining why Miller had so much difficulty with this work and why it remained so long out of print.

b. **Vladimir Nabokov.** It sometimes seems rather anomalous to include Nabokov in this section so dominated by so-called proletarian and southern writers, because in Nabokov we enter the realm of the postmodern, of reflexivity and signifiers in abundance. Patrick O'Donnell sets the tone for Nabokov criticism this year when he confesses in "Watermark: Writing the Self in Nabokov's *Pale Fire*" (*ArQ* 39: 381–405) that "the effort may seem Kinbotean. . . ." Nabokov seems to insist, in fact, that our efforts are Kinbotean. O'Donnell begins his quest for Nabokov by attempting to differentiate between "a concept of the self-critical" and the "mere self-conscious" as a means of understanding reflexivity in Nabokov's work. Self-critical fiction, O'Donnell points out, is "radically reflexive" and "more specifically raises questions about its own language, the substance and vehicle of its expression," questionings that "decompose the language by which they are articulated through the disruptions and ironies they generate." The subject of this novel, says O'Donnell, is "the subject, Kinbote, seen watermarking the text with the sign of his own identity," a thought that does not appear here for the first time but which is eloquently stated and leads to this critic's declaration that "Nabokov thus creates in *Pale Fire* the visible effect of 'intertextuality'. . . ." Amidst the deconstructionist verbiage, no one has yet put more eloquently the subject of this "game of self-creation": "Its 'subject' is the blazoning of the self into time and narrative. . . ." Less eloquent and perhaps more brilliantly Kinbotean is Annapaola Cancogni's " 'My Sister, Do You Still Recall?': Chateaubriand/Nabokov" (*CL* 35, ii:140–66). Nabokov's *Ada*, Cancogni declares, "is a novel's novel in the most literal sense of the expression." She goes on to examine the "intertextual frequencies of the novel, its literary ghosts," focusing on the "intricate dialogue" between *Ada* and the works of Chateaubriand and elucidating at length for us the figures of parody, pastiche, plagiarism, translation, and citation as they impinge upon this novel. This lengthy and weighty essay illuminates with some brilliance the particles of *Atala, René, Les Adventures du dernier Abencérage*, and *Mémoires d'outre-tombe* afloat in *Ada*, but the brilliance comes with much sound and fury and the signified, while certainly not nothing, is ore mined at considerable cost.

Nabokov as the "quintessential modernist" is the subject of Walter Cohen's "The Making of Nabokov's Fiction" (*TCL* 29:333–50). Noting what he considers the unfortunate narrowness of most Nabokov criticism, Cohen examines the historical and social context of Nabokov's fiction, his debt to Russian formalism, and the influence and importance of both Russia and America in his fiction. Cohen devotes most of his critical attention here to *Lolita*, concluding that this novel "constitutes a pessimistic vision of the human possibilities offered by the industrial capitalist West in general, and its most dynamic nation-state in particular." More ambitious than Cohen is Susan Strehle, whose "Actualism: Pynchon's Debt to Nabokov" (*ConL* 24: 30–50) is designed to provide us with a new and more useful handle for Nabokov's and Pynchon's fiction. "Actualism" Strehle defines as a "new mimetic mode" that "arises in response to the need for means to reflect the contingent world of the late twentieth century; it develops in postmodern fiction because reality has changed." The term itself Strehle derives from Heisenberg, whose Uncertainty Principle underlies her approach and, according to Strehle, postmodern fiction. In the course of her essay, Strehle examines Nabokov's Cornell lectures, supposing Pynchon's exposure to and interest in both the lectures and Nabokov's fiction, and goes on to explore Pynchon's debt to the master actualist, particularly in *V*.

The outstanding Nabokov study this year is Lucy Maddox's *Nabokov's Novels in English* (Georgia), a cogent reading that marks no radical departure in Nabokov criticism but provides thoughtful and thorough examinations of the major novels. "The real conflict in a Nabokov novel," Maddox declares, "can be said to take place between the narrator and his narrative, and if there is a winner, it is the narrative." Maddox sees Nabokov's characters as "consistently frustrated by the sense of living on the edge of meaning, of being part of a complicated pattern that they get only glimpses of but that must surely make wonderful sense to someone, somewhere." The study begins with *Pale Fire*, which Maddox places "squarely in the center" among Nabokov's novels both thematically and structurally, an approach that allows her to use *Pale Fire* as a touchstone throughout the study, as "the book to which the others point, in anticipation or in retrospect."

iii. Southerners

a. **Robert Penn Warren—Agrarians and Others.** The major event in Warren criticism this year is *Robert Penn Warren's "Brother to Dragons": A Discussion,* edited by James A. Grimshaw, Jr., (LSU). Grimshaw brings together twenty-six pieces on *Brother to Dragons,* including a number of familiar commentaries on the 1953 edition by such figures as Cleanth Brooks and Victor Strandberg, as well as outstanding reviews of that edition by writers such as Randall Jarrell, Robert Lowell, Harold Bloom, and William Van O'Connor. To these reprints, Grimshaw adds a half-dozen original essays and appendix material, and it is this previously unpublished material (derived to a large extent from the 1979 MLA session on *Brother to Dragons*) that I will consider here, beginning with C. Hugh Holman's "Original Sin on the Dark and Bloody Ground" (pp. 193–99). Holman admits the historical inaccuracies in *Brother to Dragons* pointed out by Boynton Merrill, Jr., and then goes on to argue incisively that such discrepancies are irrelevant because Warren is interested in "what is eternal not temporal." According to Holman, "Questions of accuracy pale to nothingness before such a purpose, for the author intends his readers to grieve on universal bones." In *"Brother to Dragons* and the Craft of Revision" (pp. 200–10), Victor Strandberg takes advantage of his access to the Warren manuscripts at Yale to compare published and unpublished versions of the poem, noting Warren's early interest in a ballad version among other points. Directing attention to revisions in diction in the different versions, Strandberg suggests that "by far the greater number had the effect of elevating the tone of the poem." He also notes a "softening of expletives" and the influence of "new American Poetry" in the 1953 version's greater freedom from the blank verse tradition as compared to the *Kenyon Review* typescript. After giving evidence of Allen Tate's influence upon the *Kenyon Review* typescript, Strandberg concludes that Warren reshaped the poem "toward an even higher standard of excellence" in the long process of revision leading to the 1979 edition. In contrast to this last view, in *"Brother to Dragons* or *Brother to Dragons, A New Version?* A Case for the 1953 Edition"

(pp. 211–25) Richard N. Chrisman argues for the 1953 edition for
both historical and aesthetic reasons. Chrisman finds the changes in
the 1979 edition to be "in large part superficial" and contends that
Warren's deletions of philosophical reflections, his truncation of the
character of Laetitia, his revisions for the ostensible purpose of
clarity, and his "reshaping of individual lines" all had deleterious
effects on the poem and were prompted by Warren's unfortunate
desire to "dramatize" the poem. In the longest and perhaps least
effective of the original essays collected here, "Versions of History
and *Brother to Dragons*" (pp. 226–43), Margaret Mills Harper disagrees with Chrisman. After a long windup discussion of the Lewis
axe-murder upon which Warren based the poem, Harper declares
that the verse in the 1979 version "has been made simpler and more
direct, and is much more rhythmically engaging." In contrast to
Chrisman, she finds that Warren's experience with the play version
of the poem indirectly improved the 1979 edition. Harper documents
historical facts in the 1979 edition that replace the "half-truths and
little inaccuracies" of the 1953 version with "certainties, either of
fact or fiction," and she professes doubt about Warren's assertion that
his revision was not influenced by Boynton Merrill's work.

In "The Concept of the Historical Self in *Brother to Dragons*"
(pp. 244–49), Lewis P. Simpson very briefly records his belief that in
the 1979 edition "a subtle reduction . . . in [Warren's] allowance for
. . . 'hope' " has taken place. Simpson skims the evolving concept of
self in Western civilization for our edification and concludes that
"underlying the conception of *Brother to Dragons* . . . is a movement
toward a reconcilation of the vision of America as the land of hope
. . . and the recognition of hope's illusory nature." The poem, Simpson
declares, is "primarily a struggle for the meaning of the American
self." In a final essay here, one especially valuable for its illumination
of the role of the father in the poem, " 'Doom Is Always Domestic':
Familial Betrayal in *Brother to Dragons*" (pp. 250–62), Richard G.
Law reads the poem as a domestic tragedy built around the "harsh
paradigm of double betrayal." The "familial clawing" epitomizes
relations between father and son, mother and child, in which birth is
a kind of betrayal and "each character in the work wears two masks:
the mask of victim and the mask of betrayer." An excellent discussion
of the character of the father, who "is an emblem" of the "*fact* of the

past." Appendixes to this volume include Boynton Merrill's discussion of the murder upon which the poem is based (pp. 283–93), Merrill's genealogical chart for the Jefferson family (p. 294), Warren's "Foreword to *Brother to Dragons: A Play in Two Acts*" (pp. 295–300), and a Selected Bibliography.

Allen Tate is the subject of a book-length study this year, Robert S. Dupree's *Allen Tate and the Augustinian Imagination: A Study of the Poetry* (LSU). Because the work is, as the title indicates, only indirectly concerned with Tate's fiction, it bears only passing mention here for its approach to Tate's *The Fathers* as a "reflection on history," and Dupree's declaration that the novel "comes closest to answering Tate's urgent questions about the proper kind of action to take in a period of crisis." Dupree labels Tate, like his character Lacy Buchan in *The Fathers*, "skeptical of the things of the world." This novel also comes in for attention in Nicholas Phillips's "A Note on Allen Tate's *The Fathers*" (*AN&Q* 21,v-vi:74–75), in which Phillips points out that "A heretofore unrecognized anachronism in Allen Tate's novel *The Fathers* is a passage he quotes from the 1928 version of the Protestant Episcopal *Book of Common Prayer* for a prayer service that took place during the Civil War." According to Phillips, that particular prayer was added to the *Book of Common Prayer* in 1928 and wasn't included in the 1789 version found in the novel. We are reminded of another of the Agrarians this year in Lewis P. Simpson's "Andrew Lytle: Artist and Critic" (*SoR* 19:833–35), the text of Simpson's tribute to Lytle on the occasion of a dinner honoring Lytle's eightieth birthday. Simpson lauds Lytle as a "man of letters" and goes on to suggest the splendid quality and value of Lytle's critical writings in spite of Lytle's own reservations about them.

Conrad Aiken serves as an "Other" here this year, brought to our attention chiefly by a new biography, *Lorelei Two: My Life with Conrad Aiken* (Georgia) by Clarissa M. Lorenz. Lorenz, Aiken's second wife, gives us the inside scoop, as much concerning her own life as Aiken's. This story of initial poet-worship and infatuation evolving quickly into jealousy and neurotic obsession will make interesting reading for Aiken fans. Just as last year's *Conrad Aiken: A Bibliography (1902–1978)*, by F. W. and F. C. Bonnell (Huntington Library) reminded us of the diversity and depth of Aiken's art and audience, Lorenz's book adds to the developing picture of Aiken's personal and artistic complexity. In "Aiken, Agee, and Sandburg: a Memoir" (*VQR* 59:299–315), Bernard C. Schoenfeld pays a warm tribute to Aiken, the young Schoenfeld's tutor at Harvard.

b. **Eudora Welty.**   Welty is again a primary focus of serious critical attention this year, with Albert J. Devlin's *Eudora Welty's Chronicle: A Story of Mississippi Life* (Miss.) the most auspicious undertaking. In attempting to "define the structure of her historical imagination," Devlin embarks here upon what he terms a study of "the substantial, weighty, unitary quality of Welty's extended reflection upon her southern homeplace." Devlin's comprehensive approach can best be summed up in his statement that the "entire history of Mississippi, reaching from territorial days in the early nineteenth century until the present, resounds throughout Welty's fiction, but this constant presence has scarcely, if at all, been recognized by her many diligent readers." In Chapter One, Devlin focuses on *A Curtain of Green* and *The Robber Bridegroom*, introducing as he does so his view of Welty's "profound historical imagination." "The Whistle" Devlin defines as "a subtle critique of regional planning," while "Death of a Traveling Salesman" he contends in a somewhat "slant" reading "would seem to posit a more radical pastoralism than the Agrarians usually sanctioned." In *Bridegroom*, Devlin recognizes the process of civilization a lá Turner with a twist. Chapter Two discusses *The Wide Net* and Welty's use of historical resources for "A Still Moment" and "First Love" with these stories' depictions of Aaron Burr, John James Audubon, Lorenzo Dow, and the bandit James Murrell. The chapter provides an excellent index to what Devlin refers to as Welty's "latent historiographical attitude that shifts the ground from a consideration of the content of history to its inherent structure and value." In the third chapter of this volume, Devlin examines Welty's first novel, *Delta Wedding*, with its use of plantation as "scene and mythos." This discussion is replete with historiographical background, with appearances by such figures as George Tucker, William Gilmore Simms, Harriet Beecher Stowe, and John Crowe Ransom. In the remaining chapters, Devlin carries his historiographical approach through discussions of *The Golden Apples*, *The Optimist's Daughter*, and *Losing Battles*. Devlin's study as a whole makes an outstanding contribution to our understanding of Welty's sense of place and history and of the continuity of such influence throughout her work.

When he is not reminding us of what he has just told us or is about to tell us, he writes with admirable skill and insight.

Peggy Whitman Prenshaw's *Eudora Welty: Thirteen Essays* (Miss.) is a paring-down of the twenty-seven essays published in 1979 as *Eudora Welty: Critical Essays*. Prenshaw asserts that her guide in this selection has been "to select essays that fairly represent the breadth of subject and approach that marked the earlier volume." The list of contributors who reappear here attests to the value of this continuation: Chester E. Eisinger, Albert J. Devlin, Warren French, Robert B. Heilman, Seymour L. Gross, Michael Kreyling, Ruth M. Vande Kieft, among others.

Two excellent articles appearing in the same issue of *Southern Review* examine Welty's "The Wide Net" and "June Recital." In "*The Aeneid* of the Natchez Trace: Epic Structure in Eudora Welty's 'The Wide Net'" (*SoR* 19:511–18), Nancy Anne Cluck explores "Welty's consistent play on the epic genre" in this story, particularly the "integration of mythical and comic elements." In an admirably well presented essay, Cluck notes the story's "epic catalog of warriors"; the "Epic spatial dimensions" suggestive of a "transcendent world as well as an underworld"; the allusions to such Classical, Christian, and folk epic elements as Carthage, Beulah, and William Wallace; the presence of a Virgil in Virgil Thomas; suggestions of Classical and Christian gods in old Doc; birds as signals of divine guidance; and Wallace's transformation within the river. Although not everything here is new to Welty criticism, and although Cluck gratuitously points out that "a short story cannot achieve the scope required by the epic," this is a solid contribution. Also well written and valuable is Daniele Pitavy–Souques's "Watchers and Watching: Point of View in Welty's 'June Recital'" (*SoR* 19:483–509). Translated by Margaret Tomarchio, this essay asserts that "June Recital" represents "a unique experience in the work of Eudora Welty," and goes on to discuss the visions of Loch and Cassie as "symbols of the double vision of the artist and as generators of that vision." For Loch peering through his telescope and hanging from the tree, "the world is a stage on which puppets gesticulate in a meaningless [and a sensuous] performance." For Cassie, remembering and passing moral judgment, the world is "an arena, strangely empty, which enables *regards* to fight deadly battles." In *regard*, the French word that is, Pitavy-Souques wants to suggest both perception and critical judgment, "a judgment which is both evaluative and selective." The essay provides a nice regard for the complexity and uniqueness of Welty's point of view. A less significant essay is Carol S. Manning's "Little Girls and Sidewalks: Glasgow and Welty on Childhood's Promise" (*SoQ* 21,iii:67–76). Manning discusses the "age of self-discovery" for the young girls Jenny in *The Sheltered Life* by Glasgow and Eudora Alice in Welty's "The Little Store" and Josie in Welty's "The Winds." For each of the prepubescent girls, adventure into the world represents a search for freedom "that is also a grasping for knowledge." Manning makes a significant distinction between the young girls in Glasgow's novel and Welty's stories: "Like Jenny Blair, Josie soaks up experience, but unlike Jenny, she grows from all her observations."

A note worth noting is Nancy B. Sederberg's "Welty's 'The Death of a Traveling Salesman'" (*Expl* 42,i:52–54), in which Sederberg claims that the name of R. J. Bowman in this story "evokes meanings beyond those suggested either by Welty herself or prior critics." The meanings evoked, according to Sederberg, are those alluding to "another ancient archer—Cupid," a reference particularly apt because "Bowman's troubles are . . . of the heart"; and to the act of bowing. Bowman bows before the woman in the story as before "Uroboros or archetypal Great Mothers," an act that "represents a positive acceptance of life-giving sources and an act of faith." The *Eudora Welty Newsletter* this year contains the usual blurbs and miscellany in addition to some valuable bibliographic work, including "Welty's Current Reception in Britain: A Checklist of Reviews" by Mary Hughes Brookhart (7,ii:1–5) and two checklists by W. U. McDonald, Jr.: "Works by Welty: A Continuing Checklist" (p. 8) and "A Checklist of Welty Scholarship, 1982–83" (7,ii:10–15). Another issue (*EuWN* 7,i) offers O. B. Emerson's "Reviews of *Collected Stories: A Primary Checklist*" (pp. 4–6) and McDonald's "A Checklist of Revisions in Collected Welty Stories: Phase I" (pp. 6–10) and "Works by Welty: A Continuing Checklist" (pp. 11–12), listing English reprints of Welty's works in the last two years.

c. **Flannery O'Connor, Katherine Anne Porter, Carson McCullers.** Flannery O'Connor attracted attention from several critics this year. In "From Sermon to Parable: Four Conversion Stories by Flannery O'Connor" (*AL* 55:55–71), A. R. Coulthard points out that despite

O'Connor's declaration that "all good stories are about conversion, about a character's changing," many of O'Connor's stories "leave the question of salvation unanswered." Coulthard considers four stories that do not leave the question unanswered. In "A Temple of the Holy Ghost," "The Artificial Nigger," "Revelation," and "Parker's Black," according to this critic, O'Connor "subjected herself not only to the challenge of making grace believable but to depicting its immediate effect on her protagonists." The results Coulthard finds uneven. "Temple," Coulthard says, "begins as a satire with moral undertones and degenerates into a morality play," and the collision between O'Connor's dramatic and moral senses dooms the story to failure. "The Artificial Nigger" is a better story but also ultimately a failure because it does not succeed in "dramatizing conversion." The "delightful comedy" of this story turns to "ponderous melodrama." "Revelation" Coulthard finds a still better story because of its interweaving of "the comic and the serious throughout" and because of its "profound dramatization of redemption" in the character of Ruby Turpin. Finally, Coulthard cannot find enough good things to say about "Parker's Black," the best of the four according to Coulthard and perhaps the best of O'Connor's stories. The greatness of "Revelation" and "Parker's Black," says Coulthard, belies the commonly held belief that O'Connor developed little as a writer during the later stages of her career. The strength of Coulthard's essay lies in the light it sheds not only on these four stories but on such more problematic stories as "Good Country People."

In a second essay to appear this year, "Flannery O'Connor's Backtracking Muse" (*SAF* 11:247–53), Coulthard asserts that O'Connor did repeat herself with a frequency that seems inconsistent with her otherwise fertile imagination. Coulthard supports this assertion with a somewhat tedious listing of similar persons, places, and themes in O'Connor's work. Beside the previously noted essay, this effort by Coulthard seems a bit pointless. Somewhat more to the point is William J. Scheick's "Flannery O'Connor's 'A Good Man is Hard to Find' and G. K. Chesterton's *Manalive* (*SAF* 11:241–45), though still not a particularly indispensable piece. Scheick goes source/influence hunting and finds that Chesterton's *Manalive* "figured in the germinal stages of 'A Good Man is Hard to Find.'" The argument seems stretched when Scheick asserts that O'Connor's story "appears to be in part a deliberate revision of Chesterton's novel." He bases his argu-

ment primarily upon resemblances between Chesterton's Innocent
Smith and O'Connor's Misfit, but the conclusion is undercut both by
the usual possibilities of coincidence and by his own confession that
differences between the two works and authors are "striking." Of considerably more interest is M. A. Klug's "Flannery O'Connor and the
Manichaean Spirit of Modernism" (*SHR* 17:303–14), in which Klug
declares that O'Connor "attacks the central assumptions of literary
modernism as vigorously as those of our social and economic life and
for the same reason." That reason is the predisposition of the modern
consciousness to separate spirit and matter, as O'Connor herself de-
clared. Focusing upon O'Connor's opposition to the modern notion
of the alienated artist and the modernist idea of the fabrication of
one's "own essential self," Klug traces O'Connor's attack on this modernist version of the "romantic artist of the self" in *Wise Blood* and
The Violent Bear It Away, finding Hazel Motes and Tarwater in
these two works "possessed by the same Manichaean predisposition
as the recurrent spiritual hero of our fiction." On a different track is
Arthur F. Kinney's "In Search of Flannery O'Connor" (*VQR* 26:
272–88), a leisurely account of Kinney's visit to Milledgeville to catalog the library O'Connor left behind and to record in eloquent detail
the tone and texture of O'Connor country.

A work that arrived too late for review last year but deserving
mention this year is Joan Givner's outstanding biography, *Katherine
Anne Porter: A Life* (Simon and Schuster). Givner's impressive research and loving attention to sharp detail give us the Porter behind
the figure Katherine Anne Porter wanted her public to know. The
author follows Callie Porter from a log house in Texas to the world
of international culture, showing in absorbing detail how an artist is
molded by incident and environment and, in Porter's case especially,
by self-willed platonic conception. Since this is not the place for a
full-blown book review, suffice it to say that Givner's is one of the
finest biographies to come along in a while, ranking this year with
Gilbert Harrison's work on Thornton Wilder and surpassing in style
and eloquence, though not in thoroughness and usefulness, Benson's
Steinbeck biography. Porter is also the subject of Mitzi Berger Hamovitch's "Today and Yesterday: Letters from Katherine Anne Porter"
(*CentR* 27:278–87). In these few pages, Hamovitch recounts her
exchanges of letters with Porter during six months of 1975, when
Hamovitch was editing *The Hound & Horn Letters* for the Univer-

sity of Georgia Press. Beginning with Porter's letter to R. P. Blackmur of *Hound & Horn* offering "Flowering Judas" to that journal, and Bernard Bandler's enthusiastic response accepting the story, the article is most interesting for Porter's denial of her "view of life as black," and for her response to a batch of Pound letters sent her by Hamovitch, letters which, according to Porter, constituted "a heavy fall of brickbats" for one who had long admired and defended Pound.

The signal critical work on Porter this year is undoubtedly Jane Krause DeMouy's *Katherine Anne Porter's Women: The Eye of Her Fiction* (Texas). Operating under the influences of Freud and Jung, DeMouy does a fine job of locating thematic threads that unify Porter's work, finding that from the first stories to *Ship of Fools*, a conflict operates in Porter's women: "a desire, on the one hand, for the independence and freedom to pursue art or principle regardless of social convention and, on the other, a desire for the love and security inherent in the traditional roles of wife and mother." DeMouy further boils this conflict down to a "conflict in female identity," and she examines in all of Porter's major works the impossibility of full integration or individuation for woman. After very slight readings of the early stories—"María Concepción," "The Martyr," "Virgin Violeta," "He," "Magic," and "Rope"—in which she spotlights the feminine conflict especially well in "He," DeMouy moves into the territory that interests her the most: the psychological battle of Granny Weatherall and the major stories such as "Flowering Judas." Although references to Emily Dickinson's poetry add little to the reading, DeMouy provides a valuable guide to "The Jilting of Granny Weatherall" by focusing on the protagonist's three deaths: her jilting by the faithless lover, with the ensuing loss of faith; the loss of her matriarchical role as her children grow independent; and her actual death, at which point "she has once more been betrayed into accepting mortality." Following out her thesis, DeMouy finds Laura in "Flowering Judas" to be "her own worst enemy," and she pronounces *Ship of Fools* less than a complete success, declaring of Porter: "Her eye is on the microcosm but her mind is on the macrocosm. . . . she cannot decide whether she is writing short fiction or a novel." DeMouy lays out her tools in her introduction, explaining (overexplaining perhaps) the mythical double figure of the "Great Mother and Terrible Mother" and the resulting "separation of the parts of the feminine character." Though this study may be slightly reductionist in its narrow focus, it is nonetheless an excellent addition to Porter criticism.

Women's studies gets another boost this year from Linda Huf's *A Portrait of the Artist as a Young Woman: The Writer as Heroine in American Fiction* (Ungar). Noting that "unlike men, women have only rarely written artist novels: that is, autobiographical novels depicting their struggles to become creative artists," Huf examines half a dozen women who have. Huf points out to begin with that the only book-length general study of the artist novel thus far is Maurice Beebe's *Ivory Towers and Sacred Founts*, a work she criticizes for its "sleight of hand which removes the creative heroine from sight," a criticism she also reserves for Joseph Campbell's *The Hero with a Thousand Faces*. The woman as artist in fiction is torn, says Huf, "not only between life and art [as are men] but, more specifically, between her role as a woman demanding selfless devotion to others, and her aspirations as an artist, requiring exclusive commitment to work." The woman as artist heroine "must choose between her sexuality and her profession, between her womanhood and her work." In her chapter on Carson McCullers's *The Heart Is a Lonely Hunter* (pp. 105–23), Huf admits that the novel does not fit her thesis precisely, but by focusing on the character of Mick Kelly as the author's portrait of the artist as a young girl, Huf gives us a sensitive and revisionist reading of the novel that contradicts the conventional (male) point of view. In contrast to the accepted view that Mick does the proper thing in giving up her farfetched dreams of becoming a famous composer to support her family in a dimestore, Huf sees Mick's acceptance of the job as her defeat as an artist. "Mick's story," Huf contends, "is the story of her increasing betrayal of art for heart's sake."

d. **Thomas Wolfe.**   Thomas Wolfe merits several book-length works this year, two of which originate with the familiar source of Richard S. Kennedy. In *Thomas Wolfe: A Harvard Perspective* (Croissant & Co.), Kennedy brings together a "collection of essays and presentations" as he calls it, stemming from the two-day meeting (May 7–8, 1982) of the Thomas Wolfe Society at Harvard. As should be expected, the collection has a definite in-house quality, beginning with Kennedy's chatty review-of-the-minutes introduction and ending with Paul Gitlin's brief talk on the "Problems and Policies of Administering the Estate of Thomas Wolfe" (pp. 81–86) and Kennedy's review of an exhibition of Wolfe material entitled "Editorial Influence and Authorial Intention: A Manuscript Exhibition" (pp. 87–108). As should also be expected, Kennedy takes advantage of the opportunity to enlarge upon his refutation of John Halberstadt's charges regarding Wolfe and Wolfe's editor Edward Aswell. Also to be included in the casual category here is John L. Idol, Jr.'s "Thomas Wolfe Attends a Performance of Alexander Calder's Circus" (pp. 43–52), which documents Wolfe's dismay upon attending Calder's performance at the apartment of Aline Bernstein, Wolfe's mistress. Wolfe supporters often tend to be somewhat defensive, and this is the dominant tone of the three serious critical essays in this volume, a tone suggestive of the converted preaching to the converted. Foremost among the three is John Hagan's "Thomas Wolfe's *Of Time And The River*: The Quest for Transcendence" (pp. 3–20). Hagan nods immediately to the structural difficulties in this novel and then sets out to argue that the book is more tightly structured than we have commonly been led to believe and that this structure hinges upon the theme of the Quest, in this case Eugene Gant's quest "to transcend the limits of mortality." Hagan supports his thesis in a well-argued essay. Less enlightening, though not less persuasive, is Klaus Lanzinger's "Thomas Wolfe's Modern Hero—Goethe's Faust" (pp. 21–30), in which Lanzinger cites Wolfe's reaction to a Vienna performance of the play and the subsequent effect of this experience in Wolfe's fascination with and use of the Faust legend in his fiction. "The Development of Form in Thomas Wolfe's Short Fiction" (pp. 31–42), by James Boyer, sets out to rescue Wolfe from the ubiquitous criticism that he was a "writer of formless autobiography." Boyer attempts to accomplish this task by focusing on Wolfe's short fiction, dividing it into early, middle, and late periods, and documenting Wolfe's increasing interest in and ability with form in the stories. Finally, in the late stories, Boyer claims, Wolfe not only deals in dramatic development but "has become more careful, too, in the use of images" and "is developing characters in conflict" in stories that possess "organic unity." Boyer gives a hint of damning with rather faint praise, however, when he argues that "his later writing shows genuine improvement in his craft."

Richard S. Kennedy is also the editor of *Beyond Love and Loyalty: The Letters of Thomas Wolfe and Elizabeth Nowell* (N.C.), a collection of letters primarily between Wolfe and his agent, friend,

editor, and advisor Elizabeth Nowell. Kennedy's introduction here
reappears following its publication in 1982 as "Thomas Wolfe and
Elizabeth Nowell: A Unique Relationship" (*SAQ* 81:202–13), and
stresses again Nowell's active role in the development of Wolfe's
style, an assertion readily supported by the letters themselves. Adding to the value of this collection is the inclusion here of a previously
unpublished Wolfe story, "No More Rivers," a work that caused
considerable frustration for Wolfe, Maxwell Perkins, and, especially,
Elizabeth Nowell before its appearance here. A second collection of
Wolfe's voluminous letters this year is *My Other Loneliness: Letters
of Thomas Wolfe and Aline Bernstein* (N.C.), edited by Suzanne
Stutman. Billed in the introduction as "the record of a love affair
between two great twentieth-century figures," this collection of nearly
400 pages does, as the editor suggests, "reveal the vast, kaleidoscopic
spectrum of his thoughts and a rich body of creative writing." These
letters also reveal, as Stutman also points out, Wolfe's unrelenting
emotional immaturity and painful egocentricity. Stutman has done a
fine job of editing and has produced a valuable addition to Wolfe
scholarship.

e. Margaret Mitchell, Marjorie Kinnan Rawlings.   Another indis-
putably southern writer to receive substantial attention this year is
Margaret Mitchell, the subject of a fine biography by Anne Edwards,
Road to Tara: The Life of Margaret Mitchell (Ticknor & Fields).
Edwards—novelist, biographer, and Hollywood writer—has produced a very well written and thorough account of the phenomenon
of this one-novel author, illuminating the genesis of both *Gone with
the Wind* and Mitchell herself, from tomboyish child immersed in the
Civil War period to somewhat paranoid best-selling novelist striving
as subtly as possible to keep her name before the world audience.
Edwards balances an obvious fondness and sympathy for her subject
with candor that displays Mitchell in not always favorable light.
While not a momentous contribution to our understanding of major
American fiction, this book goes far toward explaining one of the
most amazing phenomena of American publishing: a novel that continues to sell 100,000 hardback and 250,000 paperback copies a year
more than a half century after its initial appearance. Michell is also
the subject of a book-length piece of revisionism in *Recasting: Gone
with the Wind in American Culture*, edited by Darden Asbury Pyron

(Florida). Pyron admits in his introduction to being piqued by the "gap between popular acclaim and academic disdain" in response to this novel and the major film based on the novel. The argument here is broadly that "the work is worth studying," and the essays gathered in this volume make that fact abundantly clear, whether they implicitly favor or slight the novel's artistic merits. Pyron has, as others are beginning to, the sense to see that a novel that has sold millions of copies worldwide and been translated into twenty-five languages bears looking into for its relations to and influence upon what is accepted as serious fiction. Pyron divides this collection into three parts—"The Critical Setting," "*Gone with the Wind* as Art," and "*Gone with the Wind as* History"—and adds a valuable Bibliographical Essay at the end.

In addition to previously published essays and reviews by such writers as Malcolm Cowley, Henry Steele Commager, Richard Harwell, James Michener, Louis Rubin, Jr., Anne Jones, and Darden Asbury Pyron, the editor has included several original essays that I will focus on here, beginning with Thomas Cripps's "Winds of Change: *Gone with the Wind* and Racism as a National Issue" (pp. 137–52). Cripps, in a well-researched essay, examines the social/ racial impact of, reaction to, and lasting results of the movie based on Mitchell's novel. Cripps makes the point that the "half-formed liberal assumptions" of Mitchell and producer David O. Selznick "anticipated the more sharply focused racial liberalism of World War II," and, noting the mixed reaction by black critics and activists, he points out the positive "shift in black political and aesthetic attitudes" generated by reaction to the movie, including the Oscar awarded actress Hattie McDaniel for her role as Mammy. In "Race, Romance, and the Southern Literary Tradition" (pp. 153–66), Kenneth O'Brien has little good to say about Mitchell's talent and artistry, but O'Brien points out that *Gone with the Wind* differs markedly from the tradition of the Confederate Novel. Admitting to the similarities between Mitchell's work and the southern convention, such as the "incapacity for independent thought" in Mitchell's black characters, O'Brien stresses nonetheless Mitchell's relegation of race and politics to the sidelines while Scarlet O'Hara takes center stage with the myth of southern womanhood and the development of a postwar urban business center foremost in the author's concerns. Richard King, in "The 'Simple Story's' Ideology: *Gone with the Wind* and the

New South Creed" (pp. 167–83), looks at the novel in the context of
the southern Renaissance and the southern "family romance," finding
the novel "a complex, often confused expression of the Southern
cultural tradition in crisis," one which falls between the "monumen-
talist and modernizing" camps and which both conforms to and
challenges the tradition of the family romance. Stronger support for
Mitchell's power as artist comes in this volume from two other voices.
In "The Case of the Cool Reception" (pp. 21–31), Richard Dwyer
champions the "narrative power and unsurpassed readability" of the
novel while attempting to comprehend the overwhelmingly cool response by academics toward *Gone with the Wind*. Dwyer's conclusion
is that it was the novel's popularity that turned the ivory tower
against it, particularly Macmillan's "McDonald's millions of burgers
served" approach to advertising the novel, and that "its popularity
is the *only* criterion by which *Gone with the Wind* is still being
judged."

Attempting a serious critical approach to this novel is Helen Deiss
Irvin in "Gea in Georgia: A Mythic Dimension in *Gone with the
Wind*" (pp. 57–68). Irvin contends that critics have "failed to see
beyond the surface narrative" of the novel and that the "mythic
evocations in *Gone with the Wind* may be one source of the novel's
long-lasting popularity." Irvin dwells on the importance of the Earth
Mother archetype here, with Scarlett O'Hara the "child of the earth"
like Antaeus, child of Gea. In this reading, Scarlett's enduring strength
comes from her relationship with the earth. Given Rhett Butler's explicit comparison of Scarlett to Antaeus, it would be difficult to argue
against Mitchell's interest in this ubiquitous myth, particularly in a
novel written in the wake of the great myth-conscious novelists of
the twenties and thirties. Irvin makes a good case and a good beginning toward serious criticism of *Gone with the Wind*. Finally, in
"From *The Clansman* and *Birth of a Nation* to *Gone with the Wind*:
The Loss of American Innocence" (pp. 123–36), Gerald Wood explores the social appeal of these two pairs of novels and films, their
"power to seize the imagination." In contrasting the two, Wood finds
that "*The Clansman* and *Birth of a Nation* represent a positive, progressive, and moral vision of the world and of American destiny"
[albeit a racist one], while "both versions of *Gone with the Wind*
record the loss of this late Victorian innocence." Both novels are
"domestic melodramas which express popular myths of history," but

Gone with the Wind differs from its predecessor by seeing American history as "a fall from innocence and imagination into experience and reality." In offering perhaps another reason for the latter novel's popularity, Wood asserts that *Gone with the Wind* "offers the past as a refuge from a hopeless present."

Stretching the fabric of our rubric somewhat allows the inclusion of one final quasi-Southerner here: Marjorie Kinnan Rawlings. In *Selected Letters of Marjorie Kinnan Rawlings* (Florida), Gordon E. Bigelow and Laura V. Monti have done a fine job of editing, remaining unobtrusive and providing an effective though minimal preface sketching the outlines of Rawlings's life. The nearly 200 letters included pale in comparison to the lavish outpourings of a Thomas Wolfe, but they display this author's sensitivity, good sense, and above all her determination to be a writer.

iv. Detectives, Westerners and Others

Detective fiction came under scrutiny this year in biography, book-length critical study, and a special number of *Modern Fiction Studies*. Certainly the premier event in this area this year is Diane Johnson's *Dashiell Hammett: A Life* (Random House). A biography of a figure such as Hammett by a novelist of Johnson's talents should be expected to be outstanding, and this one is. Advertised on the dust-jacket as "the definitive biography" of Hammett and "the first and only book on Hammett written with the full cooperation of . . . Lillian Hellman, Hammett's late wife Josephine and his daughters," Johnson's book gets off to a slow start but improves quickly. In the opening pages, Johnson's self-conscious manipulation of point of view makes for rather turgid going, but as she becomes more comfortable with her material the book moves along surely and absorbingly, documenting Hammett's life in precise and often stark detail. Johnson refrains wisely from too much reading between the lines or biographical speculation, allowing Hammett's amazing life to speak for itself with a depth made newly possible by the newly available Hellman material. Here Johnson makes available such indispensable information as the fact that Hammett had himself steamed into delirium as a cure for one of his bouts of gonorrhea. Less gripping is William Marling's *Dashiell Hammett* (TUSAS), which, like most works in this series, will serve as a practical general introduction to Hammett, offering little depth or originality but a good deal of summary with a touch of biography. Marling is content to offer general comments when he moves into the realm of criticism, and he does little with the unifying elements of "certain chivalric conventions" and "motifs of the quest" noted in his Preface; nor does he offer much to "rectify the critical mistreatment of *The Dain Curse*" as he promises to do in the Preface.

In his leadoff essay for the special issue of *MFS* 29:3, Peter Wolfe furnishes in "The Critics Did It: An Essay-Review" (pp. 389–433) a hard-hitting, no-nonsense review of recent criticism on detective fiction. Students of this genre will profit greatly from Wolfe's essay. Raymond Chandler gets some attention in another essay in this issue, Thomas M. Leitch's "From Detective Story to Detective Novel" (pp. 475–84). Leitch begins by pointing out the fact that the detective story is "the most resolutely end-oriented of narrative modes," but that "given the financial pressures of writing . . . it is hardly surprising that authors of detective stories should occasionally seek to postpone that end by turning their short stories into novels." Leitch sets out to discover how a detective writer turns short story into novel, and his answer regarding Chandler is that this author simply takes the most obvious way and builds his detective novel out of several detective stories. Leitch focuses particularly on *The Big Sleep* to support this contention, pointing out that in the process of combining Chandler not only turns stories into novel but that the author also "achieves wider social reference." Leitch's brief study takes him on a trail of clues from Chandler to Agatha Christie and Anthony Berkeley and even into the territory of Henry James and Hemingway, and raising the shadow of Aristotle and *anagnorisis* Leitch concludes that such detective novels "call into question the foreordained revelations which allow us to read them at all."

"Westerners" as a category here has a faintly reductionist ring to it in its suggestion of the darker aspects of regionalism (should we not have a category entitled "Easterners"?), but it is such a useful grab bag for a variety of writers this year that I have decided to retain it. How else to encompass such disparate figures as Sandoz and Saroyan, Mable Dodge Luhan and Sophus K. Winther? And with the addition of "Other," we can consider some even more difficult to categorize authors. Mari Sandoz continues to draw attention in the pages of *Western American Literature* this year, following new editions of *Capital City* (1982) and *Old Jules Country* (1983) by the University of Nebraska Press. Of particular note here is *Old Jules Country*, subtitled *A Selection From Old Jules and Thirty Years of Writing Since the Book was Published*. This edition includes, in addition to the title piece, selections from Sandoz's Great Plains Series and a section of shorter pieces entitled "Miscellany." In the latter category are such essays as "The Lost Sitting Bull" and "The Homestead in Perspective." Melody Graulich's essay "Every Husband's Right: Sex Roles in Mari Sandoz's *Old Jules*" (*WAL* 18:3–20), complements very effectively the Linda Huf volume mentioned above, examining *Old Jules* as a document attesting to "the widespread physical and emotional abuse of pioneer women." Graulich calls the work a "catalogue of male-caused tragedies in women's lives," and she supports this reading persuasively with examples from the work. Graulich concludes that this Sandoz work is particularly valuable because it "explores the power dynamics within the pioneer marriage and undercuts the myth of the heroic frontiersman" and also because it "reveals the difficulties of writing about women while aspiring to male freedom." Sandoz's style is of greatest interest to Helen Stauffer in "Narrative Voice in Sandoz's *Crazy Horse*" (*WAL* 18:223–37), a solid article demonstrating the way in which Sandoz "developed an impeccable language form, carefully integrated with the story material" to create the narrative voice of *Crazy Horse*. Stauffer is at pains to demonstrate Sandoz's reliance upon historical and published material and her transmutation of that material into a unique creation clearly anticipating Truman Capote's "non-fiction novel."

A transplanted Easterner's idealization of Taos and the Southwest is the center of interest in Lois P. Rudnick's "Mabel Dodge Luhan and the Myth of the Southwest" (*SWR* 68:205–21). Rudnick examines Luhan's role in "promoting the utopian myth of the Southwest as a garden of Eden," underscoring Luhan's subsuming of the American Myth into a new myth which placed Taos at the "beating heart of the universe." Rudnick catalogs the artists whom Luhan attracted to her colony at Taos and makes a plea for Luhan's *Winter in Taos* (1935) as a "much neglected work that should become a classic of regional literature." One bothersome fact of this essay is that it never really answers D. H. Lawrence's feeling that Luhan's vision constituted a kind of ethnic colonialism or, as Rudnick puts it, "a particularly American form of corruption." A far different western writer is the subject of a Western Writers Series monograph, *Sophus K. Winther* (*WWS* 60) by Barbara Howard Meldrum. Meldrum provides the usual brief biographical introduction to Winther, which turns out to be the most interesting portion of the monograph. Meldrum declares that "for all of Winther's hardcore naturalism, his agnosticism and practical realism, he is a romantic at heart." She then proceeds to devote much of the monograph to summary and extremely brief critical commentary on Winther's Grimsen trilogy: *Take All to Nebraska* (1936), *Mortgage Your Heart* (1937), and *This Passion Never Dies* (1938). Comparing Winther's novels to the fiction of Rolvaag and Sandoz, in contrast to Cather's Nebraska writing, Meldrum declares, "Like Fisher, Rolvaag, and Sandoz, Winther realistically reveals the harsh environment and the unending struggles of individuals seeking to survive, to endure, and to make of their lives something meaningful." Meldrum also summarizes and comments in passing upon Winther's final novel, *Beyond the Garden Gate* (1946) noting the author's interest here in the "cosmic trap" of existence.

A small flurry of interest in William Saroyan continues to build following his death, with two more book-length works on Saroyan appearing this year along with another posthumous collection of his prose. In *William Saroyan* (Harcourt), Aram Saroyan follows up last year's *Last Rites: The Death of William Saroyan* with a biography of his father. The picture Aram Saroyan gives us here, underscored by a pervasive sense of distance between father and son, is again one of genius lapsing quickly into a kind of despair, a quality Saroyan traces to what he terms his father's "psychic freeze" when at age three William Saroyan was placed in an orphanage following the death of his father. This is another discussion of a strange life made stranger by the son's unrelenting third-person treatment of the father, but one that offers genuine insights into William Saroyan's mind, as in Aram Saroyan's explanation of the incredible speed at which his father wrote and lived as "a delight in accelerated physical *mobility* in general," a delight that might well have stemmed from the childhood "immobilization of his deeper reality." Critical evaluation and revision of the critical consensus is the aim of David Stephen Calonne's *William Saroyan: My Real Work Is Being* (N.C.). Dickran Kouymjian sets the tone in his admiring foreword, claiming that "Reviewers too often failed to understand both the formal structure of his work, especially the plays, and their wondrous nature." As Kouymjian makes clear, Calonne sets out to rectify this oversight, and Calonne does a pretty good job of it, responding energetically to the "outrageous" charge that Saroyan "was a simple-minded, sentimental romantic whose naive optimism did not reflect the terrible realities of the age." That Saroyan was deeply aware of and dealt with such terrible realities in both fiction and drama Calonne makes abundantly clear as he leads us through the early stories, the dramas, and the novels, tracing Saroyan's search through art "toward health, toward reconciliation, toward psychic regeneration." One discordant note here is Calonne's obsessive attempts to link Saroyan to major figures, a desire that leads to almost incessant dropping of such names as Whitman, Beckett, Henry Miller, Kerouac, even John Donne and Rilke. Nonetheless, this study is a good indicator of possibilities for serious consideration once again for Saroyan. Unfortunately, the publication of William Saroyan's *Births* (Creative Arts) will do little to enhance the writer's reputation. This rambling series of reflections has the expected moments of Saroyan brilliance but also suffers lapses into banality and incoherence.

Under "Others" here I have chosen to include authors who usually merit such epithets as "serious," "popular," and "weird." Under the last category falls H. P. Lovecraft, the focus of attention in *H. P. Lovecraft: A Critical Study* by Donald R. Burleson (Greenwood). In the Preface to this study, Burleson contends that he will use a "blended variety of critical approaches," citing formalist, philosophical, biographical, Jungian and mythic-archetypal "schools of criticism." Unfortunately, in this the first full-length study of Lovecraft's fiction, and the fifth in Greenwood's Science Fiction and Fantasy Series, Burleson provides very little critical insight in spite of such elaborate preparations. Instead, as is too often the case, Burleson offers extensive summary of Lovecraft's short stories and novels. The reader new to Lovecraft will come away with a fairly thorough understanding of the content of Lovecraft's fiction but with little critical understanding in spite of Burleson's occasional reminder of the Jungian elements in the works. A writer usually included under the heading of "Popular" is S. J. Perelman, subject of Douglas Fowler's *S. J. Perelman* (TUSAS). Fowler prefaces his study with the concession: "I would immediately agree that it would be a mistake to claim for Perelman 'major' status." Fowler labels Perelman "a toymaker" and goes on to chronicle a great deal of literary gossip, especially when dealing with Perelman's Hollywood escapades. Although he does attempt to distinguish Perelman from the American humorist tradition represented by such figures as Artemus Ward and to place Perelman in a "very subtle form [of] a European and New World Jewish tradition," Fowler is content for the most part to offer documentation and commentary in place of the serious critical examination that would serve more adequately to define Perelman's place in American humor and American literature.

Far more secure in his place among "serious" American writers is Nathanael West, the focus of Gordon Bordewyk's "Nathanael West and *Seize the Day*" (*ES* 64:153–59). Bordewyk argues here that in addition to the numerous allusions already traced in *Seize the Day*, Bellow's novella is "profoundly indebted to Nathanael West's *Miss Lonelyhearts* and *The Day of the Locust*." He cites similarities between the "grotesques" who populate both *Miss Lonelyhearts* and *Seize the Day*; between Tommy Wilhelm and Miss Lonelyhearts, both of whom "are caught in an ambiguous tension between narcissism and altruism"; and between the city in both novels as "a chaotic, entropic environment" from which Tommy and Miss Lonelyhearts both attempt to flee. The parallels are indisputable, but Bordewyk fails to provide significant new insight into the work of either writer by way of this exercise.

University of New Mexico

15. Fiction: The 1950s to the Present

Jerome Klinkowitz

The quality of scholarship and criticism accorded to contemporary fiction is rising in direct proportion to our knowledge of and facility with new critical theory. It is no accident that the innovations of recent decades were derided by commentators who preferred to plod along at the level on which plot and characters are rehearsed and admired for their "reality," without ever seriously investigating what that term means for a text. Certain novels and stories allow one to function as a priest or counselor rather than an analyst, but they are the product of an earlier era—and even in their own times such works offered much more than the reductively moralistic readings some critics give them today. Fiction of our own age demands a critical intelligence equal to the times, and among 1983's publications we can see how those that have mastered contemporary theory do a much better job than those that approach their tasks with either innocence or obsolete standards.

i. General Studies

A quantum leap forward is provided by Charles Caramello in his *Silverless Mirrors: Book, Self and Postmodern American Fiction* (Florida State). Caramello is among the first generation of scholars to receive their undergraduate and graduate training after both the period's revolutionary theorists and innovative fictionists had made their impact. His title plays upon the tension he perceives between theoretical postures (particularly the death-of-the-author/birth-of-the text) and residual habits of tradition. As Caramello explains, "the historical being known as the author remains as the ghost of a concept that has been destroyed." Thanks to the pervasive inter-textuality of our age, there is "no discrete self left to perform," but "yet it is precisely from the conditions of this absence . . . that postmodern American fiction generates its desire to perform a self, to shape a presence, to create in the language of the book an environment in which that performed and shaped self can be placed." Caramello's pantheon includes authors who are for conventional critics beyond the pale: William H. Gass, whose *Willie Masters' Lonesome Wife* plays with intertextuality itself; John Barth, whose own texts disappear in the mirrors of multiform allusion; Raymond Federman, whose *The Voice in the Closet* has its central event erase itself and so form a text of emptiness; Kenneth Gangemi, whose *The Volcanoes From Puebla* uses a guidebook form for textual self-exploration; and Walter Abish, who in *Alphabetical Africa* explores not the continent but rather his own representation of it.

Alan Singer's *A Metaphorics of Fiction: Discontinuity and Discourse in the Modern Novel* (Florida State) applies the theories of Roland Barthes, Jacques Derrida, Jacques Lacan, and Paul Ricoeur to a group of American fictionists compatible with Caramello's: Ronald Sukenick, John Hawkes, Donald Barthelme, and (again) Barth and Federman. To avoid the pitfalls of referent-based rhetorics, Singer appropriates the deconstructionists' notion of "textual productivity" to explain Federman's *surfiction*, which produces meaning instead of reproducing a preexisting meaning. *Metafiction* is only a subcategory, a specific technique by which mimesis is thwarted when the formal structures of a work call attention to themselves. The larger and more important issue is the "rejection of cultural tyrannies" that a writer such as Sukenick undertakes within the surfictionist aesthetic, a more interesting and more deeply human task than many opponents of deconstruction anticipate. Narrative is not abstract game playing but rather a combination of event and act: John Hawkes's *Second Skin* incorporates these activities within language itself, as his metaphors "force the habitual to disclose new meaning by giving free play to otherwise repressed discursive contingencies." Only by risking the established meaning-relations can innovative writers such as Sukenick and Hawkes achieve the creation of something genuinely new (and not a shadow of something else).

The movement of narrative as it frames events is Richard Pearce's subject in *The Novel in Motion: An Approach to Modern Fiction* (Ohio State). Rather than turning to French theorists, he looks back to the evolution of cinema for his keys to narrative, and finds that they imply a shift from representation of story to a focus on the act of seeing itself. Seeing is a form of action that when transposed to fiction is taken up in the act of reading itself. Thomas Pynchon, Robert Coover, Sukenick, Abish, and Federman all excel at creating a narrator whose posture is not as a storyteller but "as a witness who has imposed his frame upon reality," with the resultant gaps between narrator and story asserting themselves "as a dramatic part of the novel's fabric." Pearce agrees with Caramello and Singer that when "pure motion" is achieved, as in *Alphabetical Africa* and Sukenick's *98.6*, content becomes self-canceling.

Among the critics who have done their work with an eye toward theory, there has evolved a clear canon of contemporary fiction for study. From the thousands of novels and hundreds of serious, estimable authors at work, a few texts and authors emerge as central: *Out* and *98.6* by Ronald Sukenick, Walter Abish's *Alphabetical Africa* and Raymond Federman's writerly-autobiographical cycle of novels, the dialogue stories of Donald Barthelme (particularly in *Great Days*), and John Barth's *Lost in the Funhouse*. How works like these demand a new fictional theory is Thomas Docherty's thesis in *Reading (Absent) Character: Towards a Theory of Characterization in Fiction* (Clarendon/Oxford). Most British and American theory up to now, he points out, had ignored the French *nouveau roman*; moreover, its own bias towards realism led to the belief "that 'life' or 'reality' exists anterior to any language that purports to describe or define 'life' or 'reality.'" However, "Post-Modern experimental writers such as ... Sukenick, Federman, Barth, and many others react against this kind of understanding of fiction and language." Their writing "is itself the reality with which we must deal." Docherty finds that their consistent turning point against tradition is with the function of character. In conventional fiction, "we make the leap from an understanding of the meanings of singular characters to the truth or message meaning expressed by the author," and "with this leap, the activity of the reader is actually erased." But by keeping their characters indefinite and having all their action take place upon the surface of linguistic creation, Sukenick and his colleagues once more give the readers a field of action in which they can participate as co-creators of meaning." It is the interaction of the writer's language with the positions it affords the reader that the element of the text which we call 'character' is produced," Docherty explains, and cites Barthelme's "degree zero" of characters whose dialogues are informed

by language itself rather than by its referents, Sukenick's "democrati-
zation of character" that prohibits "existent entities with which the
reader can enter into relation," and Barth's reshaping of narrative
time into a purely textual phenomenon (which nevertheless still
motivates characters, albeit in a metafictionally self-apparent way).
A clarifying parable for all this may be found in the protagonist's
situation in *Being There* by Jerzy Kosinski: "for all the other characters in the novel, his being must imply a meaning, and the meaning
is always their own meaning which is imposed upon Chance and thus
'objectified' for them."

Three major overviews of contemporary fiction published this
year by leading critics try to make their way through both innovations and traditions without recourse to the sophistications of theory
evident in Caramello, Singer, Pearce, and Docherty. The best among
them is Malcolm Bradbury's *The Modern American Novel*, which
relies upon a strong sense of literary history for its structure and
specific insight. Bradbury, of course, knows the latest theory, sufficiently to chide it in the epigraph to his own novel, *Rates of Exchange*
(Knopf), written concurrently with his study: "You have a quarrel
on hand, I see," he quotes from Poe's "The Purloined Letter," "with
some of the algebraists of Paris; but proceed." And proceed he does
to show that much of what Derrida & Cie claim as innovations have
been present within the experimental aspects of American fiction
since the 19th century. Even then, "fiction was becoming less the
expression of a common reality all could recognize, more a response
to the uncommon realities and systems that lay behind modern life
and called for revelation." In our own times Bradbury can cite the
new gnosticism and mysticism evident in Saul Bellow's *Humboldt's
Gift*, Kurt Vonnegut's claim that the system has entered into the very
heart of the self, and Richard Brautigan's fusion of mind and metaphor so that the animate may be found deep within the alienating
inanimate. Bradbury agrees with Singer that one of the key figures
in this movement is John Hawkes, once more because he can de-
materialize both the naturally seen universe and our usual ways of
talking about it "in order to recreate these anew according to the laws
of imaginative and psychic intensity." Barthelme is praised for "generating new combinatory systems while confusing the levels of story,"
Thomas Pynchon is acknowledged as allowing writing itself to be the
dominant interest in his novels, and Robert Coover is seen as giving

most attention to "the reconstitution of forms for reality's sake." Bradbury uses the term "post-realist" to describe Sukenick, Federman, Steve Katz, and others whose "response to the contemporary historical situation has driven them into essential questions about the nature of story and modern stylistic citizenship." Bradbury's most successful novel, after all, was titled *The History Man*, and it is the overt pressures of history rather than purely theoretical matters that motivate his critical investigations.

A specific notion of history informs John W. Aldridge's *The American Novel and the Way We Live Now* (Oxford), but it is a deplorable irritation with present values and life-styles that cripples Aldridge's ability to read insightfully. Little can be said for the scholarship of this volume, since most of it appeared as back-page fumings from *Harper's*, *Saturday Review*, and other coffee-table magazines. Since his first book in 1951, Aldridge has been claiming that "American writing was now too bereft of moral or mythological community to generate art," and three decades later the state of our nation looks even worse to him. Rather than study fiction's textual self-apparency, he prefers to view it pathologically as evidence of a solipsistic retreat to the personal self; therefore Hawkes is seen as a poor writer who cannot distinguish objective from subjective (as opposed to Singer's praise of his defamiliarization and Bradbury's appreciation of his dematerialization of the previously self-evident, both of which are fundamentally recreative acts). "Reality, having become whatever one wishes to name it, soon disappears behind the words employed to misname it." Aldridge is the type of critic who decides that we must "measure the worth of a novelist by the depth of his perception of human character and sensibility"—the old priest-counselor routine—rather than by examining how he or she *writes*, and therefore there is very little attention in his book to the forms of fiction in our age. Instead, he checklists its topics, and in so doing commits egregious misreadings (such as calling Gilbert Sorrentino an imitator of Barth, when in fact Sorrentino is formally critiquing and rejecting Barth's aesthetic). Throughout he rails against contemporary values (or what he sees as a lack of them) and yearns for the better influence of "provincial and small-town America" to save us. His study concludes with a disgraceful polemic against what he calls our age's acceptance of "Blacks, Chicanos, Navajo Indians, paraplegics, defrocked lesbian nuns from Idaho, and other homosexuals."

When Cabinet officers speak in such terms, the President asks for their resignation; but in American academics, such sentiments are published by the leading university press and moreover (as Richard Kostelanetz has described in *The Grants Fix* [Erickson]) determine the conservative policies of grants organizations both public and private (an acknowledgement indicates that these high-paying *Harper's* columns were written on a Rockefeller Humanities Fellowship).

A more levelheaded and critically responsible work is Frederick R. Karl's massive *American Fictions 1940–1980*. He disregards contemporary theory, in fact claiming that there is no "postmodernism" at all; what has been accomplished in our age is simply a refining of modernist practice. Karl is best when he sets aside his own sweeping, epochal notions (the pastoral, the "counterfeit decade," and the like) and concentrates on specific writers and texts. Like most of this year's critics, he finds John Hawkes to be a good index no matter which epoch is at hand, from the 1940s through the present, since "his fiction is an adversary force, still within the terms of the traditional novel, but extending its countering potentialities to the inner reaches of time and space." Karl senses that systems are at work (as do the deconstructionists) but prefers to treat them thematically, seeing Pynchon's overload of stories (in place of narrative) and people (in place of characters) and locations (instead of place) as more of a topical interest than a determining structure. He quite frankly dislikes the "surfiction" of Sukenick and Federman, preferring instead the style of work which in Joseph Conrad's words "make us see." Such seeing, however, is directed to what the fiction writer has represented—in this case a presentation of the outside world—and so of course the innovations of the surfiction group fail to register on Karl's Conradian scale, attending as they do to the work as process and not as product. Here is just the failure to make theoretical adjustment to an age's shift in aesthetic value—a situation Thomas Docherty thought it necessary to correct.

The year's best contribution incorporates the best features of both the theory-minded and tradition-oriented critics. In *Anything Can Happen: Interviews with Contemporary American Novelists* (Illinois) Tom LeClair and Larry McCaffery do all the work expected of scholars—surveying the field to identify trends, sorting out the important books and authors, studying them for influences and developments, examining the theory that informs the texts, and eliciting from the authors themselves comments that add up to cogent essays on the subject. A certain aggravation with the inappropriate standards of an earlier day (when fiction such as that under discussion did not even exist) prompts LeClair and McCaffery to set the story straight. For them, Alfred Kazin is the representative complainer who feels that contemporary writers are "confused and abstracted, corrupted by commerce, unable to imagine the impact of science, business, history, and the media on the American present." Reading widely, then seeking out and listening to what such writers as Barth, Hawkes, Gass, Barthelme, Federman, Katz, Sukenick, and others had to say, LeClair and McCaffery explain that "we found just the opposite to be true: both visible and invisible artists are confidently creating imaginative worlds wide with history and politics, dense with commerce, media, and technics." There is now "an imagination equal to the complexities of the times." LeClair's thesis, familiar from his many previous essays on the subject, is that "the inventive energy and substance of the decade are most obvious in its encyclopedic novels—*Gravity's Rainbow*, by the absentee Mr. Pynchon, Coover's *The Public Burning*, [Joseph] McElroy's *Lookout Cartridge*, [Don] DeLillo's *Ratner's Star*, and Barth's *Letters*—each of which has all of Kazin's subjects in artful collaboration." None of them is conventionally realistic, and hence they escape the older critic's notice and appreciation; instead, they offer a kaleidoscopic view of what realism itself often misses. "In these novels the midrange of ordinary life has been narrowed to show how codes and signals, myths and formulas, gravity and fancy—all the invisible realities, sure as air and DNA—surround and engrave our lives." McCaffery, building on his own previous work, favors the more imaginatively exuberant writers—Barthelme, Katz, Federman, and Sukenick—and from each draws both theoretical and practical commentary. As Katz describes Sukenick's achievement, "everything he writes has an immediacy that invents the moment you read it," and describing how this energetic style of fiction works makes *Anything Can Happen* the year's most valuable piece of criticism. LeClair especially has done much work to make the high-quality colloquy of this book happen, organizing an ongoing fiction symposium at the University of Cincinnati that yielded extensive discussions between John Barth and

John Hawkes and then between William H. Gass and John Gardner that begin the volume.

The pertinent relationship between new literary theory and innovative fiction also dominates the year's general essays. In "White on White: Contemporary American Fiction/Current Theory" (*ArQ* 39:293–311), Robert Con Davis cites Raymond Federman's *Surfiction* to show how the primary focus of fiction will be to unmask its own fictionality. "Thus," Davis concludes, "a distinct *critical* destiny for current fiction is voiced repeatedly by Ronald Sukenick, John Barth, William Gass, Joyce Carol Oates, Donald Barthelme, Max Apple, Guy Davenport, among many others." Realism, a writer such as Barth discovers, is always tied to myth, and therefore will never purge itself of a romantic residue. Yet as Barth attempts to dismantle these archetypes, he ties himself to mimetic realism—a project that critical self-consciousness reveals at every stage. Leigh Hafrey also uses Barth to focus her more general arguments in "The Gilded Cage: Postmodernism and Beyond" (*TriQ* 56:126–36). "Text-consciousness" is her term for the affair, and while she admits that it can be found in 19th-century works such as *The Scarlet Letter* and *Moby-Dick*, postmodern writers approach it antithetically, favoring the mechanistic over the inspirational. Barth especially views creation as mechanical, a result of forsaking the possibility "of significant verbal communication." A way out of this dilemma can be found in the work of the New Journalists, who realize that "truth is not just a matter of presentation, but it can never be a matter of all the facts, either. It is a process, an encounter with and expression of the object, the other, and the gradual incorporation of it and the observer into a coherent world view." Michael Herr accomplishes this in *Dispatches* and in *Enormous Changes at the Last Minute*. Grace Paley adopts the style for fiction. "Whether consciously or not," Hafrey advises, "Paley and Herr share the conviction of having something to say, an urgency that can take the form of humor or despair, but always assumes that language does not mediate between object and subject, between the world and the perceiver."

Mixing biography and fantasy sets up a competition between writer and reader that "has at its center a tacit agreement to test the strengths and limits of the imagination"—so argues Augustus M. Kolich in "Does Fiction Have To Be Made Better than Life?" (*MFS*

29:159–74). Distinctions among the many kinds of "realism" is also the concern of Douglas Messerli in the Introduction, "Synchronic Fictions" (pp. 3–10) to his anthology *Contemporary American Fictions* (Sun & Moon). The fact that in recent years storytellers have once again used chronology, objectivity, and realistic characters does not signal a return to modernism or realism; instead, such elements of realism are simply options. "Behind the 'real' worlds presented in these tales," Messerli argues, "there is authorial acknowledgement of other realities which in their very inexplicability are alluring and perilous both." There is a new style of realism, as practiced by Ann Beattie, Raymond Carver, Gordon Weaver, and others, which does not grant the reader other options, and in "Fictions of the New Realism" (*AmBR* 6,i:27–28) Mas'ud Zavarzadeh faults it for its falsely reassuring sense of totality and coherence. These are the ploys of escapism, he argues, a dishonest compression of experience and expression. Western logocentrism has always longed after such voice and presence, in the process missing out on the true drama of human existence that resides in the area of "free play" between signifier and signified. "Experimental Realism in Recent American Painting and Fiction" (pp. 149–62 in *Representation and Performance in Postmodern Fiction*, ed. Maurice Couturier [Montpellier, France: Delta]) is Jerome Klinkowitz's demonstration of how formerly realistic conventions become, in the hands of Walter Abish, Stephen Dixon, Kenneth Gangemi, and Clarence Major, not transparent windows upon a signified reality but rather opaque screens that indicate their own materiality of signification (his analogy is to the surface-conscious work of the Super-Realist painters: Richard Estes, Ralph Goings, Robert Bechtle, and Chuck Close, whose apparent realism actually parallels point-by-point the processes of abstract expressionism).

How all of this critical activity helps determine a canon of fiction is Richard Ohmann's aim in "The Shaping of a Canon: U.S. Fiction, 1960–1975" (*CritI* 10,i:199–223). His thesis is that all the theoretical rumblings described in the previous pages of this chapter have not had any significant effect on the fiction that has become representative of our age. To prove this point, however, Ohmann simply chooses not to count for credit the innovative fictionists first backed by revolutionary critics who have now achieved mainstream prominence (such as Vonnegut, Barthelme, Brautigan, Kosinski, and Coover).

Such a practice seems more like big city machine politics than dispassionate scholarship, and readers should be warned against Ohmann's rigged election.

ii. Saul Bellow and Other Jewish-Americans

Thanks to his international eminence and long tenure as a writer of major intellectual stature, Saul Bellow now finds himself treated as a larger-than-life figure. Much of this year's criticism links him with other such eminences (such as Hemingway) or with the larger traditions of myth and romance. In *A Sort of Columbus: The American Voyages of Saul Bellow's Fiction* (Georgia) Jeanne Braham sees Bellow's work as part of a larger American tradition, and she systematically matches up its features and his canon point by point. The romantic influence is traced to both the classic and the contemporary, using the typologies of Richard Chase (*The American Novel and Its Tradition*) and Jonathan Baumbach (*Landscape of Nightmare*) respectively. In Bellow's work an emphasis on the protean, moral, and allegorical helps make possible a bridge between the actual and dreams. Braham describes his typical hero as a protagonist of thought (as opposed to Hemingway's hero of action) whose vision creates meaning and then articulates it as it is felt in life (as opposed to pure ideation). An obverse approach, showing how "Bellow has continually dissociated himself from the dominant literary tradition of the modern age" (which is "a dark literature, a literature of victimization, of old people sitting in ash cans waiting for the breath of life to depart"), yields many striking insights in Allan Chavkin's "*Humboldt's Gift* and the Romantic Imagination" (*PQ* 62:1–19). Bellow counters this darkness with "a romantic sensibility, a Wordsworthian faith in the power of the imagination to renovate the individual who has lost 'the visionary gleam'; and is suffering from boredom and fear of 'the darkness of the grave.'" The genius of *Humboldt's Gift* is that it reveals a romantic sensibility "but one modified to accommodate the harsh turmoil of a contemporary society moving toward nihilism," a posture whose development Chavkin can trace through the earlier novels as well.

Like Braham, Chavkin sees Hemingway as a figure influential on Bellow, simply because "Hemingway was the domineering 'Papa' that Bellow felt he had to reject when he began writing." In "Fathers and Sons: 'Papa' Hemingway and Saul Bellow" (*PLL* 19: 449–60), Chavkin believes it is a distorted reading of Hemingway that in fact shaped Bellow's work, overlooking all but his "hard-boiled" aspects and thus putting him into the tradition of "victim literature" each writer in fact deplores. Bellow's innovation is to replace toughness with tough-mindedness, all tempered by an essentially comic spirit. Norman Mailer is the figure of comparison in Susan Glickman's "The World as Will and Idea: A Comparative Study of *An American Dream* and *Mr. Sammler's Planet*" (*MFS* 28:569–82). Both novels were written as a satirization of the authors' own popular images, and how those protagonists behave (from their wartime experiences through their behavior in contemporary America) underscores the radical differences between Mailer and Bellow "on the issues of man's place in nature and society, the character of the religious quest, the function of evil, and the roles of will and intellect," making them respectively "the Blake and Wordsworth of modern American letters."

Three briefer studies take Bellow on his own terms, each to good effect. In "Saul Bellow's Henderson as Mankind and Messiah" (*Renascence* 35:235–46), Eusebio L. Rodrigues studies the protagonist on four levels, reaching from simple humanity to "urban man," "twentieth century man," and finally messiah. "Spatial Dialogue in Bellow's Fiction" (*Mosaic* 16,iii:117–25) is Gregory Allen Johnson's demonstration that a conflict between the needs for communal and private space create a nonverbal form of dialogue in *Dangling Man, Seize the Day, Mr. Sammler's Planet*, and *Humboldt's Gift*. Sanford Pinsker shows how water imagery pervades and directs the theme in "Bellow's *Seize the Day*" (*Expl* 41,iii:60–61).

In the three years since its founding, the *Saul Bellow Journal* has developed into a first-class scholarly magazine, and among its contributions in 3, i are informative readings of *Henderson the Rain King, Seize the Day*, and *The Dean's December*. In "Saul Bellow's Heroes in an Unheroic Age" (pp. 53–58) Joseph Cohen shows how this latest novel is essentially different from the author's previous work. "Without sacrificing any of his imaginative power," Cohen argues, "Bellow has exercised sufficient restraint to keep his new protagonist from indulging in those excesses verging on lunacy, which were a hallmark of his previous characterizations of his heroes, diminishing if, indeed, not obliterating what heroism they might otherwise exhibit." The author's personal experience is responsible to this new equilibrium in Albert Corde, a protagonist who undergoes a role reversal that significantly lowers the conflict level in his life. In the process Bellow's own views on women and blacks have changed, yet a fundamentally Covenantal acceptance characterizes Albert Corde (even though his background isn't Jewish). The behavioral extremism from which Corde departs is Ted Billy's subject in "The Road of Excess: Saul Bellow's *Henderson the Rain King*" (pp. 8–17). The model for Henderson's excess is the poet William Blake, whose dynamic philosophy informs the novel's action, imagery, and characterization. "Exuberance is beauty," Blake wrote, and Henderson fulfills the definition, who follows the road of excess to the palace of wisdom. In recent years critics such as Ihab Hassan and Charles Caramello have been suspecting that Saul Bellow has been turning into a postmodernist, but in "The Seduction of Tommy Wilhelm: A Post-Modernist Appraisal of *Seize the Day*" (pp. 18–27), Gloria L. Cronin finds evidence much earlier in his career for challenging the orthodoxies of modernism, particularly those that stifle the individual.

Bernard Malamud is given a bit of the epically moral treatment by Helen Benedict in "Bernard Malamud: Morals and Surprises" (*AR* 41,i:28–36). His "preoccupation with the question of how man uses his freedom, how he tries to 'outrun' his fate, is expressed in many of his books through the metaphor of a prison"—the grocery store in *The Assistant*, for instance. In his latest work, *God's Grace*, he elevates fate to the level of nuclear destruction, and is consequently much harder on his protagonist. Another protagonist for whom time is running out is Mendel of "Idiots First," and in "The Tree-Clock in Bernard Malamud's 'Idiots First'" (*SSF* 20:52–54), Earle V. Bryant shows how the visual image of a tree's reversed branches provides both the story's theme and structure.

Two studies of Philip Roth's latest novels will keep readers up to date. Charles Berryman's "Philip Roth: Mirrors of Desire" (*MarkhamR* 12,ii:26–31) suggests that Bellow's influence is apparent in so many protagonists being victims of themselves; *The Professor of Desire* climaxes this development in Roth's fiction, and highlights it with the dramatic monologue that shows the hero trapped between desire and respectability (as lecture notes for the professor, they are uniquely revealing). Patrick O'Donnell moves along to "The Disappearing Text: Philip Roth's *The Ghost Writer*" (*ConL* 24:365–78), a novel that challenges our accepted notions about artistic inspiration. Its narrative structure is built around a series of texts, thus suggesting an infinite text (the search for a missing parent signals a search for textual authority).

Norman Mailer's *The Executioner's Song* is praised by Joseph Epstein in "Mailer Hits Bottom" (*Commentary* 76,i:62–68) for almost becoming a novel, thanks to its naturalistic techniques and avoidance of the journalism that had become customary in Mailer's work. But with *Ancient Evenings* the author surrenders to visual obsessions that disrupt the book's plot and clutter up its pacing.

iii. Flannery O'Connor, William Styron, Walker Percy, and Southerners

The strongest work on O'Connor this year comes from an unexpected place: Alice Walker's collected "womanist prose" in *In Search of our Mothers' Gardens* (Harcourt). In "Beyond the Peacock: The Reconstruction of Flannery O'Connor" (pp. 42–59) Walker looks beyond the facile truisms of so many vita-padding essays to perceive this writer's strength by comparing her environment with Walker's own childhood home just two miles away. Walker adds a dimension to the appreciation of O'Connor that traditionalist critics never achieve by reconsidering such facts as the brick of her townhouse having been made by hand by slaves. "O'Connor's biographers are always impressed by this fact," Walker notes, "as if it adds the blessed sign of aristocracy, but whenever I read it I think that those slaves were some of my own relatives, toiling in the stifling middle-Georgia heat, to erect her grandfather's house, sweating and suffering the swarming mosquitoes as the house rose slowly, brick by brick." O'Connor's brilliance is in achieving a clear sense of history in a land that has so divided itself from reality that little "real" sense of it prevails; especially well-drawn are her southern ladies, none of whom is allowed to be written off in a cloud of magnolia fragrance. Yet as Walker's mother observes on this same visit home, peacocks are lovely "but they'll eat up every bloom you have, if you don't watch out." Mrs. Walker, it turns out, had preferred the flowers in her own more humble yard.

An interesting "French connection" sheds some welcome new light among other O'Connor scholarship. Jefferson Humphries's *The Otherness Within: Gnostic Readings in Marcel Proust, Flannery*

O'Connor, and François Villon (LSU) notes the bodily distance between bodies themselves and the spirits within them; O'Connor's work mirrors this opposition by viewing writing as transgression, as she attempts to transcend both words and selves. Like John Hawkes, she rejects positivism in favor of portraying her characters dualistically. In "Flannery O'Connor and Flaubert: A French Connection" (*NConL* 13,v:2–4), Jan H. Logan traces interest in the grotesque to Flaubert's *Trois Contes*; the symbols and color schemes of the Flaubertian stories in *Everything That Rises Must Converge* are borrowed at large to enhance this effect.

Sophie's Choice is the choice for both major essays on William Styron this year. Frederick C. Stern cites it as an example of Styron's disregard for his status as a southern writer; "Styron's Choice" (*SAQ* 82:19–27) argues that the southern experience prevails in Styron's novel not as place but when characters are seen as both victims and as victimizers. In "God's Averted Face: Styron's *Sophie's Choice*" (*AL* 55:215–32), John Lang describes the central issue of Styron's novel as the problem of belief, specifically of religious faith in a post-Holocaust world where the individual is alienated from God. Religious issues of evil, guilt, and salvation frame the character's choice. Richard Rubenstein's *The Cunning of History: The Holocaust and the American Future* influenced Styron's own belief that the World War II experience for the Jews and other prisoners extended slavery and bureaucratic expendability of human beings into modern times.

SLJ 15, ii features two essays on Percy and a third on a writer deserving of wider notice than he usually receives, Cormac McCarthy. In "A Manner of Speaking: Percy's *Lancelot*" (pp. 7–18) Bill Oliver notes how Percy's hero may be schizophrenic, a duality evident in his first-person narration. These two styles of the "univocal and the equivocal" are in the end rejected for a different voice "based on a different view of human nature . . . that *something is wrong*." Man is essentially incomplete, just as a materialistic faith in empirical science and capitalism is incomplete—this latter observation anchors Mark Johnson's analysis in "*Lancelot*: Percy's Romance" (pp. 19–30). Vereen M. Bell writes in "The Ambiguous Nihilism of Cormac McCarthy" (pp. 31–41) that traditional Cartesian predispositions toward theme and character must yield to "some primal state of consciousness prior to its becoming identified with thinking only." In McCarthy's fictive world existence both precedes and precludes essence

—"Walker Percy turned inside out," in other words, a style more in common with innovative fiction.

Conjunctions No. 5 is distinguished by Larry McCaffery and Sinda Gregory's deep-reaching "An Interview with Barry Hannah" (pp. 193–205). Hannah begins by rejecting all questions on his "southern heritage" since they detract from the interior dimensions of his work. "Intensity is all," he confesses, and describes sex and violence as palliatives against the more difficult business of simply living. Situations concerning death and violence lend themselves to dramatic treatment, and therefore Hannah favors them in his work. Writing screenplays had added a tighter discipline to his fiction, he explains.

iv. Older Realists and New Mannerists: Capote, Updike, and Cheever

A valuable addition to Truman Capote's ongoing biography has been supplied by his Aunt, Marie Rudisill, in her book written with James C. Simmons, *Truman Capote* (Morrow). In his boyhood years young Truman is seen as an especially weak male, living in a world dominated by women—especially after his mother's suicide. Rudisill is especially adept with her detail of the quotidian aspects of early 20th-century life in the South.

In "The Word as Scandal: Updike's *A Month of Sundays*" (*ArQ* 39:351–80), John T. Matthews provides both a deep and wide-ranging study of this often neglected novel. Like the *Bech* books, it meditates on writers and on writing; but unlike them, "it concentrates on the theological contexts for the author's incarnate word." The compulsion to write leads to a reconsideration of faith, particularly of the blind *Totaliter Aliter* belief Updike had favored in his earlier protagonists; Reverend Marshfield learns that the Divine Word does not overpower or make impossible the human word. Discourse is fulfilled bodily in the novel's conclusion, yet Mrs. Prynne remains as much book as body, emphasizing the writer's vocation and not just the mortal man's lust. *The Centaur* is given similar writerly treatment by John B. Vickery in *Myths and Texts: Strategies of Incorporation and Displacement* (LSU, pp. 149–65). Although the novel's thematic dimensions are the first to attract a reader's interest, the book's organic connection to history (with myth disguised as experience) works to suspend its resolution, creating a sense of perpetual motion.

Peter's telling of the story, then, invites a self-examination of how the narrative works.

George W. Hunt, S. J., whose own book on Updike (*ALS 1980*, p. 324) was a levelheaded contribution, harms his own subject in *John Cheever: The Hobgoblin Company of Love* (Eerdmans) by denigrating presumed rivals. These attacks become absolutely silly in their ignorance: Hawkes, Pynchon, and Vonnegut—three quite dissimilar authors—are lumped together as offering "nightmare visions," "which probe the deepest of our apocalyptic fears," while the authors of *Trout Fishing in America* and *Snow White* are transformed into a two-headed monster named "Richard Barthelme" who can be dismissed as an ironist. As for Cheever, he is praised for "reconstructive irony," the Kierkegaardian notion that informed Hunt's book on Updike. Cheever is a writer of comic and abrupt shiftings, a man caught between two worlds who can often be illuminated by a quote from Auden or Yeats. But "Richard Barthelme"? One wonders who refereed this book in manuscript, and who edited it. It is a great pleasure to turn to Malcolm Cowley's "John Cheever: The Novelist's Life as Drama" (*SR* 91:1–16) for this eminent critic's reminiscence of Cheever from the beginning of a literary career to its end in an untimely death.

v. Realists From Berger and Doctorow to Oates, Gardner, and Dickey

Two substantial essays bring welcome attention to the work of Thomas Berger. Gerald Weales's "Reinhart as Hero and Clown" (*HC* 20,v:1–12) focuses on the Reinhart novels to show "the fool striving for self-identity as poet-philosopher hero." Weales shows that what is common to all four novels, even though they were not originated as a unit, are similar aspects of plotting, characterization, and narrative method. Filtering the third-person narration through Reinhart reveals the limitations of perspective Berger proposes as a theme, and the bizarre manner of overstatement suggests the comic strip and movie farce. In "Acts of Definition, or Who Is Thomas Berger" (*ArQ* 39:312–50), Alan Wilde shows how Berger's detective novel, *Who Is Teddy Villanova?*, combines the condition of disorderliness with the textual compulsion for order. A phenomonological approach to contemporary fiction locates the author in the text "as the initiator of a meaning his acts create," thus allowing both order and disorder.

E. L. *Doctorow: Essays and Conversations*, edited by Richard Trenner, inaugurates the Ontario Review Press Critical Series (Princeton). Doctorow himself begins the collection with commentaries on government support for writers and on his own belief that there are no genres beyond narrative. These, however, are reprints, as are all but three of the essays and interviews that follow. The best of the new work is by Arthur Saltzman, whose "The Stylistic Energy of E. L. Doctorow" (pp. 73–108) sums up the canon as one devoted to confirming suspicions about the American Dream; the ironic sensibilities of Doctorow's narrators cut through social levels and create surprising confrontations between fiction and reality, reinforcing the notion that accounts within either category are equally narratives. Cross-indexing of the volume as a whole plus the addition of more genuinely synthetic pieces such as Saltzman's would make this series a more useful contribution to scholarship.

Joyce Carol Oates's formidable powers as a symbolist are established by Doreen A. Fowler in "Oates's 'At the Seminary'" (*Expl* 41, i:62–64). Her apparent heir in style and content is Ann Beattie, but as Pico Iyer shows in "The World According to Beattie" (*PR* 50: 548–53) a disconcerting life of "quiet desperation" underlies each of her characters, a shorthand device that allows Beattie to escape the rigors of art. Her young men and women live in a limbo where there is "nothing holding them down or keeping them in place," and their dialogues are often "dangling conversations between people deaf to one another's griefs." The most typical respondent to a Beattie conversation is an answering machine, and although this circumstance may be appropriate to the age, its fey hipness allows the author to slip out from underneath her responsibilities to character and action. "Beattie's tales seem almost mass produced," Iyer concludes, according to a pat formula: choose some upper-middle-class names, affix them to people with trendy occupations, find them at home over coffee on a gray winter's day. "Let there be a phone call from a former lover, a child from a sometime marriage. Ensure that someone takes Valium and someone refers to a gynecological operation. Write in a withered present tense and end before the conclusion."

Shortly before his death in September 1982 John Gardner recanted his beliefs on the "immorality" of innovative fiction, telling a reporter for the *Washington Post* (July 25, 1982, pp. H1, H8–9) that *On Moral*

Fiction in fact dated from 1964 when he was unpublished and envious of the innovators' successes. One would therefore expect his *On Becoming a Novelist* (Harper) to be a more balanced and insightful work. But by reducing Vonnegut to a technical science fictionist and innovators such as Barthelme and Gass to the status of "stand-up comedians like Bill Cosby or comic actors like W. C. Fields," Gardner reminds us that personal animosity kept an upper hand over reasoned aesthetic judgment. That such judgment never had a chance is displayed by his misunderstanding of the innovationists' aim, which he insists is after all representational and therefore liable to be judged "by the consistency and accuracy of observation with which they present to us their staged selves, their friends, enemies, memories, peculiar hopes and crank opinions." What Gardner proposes instead is the arid style of Workshop Modern exploited by his first generation of protégés, including Ann Beattie, Raymond Carver (who prefaced this book), and Gordon Weaver. As an introduction to the craft, it is severely limited, but as a critical document it is redeemed by Gardner's astute analysis of his own works, particularly *October Light, The Sunlight Dialogues,* and *Mickelsson's Ghosts.*

Gardner also speaks his personal piece for editor Stephen Berg's *In Praise of What Persists* (Harper). "Cartoons" (pp. 125–34) identifies his chief interests as his father's oral recitations of poetry and the "nonrealistic" books of his youth: the Bible, Dickens's novels, and the comic books based on Disney cartoons. The ease of these sources, and especially the ease with which they are taken up by critical advocates who wish to cast Gardner as a wholesomely mellow narrativist, makes one doubt that this author will survive such enshrinement. It is one thing to recognize Gardner's "affirmation," but quite another to ride the concept into the ground much as certain Faulkner critics did in the wake of his Nobel speech. Although Gardner is an affirmative writer, it is not that aspect of his work that is interesting or even in need of critical explication. More important for scholars is how he works toward that affirmation and keeps it balanced against the very real opposite tendencies he knows are in the world. One suspects he came down so hard upon the postmodern innovationists because he recognized the same artistic tendencies in himself. Books and essays that sound the party line of "moral fiction"—especially on the level of introduction to this most self-apparent author—are less than super-

fluous, for they imply that there isn't all that much there to begin
with.

The short title of David Cowart's *Arches and Light: The Fiction
of John Gardner* (So.Ill.) is another worrisome example of the familiar critical chorus. Like an angel of creation, Gardner builds a floor
over the ancient abyss, as a moral artist reacting against the modern
failure to make meaningless life meaningful. Cowart stops short of
seeing how *On Moral Fiction* collapses modernist nihilism into postmodernist play. However, his readings of the novels are especially
illuminating because they show how Gardner's theory is put into
practice. A similar tendency to memorialize flaws the essays assembled in *John Gardner: True Art, Moral Art,* ed. Beatrice Mendez–
Egle (Pan American University Living Author Series, No. 5). Angela
A. Rapkin's "John Gardner's Novels: Post-Modern Structures in the
Service of Moral Fiction" (pp. 1–12) excuses Gardner's attack by
misconstruing non-referential fiction as a psychological self-reference
in disguise; Leonard Butts's "The Process of 'Moral Fiction': Protagonist as Artist in John Gardner's Novels" (pp. 13–24) concludes
by making the author more of a religious tester of values than a true
literary artist. The tenor of the remaining essays on specific novels is
that "Gardner will not wander, lost in the funhouse of fiction, creating ending after ending. He will work until he has found something
to affirm." Such an attitude misreads innovative fiction and belittles
Gardner's own achievement at the same time, all thanks to the presumed approval of such words as "affirmation" and "value." If Gardner critics were to program their word processors not to accept
these overused terms, the value of their scholarship would increase
dramatically.

Jeff Henderson and Robert A. Morace show more respect for their
subject's depth and complexity. In the former's "The Avenues of
Mundane Salvation: Time and Change in the Fiction of John Gardner" (*AL* 55:611–33), time is the basis of Gardner's optimism. The
repeated use of ghosts reminds us that there is no certain notion of
what time is, and psychic mobility offers the promise of mastering
its limiting factors. The future may have already taken place, the
highest goals of evolution may have already been reached; for Gardner this means that all potential is real and everything is at some level
true at least for psychics. Robert A. Morace shows similar critical
acumen in his several studies, which this year include a major entry

in the *Critical Survey of Long Fiction* (Salem, pp. 1067–82), an exhaustively complete *John Gardner: An Annotated Secondary Bibliography* (Garland), and major essays on "The King's Indian" and *Freddy's Book*. The Salem Press piece begins with an acknowledgment that Gardner ably works both sides of the moral fiction issue, with many of his innovations equal to those of the surfictionists. He puts their tricks to higher thematic purpose, Morace insists; yet there is no misreading of metafictional intent, just an agreement that Gardner (without aid of the critic's misconstruction) has a different purpose in mind. In *"Freddy's Book*, Moral Fiction, and Writing as a Mode of Thought" (*MFS* 29:201–12), Morace explains that moral art need not be didactic art. Instead it is a mode of thought that employs fiction as a medium for exploring and testing ideas and values. *Freddy's Book* successfully equates fiction with thought process, thanks to its two-part textual structure that contrasts different modes of thinking and creating. "The Moral Structure of John Gardner's 'The King's Indian'" (*MQ* 24:388–99) suggests that Gardner mastered the techniques of innovative fiction before critiquing them in his later novels and in *On Moral Fiction*; principal among these devices are parodic inside narratives, contrasting levels of function, and metafictional self-consciousness.

The enormous staying power of a popular novel is demonstrated by John E. Loftus in "Technique as Metaphor in James Dickey's *Deliverance*" (*SCR* 16,i:66–76). Technical expertise contributes to the theme, by which some characters are limited and others are liberated. When technique inhibits one's life, it is damaging (as with Lewis Medlock), but it is an enlightening exercise for Ed Gentry, signifying real growth. As Loftus concludes, "If moral certainty is impossible in Dickey's world, art is possible. Technique and inspiration, resulting in art, account for that world and make it tolerable."

vi. The Beats: Jack Kerouac and Others

Literary history has now reached that point in its cycle where a movement once shunned for its antiacademic bias and nontraditional obscurity can be embraced for serious study. In other words, it is safely inert and no longer a cultural influence. Because of this, even certain artists are anxious to jump on the now static bandwagon; whether for reasons of youth, timidity, or economics, they held back from the movement, but are now anxious to affiliate themselves with its memory.

This "I liked it too" temperament pervades Gerald Nicosia's *Memory Babe: A Critical Biography of Jack Kerouac* (Grove). This celebration of Kerouac's early life in Lowell and his vibrant sense of community among the Beats takes on legendary proportion, justifiably so because Kerouac's own sense of legend was what fueled his best work. His friend Neal Cassady supplied both the subject and rhythmic style for his work. Unhappily, Nicosia's criticism is not equal to the documentary rigors of his history; much of the analysis is on the level of "Like Shakespeare, Kerouac mingles starkly contrasting characters and diverse settings" and "That *The Subterraneans* ends less tragically than *Oedipus Rex* is due to the narrator's acceptance of his own strange vision. . . ." How Kerouac's own life resisted his attempts at literary legendizing still demands more investigation, with facile references to the Great Books kept out of the way.

Kerouac's previous biographer, Ann Charters, has edited the two-part *DLB* volume 16 entitled *The Beats: Literary Bohemians in Postwar America* (Gale). George Dardess files the report on Kerouac (I:278–303), noting that the author's literary reputation has been sacrificed in order to make him a spokesman for the movement. It is far better, Dardess believes, to examine the contradictions within Kerouac himself and see how they were resolved in Buddhism (itself an "annihilation of paradox"). *On the Road* celebrates ecstasy and death as releases from spatial and temporal limits; its spontaneous vitality of composition creates a life in itself (*Visions of Cody* is then studied as having once been a part of this larger manuscript). Within this two-part volume (II:621–25) and also in her memoir *Minor Characters* (Houghton Mifflin), Joyce Johnson details her own life with Kerouac and the Beats as a thankless, sexist captivity best summarized by the words of Billie Holiday's "God Bless the Child." Carolyn Cassady's "As I See It" (II:607–20) grants the Beats their "honesty" and gives a stylistic sense of their daily life. Most noteworthy among the entries on other figures are Richard Kirk Ardinger's on John Clellon Holmes (I:247–62), which appreciates Holmes's sober novelistic picture of the Beats, and Jennie Skerl's on William S. Burroughs (I:45–69), which locates his formal achievement in revolt and his thematic innovation in the realms of controlling sexuality and death. Most helpful is Skerl's "Beat Chronology" (II:593–606) dating from 1944 through 1969, the first twenty-five years of this movement.

A valuable study of Kerouac's religious beliefs is found in Beong Cheon Yu's *The Great Circle: American Writers and the Orient* (Wayne State). As opposed to J. D. Salinger's style and behavior, Kerouac embraced not Zen but the original Buddhism as a serious affirmation of his original Catholicism (life as pain and suffering, redeemed by charity and compassion). His earlier novels show no such influence, but beginning in January of 1954 Buddhism becomes central to his work. His narrators search for wisdom instead of pursuing reckless movement (*The Dharma Bums* versus *On the Road*). The most important contribution to Kerouac scholarship for the past several years is the special issue John O'Brien has prepared of the *Review of Contemporary Fiction* (III,ii). From William S. Burroughs's opening analysis through the 20 essays and memoirs (all original) that follow, O'Brien's collection covers all of Kerouac's major works and adds new historical material on the author's life. Unique among these contributions are reactions by several younger artists at work today; how they have come to terms with Kerouac's legend is a clear indication of how the Beats will be incorporated in the ongoing literary history of America.

vii. Innovative Fiction

a. **General Studies.** Since its inception in 1981, the *DLB Yearbook* (Gale) has kept its pages open to the new and innovative fiction writers just emerging into academic reputations. The *1983 Yearbook*, however, edited by Mary Bruccoli and Jean W. Ross, has begun to exercise some exclusionary tendencies, passing over such genuine innovationists as Walter Abish (at work since 1970) and Clarence Major (first published in book form the same year) to give more than warranted space to such Writers Workshop products as Jonathan Penner (just two full-length books to Abish's five and Major's thirteen, and dating only from 1977) and Douglas Adams (who writes novelizations of his comic science fiction scripts as seen on BBC-TV). This new trend toward the academically slick and commercially successful is revealed in George Garrett's "The Year in Fiction: A Biased View" (pp. 92–99), which takes its keynote from the best seller lists and discusses Bette Midler's *The Saga of Baby*

Divine and various works by Stephen King, the Reverend Andrew Greeley, and Trevanian. Most biased and offensive is Garrett's glib sense of metaphor; he finds it comical to contrast himself with "the proles of literature," and slaps his knees with hilarity when considering labor in the cotton fields compared to "the cooler comfort of the living room and dining room of the big house" (descendants of slaves take note: your great-grandfathers' and mothers' suffering is, in this Southerner's view, equivalent to his lacking a tenured professorship and going ten years between best-selling books). Yet a number of important entries can be found in *DLB '83*, and will be noted below.

Thomas LeClair advances his thesis on "the novel of excess" (see *ALS 1981*, p. 280, and *ALS 1982*, p. 294) in "Post-Modern Mastery" (*Representation and Performance*, pp. 99–111). If fiction is the only way we know reality, then it better be good and it better be big, LeClair insists—hence advocacy of those massive novels by Coover, Gaddis, McElroy, Pynchon, Barth, and DeLillo. Demands are exceeded, expectations are exhausted, and outstrip conventional communication, all as a way of mastering a supposedly unmanageable reality. Zoltán Abádi–Nagy's model for this same period is more familiar, as named in his "Ironic Historicism in the American Novel of the Sixties" (*JOHJ* 5:83–90); these novels consider "the entropic system of the present age as being determined by various laws and patterns of historical 'development'" in an ironic way, with chaos increasing and history itself wearing down. History has turned into entropic mechanism, Abádi-Nagy believes, and cites the work of Vonnegut and Pynchon to make his case. Making this argument on level of characterization, John Z. Guzlowski in "Hollow Gestures and Empty Words: Inconsequential Action and Dialogue in Recent American Novels" (*MarkhamR* 12:21–26) sees their exchanges as revealing characters' alienation from themselves and their environment. The break between inner and outer reality leads to action for its own sake in Barth, Gaddis, Hawkes, and Pynchon. Neil Schmitz sees quite another outcome for these works in *Of Huck and Alice*. His "Epilogue: In the Snare of Mother-Wit" (pp. 241–58) finds Barthelme, Vonnegut, Brautigan, and Roth all seizing the humorous impulse rather than surrendering to the entropic and alienative forces Guzlowski and Abádi-Nagy describe. In "Pynchon, Hawkes, and Updike: Readers and the Paradox of Accessibility" (*SCR* 16,i:45–51),

Donald J. Greiner strikes a balance between these camps by considering the common reader's complaint of inaccessibility and reminding us that such inaccessibility is not necessarily "immoral" (in John Gardner's sense). "The tendency for literature to become momentarily inaccessible merely illustrates the tendency for a culture to become more complex," and innovative writers are more often varying their notion of verisimilitude rather than violating it. With once-stable norms now in flux, the artist must trust his or her art more than convention.

How fiction generated by the Vietnam War demands its own new set of conventions is demonstrated once again by the essays in *Crit* 24, ii. Here the favorite texts are Robert Stone's *Dog Soldiers*, Tim O'Brien's *Going After Cacciato*, and Michael Herr's *Dispatches*. The popularity of these works with critics suggests that a canon of Vietnam war fiction has been formed. As Marshall Van Deusen shows in "The Unspeakable Language of Life and Death in Michael Herr's *Dispatches*" (pp. 82–87), experience generates stories, and stories generate models—but at a certain point new experience outstrips the old models and literature must be reinvented, just as narrative invention in the first place was a way of articulating the unspeakable.

b. **Heller, Kesey, Vonnegut, Kosinski, Fariña, and Brautigan.** The major work on Joseph Heller this year may be found in *Contemporary Authors* (Gale, New Revisions Series 8:237–44, Ann Evory and Linda Metzger, eds.). In a 1981 phone interview Heller describes his writing method as assembling files and writing chronologically, even though the novel's resultant action isn't chronological.

Ken Kesey receives broader treatment thanks to essays on each of his novels and the publication of Stephen L. Tanner's *Ken Kesey* (TUSAS 444). Elements of the West are examined in both the writer's biography and his writing; elements of myth and legend inform *One Flew Over the Cuckoo's Nest*, making it far more than a gesture of anarchic rebellion, and with *Sometimes a Great Notion* Kesey presents a many-faceted story, expanding his repertory of narrative techniques. Tanner is especially sensitive to Kesey's subsequent role as a cultural "lightning rod," sensing in this failed attempt to use his life as a work of art a reminder of the word's primacy (as studied in his work in progress). Virginia Valentine's "Kesey's *One Flew Over the Cuckoo's Nest*" (*Expl* 41,i:58–59) and Elaine B. Safer's "The

Absurd Quest and Black Humor in Ken Kesey's *Sometimes a Great Notion*" (*Crit* 24:228–40) show respectively that notions of victory in death and the absurdities of black humor unify Kesey's work.

Kurt Vonnegut's life and work are given feature treatment in the *DLB* Documentary Series, 3: 321–76 (Gale, edited by Mary Bruccoli). Especially valuable are two student columns by Vonnegut reprinted from the *Cornell Sun* and the transcript of Harry Reasoner's 1970 interview (at the time of *Happy Birthday, Wanda June* on Broadway) with the author from *Sixty Minutes*. *Putting Dell on the Map: A History of the Dell Paperbacks* (Greenwood) by William H. Lyles identifies the high editorial standards of Knox Burger as one of the reasons Vonnegut's *The Sirens of Titans* was acquired as a paperback original. Vonnegut's affinities with Twain are explored by Frank Ancone in "Kurt Vonnegut and the Great Twain Robbery" (*NConL* 13,iv:6–7), centering on their ambivalent notions toward America and their resolutions to this problem by stopping time (in *A Connecticut Yankee* and *Slaughterhouse-Five*). A batch of science fiction essays also treat Vonnegut, most of which are best summarized by their titles as they appear in *MLAB*. The best of these is Lawrence Broer's "Pilgrim's Progress: Is Kurt Vonnegut, Jr., Winning His War with Machines?" included in *Clockwork Worlds: Mechanized Environments in SF*, edited by Richard D. Erlich and Thomas P. Dunn (Greenwood, pp. 137–61). Instead of wishing a simplicity of form upon Vonnegut, as some other SF commentators have done, Broer appreciates the author's complexity, especially as it grants primacy to "human awareness" and the richness of imagination. The year's best essay, however, is Kathryn Hume's "Kurt Vonnegut and the Symbols of Meaning" (*TSLL* 24[1982]:429–47) that resolves the problem of his pessimism by examining its symbolic structure; new mythostructures that Vonnegut explores lead to a sense of otherness in which he finds salvation.

Because of the very special way in which he lives and works, Jerzy Kosinski's biography has finally stolen center stage interest from his often spectacular fiction. This movement has been growing since critics first confronted the autobiographical hints in his first novel, *The Painted Bird*, and has swelled as Kosinski added a historically revealing preface to the book's second edition (1976) and proceeded to use widely known stories about himself as the basis for plots in his more recent novels—notably *Cockpit*, *Blind Date*, and *Pinball*.

In "The Disconnected Eye: Vision and Retribution in Kosinski's *The Painted Bird*" (*par rapport* 5 and 6: 67–70), Robert E. Ziegler shows how the protagonist's vision, expressed directly through his eyes, is the vehicle for reestablishing the wholeness of identity and security of the self. How Kosinski ran afoul of the American press is detailed by Jerome Klinkowitz and Daniel J. Cahill in "The Great Jerzy Kosinski Press War: A Bibliography" (*MissR* 6,iii:171–75) with annotations from the first biographical controversies in the *New York Times Magazine* through their exposure in *The Village Voice* to the affair's climax as parody in the pages of *The Nation, The New Yorker,* and *New York* magazine. "Betrayed by Jerzy Kosinski" (*MissR* 6: 157–71) is Klinkowitz's own account of Kosinski's manipulation of himself and other critics—a tactic that is excused for being an integral part of his fictive method by which he creates layers of textuality between his novels and himself. Kosinski's working method sometimes includes having writers native to other languages than English rewrite a narrative so that Kosinski can compare how their different linguistic backgrounds influence the prose. Critical misunderstanding of this technique has led to charges of plagiarism, which are untrue.

Richard Fariña and Richard Brautigan constitute the "aging hippie" wing of innovative fiction. And although the former died in 1966, his work and even more importantly his reputation live on; Brautigan, of course, has continued to write through succeeding decades and within radically different cultural contexts, yet his stature has never been in question. For a new edition of *Been Down So Long It Looks Like Up to Me* (Penguin), novelist Thomas Pynchon has stepped out from his customary obscurity and anonymity to write an Introduction (pp. v–xiv) about Fariña and himself (who shared a student background at Cornell). Even then Fariña was a legend, which Pynchon believes allowed the easy melding of biography and imagination in his novel. Cosmic humor among many dark scenes is Fariña's success, while his own death in a motorcycle accident enshrined him in cultural history as effectively as the misadventures of his protagonist.

Two superb series books on Richard Brautigan once again eclipse the limitations of their form to be major contributions to scholarship. Edward Halsey Foster's *Richard Brautigan* (TUSAS 439) seizes a possible critical weakness—the author's tendency to be subsumed beneath his definition as a sixties counterculture phenomenon—and explores it for the true strength of his work: how Brautigan fashioned a new aesthetics from the elements of cultural revolt in his times. From first to last Brautigan opposes convention and custom, and within this gesture of revolt finds space for true freedom of life and of expression. Essentially Emersonian, Brautigan combines a western liveliness and exuberance with eastern questioning and insight, re-inventing both life-style and fictional form for our times. In another *Richard Brautigan* (Methuen, Contemporary Writers Series) Marc Chénetier favors a textual approach that reveals even more of the author's talent. There is a dialectical opposition between motion and immobility that gives his early texts a fundamental tension that "pushes the reader beyond the referential toward a metafictional reading of the structural," Chénetier notes, and finds that this practice extends to the use of similes whose radical clash of elements escape from "the logic of the original oppositions"—another example of Brautigan's escape from the trap of referentiality. "Never taken up again, they simply wrench the reader's attention away from the apparent subject and destabilize the system of reference." Free creation is thus generated on the narrative margins, with a verbal rather than referential plot structuring his work.

c. Pynchon, Barth, and Hawkes. A very good year for Pynchon criticism, with two excellent books and a strong book-length collection of original essays on this writer who lends himself to academic study. Molly Hite's *Ideas of Order in the Novels of Thomas Pynchon* (Ohio State) is the strongest book on Pynchon in years, largely because the critic here eschews treating him as a "philosophical novelist" in favor of confronting the imbedded assumptions in all narratives (philosophical included) that his experiments reveal. His novels are about order at the same time they experiment with ordering devices themselves; by contrasting external authority with internal chaos, Pynchon "generates a myth of origins for both freedom and language," which he then plays against reader expectations to show how meanings often create themselves. His ultimate interest is in systems, as most previous critics have understood. But Hite's treatment of entropy is more literary than physical, reminding us that her subject is an artist, not a scientist or philosopher.

The value of Peter L. Cooper's *Signs and Symptoms: Thomas Pynchon and the Contemporary World* (Calif.) is in its first chapter,

"Pynchon's Literary Context." Here Cooper identifies the "counter-realists"—Barth, Kesey, Vonnegut, Barthelme, Hawkes, Ishmael Reed, and others—as those who oppose the social plausibility of the "neorealists"—Bellow, Updike, Roth, James Baldwin, and Joyce Carol Oates among them. Pynchon belongs in the former camp, where his talent for the grotesque and the absurd makes him an artistic leader. Cooper continues through the catalog of antirealistic techniques, each point showing how a feature of Pynchon's work that might be baffling in itself becomes the new norm when viewed within his literary historical context. A strong amount of literary and scientific history informs Charles Clerc's important collection, *Approaches to "Gravity's Rainbow"* (Ohio State). Here are all the superstars of Pynchon criticism, in many cases expanding on the essay topics that distinguished them among the first wave of scholarship. Khachig Tölölyan covers the history of World War II as it is reimplemented in the novel; Clerc himself provides a cinematic study of its devices at work; Alan J. Friedman reviews the history of science; and Charles Russell, in the volume's most original contribution, shows how the system of language works on multiple levels (signifier, signified, and sign, as the deconstructionist theory that informs this essay parcels it out), thus allowing the reader to participate in the novel self-reflexively. Five other essays, all worthwhile, round out this original collection.

PNotes as edited by John M. Krafft and Khachig Tölölyan is itself a road map to current Pynchon studies, but it has also become the first place to look for ground breaking studies. From its three issues this year, scholars of contemporary literature in general should be sure to note Steven Moore's "'Parallel, Not Series': Thomas Pynchon and William Gaddis" (No. 11, pp. 6–26), an instructive comparison of the two authors' use of entropy, German culture, and the occult; Mark E. Workman's "*Gravity's Rainbow*: A Folkloristic Reading" (No. 12, pp. 16–25); David Seed's "Pynchon's Textual Revisions of *The Crying of Lot 49* (No. 12, pp. 39–45), which examines first serial previews to show that Pynchon was scrupulously careful about "the smallest details of phrasing" and tightening up his subject to the point that it becomes "a self-contained system"; and J. O. Tate's exhaustive study of the popular culture elements, "*Gravity's Rainbow*: The Original Sound-track" (No. 13, pp. 3–24). Issue No. 13 in general, with substantial essays by Thomas A. Bass on this same novel and by Stephen P. Schuber on the story "Entropy," should cause major journals such as *AL* pause—why should the best scholarship on this most complex of current authors be slipping away from their rightful place on center stage of our profession's major journals to a typewritten, photocopied newsletter? The excellence of *PNotes*'s contents proves that when establishment doors close, alternative publications flourish. *ConL* 24: 30–50 includes Susan Strehle's excellent "Actualism: Pynchon's Debt to Nabokov," in which the term is coined to describe the depiction of external reality without benefit of conventionally realistic techniques.

The first substantial book on John Barth in nearly a decade can be credited to Charles B. Harris with his *Passionate Virtuosity: The Fiction of John Barth* (Illinois). Harris chooses to emphasize the humanizing elements, such as closeness to life, affirmations of humanistic values, and roots in myth in order to present the sage of Maryland's Eastern shore as an essentially conservative author. For Barth, love is a primordial experience in the Jungian sense, as contact is made with the archetype. Fiction becomes mythopoeic as it suggests cosmic harmony, and although Barth's first two protagonists retreat from this possibility, his later heroes such as Henry Burlingame seek it. *Lost in the Funhouse* and *Chimera* address problems of expression, while *Letters* returns Barth's narrative interest to the world. Throughout his mythopoeic imagination constantly expands, inventing alternative realities that exist not in but through the world. One wishes Harris had delayed his study for one more year so that the climax of this development could be celebrated in the immensely more readable *Sabbatical*.

Earlier Barth criticism has stressed the mythic dimension, and in *Myths and Texts: Strategies of Incorporation and Displacement* (LSU) John B. Vickery's pages on Barth (pp. 166–83) show how he joins myth and narration by exploring the origins of story in nature. The act of telling and of self-criticizing that telling are featured in *Chimera*. Sex, myth, value, and fiction—all are invested with the values of storytelling itself (Vickery uses this term as more encompassing than "the novel"). By granting a primacy to point of view and narration, the parodic becomes the real. How minor interests help form novels are the subject of Linda S. Bergmann in "The Why's

and Wherefore's of 't': History and Humor in *The Sot-Weed Factor*"
(*MarkhamR* 12:31–36) and of John Budd in "Gardner vs. Barth"
(*NConL* 13,i:6–7). Barth's characters rewrite history to suit their
own needs, and his novel's location is a region whose true past has
been obscured by such rewritings; the history that does come through
is just like the present: meaningless fragments. Barth himself appears
as the character Tillson in John Gardner's *Mickelsson's Ghosts*, with
Gardner as the title figure who finds security in rejecting Barth's
methods.

    The John Hawkes special number of *RCF* 3, iii presents an in-
terview plus fifteen essays on the full range of Hawkes's fiction. Of
special value to American readers are the contribution by several
European Americanists (described as the "Trilaterals" in *ALS 1981*,
p. 279 and *ALS 1982*, p. 274). Their method is unobtrusively textual
and is especially suited to this most self-reflective and intertextual
of authors. In "'The Pen & the Skin': Inscription & Cryptography in
John Hawkes's *Second Skin*" (pp. 167–77), Marc Chénetier examines
"the conspicuous presence of the writing act and of its products" to
show how Hawkes maintains "a sustained continuo of print and trace
that keeps alive and ariaing at all times the chords of inscription
and flesh," only to strip it away at the very end. Christine Laniel's
"The Rhetoric of Excess in John Hawkes's *Travesty*" (pp. 177–85)
studies "the dialectics of desire as presence/absence and the inner
destructiveness of the poetic language." "From the Zero Degree of
Language to the H-Hour of Fiction: Or, Sex, Text, and Dramaturgy
in *The Cannibal*" (pp. 185–92) is André Le Vot's demonstration of
how a text is dramatized by its lines of force; this force derives from
the narrator's desire and takes shape as a proliferation of signs—in
Hawkes's case, by signs connoting aphasia, impotence, mutilation,
and chaos. How the Hawkes canon provides a developmental example
of textual theories is demonstrated by Heidi Ziegler in "Postmodernism as Autobiographical Commentary: *The Blood Oranges* and *Vir-
ginie*" (pp. 207–13), in which the latter novel parallels developments
in the genre from the 18th century to the present. The many fine
American contributions help make this number the most substantial
repository of Hawkes scholarship presently available. That "John
Hawkes is the Edgar Allan Poe of the twentieth century" is proven by
Charles Berryman in "Hawkes and Poe: *Travesty*" (*MFS* 29:643–54)

points of comparison being gothic revenge against trauma and what unfriendly critics claim is a "contemptible imagination."

d. Irving, Elkin, Coover, and Gass. After several years of bestsellerdom and interviews, John Irving is finding himself to be a regular topic in scholarship. Impressively, his full *oeuvre* and not just a few "big" novels or anthology chestnuts interest his critics. In "John Irving's Aesthetics of Accessibility: Setting Free the Novel" (*SCR* 16,i:38–44), Jane Bowers Hill surveys all his works as an ongoing struggle with the novel's alleged obsolescence for our age. Irving's own ideals are found in his essays in defense of Vonnegut's popular accessibility and Dickens's sentimentality—two qualities that keep the novel alive for readers but that scare away serious critics. "Most good novels are intelligent soap opera," Irving claims, and is justified in this case because his novels themselves examine the counterpulls between high and low art. These are novels of "ecstatics" that "transcend all rhetorical rules in order to dissolve the normal limits of flesh and spirit." Edward C. Reilly looks at Irving's first and two most recent novels in "Life Into Art: Some Notes on Irving's Fiction" (*NConL* 13,iv:8–9), noting their success at transforming the author's autobiography into fictive events capable of carrying strong meaning (destruction of the old, initiation to violence). Randolph Runyon takes the opportunity in 'Of Fishie Fumes and Other Critical Strategies in the Hotel of the Text" (*Cream City Review* 8,i-ii:18–28) to say that recurring elements in *The Hotel New Hampshire* perform the function of criticism, even to the extent that criticism is a parasite in the body of the text (by the same reasoning that language is not an instrument that man uses but rather something that thinks man and his world). How recurring elements from the world at large are accented differently in each of the novels is explained by Zoltán Abádi-Nagy in "From Graff to Garp: The World According to John Irving (Part Two)" (*HSE* 16:23–42). Irving begins with one man's relation to history, but with *The Water-Method Man* enlarges his focus to include "the human psychology of social existence"; by the time we reach Irving's latest work, history as an abstract subject has yielded to a larger concern with the contemporary social environment, climaxing in Garp's relationship to the world as an artist.

This year Stanley Elkin is his own best critic, telling Jay Clayton in "An Interview with Stanley Elkin" (*ConL* 24:1–12) that *The Living End* came to him in the form of a premise: that every idea we've ever had about God is absolutely correct and precise. But rather than satirizing the world, Elkin claims he embraces it; his characters are under the illusion that they have a special destiny, and this illusion is enough to last a lifetime. "God is all of the characters writ largest." A strong sense of Robert Coover's craft comes through in Robert A. Morace's entry on him in the *Critical Survey of Long Fiction* (Salem, pp. 617–25); with man not as the center of the universe but as the center of fiction he himself creates to explain his interest, metafiction is a natural result. Distrust of the reasoning process and distrust of the fiction making process itself leads to Coover's innovations, which in turn welcome the reader's participation (as in viewing a Cubist painting). The special issue of *Les Cahiers de Fontenay* (Nos. 28–29) devoted to new voices and visions in contemporary American fiction is distinguished by Marc Chénetier's "Robert Coover's Wonder Show" (pp. 9–22), which examines Coover from various biographical, bibliographical, and textual perspectives to conclude that "there is no History without preconceived vision and the only alternative might be defined as some sort of existential and anarchic cubism, an a-historical humanism" which is Coover's métier. Often a disruptive force will pit itself against mythical discourse to bubble up through the text's apparent surface: this is Coover's method at its best.

The best material on William H. Gass this year is found in two extensive interviews, "A Colloquy with William Gass" (*MFS* 29: 587–608) conducted by Brooke K. Horvath et al., and Bradford Morrow's "An Interview with William Gass" (*Conjunctions* No. 4, pp. 14–29). In the former piece Gass agrees with the deconstructionist separation of author from work to the extent that the work has already been given a certain perspective of its own; art enhances life through structure, not by description. To Bradford Morrow Gass describes progress on his novel *The Tunnel* as "an adaptation of the monologue in *Omensetter's Luck* in the [Jethro] Furber mode." Use of history and the forms of narrative structure are discussed, plus the philosophy of literature as he teaches it. Also described is the theft and rewriting of his first novel. An excellent analysis of "Order of Insects" is found in Susan Lohafer's *Coming to Terms with the Short Story* (LSU, pp. 135–43), where the story is seen as a com-

plex arrangement of sematics whose density is due to the interref-
erentiality of words—"deferred cognitive disclosure," as Lohafer
puts it.

e. Katz, Sukenick, Federman, and Abish. Steve Katz is respected
by his fellow innovative fictionists as the most pure and uncompro-
mising of the group, and two essays now help establish his reputation with critics. In the *DLB Yearbook: 1983* (pp. 271–79) Sinda J.
Gregory and Larry McCaffery survey Katz's biography and artistic
development before providing full analyses of his eight books of
fiction. The full-blown experimentation of his early work is shown
as preparation for his mature style, in which he "allows his imagination freedom to create scenes, characters, and events restricted not
by the validity of their human 'truths' or the accuracy of their psychology but generated by spontaneous and private rules of transformation. These rules serve to organize and direct certain aspects
of the novel" for Katz, and undergo a metafictional test in his work
Moving Parts, which is studied by J. Kerry Grant in "Fiction and the
Facts of Life: Steve Katz's *Moving Parts*" (*Crit* 24:206–13). Grant
shows how Katz's work explores the way fiction shapes our identity.
A four-part structure combines journal documentaries with travel
narrative, autobiography, and fiction, climaxing with a speculation
on numerology. Katz emphasizes throughout the need for individual
as well as collective fictions and the danger of seeing fictions as
rigid descriptions of objective reality.

Ronald Sukenick has been one of the most studied of the radically
innovative fictionists because his fiction presents such a high theoretical profile. No wonder, since his first book was a theory-based
study itself, *Wallace Stevens: Musing the Obscure* (NYU, 1967). In
"Fiction, Truth, and the Character of Belief" (*GaR* 37:835–46), C.
Barry Chabot takes the opportunity to investigate the impact of
Stevens's poetry and his aesthetics upon Sukenick's fiction. Chabot's
bias is conservative, claiming that the poet always "cautions to the
effect that the bedrock of things nonetheless be respected," warnings
that Sukenick disregards. A more sympathetic reading may be found
in Janusz Semrau's excellent "Flying a Kite: Ronald Sukenick's *Up
and Out*" (*Studia Anglica Posnaniensia* 16:255–63). Sukenick's first
two novels "offer a therapeutic clearing of the ground"; his more
recent works "generate new meanings and create new fictional re-

alities." Kite flying and the nebulously changing shapes of clouds
in the earlier work presage this development toward the writing of
"a book like a cloud that changes as it goes." Therefore Sukenick's
early novels "suggest a sequel and thus lend themselves to collective treatment."

Critics flock to the innovative fictionists for interviews. Articulate, self-conscious, and often doctoral-trained theorists themselves,
they are the first to offer convincing explanations for their work—
much as the modernists were spokesmen for a literary generation
before. Zoltán Abádi–Nagy's "A Talk with Ronald Sukenick" (*HSE*
16:5–22) selects the key notions from this author's fictional aesthetic
and subjects them to critical examination: how is reality reinvented
and why should it be? Why is defamiliarization preferable? What
new rules for readers are needed when fiction is simply "more experience"? How does improvisation create structure? Charlotte
Meyer's "An Interview with Raymond Federman" (*Story Quarterly*
Nos. 15/16, pp. 37–52) complements her talk with Ronald Sukenick
(*ALS 1982*, pp. 295–96) by touching many of the same subjects (fiction versus life, the interpenetration of imagination and factuality)
but also explores Federman's remarkable biography that often provides subject matter for his novels. Against modernist concern with
the Self, Federman posits postmodernist interest in the surface play
of fictionality; critics call his texts unreadable because they demand
coherence beneath this surface, whereas in fact his fascination with
language provides its own apparent legibility. "Because the new
fiction calls for a different mode of reading," Federman explains,
"many of these novels contain their own critical instructions on
how to read them." Federman's wealth of information and analysis
flows over into two interviews with Larry McCaffery. In *ConL*
24: 285–306 he tells the full story of his early life in Paris, and how
the artistic work of his father (as a painter) supplied some of the
structural modes used later in *Double or Nothing*. Federman's
scholarly and personal relations with Samuel Beckett (on whom
he wrote a UCLA doctoral dissertation and with whom he became
close friends) are again related to both of their fiction, and Federman explains how he revisited Paris to write his first published novel
(centering on his emigration to the States as a teenager). McCaffery's talk with Federman in *Anything Can Happen* focuses on
aesthetic issues, specifically as they relate to his practice of com-

position; this leads to a discussion of how *Take It or Leave It* was composed in French (a first for Federman) and then completely rewritten in English, making it a radically different novel. Lori Chamberlain's "*The Two-Fold Vibration*" (*ChiR* 34,i:117–23) shows how a line from Beckett's *The Lost Ones* provides the central image for Federman's most recent novel: alternating patterns of heat and light that never coincide keep Beckett's characters in a continual state of motion and anxiety, which in Federman's novel is paralleled by the old man's uncertain future. Digressions into the past pull the past and present together toward the future, with holocaust as a common theme (recalling the first sentence of Gabriel García Márquez's *One Hundred Years of Solitude*).

Walter Abish continues to stimulate interest among European Americanists. Richard Martin (Aachen) chooses Abish's two novels as examples of language and perception in "Walter Abish's Fiction: Perfect Unfamiliarity, Familiar Imperfection" (*JAmS* 17:229–41). "This is a familiar world. It is a world crowded with familiar faces and events," Abish's fiction tells us. "Thanks to language the brain can digest, piece by piece, what has occurred and what may yet occur. It is never at a loss for the word that signifies what is happening this instant," yet within this action lies immense fields of action for fiction. In "The Disposition of the Familiar" (*Representation and Performance*, pp. 73–83) Régis Durand (Lille) shows how Abish's texts exist in the presence of ghosts of former texts (by Proust and James) and exploit the complexities and ambiguities that exist between the self and the other. James saw the familiar as problematic, and Abish chooses to explore its surfaces to show how much disjunction exists within the sign (that is, between signifier and signified). "Reality testing," Durand concludes, "by making distinction possible, permits the constitution of a self that differentiates itself from external reality in the very process that establishes it as external reality."

f. **Sorrentino and Eastlake.** *In Praise of What Persists* (pp. 252–55) includes Gilbert Sorrentino's appraisal of his own influences: James Joyce, Flann O'Brien, and his parents' Italian and Irish heritage, all of which adds up to a "collaborative band" of culture. Italian art is the art of layering, to the point that the original impetus is unrecognizable; from the Irish comes an understanding of "the idiocy of

living." Both cultures "hold reality cheap, and the brilliance of the
art produced by these peoples is, by and large, the brilliance of formal invention used to break to pieces that which is recognizable to
the quotidian eye."

To *Representation and Performance* (pp. 113–29) Johann Thiel-
mans contributes "The Voice of the Irresponsible: Irresponsible
Voices," proposing that Sorrentino's *Mulligan Stew* replaces characteristics of traditional fiction with more self-apparently emphatic
effects on the reader: "It engages him in a discourse exhibiting the
freedom of pleasure and desire. . . . It wants to make him laugh or
smile constantly" as the techniques of fiction, even innovative fiction,
are deliberately exhausted. In "Blues Without Blues: Gilbert Sorrentino and the Subversion of the Novel" (*Boston Phoenix*, July 5, section
3, pp. 1–2, 4), John Domini notes how *Blue Pastoral* begins by mocking novel writing but ends up gracing the genre with verve and
panache. This dedication makes him the boldest of the innovationists, for he questions his material at the same time he uses it for
spectacular effect.

The William Eastlake special number of *Review of Contemporary
Fiction* (3,i) is noteworthy for its success in covering all aspects of
this writer's diverse career. Some consider Eastlake a western writer
(favoring *The Bronc People*); others see him as especially sensitive
to sixties politics (*The Bamboo Bed* and his reports from Vietnam);
the best appreciate that he is from start to end an innovative fictionist
who no matter what material confronts him can accomplish successful art. Editor John O'Brien's interview (pp. 4–17) covers the realistic
versus imaginary components of *Castle Keep* (just opposite of what
one might presume) and the impressionistic writing from his reporter's experience in Vietnam. "A writer fails if he cannot communicate
through the poetry of his language," Eastlake insists, and Larry Mc-
Caffery shows how this language sometimes disconcerts critics who
cannot take a joke (pp. 31–41), while James R. Lindroth finds in
Portrait of an Artist With 26 Horses that "Eastlake's poetic vocabulary corresponds to the idiom of color and shape employed in surrealism and abstract art" (pp. 27–31). As for characterization, McCaffery
reminds us that "the people he describes often *are* cliches, that they
are as shallow and two-dimensional as he draws them." The best of
his people try to escape from "the white man's trite, overly familiar
language system," thus placing Eastlake's work once more off the con-

ventional critic's graph. "The Southwestern Novels of William Eastlake" (pp. 20–27), as Gerald Haslam considers them, direct their
themes as well toward "exposing negative aspects of contemporary
American civilization," particularly as played against nature and the
environment. Delbert E. Wydler (pp. 42–49) surveys all the novels
to show how Eastlake's voice has never been "Western," but tends
instead toward experiment and satire. His ever-shifting form and
surprising characterizations sometimes lead to bad habits, but *The
Bronc People* and *Castle Keep* are lasting successes. The former novel
analyzes the Native American West as an artifice (says Barbara E.
Barnes, pp. 62–68), while the latter is more a story about artists than
of soldiers (argues George Bowering, pp. 55–62). Eric Mottram
studies the humor (pp. 68–83), while biographical and bibliographical (primary and secondary) pieces are supplied by Robert Creeley,
Edward Abbey, Albert Wachtel, and William McPheron.

viii. Subgenres

a. **The New Journalism.** In the wake of major books by Mas'ud
Zavardazeh and John Hellmann, few critics have added new topics
for study. Barbara Lounsberry, presently at work on a new edition
of the Tom Wolfe–E. W. Johnson anthology *The New Journalism*
(1973), has filed one essay this year on a major figure, "Personal
Mythos and the New Journalism: Gay Talese's *Fathers and Sons*"
(*GaR* 37:517–29). Talese is her occasion for discussing "the subjectivity of writers applying fictional techniques to nonfictional subject matter," which is a definition of The New Journalism itself. But
for Lounsberry the "personal mythos" of a writer transcends literary
invention, and the degree to which experience, traits, values, and
influence shape stories becomes the real issue, as demonstrated by
Talese's focus on father-son relationships in many of his stories.

b. **Detective and Suspense Fiction.** *MFS* 29, iii is devoted to this
topic, and among the several essays most notable are Frederic Svoboda's "The Snub-Nosed Mystique: Observations on the American
Detective Hero" (557–68) and Larry E. Grimes's "Stepsons of Sam:
Re-Visions of the Hard-Boiled Detective Formula in Recent American Fiction" (535–44). Svoboda chooses the hard core of writers—
John D. MacDonald, Russell Nye, Ross Macdonald, and others—to

establish parallels between the detective and the classic American
western hero. Both live at the edge of a moral frontier, but where the
western hero can cleanse a town and leave, the detective's work is
never done. Both forms are action centered, but the detective story
reconstructs a crime (backward from a key pivot) whereas the western looks forward from dilemma to solution. Grimes looks at three
innovationists—Jules Feiffer, Richard Brautigan, and Thomas Berger
—who have tried detective novels, and sees in their work a re-
envisioning of the formula. Though settings are the same, the point
of view has become absurdist instead of existential. Actions are seemingly causeless, and the hero is no longer rational; as a result, there
is a search for self that occupies the hero more than the pursuit of
any villain can do.

c. Science Fiction.   Thanks to Marshall Timm and others SF has its
own annual reviews of scholarship, but two trends which should be
noted here are a reexamination of fantasy with regard to SF and a
new vision of utopias in the subgenre. In *The Impulse of Fantasy
Literature* (Kent State) C. N. Manlove finds that Ursula Le Guin's
conservative fantasy allows her to see magic as not transforming
things but rather as preserving them; this is contrasted to Peter S.
Beagle's self-indulgence of wonder, an escapism due to the lack of
dialectical conflict. How fantasy often eclipses language's ability to
express is explained by Robert J. Branham in "Fantasy and Ineffa-
bility: Fiction at the Limits of Language" (*Extrapolation* 24:66–79);
the reader of fantasy is forced to assemble meanings from a fictional
atmosphere rather than from individual words and sentences. From
Hazel Beasley Pierce's *A Literary Symbiosis: Science Fiction/Fantasy
Mystery* (Greenwood), we learn that SF is idea oriented and hence
futurological, whereas fantasy mystery is action and situation oriented, focusing on the here and now. Yet each plots human reaction
to disruptions of the status quo, and drawing upon fantasy's enhance-
ment of character shores up SF at its weak point. Boris Eizykman's
"Chance and Science Fiction" (*SFS* No. 29, pp. 24–34) shows how a
perfect utopian system would have to abolish chance, because chance
destroys any vision of an ordered world. Science-fiction writers, however, have integrated randomness into the machinery of society in
order to neutralize chance's power. Robert Silverberg's *The Stochas-
tic Man* shows how extreme attempts to rid the world of chance lead

to robot life. SF shows that reason and predictability are only one side of reality, to which there are alternatives.

The Starmont Reader's Guide series as published by Starmont House continues to attract first class scholarship. No. 18 is *Robert Silverberg* by Thomas D. Clareson, whose thesis is that Silverberg has transcended the "science fiction factory" of stock techniques to fulfill Lester del Rey's assertion that "science fiction is the myth-making principle of human nature today."

d. **Fiction by Women with Women as an Issue.** "Ambivalence in Utopia" (pp. 157–80) sounds an important theme in Sheila Delany's *Writing Woman: Woman Writers and Women in Literature Medieval to Modern* (Schocken). Marge Piercy's *Woman on the Edge of Time* runs against the grain of contemporary skepticism to fashion a utopia out of realistic materials. Much of her impetus comes from the counterculture, helping emphasize the transitional nature of her utopia. The result is "a delicate suspension—utopian particles suspended in the medium of a realistic novel" that forces us to choose a different interpretation than the established order presents.

Women Writers Talking, edited by Janet Todd (Holmes & Meier), includes interviews with Erica Jong (by Wendy Martin, pp. 21–32) and with Grace Paley (by Ruth Perry, pp. 35–56). Jong discusses writing *Fanny* and sexual subjects in general; Paley describes her antiwar activities and reactions to men's power in the world, the role of women in her parents' families, the early influence of W. H. Auden as poet and teacher (at The New School), how she grew beyond the academic voice of her early fiction, and the writer's art of illumination as a political act. Rose Kamel's "To Aggravate the Conscience: Grace Paley's Loud Voice" (*JEthS* 11,iii:29–49) studies the mix of Yiddish, New York slang, and ethnic rhythms and syntax in Paley's "collage" technique. Relations with males involve bondage, but bonds between women are free of this, being sufficiently healthy to encompass death as well as life. The openness of these stories underscores her hopeful style, a utopian tone sounded by two other essays this year, Lucy M. Freibert's "World Views in Utopian Novels by Women" (*JPC* 17: 49–60) and Margaret Miller's "The Ideal Woman in Two Feminist Science-Fiction Utopias" (*SFS*, No. 30, pp. 191–98). The world views come from Ursula Le Guin (anarchy), Marge Piercy (personhood), and Salley Miller Gearhart (sisterhood). The ideal woman as portrayed in Suzy McKee Charnas's *Motherlines* has discarded many previous ideals of peaceful maternity.

Single-author studies are highlighted by Victor Strandberg's "The Art of Cynthia Ozick" (*TSLL* 25:266–312), which examines Ozick's use of Jewish identity and the lure of paganism throughout her four books of fiction. In "Family as Fate: The Novels of Anne Tyler" (*SLJ* 15,iii:47–58), Mary Ellis Gibson proposes "a sense of distance" as the key to Tyler's structure. "*Play It as It Lays*: Didion and the Diver Heroine" (*ConL* 24:480–95) is Cynthia Wolff Griffin's consideration of the emotional as a vehicle for describing a protagonist's larger search for American heritage. Eternal youth versus a Puritan sense of death and predestination are Didion's elements. Joanne S. Frye makes a convincing case in "Narrating the Self: The Autonomous Heroine in Gail Godwin's *Violet Clay*" (*ConL* 24:66–85) that Godwin uses first-person narrative as a vehicle for self-analysis and definition. Because narrative is a process of selection, her protagonist can choose which parts of her life to use in the story—parts which will not limit her in the future. Ready-made plots are learned to be rejected, freeing her from the traditional conflict between conventional female life and the expectations of the artist's existence. Rather than rejecting plot as a fixation of reality, Godwin uses a complex plot in this novel to actively shape reality.

e. Native American Fiction and the American West.   N. Scott Momaday, James Welch, and Leslie Marmon Silko continue to attract the most attention among scholars of the contemporary Native American, and despite their master status one fears that the field may be suffering from the style of tokenism that for years retarded the study of Black Literature: that of one such author at a time, and with his or her writing being studied as an anthopological curiosity. Yet for as far as they go, there are no weaknesses in the critiques of these authors. In *Native American Renaissance* (Calif.) Kenneth Lincoln grounds his study in tribal relatedness, stretching from the family and clan to tribe and Nature. Thus Momaday becomes a "word-sender" of preverbal reality, Welch a citizen of a dialectical world whose severe climate helps lead a movement toward reintegration with nature as it is, and Silko as a storyteller whose strength is her personal inflection within the community tradition. Jarold Ramsey's *Reading the Fire: Essays in the Traditional Indian Literatures* *of the Far West* (Nebraska) chooses the same three writers, praising Welch's songlike repetition, Momaday's use of the trickster figure and his sense of exclusion, and Silko's ceremonial drawing upon tradition—a mythic pre-text that creates heroic roles.

Silko's protagonist, Tayo, is a modern version of Black Elk, Marion W. Copeland asserts in *"Black Elk Speaks* and Leslie Silko's *Ceremony*: Two Visions of Horses" (*Crit* 24:158–72); the same paralytic spells and the same vision lead Tayo to a fulfillment of the mission Black Elk fails, with the novel itself as a healing ceremony. A key difference is that Tayo recognizes the feminine force (symbolized by the she-elk). In "Momaday's *House Made of Dawn*" (*Expl* 41, i: 60–62), William M. Clements finds a circular narrative beginning and concluding with the same scene; details support the belief that the ritual race is an actual one, not a figment of the imagination. Peter Wild's *James Welch* (WWS 57) is a sensitive and intelligent reading; too often critics treat Welch's themes at the expense of his language, but Wild (a poet himself) prefers to treat him as a literary artist (downplaying Welch's "Indianness" that has often led to misreadings). Interestingly, *The Death of Jim Loney* is dismissed as slick melodrama; it is to Wild's credit that he knows "series studies" such as his need not be uncritical celebrations.

Frederick Manfred is the dean of western American writers, and Mick McAllister is not about to challenge that ranking in "'Wolf That I Am . . . ! Animal Symbology in *Lord Grizzly* and *Scarlet Plume*" (*WAL* 18:21–31). As the protagonists are pursued respectively by a bear and a wolf, Manfred endows these creatures with thematic suggestiveness. The first indicates solitude and the healing power of Nature, while the second represents the wilderness's potential to accommodate man and his civilization.

University of Northern Iowa

16. Poetry: 1900 to the 1940s

James K. Guimond

This proved a good year for book-length studies of the poets of these decades including Allen Tate, Yvor Winters, Robert Frost, Robinson Jeffers, John Wheelwright, and Sherry Mangan. There were several good books on Stevens, some interesting essays on H. D. and Cummings, and many items on William Carlos Williams, a large number of these celebrating the centennial of his birth.

i. Yvor Winters, Allen Tate

The period between 1900 and 1940 was a revolutionary one in American literature, and so it is not surprising that it produced a fair number of counterrevolutionaries as well. Two of the period's more important reactionaries, Yvor Winters and Allen Tate, are the subjects of a pair of soundly written and well-researched studies. In his *Wisdom and Wilderness: The Achievement of Yvor Winters* (Georgia), Dick Davis—unlike some of Winters's other admirers—does not treat his subject's "wisdom" as a species of divine revelation. Instead, he deals with the question of how Winters's ideas developed, and how he changed from an experimental, imagist poet in the early 1920s into an avowed "reactionary" by the 1930s. To do this, Davis emphasizes his perception that virtually all of Winters's writings, including both his criticism and his poetry, were inspired by his vision in the mid-1920s that human life existed on the brink of a "horror," a chaotic "wilderness" that lurks both beneath human consciousness and outside of it in an external reality that is "an invading chaos." Like Marlow in *Heart of Darkness*, Winters "had peeped over the edge," and what he saw there had changed his life and poetry. Davis also shows how this vision is expressed in Winters's short story, "The Brink of Darkness," which is probably his best piece of writing. He then analyzes how this vision led Winters to adopt a kind of negative

mysticism—he believed in demons but not in God—that heavily influenced his criticism by making him a virulent antiromantic who was
almost obsessed with the need for technical discipline and an equally
severe, rationalistic morality in literature that would keep the "horror" at bay. Davis reminds us, however, that Winters was not a total
critical curmudgeon, that he was surprisingly fair to poets like Pound,
Williams, Crane, and Stevens in some of his early criticisms of their
poems, and that it was not until near the end of his life that he made
many of his hopelessly intolerant attacks upon their reputations. Davis
also analyzes how Winters's vision was expressed in his own poetry,
and he has particularly good readings of the poems based on mythological subjects in which he shows that these works are allegorical
versions of the conflict between order and chaos in which intellect is
opposed to and eventually triumphs over the "flux of life" that Winters considered so alarming.

Allen Tate's contributions, and debts, to Southern Agrarianism
have been discussed in great detail. In his *Allen Tate and the Augustinian Imagination* (LSU), Robert S. Deupree shows that Tate's
European and religious sources were almost equally important to his
development. "No person," Deupree writes, "made aware of the intolerable demands placed on the modern soul, could face them alone
without despairing," and he demonstrates convincingly in the first
half of his book that Augustine was one of Tate's intellectual companions who did a great deal to keep him from despairing. His
analyses of Tate's readings and his intellectual milieu are succinct
and intelligent as he surveys the influence on him of writers as diverse
as Dante, Spengler, and Rahv (as well as Poe, Baudelaire, and Eliot).
He emphasizes how *The City of God* enabled Tate to avoid having a
sentimental and nostalgic view of the "Old South," and he demonstrates that it was from *The City* and Virgil's *Aeneid* that the poet
achieved the detachment toward the present—expressed in poems
like "Aeneas at Washington" and "Ode to Our Young Pro-consuls of
the Air"—which enabled him to warn against the pretensions of a
more recent imperial city of man. In his final chapters Deupree argues
that Tate adopted what he calls an "Augustinian vision" of humanity
and culture that is embodied in both his prose and his poetry. He
does this most successfully in his chapter on "The Augustinian Perspective" in which he shows the influence of Augustine's thought
upon Tate's cultural criticism and several of his poems, particularly

"The Mediterranean." Deupree is less persuasive in the chapters that follow in which he tries to show that several of the important themes in Tate's mature poems are derived from the Augustinian triad of memory, light, and love. Overall, however, Deupree's book is a sound, well-written one that has many good insights into how Tate's intellectual, religious, and historical readings may be related to his poetry.

Richard Law's "'Active Faith' and Ritual in *The Fathers*" (*AL* 55:345–66) is devoted mostly to a close reading of Tate's novel and not his poetry. But his essay does have relevance to Tate's "Ode to the Confederate Dead," and Law's analysis of the novel fits in very well with Deupree's comments on Tate's unsentimental attitude toward the southern "Romantic Traditionalists."

ii. Wheelwright, Mangan, Jeffers

Alan M. Wald's *The Revolutionary Imagination: The Poetry and Politics of John Wheelwright and Sherry Mangan* (N.C.) is really not one but two good books. Wheelwright and Mangan—whose full fore name was John Sherry—were members of the same Boston litterary circles, friends who worked together to publish a series of radical poems as "Vanguard Verse" in the 1930s. They also both belonged to the Trotskyist Socialist Workers Party. But Mangan, unlike Wheelwright, never became a very good creative writer, and he wasted many of his talents by drinking too much and by working as a Time-Life correspondent for ten years. Wald's chapters on Mangan's colorful personality, adventures, and travels read like a good novel, or even a thriller at times, as he describes Mangan's struggles to keep his assorted identities as a sybarite, a political radical, a professional journalist, and a creative writer all functioning together in some kind of harmony. Even though he acknowledges Mangan's limitations as a poet, however, he might have tried harder to have written more of a literary biography about him. He might, for example, have compared him in more detail to a number of other writers of his generation like Robert McAlmon or James Agee who succumbed to the lures of demon rum or Luce journalism. (In fact, when Mangan did go to Paris in the 1920s, he went on "drinking marathons" with McAlmon.) Or Wald might have given more information about his unfinished "revolutionary" novel about the exploitation of Indian tin miners, since Mangan seems to have—almost deliberately—ruined his health trying to do the research for it in Bolivia in a final, pathetic effort to unite his political loyalties and his creative abilities.

Wald's chapters on Wheelwright contain more literary analysis, since Wheelwright was a more capable and dedicated writer, and he makes a good case that—before his death in 1940 in a car accident—Wheelwright had managed to achieve a creative synthesis between poetic modernism and political radicalism. Wald reviews Wheelwright's Massachusetts ancestry to show how it influenced his attitude toward modern New England, and he points out how—in Wheelwright's case—this ancestry served to legitimatize his nonconformity and his radical politics. For him, modernism *and* Marxism were both ways to challenge the 19th-century New England conservatism of the genteel tradition and to return to the radicalism of the Reverend John Wheelwright, who was a leader of the Antinomian rebellion in the 1630s. Wald also emphasizes Wheelwright's bohemian dandyism—another way to smite the genteels—and he includes several fine anecdotes illustrating Wheelwright's sincere—but very self-conscious—efforts to espouse the cause of the proletariat despite his Brahmin accent and affectations.

Wald has a thorough, intelligent analysis of Wheelwright's religious poetry of the 1920s, and his attempts to create a revolutionary political myth in his poetry, which was a mixture of humanism and socialism. As described by Wald, both Wheelwright's poetry and his behavior disprove the old cliché that writers with Marxist beliefs must be drab materialists or degenerate into social-realist hacks. In the case of Wheelwright (though not Mangan), he successfully shows that his subject deserves to be read more widely and taken seriously as representing a significant version of modernism.

Robert Zaller's *The Cliffs of Solitude: A Reading of Robinson Jeffers* (Cambridge) is an attempt to improve Jeffers's reputation by analyzing how the Oedipal themes in his poetry are related to one another and to Jeffers's life. Zaller demonstrates how these themes exist in virtually everything Jeffers wrote; and as his chapter titles indicate (e.g., "The Bloody Sire," "Fathers and Sons") he emphasizes how the various poems express different aspects of the Oedipus myth as they would be experienced by different actors or characters in that myth. Zaller also discusses, more briefly, Jeffers's religious attitudes and his ideas about politics, history, and culture. What is almost entirely lacking in this study is any commentary on the quality of Jeffers's poetry. Zaller suggests that Jeffers has been unfairly ignored or downgraded by modernist critics because he wrote narrative poetry, a "form . . . which fashionable criticism held to be bankrupt," but Zaller himself does not even raise the issue of whether Jeffers was a good or a bad poetic narrator. Instead, at the end of his book, he makes a provocative point that perhaps Jeffers should not be read as a poet at all but as a prose writer and that he should be compared with Faulkner and O'Neill. Zaller briefly sketches in a few of the issues that such a study would consider; however, he then, strangely enough, concludes, "But that is someone else's book."

iii. H.D., Cummings, Hart Crane, Marianne Moore, Elizabeth Bishop

Susan Stanford Friedman published a feminist developmental study of H.D. two years ago, and she has now applied these insights to the relationship between H.D.'s and Adrienne Rich's works in her " 'I go where I love': An Intertextual Study of H.D. and Adrienne Rich" (*Signs* 9:228–45). Friedman shows that Rich has chosen H.D. as one of the women poets to influence her as a foremother, and she emphasizes the analogies that exist between certain of their works, particularly H.D.'s "Trilogy" and Rich's *The Dream of a Common Language*, which indict patriarchy as a source of the violence that is so characteristic of modern civilization. Friedman also emphasizes how H.D.'s and Rich's visions of a regenerated feminine culture diverge on the role of men in such a culture: Rich has become a lesbian feminist, whereas H.D. "never gave up her search . . . for the masculine form of divinity that she balanced with the woman symbols he had resurrected."

Sandra M. Gilbert's " 'H.D.' Who Was She?" (*CL* 24:496–511) is a slightly polemical but definitely useful guide through the H.D. biography industry that has been so busy for the past few years. She strongly attacks Janice S. Robinson's *H.D. The Life and Work of an American Poet* (Houghton Mifflin, 1982), which probably should have been entitled *Life and Loves*, since Robinson's great *clef* is her claim that H.D. was the original of Connie Chatterley and that her daughter was Lawrence's child. Gilbert spends most of her essay demolishing Robinson's "soap opera" by arguing, among other matters, that Lawrence was living too far from H.D. and was probably too poor to have had the train fares he would have needed to be her lover at the time in question. In the remainder of her essay, however, Gilbert raises the more important critical questions of the influences which Lawrence and H.D. may have had on one another's *literary* creative activities, and she also raises the issue of what H.D. might have learned from Freud that would have influenced her as a writer. Gilbert's essay is a good reminder that H.D. still deserves to be studied as a significant modern writer in her own right.

The use of Freudian theories for analysis of a poet, which Gilbert recommends for H.D., is the subject of Milton A. Cohen's "Cummings and Freud." (*AL* 55:591–610). Cohen briskly integrates biographical details, with material about Cummings's prose of the 1920s and his readings in Freud's works into an unusually well-organized essay. He also skillfully relates these materials to Cummings's poetry of the period, including its techniques, and to his interest in painting. Cohen emphasizes how Cummings's understanding of Freud probably caused him to use oxymorons frequently in *Tulips and Chimneys*, influenced his poems about sex, and also explains the conflicts and tensions in his personal life as he struggled with his responsibilities as a lover, father, and husband. Cohen ends the essay with a psychoanalytical and biographical reading of Cummings's 1927 play *Him*. A very good piece of criticism.

Joseph Schwartz's *Hart Crane: A Reference Guide* (Hall) is a very useful compilation of Crane's writings and of writings about him. In his Introduction Schwartz gives a brief, helpful survey of the criticism Crane's poetry received in his lifetime and in the decades after his death, and he summarizes some of the important critical issues. His survey of the writings about Crane (including reviews of books about him) is arranged by year from 1919 to 1980 and includes abstracts of the books and essays. Since Crane's reputation and poetry have been the fields for so many battles about modernism, the abstracts are particularly valuable. The book's index includes the names of the critics, the titles of their works, and the titles of Crane's poems.

There were two disappointing articles on Marianne Moore's relationships with other writers. Glenway Wescott's "A Succession of Poets" (*PR* 50:393–406) is a succession of dreary anecdotes about Wescott's encounters with E. A. Robinson (drunk and depressed), Maxwell Bodenheim (drunk and obnoxious), and Robert Frost (deaf but sober). Wescott then gives a longer series of comments on

Moore's personality and poetry, which contains one interesting detail—Moore told Wescott she had learned more about writing from
Louise Bogan than she had from anyone else—and some commonplace generalities about Moore's precision, sense of humor, and sincerity. Lynn Keller's "Words Worth a Thousand Postcards: The
Bishop/Moore Correspondence" (*AL* 55:405–429) is far more promising. Keller has read and analyzed the hundreds of letters that
Moore and Bishop sent one another that have survived (approximately 150 of Bishop's and 200 of Moore's), but she has devoted
most of her study to a detailed analysis of Bishop's emotional attitudes and her apprentice-mentor relationship to Moore. For this
reason, she often seems to slight Moore's side of the relationship as,
for example, she does when she quotes a request by Bishop for a list
of three or four books of modern French poetry to illustrate her
"extreme humility" but does not even mention whether or how Moore
responded to that request. Moreover, even though Keller points out
that Moore was acting virtually as Bishop's editor between 1935–40,
"for Bishop was then sending most of her manuscripts to Moore for
criticism before submitting them to publishers," she gives only a
relatively small number of specific examples of the changes that
Moore suggested as a result of her "minute and painstaking" scrutiny
of the manuscripts. She does, however, have a good—though rather
brief—analysis of the change that Moore demanded for Bishop's
"Roosters." Perhaps at some time in the future, hopefully the near
future, Keller will do an additional study of the correspondence with
more specific information about the two poets' poems and how
Moore may have responded in her poetry to the stimulus of seeing
the work of so talented an apprentice.

iv. Sandburg, MacLeish

Carl Sandburg's *Ever the Winds of Chance* (Illinois) is presumably
one of the last books *by* a poet from the 1900–1940 time period to be
published. Originally written in the form of a rough draft by Sandburg in 1955, the fifteen chapters of *Winds* were meant to be a sequel
to his earlier autobiography, *Always the Young Strangers*, which he
published in 1953. Sandburg's age and his other commitments prevented him from revising or finishing this book, and now his daughter Margaret and George Hendrick have put it into publishable

form. In their "Introduction" they imply that *Winds* might have been a better book if Sandburg had completed it. This may be true, but *Winds* can also be read as a representative work by Sandburg that has most of the virtues and vices of his other writings, including his poetry. It is a pleasant book that is easy to read, but it is often banal and plodding. Twelve of its chapters are about the years (1898–1902) he spent at Lombard College in Galesburg, Illinois. Lombard was founded by members of the Universalist Church, a vehemently anti-Calvinist sect, who believe that everyone will be saved, and it is not difficult to imagine how this idea might have influenced Sandburg, the poet, who wrote *The People, Yes*. But Sandburg the autobiographical writer does not speculate on such matters, and most of the Lombard chapters are accumulations of capsule biographies of Sandburg's professors and classmates, quotes and paraphrases from his college writings, lists of speakers at Knox College, and a great deal of information about the odd and part-time jobs that he used to support himself. In the last three chapters, he describes his wanderings after he left Lombard and his growing determination to become a writer. There are some political reminiscences in these chapters as Sandburg leads up to his brief career as an organizer for the Social Democratic Party; but he describes his experiences during this period, including the ten days he spent in the Pittsburgh jail and his meetings with anarchists, in such benign terms and with so little passion that it is difficult to imagine how he could have become a socialist or have written the poetry in *Chicago Poems*. Perhaps the most revealing detail in *Ever the Winds of Chance* is one of Sandburg's college papers, a very moral analysis of Stevenson's "Dr. Jekyll and Mr. Hyde" in which he claims Stevenson's message is "that the tendency toward evil in a person must not be acknowledged in one's self, much less indulged in." "I didn't," he commented, "put it in the paper that I [had] searched myself for the Jekyll and Hyde streaks in me and found several Hyde streaks that it wouldn't do to write about." Over fifty years later, he still was not writing about his "Hyde streaks"—which may account for both his popularity and his limitations as a poet.

The *Massachusetts Review* published a tribute to Archibald Mac-Leish, who died in 1982, in its Winter, 1982 issue (23:657–704). The tributes to MacLeish by Henry Steele Commager and John Ward contain little commentary on his poetry; the one by Joseph Langland is a pleasant survey of MacLeish's works, their relation to his politics, and their various poetic merits. But the best part of the tribute is a transcription of an interview with MacLeish (by William Heyen and Anthony Piccione) at a reading he gave in 1974. In it he gives many lively, interesting comments on the writers, particularly the poets, whom he admired and the effects that their poems had on him. His mixed emotions about Ezra Pound—admiration for his poetry, hatred of his politics—are particularly revealing and remind us that even poets can have feelings about war, peace, and politics.

v. Frost

A student of numerology might be intrigued by the arcane significance of the triadic patterns formed by certain critical comments on Frost that were published in 1983. In one issue of *The Explicator* there are three items by Laurance Perrine interpreting passages from 'The Tuft of Flowers," "Revelation," and "Nothing Gold Can Stay" (42:36,36–38,38–39); and during one year *The South Carolina Review* published exactly three articles on Frost. In "Markin' the *Frost Line*" Robert F. Fleissner claims that certain of Frost's poems, particularly "The Objection to Being Stepped On," should be read as a commentary on Edwin Markham's famous "The Man with the Hoe" (*SCR* 16:120–24). Marjorie E. Cook's "The Serious Play of Interpretation" is an analysis of the "serious play" of irony in Frost's writings in which she emphasizes that this irony is poetic or metaphorical in nature rather than "philosophical irony" (*SCR* 15:77–87). Finally, in an article with the ponderous title, "I Always Keep Seeing a Light as I Talk with Him': Limning the Robert Frost/Ridgely Torrence Relationship"—George Monteiro deals with the probable influence of Torrence's poem "The Lesser Children" upon several of Frost's works. Monteiro shows how Frost's personal relationship to Torrence—like so many of his other literary "friendships"—was clouded by Frost's vanity and his chronic opportunism. (Torrence was poetry editor of the *New Republic* from 1920 to 1934, and he published many of Frost's poems in that magazine.) He then claims that his poetic relationship to Torrence included incorporating and adapting—"perhaps without Frost's full, conscious knowledge"—a number of images, themes, and words from Torrence's 1906 "The Lesser Children" in his own "Mowing," "A Leaf-Treader," "Nothing Gold Can Stay," and "Desert Places" (*SCR* 15:32–43).

William W. E. Slights's "The Sense of Frost's Humor" (*CP* 16: 29–42) is an application of various theories of comedy, by classical and modern authors, to a number of Frost's poems. Slights begins with commentaries on several of the poet's works that are obviously comic or satiric in intention, such as "Haec Fabula Docet" and "My Aunt Jerry," and he then shows it is helpful to apply a comic perspective to several of Frost's more serious poems, like "West Running Brook." Sandra W. Tomlinson analyzes "Frost's 'The Draft Horse'" (*Expl.* 42:28–29) from an existentialist perspective to point out what its landscape, imagery, and action have in common with themes in such works as Beckett's *Waiting for Godot* and Camus's "Myth of Sisyphus." And finally, in the article that inspired this trio of reviews, Jere K. Huzzard has analyzed the triadic patterns in "Frost's 'Design'"—grammatically and otherwise—to discover that the final couplet may be read so that it implies a trio of possibilities: certainty, uncertainty, or "deliberate ambiguity." (*Expl.* 42:26–27).

Dorothy Judd Hall's *Robert Frost: Contours of Belief* (Swallow) is not exactly a work of literary criticism. Instead it is essentially a collection of religious reassurances on various topics that have been illustrated with excerpts from Frost's poems, notebooks, letters, lectures, his "offhand remarks during his readings," and his private conversations. Hall clearly does not accept the position, advanced by some of Frost's critics, that he expressed disturbing doubts about humanity and its relation to the divine. Her technique is to quote from his poems—including some that might be interpreted as expressing skepticism—and then to discuss them in the context of passages from other poems, Frost's prose, and his conversational remarks until they can be interpreted in an affirmative way.

vi. Stevens

Peter Brazeau's *Parts of a World: Wallace Stevens Remembered: An Oral Biography* (Random House) is a rather long, diffuse book composed of selected passages from the tape-recorded interviews that Brazeau made with more than 150 of Stevens's assorted business colleagues, literary acquaintances, neighbors, nephews, and nieces.

(Approximately 90 of the people interviewed made the "final cut.") The interviews are interspersed with extensive comments by Brazeau that identify who the people are and what were their relationships to Stevens or to his family. Like most oral histories, this one is rather repetitious, and Brazeau might have improved it a little if, for example, he had cut a few of the many references to Mrs. Stevens's withdrawn personality and the dreary details of Stevens's domestic life. The book would also have been better if Brazeau or his editors had discovered another format for presenting the extensive information, from letters and other interviews, that is contained in notes that sometimes are longer and more complicated than the interviews they are meant to explain. But despite these faults, the book is still a very worthwhile contribution to our understanding of Stevens's personality and some significant "parts" of his world.

Brazeau's book has a few surprises. According to several of the people whom he interviewed, including the hospital chaplain, Stevens became a convert to Roman Catholicism as he was dying, and he confided to them that he had loved to meditate in St. Patrick's Cathedral when he was in New York. It is hardly what one would expect from the author of "Sunday Morning," but it would have been in keeping with his other profession—a final insurance policy, so to speak, just in case . . . (Stevens's daughter strongly denies that her father did become a convert, however, and he did not receive—or ask for—a Catholic burial service, so there are still some questions about his final religious feelings that need to be explored.) Another, milder surprise is that—far from being a secret—the fact that Stevens wrote poetry was very well known at the Hartford; he had his secretary type his poems, on company time; but his business colleagues were not exactly an appreciative audience—one called his poems "the biggest bunch of gobbledygook," and another told Stevens that he liked Robert Service's poetry better.

As its subtitle indicates, Glen G. MacLeod's *Wallace Stevens and Company: The Harmonium Years 1913–1923* (UMI) refers to Stevens's early career, and the "company" MacLeod describes were his early literary associates and influences. In Brazeau's oral history, several of Stevens's insurance colleagues spoke of him as a "loner," but MacLeod's brief, intelligent, and well-researched study shows that Stevens the poet was slightly more gregarious, at least when he was writing the *Harmonium* poems. His contacts were mostly with the New York avant garde of the period that included Donald Evans, Louise Norton, Carl Van Vechten, Walter Arensberg, Marcel Duchamp, and William Carlos Williams. Because so many of these modernists were minor and sometimes rather eccentric figures, some scholars have ignored their existence almost entirely and treated Williams and Stevens as if they concocted their early poems out of thin air, some letters from Pound, and a few anthologies of French poetry. MacLeod shows that when they are considered as a group these avant-garde artists and literati did have some creative vitality, and he demonstrates what Stevens learned from them and how he adapted it to his own purposes. He has particularly good passages analyzing the literary relationships that existed between Stevens and Arensberg and Stevens and Williams.

Leonora Woodman's *Stanza My Stone: Wallace Stevens and the Hermetic Tradition* (Purdue) is a good counterweight to Brazeau's oral history. Brazeau's interviews often, in effect, domesticate Stevens and make him seem like "one of the boys" at the Hartford who was as ordinary as any evening in New Haven. Woodman sees Stevens as a wonderfully arcane poet as she attempts to show that he may have been a secret, very secret, student of alchemy and that many of his most important poems can be read as expressing various aspects of the alchemists' "hermetic philosophy." The hard evidence that she is able to offer for this theory is very conjectural, and at one point she admits that "the effort to reconstruct Stevens's spiritual education, as well as to suggest the means by which he came to know the Hermetic vision, must, ultimately, remain speculative." She does not show that Stevens read any particular books on alchemy, and many of the commentaries on hermeticism that she uses to elucidate his poems actually were published and/or translated years after the poems were written. So instead of showing that Stevens was influenced by any readings, Woodman speculates in her last chapter that he may have been acquainted with the ideas of a group of German pietists who had a community at Ephrata, in eastern Pennsylvania eighteen miles from Reading, in the 17, 18th and 19th centuries. The pietists at the Ephrata Cloister seem to have been Rosicrucians, they may have tried to do a bit of alchemy, and it is remotely possible that Stevens may have heard about their doctrines from people who were descended from the "last initiates" when he was a young man in Reading. Stevens did mention these pietists in an essay on Williams, and he also mentioned Ephrata in a poem; however, there does not seem to be any evidence that he had much interest in the Cloister.

On the other hand, Woodman does find an interesting assortment of analogies between alchemical doctrines and certain phrases and themes in Stevens's poems. Some of these analogies are far-fetched. Some of her other connections are more convincing as she points out similarities between the alchemists' vaguely transcendental theories and the vaguely oracular language that occurs in the poems when Stevens uses terms like "supreme fiction" and "ultimate poem." Her readings of poems like "Owl's Clover" and "Large Red Man Reading" do suggest that he may have had more interest in mysticism (and less in systematic philosophy) than earlier critics have realized. Thus, even though Woodman may not be correct when she claims that his writings were "informed by a view of spiritual correspondence" that was "a received system drawn intact from a coherent and codified symbolic tradition," she does demonstrate that it is possible to interpret Stevens's poetry in at least semireligious terms.

The Fall, 1983 *Wallace Stevens Journal* is a special issue on "Stevens and Postmodern Criticism," edited by John Serio. Joseph Riddel's "The Climate of Our Poems" (7:59–75) and Patricia Parker's "The Motive for Metaphor: Stevens and Derrida" (7:76–88) deal primarily with theoretical issues. Riddel, in an energetic and witty essay, reviews theories of postmodernism (mostly Lentricchia's) in relation to the criticism of Stevens's poetry by Bloom, Miller, et al. Parker's essay is rather scholarly as she analyzes assorted classical and neoclassical descriptions of metaphor and relates them to Derrida's theory and Stevens's poems. Joseph Kronick's and Michael Beehler's essays are less theoretical and more concerned with showing how Stevens can be read as a postmodernist in his essays and poetry. Kronick's "Large White Man Reading" (7:89–98) deals mostly with his religious ideas in relation to Nietzshe's—Kronick considers Stevens's "giant" to be a Nietzchean poet—but he includes some asides about Heidegger and Derrida. Michael Beehler's "Stevens' Boundaries" (7:99–107) is an explication of Stevens's 1937 essay "The Irrational Element in Poetry" and passages from several of his poems to show how the poet was aware of one of the most important concepts in postmodernist poetics—that language is a boundary or a horizon and therefore we cannot "move outside its foreshortening constraints."

R. D. Ackerman has written two analyses of important motifs in Stevens's poetry. In "Death and Fiction: Stevens' Mother of Beauty" (*ELH* 50:401–14), he discusses the significance of the "mother" in "Sunday Morning," where she is a solar earth mother uniting life and death in a natural creativity cycle. In other poems by Stevens, Ackerman says, the mother is a nocturnal muse who inspires fictions, and the poet's own thought processes; and therefore she can no longer give "access to nature's unifying domain." Thus, instead of signifying the "Sunday Morning" poet's faith in a kind of romantic natural supernaturalism, she becomes a source of skepticism in Stevens's mature poems. In his late poems she becomes a less important figure who makes the poet ironically aware of the "illusion" that he was ever part of the natural cycle. In "Desire, Distance, Death: Stevens' Meditative Beginnings" (*TSLL* 25:616–31), Ackerman deals with Stevens's poetic awareness of a "break with nature" in the context of his early poems. In "Peter Quince at the Clavier" he dramatized the "fall from natural time (lessness) into human temporality" and the failure of romantic desire, but in "Le Monocle de Mon Oncle" he transformed these losses into a heightened sense of his identity as a reflective poet, a "rose rabbi," who is able to possess reality meditatively and thus defend himself against "lost youth, lost love, and lost belief."

In her "Wallace Stevens' 'The Rock'" (*CP* 16:45–56), Janet McCann claims that this poem, which is usually read as a pessimistic one expressing resignation to death, is not completely bleak and that it possesses a sense of mysticism. She interprets the parts of the poems as moving from a rational, pessimistic idea of existence as a mere "illusion that we were ever alive," to a more optimistic but hypothetical belief that the artist as "icon-maker" can create meanings for existence that heal the split between mind and world; however, she claims that in the final part of the poem Stevens "backs off from [this] ultimate affirmation" by saying that though we may know the "rock of reality gives meaning to life ... we cannot read this meaning."

Pam Pugsley's analysis of "To the One of Fictive Music" (*Expl.* 42:42–45) is an attempt to explain that poem, not as an inconclusive work about the "debate between reality and the imagination," but as an exploration of ideas about the subject. Applying Stevens's comments on music in "Peter Quince" to "One of the Fictive Music," she concludes that in the latter poem he is suspicious of the imagination because, even though we cannot live without it, it may still insidiously betray our grasp on reality.

vii. William Carlos Williams

1983 was the centennial of Williams's birth, and as one would expect, there were many publications about him during that year—some of them good and a few of them bad.

That Williams was very interested in, and influenced by, the visual arts has been well known and well discussed by many critics and scholars. In *The Visual Text of William Carlos Williams* (Illinois), Henry M. Sayre tries to go a step farther by claiming that Williams was essentially a visual artist rather than a verbal one and that he "has been mistakenly canonized by an entire generation of poets and critics" who have emphasized his works' verbal qualities. Sayre's argument is undermined by his selection and his interpretation of many of his materials. Thus, when he wants to discount Williams's comments on the verbal qualities of his poetry, Sayre is quick to warn the reader about the poet's limitations as a self-critic ("Williams's discussions of his measure are notoriously inadequate"), but when Williams's criticism supports Sayre's theories he quotes from it copiously and without caveats. To show that Williams was influenced during the 1920s by the visual arts, Sayre heavily emphasizes what he could have learned from Juan Gris and the "Steiglitz circle." But he scarcely mentions that Williams was also learning a great deal about modernism during the same period from Pound and Joyce, and that Williams was not exactly an admirer of Steiglitz and some of his ideas.

Sayre's thesis is also undermined by the publication of the correspondence between Williams and Richard Eberhart in "Making Poetry a Continuum" (*GaR* 37:533–64), with an introduction by Stephen Corey. In these letters Williams never mentions the visual patterns that Sayre considers so significant, but he comments frequently on the verbal qualities that he considers very important to modern poetry. (E.g., "I am as you know a stickler for the normal contour of phrase which is characteristic of the language as we speak

it. It gives to a poem a distinction which it can get in no other way.")
Reading such remarks, it is hard to believe that Williams was primarily concerned with how his poems looked on the page rather than
how they sounded or that (as Sayre claims) his "late poetry is to
American poetry what Jackson Pollock's monumental drip canvases
are to American painting."

The Eberhart-Williams correspondence is lively and interesting,
particularly when they debate "what is it that makes a poem now-a-
days?" (Williams's phrase). Both poets defended their viewpoints
ably, and, in the process, they also defined their conceptions of how
poems should be constructed and how they should be related to language. The letters also contain some references to other poets, and in
one of them Williams urges Eberhart to read Allen Ginsberg's *Howl!*
because "it will do you good to find out how this Jew raises his voice."
In "Documents of Presumption," (*AL* 55:1–23), Gay Sibley expounds
upon the Williams-Ginsberg relationship to argue that Williams was
offended by Ginsberg's "presumption," and that he included his
letters in *Paterson* to satirize him. Like the editors of *Time* back in
the 1950s, Sibley does not approve of Ginsberg's manners, and he
tries to show that Williams must have shared his disapproval by
analyzing *Paterson*, by quoting from several of Williams's biographers, and by interpreting some of Williams's comments on Ginsberg
so that they seem relatively derogatory. He alludes to, but does not
quote from, Williams's laudatory introduction to *Howl!*, and he makes
no effort to discuss Ginsberg's poetry or to understand why Williams
might have praised it and been interested in Ginsberg. Nor does he
try to compare Williams's pater-son attitude toward Ginsberg with
his attitude toward a number of other younger poets like Kenneth
Rexroth and Gilbert Sorrentino. As an exercise in 1980s genteel social
criticism, Sibley's essay is revealing, but it is not very successful as
literary analysis.

One of the best books published on Williams (and also Pound)
has been edited by Daniel Hoffman, *Ezra Pound & William Carlos
Williams: The University of Pennsylvania Conference Papers* (Penn.).
The conference was held in 1981 to celebrate the 75th anniversary of
the date when Pound (M.A.) and Williams (M.D.) received their
degrees from Pennsylvania. The essays on Williams include Emily
Mitchell Wallace's "Poets at Pennsylvania," a biographical study of
Pound's and Williams's academic and extracurricular activities—with

photographs of Pound costumed as a Greek maiden for a production of *Iphigenia* and Williams costumed as Polonious for a musical comedy version of *Hamlet* (plus a photograph of Marianne Moore dressed as a Renaissance lady-in-waiting for the 1906 Bryn Mawr May Day).

Theodora R. Graham's "'*Her Heigh Compeynte*': The Cress Letters of William Carlos Williams' *Paterson*" is an extremely important analysis of the letters from "Cress" (Marcia Nardi) that Williams included in *Paterson*. Graham has corresponded with Nardi and interviewed her to discover her viewpoint of her difficulties with Williams and the letters he used in his poem. Graham narrates the development of the painful relationship that developed between Williams and Nardi, and she scrupuously analyzes all of the letters they exchanged that are extant and available in collections. She shows how Williams created his portrait of "Cress" by selecting and editing Nardi's letters, she reviews the formal difficulties created by Williams's inclusion of the letters in *Paterson*, and she concludes with a discussion of Williams's reactions to the episode as expressed in *Paterson* and his theories about women and poetry.

Other valuable items on Williams from this conference include "The Ideas in Things," a discussion of Williams's poetry by Denise Levertov; a good paper on "William Carlos Williams in the Forties: Prelude to Postmodernism" by Paul Christensen; some passages from the poet's letters to James Laughlin, from Laughlin's gold mine of Pound-Williams correspondence, with Laughlin's comments on them; and a listing of assorted items, mostly letters, by and about Williams that are in the University's Archives and Collections. There are also some brief, but very useful speculations by Hugh Kenner on the effect on Williams's writing by his medical studies and the kind of writing he had to do for them: "The case history is dense, it is cryptic, it is crisp, and it is factual. That is not a bad way to be writing day in, day out if God is determined to drive Keats from your mind."

Even though he uses a prose work, Williams's *In the American Grain*, as his case study, Paul L. Jay's "American Modernism and the Uses of History: The Case of William Carlos Williams" (*NOR* 9: 16–25), raises issues that are relevant to other modernist writers of the period such as Crane, Tate, Pound, and Eliot. He compares Williams's cultural concerns during the early 1920s with those of Pound, Eliot, and Crane by pointing out that they all were writing works in which history becomes a "topic of literature because it is deemed to

possess a kind of recuperative value." He relates this idea to the crisis
in historical studies that was articulated by Henry Adams in *The
Education*, and he points out that the creative principle behind this
approach to history lies in its emphasis upon the "metaphorical" connections that the writer discovers between figures who would not be
considered related to one another by other kinds of historical studies.

Another study of Williams's early writings is Roy Miki's *The
Prepoetics of William Carlos Williams: Kora in Hell* (UMI). Miki
does not deal primarily with Williams's poetry, which is written in
lines, but with the poetic prose of *Kora*. In the course of his analysis
of that work, however, he relates it very well to Williams's biography,
the cultural context of early 1920s modernism in the United States,
and the themes and techniques of his poems—particularly those in
Spring and All. What Miki manages to convey is a sense of how Williams might have felt as he discovered modernism, those moments
when he became aware that he was not merely "—the artist, good or
bad—but a new creature." In a decade in which journals are becoming increasingly glutted with anecdotes about trivial personal encounters with the great modernists of the 1920s, it is important, now
and then, to read a book that emphasizes how exciting and lively
20th-century modern poetry and art were to the poets and artists
who actually created it.

William Carlos Williams: Man and Poet, ed. Carroll F. Terrell
(National Poetry Foundation/Univ. of Maine) is a big, miscellaneous
collection of all kinds of information, reminiscences, criticism, and
bibliographies about Williams. Among the poets who discuss Williams's poetry and personality are Ginsberg, Creeley, Carruth, Levertov, and Sorrentino (writing on Williams's prose), and there are
also two reprints of Pound's comments on Williams, originally written in 1913 and 1928. There are critical articles on Williams's free
verse, *Paterson*, *Sour Grapes*, his early and late poetry, his short
stories, and his novels. Finally, there is a long, detailed useful "Annotated Bibliography" by Joseph Brogunier of works about Williams
published between 1974 and 1982. The Centennial Issue of the *William Carlos Williams Review* contains reminiscences about Williams
by his son William Eric Williams and Mary Ellen Solt. Cecelia Tichi's
"Twentieth Century Limited: William Carlos Williams' Poetics of
High Speed America" (9:49–72) is a survey of comments about the
"fast-paced" quality of life in the United States, primarily in its popu-

lar culture, in relation to Williams's poetry and his desire to avoid "obsolescence" in his writing and his medical career. Peter Schmidt has an analysis of Williams's poem "These" in relation to his early fascination with Keats's poetry, and Henry Sayre and Emily Mitchell Wallace comment on Williams's "Tribute to the Painters" (9:74–90, 125–55).

A rather different centennial tribute to Williams is the September, 1983, issue of the *Journal of the Medical Society of New Jersey*, edited by Geraldine Hutner, Dr. Avrum Katcher, and Dr. Arthur Krosnick (both M.D.s). Perhaps someday organizations like the New Hampshire Grange or the Connecticut Surety Bond Association (if such groups do exist) will make similar efforts on behalf of Frost and Stevens. The New Jersey doctors did a fine piece of work for Williams. Besides the traditional reminiscences—one by artist Henry Neise, one by a former writer for the *Bergen County Record*, and another one by William Eric Williams—the issue contains several articles on Williams by critics and one by a medical doctor. It also contains reprints of many of Williams's poems and stories and an excellent selection of reproductions of paintings by artists who influenced him, such as Brueghel, Marin, Demuth, and Matisse. A final fascinating aspect of this issue, as a text, is its advertisements; it is an unusual experience to read poems, fiction, and literary criticism interspersed not with ads for University Presses and Reviews, but with pages of images and language proclaiming the virtues—many in vivid color—of "Propraholol HCl long lasting capsules," "Fluoxymesterone U.S.P. Tablets, 10 mg," and something called "a peripheral vasodilator"—all accompanied by tiny print columns of "Indications" and "Side Effects." Perhaps someone will speculate upon the side effects *these* texts had upon Williams's prose and poetry?

Rider College

17. Poetry: The 1940s to the Present

Lee Bartlett

This year saw little relief from our outbreak of critical tarantism as once again myriad books and articles on the postmoderns forced their way into the dance. Yes, another fifty-odd volumes and scores of essays (excluding even the most extended reviews) of just about every type: biography, explication, theory, comparative and source studies, collections of interviews and primary pieces, and reference works. Additionally, 1983 gave us the first issues of Cid Corman's *Origin* (fifth series, now published by Terry Terrell's National Poetry Foundation), the "language-oriented" *Poetics Journal, American Poetry: a critical triquarterly*, and the charming monthly of opinion and reviews, *Exquisite Corpse*.

i. Groundwork

Two years ago, M. L. Rosenthal and Sally M. Gall argued in an essay in *CL* that "the modern sequence is the decisive form toward which all developments of modern poetry have tended." Set against the epic, they pointed out, the sequence seems to cry out for subjectivity, while solving the problem of the "encompassment of disparate and often powerfully opposed tonalities and energies," which is beyond the lyric. Now Oxford has published a 500-page study of the nature and evolution of this "new anatomy," *The Modern Poetic Sequence: The Genius of Modern Poetry*, and it is an impressive book. Many of the volume's chapters have been reviewed in earlier numbers of *ALS*, and three quarters of the work (including discussions of a number of British poets, as well as Williams, Dickinson, Masters, Eliot, Pound, Whitman, and Crane) will be touched upon in earlier sections of this number. I'll limit comment here to the coauthors' examination of more recent figures. Calling Hart Crane and Charles Olson "two American models," Rosenthal and Gall see the first three volumes of *Maximus* as indicative of Olson's turning "toward pure faith in the magnetic, implicitly form-discovering autonomy of the associative process," a movement that eluded Crane, finding it shaped by the elegiac. Robert Lowell's *Life Studies* and *Day by Day*, W. D. Snodgrass's "Heart's Needle," John Berryman's *77 Dream Songs*, Allen Ginsberg's *Kaddish*, Sylvia Plath's "last poems," and Anne Sexton's "Divorce Papers" are all discussed in the context of the "confessional mode." Taking Lowell's *Life Studies* as the *"locus classicus* of confessional poetry in the last generation," Rosenthal and Gall suggest that the "psychological pressure" that called these various sequences into being was, unlike the meditative sequences of their precursors Stevens and Auden, the "active element"; here "the chaos of the psychic situation becomes the ground of a reorientated art in which the beset self is the testing-ground and embodiment of all human possibilities." Sensing Ramon Gutherie's *Maximum Security Ward* to be "neglected," the authors argue for the "lyrically evocative element" in the sequence, while reading Galway Kinnell's *The Book of Nightmares* as "dominated by a meditating sensibility that appears completely consistent and localized in time and place." Finally, Muriel Rukeyser's "Waterlily Fire" evinces "a rhetoric of secret emotions" and Adrienne Rich's "The Phenomenology of Anger" is "dynamic," yet both poems display a didacticism that diminishes "the affective purity and authority of the work."

Throughout the study, readings of the individual poems are generally sensitive, and while maintaining their overarching concern, Rosenthal and Gall never seem guilty of thesis-mongering. Further, the very attempt to draw attention to the prevalence of the sequence in the 20th century is commendable. However, for all the book's virtues it seems to me that at most every turn *The Modern Sequence* is far too predictable, a fine synthesis but hardly breaking any new ground. Once the thesis has been established do we, at this point, really need sustained general discussions yet again of, for example, *The Waste Land, The Cantos, Paterson, Maximus, Life Studies*, the *Dream Songs*, and so forth? Maybe I've simply been reading far too much on these poems for far too long in the service of *ALS*, which is hardly the fault of either Rosenthal or Gall. However, the book's subject offered such possibilities for opening up the canon: Kenneth Rexroth's early *The Homestead Called Damascus* (or, really, any of the longer poems), Gertrude Stein's *Tender Buttons*, Melvin B. Tolson's *Harlem Gallery*, Ed Dorn's *Slinger*, Charles Reznikoff's *Testament*, Robert Duncan's *Passages*, Diane Wakoski's *Greed*, Louis Zukofsky's *A*, Maxine Kumin's "The Kentucky Poems," Robert Creeley's *Daybook*, William Everson's *Rose of Solitude*, Gary Snyder's *Myths & Texts*, Robert Kelly's *Loom*, Nathaniel Tarn's *A Nowhere for Vallejo*, Clayton Eshleman's *The House of Ibuki*, Theodore Enslin's *Synthesis*, Diane DiPrima's *Loba*, Shirley Kaufman's "Jerusalem Notebook," and on and on. It is of course unfair to ask the authors to cover every inch of ground opened up by their rubric, but it is difficult to understand why *none* of the works or poets above are even mentioned in the text. Would the objectivists, for example, raise difficulties for the thesis, or would truly experimental work? Do the authors have a grudge against West Coast poets? How, even by the most conservative standards, can such a study bypass Stein, Zukofsky, and Rexroth (or on the British side J. H. Prynne) without even a nod? Thus, while *The Modern Poetic Sequence* is obviously the year's most important single volume, my enthusiasm must be tempered by an honest disappointment.

The long poem is also the subject of a series of short (and charmingly reactionary) pieces in *KR* (5,ii): in "The Dilemma of the Long Poem" (pp. 19–23) Dana Gioria argues that the form courts failure, that "American Literature needs a more modest aesthetic," and a "less chauvinistic theory" of the epic; Frederick Feirstein's "The Other Long Poem" (pp. 52–56) rages in a rather ill-informed fashion against the supposed loss of "plot and character" in contemporary poetry; Emily Grosholz ("Imagining Human Action," pp. 64–66) asks poets like John Ashbery, in whom "incoherence is writ large," to "go back to the old masters"; finally, and more interestingly, in "The Forest for the Trees" (pp. 78–82) Dick Allen sees the "noble failures of the long poem in our century" sourced in "the poets trying to write the long poem as if it were an extended imagist lyric."

In a second important book-length study this year, *Poet's Prose: The Crisis in American Verse* (Cambridge), Stephen Fredman devotes chapters to close readings of three extended "prose poems": Williams's *Kora in Hell*, Creeley's *Presence: A Text for Marisol*, and Ashbery's *Three Poems*, with a concluding section focused refreshingly on four younger avant-garde poets (David Antin, David Bromige, Ron Silliman, and Michael Davidson). The crisis Fredman alludes to in his subtitle is the shift "from the choice of the matter

and meter to the decision as to whether poetry, under present conditions, is possible." He sees the fullest articulation of this crisis to
have arisen in Emerson's "ethic of discovery" that promotes a stance
of simultaneous "appropriation and accommodation." The first aspect
of this stance is worked out through the long poem, "a paradigm of
heroic imposition"; the second through the "prose poem," wherein
the poet creates through the receptivity of the form "a space of per-
mission in which the world is allowed to appear as it is." Williams's
Kora, Fredman argues, demonstrates the poet's "highly inventive de-
ployment of the sentence as poetic form"; Creeley's *Presences* (which
plays through a series of improvisations upon Marisol's work and
life) "interrogates" the notion of completeness, exploring process as
"a means of access to presence"; Ashbery's *Three Poems* are "a predominantly meditative prose," a Steinian "translative writing" that
aspires finally to "pure language" in a movement toward Emersonian
accommodation. While the younger poets "adopt some of the hermeneutic practices and phenomenological attention of Creeley and
Ashbery, these poets focus more relentlessly upon the ability of language to predicate." Fredman here has not exhausted his subject
certainly; rather he has attempted to look carefully at a few difficult
and unfamiliar, though central, texts that do much to illuminate what
is perhaps currently the most fascinating impulse in American verse.

The questions Fredman raises—reference, absence, disjunction,
the nature of the sentence, a pure language—are those that seem to
preoccupy a wide range of poets more or less associated with Bruce
Andrews and Charles Bernstein's $L=A=N=G=U=A=G=E$ magazine. While each poet is in the process of generating a personal
aesthetic, still taken together enough of them share common interest in what Bernstein calls "the resonating of the wordness of
language" to make a loose group or movement. Through their own
presses (Figures, Tuumbra, This, Jordan Davies) and journals
($L=A=N=G=U=A=G=E$, $A^*BACCUS$, *Hills*, *The Difficulties*)
many of these writers have infused the American poetic avant-garde
with a new vitality and intelligence, forcing even the most conservative of us to give both their verse and their poetic a hearing. *Hills*
(6/7), which I unfortunately overlooked in 1980, gives over a full
issue to "Talks" by a number of the more important "language-
oriented poets" given between 1977 and 1980 in San Francisco: Bill
Berkson, for example, discusses the influence of Frank O'Hara, Clark

Coolidge, and others; David Bromige examines "intention"; Michael Davidson's analysis of "the prose of fact" directly anticipates Fredman's thesis; Ron Silliman ranges through linguistics in his attempt to both define "the new sentence" and explain its lack of "legitimacy" among a number of editors and critics. Other participants include Fanny Howe, Barrett Watten, Steve Benson, William Graves, Warren Sonbert, Douglas Woolf, and Bob Perelman.

Last year I missed a second collection of theoretical essays by many of the same writers in *Open Letter* (Toronto, fifth series, 1), which doubles as the fourth issue of *L=A=N=G=U=A=G=E*. The 31 pieces gathered here vary in both length and quality of argument, but even the slightest is worth a glance. Stronger analyses include Bernstein on " 'thinking' as a means of locating the materials of language and writing," Jackson MacLow's discussion of the inadequacy of "language-centered" as a critical term, Ron Silliman's Marxist "The Political Economy of Poetry" (Marx's sense of "commodity fetishism" seems to be central to the aesthetic of a number of these poets), and Barrett Watten's talk on "Method and Surrealism: The Politics of Poetry"; other notes of interest are Tina Darragh on Susan Howe, Steve Benson on Kathy Acker, and Robert Grenier on Creeley.

Barrett Watten and Lyn Hejinian's *Poetics Journal* and Michael Palmer's anthology *Code of Signals* bring us current. Watten published *This* magazine for over a decade, while Hejinian's Tuumbra produced chapbooks; both dedicated to the "language-centered" project. Now together they have given us the first three issues of *Poetics Journal* (Berkeley), which seeks to become, I suppose, the theoretical arm of this "movement." Again, a number of these pieces are rather obscurantist and underdeveloped (and because often these poets—most practice as well as theorize—seem to be writing simply for each other, they employ a kind of shared code that suggests, rather fairly, an in-group preciousness); still, generally even these hint at important issues. Bob Perelman's "Plotless Prose" (pp. 25–34), David Ploke's "Language and Politics Today" (pp. 35–47), and Watten's "The Politics of Style" (pp. 49–60), all from issue 1, can be especially recommended. Issue 2 is devoted to "close reading," and Watten's discussion of Hart Crane and Larry Eigner (pp. 12–26), Ron Silliman's analysis of "the parsimony principle" (pp. 27–41), and Steve Benson's "Leavings and Cleavings" (pp. 75–81) open interesting territory. "Philosophy & Poetry" is the focus of *PJ* 3, which

includes Bernstein's "Writing and Method" (pp. 6–16) and Delphine
Perret's examination of irony (pp. 33–45), as well as pieces by Bromige, Rae Armantrout, Jed Rasula, and others. Michael Palmer, who
is certainly the most consistently interesting *poet* of this very loosely
defined group, has drawn together 28 additional original prose writings in *Code of Signals: Recent Writings in Poetics* (North Atlantic
Books, *No.* 30). The title of the collection is apt, and often the code
is difficult to break. Charles Stein's brief outline of Charles Olson's
sense of Jungian "projection" (pp. 67–78), David Levi Strauss's reading of Zukofsky's *80 Flowers* (pp. 79–102), Aaron Shurin's reflections
on the "third person" (pp. 185–95), Susan Howe's discussion of Emily Dickinson (pp. 196–218), two extended lectures by Bob Perelman
(pp. 224–41) and Michael Palmer (interestingly on duration; pp.
243–314) are all usefully accessible, however. Finally, the year's
Sulfur (numbers 6, 7, and 8) continues an ongoing dialogue on the
work and method of many of these writers in its "Notes, Correspondence, Reviews."

Four other extended essays taking on many of the same concerns
appeared this year. Henry M. Sayre continues his investigation into
the avant-garde with "The Object of Performance: Aesthetics in the
Seventies" (*GaR* 37:169–88). Beginning with a brief history of the
"aesthetics of absence" (ie., "the art object per se has become, argu-
ably, dispensable"), Sayre argues that "it has become increasingly
clear to American poets . . . that the sanctity of the written text—the
very possibility of its *possessing* any meaningful signification—is at
least questionable." With reference to Ginsberg, Blackburn, Rothenberg, and Ashbery, he sees the latter's eminence "in the decade's
critical canon" as "probably more due to its willingness simply to
problemitize—and not resolve—art's relation to its audience than
anything else."

Charles Bernstein and Jed Rasula, two of the better known
$L=A=N=G=U=A=G=E$ writers, contribute pieces to *Sagetrieb*
(2,i). Bernstein's "Words and Pictures" (pp. 9–34) explains (using Zukofsky and Olson as examples) that "much of the formally imaginative American poetry of this century flirts, oddly, with a poetics of
sight . . . the object-focused, extra temporal, single perspective that
is, in actuality, a static idealization of the experience of looking." In
"Exfoliating Cosmos" (pp. 35–71), Jed Rasula continues his examination of "composting poetry": without history, "American poetry—

books and all—recognizes its public domain as the entire unacknowledged history of the world." A third recommended essay, "The Poetry
of Production" (*Sagetrieb* 2,ii:1–43) by Don Byrd, looks at work by
Pound, Stein, Williams, Zukofsky, Olson, and Duncan as tending
towards "quantity of consciousness," action, the asymmetric and un-
stable—"it is a sustained glorification of the powers of consciousness
to disrupt, to create discontinuities . . . to create conditions in which
action is not only possible but unavoidable." With reference to Hegel,
Nietzsche, Marx, Freud, Derrida, and Lacan, Byrd demonstrates how
a "nomadic criticism" evolves as "critics commit themselves to following works through the fields of language, so they will be nourished
in its on-going production." Three creative and productive pieces.

Five solid studies centering on influence appeared this year, one
focusing on Yeats, another on the Orient, two on Native American
literature, and a fifth on a variety of ethnopoetics. The last thirty
pages of Terence Diggory's *Yeats & American Poetry: The Tradition
of the Self* (Princeton) locate Yeats's sense of the "creation of the
self" (as opposed to Wordsworth's *expression* of the self) as culminating in the work of the "confessional" poets, especially Theodore
Roethke, John Berryman, and Robert Lowell. Unlike Yeats, however, these poets suffer a deep despair "founded on the suspicion that
the coherence that Yeats discovered in the self no longer resides
there, or anywhere." Roethke suffered an anxiety of influence in his
struggle with the elder poet, Diggory suggests, attempting to come
to terms with "the authority of the father"; Berryman uses Yeats as a
"counter-balance" to Pound and Eliot, and later Auden as a counter-
balance to Yeats; while distrusting influence, Lowell looked to Yeats
for the example "of private rather than public speech" and, further,
the poet as self-made hero.

Beongcheon Yu's wonderful study of *The Great Circle: American
Writers and the Orient* (Wayne State) traces the hold orientalism
has held on the American writer's imagination since Emerson (with
examinations of Thoreau, Whitman, Fenollosa, O'Neill, Pound, and
others). In his epilogue on the Beat Generation, Yu rather briefly
locates Gary Snyder's sensibility as being sourced in the Chinese
rather than the Japanese, looking at a few of his Buddhist-influenced
poems. Certain to be discussed at greater length in the appropriate
essays in this volume, *The Great Circle* is a book long-needed, one
that is clearly written and thoroughly researched.

Each year Native American literature and its influence on other American poets commands more of our attention. Michael Castro's *Interpreting the Indian: Twentieth-Century Poets and the Native American* (N. Mex.) traces first the early attempts by poets and ethnologists to "bring Indian poetry to non-Indian Americans," then examines the influence of that work on Charles Olson, Jerome Rothenberg, and Gary Snyder. Each of these chapters is, it seems to me, a little sketchy, though Castro's comments on Olson's "Kingfishers" and Rothenberg's "total translation" are interesting. Of more use is the volume's last section on the emergence of younger Native American poets like Marnie Walsh, Ray Young Bear, and Simon Ortiz. *Studies in American Indian Literature: Critical Essays and Course Designs* (MLA), edited by Paula Gunn Allen, is, however, the place to start if you are unfamiliar with this material, as it provides a wealth of information on the subject. Of most interest to readers of this essay will be Patricia Clark Smith's "Ain't Seen You Since: Dissent Among Female Relatives in American Indian Women's Poetry" (pp. 108–26) and "Coyote Ortiz" (pp. 192–210), and "Bear and Elk: The Nature(s) of Contemporary American Poetry" (pp. 178–91) by Kenneth M. Roemer, a very good quick introduction to material that currently is generally undervalued.

In the late 1960s, Jerome Rothenberg introduced the term "ethnopoetics" to mark a recognition of what Nathaniel Tarn called the "intersection between poetry and anthropology," and through his various anthologies, essays, translations, and the journal *Alcheringa* the poet has continued for the past 15 years seriously involved in this project. *Symposium of the Whole* (Calif.), edited by Jerome and Diane Rothenberg, "is an attempt to present some highlights of that discourse—both over the last two decades and in relation to its own history—and to show as well how ethnographic revelations can change our ideas of poetic form and function." Like the Gunn volume above, this symposium is a rich sourcebook, with contributions by writers from Blake, Marx, Jung, and Eliade to Tarn, Olson, Snyder, and Eshleman. My only reservation is that the tone of the book is rather too celebratory; as the whole question of the validity of ethnopoetics as an approach is still open, perhaps a more negative note (like Geary Hobson's "'The Rise of the White Shaman as a New Version of Cultural Imperialism" or Leslie Silko's "An Old-Time Indian Attack Conducted in Two Parts") would have furthered the editors Rothenberg's call for an ongoing dialogue.

The relationship between contemporary American poets and writers from other shores also drew the attention of journals this year. Julian Gitzen's "Transatlantic Poets and the Tradition Trap" (*CritQ* 25,ii:53–71) is an interesting (though thoroughly British) attempt to "identify the distinct traditional qualities which lend differing character to English and American poetry." Gitzen argues that formal metrics versus free verse is no longer a criterion in such a discussion; rather, English poets long for links to the past and reach for myth, as opposed to Americans who reject myth. While the English have a fondness for history, the Americans have a love of place. Finally, when writing nature poems, Gitzen suggests, the British give emphasis to "determinism on the operation of physical laws" (Ted Hughes, Jon Silken), while the Americans emphasize "a recognized bond between man and nature" (Roethke, Snyder). Here we learn, by the way, that American Blacks are "forcefully succinct but wily and grimly amused." *Studies in Twentieth Century Literature* (8: 101–27) presents a symposium, "Encounters: American Poets on Paul Celan," in its special Celan issue. Jerome Rothenberg asked a dozen poets to write on Celan's influence on their work; Paul Auster, Jed Rasula, Cid Corman, Clayton Eshleman, Jack Hirschman, and David Meltzer respond, plus Rothenberg's own "Celan: A Memoir and a Poem."

Two other general symposia are of note. In "Sexual Poetics: Notes on Genre and Genre in Poetry by Women," *AmerP* (1,i:72–80) prints two addresses on the subject given at the 1982 MLA convention by Denise Levertov and Ruth Stone, as well as two solicited essays by Shirley Kaufman and Diane Wakoski; Wakoski's piece is particularly lively, as the poet advises us to "accept that some of the theatrics, rebellious statements, and dramatic finger-pointing actions, no matter how sincere, are only part of one stage of reality: the adolescent." In "The Role of the Critic, the Role of the Reviewer" (*MissR* 7,i: 263–86), Robert B. Heilman, Ronald Hayman, Betsy Kline, Richard Rupp, Seymour Krim, and Keith Opdahl discuss the nature of the differences between the critic and the reviewer, as well as the effect each has on the fortunes of poets and others.

In "The Paradox of Achieved Poetic Form: The Problem of Aesthetic Distance in a Personal Poetry" (*PoetryR* 1,i:48–61), Jonathan Holden refers to John Ashbery, Richard Hugo, John Logan, and Stephen Dunn as he briefly explores "how any fully achieved poem must, by its very nature, be deeply and inherently contradictory." Tinged with a sense of born-again Republicanism, Mary C. Williams's "The Aesthetics of Accessibility: Contemporary Poetry and its Audience" (*SCR* 16,i:58–65) presents a review of "the barriers on the way to an aesthetics of accessibility" with reference to Jonathan Culler and others, asking for "a restoration of clarity and rationality as critical standards."

This year both business and ambition were attended to. "Sodomy, incest, pedophilia, and homosexuality have been no less domesticated by our domineering national Muse," Dana Gioia explains in "Business and Poetry" (*HudR* 36:147–71), "than have skunks, armadillos, tarantulas, hoptoads, and at least one warthog. But somehow this same poetic tradition has never been able to look inside the halls of a corporate office" with intensity. With reference to Louis Simpson, William Bronk, Allen Ginsberg, and others, Gioria decides that working in business has given some poets "a healthy perspective on their careers as writers." In "Poetry and Ambition" (*KR* 5,iv:90–104), Donald Hall meditates on a variety of complaints, including the lack of "serious ambition," egotism, poor education, and complicity in an aesthetics of mass consumption among current poets.

Good collections of essays by poets appeared in 1983. Canadian writer Margaret Atwood's *Second Words: Selected Critical Prose* (Ananse) reprints a number of exemplary reviews of assorted American women poets, including Adrienne Rich ("one of America's best poets"), Erica Jong ("seemingly inexhaustible verbal dexterity"), Marge Piercy ("her literary ancestor is not Dickinson but Whitman"), Anne Sexton ("one of the most important American poets of her generation"), and Sylvia Plath ("an incandescent poet of drastic seriousness"), written over the past decade; an important gathering by a major writer. A second volume, Wendell Berry's *Standing By Words* (North Point), collects six essays that focus on the poet's impression that "we have seen for perhaps one hundred and fifty years a gradual increase in language that is either meaningless or destructive of meaning," and parallels the destruction of community. Especially recommended are the title essay (pp. 24–63) and "Poetry and Place" (pp. 92–199), two meditations on the relationship between language and landscape. *Vectors and Smoothable Curves: Collected Essays* (North Point) collects William Bronk's prose pieces written over the past decade on subjects ranging from Macchu Picchu, costume, and desire to Thoreau and Whitman; interesting meditations by the winner of the 1982 American Book Award for Poetry. Finally, William Everson's *On Writing the Waterbirds* (Scarecrow), edited by Lee Bartlett, draws together the poet's forewords and afterwords written between 1935 and 1981. Divided into three parts, following an introduction by the editor, the volume collects pieces written on Everson's own poetry and prose, essays on handpress printing, and a substantial section of material on Robinson Jeffers.

Interviews with poets continue to capture the literary imagination, and while pieces on individual writers are noticed in appropriate subsections later, I should mention three useful volumes that appeared in 1983. L. S. Dembo's second series (1972–82) of *ConL* interviews, *Interviews with Contemporary Writers* (Wis.) continues the high standard of the first. Besides important discussions with Paul Blackburn and Robert Duncan, readers will have an interest in interviews with Stanley Kunitz, James Dickey, Ed Dorn, A. R. Ammons, and Richard Hugo, though they may wonder at the lack of any American women poets here. *Acts of Mind: Conversations with Contemporary Poets* (Alabama), by Richard Jackson, reprints a full 30 brief discussions with poets that all appeared first in *Poetry Miscellany*; Stanley Plumly, Mark Strand, Carol Muske, Heather McHugh, John Ashbery, William Stafford, Robert Creeley, Linda Pastan, and Michael S. Harper are a few of the writers who participate. The third volume, *Women Writers Talking* (Holmes & Meier), edited by Janet Todd, is a wide-ranging collection of discussions with a number of women writers (both American and foreign); includes interviews with May Sarton by Todd, Erica Jong by Wendy Martin, and Robin Morgan by Helen Cooper. According to Todd, her collection is to remind us of "a party": "its purpose is to juxtapose voices."

Finally, I'll close by calling your attention to two general reference works. *The Peters Black and Blue Guide to Current Literary Journals* (Cherry Valley Editions) is a collection by perhaps the most entertaining reviewer in America, Robert Peters. Here he takes on 28 of the leading American literary journals (from *Abraxas* and *APR* to *Wormwood Review*), devoting a few pages to each, then (shades of Michelin!) rates them. As with just about anything from

Peters, this makes for lively reading. Volume 41 of Gale's Information Guide Series is devoted to *Contemporary Poetry in America and England, 1950–1975,* compiled by Martin E. Gingerich. A full 1637 annotated entries describe bibliographies, cultural studies, general critical studies; further, there are primary checklists and brief annotated secondary bibliographies for over 100 American and British poets. Generally, this book will be useful for quick reference, though it should be used with caution. A quick glance uncovered Duncan's *The Truth and Life of Myth* as *The Truth and Life of Myrtle* (!); David Meltzer's listing inexplicably ends abruptly at 1965 with his first four books of poetry (he's published over a dozen); Ginsberg's *The Gates of Wrath, First Blues,* and *Poems All Over the Place* are omitted. Still, any such undertaking is bound to suffer from a few gaffes, and Gingerich's industry must be commended.

ii. The Middle Generation

a. **Robert Lowell.** Of the "middle generation" poets, this year Robert Lowell attracted by far the most critical attention, with two full-length studies, part of another, and a variety of essays centering on his work (in fact, this year about the only writer to rival Lowell for attention was, interestingly, Robert Duncan). Vereen M. Bell's *Robert Lowell: Nihilist as Hero* (Harvard) takes as its thesis Bell's sense that Lowell's "poetry is identifiable by nothing so much as its chronic and eventually systematic pessimism," as the poet "becomes increasingly problematic to himself, as an artist and as a human being." Lowell was generally, according to Bell, refused consolation (his movement from Christian theism, his disinterest in "romantic supernaturalism" and eastern religion, an antimelioristic view of history, the lack of regeneration out of sexual love) by his muse, and "the allure of posterity is mocked repeatedly." Further, for the poet "the inner life cannot displace the external, and the external in fact introjects so deeply that it infects the very language that might be used to displace it." It is Lowell's continuing battle against this nihilism that Bell maps, reading with sensitivity well-chosen passages from the earlier work and, especially, *Notebook.*

Mark Rudman's *Robert Lowell: An Introduction to the Poetry* is the first of three volumes to appear this year in Columbia's revitalized "Introductions to Twentieth-Century American Poetry" series, ed-

ited by John Unterecker (who writes a preface for each volume).
Unlike Burton Raffel's *Robert Lowell*, published in a similar series
two years ago, this handbook excludes any extended discussion of the
drama or other nonpoetic work; also, occasionally Rudman's enthusiasm ("There's hardly any poetry that has so many signifiers, so many
details, so much data, as Lowell's"—Olson? Zukofsky? Silliman?
Prynne?). Still, there is a good mix of biography and explication
here, and at the very least the study is a good student introduction
to Lowell's verse. As its title indicates, Lachlan Mackinnon's *Eliot,
Auden, Lowell: Aspects of the Baudelarian Inheritance* (Macmillan)
attempts to set these three modern poets in Baudelarian relief. Like
Bell, Mackinnon sees Lowell haunted by self-doubt, a poet in the
tradition of the dandy in search of transcendence. "Waste," he argues
to good purpose, "is Lowell's method."

Bruce Michelson pursues similar concerns in "Lowell versus Lowell" (*VQR* 59:22–39). Taking off from the conclusion of "Ulysses and
Circe," Michelson argues that "Lowell's poetry depends very much
upon the repeated destruction of his own wake, a sequence of dramatic insurrections against and denials of his own public and artistic
identity" in the manner of Yeats's self-transformations counterbal-
anced by New England Puritanism. In " 'Day By Day': Lowell's
Poetics of Imitation" (*ArielE* 14,i:5–14), Norma Propcopiou briefly
examines Lowell's last book as an "imitation" of his earlier poetry,
with its "elegiac tone, its wistfulness for old friendships, its continuing search for consummate love" in a style that "bemoans its own
inadequacy." Heather Dubrow's "The Marine in the Garden: Pastoral
Elements in Lowell's 'Quaker Graveyard' " (*PQ* 62,ii:127–45) asserts
that "Lycidas" is an obvious model for Lowell's "Quaker Graveyard
in Nantucket," as the latter poem "is at once a systematic adaption
of certain pastoral conventions and a strident renunciation of others";
a close and graceful reading with reference to Lowell's unpublished
notebooks. In "Saving the State in Lowell's 'For the Union Dead' "
(*AL* 55:639–42), William Nelles discusses the epigraph to the poem,
focusing on the translation of the Latin *servare*, which he feels other
critics have mistaken.

b. **Randall Jarrell, Elizabeth Bishop, John Berryman.**   Suzanne Ferguson has this year added a volume on Randall Jarrell to G. K. Hall's
"Critical Essays on American Literature" series. *Critical Essays on*

Randall Jarrell collects primarily partisan material on the poet, and
it is usually very good: eighteen reviews by Delmore Schwartz,
Karl Shapiro, Robert Lowell, and others; four "general essays" by
Sister M. Bernetta Quinn, Jerome Mazzaro, Helen Hagenbuchle, and
William H. Pritchard; ten essays on the poetry by Parker Tyler,
Richard Fein, Mary Kinzie, and others; Janet Sharistanian and Keith
Monroe on the criticism, Sylvia Angus, Suzanne Ferguson, and Kathe
Davis Finney on the fiction; two closing essays by Ingo Seidler and
Richard K. Cross on Jarrell's translations. An informed and attrac-
tively produced gathering. In "Randall Jarrell and German Culture"
(*Salmagundi* 61:71–89), Jeffrey Meyers looks at a number of Jarrell's
poems and translations, continuing his work on the poet in a dis-
cussion of his retention of "his belief in an ideal German culture"
following the war.

Carolyn Handa's "Elizabeth Bishop and Women's Poetry" (*SAQ*
82:269–81) examines reasons that "keep us from considering Bishop
a woman's poet"—her refusal to appear in "all-women anthologies"
and her freedom "from overt doctrinal affiliations." Reading poems
from *A Cold Spring*, Handa argues that Bishop's true feminism has
its source in her "artistic independence and self-definition." In
"Words Worth a Thousand Postcards: The Bishop/Moore Correspondence" (*AL* 55:405–29), Lynn Keller surveys the 350 pieces of
correspondence exchanged between the two writers "bound by common tastes and extraordinary alertness." Charles Sanders notes that
Bishop's "The Gentleman of Shalott" (*Expl* 42,i:55–56) is a "descen-
dental" argument "with design in rebuttal to Emerson's Yankee
'Merlin.'"

About the only piece on John Berryman to catch my attention
this year was "*Berryman's Sonnets*: In and Out of the Tradition" (*AL*
55:388–404), by David K. Weiser. In a close reading, Weiser sees the
poems as illustrative of "the process of creative imagination, in which
old forms are deliberately reshaped to express new attitudes," making
use of the theory of *inventio* from the Renaissance.

iii. A Kind of Field

a. **Charles Olson.**   A good year for Olson studies, thanks yet once
again to George F. Butterick. The University of California Press,
which last year published the collected Creeley, this year gives us

The Maximus Poems, edited by Butterick, complete in a single volume. The importance of this project is obvious, and it is long overdue. The press is to be congratulated on two scores—undertaking the task itself and, as with the Creeley volume, providing the kind of production quality the poems call for, especially (i.e., in these days of severe budget cuts forced upon university presses) 652 oversized pages that fully open up the field. As a supplement to his volume, Butterick also this year released his *Editing the Maximus Poems* (Storrs: University of Connecticut Library). In his introduction he explains the addition of 29 "previously omitted or inaccessible poems" to the third book of the California edition. Following are numerous notes on *Maximus* as an addition to Butterick's *Guide,* plates of manuscripts of "difficult poems," and poems rejected from the final edition. Finally, the fifth volume of Butterick's *Charles Olson and Robert Creeley: The Complete Correspondence* (Black Sparrow) covers once again just a few months of this important exchange, from February 13 through April 26, 1951. It was during this period that Olson was in Yucatan, and Butterick here presents definitive transcripts of various letters that appeared in *Mayan Letters.* In terms of scholarship it is not an exaggeration to suggest that Butterick's decade-long devotion to Olson has raised the poet's stock immeasurably, and the scholar has emerged as one of the most diligent and judicious editors of the current time in the process.

Olson scholarship (which has moved rapidly from a cottage to heavy industry) is served with more mixed results in Thomas F. Merrill's handbook *The Poetry of Charles Olson: A Primer* (Delaware). Merrill makes no claim to do much more than read through the poetry more or less chronologically, providing explication and setting various aspects of Olson's aesthetics into a larger cultural context—in itself no mean feat. He is generally quite successful when discussing the shorter work, especially poems from *The Distances.* There are a number of problems (some factual, others interpretive) with his study, however, and one might be advised to read Butterick's extended enumeration and discussion of these in *AmerP* (1,i:87–93), where he concludes that "it is necessary that the prospective reader has some sense of the degree of error in the book since there is also some value to be found in it, but emphatically not as a 'primer.'"

A second group of Olson's letters, "The start of ORIGIN: letters" (*Origin* fifth series, 1:78–106), is edited by George Evans; a fascinating exchange between Olson and Cid Corman from late 1950, prompted by young Corman's plan to start *Origin*. Percilla Groves contributes "Archival Sources for Olson Studies" (*Line* 1,i:94–102), listing with annotations Olson materials in the Contemporary Literature Collection at Simon Fraser University. Finally, in "One and Many: The Paradox of 'Methodology' in Charles Olson's *Maximus*" (*MSE* 9,i:1–21), Dibakar Barua examines the paradox of the "one and many" with good purpose, ranging through both Whitehead and a number of passages from *Maximus*.

b. **Robert Creeley, Edward Dorn.** Work on both these poets was limited this year. In "Creeley, Duncan, Zukofsky 1968—Melody Moves the Light" (*Sagetrieb* 2,i:97–104), William Sulvester briefly argues that these three poets "did not respond to the times as much as the times responded to them." Kathryn Shevelow's "Reading Edward Dorn's *Hello La Jolla* and *Yellow Lola*" (*Sagetrieb* 2,ii:99–109) attempts to demonstrate that while after *Slinger* these two recent volumes may "appear constricted and slight," they in fact continue to "test" Dorn's readers. Sarcasm is the dominant tone of both books, Shevelow feels, as they indicate a movement "into an explicitly didactic mode."

c. **Louis Zukofsky, George Oppen.** First *The Cantos*, then *Paterson*; most recently *The Maximus Poems*. If you enjoy investing in long poem growth stocks, the indication this year is that Louis Zukofsky's *A* would be a good bet. Barry Ahearn's *Zukofsky's "A": An Introduction* (Calif.) clears a good bit of the ground as it moves rather carefully through Zukofsky's autobiographical maze. In his first chapter, Ahearn dips into biography in an attempt to "reveal more of the man behind, and in, the work," tracing as well the poet's influences and his developing aesthetic. He then devotes four chapters to reading the poem's 24 "movements," arguing in a final chapter for *A*'s "unities." An appendix discusses the "mathematical configuration" in the poem, with reference to sections 8 and 9. Book-length examinations of this important poem without doubt will proliferate, though Ahearn's first study will remain seminal.

Zukofsky was the subject of a number of other inquiries in 1983. In "The Poetry of Louis Zukofsky: To *Draw* Speech" (*Origin* fifth series,

1:44–55), Michael Heller argues that the poet's power comes from the "display of the imagination reaching toward and into existence," and the belief that "the music of verse is the embodiment of conviction." Linda Simon's "A Preface to Zukofsky" (*Sagetrieb* 2,i:89–96) discusses the poet's "Preface—1927" and "Poem beginning 'The'" in terms of their influences, while in the same issue of that journal Ahearn provides transcripts of "Two Conversations with Celia Zukofsky" (pp. 113–32), taped in 1978. David Gordon's "A Note on LZ's Catullus LXI: Theme and Variations" (*Sagetrieb* 2,ii:113–22) reminds us with reference to the original that Zukofsky "decidedly does not forget the meaning as he brings over the almost pure sound of Latin into the almost pure sound of English."

Sylvester Pollet's explication of "Oppen's 'Return'" (*Sagetrieb* 2,i:123–28) argues for reading the poem as embodying "the theme of alienation between urban poet and raw nature," wherein Oppen opts finally for his home ground, "the city street."

iv. The Autochthonic Spirit

For the past three years I've been complaining about the slight critical effort devoted to writers associated with the San Francisco Renaissance/Beats in these pages. This year the news is far better, as an important reference work, a biographical study of Robert Duncan and a Duncan "special issue" of *Ironwood*, critical studies of Lawrence Ferlinghetti and Gary Snyder, and numerous essays appeared.

Volume 16 of Gale's ongoing "Dictionary of Literary Biography" series focuses on *The Beats: Literary Bohemians in Postwar America*, 718 pages in two volumes edited by Ann Charters. Although there are a few problems with the project, in general it is a treasure. Almost all of the entries are extended (heavily illustrated, critical as well as biographical, with good primary bibliographies) and written by commentators fully up to the task—Michael Davidson on Duncan, for example, Paul Christensen on Ginsberg, George F. Butterick on Ed Sanders. Further, an appendix that runs almost half the length of the second volume gives us Jennie Skerl's "Beat chronology," essays by Carolyn Cassady, Joyce Johnson, John Clellon Holmes, and Kenneth Rexroth, and George F. Butterick's list of "periodicals of the Beat Generation" complete with 30 pages of plates of journal covers.

I'm not sure that a number of the entries are really appropriate, added perhaps to fill out the two volumes—Williams, for example, is certainly an influence but doesn't really belong here; Janine Pommy Vega, Bob Dylan, and even to a great extent Charles Olson among others are very problematic. Nancy J. Peters on Philip Lamantia, Nettie Lipton on Lawrence Lipton, and Michael McClure on Joanna McClure are probably too close to their subjects to be of great use. Finally, at over one hundred and fifty dollars, the volumes are obviously headed primarily for library shelves. Still, this is the best single reference source on these writers, very likely to remain unsurpassed.

a. Robert Duncan.   Perhaps in anticipation of his first book-length collection in 15 years, *Groundwork*, to be published next year by New Directions, interest in Robert Duncan remains this year high. Ekbert Faas's much anticipated *Young Robert Duncan: Portrait of the Poet as Homosexual in Society* (Black Sparrow) finally appeared. As the subtitle indicates, this 361-page study attempts to see the development of Duncan's aesthetic in terms of his homosexuality, though, in tracing the poet's life from childhood through age thirty, the study is not thesis-ridden. On the contrary, despite its sometimes turgid prose (English is not Faas's first language) this first book-length treatment by a single author of one of the most continually fascinating minds in contemporary American letters is an example of excellent biographical scholarship. Extremely well-researched, *Young Duncan* is certainly the most substantial book yet on any poet of the first San Francisco Renaissance, with a wealth of information on Robin Blaser, William Everson, Pauline Kael, Henry Miller, Anaïs Nin, Charles Olson, and Jack Spicer integrated into the narrative. In a word, indispensable.

   Ironwood 22 is a 200-page special issue on Duncan, edited by Michael Cuddihy. The poet contributes a number of poems, as well as a chapter from the in-progress *H.D. Book* and the valuable "*H.D. Book*: Outline & Chronology." The 11 prose pieces on Duncan include Hayden Carruth's "Duncan's Dream," Wendy MacIntyre's "Psyche, Christ and the Poem," and Bruce Boone's "Robert Duncan and the Gay Community," as well as essays by Hugh Kenner, Michael Davidson, Charles Molesworth, Carl Rakosi, John Matthias,

Mark Rudman, Mark Johnson, and John Taggart. Additionally, Gary Burnett edits a selection of letters by Duncan to Robin Blaser and Jack Spicer. This is, unlike a number of such projects that often fall into mere celebration, a substantial gathering; a first-rate critical companion to Faas's biography.

Norman M. Finkelstein's "Robert Duncan, Poet of the Law" (*Sagetrieb* 2,i:75–88), argues that the poet represents "the first real synthesis of Romantic and Modernist modes" with its fragmentation merging with visionary hermeticism. In his discussion of various aspects of Duncan's poetics (concluding that while his "best work *arises out* of field poetics," its power is that of the controlled lyric), Finkelstein finds that his poetry "may be regarded as either a celebration of the Law or a defense of it in the face of political and cosmic disorder." In "Robert Duncan's 'Momentous Inconclusions'" (*Sagetrieb* 2,ii:71–84), Mark Johnson closely examines two aspects of the poet's "unfinished" verse: "vision" over "revision" and the impossibility of "conclusion."

b. **Kenneth Rexroth, Gary Snyder, William Everson.** *Sagetrieb* 2,iii is a Kenneth Rexroth issue, edited by Burton Hatlen. The volume begins with three previously unpublished excerpts from the poet's autobiography, followed by a number of appreciations by Carol Tinker, Sam Hamill, Bradford Morrow, Michael McClure, Nathaniel Tarn, Doren Robbins, Edouard Roditi, James Broughton, and Thomas Parkinson. Eliot Weinberger meditates on Rexroth's reputation at his death, while Sam Hamill remembers hearing the poet read to jazz. Lee Bartlett's "Creating the Autochthon" discusses the relationship between Rexroth and William Everson, with special reference to Rexroth's role in the publication of Everson's first New Directions volume, *The Residual Years.* In "Rage and Serenity" George Woodcock examines "the poetic politics" of Rexroth, finding in "Towards an Organic Philosophy" a capsule of the poet's thought, while Morgan Gibson (in "'Poetry is Vision'—'Vision Is Love'") sees Rexroth's "theory of literature" as an "*act*, a dynamic transformation" towards "communion." In "Love Sacred and Profane," Donald Gutierrez discusses the poet's love poetry, arguing that "the hub of love verse in the context of his jeremiads functions in effect as his 'solution'" to the problem of modern fragmentation. William J. Lockwood's "Toward a Reappraisal of Kenneth Rexroth" looks at the middle and late poems with "the geographer's phenomenologically-oriented attentiveness" as a "life-time's journeying toward self-realization." Finally, Rexroth's literary executor, Bradford Morrow, provides an annotated "Outline of Unpublished Rexroth Manuscripts, and an Introductory Note to Three Chapters from the Sequel to *An Autobiographical Novel.*" Like the Duncan *Ironwood,* highly recommended.

Donald Gutierrez in "Natural Supernaturalism: The Nature Poetry of Kenneth Rexroth" (*LitR* 26:405–22) contends that the typical Rexroth "nature poem", set in or near the San Francisco Bay Area, is "often comprised of a movement from one crisply precise detail of knowledgable observation to another," and ends in an epiphany. For Rexroth, "nature and its phenomena *are* themselves." In the same issue appears a snippet from Linda Hamalian's longer interview with William Everson on the subject of Rexroth (pp. 423–26).

Charles Molesworth's *Gary Snyder's Vision: Poetry and the Real Work* (Missouri) reads through the poet's major texts, seeing them as offering "a countercultural matrix of social values and historical vision." As a brief introduction to Snyder's work, the 128-page volume will be of more use to newer readers than old. However, Molesworth's sense that "Snyder's grounding in myth must be read as a way of seeing the political in some larger context" adheres throughout his analysis, as he traces the poet's movement from an objectivist poetic to an overriding concern with the social. From that perspective the brief volume is more of a contribution than its format implies. Katherine McNeil's long-awaited *Gary Snyder: A Bibliography* (Phoenix Bookshop) appeared this year. Fully descriptive, the well-researched volume lists primary and secondary material (though the checklist of criticism is unannotated); there are numerous plates of title pages, as well as an index of first lines. A worthy end to a long adventure. Lee Bartlett's "Gary Snyder's Han-shan" (*Sagetrieb* 2, i:105–10) discusses the poet's sense of translation, setting Snyder's Chinese translations from Han-shan next to other versions.

Bartlett also examines William Everson's relationship to Jung this year in "God's Crooked Lines: William Everson and C. G. Jung" (*CentR* 28:288–303). While most postmodern poets have probably been influenced by depth psychology to some extent, he argues, Everson comes closest to being a Jungian disciple; this article traces the evolution of the poet's interest in Jung, with specific reference to the notions of vocation and androgyny.

c. **Lawrence Ferlinghetti, Allen Ginsberg.** In *Lawrence Ferlinghetti: Poet at Large* (So. Ill.) Larry Smith approaches Ferlinghetti as "the contemporary poet-prophet of engagement and wonder" as he examines his various guises: "oral poet, poet of the streets, super-realist, actualist of the public nightmare, political poet, poetry-and-jazz poet" and etc. As a handbook to Ferlingheti's achievements as a poet, playwright, and novelist this study succeeds, touching all the important bases of the life and aesthetic of the owner of "America's first all-paperback bookstore," City Lights in San Francisco. Like Molesworth on Snyder, Smith finds Ferlinghetti's political vision to be his primary motivating force, in the poet's attack on "simple-minded nationalism, institutionalized authoritarianism, the hypocrisy of moralistic sexual attitudes, military aggression, and a general waste of modern life."

In "Documents of Presumption: The Satiric Use of the Ginsberg Letters in William Carlos Williams' *Paterson*" (*AL* 55:1–23), Gay Sibley sorts through the possibilities of the "Pater/Son relationship" of the poets: "a friendship, a business deal, a territorial struggle, a comradery in iconoclasm or delusion on one or both sides."

v. Dream of a Common Language

In one of the more fully realized essays I've run across on a group of poets in some time, Mary J. Carruthers's "The Re-Vision of the Muse: Adrienne Rich, Audre Lorde, Judy Grahn, Olga Broumas" (*HudR* 36:293–322) examines four volumes of verse (one by each poet) published in 1977 and 1978. Carruthers argues that the books "articulate a distinctive movement in contemporary American poetry"— 'Lesbian poetry'—because the 'naming and defining' of this phrase is its central poetic preoccupation." At the core of these four poetic projects is the decision to "deal with life at the level of metaethics ... articuable only in myth," structured from a "complex poetic image of lesbian relationship."

Adrienne Rich is given a chapter in Wendy Martin's study, *An American Triptych* (N.C.), following discussions of Anne Bradstreet and Emily Dickinson. Martin sees each of these poets as bound to her "historical moment," though each has "resisted the prevailing ethos of her time." Bradstreet's universe, Martin argues, was theocentric, Dickinson's gynecocentric; Rich "extends Dickinson's woman-centered vision beyond the private sphere to encompass the public world." Tracing Rich's evolution from elegant traditionalist to radical lesbian, Martin concludes that the poet "has evolved a female aesthetic-ethic based on shared relationship, emotional reciprocity, and emphatic identification." Susan Stanford Friedman ("'I go where I love': An Intertextual Study of H.D. and Adrienne Rich," *Signs* 9:228–45) also attends to Rich, explaining that H.D. has been a profound influence on Rich's development, as the younger poet "has seen in H.D.'s work a comprehensive critique of the violence at the core of patriarchy, a quest for the personal and mythic maternal principle to counter the patriarchy, and a desire to strengthen those bonds between women as friends and lovers." Further, she argues for a close relationship between H.D.'s *Trilogy* and Rich's *Dream of a Common Language* in terms of "matriarchal prehistory"; Friedman sees, however, a parting of the ways between the two poets on the question of men—H.D. opting for "a context that included men," Rich growing into radical lesbianism.

In "Sylvia Plath's Narrative Strategies" (*IowaR* 13,ii:1–4), Margaret Dickie describes her sense that Plath's energy in fiction "opens up the possibility that the acknowledged narrative bent in her poetry may derive from her experience as a fiction writer, and, if so, that her poetry should be read in that context as social commentary rather than rantings of an isolated victim." A chapter in Linda Huf's *A Portrait of the Artist as a Young Woman* (Ungar) is devoted to *The Bell Jar*, while in two notes Daniel J. Beirne and Leonard Sanazaro look at two poems. Beirne argues that in "Two Campers in Cloud Country" (*Expl* 42,i:61–2) Plath's "reference to Lethe is not a suicidal shadow, but rather an allusion to the benefits of vacation and the powers of sleep"; Sanazaro sees "Lady Lazarus" as perhaps having its source in Leonid Andreyev's short story "Lazarus" (*Expl* 41, iii:54–7). Finally, Susan R. Van Dyne introduces the 32-page pamphlet *Stings: Original Drafts of the Poem in Facsimile, Reproduced from the Sylvia Plath Collection at Smith College* (Northhampton, Mass.: Smith College Library Rare Book Room).

vi. A Complex of Occasions

The two additional volumes to appear this year in the Columbia "introduction" series are sensible handbooks. Howard Nelson's *Robert Bly: An Introduction to the Poetry* tries "to strike a balance, commenting on a substantial number of individual poems, and at the same time giving a sense of the ongoing themes and developments of Bly's poetry as a whole, book by book," and it does, I think, succeed. Drawing on Bly's major poetry from *Silence in the Snowy Fields* to *The Man in the Black Coat Turns*, as well as the poet's essays and interviews, Nelson is sympathetic with his subject but not in awe of him (as are a few of Bly's earlier commentators). One major drawback to the volume is that there is no real discussion of either Bly's editorial strategies or his sense of translation, two aspects of the poet's work that are central to his project. Still, Nelson is very good on the poems, and an 11-page biographical chronology and a thorough index round out the book. Both Lawrence Kramer and Walter Kalaidjian attempt to dissociate Bly to a certain extent from questions of "deep image" this year. In "A Sensible Emptiness: Robert Bly and the Poetics of Immanence" (*CL* 24:449–62), Kramer sees Bly as inheritor of a "specifically American" poetic tradition, "a feeling for the numinous value of objects divorced from all transcendental glamor," *This Tree* marks, according to Kramer, a return to Bly's early "will to subtration," which constitutes the poetics of *Silence*. Kalaidjian's "From Silence to Subversion: Robert Bly's Political Surrealism" (*MPS* ii:289–306) takes a different track, arguing that Bly's "later surrealist strategy" foregoes his earlier "transparent privileging of immanence to develop a more rhetorically based poetic style" as he exploits "more self-reflexive meditations of discourse." William H. Roberson's "Robert Bly: A Primary Bibliography" (*BB* 40:5–11) lists all books, chapbooks, and broadsides, as well as translations, editions, and recordings.

Portions of Judith Moffett's *James Merrill: An Introduction to the Poetry* (Columbia) have appeared previously in journals and are reviewed in earlier *ALS* chapters. Like Nelson's study, this volume reads through the important collections, dividing its attention pretty equally between the shorter poems and the Ouija trilogy. Moffett agrees with other critics that love and family relationships are Merrill's "best subjects," arguing that "rather than bewail the certainty that love doesn't last, he chooses to be grateful to masks for making intervals of love possible." A second volume to appear on Merrill this year, *James Merrill: Essays in Criticism* (Cornell), is edited by David Lehman and Charles Berger, and is much like Lehman's earlier edited collection of essays on John Ashbery. Lehman in his introduction sees Merrill as Auden's heir: master craftsman, well read, clever, reserved, ironic; he is probably right. Essayists include Lehman, J. D. McClatchy, Samuel E. Schulman, David Kalstone, Rachel Jacoff, Peter Sacks, Willard Spiegelman, Richard Saez, Stephen Yenser, Charles Berger, and David Jackson. Merrill afficionados will enjoy this collection, and readers new to the work will find much of use. While both Moffett and Lehman turn in rather safe and perhaps workmanlike books, these two studies serve Merrill well.

Peter Stitt provides a first-rate interview with John Ashbery this year as "Art of Poetry XXXIII" (*ParisR* 90:30–59); as with Merrill, Auden is again an influence, as Ashbery remarks that "I particularly admired Auden, whom I would say was the first big influence on my work, more so than Stevens." Further, Imre Salusinsky examines "The Genesis of Ashbery's 'Europe'" (*NMAL* 7:item 12), discussing the poet's adaption of William La Queux's charming *Beryl of the Biplane*.

Frank Bidart seems to be attracting progressively more attention, and Brad Crenshaw's "The Sin of the Body: Frank Bidart's Human Bondage" (*ChiR* 33,iv:57–70) is a good introduction to his work. According to Crenshaw, Bidart "has taken the dualism inherited from his modernist fathers, has accepted the separation between what he can say and what he can know, and has sexualized it, so that the felt mode of his alienation is at once anxious and static." Hence, characters in his work tend to be "profoundly troubled" and "inarticulate," tormented by "a moral ambiguity regarding the flesh."

Randall Stiffler looks at W. S. Merwin's sequence of 21 poems about the sea that run across *Green With Beasts* and *The Drunk In The Furnace* in "The Sea Poems of W. S. Merwin" (*MPS* 11:247–66): "The sea is everywhere, he says, and to forget that is dangerous. We sail in this sea not by choice but by necessity, all of us, ignorant of our own interior oceans." As we are all doomed to fail, or "drown," the sequence ends "with an aura of despair." In " 'The Annunciation' of W. S. Merwin" (*CP* 16,ii:55–63), Stiffler argues that the early poem (and his longest) maps out Merwin's "spiritual quest," as well as constituting "a theoretical turning-point" in the development of his poetic. Jack Myers and Michael Simms offer "Conversations with W. S. Merwin" in *SWR* (68:164–80).

In "The Listener: William Stafford" (*MPS* 11:274–86), Julian Gitzen sees Stafford's poetic as founded in a "passive but alert receptivity"; interestingly, Gitzen sees the poet's most original contribution as his sense of "depth . . . an interior richness contributing to each locale." A. K. Weatherhead's "William Stafford's Recent Poetry" (*CP* 16,i:71–78) agrees with Gitzen, noting that "to the artist who abandons convention, a world of transcendental experience is open." Michael Graves's "A Look At the Ceremonial Range of James Wright" (*CP* 16,ii:43–54) places Wright with poets of "the new subjectivity" and argues that his "conscious craftsmanship and ceremonial qualities . . . set him head and shoulders above his contemporaries." Mark Allen's "Theodore Roethke's 'Frau Bauman, Frau Schmidt, and Frau Schwartz' " (*NMAL* 7,iii: item 19) discusses the significance of the choice and arrangement of these names."

James Dickey (TUSAS 451), by Richard J. Calhoun and Robert W. Hill, follows the usual Twayne format, as it opens with a chronology and a biographical sketch, then reads through the poetry chronologically, closing with chapters on the fiction and the literary criticism. Given the limitations of the volume's series, Calhoun and Hill have produced a sound introduction to a poet of far more complexity than is generally acknowledged. The work of James Dickey also concerns Ronald Baughman this year. In "James Dickey's War Poetry: A 'Saved, Shaken Life' " (*SCR* 15,ii:38–48), Baughman reads a number of Dickey's war poems as progressions "from an initial, relatively distant recollection of the experiences of others towards a deeper concentration on the role of the Self." A second Twayne book deals with *Three Contemporary Poets of New England: William Meredith, Philip Booth, and Peter Davison* (TUSAS 437) by Guy Rotella. Rotella sees the inclusion of these three figures in one volume as sensible, as they share a movement from "academic to experimental norms," as well as "use of New England settings and of aspects of the New England literary tradition." Again, each writer is represented by a brief biographical sketch, followed by brief readings of the major poems, and the result is successful enough that general editor Warren French might well consider contracting for other multiauthor volumes.

Another series of note is Boise State's "Western Writers Series" pamphlets, 50-page introductions to the lives and works of Western writers. This year, *James Welch* (*WWS* 57) by Peter Wild and *Richard Hugo* (*WWS* 59) by Donna Gerstenberger appeared; consistent with most of the other numbers in the series, both provide clear and concise readings of the more important poetry and enumeration of major themes. Further, Paul J. Lindholt's "Richard Hugo's Language: The Poem as 'Obsessive Musical Seed' " (*CP* 16,i:67–75) uses the work of Danish linguist Otto Jespersen to illuminate Hugo's "masculinity." James Bense's "Richard Hugo: A Bibliography" (*BB* 40:148–62) provides a very thorough chronological listing of primary and secondary sources.

Daniel Hoffman discusses at some length both the circumstances of composition and metric of his long poem *Brotherly Love* in "The Exactions of Clio: History into Poetry in *Brotherly Love*" (*PAPS* 127:330–38)—a fascinating look into the poet's workshop. Discussion of poetics of a different order is carried on between Charles Bukowski and Al Purdy in *The Bukowski/Purdy Letters, 1964–1974* (Paget Press), edited by Seamus Cooney. I have a real weakness for collections of letters, and this volume is wonderful—the 37 letters are informative yet full of vigor, cleanly edited, and attractively reproduced. As Cooney comments in his brief introduction, the letters trace the decade in which each poet moves into fame, and here is a record of no small moment as each "improvises tipsily and copiously on matters personal and literary."

Finally, readers of contemporary writing will not want to overlook the second half of an extended *ParisR* interview with James Laughlin in "The Art of Publishing" (90:110–51), conducted by Richard Ziegfield. Laughlin is *the* major publisher of our time; he is always an engaging conversationalist, and in this discussion offers an insider's comments on the lives and works of Thomas Merton, Delmore Schwartz, Gary Snyder, and Kenneth Patchen.

The University of New Mexico

18. Drama

Walter J. Meserve

In an editorial for the *Performing Arts Journal* (7:4–6), entitled "The Drama in American Letters," Bonnie Marranca and Gautarn Dasgupta write: "The real history of theatre is the history of dramatic literature and the ongoing critical responses it generates. Our greatest desire is to see theatre overcome the anti-theatrical prejudice in American letters." They were responding to an editorial in the *New York Times Book Review* of December 26, 1982, in which American dramatic literature, dramatic criticism in America and American theater had been taken to task; and it is a revealing comment on all three areas of endeavor that the editors of the *Performing Arts Journal* should have the wisdom and courage to make the first statement quoted above. The distinctive interests of playwrights, critics and theater artists have ever been in contention—as the editors suggest in their second sentence quoted above. A hundred and fifty years ago in America, editors complained about the conditions of dramatic literature and blamed critics, English theater managers, audiences that demanded only spectacular melodrama and the fact that playwrights "must compose pieces not so much for the purpose of 'holding the mirror up to nature' as to suit the fancies of actors, a thing about as ridiculous as would be the writing of books to suit the taste of compositors" (*American Masonic Register and Literary Companion*, V, June, 1844, p. 62).

i. Histories, Anthologies and Reference Works

It is undeniable that critical interest in American dramatic literature is considerably less than scholarly interest in American poetry or fiction, although the number of articles and books concerned with American drama and theater grows yearly. Charles H. Carpenter's perceptive work entitled "American Drama: A Bibliographical Essay" (*American Studies International*, 21,v:3–52) shows clearly that American drama is a neglected area of scholarship. Using only book-length studies, Carpenter misses a lot of important scholarship, but his critical comments are honest and astute. As the bibliographer for *Modern Drama*, Carpenter adds to his essay with "Modern Drama Studies: An Annual Bibliography" (*MD* 26:150–233). Articles dealing with American drama appear on pages 155 through 164. Volume 7 of Jacob Blanck's momentous undertaking, *Bibliography of American Literature* (Yale), edited and completed by Virginia L. Smyers and Michael Winship, includes entries on five writers who contributed to the development of American dramatic literature: James Kirke Paulding, John Howard Payne, Robert Penn Smith, Epes Sargent and William Gilmore Simms. Barbara C. Gannon's "Little Theater in America, 1890–1920" (*BB* 40,iii:189–92) purports to be the only "published or indexed bibliography on the rise of the independent theater." It includes books, periodicals and dissertations.

Phyllis Hartnoll's fourth edition of *The Oxford Companion to the Theatre* (Oxford) appeared this year; the third edition was published in 1967. The type used in printing this new volume is easier on the eye, and the book is better illustrated. Throughout, contemporary dramatists and theaters are emphasized, and most items have been revised; consequently, many items have been dropped or reduced in length. This is particularly true with American entries in a work generally slanted toward England. Entries on Nathaniel H. Bannister, Nathaniel Parker Willis, Charles Hoyt and Archibald MacLeish that appeared in the third edition, for example, are missing from the fourth edition. A minor British actor named John Bannister has been added. The long essay on negroes in the American Theater has been removed and the material distributed elsewhere. Entries on Bronson Howard, Anna C. Mowatt, Booth's Theatre and Augustin Daly are reduced along with numerous other entries. The drama and theater of other countries has also been rewritten with a view to saving space. The entry for China was cut and the transliteration modernized. Individuals lost stature in some instances, as Hungary's only major dramatist, Imre Madách, was absorbed into the general essay on Hungary. Obviously, editorial decisions for compressing information had to be made as the emphasis changed. Edward Albee now has an entry in his own right rather than as a part of the Albee information. Robert Anderson has been added along with African Theater and a large number of named theaters in America. "Acoustics" has been greatly reduced; "Revue" has been expanded. These items, of course, indicate only a selected thumbing of the long text. This new edition remains an extremely valuable resource for students and scholars.

With the assistance of a grant from the National Endowment for the Humanities, Vera Jiji of Brooklyn College has established the Program for Culture at Play, Multimedia Studies in American Drama, in which she is "Showcasing American Drama." Thus far she has published through the CUNY Research Foundation *A Handbook of Source Materials on "The Lion of the West" by James Kirke Paulding* and a similar work on the George J. Aiken dramatization of *Uncle Tom's Cabin*. Each thin paperback volume provides background information on the playwright, the theater, the contemporary reception of the work and the criticism of the period. There are also study notes and questions that indicate the audience Professor Jiji has in mind, but the essays are well researched and written by substantial scholars such as Daniel Gerould and Glen Loney with Professor Jiji. Well illustrated and organized, these two works are helpful references for anyone teaching or writing about these plays.

One of the most interesting drama-theater books published this year is *Ethnic Theatre in the United States* (Greenwood), ed. Maxine Schwartz Seller. This scholarly volume contains abundant notes, a good bibliography and essays on twenty ethnic theaters in America, each written by an expert with attention to origins, literature, playwrights and the relationship of the work described to mainstream American drama. The first essay on "Armenian-American" theater (pp. 19–135) by Nishan Pariakian is typical of the style and format and suggests its interest with comments on a comedy *Go Die, Come I Love You* (1979) by Aram–Ashot Babayan. One expects essays on Danish, French, German and Italian, for example, but not on "Byelorussian-American Theatre." The essay on "Native American Theatre" by Jeffrey F. Huntsman (pp. 355–85) makes the distinction that "Indian events assert a present and eternal reality; Western ones celebrate past realities or seek to involve realities to be." Maureen Murphy's essay on "Irish-American Theatre" is the least exciting. The volume, however, provides an excellent view of some of the hidden corners of the American theater. A minor classic in the study of American theater and drama—Harold Clurman's *The Fervent Years*

(De Capo) with a new introduction by Stella Adler—has been reprinted.

Among new anthologies this year the most useful will be *Best American Plays, Eighth Series, 1974–1982* (Crown) ed. Clive Barnes, which includes 17 plays. Few of the dramatists had been listed in previous volumes, but Barnes included Neil Simon's *Chapter Two* and *A Lovely Sunday for Creve Coeur* by Tennessee Williams. *The Best Plays of 1981–82* (Dodd Mead), ed. Otis J. Guernsey, Jr., offers the usual excerpts of the "ten best plays" along with reviews of the New York season and lists of produced plays. *Three Plays for a Gay Theater & Three Essays* (Grey Fox), ed. Richard Hall, includes rather basic essays on identity and homosexual activity. The plays seem too self-conscious and defensive. *Swords Into Plowshares* (Elgin, Ill.: The Brethren Press), edited by Ingrid Rogers, collects 27 short plays and skits for classroom or church study and production. The viewpoint is strongly Christian; the motivation is persuasion. More useful for courses in American drama is Daniel Gerould's *American Melodrama* (PerfAJ). The difficulty of finding 19th-century American plays in print mounts yearly, and perhaps spectacular melodrama may be all that survives. Gerould includes *Uncle Tom's Cabin* (1852), *Under the Gaslight* (1867) by Augustin Daly, *The Poor of New York* (1857) by Dion Boucicault and David Belasco's *Girl of the Golden West* (1905).

The Theatre Communications Group (TCG) started some twenty years ago with objectives that are now limited to serving the professional, not-for-profit theaters in America. In this national capacity it is admired and well known to theater managers and artists. It has publications, however, that are valuable reference sources for playwrights, drama critics and theater historians. *Dramatists Sourcebook* (TCG), an annual edited by M. Elizabeth Osborn, is a "bible" for playwrights. The introductory essay, "Playwrights' Little Crimes" (pp. i–viii), should be read by all aspiring playwrights. TCG also publishes, on an annual basis, a *Theatre Directory*, *Theatre Facts* dealing with finances and productivity of its constituent theatres, and *Theatre Profiles*. In 1982 it initiated *New Plays USA*, a series that is being continued. *American Theatre*, a "monthly forum for news, features & opinions" begins publication in 1984 and promises to be a major journal for drama and theater history and criticism in America.

Every year there are a number of books that provide basic information about theaters, theater artists, playwrights and their plays. They are seldom scholarly but frequently interesting and well illustrated as well as being valuable sources for bits of information and theater relationships. *Great Actors and Actresses of the American Stage in Historic Photographs* (Dover), edited by Stanley Appelbaum, provides 332 black and white photographs with short biographies of Broadway stars during the 1850–1950 period. In *Stars of the Broadway Stage, 1940–1967* (Dover) Fred Fehl has collected 240 photographs of stars taken during performance. Linda Lee Koenig has written a history of *The Vagabonds, America's Oldest Little Theater* (Fairleigh Dickinson), Baltimore's little theater that dates from the 1920s. *Broadway Babies, The People Who Made the American Musical* (Oxford) by Ethan Mordden shows this critic's easy style of storytelling in an area of theater where he has some authority. On a broader spectrum, Sarah Blacker Cohen has collected a large number of images depicting the contributions of Jews to American stage and screen. Titled *From Hester Street to Hollywood* (Indiana) it is the first volume in a series on Jewish literature and culture edited by Alvin H. Rosenfeld. The number of major American playwrights is revealing: Elmer Rice, Clifford Odets, Lillian Hellman, Arthur Miller, Paddy Chayefsky, Neil Simon, Jules Feiffer, Saul Bellow, Isaac Bashevis Singer. Not all, however, emphasized their Jewish heritage in their work, and the essayists concentrate on their Jewish contributions to American letters. *Women in Theatre* (Drama Books) ed. Karen Malpede, founder of the New Cycle Theatre, excerpts past publications on playwrights and theater artists. The item on Lorraine Hansberry is particularly good, and there are essays on Susan Glaspell and Gertrude Stein. *We Are Strong, A Guide to the Work of Popular Theatres Across the Americas,* volume 1 (Mankato, Minn.: Institute for Cultural Policy Studies) should be noted along with the *California Theatre Annual,* edited by Barbara Isenberg, and other publications of the Performing Arts Network of Beverly Hills, California. All such publications provide the theater and drama historian with necessary facts about theaters and notes on productions.

A new introduction to theater history by Edwin Wilson and Alvin Goldfarb, *Living Theater* (McGraw-Hill) pays scant attention to America. Only Edwin Booth and Edwin Forrest among American actors and actresses of the 19th century are even mentioned. Anna Cora Mowatt and William Dunlap are the only American dramatists mentioned prior to O'Neill. Belasco is included in a listing; Augustin Daly is omitted; Steele MacKaye's stage innovations are mentioned. The chapter on Asian Theater lacks critical specificity and, as a strictly historical recounting of events, is out of phase with the rest of the book. Although the chronological charts throughout the volume are valuable, the limited illustrations and sparse bibliography detract from its value.

ii. 19th-Century Plays, Playwrights, and Theaters

The study of a dramatic literature and its place in the history of American theater remains the most neglected genre of American letters for serious scholarship. Any evaluation or commentary on theater or drama prior to 1915 is frequently made to appear woefully esoteric. Fortunately, there are those researchers and scholars who persist. All students of early American drama have heard of *Androborus*, the satiric farce through which Governor Robert Hunter of colonial New York purged himself of his frustrations and anger. In the words of Mary Lou Lustig, *Robert Hunter, 1666–1734* (Syracuse), the play was "cathartic to Hunter" who used the satire to murder three of his most annoying enemies. On pages 136–40 Lustig provides a full plot and commentary. An article by Lewis Leary should encourage young scholars. His "William Charles White, the American Garrick; A Footnote to the History of Early American Drama" (*EAL* 18:84–94) provides a biographical sketch of White focusing on his playwriting and theater interests.

One of the most interesting essays of the year was Rosemarie K. Bank's "Theatre and Narrative Fiction in the Work of the Nineteenth-Century American Playwright, Louisa Medina" (*Theatre HS* 3:55–67). A very bright young woman, who provided some of the most popular melodramas for Thomas Hamblin's Bowery Theatre in New York, Medina had a mysterious and brief life as a playwright. Mainly, she adapted contemporary fiction for the stage with an astounding success during the 1830s. Basing his article on John Banvard's fragmentary and unpublished autobiography in the archives of the Minnesota Historical Society of St. Paul, John Hanners provides new commentary on the Chapman Family's *Floating Theatre* as well as Banvard's own experiences in "It Was Play or Starve: John Banvard's Account of Early Showboats" (*Theatre RI* 8:53–64). *Selected Letters of P. T. Barnum* (Columbia), edited by A. H. Saxon, provide some insights into the philosophy and practice of a mid-19th-century theater manager. "Dan Rice" (*Theater* 14,ii:86–92) discusses this actor's appeal to audiences. The author, Ron Jenkins, had access to scrapbooks and other materials owned by Rice's descendents in Long Branch, New Jersey and Girard, Pennsylvania. Pat M. Ryan's "The Hibernian Experience: John Brougham's Irish-American Plays" (*MELUS* 10,ii:33–47) offers little that Ryan has not published previously. The difficulty in identifying actors, actresses and actor-playwrights in the 19th century is illustrated in *Victorian Actors and Actresses in Review* (Greenwood), compiled by Donald Mullin who includes excerpted reviews that are helpful for the historian. Kate Bateman (1843–1917) is identified as an American-born English actress. Dion Boucicault, who went back and forth across the Atlantic but spent nearly the last 20 years of his life in America, is called an English-born Anglo-American actor and playwright. John Brougham, who came to America in 1842 and remained, is termed an Irish-born Anglo-American actor, actor-manager and playwright. As critics and countries begin to claim their successful artists, accurate identification becomes a problem.

Not too many scholars identify Hamlin Garland as a playwright, but he did write plays as well as dramatic criticism and showed a certain fascination with the theater and its playwrights. Warren Motley makes significant claims for Garland's work in a well-written and carefully argued essay: "Hamlin Garland's *Under the Wheel*, Regionalism Unmasking America" (*MD* 26:477–85). Motley emphasizes Garland's best known play but also contends that his work "influenced Herne's more successful plays and represents a step toward the distinctive qualities of American realism."

iii. Eugene O'Neill

With the exception of Tetsumaro Hayaski's *Eugene O'Neill, Research Opportunities and Dissertation Abstracts* (McFarland), which provides a checklist of the items indicated in the title, there were no book-length studies of O'Neill this year. The *Eugene O'Neill News-letter* continues to publish notes of somewhat uneven quality. Of particular interest is Louis Scheaffer's article (*EON* 6,ii:13–24) concerned with mistakes in O'Neill scholarship that Scheaffer also republishes with additional information as "Correcting Some Errors in Annals of O'Neill" (*CompD* 17:201–32). Frederick C. Wilkins examines "one of the major public responses" to O'Neill's death in "Lawson and Cole Revisited" (*EON* 7,ii:17–23). Lester Cole responded to John Lawson's article in *Masses and Mainstream*, and Lawson replied. Two essays on O'Neill deal with film versions of his plays. In "From Stage to Screen, *The Long Voyage Home* and *Long Day's Journey Into Night*" (*EON* 7,i:10–14), William L. Sipple analyzes the different directorial approaches of John Ford and Sidney Lumet. Linda Ben-Zvi looks at "Eugene O'Neill and Film" (*EON* 7,i:3–10), particularly *Before Breakfast* and *The Emperor Jones*, and finds that O'Neill's plays were rarely given adequate treatment. For Brenda Murphy, *The Iceman Cometh* is O'Neill's first fully developed realistic play. In "O'Neill's Realism: A Structural Approach" (*EON* 7,ii:3–6), she argues that *Iceman* and later plays demonstrate a final achievement in which realistic form and structure "represent his dynamic realism of character."

One of the most formidable essays appearing this year in the *Newsletter* is Peter Egri's "Beneath *The Calms of Capricorn*: O'Neill's Adoption and Naturalization of European Models" (*EON* 7,ii:6–17). After examining briefly a variety of European models that influenced O'Neill, Egri states that O'Neill's originality lies in "transforming them by subjecting them to the requirements of the crucial conflict treated in the cycle of possessors self-dispossessed." Looking East rather than West, Sheng-chuan Lai tries to show that O'Neill's work reveals a strong affinity with the form and mechanics of *noh*. The article is "Mysticism and Noh in O'Neill" (*TJ* 35:74–87), and Lai's argument is wholly unimpressive, particularly in the explanation of *Yugen* and the circumstantial linking of Noh to *Long Day's Journey*. The comments on *Fight in the Path* sharply divide the writer's application of mysticism and Noh to O'Neill. In "A Note on O'Neill, Nietzsche, and Naturalism: *Long Day's Journey into Night* in European Perspectives" (*MD* 26:331–34), Reinhold Grimm appears to argue all sides as he sees the play as a "unique acceptance and combination as well as rejection and revaluation of those two determining forces [Ibsen and Nietzsche] and their overpowering heritage."

iv. Anderson, Hellman, Saroyan, and Wilder

As one of America's most admired dramatists, Maxwell Anderson worked hard to keep his private life out of print. That is now changed with the publication of *The Life of Maxwell Anderson* (Stein and Day) by Alfred S. Shivers, who has researched Anderson's life in an extremely thorough manner. He appears to have all the facts as he carefully traces Anderson's life and relationships with wives and friends. Good books, however, require more than facts. In a prose style that is romantic and anecdotal, Shivers tends to wander through Anderson's life with witty and gratuitous observations. On occasion there is a "you are there" editorial point of view as the reader waits at the theater for the opening of *What Price Glory?* Ten pages later Shivers explains the play in less than a page, an approach that suggests a major problem with the book. There is no assessment of Anderson's work as a playwright. Shivers is great on facts, intrigues and infidelities but shows no real understanding of his subject or insight into his work. The mystery surrounding Anderson the dramatist and artist still exists.

Linda W. Wagner argues a fascinating thesis in "Lillian Hellman: Autobiography and Truth" (*SoR* 19:275–88) by challenging the notion that recollection equals truth. There is value in Hellman's four autobiographical volumes, however, that Wagner states may even bring about a "credible account of her life." *William Saroyan* (Harcourt) by Aram Saroyan turns out to be, unfortunately, another book in which a child strikes back at a parent. Expressing great sympathy for his mother, Aram Saroyan explains the less admirable characteristics of his father's life and art. He is particularly distressed that his father created and left his money to the William Saroyan Foundation. Harry Keyishian underscores this hostile relationship in "Who Was William Saroyan?" (*LitR* 27:153–58), a discussion of Saroyan's last work, *Births*, and Aram Saroyan's two books on his father, *Last Rites: The Death of William Saroyan* and *William Saroyan. The Enthusiast: A Life of Thornton Wilder* (Ticknor and Fields) by Gilbert A. Harrison is written in a style that will entrance both the scholar and the casual reader. It provides that well-tempered portrait of a man that Leon Edel applauds as it illuminates the thoughts and actions of an artist who found a fascination with both living and dying. Carefully using Wilder's works and words and all that people know about him, Harrison tells a fine story and adds considerably to critical thought with ideas that will enlighten students of Wilder's plays.

v. Arthur Miller

In 1961 Dennis Welland, the English critic and professor now teaching at Victoria University in Manchester, England, wrote the first book-length study of Arthur Miller. In 1979 he published *Miller: A Study of His Plays*. His latest book, *Miller, The Playwright* (Methuen), supersedes *Miller: A Study of His Plays* by covering works since 1979 and providing an accurate up-to-date chronology. Chapter 12 entitled "The Passage of Time" (pp. 144–57) treats *The American Clock* and *Playing for Time* and places them in perspective among Miller's works. "Arthur Miller at New Haven" (*Drama* 147:41) by E. Shorter notes Miller's visit to Yale. Richard T. Brucher tries to bring Willy Loman into the high-tech age with "Willy Loman and *The Soul of a New Machine*: Technology and the Common Man" (*JAmS* 17:325–36).

vi. Tennessee Williams, 1911–83

Scholarship this year suggests the forthcoming interest in a major 20th-century American dramatist whose macabre death startled the theater world. *Twentieth Century Interpretations of "The Glass Menagerie"* (Prentice-Hall), edited by R. B. Parker, reprints 15 essays on productions, influences, dramaturgy, characters and themes by major scholars. Parker's "Introduction," (pp. 1–13) outlines the problems critics faced with this play and concludes that "scholarship on Tennessee Williams is still only just beginning." Tetsumaro Hayashi has provided another resource volume on *Arthur Miller and Tennessee Williams* (McFarland). Asserting that Williams's plays must live as *plays*, not as a reflection of Williams's life in *scripts*, Glen Loney surveys Williams's achievements in "Tennessee Williams, the Catastrophe of Success" (*PerfAJ* 7:73–86).

Most of the essays on Williams's plays are relatively slight in terms of lasting scholarship. William J. Free's "Camp Elements in the Plays of Tennessee Williams" (*SoQ* 21,ii:16–23) is a good example. "A Study of Illusion and the Grotesque in Tennessee Williams' *Cat on a Hot Tin Roof*" (*SoSt* 22:359–65) by Susan Neal Mayberry also has limited value. In "The Blind Mexican American Woman in Williams' *A Streetcar Named Desire*" (*NMAL* 7,ii: item 14), Bert Cardullo provides a two-and-a-half-page note on the individuality of this character. Having directed *Camino Real*, Dawning Cless relates this play to Brecht's theories in "Alienation and Contradictions in *Camino Real*: A Convergence of Williams and Brecht" (*TJ* 35:41–50). In an extremely thorough study of his subject—a fact revealed by the profusion of notes, six of his twenty-one pages—Gilbert Debusscher tries to prove the influence of Hart Crane upon Williams: "Minting Their Separate Wills: Tennessee Williams and Hart Crane" (*MD* 26:455–76). Much of his argument is compelling, but he also must rely upon "striking similarity."

vii. Some Contemporary Playwrights

Edward Albee An Interview and Essays (Houston, Texas: University of St. Thomas), edited by Julian N. Wasserman, draws attention to a major dramatist of a past generation whose current plays—*The Man Who Had Three Arms*, for example—have not attracted scholars. The volume begins with "An Interview with Edward Albee, March 18, 1981" (pp. 1–27) that elicits some interesting dalliance with Albee but nothing worth repeating. Wasserman's essay entitled "The Pitfalls of Drama, The Idea of Language in the Plays of Edward Albee" (pp. 29–53) concentrates on the imitative aspects of language—mainly with reference to *Tiny Alice* that are related to the importance of realism in the theatre. "Disturbing Our Sense of Well-Being" by Virginia Perry (pp. 55–64) argues the obvious point that *A Delicate Balance* disturbs the audience in order to explain Albee's thesis. In "On Death, Dying and the Manner of Living, Waste as Theme in Edward Albee's *The Lady from Dubuque*" (pp. 65–81), Mathew C. Roudané states that the value of this play is illustrated through the life of waste endured by everyone but the dying Jo. For Leonard Casper, "*Tiny Alice*, The Expense of Joy in the Persistence of Mystery" (pp. 83–92), the play encourages one to persist even if there is risk. Jerry is the guide in Albee's ritualistic confrontation with alienation and death in "Ritual and Imitation in *The Zoo Story*" (pp. 93–100) by Mary C. Anderson. Thomas D. Adler explores "The Pirandello in Albee, The Problem of Knowing in *The Lady from Dubuque*" (pp. 109–19). "*Counting the Ways*, The Ways of Losing Heart" (pp. 120–40) by Philip C. Korn is concerned with a perceived tension between form and content. In "The Limits of Reason, Seascape or Psychic Metaphor" (pp. 141–53) Liam O. Purdom elaborates on Albee's use of metaphor as a means for cognition. One misses an essay on *Virginia Woolf* in this volume, but all of the essays here strike one as esoteric arguments about pins and pennies. They defend Albee against all critics but themselves.

According to June Schlueter and Elizabeth Forsyth, David Mamet sees "the decadence of the American dream" as "directly attributable to the dominance of the American business ethic." Their argument is entitled "America as Junkshop: The Business Ethic in David Mamet's *American Buffalo*" (MD 26:492–500). Western Writers Series now has a volume on *Preston Jones* (WWS 58) written by Mark Busby who shows considerable sensitivity to Jones's problems as a dramatist from New Mexico, as well as Texas, who was never a great success in New York. The book provides a good description of Jones's plays and an honest defense of his reputation as a poet dramatist who died young. N. Carroll's "Select View of Earthlings: Ping Chang (U. S.)" (DR 27:72–81) discusses the multimedia characteristics of Chang's "bricolages," such as *Lazarus* and *The Articulated Man*. In his all-seeing way, Timothy Murry reduces Marsha Norman's *Getting Out* to a bad joke on the audience in "Patriarchal Panopticism, or the Seduction of a Bad Joke: *Getting Out* in Theory" (TJ 35:376–88). Suzanne Dieckerman and Richard Bradshaw follow a subjective metaphor in "Wings, Watches and Windows: Imprisonment in the Plays of Arthur Kopit" (TJ 35:195–211).

Criticism of individual dramatists seems particularly scattered this year: books on Wilder and Saroyan, a collection of essays on Albee, a few essays on O'Neill and fewer on Miller, growing attention for Williams. Even Sam Shepard, who seduced the minds of a number of scholars last year, attracted only two this year. In a pithy comment Bert Cardullo explains "Shepard's *Curse of the Starving Class*" (Expl 42,i:64) in terms of the "eagle and the cat" story in Act III that stands as a metaphor for the action of the entire play. In "Sam Shepard's *Buried Child*: The Ironic Use of Folklore" (MD

26:486–91), Thomas Nash presents a compelling argument that Shepard has borrowed heavily from *The Golden Bough* to produce a modern version of the death and rebirth of the Corn King. Nash strengthens his argument with some comparisons to Shirley Jackson's "The Lottery" and concludes that the seemingly trivial mishaps of Shepard's midwestern family masks "the shadows of sacrificial rites and the shades of dying gods."

viii. Black Ethnic Drama

Scholarly attention to theater and drama in America has been jeopardized by many prejudices in the past. Religious sanctions, the self-imposed mystique of theater artists, the snobbish preference of literary writers and critics for foreign drama and theater, the backlash of literary nationalism campaigns—all have contributed to the current attitudes toward American dramatic literature and the lack of a substantial body of dramatic criticism and theory. In America of the present day, however, there is a concerted effort among critics to avoid one prejudice and publicize black drama and theater. No single minority effort in America attracts the attention that surrounds black drama, and one of the best books published this year is concerned with contemporary Afro-American theater.

Drumbeats, Masks and Metaphor (Harvard), written by Genviéve Fabre and translated by Melvin Dixon, presents a clear if brief history of black theater and the playwrights who create for it, followed by a chapter entitled "The Militant Theatre" that stresses the work of LeRoi Jones/Amiri Baraka and those who followed his philosophy. She also writes of "The Theatre of Experience," the black Experience in which the needs and practices of black theaters are presented in a strong argument describing the conflicts of blacks against blacks and blacks in an America that has no place for them. The author concludes with a discussion of "Theatre and Culture" and the problems of black theater and drama for the black people and within the larger community in America. Afro-American theatre, Fabre argues, has reached a crossroad. Will it serve a racial community or seek recognition in the dominant society? Will it be a part of a broad culture in a competitive world or will it remain in the hands of black people? Fabre writes a thoughtful book in a provoking and persuasive manner.

Among current periodicals the *Black American Literary Forum* publishes a large number of very short articles on black theater and drama. A. Peter Bailey provides a broad view of the Black Theater movement starting with Amiri Baraka in 1964: "A Look at the Contemporary Black Theater Movement" (*BALF* 17:19–21). "Witness to a Possibility: The Black Theatre Movement in Washington, D. C., 1968–1976" (*BALF* 17:22–26) by Taquiena Boston and Vera Katy focuses on the contributions of 11 people. Other articles in the same issue include Margaret Wilkerson's "The Sighted Eyes and Feeling Heart of Lorraine Hansberry" (17:8–13), a revision of an earlier article; Andrej Ceynowa's "The Dramatic Structure of *Dutchman*" (17:15–18), an attempt to explore the structure and show how it helps one appreciate "more generally" Jones the artist; E. H. Freydberg's "Concealed Dependence Upon White Culture in Baraka's 1969 Aesthetic" (17:27–29), an examination of the failure of plays written under the influence of Baraka's aesthetics; Anthony Hill's "Rituals of the New Lafayette Theater" (17:31–35), an interview with Robert Macbeth. All of the articles are brief and slight, and some are excerpted reprints. One essay of interest in the summer 1983 issue was Baraka's attack on Charles Fuller's *Zooman* and *A Soldier's Play* and his condemnation on the Negro Ensemble as a "skin theatre" (17:51–54). Other topics in this summer issue are the Free Southern Theatre, "Theatre and the Afro-American Rite of Being," the Kennedy Center Black Theater Project, Rosetta Le Noire, the "conflicting impulses" in the plays of Ntozake Shange, the linkage of the theater in South Africa with black theater in America, and the black theater organizations in America from 1961 to 1982.

Allen Woll's *Dictionary of the Black Theatre* (Greenwood) includes a three-page history of black theater, two major sections describing "The Shows" and "Personalities and Organizations," a brief chronology of black theaters from 1898 to 1919 and a pathetic three and a half-page bibliography. It would appear to have little value for scholars. Faith Berry's biography of *Langston Hughes Before and Beyond Harlem* (Lawrence Hill) is a fine study of a persevering artist. Faced with problems in getting his plays produced, Hughes said: "I'm afraid there is nothing left for me to do except start a theatre and produce plays." And he did—the Harlem Suitcase Theater—with a production of *Don't You Want To Be Free?* Berry provides a thorough discussion of Hughes's problems as a playwright, his confrontations with prejudiced theater managers and his stalwart reactions and accomplishments.

ix. Final Comments

The world of theater and/or drama is extremely complicated. From the various parts of this world—carefully portioned and proportioned by dominating people—there are innumerable advocates proclaiming that whatever exists, under the name that is most clearly understood by the public, would not come into being without their particular creativity. Although Zelda Fichandler talks about the "Humanist View of Theater" (*PerfAJ* 7,ii:88–99), she refers to a tradition "rooted in our capacity for empathy and identification" from a viewer's position in a theater, not a reader's reaction through an inspired imagination. From the literary point of view, the playwright is the keystone, but not all people agree with this simple observation, nor has history always properly appreciated the playwright. He or she is, however, part of the theater world and is always instructed by other parts of that world. One of the few fine books in this area is Raymond Hill's *How to Write a Play* (Cincinnati, Ohio: Writer's Digest Books) that is easily read and contains many helpful exercises for the aspiring playwright. Yet Hill writes: "A script cannot really be called a play until it has been produced." Language problems again. Bonnie Marranca interviewed four playwrights on the subject of "American Playwright: Insider or Outsider?" (*PerfAJ* 7,ii:36–47) without reaching any conclusions regarding his or her position in that theater world.

Where does the playwright fit in the American theatre? As the play is produced upon the stage with the help of the playwright and the theater artists—actors, directors, designers—theater companies are continuing their long tradition of taking what they will from English and European theaters by employing a dramaturg who has a new influence upon the playwright. The dramaturg, however, is not universally accepted, and Peter Hay, "American Dramaturg, a Critical Re-Appraisal" (*PerfAJ* 7,iii:7–42) argues the need for one. Another source of instruction for the playwright is the critic or reviewer, that person who tries to decide where the playwright does, in fact, belong in the theater. In "The Last Word" (*Plays & Players* 356:16–17), Clive Barnes explains what he considers the critic's task: "The artist works with synthesis. He takes in genetic constitutions and life experience and from those creates with his sensibility a work of art. The critic—his is the craft of analysis—reverses the process. Using his own genetic constitution and life experience, he tries to take the work apart to display it to his public." America does not have a rich tradition of dramatic criticism, although the history of what exists is slowly being compiled. Tice L. Miller adds more with "George Jean Nathan and the 'New Criticism'" (*Theatre HS* 3:99–107).

As this yearly essay attempts to show, critics and historians continue to write about all aspects of the drama-theater process in an attempt to clarify that humanist tradition for immediate audiences and to define it for cultural historians. It is an extremely broad picture to illuminate. Ibsen's *Hedda Gabler*, for example, has now been transformed into a musical set in Charleston, South Carolina. Carl L. Anderson discusses the libretto in "Hedda Gabler as Musical Drama: Robert Ward's *Claudia Le Gare*" (*SoQ* 21, iii:44–55). James S. Moy describes "The Folies Bergère in New York City in 1911" (*Theatre RI* 8:146–56). One of America's great modern directors is Elia Kazan, an outstanding figure in American theater who was particularly responsible for productions of Arthur Miller's plays and also directed plays by Williams, Maxwell Anderson and Robert Anderson, among others, for the New York stage. In *An American Odyssey, Elia Kazan and American Culture* (Temple) Thomas H. Pauly provides a reasonable and frequently exciting assessment of Kazan's achievements. Meanwhile, playwrights also reveal their cycles of interest, or critics attempt to show that they do. One of the more imaginative book-length discussions of plays this year is Carol Rosen's *Plays of Impasse, Contemporary Drama Set in Confining Institutions* (Princeton). Arguing that plays are a metaphor for contemporary conditions, Rosen has discovered "a mode of serious plays relentlessly depicting characters at the edge of despair, characters lost in a situation of pain, anguish, and powerlessness, characters cornered, subjected to the will of an overwhelming social setting." (p. 6) Her chapters include analyses of Kopit's *Wings*, Kenneth Brown's *The Brig*, and David Rabe's *Basic Training of Pavlo Hummel* and *Streamers*.

Every year is a year of review—even as this review provides one more. The editors of the 100th issue of *The Drama Review* attempted to look forward after this recognized milestone but included Brooks McNamara's "TDR: Memoirs of the Mouthpiece, 1955–1983" (*TDR* 27,iv:3–21). Robert Asahina reviewed *Cats, Angel's Fall* and *True*

West in his "Theatre Chronicle" (*HudR* 36:229–31), and C. Hughes discussed a cross section of New York productions in various issues of *Plays & Players* under the heading of "New York Report." Always one of the more substantial and perceptive critics of any drama season, Gerald Weales in his annual "American Theater Watch, 1982–1983" (*GaR* 37:601–11) mentions new plays by Shepard, Ribman, Mamet and Albee, but finds only Marsha Norman's *'night, Mother* outstanding. This year, it is likely that a number of the books and articles on various dramatists and their work will be considered more important in theater annuals than the season's plays.

Institute for American Theatre Studies
Indiana University

19. Black Literature

John M. Reilly

In previous years I have opened this report by noting the general expansion of black literary studies and by commenting on the critical agenda that seemed to be implied in the year's work. At times the agenda has shown a general concern for literary history, particularly the problems of period definition and genre formation. This year I am impressed most by the number of critics exploring the issue of black control of discourse that must necessarily draw for sources upon language and literary forms that are shared with the entire American culture. In some respects this concern with the integrity of discourse is evidence that the Black Aestheticians continue to influence us, for it was they who first made the politics of literary language a programmatic point. Of course, feminist criticism can also take responsibility for increasing our sensitivity to character stereotype and the latent assumptions burdening the language. Still, what is most significant about current attention to discourse control is the understanding that black writers have always been aware of the questions of dominance and control. As critics proceed to explore the ways writers have reacted to white dominance of the received literary forms, they are establishing a new imperative for criticism. For too long it has been assumed that the way to gain room for Afro-American writers in the literary canon, or to establish the legitimacy of black literary studies in the first place, was through skillful interpretations that would reveal the depth and complexity of black writing. Depth and complexity are there to be sure, but interpretation seems less and less the primary role of critics. Writers have known all along that the transactions in language, the control of discourse, determine the way we know reality. So, then, critics are adjusting their agenda to attend also to this larger, more fundamental issue. Certainly a good deal of the work for 1983 recorded here suggests that this is the case.

i. Bibliography

Gregory S. Sojka contributes "Black Slave Narratives—A Selected Checklist of Criticism" to the *The Art of Slave Narrative*. The volume results from sophisticated critical work on the genre, and Sojka's listing provides an indispensable guide to those wishing to study the exciting field. Sojka categorizes items into bibliographical sources, major library holdings of primary materials, published collections of slave narratives, book-length studies, sections of books, articles and introductions dealing with the narratives, articles on individual narratives (there are 15 authors who are subjects of these studies), and unpublished dissertations. To compile *Index to Black American Writers in Collective Biographies* (Littleton, Colo.: Libraries Unlimited), Dorothy W. Campbell searched 267 titles published from 1837 to 1982. Her listings refer to approximately 1,900 writers arranged alphabetically in entries that include variant names and cross-references. References include anthologies where the information is slight, but all works cited include notice of at least two writers. Notations indicate works designed for children.

The Black History Museum of Philadelphia is responsible for *Sterling A. Brown: A UMUM Tribute* (1982). In addition to remembrances and photos the volume contains a bibliography up to 1975 (pp. 89–101) listing books by Brown with notes of reviews they received; critical reviews written by Brown; his essays on cultural, social, economic and other issues; other media treatments; selected poems; short stories; articles about Brown; and books of interest as background. The volume as a whole is quite useful. For scholarly purposes of identifying Brown's full poetic output, however, the bibliography should be supplemented with reference to the one compiled by Robert O'Mealley for *Callaloo* (see *ALS 1982*, p. 384).

Yoshinobu Hakutani's "Richard Wright in Japan: An Annotated Checklist of Criticism" (*RALS* 10[1981]:241–56) opens with an introduction on the critical reputation of Wright and the phases of interest in his work since the first translation of *Native Son* in 1940. Hakutani points out that of the 69 secondary sources he identified only two are listed in the *MLA International Bibliography*. The 57 items he lists and annotates in chronological order include all with substantial commentary. Most are in Japanese, with titles translated by Hakutani, and only one is book length—Masao Takahashi's *The Tragic Wanderer* (1968).

The two *BALF* issues on black theater will be discussed later, but here it is appropriate to single out for mention two contributions that resemble bibliographical resources more than critical essays. Neil Conboy and James V. Hatch's "An Index of Proper Nouns for 'The Place of the Negro in the Evolution of the American Theatre, 1767 to 1940,' a Dissertation by Fannin Saffore Belcher, Jr. (Yale University, 1945)" (*BALF* 17:38–48), is designed to increase access to "the monument in Black theatre research." Andrezej Ceynowa's "Black Theaters and Theater Organizations in America, 1961–1982: A Research List" (*BALF* 17:84–93) assembles basic information on organizations that often had meteoric existence. Entries include the name of the theater or organization, any institutional affiliation, the name of founder or director, and address. If groups changed names all are included, and Ceynowa has attempted to fix the dates for each group by indicating its inclusion in *Black Theater Directory* published by the Kennedy Center (1981) or *Black Theaters*, edited by Marc Primus (1973).

ii. Fiction

a. **Wilson, Chesnutt, Griggs, Corrothers, Micheaux.** Though Harriet E. Wilson was never exactly as "lost" as some newspaper accounts made her out to be upon the publication of a facsimile edition of her novel, she certainly was obscure and almost overlooked. In any case, through the enterprise of Henry Louis Gates, Jr., and the good offices of Random House we now have a new edition of *Our Nig; or, Sketches from the Life of a Free Black, in a Two-Story White House, North, Showing that Slavery's Shadows Fall Even There.* This is the first Afro-American novel published in the United States (William Wells Brown's *Clotel* was originally issued in London), and, as its title indicates, it enters a dissenting view to those that represented the North in 1859 as a promised land. In his introduction to the edition Gates relates *Our Nig* to the sentimental novel, applying Nina Baym's concept of "overplot," but noting that Wilson invents her own structure and, thus, deserves recognition for formal inauguration of a black tradition in fiction. Despite literary innovation, however, the novel, in a manner characteristic of its time, carries appended testimony on the author suggesting an autobiographical basis for the narrative, and in his notes to the text Gates pursues this possibility.

In last year's report (pp. 385–86) I noted Sally Ann H. Ferguson's study of the failure of Charles W. Chesnutt's ideal of assimilation in his first novel. In an article presumably written around the same time but only recently published Ferguson pursues the theme through a close reading of short fiction. "Chesnutt's 'The Conjurer's Revenge': The Economics of Direct Confrontation" (*Obsidian* 7,ii–iii[1981]: 37–42) interprets the story as a duel of epistemologies in which Julius "cons his employer by using language that plays to the perceptual biases of the white world." The success is shortlived, however, for the white employer is backed by the force of capitalism as it invades the Reconstruction South.

As part of his ongoing project on black literature from the turn of the century James Robert Payne has published "Griggs and Corrothers: Historical Reality and Black Fiction" (*ExES* 6:1–9). Where modern readers may see fantasy in the accounts of black alliances rendered by Sutton Griggs in *Imperium in Imperio* and by James D. Corrothers in the short story "A Man They Didn't Know," published in *Crisis*, Payne argues that visions of multi-ethnic organizations project radical historical alternatives to the racism of the Spanish-American War and the "yellow peril."

In "Oscar Micheaux, Black Novelist and Film Maker" (*Vision and Refuge: Essays on the Literature of the Great Plains*. Eds. Virginia Faulkner and Frederick C. Lubke. Nebraska, 1982, pp. 109–125) Chester J. Fontenot, Jr., examines the trilogy of autobiographical novels in which Micheaux sought to counter the recommendation of Booker T. Washington that blacks remain in the South and the encouragement W. E. B. DuBois gave to urban resettlement. Micheaux portrays, in the manner of realism, the possibilities for middle-class life on the western plains.

b. **Toomer, Wright, Hurston, Baldwin, Ellison, Demby.** The year's two articles on Jean Toomer focus on the verse published in *Cane*. In the first, "Repeated Images in Part One of *Cane*" (*BALF* 17:100–105), Herbert W. Rice follows the image patterns suggested by the lines Toomer wrote for his title page. By Rice's reading, each story or poem in part one of the novel is analogous to an image in these opening lines. The second article, "Jean Toomer: A Cubist Poet," by Ann Marie Bush and Louis D. Mitchell (*BALF* 17:106–108) offers diagrams and explication of "Nullo" and "Storm Ending" on behalf of the argument that Toomer's images are not metaphors, but rather objects or subjects compressed into a moment in which readers react with intuitive perception. Bush and Mitchell are so impatient with critics who fail to read Toomer correctly that they overlook the fact that more than a decade ago Bowie Duncan introduced to criticism the idea that Toomer's multi-dimensional techniques bear close relationship to cubism (see *CLAJ*, March 1972). Still, despite the tone and an unaccountable introduction of allegory into their interpretations, Bush and Mitchell are suggestive about Toomer's technique.

Speaking of materials overlooked, I must mention that in last year's report I did not take notice of two contributions on Richard Wright. Sherley Anne Williams in the allusively titled essay "Papa Dick and Sister-Woman: Reflections on Women in the Fiction of Richard Wright" (*American Novelists Revisited*, pp. 394–415) charges the founder of modern Afro-American literature with fathering also a misogynist line. Because, in Williams's judgment, Wright never moved beyond his earliest portrayals of women, she concentrates on the male-centered narratives of *Uncle Tom's Children*, indicating how females are kept in the background and how assaults upon them, as in "Long Black Song," are treated as affronts to their men. Even Aunt Sue in "Bright and Morning Star" is by Williams's reckoning linked to stereotypical views, though in this case she carefully specifies the complex reimagining on Wright's part of the black "Mammy." Williams supports her argument with brief discussion of later works and consideration of Wright's autobiographical record. The result is a thoroughly convincing study of a subtext of Wright's canon. The second item omitted from last year's report is Jack B. Moore's "The View from the Broom Closet of the Regency Hyatt: Richard Wright as a Southern Writer" (*Literature at the Barricades*, pp. 126–43). Taking his title from remarks by Hugh Holman cautioning against monolithic representation of southern writing and focusing attention on the short stories in which Wright is most explicitly concerned with the southern scene, Moore contrasts Wright's narratives with features of the Agrarian myth and compares the black writer's treatment of such subjects as lynching with their appearance in the white literature of his time.

In his critical essays Wright spoke of the blues as an affirmative, sensual expression of black culture, but it is the contention of John McCloskey, Jr., in "Two Steppin': Richard Wright's Encounter with Blue Jazz" (*AL* 55:332–44) that Wright was reluctant, or unable, to explore blue jazz "as an ethic capable of informing his protagonists about layers of experience." Wright sought his precedents in Euro-American writing, and his strategy of representing his characters in isolation works against invocation of folk culture in his fiction. So far as the broad patterns of Wright's fiction are concerned, McCloskey's point is a strong one; yet, Eugene E. Miller in "Folkloric Aspects of Wright's 'The Man Who Killed a Shadow'" (*CLAJ* 27:210–23) indicates that more localized features such as motifs and tone may be found to parallel usage in stories collected by folklorists. Miller's work is exemplary because it seeks the features of a mode rather than single coincidences and because it calls upon unpublished materials from the archive to help present the possibility that Wright thought the surreal manner of his narrative to be closely related to vernacular storytelling.

Since publication of the new edition of *American Hunger* critics have undertaken a rereading of the seemingly optimistic conclusion of *Black Boy*. Robert J. Butler addresses the issue in "The Quest for Pure Motion in Richard Wright's *Black Boy*" (*MELUS* 10,iii:5–17) to establish a distinction between the plot of outer motion—a series of random physical movements and geographical relocations—and the inner, emotional freedom engendered by the journey. In moving North, Butler maintains, Wright sought a symbolic space; the city of Chicago and the actual events that would occur there were not his goal. Butler is no doubt correct in his reading and helpful in enforcing a sense of the dynamics of the narrative. Correct, too, but less significant for further study because much of its argument is already familiar, is Earle V. Bryant's "Sexual Initiation and Survival in Richard Wright's *The Long Dream*" (*SoQ* 21,iii:57–66), which provides an exposition of the racism under a sexual aspect in the novel.

If the use of folklore is problematic in the work of Wright, it is self-evident source and substance for another writer. In "Zora Neale Hurston: Changing Her Own Words" (*American Novelists Revisited*, pp. 371–93) Cheryl A. Wall attends to the tropes and rhythms Hurston adapted from her informants in *Mules and Men*, the priority given lyrical language in *Their Eyes Were Watching God*, and the significance the linguistic qualities of Hurston's writings have in the tradition now sustained by writers such as Toni Morrison and Alice Walker. Missy Dean Kubitschek's " 'Tuh de Horizon and Back': The Female Quest in *Their Eyes Were Watching God*" (*BALF* 17:109–15) develops the role of Janie by adapting Joseph Campbell's quest scheme to interpret the basic narrative and by proposing a merger of that quest within the frame story, so that Janie is seen as preparing the way for what Robert Stepto terms a narrative of ascent, which in this case involves the whole community; thus, while Kubitschek indicates there has been critical hesitancy to accept Janie's quest as central to the novel, she has none in calling Janie a true heroine. Another, more peripheral, way of evaluating Hurston's use of folklore can be found in Miriam DeCosta Willis's "Folklore and the Creative Artist: Lydia Carbrera and Zora Neale Hurston" (*CLAJ* 27:81–90). The contrast between the Cuban and American writers shows that Hurston's work evidences shifting voices and perspectives, signs of a nonscientific but decidedly novelistic sensibility.

The year's work on James Baldwin may be considered as largely defense and amplification. The defense appears most clearly in John T. Shawcross's "Joy and Sadness: James Baldwin, Novelist" (*Callaloo* 6,ii:100–11), which charges critics with extrapolating characters' views from the novels as though they were Baldwin's own. To counter the tendency to sociology, Shawcross examines the structures of inner being and outer demands governing characters in *Go Tell It On the Mountain* and *Giovanni's Room*. Dorothy H. Lee's "The Bridge of Suffering" (*Callaloo* 6,ii:92–99) provides amplification by covering such characteristic features of Baldwin's fiction as retrospective viewpoint, the connection of physical and internal travel, the metaphor of the bridge, and the transforming power of sexuality as they appear in the recent novel *Just Above My Head*. Emmanuel S. Nelson's "James Baldwin's Vision of Otherness and Community" (*MELUS* 10,ii:271–31) gives particular attention to scapegoating and the failure of self-knowledge while reviewing the conditions Baldwin posits as necessary for achieving identity. As these articles treat prevailing views of Baldwin, one by Trudier Harris entitled "The South as Woman: Chimeric Images of Emasculation in *Just Above My Head*" (*SBAL 1*, pp. 89–109) introduces a new area of discussion. Advancing her argument through skilled use of feminist criticism, Harris points to the similarity in Baldwin's works between the South as an area to avoid because of its unpredictable destructiveness and the portrayal of women as vindictive emasculaters. The value of Harris's work lies particularly in the linkage she develops among the themes of sexual violence, homosexuality, and characterization. Previous treatments of sexuality in Baldwin have focused on one or another of those elements. Now we have the way cleared for a dialogue that promises to be comprehensive.

"To Move Without Moving: An Analysis of Creativity and Commerce in Ralph Ellison's Trueblood Episode" (*PMLA* 98:828–45) by Houston A. Baker, Jr., is a brilliant exploration of a troubling, multi-layered episode in *Invisible Man*. Discerning the parodic Freudianism, relationships to anthropological records of racial rituals, and the ideological infrastructure of the episode, Baker establishes it as a metacommentary on Ellison's treatment of folklore and the system out of which the narrative is generated. Per Winther, who published an article last year on Ellison's narrator giving form to chaos, this year discusses ways the reader is implicated in the narrator's struggle. In "Imagery of Imprisonment in Ralph Ellison's *Invisible Man*" (*BALF* 17:115–19) Winther comments on metaphors of the cage and images of victimization, showing how they function simultaneously as indications of the narrator's need to uncover the truth about manipulation and challenges to readers' interpretation.

Jay R. Berry's "The Achievement of William Demby" (*CLAJ* 26: 434–51) characterizes Demby's stylistic techniques, noting that his most recent novel, *Love Story Black*, is the first fully immersed in the black community as well as the most linear in style. It is also, in Berry's judgment, the most shallow of Demby's three novels.

c. **Marshall, Morrison, Bambara, Walker, Major, Reed, Wideman.** Paule Marshall receives extended treatment this year through the efforts of Charles H. Rowell, editor of *Callaloo*, who devotes a special section of the Spring-Summer issue to publication of the autobiographical essay "From the Poets in the Kitchen," which will appear as the preface to a reissue of Marshall's short fiction forthcoming from Feminist Press, and to five critical essays and an extended review. Dorothy L. Denniston's contribution is "Early Short Fiction by Paule Marshall" (6,ii:31–45), which examines "The Valley Between" as announcement of the problem of sex roles in a white marriage and

"Reena" as the answer to the problem for Marshall. The latter story affirms the female position and, according to Denniston, in working out the techniques for her position in "Reena" Marshall found her voice as a black writer. Marilyn Nelson Waniek's "Paltry Things: Immigrants and Marginal Men in Paule Marshall's Short Fiction" (6,ii:46–56) examines the representation of alienated men in *Soul Clap Hands and Sing*, concluding that while no character is without blame Marshall's sympathy includes them all. In "No Outlet for the Blues: Silla Boyce's Flight in *Brown Girl, Brownstones*" (6,ii:57–67) Trudier Harris exhaustively studies the character usually treated as only an obstacle in her daughter's story. By Harris's account Silla Boyce is living an intense form of the blues but can only turn her pain inward. Sandra Y. Govan in her review of the new Feminist Press edition of *Brown Girl, Brownstones*, entitled "Woman Within the Circle: Selina and Silla Boyce" (6,ii:148–52), also elevates the significance of Silla, asserting that she and her daughter generate concentric circles of experience within which readers find a collage of black women and an insider's perception of the West Indian community. In "Paule Marshall and the Crisis of the Middle Years: *The Chosen Place, The Timeless People*" (6,ii:68–73), Joseph T. Skerrett, Jr., uses the Eriksonian concept of a crisis of generativity to explain the experience of Merle Kinbona struggling with unresolved shame and eventually divesting her self of the impediments of the past. From this perspective, Skerrett shows us that by portrayal of protagonists in three published novels Marshall has traced a history of human psychosocial development. Selina Boyce is the example of youth, Merle Kinbona of middle age, and Avey Johnson of age. Barbara T. Christian treats Johnson at length in "Ritualistic Process and the Structure of Paule Marshall's *Praisesong for the Widow*" (6,ii: 74–84). Through juxtaposition of dream and reality Avey Johnson is led to personalize Afro-American story and to proceed through rituals that reunite her body and spirit.

Toni Morrison is rapidly becoming for critics an artist to measure others by; thus, Sanford Pinsker in "Magic Realism, Historical Truth, and the Quest for Liberating Identity: Reflections on Alex Haley's *Roots* and Toni Morrison's *Song of Solomon*" (*SBAL 1*, pp. 183–97) lambasts the Haley novel for poor writing and proceeds to designate *Song* a triumph that exhibits a more natural use of folklore than is evident in the too "literary" Ralph Ellison. In development the essay amounts to an update of the assertion that poetry, manifest in Morrison's multiple levels of meaning, contains more truth than history. For a more substantial application of concepts there is Cynthia A. Davis's "Self, Society and Myth in Toni Morrison's Fiction" (*ConL* 23[1982]:323–42), which examines Morrison's first three novels with reference to the power to name reality, Sartre's idea of "the look of the other" that represents bad faith when internalized, and the functional means employed to deny mythic power in the novels to rituals of oppression. Where Davis enriches our discussion of the novels by the introduction of additional concepts to organize readings, Grace Ann Hovet and Barbara Lounsberry add to our appreciation in "Flying as Symbol and Legend in Toni Morrison's *The Bluest Eye, Sula,* and *Song of Solomon* (*CLAJ* 27:119–40) by categorizing the pervasive images of flight in a way that establishes them as a dominant metaphor. In view of the critical devotion to Morrison's rich art, it must be noted that some of the most suggestive remarks on that art, and on critical approaches, are made by the author herself in "An Interview with Toni Morrison" conducted by Nellie McKay (*ConL* 24:413–29) and in the volume by Claudia Tate on black women writers, discussed later.

Nancy D. Hargrove's contribution to the special issue of *Southern Quarterly* on contemporary southern writers, "Youth in Toni Cade Bambara's *Gorilla, My Love*" (22,ii:81–100), treats seven of the 15 stories in the collection, noting the skill in stimulating speech and relating urban situations. Enthusiastic about Bambara's success, Hargrove remarks on the "universality" of themes and classes the writing with such other works on "youth" as *Portrait of the Artist* and *Huckleberry Finn*! Bambara's work besides *Gorilla* has received so little attention that we are grateful to Gloria T. Hull for the companion guide she provides in "What It Is I Think She's Doing Anyhow: A Reading of Toni Cade Bambara's *The Salt Eaters*" (*Home Girls*, pp. 124–42). Hull offers the notes on characters, diagrams and exposition of structure, and the materials of spiritual arts required by readers who are daunted by the experimental novel.

"Alice Walker's Celebration of Self in Southern Generations" (*SoQ* 21,iv:39–54) by Thadious M. Davis, another contribution to the issue on contemporary writers, organizes Walker's commentary and other evidence of the consciousness of her role as an artist to elucidate the leading themes of family and self, violence and reparation. Each of the year's two essays on Clarence Major provides an exposition of technique as aesthetic statement. In "The Self-Apparent Word: Clarence Major's Innovative Fiction" (*SBAL 1*, pp. 199–214) Jerome Klinkowitz shows Major's understanding that all the "devices of human interest" demanded by realists raise problems of language for the writer, problems laid open by the methods of *Reflex* and *Bone Structure* and *Emergency Exit*. Larry D. Bradfield focuses tightly on a single novel in "Beyond Mimetic Exhaustion: *The Reflex and Bone Structure* Experiment" (*BALF* 17:120–23), effectively explaining how it becomes an account of Major's imaginative interaction with the contingencies of his story. Ishmael Reed and John Wideman are represented in the year's work through interviews. Peter Nazareth directs his "Interview with Ishmael Reed" (*IowaR* 13,ii:117–31) toward discussion of many of Reed's publishing projects and his interest in popular culture, while in "Going Home: A Conversation with John Edgar Wideman" (*Callaloo* 6,i:40–59) Wilfrid D. Samuels encourages Wideman to amplify the biographical background of the insider/outsider views he develops in fiction.

d. **General Criticism of Fiction.** This general category may be subdivided into works contributing the materials for black literary history and works representing methods for the writing of such history. James Robert Payne broadens the scope of the study noted earlier to write "Afro-American Literature of the Spanish-American War" (*MELUS* 10,iii:19–32) in which he treats the ways works are shaped by the idealism of the tradition of black military experience and the disillusion fostered by betrayal of black service. The essay has the merits of an excellently planned historical survey. It clearly outlines the social context, refers in detail to many works, and presents an appropriate scheme for their classification. Also valuable as an overview, and a highly suggestive one, is Joe Weixlmann's "The Changing Shape(s) of the Contemporary Afro-American Novel" (*SBAL 1*, pp. 111–28). Taking *Invisible Man* as the prototype of the "exploratory" black novel, Weixlmann describes the principal directions followed by writers disaffected from the status quo. While he resists specification of schools, he identifies as major projects the development of surrealism evident, for example, in the writing of Amiri Baraka and Samuel Delany; the exploitation and deconstruction of popular cultural forms by such authors as Reed, Major, and Morrison; and the

attempts at metafiction by Demby and Major. Urging his readers to
re-view the innovative novel of the 1960s and 1970s he posits *Flight
to Canada* as exemplary. "A Cultural Legacy Denied and Discovered:
Black Lesbians in Fiction by Women" by Jewelle Gomez (*Home
Girls*, pp. 110–23) makes its contribution for literary history through
an examination of character portrayal and persona by Ann Shockley,
Alice Walker, Audre Lorde, Barbara Smith and others. The plausible
point of this survey is to end treatment of black lesbians as exotics
and to return them to the culture in which they live along with
everybody else.

Two of the six writers treated by Kristin Herzog in *Women,
Ethnics, and Exotics: Images of Power in Mid-Nineteenth-Century
American Fiction* (Tenn.) are the black novelists William Wells
Brown and Martin R. Delany. The burden of the book is study of
characterization that recovers the wholeness of human nature by
amplifying stereotypes and reversing the values assigned to them.
Herzog directs her study toward the end of gaining admission to the
canon for fiction running contrary to the dominant strains of individualistic, ethocentric American writing. Given this purpose Herzog's book may be seen as proposing a well-established method for
use in reconstructing literary history. Two essays in *SBAL 1* also
proposing a new history bring to the surface of their arguments
methods for writing the history in terms of formal properties. In the
one, "Visionaries, Mystics, and Revolutionaries: Narrative Postures
in Black Fiction" (pp. 63–87), Chester J. Fontenot draws upon
Northrop Frye to disentangle strands of utopian thinking so that they
may be distinguished, and seen combined, in treatment of language
by Frantz Fanon. While the essay is highly expository, it serves also
as suggestion because the matter of utopian language is at the heart
of black writers' attempts to recover the past and, through protest
and other means, to project new social arrangements. The second
blueprint essay, entitled " 'The Blackness of Blackness': A Critique
of the Sign and the Signifying Monkey" (pp. 129–81) and written by
Henry-Louis Gates, Jr., exhaustively explores "signifying" and parody
with particular reference to Ralph Ellison signifying on *Native Son*
and Ishmael Reed struggling for a place in the canon by his parodic
critique of the received tropes peculiar to that canon. Contending
that the whole of Afro-American literature can be read as successive
attempts to create new narrative space for representation of "so-

called black experience," Gates undertakes to show that inter-textual critical theory, sometimes called antithetical criticism, at the very least provides the framework for the new black literary history so often announced and so long in coming. It is a contention that must be met by all serious critics of Afro-American literature.

iii. Poetry

a. **Horton, Dunbar.** Sondra O'Neale's "Roots of Our Literary Culture: George Moses Horton and Biblical Protest" (*Obsidian* 7, ii–iii [1981]:18–28) starts with the dubious idea that the wide range of Biblical allusion in Horton's verse was intended to go above the heads of pro-slavery readers. Still, the reading of "The Slave" with reference to contemporary Methodism usefully recreates the network of allusion. "Paul Laurence Dunbar: Master Player in a Fixed Game" by Ralph Story (*CLAJ* 27:30–55) speaks to the perennial issue of the motives for Dunbar's dialect and raceless works. Though one might think there could hardly be anything left to say on the subject, Story's examination of Dunbar's reception and reputation reminds us that the issue remains a live one, because it is, after all, a matter of determining who controls the writer's discourse.

b. **Brown, Hughes, Tolson.** The Black History Museum Committee's publication *Sterling A. Brown: A UMUM Tribute* requires mention once more, because in addition to the bibliography, it contains tributes by 24 writers and reprints a small selection of Brown's poems and essays. The tributes are all brief, but in collection they serve to situate Brown in terms of his influence on other writers and his contributions as a pioneer critic. There are also insights to be gained from the recollection of experience in the segregated District of Columbia.

Faith Berry's biography *Langston Hughes: Before and Beyond Harlem* (Westport, CT: Lawrence Hill) was written with the help of materials at the Moorland-Spingarn Research Center at Howard University, papers at Fisk University, items secured under procedures of the Freedom of Information Act, and documents in the James Weldon Johnson Collection at Yale, though restrictions prevented full examination of the papers in the Beinecke Library. Despite these resources, Berry has not chosen to write a definitive or critical biography. Instead, she "corrects" and fills out the record of the autobiographical volumes, concentrating on the time before Hughes's permanent move to Harlem in the 1940s. The work satisfies because it assembles and re-presents in continuous narrative previously scattered information about Hughes's relationship with his parents and the infamous patron, and because it is more explicit than other sources about details of personal life and about such episodes as the McCarthy Committee testimony. The "Life," however, remains to be written.

With "Point and Counterpoint in *Harlem Gallery*" (*CLAJ* 27: 157–68), Patricia R. Schroeder addresses the complexity of the poem by isolating significant movements in its narrative structure. The language of metaphor, puns, and bifurcations shows the Curator demonstrating the art of integration of opposites. Moreover, Schroeder explains, the poem appears to have a linear progression because of the presence of the Curator but is also dialectical as a result of its revolving around three Harlem artists.

c. **Brooks, Randall, Knight, Wright, Jeffers, Lorde, Jordan.**   Both of the year's essays on Gwendolyn Brooks demonstrate the insights that can be gained by adoption of a feminist critical outlook. Gary Smith's "Gwendolyn Brooks's *A Street in Bronzeville* and the Mythologies of the Black Woman" (*MELUS* 10,iii:33–46) addresses the question of Brooks's relationship to the Harlem Renaissance and concludes that in profound ways she was its critic. Demystifying romantic love she debunked the general optimism of the period's writing; observing intraracial color discrimination she countered the idealization of women; and by concern for victimization she demythified such figures as women blues singers. "Rage and Silence in Gwendolyn Brooks' *Maud Martha*" by Mary Helen Washington (*MR* 24: 453–66) is an exercise in what might be termed reading beyond the author. Commenting on the autobiographical writing Washington identifies the silences of Maud as also Brooks's silences. The tight passages withholding information, the stiff, declarative sentences and broken utterances are evidence of a muted rage in the author and her protagonist. Re-contextualizing these details Washington, then, addresses Brooks's critical reception indicating that reviews have embodied, in their approval of feminine values, the sexism against which Brooks rages.

"Dudley Randall: A Humanist View" by D. H. Melhem appears in *BALF* (17:157–67) along with nine poems by Randall to mark a new period of vigor in which he is again editor and publisher of Broadside Press. Melhem's essay written as a chapter for a forthcoming book on black poets in "the new heroic genre" presents an overview of the career and commentary on the technical development in Randall's major collections. Writing on Etheridge Knight both Patricia Liggins Hill and Craig Werner discuss his relationship to popular sources. Hill's essay, " 'Blues for a Mississippi Black Boy': Etheridge Knight's Craft in the Black Oral Tradition" (*MissQ* 36: 21–34) explores Knight's development of his own version of toasts by comparing the Shine toast to "Dark Prophecy: I Sing of Shine" and explains the search for heritage in Knight as adaptation of the pulse structure from African music and the blues structure from American. In "The Poet, The Poem, The People: Etheridge Knight's Aesthetic" (*Obsidian* 7,ii–iii[1981]:7–17), Werner generalizes the implication in such findings as Hill's by presenting Knight as a representative of the populist tradition in black expression. Associating Knight with Brooks and Hughes and the "new Black aesthetic" with populism, Werner indicates the complexity of Knight's practice of the tradition by analysis of jazz rhythms and the inversion of conceits.

Werner's article proposing a populist tradition in contrast to a more specialized one was occasioned by the apparent designation in *Chant of Saints* (1979) of Michael Harper, Robert Hayden, and Jay Wright as the major contemporary black poets. As it happens, both traditions have representation in this report, for a major event of the year is the special issue of *Callaloo* given over to treatment of Jay Wright. This issue includes three poems by Wright, the play "Love's Equation" (1983), an interview conducted by Charles H. Rowell, and three critical essays. The interview, " 'The Unraveling of the Egg' " (6,iii:3–15) concentrates squarely on Wright's poetic theory, which he relates to myth and history, by contending that it has the same creative ground. The first of the critical essays is " 'The Aching Prodigal': Jay Wright's Dutiful Poet" by Robert B. Stepto (6,iii:76–84). Addressing the question of how one prepares to read "a truly New World poet," Stepto creates a simulacrum of the poems, thus, illustrating that the tradition Wright seeks does not readily align with one cosmology, but, like a genuine modern community, is beyond geography. The subject for Gerald Barrax is "The Early Poetry

of Jay Wright" (6,iii:85–102). Observing that for Wright the basic
technical unit is the phrase and that nearly every line is indebted to
another text, Barrax reads in the five volumes published between
1967 and 1980. Through close attention to ambivalence and the rich
variety of subject, he establishes the central concern of the corpus as
a religious quest, which he characterizes as akin to the process of
self-discovery in Whitman's poetry. The third essay in the special
issue, Vera M. Kutzinski's "The Descent of Nommo: Literacy as
Method in Jay Wright's 'Benjamin Banneker Helps to Build a City'"
(6,iii:103–18) successfully develops Robert Stepto's ideas about the
animation of Afro-American literature by the drives for freedom and
literacy into an examination of the Afro-American preoccupation
with a history of subjection to the dominance of the written word.
Against the background of ambiguity regarding literacy Kutzinski
reads the Wright poem as one that unsettles the fiction of new
beginnings.

To correct another omission in a previous report I must acknowledge here the carefully prepared materials published by the Reno
company, Women-In-Literature. *Woman Poet-Volume 2—The East*
(1981), edited by Marilyn Hacker, includes a section on Audre
Lorde containing three poems, a discussion by Joan Larkin of the
plain-spokenness of Lorde ("Full Stature: Audre Lorde," pp. 15–17)
and an interview conducted by Adrienne Rich (pp. 18–21) in which
Lorde discusses the origin of her impulse to write. In the same volume
there is also a section on June Jordan including four poems, an essay
by Sara Miles ("The Poetry of June Jordan," pp. 87–89) treating
Jordan's critical reception and the complex politics that account for
it, and an interview conducted by Karla M. Hammond (pp. 90–94)
that permits Jordan to explain both her politics and her literary influences. Both sections also include biographical notes on the poets.
Another interview, this one from 1983, appears as Doris L. Laryea's
"A Black Poet's Vision: An Interview with Lance Jeffers" (*CLAJ*
26:422–33). In this Jeffers characterizes his own verse and offers
general commentary on poetry.

d. **General Criticism of Poetry.**   L. L. Dickson's "'Keep It In the
Head': Jazz Elements in Modern Black American Poetry" (*MELUS*
10,i:29–37) gives special attention to Al Young, but devotes most
attention to identifying two manifestations of jazz: the use of synco-

pated rhythms, detailed in the verse of Hughes and Brooks, and the use of jazz performers as symbols by Baraka and A. B. Spellman. "The Afro-American Sensibility" by Craig Werner in *Magill's Critical Survey of Poetry* (Salem Press, 1982, pp. 3395–3404) deserves attention as an excellent job of surveying the generations in black poetry, but beyond that the essay makes the unusual effort, for a reference article, of distinguishing the historical and cultural sources for the complex pluralism of an art form that transforms "the burden of double consciousness, as manifested in the traditions of masking and ironic voicing, into sources of aesthetic power."

iv. Drama

a. Hansberry, Baraka, Fuller, Shange. In preparation for a New American Library edition of Lorraine Hansberry's plays, Margaret A. Wilkerson has revised her 1981 essay "The Sighted Eyes and Feeling Heart of Lorraine Hansberry." Appearing in a special theater issue of *BALF* (17:8–13), the essay implicitly defends the playwright against her detractors by representing her as a forerunner of the Black Arts Movement and offering an exposition of the social criticism in her plays, including the television drama *Drinking Gourd* that remains unproduced and the surviving draft of *What Use Are Flowers?*

The impending twentieth anniversary of the opening production of Amiri Baraka's *Dutchman* provides the occasion for the two special theater issues of *BALF*, occasion also for some reconsideration of Baraka's work. One such essay, "The Concealed Dependence Upon White Culture in Baraka's 1969 Aesthetic" by Elizabeth Hadley Freydberg (17:27–29), begins from the observation that most plays written under the influence of Baraka's aesthetic have not lasted because white audiences have exhausted their capacity for self-flagellation. Developing her point about dependence, Freydberg asserts that despite their rhetoric of self-determination many of Baraka's revolutionary plays rely for intelligibility upon the presence of whites. Moreover, she says, the method of the plays affirms that blacks require simple didactic drama. According to the argument, the more successful black theater does not need to flaunt race; rather it uses, as for example does Lonne Elder's *Ceremonies in Dark Old Men,* a black frame of reference. Clearly the issue is political as well as aesthetic. Indicating how closely linked those are in Baraka is Andrzej Ceynowa's "The Dramatic Structure of *Dutchman*" (17:15–18), a study that departs from the usual critical interest in the semantic aspects of the play and its external forms. Ceynowa's analysis of the thought content of the play shows that Lula's catechismic questions to Clay open a black revolutionary perspective from which he retreats into individualistic defense. By this analysis Lula presides over the trial of a traitor. The immediate response to such a reading is shock, since Clay is black, Lula white, but Ceynowa testifies that when the play is performed in Europe with an all white cast the point comes through clearly. The reading also provokes by showing that Baraka's development is more of a piece than is usually assumed, for the catechismic technique and lecturing in *Dutchman* also characterize his later plays.

The politics of Baraka's theater are evident in the essay he entitles "The Descent of Charlie Fuller into Pulitzerland and the Need for African-American Institutions" (17:51–54). Treating the author of *The Brownsville Raid* and *Soldier's Story* Baraka finds Charles Fuller to be a voice of the most reactionary part of the black middle-class, especially in the latter play. The ideology of the play Baraka terms anti-masses, and he relates its presence to the white corporate support of the Negro Ensemble Company that produced the play.

"Conflicting Impulses in the Plays of Ntozake Shane" by Sandra L. Richards (17:73–78) examines a dialectical relationship between awareness of the need to struggle against oppression and a desire to transcend the limits of human existence. Borrowing the label "combat breath" from Frantz Fanon for the thesis and a concept of will to divinity from African religion for the antithesis, Richards explains the dialectic operating in *spell #7*. In the process she indicates also how Shange has drawn upon the dramaturgy of Brecht, Artaud, and Baraka, as well as an older African philosophical tradition that attributes power to all things including the props and costumes of theater.

b. **General Criticism of Drama.**   A major publication enriching the list of books on black drama is Geneviève Fabre's *Drumbeats, Masks and Metaphor: Contemporary Afro-American Theatre* (Harvard). (See also Chapter 21, "French Contributions," Sec. g, below). Translated by Melvin Dixon, the work is an abridgement of *Le Théâtre noir* *aux Etats-Unis* (Paris 1982). Providing an historical account as well as a typology of drama, the book is divided into three large sections. The first treats historical precedents in the Federal Theater Project, the American Negro Theatre, and other companies but locates the theoretical foundations of contemporary black drama in Baraka's "The Revolutionary Theatre" and in the synthesis of concepts that emerged in the Black Arts Movement. While the militant theater, Fabre's concern in the second large section of the book, has beginnings in such works as Ossie Davis's *Purlie Victorious* and James Baldwin's plays, Baraka presents the template for this manner of drama. In the third section, theater of experience, it is Ed Bullins whose work is template for a non-Aristotelian, convincingly ethnic drama. Fabre cautions that though her presentation is diachronic the dramatic language and forms she discusses are not easily contained in periods; thus, it is appropriate that as the book proceeds it becomes increasingly expository of the dramatic action of individual plays and increasingly analytical of their semiotic importance. The analysis is particularly strong in discussion of the modes of discourse engendered in the dramas, proceeding in the militant theater from a call to a liberal audience to denunciation and then to consecration of the choice to become righteous, and in the theater of experience developing a version of social science discussion moving between poles of determinism and autonomy until it makes way for an Africanized language. The persistent problem of gaining legitimacy in the mainstream for black theater, while retaining freedom for art that is not commodified, conditions Fabre's entire project, just as we see it conditioning all other critical commentary on black theater. Consequently, the book also contains extensive discussion of ideology along with the ritual forms and archetypes designed to enact the playwrights' conception of the theater's struggle.

What Fabre's book does not cover as an essential part of its study is the role of theater companies and performers in black drama. For such a focus one turns to those two special issues of *Black American Literature Forum* coedited as the spring and summer numbers of the journal by James V. Hatch and Andrzej Ceynowa. For the time being this concludes the project begun in 1982 with a concentration on historical figures and productions in the first *BALF* issue on drama. Many of the items presented this year constitute materials for a contemporary history. Among them are Geneviève Fabre's "The Free

Southern Theatre, 1963–1979" (17:55–59), which describes the organization, productions, and repertory of a company conceived as a
political and cultural tool; A. Peter Bailey's "A Look at the Contemporary Black Theatre Movement" (17:19–21), which retrospectively
outlines the general topics of drama and outstanding plays from the
1960s to the present; George Houston Bass's "Theatre and the Afro-
American Rite of Being" (17:60–64), an exposition of the principles
developed by Bass and Rhett S. Jones for Rites and Reason, the research theater and performing arts component of the Afro-American
Studies Program at Brown University; Taquiena Boston and Vera J.
Katz's "Witnesses to a Possibility: The Black Theater Movement in
Washington, D.C., 1968–1976" (17:22–26), an historical account of
the persons, many of them associated with Howard University, and
organizations responsible for productions in the mode of black ritual
theater; Vivian Robinson's "The First Ten Years of AUDELCO"
(17:79–81) in which the founder of the Audience Development
Committee relates the means she devised to popularize the theater,
including a series of awards which are chronologically listed; and
Winona L. Fletcher's "A Slender Thread of Hope: The Kennedy
Center Black Theatre Project" (17:65–68), which describes black
participation in outreach programs. In addition, the special issues
also contain "Rituals at the New Lafayette Theatre" (17:31–35), an
interview conducted by Anthony D. Hill with Robert Macbeth, the
artistic director of the New Lafayette, who recollects performances
and provides production details; Linda Kerr Norflett's "Rosetta Le-
Noire: The Lady and Her Theatre" (17:69–72), which draws upon
the resource of three interviews with the founder of Amas Repertory
and the originator of *Bubbling Brown Sugar* to discuss the challenges
of developing new musical theater off-Broadway; and Brenda Dixon–
Stowell's "Dancing in the Dark: The Life and Times of Margot Webb
in Afroamerican Vaudeville of the Swing Era" (17:3–7), which illuminates a sector of black participation in popular culture by its
account of the career of the ballroom dancing team Norton and
Margot.

v. Slave Narratives and Autobiography

During the past decade historians have learned to use the autobiographical narratives written by fugitive slaves as a basic source

for recreation of the institution of slavery. More recently literary critics have begun to follow the lead of such pioneers as Marion W. Starling, Charles H. Nichols, Margaret Young Jackson, each of whom wrote doctoral dissertations on the narratives, and others such as Sidonie A. Smith and Stephen T. Butterfield, who wrote book-length studies of black autobiography, in drawing attention to the genre's significance in founding the Afro-American literary tradition. This new interest will be greatly advanced in the classroom as well as in journals by publication of *The Art of Slave Narrative*, a collection of original essays. Of course, the ten essays in the volume make up the bulk of contributions noted in this report.

In "The First Fifty Years of the Slave Narrative, 1760–1810" (pp. 6–24) William L. Andrews characterizes the early narratives as renderings of struggle for freedom *from* the self more than examples of self-actualization. Before 1810 there is no evidence that narrators were involved in the transcription, editing, or publishing of their adventures. They gave the "facts," editors selected and arranged them, most often in accordance with the paradigm of conversion, captivity, or confession stories. Andrews also deals with the narratives in "The First Century of Afro-American Autobiography: Theory and Explication" (*SBAL 1*, pp. 4–42), this time with attention to the routes for investigation that appear promising for future study. Concentrating on such problems as the authors' initial selection of genre, their contest with positivistic epistemology in works deeply concerned with reportage, their search for linguistic integrity, etc., Andrews seeks the critical theory that will address the unique features of the genre. This excellent discussion is especially valuable for its resolution of the problem facing the analyst of a text that has been edited by hands other than the authors'. Because ontology is so problematic, Andrews says, it is better to reserve close reading for autonomously authored texts that may unquestionably be understood as verbal emblems of the self. Instead, he advises, consider the slave narratives to be linguistic acts in a discursive field for which speech-act and reader-response theory has more relevance.

Andrews might consider the narrative of Olaudah Equiano an exception to his recommendations for critical method, because in the essay on "The First Fifty Years" he puts the Anglo-African narrator forward as an example of one who has come to terms with a bicultural perspective to the extent that his narrative becomes an

analysis of acculturation. Chinosole in "Tryin' to Get Over: Narrative
Posture in Equiano's Autobiography" (*The Art of Slave Narrative*,
pp. 45–54) seems to disagree with Andrews about the level of control
Equiano exercises over the text. In her reading, oppositions appear
as bifurcations of the self. In developing the idea that Equiano enacts
a double vision, she explores his use of multiple identities and multiple voices, along with the shifts from psychological realism to situa-
tional irony.

The slave narrator continuing to receive most critical attention is
Frederick Douglass. John Sekora's "The Dilemma of Frederick Douglass: The Slave Narrative as Literary Institution" (*ELWIU* 10:219–
26) examines the literary dimension of Douglass's quarrel with the
Garrisonians to illustrate the implications of editorial control. Aboli-
tionist sponsors of fugitive slaves stressed fact and collective experience over individual voice. Charging that blacks were viewed only as
victims, Douglass raised the question of who owned the slave's narrative, who informed the facts with philosophy. Thomas DiPietro
develops the answer Douglass gave to his question in "Vision and
Revisions in the Autobiographies of Frederick Douglass" (*CLAJ* 26:
384–96). This fine essay points to the contrasts among Douglass's
three versions of his autobiography, showing that in *My Bondage
and My Freedom* Douglass de-emphasizes the religious meaning
present in *The Narrative* and draws out the latent sociological and
political views. *Bondage*, thus, becomes more of an intellectual biography and one that, by introduction of generalization and explanation, contextualizes the events of the life. The third autobiography,
Life and Times, DiPietro characterizes as a man-of-achievement story
and the weakest of the three. Lillie Butler Jugurtha applies an essay
by Norman Friedman from 1955 in writing "Point of View in the
Afro-American Slave Narratives: A Study of Narratives by Douglass
and Pennington" (*The Art of Slave Narrative*, pp. 110–19). The subject is the technique of participant narrators in delineating environment and detailing events.

Lucinda H. MacKethan also considers Douglass and Pennington,
along with William Wells Brown, in her study "Metaphors of Mastery
in the Slave Narrators" (*The Art of Slave Narrative*, pp. 55–69). As
aware as other critics of the exigencies of audience and sponsorship
that constrained the narrators, McKethan proposes that, nevertheless,
they created agencies that produced connection between their sub-

jective consciousness and the objective reality that were charged to present. These agencies include the metaphor of the trickster, the word as a trap finally coming to stand for freedom, and the design of the narrative. The essay is convincing and squarely concerned with the substance of the black narrator's art. Mary Ellen Doyle chooses the narratives by William and Ellen Craft and Josiah Henson as her examples in "The Slave Narratives as Rhetorical Art" (*The Art of Slave Narrative*, pp. 83–95). She distinguishes situation oriented narratives (the Crafts's) from those focusing on character (Henson) and makes satisfactory remarks on the functional features of each, but her conception of the appropriate "art" for the narratives leads her into prescriptive judgments and irrelevant statements about universal appeal.

Raymond Hedin extends ideas he developed last year in an essay on the picaro narrative (see *ALS 1982*, pp. 403–404) to treat the use of form as implicit challenge to audience assumptions. His "Strategies of Form in the American Slave Narrative" (*The Art of Slave Narrative*, pp. 25–35) focuses on the conventions of the sentimental novel as well as the picaresque, indicating how the formal problems of closure, among others, derive from historical problems faced by the writers. Keith Byerman's "We Wear the Mask: Deceit as Theme and Style in Slave Narratives" (*The Art of Slave Narrative*, pp. 70–82) also seeks to connect formal properties with historical experience. Verbal manipulation to justify theft and irony, which he describes as stylistic duplicity, are among the techniques Byerman identifies beneath the conventions of language narrators adopted in conformity with audience demands.

Annette Niemtzow brings the leading theoretical points introduced by the studies in Sekkra and Turner's volume to a conclusion in "The Problematic of Self in Autobiography: The Example of the Slave Narrative" (*The Art of Slave Narrative*, pp. 96–109). As the narrator began to write, she points out, the page was full, that is, the autobiography was predetermined by the conventions of white culture whose ruling ontology left the slave in a void. Douglass is her primary example, and considering the importance he has for students of the slave narrative it is to Niemtzow's credit that she has the nerve to choose his narrative to illustrate the proposition that by virtue of genre the slave narrative unconsciously pays tribute to definitions of the self created by whites. Niemtzow illustrates efforts to evade the control of autobiography with Linda Brent's *Incidents in the Life of a Slave Girl*, which eludes convention by changing the genre to a form resembling the domestic novel; yet, while Brent gains a form for herself, she meets new constraints also, chief among them being the sexual silence imposed by a form that transforms rape into seduction. Niemtzow may be charged with overstatement or with a demand for elaboration of the contention that a genre can be entirely white, but unquestionably hers is a challenging statement.

Martha K. Cobb's "The Slave Narrative and the Black Literary Tradition" (*The Art of Slave Narrative*, pp. 36–44) identifies three themes in the narratives: struggle for psychic and physical freedom, resolutions of opposition between order and disorder, etc., and the need to define identity. The concept of slave as victim that engenders the themes is reversed, she says, by the voice of the protagonist speaking declaratively. Expanding the range of the slave narrative beyond North America Cobb considers the Cuban texts of Juan Manzano and Esteban Montejo along with the life of the Haitian slave Pierre Toussaint, known to us through biography rather than autobiography. Marva J. Furman's "The Slave Narrative: Prototype of the Early AfroAmerican Novel" (*The Art of Slave Narrative*, pp. 120–26) is a brief presentation of the well-known relationship of slave narrative and the works of early novelists nurtured on them.

vi. Literary History, Criticism

John Sekora joins with Houston A. Baker, Jr., to expand upon the problem of genre control in "Written Off: Narratives, Master Texts, and Afro-American Writing from 1760 to 1945" (*SBAL 1*, pp. 43–62). Their highly intelligent discussion presents George White's account of his life (1810) as an exception to the exclusion of blacks from the white Protestant epic that constitutes early American writing and Richard Wright's *Black Boy* as the signal instance of a text liberated from the constraints of modern versions of genres. Developing the trope of the black hole for their critical discussion, Sekora and Baker read the image of Wright's mother's absence as a figure for gathering all lineaments of black blues life, his consuming of novels as the projection of desire to gain intersubjective community, and his entire project as illustration of zero sum language. The imaginative skill with which the essay is developed makes it exemplary of the critical work that needs to be undertaken to address the issues raised by the new studies of narrative. Since criticism gains a larger audience when it is related in the classroom than when it first appears in journals, it is also necessary to give attention to ways our critical problems and critical subjects can be adapted to teaching. Ready to hand is Darwin T. Turner's "Uses of the Antebellum Slave Narratives in Collegiate Courses in Literature" (*The Art of Slave Narrative*, pp. 127–34). which suggests the variety of courses where the narratives provide appropriate texts and outlines the structural modes that make them an incomparable subject for American literary study.

Of course, the feminist approach to black literature also yields criticism that focuses upon the issue of genre control. Cheryl A. Wall's "Poets and Versifiers, Singers and Signifiers: Women of the Harlem Renaissance" (*Women, The Arts, and the 1920s in Paris and New York*. Eds. Kenneth W. Wheeler and Virginia Lee Lassier. Transaction 1982, pp. 74–98) discusses the debilitating effects of self-consciousness on several poets while providing an overview of their work during the Renaissance. The artistry of Bessie Smith's blues presents a striking contrast. The essay anticipates a book in progress and also treats several novelists. "Black Women on Black Writers: Conversations and Questions" (*Conditions* 9:88–137) is a taped "pentalog" among Cheryl Clarke, Jewelle Gomez, Evelyn Hammonds, Bonnie Johnson, and Linda Powell. Edited to reflect the issues that most concern the participants, the conversation reveals a sense of the dilemma facing a feminist critic who may fear exposure, the practical problems surrounding the writing of reviews, and especially the difficulties in naming and elaborating lesbian aesthetics. *Home Girls: A Black Feminist Anthology*, edited by Barbara Smith, draws heavily on previously published material from *Conditions* and includes sketches, autobiography, poems, and essays that help to certify the point made by Smith in her introduction that black feminism is on every level organic to black experience. The volume is also useful because it includes lists of periodicals and presses specializing in black feminist writing. The outstanding contribution to study of women writers from this year's output is Claudia Tate's *Black Women Writers at Work* (Continuum). Tate constructed her 14 interviews so that writers would share their conscious motives for characterization, situations, and technique and provide a self-assessment. Participants include the contemporary figures most often mentioned in these reports as subjects of current criticism. Each interview is accompanied by headnotes, and the introduction usefully outlines Tate's general findings.

Ernest D. Mason's "Black Art and the Configuration of Experience: The Philosophy of the Black Aesthetic" (*CLAJ* 27:1–17) suggests the continuing relevance the ideas of the Black Aesthetic movement have for critical theory. Taking direction from Alain Locke, Mason detaches aesthetics from exclusive focus on the forms of art and, by asserting its concern with objects of perception and experience, relates aesthetics broadly to the cultural and practical world. Like other criticism I have noted in this report, Mason's also engages the issue of control of imagery and discourse, in the process arguing effectively for a diverse community of black styles and artists. *The Womb of Space: The Cross-Cultural Imagination* by Wilson Harris (Greenwood) includes Ellison, Toomer, Paule Marshall, and Jay Wright among the subjects for meditation. In contrast to criticism that locates its subject on a field of contesting cultures, Harris seeks evidence for the occurrence of unconscious mingling of cultures. Myth is the base or ground for Harris, while a text is the figure referring to other texts and through them, or sometimes despite them, touching the mythic as it emerges from beneath consciousness. On another level intertextual references are also the subject of Craig Werner's "Tell Old Pharoah: The Afro-American Response to Faulkner" (*SoR* 19:711–35). Noting that Faulkner revoices Afro-American experience as a narrative of endurance, Werner depicts a dialogue in which William Melvin Kelley, Toni Morrison, Ishmael Reed, Ernest J. Gaines, and Gayl Jones present kinetic treatments of black life to counter the stasis associated with Faulkner's.

Anyone needing further indication that the relationship between black and white arts are complex may consult Andrea Hairston's "If You Just Change the Key, It's Still the Same Old Song" (*BALF* 17: 36–37), which reiterates the point that semantically the American language is infused with the assumptions of white, heterosexual males, and Woodie King, Jr.'s "The Politics of Black Art" (*BALF* 17:30), which remarks how the political climate frustrates the goal of total acceptance of black art in the mainstream.

Steven C. Tracy's "The Blues in Future American Literary Histories and Anthologies" (*MELUS* 10,i:15–25) carefully prescribes the procedure to be followed by scholars who wish to make correct use of the blues. He points out that they must study blues as poetry in their own right, not simply as influences, and to do this must learn enough of the discipline of ethnomusicography to identify conventions and styles and to acknowledge African sources. Tracy also suggests works to be included in studies, providing a discography (pp. 26–28) as an aid, and even goes so far as to tell readers how blues may be laid out on the printed page. The cautionary note to all this appears in "Can't Even Write: The Blues and Ethnic Literature" (*MELUS* 10,i:7–14), where Paul Oliver asserts that blues are an expression of a specialized subculture not shared by all blacks. Blues singers, he points out, do not draw upon literature for ideas, since they are rarely literate, and writers who adapt the blues employ variations on form and concepts not found in the originals.

As resources for study of black creative literature grow, so do those for consideration of critical tradition. Last year I commented on the publication of the collection of essays by Charles T. Davis. This year I note acknowledgements of the place held in the record of critical writing by Alain Locke and George E. Kent. Jeffrey C. Stewart has edited *The Critical Temper of Alain Locke: A Selection of His Essays on Art and Culture* (Garland). Topically arranged into sections on Renaissance apologetics, genres of art, retrospective reviews, and scholarly articles, the 69 items record the development of Locke's theory of art as an alternative political strategy. Each section is provided notes; the whole is indexed; and 64 illustrations accompany the text. James W. Coleman and Joanne Veal Gabbin are responsible for "The Legacy of George E. Kent" (*BALF* 17:143–47), a survey of Kent's work that explains how Kent's writing followed from the conviction that "high ground humanism" does not reflect black experience adequately.

State University of New York at Albany

20. Themes, Topics, Criticism

Michael J. Hoffman

1983 was in many ways a disappointing year for this chapter, primarily because there were so few major attempts at synthetic treatments of American literature. I discovered many fewer books than usual on appropriate American topics, and the ones I did discover were, with some exceptions, only modestly ambitious. In the more general field of literary theory, however, the choices were better and included books by major authors and a number of works that I believe will be read for years to come.

Once again, I have divided the chapter into an American Literature section and one on Literary Theory. Within each subsection I treat the books in alphabetical order. In American literature I attempt to write about all the books I have received that I think relevant to the chapter and that will not be treated elsewhere in *ALS 1983*. In the other, longer section I must select, for the volume of books of theory either originally in English or translated into English is quite large. As usual, I have read in their entirety or perused with some care well over 100 books to prepare for writing this chapter. My bookshelves bulge. My brain feels cluttered.

i. American Literature

a. Thematic and General Studies. Mary Allen's *Animals in American Literature* is a study of the literal, not the metaphorical animals used in the writings of major American authors, and for that reason I hesitate to call it a thematic study. The useful introduction traces the historical attitude toward animals in literature from Greek through Christian to modern times. American literature is more interested in the wild animal than the pet, developing something like a cult of wild animals that, according to Allen, derives from the frontier experience. "If to be wild is good, to become domesticated is to sell out to a master. Pets are a rarity, and those who do live under a human's roof may yet exhibit their wildness—the cat in a deliciously fierce attack" (p. 13).

Each chapter discusses the particular significance given to wild animals by different authors. For instance, Melville and the whale; Dickinson with insects and small animals; Twain—frogs, hogs and other "lowbrow" animals; London with dogs such as Buck; Marianne Moore, such special kinds of animals as the dikdik and echidna, "controlled creatures"; and Steinbeck who puts his animals to death. Allen treats such characteristics as the tendency to anthropomorphize animals, as in Melville's treatment of his white whale. This is a well-written book, unpromising at first glance but surprisingly full of good insights.

Brief mention goes to a collection of essays edited by Winifred Farrant Bevilacqua, *Fiction by American Women: Recent Views* (Associated Faculty Press). The contributors contain such well-known names as Marjorie Perloff, Joyce Carol Oates, and Judith Fetterley, and the subjects of the essays range from 19th-century sentimentalists through *Fear of Flying*. Everything here has been published elsewhere, but the quality of the pieces is high. Especially good is a long piece on Kate Chopin's *The Awakening* by Cynthia Griffin Wolff and Oates's essay on "The Visionary Art of Flannery O'Connor." Bevilacqua's introduction contains a brief survey of contemporary feminist theory.

A lively book is Harvey A. Daniels, *Famous Last Words: The American Language Crisis Reconsidered* (So. Ill.), which indicates that while the sky may be falling on the American language, it has always been falling, with today's doomsday prophets little different from those of yesterday. Daniels takes to task critics such as John Simon, Edwin E. Newman, and William Safire for their overstatements about and their ignorance of the ways language really operates. Aside from knowing little about linguistics or the history of the language, these critics believe they are making linguistic judgments when in fact they are making social ones designed "to police the utterances of their social and intellectual inferiors" (p. 262).

Daniels finds the "current language crisis highly suspect. I do not accept its definitions, respect its promoters, believe its evidence, fear its dangers, or revile its villains" (p. 30). The promoters of the language crisis are misinformed, they trivialize the study of the language, and they threaten to bring back old, discredited teaching techniques or create new ones that have little to do with what we know about how language works. Daniels expands on these claims throughout the book in an erudite, lively, and witty style. He deals with such matters as Black English, testing, propaganda, and remedial English, shooting holes in most theories that are promulgated by both liberal and conservative guardians of the language. While often a devastating critic of the critics—through argument and evidence as well as wit—Daniels does not leave the reader with enough of a sense of the best way to deal with the difficulties students have with the language, whether the problem is a new one or not. But I do recommend the book as a corrective to the language snob in all of us—even though I too cringe when I hear someone say "hopefully," particularly at the beginning of a sentence.

The last book by distinguished folklorist Richard M. Dorson is *Man and Beast in American Comic Legend* (Indiana), which he was preparing for the press at the time of his death. The book is in two parts: the first, an account in separate chapters of some of the famous "American Legendary Creatures," such as the "Guyuscutus," the "Sidehill Dodger," the "Hugag," the "Hodag," the "Jackalope," and "Bigfoot"; the second part concerns the exaggerating storytellers, the "Munchausens," including Jim Bridger, Oregon Smith, Gib Morgan, Jones Tracy, and Hathaway Jones. Each chapter contains an account that is more descriptive than analytical and is, thereby, all the more amusing. Drawings and photographs provide illustrative materials for the various hoaxes and add much humor to this account of a peculiarly American phenomenon. The book contains a frank assessment of Dorson's career written by Alan Dundes, as well as a short memoir of Dorson written as an Afterword by his son, Jeff.

The title of historian David C. Duke's *Distant Obligations: Modern American Writers and Foreign Causes* might suggest that it is another study of American expatriates, but in fact the book is about a number of American writers "who became involved in the turmoil of foreign causes" (p. vi) out of a "blend of idealism and disillusionment" (p. 16), expressing an "idealistic sense of commitment tinged with feelings of guilt" (p. 17). The 11 writers include Ernest Fenollosa, Edith Wharton, John Reed, Louis Fischer, Ernest Hemingway, John Dos Passos, and Ezra Pound. Each chapter is organized biographically around the details of the writer's foreign commitments, and while most of the stories are familiar to students of American literature, Duke often works with new materials. The chapters on Reed, Fischer, and Pound are particularly fresh. I also enjoyed reading about how the friendship of Dos Passos and Hemingway broke apart during the filming of *The Spanish Earth*. Duke's skills are primarily narrative and empirical. Although he attempts to generalize in his concluding chapter, he does little more than fall back on some of the phrases I quoted earlier.

I shall briefly mention a collection of essays edited by Giles Gunn, *The Bible and American Arts and Letters* (Fortress Press), which is part of The Bible in American Culture series. A distinguished list of contributors includes Herbert Schneidau, Edwin Cady, William H. Shurr, and Sacvan Bercovitch, and the book covers such topics as the American novel, American painting, American folk arts, and American poetry. I particularly recommend the essay on American poetry by Schneidau and the one on painting by John W. Dixon, Jr. The editor's introduction is well-written and helpful.

A more lasting contribution to the study of American literature is Neil Schmitz's virtuoso performance, *Of Huck and Alice*, an ingenious examination of humor as a stylistic phenomenon. Schmitz compares his intentions with those of Constance Rourke's classic work, *American Humor*: "Where Rourke's study of American humor explains its relevance in terms of the national character, the American *ethos*, this study examines the stylistic character of humorous writing in American literature" (p. 25). By focusing on style, Schmitz deals with humor as a linguistic phenomenon, his interpretive tool being deconstructive analysis.

"Humor deconstructs the formal knowledge of writing—and undoes the writer. All the important humorists in the nineteenth century write behind assumed names, an alias that is their alibi" (p. 28). Thus Samuel Clemens becomes Mark Twain, and in the next century Gertrude Stein pretends to write as Alice Toklas in another work of humorous fictionality, *The Autobiography of Alice B. Toklas*. Schmitz's ingenious readings and his notion that humorous writing is written between the spaces of conventional writing place his interpretations of *Huck Finn* and *Tender Buttons* among the most original I know. While the readings of Stein are the high points of the book, Schmitz is also very good on the subject of Twain's 19th-century precursors and on George Herriman's classic cartoon *Krazy Kat.*

b. Ethnic and Regional Literatures. This section treats works about the literatures of American ethnic minority groups other than Black Literature. The MLA has published a volume edited by Pamela Gunn Allen, *Studies in American Indian Literature: Critical Essays and Course Designs,* which is designed to help instructors to set up courses in the literature of the American Indian. The book is divided into the following sections: "Oral Literature," "Personal Narrative, Autobiography, and Intermediate Literature," "American Indian Women's Literature," "Modern and Contemporary American Indian Literature," "The Indian in American Literature," and "Resources." Each section contains a series of essays written by experts and a section on teaching courses in that particular subject matter. The book was developed out of a 1977 MLA/NEH Seminar on American Indian Literature and is truly a collaborative effort. As such it is more unified in both approach and style than many other such books, and although it is written by experts in the field it is accessible to the non-specialist. It should prove useful to those charged with designing a curriculum in American Indian/Native American literary studies.

Michael Castro's *Interpreting the Indian: Twentieth-Century Poets and the Native American* (N. Mex.) is not a study of American Indian literature but rather of the use of Indians and Indian themes in 20th-century American verse. Castro, himself a poet, begins with ethnologists and translators of Indian verse, including those who transcribed that verse directly from the oral tradition. Although he does mention a 19th-century precursor, Castro avoids discussing him. This is probably a mistake, since the consciousness many of us have of American Indians stems from our contact when young with such works as *Hiawatha.* Castro believes that he relates well to the Indian oral tradition because he sees himself as part of the oral tradition of the 1960s—his poetic generation. Along the way Castro studies many American poets who used Indians as subjects, including Vachel Lindsay, Hart Crane, William Carlos Williams, Charles Olson, and Gary Snyder, as well as a number of such lesser-known poets as Jerome Rothenberg, Lew Sarett, and John G. Neihardt. Castro claims that Indian verse was influential in developing a contemporary

American poetics, particulary in the work of Olson, Rothenberg, and Snyder, and the evidence he brings to bear is convincing. The book's approach is scholarly, and the writing lively, but Castro does tend to get sentimental at times about his subject.

Kenneth Lincoln, in *Native American Renaissance* (Calif.), has attempted to establish a belletristic tradition of Native American literature that has its roots in the ethos of a variety of American Indian cultures and finds its expression in such writers as Black Elk, Scott Momaday, and James Welch. Lincoln, himself a Lakota who was raised in Nebraska, focuses on the recent "renaissance" of works written by American Indian writers and the more general public interest in the writings and culture of Native Americans. Lincoln comes to the task with sophisticated ethnographic tools and a genuine literary sensibility. He emphasizes characteristics common to folklore, such as the trickster, but the richness of reference to ancient traditions finds its expression in analyses of contemporary poems and stories. The book is a first-rate piece of scholarship, written with a sense of personal urgency, and it will be helpful not only to those interested in American Indian writings but also to those interested in discovering how to use anthropological insights when writing about literary topics.

Another book by a poet who uses American Indian materials is Jarold Ramsey's *Reading the Fire: Essays in the Traditional Indian Literatures of the Far West* (Nebraska). The 11 essays, anthropological in approach, focus on traditional Indian narratives that come directly out of the oral tradition and deal most directly with a series of powerful myths. A few chapter titles will give a sense of the subject matter and methodology: "Coyote and Friends: An Experiment in Interpretive Bricolage," " 'The Hunter Who Had an Elk for a Guardian Spirit' and the Ecological Imagination," "Uncursing the Misbegotten in a Tillamook Incest Story," and "Retroactive Prophecy in Western Indian Narrative." The final essay, "Tradition and Individual Talents in Modern Indian Writing," deals briefly with contemporary traditions among Indian writers. The book contains many lengthy quotations from Indian narratives—often seeming like an anthology—which it then analyzes. This sympathetic, well-written study, if read in conjunction with Lincoln's, will give the reader a good overview of Native American literatures.

Brief mention goes to an anthology of essays exclusively about

American Indian oral literature, edited by Brian Swann, *Smoothing the Ground: Essays on Native American Oral Literature* (Calif.). Aside from two opening essays that create the context, the book is organized into "The Question of Translation and Literary Criticism," "Focus on Stories," "Native American Culture and the 'Dominant' Culture." Anthropologists are represented (e.g., Karl Kroeber and Dell Hymes), as well as literary critics and scholars. Chapters from both Lincoln's and Ramsey's books also appear. Because of the diversity of approaches this is a difficult book for the non-specialist.

The final book in this section is about the contributions to American literature of various European immigrant groups: Robert J. Di-Pietro and Edward Ifkovic, eds., *Ethnic Perspectives in American Literature: Selected Essays on the European Contribution* (MLA). All European nations or major language groups, other than the British, are represented, and each one has an essay devoted to its major contributions, along with a history of the problems that group encountered in joining the American political and literary mainstream. The essays discuss the major sources of research materials and review the scholarship that would be helpful to anyone beginning to study that particular American subculture. They describe the genres peculiar to each group, and generally celebrate the extraordinary cultural pluralism so central to the American experience.

Two works, both produced by Don Graham, conclude this section with emphases on regionalism. The first is a large-format book called *Cowboys and Cadillacs: How Hollywood Looks at Texas* (Texas Monthly Press), which traces both the stereotypes and the history of Texas in films since the early years of our century. Graham's light touch and his continuous irony are both appropriate and funny. The opening chapter, in which he writes about his experiences as a young Texan teaching at the University of Pennsylvania, is an amusing introduction to the mixture of awe and condescension with which the rest of the country views Texas. The movies have manifested all these contradictions, and Graham has analyzed them well. The book is well made and characterized by careful scholarship, excellent photographs, and a good historical perspective. At the end there is also a year-by-year catalog of films about Texas. Cowboy movie buffs will love this book.

Graham has also edited, along with James W. Lee and William T. Pilkington, *The Texas Literary Tradition: Fiction, Folklore, His-*

tory (Texas), the proceedings of a conference celebrating the centennial of the University of Texas. The writers and speakers focus on prose rather than poetry and include some emphasis on the Mexican-American tradition. The introduction tries to establish the nature and quality of Texas fiction, and the book follows the themes laid out in the Introduction through the following categories: "The Old Guard," "The Old Order," "The Vanishing Frontier," "The Texas-Mexican Perspective," "The Texas Mystique," "The Sixties and Beyond." There is also a good selected bibliography. Uneven as most proceedings are, this one does establish some useful ways of looking at writings by Texans. It remains to be proved, however, whether there is really a Texas "tradition" in literature.

c. **Major Figures and Literary History.** This section contains works about major figures and other works whose interest is primarily literary historical. The first is a historical-sociological study of American culture in the 1960s and 1970s, *America's Quest for the Ideal: Dissent and Fulfillment in the 60s and 70s* (Oxford), by Peter Clecak. Clecak does not see a disjunction between the two decades as so many critics are prone to do. Instead, he sees continuity in the thematic and ideological concerns that carried over from one period to the next. "I view both decades," he writes, "as aspects of a single, uncompleted chapter in American civilization" (p. 6). The main social fact that distinguishes the 60s and 70s from the 50s is that "the expanding idea of personal fulfillment was diversified and extended to include significant numbers of citizens within every social category" (p. 13). Life for many members of disadvantaged groups was "more full of possibility at the end of the seventies than it had been in the quieter, more stable middle fifties" (p. 23). With chapters on many topics, the book is divided into three sections: "Defining the Framework of Nostalgia," "Searching for Fulfillment," and "Misreading the Signs." It is an erudite, pleasant work that makes a number of points similar to those of Christopher Lasch and other critics of the culture of narcissism, and although it is not primarily about literature, it is relevant to students of that period.

Another book about the culture of a period is Peter Conn's *The Divided Mind: Ideology and Imagination in America, 1898–1917* (Cambridge), which contains a selective overview of that era. Although Conn claims that generalizations are important to him, the book is not informed by a thesis so much as by a point of view. Such thesis as there is derives from Santayana's "The Genteel Tradition in American Philosophy," in which the philosopher talks about America's two "mentalities": "'one a survival of the beliefs and standards of the fathers, the other an expression of the instincts, practices and discoveries of the younger generation'" (p. 13). The book is about how the disaffection from contemporary reality leads to either reactionary responses (e.g., Henry James and the architect Ralph Adams Cram) or radical responses (e.g., John Sloan, the artist, and the poet Emma Goldman). The book contains good chapters on Henry James, black writers such as Booker T. Washington and W. E. B. Du Bois, women writers Kate Chopin, Emma Goldman, and Edith Wharton, architects Cram and Frank Lloyd Wright, and modernist painters. Conn writes well about literature, music, art, and architecture, but the book lacks a strong enough central thesis to help it supplant other books covering roughly the same period, such as those by Henry May, Howard Mumford Jones, and the progressive historians Eric Goldman and Richard Hofstadter.

Noel Riley Fitch's *Sylvia Beach and the Lost Generation: A History of Literary Paris in the Twenties & Thirties* (Norton) is a lively, though unsearching book whose primary interest for readers is described by its subtitle. The book has many deficiencies as a biography, but it does provide students of the period with some fresh and interesting factual material. The book is not forthright about Beach's lesbianism, a strategy that seems anachronistic, and for a work that depends so heavily on fact it contains a number of avoidable factual errors. For instance, Fitch confuses the "Eumaeus" chapter with the "Ithaca" chapter in *Ulysses* (p. 88) and mixes up the publishing dates of Henry Miller's *Tropics* of *Capricorn* and *Cancer* (p. 394). There is some interesting material on Hemingway and Stein, but the core of the book lies in the discussion of Beach's relationship with James Joyce. There are also a number of good photographs, some of them little known, of the book's principal actors. Had Fitch focused even more strongly on Paris as a place of literary exile the book would have been stronger.

Brief mention goes to *Writers & Politics: A Partisan Review Reader* (Routledge), edited by Edith Kurzweil and William Phillips, a collection of writings from a great diversity of poets, critics, novelists, and essayists. The political orientation is to the left, as one would expect, and the tendency is somewhat anti-Soviet and certainly anti-Stalinist. The level of work is high, for the anthology includes Hannah Arendt on "Tradition and the Modern Age," Leon Trotsky's "Art and Revolt," Daniel Bell's "Modernism and Capitalism," Stephen Spender on "Writers and Politics," Nicola Chiaromonte on "Sartre versus Camus," and many other pieces equally good. Not surprisingly, the most interesting essays are primarily from the 1930s, 1940s, and 1950s, before the intellectual decline of the American left.

The award for most contentious book in the American Literature section goes to Kenneth S. Lynn, for *The Air-Line to Seattle: Studies in Literary and Historical Writing About America* (Chicago), a collection of (mostly) review-essays published in *Commentary*, the *American Scholar, The American Spectator*, the *Times Literary Supplement*, and *Harper's*. Lynn's nasty tone often gets out of hand, although it is consistent with the angry journalese style currently in vogue at journals of opinion. Lynn is fond of accusing other writers of political bias, all of them on the "left," while he, a neo-conservative, has no bias he is willing to acknowledge. An example of his use of the gratuitous insult is a comment in an article on "Hemingway's Private War." It appears at the opening of a paragraph that ostensibly provides context for a quotation from Malcolm Cowley: "When, in 1940, Malcolm Cowley finally ceased apologizing for Stalinism, he, too, began to cast about for non-Marxist modes of continuing his assault on the moral credentials of capitalist society" (p. 110). This loading of the gun enables Lynn to overread a comment by Cowley, a reading that depends on the opening insult.

Although I had a hard time reading some of these essays, the truth is that they are often entertaining and instructive because of Lynn's tenacious skill in uncovering intellectual dishonesty—even though he is much harder on others than on himself. His dismantling of Gary Wills's thesis in *Inventing America*, for instance, is an example of Lynn at his unforgiving best. These lively, wide-ranging essays include effective pieces on Emerson, Eleanor Roosevelt, Walter Lippmann, and "The Rebels of Greenwich Village."

Final mention goes to *Literary Admirers of Alfred Stieglitz* (S. Ill.), by F. Richard Thomas, a short volume that supplements Bram Dijkstra's *The Hieroglyphics of Speech: Cubism, Stieglitz, and the Early Poetry of William Carlos Williams* (1969), by "investigating the impact of photography on modern literature" (p. xi). To estab-

lish his statement of theory, Thomas states some principles he thinks
are basic to photography. He then attempts to apply these principles
to Gertrude Stein, Sherwood Anderson, Hart Crane, and William
Carlos Williams, all of whom, Thomas claims with some justification,
were extremely influenced by the example of Stieglitz. Because he
changed how people saw the world and how that world was portrayed in literature, Stieglitz was a major force in American modernism. Along with compelling evidence from each of the authors,
there are a number of interesting photographs by Stieglitz.

ii. Literary Criticism and Theory

a. Literary Theory. The first three books here are concerned with
women in literature and feminist theory. *The Signs Reader: Women,
Gender & Scholarship* (Chicago), edited by Elizabeth and Emily K.
Abel, collects the best essays from the first years of the well-known
feminist journal, *Signs: Journal of Women in Culture and Society*,
since its first publication in 1975. The collection covers a broad range
of topics, as befits an interdisciplinary journal, but many of the essays
are relevant to students of literature. I especially recommend the
following essays, all of them engaged in questioning the premises of
a feminist critcism: Myra Jehlen, "Archimedes and the Paradox of
Feminist Criticism"; Adrienne Rich, "Compulsory Heterosexuality
and Lesbian Existence"; and particularly Heléne Cixous, "The Laugh
of the Medusa."

Elizabeth Abel also edited another anthology, along with Marianne Hirsch and Elizabeth Langland, this one entitled *The Voyage
In: Fictions of Female Development* (New England) and concerned
with applying the concept of the *bildungsroman* to the development
of the female character. The Introduction states that "a distinctive female 'I' implies a distinctive value system and unorthodox developmental goals, defined in terms of community and empathy rather
than achievement and autonomy" (p. 10). Susan J. Rosowski calls the
female *bildungsroman* "The Novel of Awakening." While many of
the essays are not about American topics, the strong theoretical
underpinning in most of them makes what they say applicable elsewhere. I especially recommend the following essays, in addition to
Rosowski's: Elizabeth Langland, "Female Stories of Experience: Alcott's *Little Women* in Light of *Work*"; Elizabeth Abel, "Narrative

Structure(s) and Female Development: The case of *Mrs. Dalloway*";
and Mary Anne Ferguson, "The Female Novel of Development and
the Myth of Psyche."

In *How to Suppress Women's Writing* (Texas) Joanna Russ attempts to update Virginia Woolf's *A Room of One's Own* and does
not wholly succeed. Part of my disappointment stems from the fact
that the book was completed in 1978, to judge from the date given
in the "Author's Note," which suggests why the tone and many
specific references seem inappropriate. The writing is lively and persuasive, and Russ has amassed much evidence that damns writers of
both sexes for fostering stereotypes about women writers. Russ's
strategy is to point out the series of "double-bind" or "yes, but"
situations in which women writers find themselves. If they are not
supposed to write a novel and they do, they won't get it published.
If they get it published, it is only because they are women; or perhaps
because they "write like men." If they write about general topics,
then they are limited in their perceptions because they are women.
If they have written a good novel, then they haven't written a whole
shelf of good novels. And so on. The idea is clever, and it is developed well, but what might have seemed fresh five or six years ago
does not work quite as well today. There is also no reference to the
good feminist works that have appeared in the interim—e.g., Gilbert
and Gubar's *Madwoman in the Attic*. Surely her editor could have
asked her to bring her references up to date.

A review of more general works of literary theory constitutes the
remainder of this section. Hazard Adams's magisterial book, *Philosophy of the Literary Symbolic* (Florida State), is more a history of a
theoretical concept than a work of theory in its own right. But rather
than attempting a comprehensive history of the "literary symbolic,"
it focuses on "moments" in that history in a tradition that runs from
Blake through Yeats to Northrop Frye. Precursors to Blake are
Goethe, Schelling, Coleridge, Carlyle, and Hegel. Followers include
Baudelaire, Mallarmé, early Yeats, and Wilde. Most of the book
focuses on the 20th Century, and the many references include Freud,
Croce, Vaihinger, Langer, and Bachelard. Adams deals at the end
with contemporary theory and with how structuralism and post-
structuralism deal with, extend, and modify the concept of the symbolic. Adams is especially good on matters having to do with dream,
myth, and symbol, and the book is well written; perhaps, in the final

analysis, however, it is more a book for dipping into than reading through.

An interesting collection of essays with an unpromising title is *Relativism in the Arts* (Georgia), ed. Betty Jean Craige. Influenced by a deconstructionist theory of language, Craige's Introduction states that the early 20th century began the abandonment of "logocentrism." Along with the corresponding abandonment of representation in the plastic arts, this moment constituted the beginning of an age of relativism, a situation that Craige does not find negative. A number of distinguished critics have contributed essays concerned with that general theme, although written from different points of view. The best essays, and well worth the reader's time, are by Arthur C. Danto, "The Appreciation and Interpretation of Works of Art"; Hayden White, "The Limits of Relativism in the Arts"; Donald B. Kuspit, "Collage: The Organizing Principle of Art in the Age of the Relativity of Art" (the most distinguished essay for its ideas, but turgidly written); and (peripherally tied to the theme, but effective anyway) J. Hillis Miller, "The Two Relativisms: Point of View and Indeterminacy in the Novel *Absalom, Absalom!*"

The year's most polemical book is Terry Eagleton's *Literary Theory: An Introduction* (Minnesota), which is not quite an introduction, requiring as it does much knowledge of contemporary theory. Eagleton's greatest virtue is his passionately lucid writing style, which combines both clarity and aphorism. The book surveys from a Marxist perspective the state of both English studies and contemporary theories of literature, and it contains some of the best discussions I know of such figures as Lacan and Saussure. While I found the book both stimulating and annoying, I also find that much of it has remained with me, particularly the trenchant, quotable critiques of various schools of criticism.

In Eagleton's view, literary theory always rationalizes a particular view of society. It is from this perspective that he surveys the schools of criticism that have cornered the academic marketplace in the past few generations. ". . . There is no such thing," he says, "as a purely 'literary' response: all such responses, not least those to literary *form*, to the aspects of a work which are sometimes jealously reserved to the 'aesthetic,' are deeply imbricated with the kind of social and historical individuals we are" (p. 89). On this score Eagleton is particularly angered by structuralism, which in its attempt to find a structure totally devoid of reference "is rather like killing a person in order to examine more conveniently the circulation of the blood" (p. 109). He is most pleased with current interest in the role of the reader, especially if it considers the reader a social creature, and a product of both history and society. Eagleton seems sympathetic to Roland Barthes who finds a text "less a 'structure' than an open-ended process of 'structuration', and it is criticism which does this structurating" (p. 139). It is an easy step to conclude from there that "literary theorists, critics and teachers, then, are not so much purveyors of doctrine as custodians of a discourse" (p. 201). While a good work for the experienced reader of theory, this "introduction" should be recommended to beginners only with great care.

Anthony Easthope's *Poetry as Discourse* (Methuen), part of the New Accents series, contains a succinct summary of the discourse theory of language and its application to poetry. Discourse theory is concerned with language beyond the sentence, taking the study of communication beyond the point where linguistics has been able to go. Easthope claims that his theory of discourse "can explain the author as product or effect of the text, whereas conventional criticism accepts the notion of the author as unquestionable and pre-given in order to be able to define how the text should be read" (p. 7). What distinguishes poetic discourse from any other kind is the fact that it "accords precedence to the signifier" (p. 17). Building on Lacan, Easthope claims that "there is no discourse without subjectivity and no subjectivity without discourse" (p. 32). Having discussed discourse as language, ideology, and subjectivity, Easthope then applies the theory to some aspects of English poetry, with a stimulating chapter on "The Modernism of Eliot and Pound."

Brief mention goes to another work in the New Accents series, *Literature and Propaganda* (Methuen), by A. P. Foulkes, a well-written discussion of how propaganda and ideology relate to language and literature. While the book makes no original contribution, it does the useful service of applying theories of reader reception to the ideological element in literature. For Foulkes, "the relevant relation is not that which obtains between a text and the way it marks its own referentiality, but rather the relation between the designata of a text and the modes of perception accompanying a particular historical act of reception" (p. 73). Along the way appear interesting discussions of such topics as "Linguistic determinism and literary freedom," "Capitalist integration myths," "Demystification," and "Fiction and reality."

Innovation/Renovation: New Perspectives on the Humanities (Wis.), edited by Ihab and Sally Hassan, is a collection that grew out of two international conferences. I mention it here because it contains a number of provocative essays from well-known contemporary theoreticians on the theme of postmodernism. Although the quality is uneven, I can nonetheless recommend Ihab Hassan, "Ideas of Cultural Change"; Geoffrey H. Hartman, "The New Wilderness: Critics as Connoisseurs of Chaos"; Ralph Cohen, "The Joys and Sorrows of Literary Theory"; Richard Schechner, "News, Sex, and Performance Theory"; Matei Calinescu, "From the One to the Many: Pluralism in Today's Thought"; Malcolm Bradbury, "Modernisms/Post-modernisms"; Jean-François Lyotard, "Answering the Question: What is Postmodernism?"

The nature and theory of composition is the subject of two books, the first of them a collection edited by Winifred Bryan Horner, *Composition & Literature: Bridging the Gap* (Chicago), and culled from a number of MLA Programs on Composition. The overall impression with which the book leaves us is that we are nowhere near a consensus on the nature of writing skills or on how to teach students to write. English departments spend at least three quarters of their teaching effort on composition courses, but the full-time faculty is by and large concerned only with literature. The struggle documented by this book is how to find ways of bridging that gap. Is writing a purely technical skill, much like learning to work a calculator, or is it intimately related to the processes of thinking and reading? Such seemingly contradictory positions are often held by the same person (p. 150). Most memorable to me is the argument of J. Hillis Miller that shows how reading and writing are intimately related (p. 41–42). There are also good essays by Horner (the Introduction), Richard Lanham, Wayne Booth, Elaine Maimon, E. D. Hirsch, and Frederick Crews.

Richard Lanham spends an entire book on this topic in *Literacy and the Survival of Humanism* (Yale), a set of his essays on rhetoric and college writing. These essays embody more a theory of culture than a theory of writing, for Lanham accepts the ancient assessment of rhetoric as one of the humane disciplines: "Humanism in our time ... will have to *include* style, not banish it. It must, that is, acknowledge the leftover evolutionary baggage, the impulses of game and play from which style emerges. The central crisis in man's management of his own affairs will be a crisis of self-consciousness rather than a crisis of ethics. We shall have to practice a kind of rhetorical judo on ourselves, learn to discipline, balance, and domesticate the various motives built into us" (pp. 12–13). In Lanham's view the "Post-Darwinian conception of man" forces humanists to concentrate on "stylistic behavior" (p. 39), and writing, as readers of *Style: An Anti-Textbook* know, is style, not technique. While the essays are often repetitious, their very emphasis on a singular set of ideas makes them seem stronger when read as a group. Lanham's wide range includes such topics as "Aristotle and the Illusion of Purpose," "The Choice of Utopias: More or Castiglione?" "*At* and *Through*: The Opaque Style and Its Uses," and "Should English Departments Take an Interest in Teaching Composition?"

I shall briefly mention *The Politics of Interpretation* (Chicago), ed. W. J. T. Mitchell, an excellent compilation of essays most of which originally appeared in the September 1982, December 1982, and March 1983 issues of *Critical Inquiry*. The editor defines this book "as a collection of essays which explores the proposition that criticism and interpretation, the arts of explanation and understanding, have a deep and complex relation with politics, the structures of power and social value that organize human life" (p. 1). The book opens with nine theoretical articles and continues with three "Critical Exchanges" in which writers respond to one another. Some of our best-known theoreticians are represented here, including Edward W. Said, Wayne C. Booth, Hayden White, Gerald Graff, Stanley Cavell, Stanley Fish, E. D. Hirsch, and Terry Eagleton. The quality of the essays is high, and the book has a unity that one does not always find in such collections.

b. **Theory of Fiction.** This section discusses the best books of 1983 in a burgeoning genre of literary theory. I begin with mention of a new edition of one of the classics in the field, Wayne Booth's *The Rhetoric of Fiction* (Chicago). The entire original text and bibliography has been published without revision. There is a lengthy new Afterword in which Booth responds to criticism of the book, expresses reservations he now has about how he did things 20 years ago, talks about the present state of fictional theory, and suggests what he might now do differently. The theorists he seems most to respect are Sheldon Sacks, Mikhail Bakhtin, and Gerard Genette, and it seems to me on looking through the book again that *The Rhetoric of Fiction* still retains a place with books by those writers. James Phelan has prepared an excellent "Supplementary Bibliography 1961–82," which contains more than 400 items.

A more topical work is Kenneth A. Bruffee's *Elegaic Romance: Cultural Change and Loss of the Hero in Modern Fiction* (Cornell), which studies that form of fiction in which the narrator expresses nostalgia for a lost "hero" who has had a major impact on the narrator —e.g., Marlow/Kurtz, Marlow/Lord Jim, Carraway/Gatsby. Bruffee defines the elegaic romance as a genre that interweaves three major "thematic strands—the quest romance tradition, the discrediting of hero-worship and heroism, and the impact of loss and change" (p. 15). The narrator maintains a belief in the 19th-century concept of the hero, and "his hero's influence remains unaccountably alive in the narrator's mind. The narrator attempts to solve this problem by coming to terms, through telling the tale, with the debilitating influence that his hero continues to exert over him" (p. 28). The tale is narrated months or years after the hero's death and mixes events that took place during the hero's lifetime with events and discussions that take place after his death. This useful discussion leans heavily on Conrad's work for models, but it also includes good readings of such American works as *The Great Gatsby, All the King's Men,* and *A Separate Peace.*

John Gardner's *On Becoming a Novelist* (Harper), completed before the author's untimely death, is not a theory of fiction so much as a book of advice to writers, and as such it is probably the best book I know for young writers. The advice is practical but quite in touch with a serious literary dimension, having the right mixture of common sense and idealism that writers need who wish to be successful without writing trash. Gardner's advice is so well put and so unpatronizing that I cannot resist sharing some sample quotations. On the subject of imitation Gardner says that "the young writer who imitates TV instead of life is essentially no different from what's wrong with the young writer who imitates some earlier writer . . . every literary imitation lacks something we expect of good writing; the writer seeing with his own eyes" (p. 25). On how writers should read he says: "The good English major studies a work to understand

and appreciate its meaning, to perceive its relationship to other works of the period, and so on. The young writer should read to see how effects are achieved, how things are done, sometimes reflecting on what he would have done in the same situation and on whether his way would have been better or worse, and why. He reads the way a young architect looks at a building, or a medical student watches an operation, both devotedly, hoping to learn from a master, and critically, alert for any possible mistake" (pp. 45–46). It can't be said much better than that.

Frank Kermode's latest book is a collection of essays entitled *The Art of Telling: Essays on Fiction* (Harvard), mostly on the interpretation of narrative or on the general theory of interpretation. While somewhat theoretical, Kermode's commonsense approach often makes him sound anti-ideological. He explains the new French theory well, but his tone is often hostile. For instance: "The inference appears to be that all the novels of the past in which we find much to admire partake of the modern precisely in so far as they are not patient of interpretation that assumes limited meaning. Barthes, under the influence of a domestic French quarrel, always talks as if establishment critics deny that position. Outside France this is, of course, untrue. In a sense he is saying, in a new way, something we have long known about the plurality of good texts" (p. 68). The essays tend to repeat similar themes, but are always driven by Kermode's erudition, thoughtfulness, and clarity. The thesis underlying the book is similar to that of *The Genesis of Secrecy*: all reading is interpretation. Narrative has a hidden dimension, and the interpreter's job is to ferret out the latent content. I found the most interesting essays to be: "Local and Provincial Restrictions," "The Use of the Codes" (about Barthes), "Secrets and Narrative Sequence," "Can We Say Absolutely Anything We Like?", and "Institutional Control of Interpretation."

Because the theory of fiction has said comparatively little about the short story, Susan Lohafer's *Coming to Terms with the Short Story* (LSU) attempts to construct a poetics of that genre. Taking off from Norman Friedman's essay, "What Makes a Short Story Short?" Lohafer attempts to add a number of points that she finds missing from Friedman. Her approach is primarily common sense, although she does use both phenomenology and reader-response criticism. For Lohafer the basic short story unit is not the word but the sentence.

She says that "we pay attention to sentences in stories because we have to, because if we dally over the nuances of a word, if we skim for the drift, either way we are missing literally the sentience of the story" (pp. 34–35). But it is on the larger scale that Lohafer tries to deal with the story's formal qualities, in exploring the "aesthetics of brevity." The ever present consciousness of the need for closure is what controls the story itself as well as both the writer and the reader. Unfortunately, Lohafer's discussion of the various issues does not go far enough. Her book is not pitched at short story writers, and not enough at the theorists of fiction. It will be most satisfying to teachers of the short story who want to read a short book in which some of the crucial issues are raised.

Concluding this section I shall mention a short work from the New Accents series, *Narrative Fiction: Contemporary Poetics* (Methuen), by Shlomith Rimmon–Kenan. This is a solid, up-to-date presentation of contemporary theories of narratology, which draws upon "Anglo-American New Criticism, Russian Formalism, French Structuralism, the Tel-Aviv School of Poetics and the Phenomenology of Reading" (p. 5). The theorist most in evidence is Gerard Genette, and the book's organization reflects that writer's work on narratology. Rimmon-Kenan focuses on story, Genette's *histoire* (events, characters); text, Genette's *récit* (time, characterization, focalization); and narration (levels and voices, speech representation). While the writing tends to be dry, the book is the best brief compendium I know of current thinking about narratology, and it would be useful in courses in the theory of fiction, if supplemented by full-length basic texts such as those by Booth, Genette, and Sacks.

c. **Major Figures.** This section reviews works about major theoreticians, an increasingly common genre in an age of critical ascendency. If critical theory is now a genre of equal status with poetry, fiction, and drama, then its practitioners deserve exegesis as much as other writers, and they often need it as much. The first work here is Jonathan Culler's brief summary, *Roland Barthes* (Oxford). Culler has always been an excellent explainer, and in this work he brings off something quite difficult. He has written an explanatory book clear enough to be accessible to beginners but interesting enough to stimulate those who have read a great deal of Barthes. Culler divides the career of Barthes into the following categories that serve

as titles for his chapters: literary historian, mythologist, critic, po-
lemicist, semiologist, structuralist, hedonist, writer, and man of letters. While some of Barthes's works overlap the categories, Culler's
schema enables him to approach his subject's multi-faceted career
chronologically.

Culler captures the flavor of Barthes in such statements as "For
Barthes, of course, interpretation should be extravagant. Criticism
that remained within received opinion would have no point or savour.
Barthes's writing has always fed controversy: its laconic pronouncements irritate those who hold other views" (pp. 67–68). Culler also
has an ability to define terms succinctly: "Semiology is based on the
premise that insofar as human actions and objects have meaning,
there must be a system of distinctions and conventions, conscious or
unconscious, that generates that meaning" (p. 72). While discussing
Barthes's brilliant reading of Balzac's *Sarrasine* in S/Z, Culler demonstrates his ability to explain difficult conceptions simply and clearly:
"Barthes's breaking up of the text in pursuit of codes enables him to
do close reading while resisting the presumption of Anglo-American
close reading that every detail must be shown to contribute to the
aesthetic unity of the whole. Interested in the 'plural' qualities of
the work, he refuses to seek an overall unifying structure but asks
how each detail works, what codes it relates to, and proves adept
at discovering functions" (p. 86). This slim volume is rich and
rewarding.

Two books on the late Michel Foucault join the ones I reviewed
last year in attempting to describe the theoretical program of this
important, problematic thinker: Pamela Major–Poetzl, *Michel Foucault's Archaeology of Western Culture: Toward a New Science of
History* (N.C.) and Karlis Racevskis, *Michel Foucault and the Subversion of Intellect* (Cornell). Major-Poetzl's book is a fairly straightforward presentation of Foucault's work and thought, written in a
more direct, accessible style than Racevskis's study. The author uses
Foucault's *Archaeology of Knowledge* as a theoretical basis for exploring his theories. She examines his work in a number of cultural
contexts to show that Foucault is part of a large movement in contemporary Western culture that is rethinking the intellectual bases
of thought, and includes, among others, Thomas Kuhn, Ferdinand
de Saussure, Georges Canguilhem, and Gaston Bachelard. In this
book it is the earlier Foucault that dominates, the writer of *Madness*

and Civilization and *The Order of Things,* and the author is less concerned than Racevskis with Foucault's works on power and sexuality. This book is probably the best description available of Foucault's notion of archaeology, which, "like field theory, has shifted attention from things (objects) and abstract forces (ideas) to the structure of 'discourses' (organized bodies of knowledge and practice, such as clinical medicine) in their specific spatio-temporal articulations" (p. 5).

In Racevskis's *Michel Foucault and the Subversion of Intellect* the study of Foucault's thought proceeds categorically rather than through a study of individual works in analyzing some of Foucault's key concepts such as the subject, archaeology, the *episteme*, discourse, power, and the Symbolic. He applies Lacan's notion of the role of the Symbolic and the Imaginary in our experience of the Real. In the beginning Racevskis focuses on the concept of the subject: "taken as the foundation of discourse, the subject is a support on which discourse is erected but . . . it is both the active agent and an object acted upon. The subject is also an object—it is a product of discourse" (pp. 25–26). But by becoming part of the dominant discourse of a culture which it is archaeology's task to discover, individuals are not only a subject of the discourse, they are objectified as part of a power struggle. Racevskis is worth quoting at length to clarify this: "Man's appearance in the field of discourse is seen by Foucault as the determining cause of a new mode of social existence: man has been subjected and reified as an object of knowledge, he has become a "body" in a field of forces, of power-knowledge strategies intent on effectively integrating the individual within the social scheme. These systems of power, Foucault shows, are products of knowledge; and power, in turn, helps constitute fields of investigation where truths are to be found" (p. 27).

The latter part of the book is concerned with exploring the postulate that knowledge is power in such chapters as "The Game of Knowledge." Racevskis also uses the work of Jean Baudrillard to do a critique of Foucault, but ends by supporting the latter. He writes with clarity and he is usually, though not always, helpful on some of the tough issues raised by Foucault.

There are also two books on another French culture hero, Jacques Lacan: Catherine Clément, *The Lives and Legends of Jacques Lacan* (Columbia), trans. Arthur Goldhammer, and Stuart Schneiderman's

Jacques Lacan: The Death of an Intellectual Hero (Harvard). Both books were written by disciples of Lacan, and both share similar limitations. Instead of taking us into Lacan's theory, a service English readers sorely need, these books are personal meditations on the father of French psychoanalysis.

Schneiderman claims that he was the only American to have taken a training analysis with Lacan, and we have a good sense when we are finished of what kind of therapist Lacan must have been. Schneiderman explains many of the difficult concepts of Lacanian therapy, such as the pass, the short session, and the insistence of the letter in the unconscious, and he covers a lot of ground in presenting Lacanian analysis as a behavioral system; but he does not give us an *intellectual* grounding in Lacan's system of thought.

Although similar in its informal style and personal approach, Clément's book makes a more serious attempt to be theoretical. Because she seems to have broken from the master late in Lacan's life, she is less tolerant of his combativeness, rudeness, and overall eccentricity. The book seems to be written by someone needing to declare her personal independence. Nonetheless it contains some interesting statements about Lacan's theories; for instance, his two "axioms of psychoanalysis": "The first axiom of psychoanalysis is not to confuse analysis with altruism. It is an unnatural axiom: for even if analysts, by delving into their own histories, discover that altruism is only a cover for sadistic impulses, it nonetheless remains true that psychoanalysis, viewed strictly in terms of its social function, offers help to its patients" (p. 94). The second axiom Clément quotes directly from Lacan's *Écrits*: "Only psychoanalysis recognizes the knot of imaginary servitude that love must either repeatedly untie or sever" (p. 95). As interesting as this book is, however, the best works in English for students of literature on the subject of Lacan are probably those of Jane Gallop and Juliet Mitchell and translations of certain works of Julia Kristeva.

I shall give brief mention to Lee Congdon's *The Young Lucács* (N.C.), a biography of Georg Lukács until around 1920. Congdon, an historian, focuses on Lukács's intellectual development, clarifying details of his life and showing how they relate to his various intellectual positions. What lends authority to Congdon's account is his thorough grounding in both Lukács's life and work and in the intellectual milieu and historical period. Congdon also documents how

Lukács developed from a Hegelian literary critic to someone involved
in politics and ultimately into a serious Marxist theoretician by the
time of the Russian Bolshevik Revolution and the Hungarian Soviet
Republic.

I shall also briefly mention *Elder Olson: An Annotated Bibliography* (Garland) edited by James L. Battersby. This is part of a new
series, the Garland Bibliographies of Modern Critics and Critical
Schools, edited by William E. Cain. Elder Olson, associated with the
Chicago School of Criticism, was a poet, playwright, scholar, and
critic, who was also noted as a "neo-Aristotelian." He is served well
by this volume. The book begins with a substantial introduction
that covers Olson's career and major publications and states his
critical principles. Two parts follow, obviously set by computer and
photographed. The first lists Olson's primary titles, including his work
in all genres. The second lists critical responses to Olson's work, including book reviews, essays, articles, and Ph.D. theses.

d. **"On the Cutting Edge."**   This section reviews works that are pri-
marily post-structuralist. Jonathan Arac, Wlad Godzich, and Wallace
Martin are all listed as editors of a volume entitled *The Yale Critics:
Deconstruction in America* (Minnesota), which is volume six of the
Theory and History of Literature. The essays contained herein were
all commissioned for this volume and take as their subject either the
"Yale School" or individual members of it. The Yale Critics are
Harold Bloom, the late Paul de Man, Jacques Derrida (who has an
appointment at Yale), Geoffrey Hartman, and J. Hillis Miller.

Wallace Martin's Introduction contains a history of how a particular point of view developed at Yale along with some trenchant
observations as to the nature and value of that point of view. "Depending upon which perspective is selected," Martin writes, "we can
view the Yale critics as iconoclasts or as wily conservatives. It is even
possible to view them as the last stage of a decadent tradition in-
augurated by Modernism, or Romanticism, or Descartes" (p. xxix).
This statement reflects a tendency throughout most of the essays to
see the Yale School as a conservative rather than radical enterprise,
designed to make literary study the province of an elite inner circle
of initiates versed in a certain hieratic lore and dogma. But Martin's
position leads him to some unfair characterizations: "Anti-formalists
such as Hartman, de Man, Miller, and Bloom have traditionally dis-

cussed the relationship of literary study to other disciplines with only one purpose in mind: They want to show why the methodologies employed in the sciences are not of any relevance to literature—after which they can return to their own methods of hermeneutic meditation" (p. xxvii). That strikes me as being a low blow.

Jonathan Arac's summary "Afterword" contains similar trenchancies, such as his claim that the Yale critics manifest "timidity." "As readers we need less of Hartman's hesitant 'patience' for ourselves and need more confidence in what Frank Kermode calls the 'patience' of great literature. We must not fear that if we make interpretive decisions rather than indeterminations—and thus try to make literature part of our future as well as our present—we will somehow destroy or violate the works we care for" (p. 196). Some of the best essays are by Wlad Godzich on "The Domestication of Derrida," Stanley Corngold on the concept of "Error in Paul de Man," and Donald Pease on "J. Hillis Miller: The Other Victorian at Yale." Readers should be warned that this volume requires extensive knowledge of texts by the Yale critics.

A French critic whose work has been connected with the Yale School is Maurice Blanchot, whose book of essays *The Space of Literature*, trans. Ann Smock, was published by Nebraska in late 1982. I can only make a few remarks about this collection, first published in French in 1955, because it came to my attention too late to be read through carefully. The translator's introduction does an excellent job of placing Blanchot's work into the proper context of 20th-century letters, particularly concerning his influence on such eminent critics as Sartre, Derrida, Foucault, and de Man. Blanchot seems most interested in exploring the process of reading and the nature of artistic creativity. I was particularly moved by the two sections that I read: "The Essential Solitude" and "Literature and the Original Experience."

G. Douglas Atkins has written a fairly effective, simple explanation of deconstruction entitled *Reading Deconstruction/Deconstructive Reading* (Kentucky), which contains an outline of deconstructive theory followed by readings of three 18th-century English poems according to that theory. The readings are less interesting than the explanatory section that contains a clear exposition of a number of difficult concepts, including definitions of "text" and "trace." His statement of what a deconstructive critic does is also succinct and clear: "The deconstructive critic thus seeks the text's navel, the moment when any text will differ from itself, transgressing its own system of values, becoming undecidable in terms of its apparent system of meaning" (p. 25). This is a good example of the jargon-free style in which Atkins writes, although his simplicity of language sometimes reflects a simplicity of content. Atkins's prose is more clear than that of such explainers as Jonathan Culler, Vincent Leitch, and Frank Lentricchia, but he is valuable primarily for someone who is reading deconstructive theory for the first time.

At this point I should like to note the publication of a new edition of a classic work of contemporary criticism, Paul de Man's *Blindness and Insight: Essays in the Rhetoric of Criticism* (Minnesota), which was published just before his death. The introduction, in which Wlad Godzich places de Man in a historical context, states a number of interesting facts about his background, and emphasizes him as a theorist of reading. None of the original essays has been changed or deleted. There are, however, five new essays, two of them originally published in French. Two of these pieces are quite important: "The Rhetoric of Temporality" and "The Dead-End of Formalist Criticism." There is also a fascinating review of Bloom's *Anxiety of Influence*, with its affinities to de Man's theory of "error." This is volume 7 of the Theory and History of Literature.

One of the year's most unusual books is a translation by Catherine Porter of Shoshanna Felman's *The Literary Speech Act: Don Juan with J. L. Austin, or Seduction in Two Languages* (Cornell). This intertextual study reads the Don Juan myth through the agencies of contemporary linguistics and philosophy. Felman draws the Don Juan myth primarily from Moliére's play and Mozart and Da Ponte's *Don Giovanni*. But the book is really a meditation on the theory that language is performance; as such it takes into account the speech act theories of English philosopher J. L. Austin and the philosophical controversy between him and the French linguist Émile Benveniste. The fundamental linguistic act of Don Juan is the promise, most particularly the promise to marry, and it is the kind of performative behavior implied by the promise that Felman wishes to examine. "On the basis, then, of a triple reading—of a literary text, a linguistic text, and a philosophical text—I want to undertake a meditation on promising, in such a way that the place of the literary will becomes the meeting and testing ground of the linguistic and the philosophical,

the place where linguistics and philosophy are interrogated but also
where they are pushed beyond their disciplinary limits" (p. 11).

Heavily laden with quotations from Nietzsche, Freud, Kierkegaard, and Lacan, the book can best be characterized by the titles
of its various sections: "I. Between Linguistics and Philosophy of
Language: Theories of Promise, Promises of Theory"; "II. The Per-
version of Promising: Don Juan and Literary Performance"; "III.
The Scandal of the Performative"; "IV. Knowledge and Pleasure, or
the Philosopher's Performance (Psychoanalysis and the Performative)." Man is defined in the Preface as "The Promising Animal,"
and Don Juan is the archetypal promiser. "Saying, for him, is in no
case tantamount to knowing, but rather to *doing:acting* on the inter-
locutor, modifying the situation and the interplay of forces within it.
Language, for Don Juan, is performative and not informative; it is a
field of enjoyment, not of knowledge" (p. 27). Felman herself treats
language as a field of enjoyment. Writing from within a deconstructive technique that emphasizes the potential free play of language,
she is extremely playful herself but surprisingly accessible and without the jargon that puts American readers off of the language of
most French theoreticians. Felman is in touch not only with her own
language but with that of the texts she is treating. This is a wise,
impudent, and stimulating book.

A good collection of essays written to illuminate the work of
Derrida is Mark Krupnick, ed., *Displacements: Derrida and After*
(Indiana). The essays seem to have been commissioned for the book,
although portions of a piece by Susan Handelman did appear in *The
Slayers of Moses*, which I reviewed last year. Other contributors include Paul de Man, Michael Ryan, Herman Rapaport, and Gayatri
Chakravorty Spivak. The modern sense of "displacement" comes from
Freud's *Interpretation of Dreams*, and, as Krupnick writes in his Introduction, "Although displacement is not theoretically articulated
in Derrida's writing, it is central to his de-centering mode of critique.
For Derridean deconstruction proceeds by way of displacement, first
reversing the terms of a philosophical opposition, that is, reversing
a hierarchy or structure of domination, and then displacing or dis-
lodging the system" (p. 1). Krupnick goes on to claim that "displacement became ubiquitous at that moment when an old poetics based
on metaphor and symbol gave way to a new poetics that privileges

metonymy" (p. 4). Other writers in the collection stress a similar point, particularly following Jakobson's definition of metonymy as embodying the principles of contiguity. Handelman claims, for instance, that Derrida is part of a Rabbinic tradition which, in contrast to the Greek notion of identity, "focused on relations of juxtaposition, contiguity, association" (p. 104). The most interesting essays are Handelman's "Jacques Derrida and the Heretic Hermeneutic," Spivak's feminist application of Derrida in "Displacement and the Discourse of Woman," and Tom Conley's "A Trace of Style," which discusses not only how to read Derrida but also the place of writing: "One must write," he says, "*in* the margin to reflect the historical perspectives of discourse; but, also, within the remainders—the discards, the leftovers in a game of cards or chance . . .—that determine one's own given (symbolical, political, and historical) conditions as a writer" (p. 80). All the essays assume a familiarity with Derrida's work.

A collection of essays by a single author is Dominick LaCapra's *Rethinking Intellectual History: Texts, Contexts, Language* (Cornell). Like Hayden White, LaCapra is an historian who is versed in contemporary thought about language, philosophy, and literary theory. All these pieces have been published in such places as *Diacritics* and *History and Theory*, their subjects including Hayden White, Wittgenstein, Ricoeur, Habermas, Sartre, Fredric Jameson, Marx, and Mikhail Bakhtin. I especially recommend the title essay for its stimulating study of the individuals LaCapra considers the crucial agents in the contemporary revision of intellectual history. The book is a set of discrete but intellectually connected forays into modern thought, written in a style that is always challenging.

If I were asked to name the one recently published book that describes most clearly the nature and history of deconstruction, I would surely name Vincent B. Leitch's *Deconstructive Criticism: An Advanced Introduction* (Columbia), which surpasses even the work of Culler and Lentriccia in providing a comprehensible overview of recent literary theory. Leitch believes that criticism since Saussure, and particularly since the Second World War, was headed irrevocably toward the dominance of deconstruction. He considers in detail the work of Heidegger, Derrida, the Yale School, Foucault, Lévi-Strauss, de Man, and many others, and if I had a bone to pick with his presentation, it would be with the way he seems to mold them into a single unitary enterprise. Nonetheless, his argument is convincing.

The argument begins with Saussure's description of the arbitrary relationship between signifier and signified, the two components of the sign, a term that is not unitary but relational or "differential" (p. 8). Because of that differential quality, the only way to talk about a sign in a unitary fashion is through the Derridean concept of the *trace*, which "is the sum of all possible relations, whether isolated or not, which inhabit and constitute the sign" (p. 28). The linguistic sign is thus *"the site of an ambivalent and problematic relation between referential and figural meaning"* (Leitch's italics) (p. 47). This ambivalence makes thematic reading questionable, and for Paul de Man "the revisionary project of criticism, therefore, is to create a nonthematic figural criticism—deconstructive rhetoric" (p. 47).

But if referentiality is potentially infinite, the concept of the "text" must be reexamined. Differences are "myriad," meanings are "infinite," and "are broadcast across textual surfaces. In deconstructive theory, such dissemination takes the place of truth" (p. 99). Still there is no escaping the constitutive nature of language, and "since language serves as ground of existence, the world emerges as infinite Text. Everything gets textualized. . . . Instead of literature we have textuality; in place of tradition, intertextuality" (p. 122). Then where does truth come from? "Truth comes forth in the reifications, the personal pleasures, of reading. Truth is not an entity or property of the text. No text utters its truth; the truth lies elsewhere— in a reading. Constitutionally, reading is misreading" (p. 122). This kind of argument leads to the logic contained in de Man's notion of error, or Bloom's of misprision. As Leitch states, "In other words, if it ruled out or refused all misreading whatsoever, a text would not be literary. A text is literary to the degree that it permits and encourages misreading" (p. 185).

The controversial nature of contemporary theory has been increased by its tendency to "elevate" criticism to the status of literary text, but by the logic outlined above, there is no fundamental difference between "literary" and "theoretical" or "critical" texts. "The new problematics concerning the processes of reading, the activities of free play, the effects of intertextuality and the practices of writing bear equivalent pertinence. Literature, criticism, metacriticism—all partake of language. All share the same resources" (p. 225). "There is nothing other than interpretation" (p. 250).

Something other than deconstructive analysis is embodied in Michael Riffaterre's *Text Production* (Columbia), trans. Terese Lyons, a book of formal analysis in the tradition of descriptive poetics. This book was published in France in 1979 and has already achieved the status of a classic. Riffaterre believes in the "literariness" of a text as distinct from non-literary texts. "The text," he says, "is always one of a kind, unique. And it seems to me that this *uniqueness* is the simplest definition of literariness that we can find." He goes on to say that "the difference between poetics and textual analysis is that poetics generalizes and dissolves a work's uniqueness into poetic language, but analysis, as I see it, attempts to explain the unique" (p. 2). The text is characterized not merely by its own existence or its relation to "reality" or to an author, but by its relationship to a reader. "*The literary phenomenon is not only the text, but also its reader and all of the reader's possible reactions to the text*" (Riffaterre's italics) (p. 3). But Riffaterre does not accept the concept of the free play of the signifier; he believes that "*the text is a limiting and prescriptive code*" (his italics) (p. 6), and that the reader's responses are thereby limited by the text.

The entire book is characterized by the kind of dry, tight, and logical argument exemplified by the above. Riffaterre treats such topics as the "Semantics of the Poem," "Literary Sentence Models," the "Poetics of Neologisms," "Paragram and Significance," and "Toward a Formal Approach to Literary History." The latter two-thirds of the book consists of readings of various literary texts in light of the author's theory of how such texts are produced. He is especially good on the subject of literary history, showing how the only attributes we can really compare between texts of different periods are their analagous linguistic and structural functions. "Literary influence or classification can be established only by the discovery of structural parallelism. This means that textual components should not be compared but, rather, their functions should be" (p. 98). We should understand further that readers contemporary to a work's composition can read it from within the same set of linguistic codes as the work was written. Later reactions are controlled by different linguistic codes which must be taken into account by the his-

torian of literature. *Text Production* is a complex work that makes
no compromise with the reader, but even though it is dry and unrelenting, it is not disfigured by jargon and it is characterized by
common sense.

A collection of essays by the prolific Edward W. Said, *The World,
the Text and the Critic* (Harvard), amplifies and to some extent extends the project outlined in *Beginnings* and *Orientalism*. Said also
strikes out in a few new directions, and for his readers that is something to be happy about. The Introduction opens with the claim that
"Literary criticism is practiced today in four major forms. One is the
practical criticism to be found in book reviewing and literary journalism. Second is academic literary history . . . Third is literary
appreciation and interpretation . . . what is taught and performed
by teachers of literature in the university . . . And the fourth form
is literary theory, a relatively new subject . . . The essays collected
in this book derive from all four forms . . ." (p. 1). The book contains
essays on Swift and Conrad (on whom Said once wrote a book), as
well as pieces on "oriental" topics and essays in literary theory such
as "On Repetition" and "On Originality." All the pieces are interesting and none are perfunctory. The best ones, however, survey the
contemporary scene in literary theory and contain the most passionate writing in the book. The Introduction subtitled "Secular Criticism," contains a good overview of that scene, as does the title essay
and a piece called "Roads Taken and Not Taken in Contemporary
Criticism." My favorite is "Reflections on American 'Left' Literary
Criticism." Said has come under some fire for his involvement in
political causes connected with the Middle East, but the kind of
passionate commitment he gives to his political activities is expressed
in a number of essays where he makes clear his belief that criticism
is an act of high cultural seriousness. He states his admiration for
such unlikely older figures as Erich Auerbach and F. O. Matthiessen
because of their intense inner involvement with their cultural situations. I find it pleasant to watch the expanding intellectual purview
of this already learned critic.

Kaja Silverman's *The Subject of Semiotics* (Oxford) is another
fine study of post-structuralist thought. Unlike Leitch, however, who
goes from Saussure into deconstruction and the breaking down of
codes, Silverman follows the other post-Saussurean line of develop-

ment that claims that all behavior is organized, even at the level of
the unconscious, systematically, like a language. In her Preface Silverman claims that her book is different from other "synthetic" books
on post-structuralism in three ways: "First, it maintains the centrality of psychoanalysis to semiotics; it proposes, that is, that the
human subject is to a large degree the subject of semiotics. . . .
Second, [it] assumes the connections between literary and cinematic
texts and theory to be at all points reciprocal . . . [Third] is its emphasis upon sexual difference as an organizing principle not only of
the symbolic order and its 'contents' (signification, discourse, subjectivity), but of the semiotic account of those things" (pp. vii–viii).

Silverman begins with a historical study of semiotics from Saussure and Peirce to Derrida, through the agencies of Freud and Lacan.
There are excellent discussions of the latter as expositors of semiotic
systems in which the unconscious is seen as a semiosis that obeys
laws similar to those of language. Silverman's summary of Lacan's
thoughts is one of the clearest and most comprehensive I know. Her
discussion of film is concerned primarily with the "suture," which she
defines as "the name given to the procedures by means of which
cinematic texts confer subjectivity upon their viewers" (p. 195). This
is a concept that Silverman believes should be applied to literary
texts, and I agree with her.

The last chapter, on Barthes's S/Z, demonstrates how the establishment of semiotic codes can isolate the oppositions that exist in a
text and thereby expose its symbolic content. That chapter contains
excellent discussions of the "readerly" text and the "writerly" one.
"The readerly or classic text strives above all for homogeneity. It organizes its materials according to the 'principle of non-contradiction,'
stressing at all points the 'compatible nature of circumstances'" (p.
243). On the other hand, "The writerly text promotes an infinite play
of signification; in it there can be no transcendental signified, only
provisional ones which function in turn as signifiers" (p. 246). This
is a useful distinction, even though a true deconstructionist would
believe that all texts are, if not writerly, at least "undecidable" and
not subject to "homogeneity."

To sum up, 1983 was a mixed year for works covered in this chapter. I repeat the disappointment I expressed in the beginning with
the lack of ambitious synthetic studies of American literature. Books

announced in 1984 look more promising. The choice in 1983 was
better in literary theory. While there were few classics, I do believe
the general level of discourse was high and that many of the best
minds in our profession are writing works of theory. This fact in
itself may not be the best thing for literary studies, but I do feel that
when the current emphasis on theory finally establishes a new methodology we shall be better equipped to read our basic literary texts.

University of California—Davis

21. Foreign Scholarship

i. French Contributions

Marc Chénetier

Anticipatory apologies may be in order as I begin, since I spent the academic year 83–84 teaching at the University of Virginia and had to rely on what material was sent me rather than being able to systematically solicit the colleagues concerned. There may, therefore, be a few "gaps," even though I do not believe they are sizable. Should I have missed a few things this year, they shall, of course, be covered in next year's report. As it is, and however brief I may try to be, the harvest is another massive one and I have had to keep commentary down to a minimum. From the authors—for excessive brevity—and from the general editor—for excessive length—let me beg double forgiveness.

a. **Bibliography.** *DeltaES,* no. 17, contains one of the only two notable bibliographies published this year—this one on Nabokov prepared by Maurice Couturier (pp. 129–35). The other follows the text of Jean Méral's book on Paris in American literature discussed in the section "General Works" below.

b. **Critical Theory.** A number of texts this year were written by French Americanists on problems of theory and critical attitudes; and even though they may or may not be illustrated by American literary texts, they do shed important light on the way the critical activity of men and women interested in this field of investigation is shaped by fundamental theoretical concerns. Thus, in "L'Activité Post-Moderniste" (*Roman,* no. 5), Régis Durand has made yet another attempt at defining a rather elusive critical concept, while Marc Chénetier, taking part in a symposium on criticism ("Complete Diversity—or disarray") organized by *The Times Higher Education Supplement* (Feb. 11, 1983, pp. 12–13) clearly favored critical theory in the classroom rather than excluding it for the benefit of a strict obeisance to "great texts."

Claude Richard spent the last few years investigating the potential value of epistemological concerns for literary studies. This year he published several papers with such theoretical scope: "Causalité et narration" (*Dires*, no. 1 [Montpellier]:43–54) and "Causation, Causality and Etiology" (*Representation and Performance*, Maurice Couturier, ed., Montpellier: DeltaES, pp. 9–20) rely mostly on examples taken from Thomas Pynchon and John Barth while "Le Graal du Référent" (*Fabula*, no. 2 [Lille]:9–27) concentrates more particularly on *Gravity's Rainbow*. "Causality and Mimesis in Contemporary Fiction" (*SubStance* no. 40:84–93) is an attempt at synthesis for the American public.

By the same token, Pascal Robert, in "Sémiotique , littérature et critique" (*Sémiosis* 30:35–41) provides a framework within which the use of semiotics applied to literary analysis may be evaluated.

Poétiques, a volume put out by the "Société des Anglicistes de l'Enseignement Supérieur" following its 1981 conference and edited by Alain Bony (Lyon: Presses Universitaires de Lyon), gathers many of the papers given at the meeting. There are several general articles dealing with literary theory written by French Americanists that might be useful to the readers of *ALS*, even though they tend to be general rather than about single authors: Noelle Batt's "De la structure à la construction" (pp. 241–50) concentrates on narratology while Christine Brooke–Rose reflects on the problems of genre posed by science fiction ("Théorie des Genres: la science-fiction," pp. 251–62).

Here may be the place to salute the birth of a journal given to problems of literary theory and critical theory as they apply to literatures written in English: *Fabula* comes out of the University of Lille and is jointly edited by Jean–Claude Dupas, Régis Durand and Henri Quéré.

c. **Translation.** A word must be said here of the growing concern among French Americanists for the problems posed by literary translation. The number of plays, novels, short stories and poems being translated is on a spectacular rise. This year's "Prix Maurice–Edgar Coindreau" was awarded to Suzanne Nétillard for her translation of Peter Matthiesen's *The Snow Leopard*, and a special issue of the

Revue Française d'Etudes Américaines (no. 17), under the editorship of Guy-Jean Forgue and Michel Gresset, was given to the problems posed by literary translation. Part II (Aspects of literary translation) contains six articles on the subject of translation, while Part I is devoted to articles on "American English" that endeavor to define a number of lexical and syntactic specificities of the American language.

d. General Works. The one important book of general scope to be published this year is the revised version of a very good "thèse d'Etat" published under the auspices of the Centre National de la Recherche Scientifique: Jean Méral's *Paris dans la Littérature Américaine* (Paris: Editions du CNRS) must be the definitive work on a theme often awkwardly belabored in a number of American articles. Basing his thematic research on a corpus of some 200 literary works, Méral first discusses the imaginary visions of the French capital in the early years of the 19th century, tracing the evolution of that image from Poe to the first real lineaments of the city as revealed by James, Wharton and Dorothy Canfield. The sequence of chapters is largely organized on a chronological basis: before 1914, the 20s, 30s and 40s, the post–World War II scene and the recent decades. But within this obvious distribution, Méral stresses a number of aspects of the city that drew the attention of American literary creators: aristocracy, revolution, bohemia on the one hand; politics, geography, literary and aesthetic movements on the other. The study of the period since 1960 makes plain a crumbling away of a once-romantic image in the eyes of permanent or temporary American expatriates, bringing Méral to the conclusion that, to coin a phrase, "Paris is not what it used to be" in the eyes of these men and women who keep flocking into a city they never relate to in exactly the same way as its natives do; this fact may well explain the disappointment of such who come over in a quest for the exotic and have trouble finding it in a city that follows —or creates—the trends of its time more than it conforms to the preset image travelers bring along with them. Paris may no longer be "a feast," as Hemingway could once put it, but Méral cannot foresee the time when the influence of Paris will decline in American literature, even though he conversely does not believe it can soon feed again a significant major work of American literature.

Portions or tangential developments of this important book have appeared in two articles by Méral: "Edith Wharton, Dorothy Canfield, John Dos Passos et la présence américaine dans le Paris de la Grande Guerre" (*Caliban*, no. 19:73–82) and "L'Aventure policière dans le Paris des écrivains américains, 1880–1914" (*EA* 37:4).

The other piece that covers far too much ground to be conveniently integrated to one of the following sections is Pierre Deflaux's synthesis on military discourse in American literature: "De l'inégalitarisme militaire dans le discours littéraire" (*All Men Are Created Equal*, Aix: Université de Provence, pp. 83–102).

e. **18th Century.** Jean Béranger, whose work on early, colonial and revolutionary America is already well known among *ALS* readers, has added two articles to his important body of research: "St John de Crévecoeur à New York en 1779–1789" (*Annales de Normandie*, 33: 161–73) and "Les Souvenirs de Saint-John de Crévecoeur sur Mme d'Houdetot" (*DHS* 14[1982]:161–73).

Also noteworthy this year is Bernard Vincent's editorial work on Thomas Paine. Curiously, concerning a "citizen of France, the United States and the world," there was no longer a French version of *Common Sense* available, and the preceding translations, going back to the 1800s and early 1900s, left much to be desired. The bilingual edition (on facing pages) prepared by Vincent ("Thomas Paine, *Le Sens Commun*," Paris: Aubier, 220 pages) combines a well-written introduction with an excellent translation—minus a couple of local flaws—and a convenient critical apparatus.

f. **19th Century.** Be the American dismay at the French passion for Edgar Allan Poe what it may, the work goes on; as an occasional foray, as in the case of André Poncet ("Le Voyage Initiatique du Héros d'Edgar Poe dans les *Aventures d'Arthur Gordon Pym*," S.F. Fantastique," *Métaphores* 7[Nice]:83–101) and Joël Shapiro ("'The Tell-Tale Heart': une parodie de Platon," *Théorie-Littérature-Enseignement*, no. 2 [1982], St-Denis: Presses et publications de l'Université de Paris VIII) or as an addition to the lifelong work of Claude Richard. I had forgotten last year to mention two excellent articles of his: "Edgar A. Poe et l'esthétique du double" (*Prévue* no. 19 [Montpellier, Janvier 1982]:60–71) examines the relationship entertained by the real and the specular double and concludes that for Poe the question of the double poses that of the madness of the artist himself; the title of the other article speaks for itself: "Destin, Design,

Dasein: Lacan, Derrida and 'The Purloined Letter'" (*IowaR*, 12 [1981]:1–11). It humorously begins: "For the second time in the rich history of Franco-American misunderstanding, Edgar Allan Poe is becoming, in France, one of the most important American writers." Needless to say, Lacan's seminar on "The Purloined Letter" and Derrida's *La Carte Postale* loom large on Richard's critical horizon. The latter also brought out this year a French edition of Poe's prefaces, with notes and an introduction, in his own translation (Edgar A. Poe, *Préfaces et Marginalia*, Aix-en-Provence: Alinéa).

If Richard's name is known as that of one of the world's best Poe specialists, Roger Asselineau's is particularly reputed for his Whitman scholarship. It will therefore come as no surprise that it should be attached to a thematic study ("Nationalism vs. Internationalism in *Leaves of Grass*") in James Woodress's collection of essays: *Critical Studies on Walt Whitman* (Hall, pp. 320–29).

But there is also, this year, a special issue of *DeltaES* (no. 16) dedicated to Walt Whitman; this was prepared by Régis Durand, who introduces the collection himself with a poem ("WW:Veduta," pp. 1–2) inspired by the American bard and contributes his own article, "Whitman, le rythme, le sujet de l'écriture" (pp. 63–78) in which, following several Lacanian thinkers but also feeding on the work of Henri Meschonnic, he argues that the Whitmanian "yawp" must be considered as "effusion," meaning, in context, that the "voice" of the poet is not so much a matter of pouring forth, following the taking in, as it is the device by which a place of passage between world and subject is created allowing, among other things, true communication between the self and the other. The second French contribution in a collection laudably including critics of very diverse national origins is that of Jacques Darras: "La langue du mythe" (pp. 39–52); his essay combines an exploration of the conditions under which the Whitmanian subject is born with an attempt at accounting for the relationships entertained by the same subject to the spatial and mythical environment.

Apparently, following the excitement generated last year by the defense of Philippe Jaworski's uncommonly brilliant "thèse d'Etat" on Herman Melville—one hopes it will soon be published and reviewed here—few French scholars have felt inclined to work on this master for the nonce. However, Patricia Bleu wrote " 'Benito Cereno' ou le fantôme de la subversion" in *Le Voyage Austral* (Presses Universitaires de Grenoble) and C. Richard, paying homage to the un-published work of Jaworski throughout his poetic and deconstruc-tionist reflexions on the letter and the celebrated 'whiteness of the whale,' demonstrates that the so-called "irrelevant" chapters in *Moby-Dick* are essential to an understanding of the novel, inasmuch as they literally program or enunciate the economy of Melville's writing in this text ("La lettre blanche de la baleine," *Ex*, Aix-en-Provence, no. 2:56–61).

Monique Pruvot's " 'L'Imposture' de Hawthorne dans 'The Pro-phetic Pictures' " (in *La Nouvelle de Langue Anglaise, visions cri-tiques*, Paris: Publications de la Sorbonne-Nouvelle) is, similarly, the only noteworthy article written on Hawthorne, bearing indirect witness to the relative and no doubt temporary dearth of 19th-century studies this year, in spite of the interest generated in the end of that period by the 1982 Paris Conference of the European Association for American Studies. Wider in scope than an exclusively literary study, but including interesting pieces on American literature by European scholars, the volume regroups the proceedings of that conference as Marc Chénetier and Rob Kroes, eds., *Impressions of a Gilded Age: The American Fin de Siècle* (Amsterdam: EAAS se-ries). Its introduction (pp. 9–20) endeavors to outline the sense of epistemological and aesthetic transition conveyed by the authors represented.

Some of the papers given at the Conference were not included in the proceedings but found their way into a special issue of the (*RFEA*, no. 17, "American Writers: 1870–1910"), ed. John Blair of the University of Geneva. Such is the case for two pieces by French scholars: "From Tom Sawyer to Penrod: The Child in American Popular Literature, 1870–1910" by Bernard Macaigne (pp. 319–31) and "William Dean Howells: Critical Leader of the Realistic Move-ment in America" by Jean Rivière (pp. 249–56).

Yves Lemeunier's "Vision of Poverty and the Poor in [Horatio] Alger's Novels" (*All Men Are Created Equal*, pp. 121–136) and Maurice Gonnaud's "Dans le Sillage Puritain: les vicissitudes du progrès à l'époque transcendentaliste" (*RSAA*, no. 2–3:32–47) would wrap up this year's list of articles on the 19th century, were it not for the usual flurry of pieces concerned with Henry James.

James provides the starting point for Régis Durand's meditation on the familiar in Walter Abish's work (see section below on contemporary fiction); but the following five articles deal with specific texts of Henry James.

Georgiana Colville's "Verena ou la voix détournée: une lecture de *The Bostonians*" (*Ranam* 15:69–82) studies the effects achieved by the superposition of voices, pointing out, particularly, that Verena's last word, the word she could "soothe" the crowd with, remains unknown to the frustrated reader. She sees in James's narrative strategies an attempt at going beyond realism and points out that Verena's voice is seductive, what it says mattering less than the effect of that organ itself. Body and desire express more than their explicit utterances. Nancy Blake, in "Le livre de l'objet" (*Ranam* 15:83–100), explores the world of objects in *The Spoils of Poynton*, seeing them as fetishes, explaining their independence and significance, pointing out the reasons for James's attempt to "say the object" and concludes on the status of the object as "trash," "leftovers," fragments of a loss.

Fabienne Durand–Bogaert's "'A vision of appearances': du paraître au même dans *The Wings of the Dove*" (*Ranam* 15:101–10) broaches her theme with the help of Jean Baudrillard, insisting on the power of the symbolic in James's novel, over and against appearances and the real. In "Jungle du temps, jardin de mort: *The Beast in the Jungle*" (*Ranam* 15:111–26), Evelyne Labbe dwells on time, fate and tense. Finally, let me add that one article on Henry James was left out from last year's report, Patricia Bleu's "Fantastique et Parodie dans 'The Aspern Papers'" (Grenoble: *Actes du Colloque du CERLI*, 1982).

g. Drama. I mentioned last year the French publication of Geneviève Fabre's wonderful book on Black Theater. Her work is now available in English: *Drumbeats, Masks, and Metaphor: Contemporary Afro-American Theatre* (Harvard). A portion of her work has also been developed and focused for another book, appearing as "Le théâtre militant noir américain" in *Théâtre d'Intervention*, Philippe Ivernel, ed. (Lausanne: Editions de la Cité).

Two short pieces by Régis Durand ("Theatre in the thinking," *AmBR* 5, iii, and "Les machineries jubilatoires de la récitation," *Théâtre Public*, no. 51) and one by Danièle Pitavy–Souques ("L'Intruse: Stratégie du désir dans *Desire Under the Elms* et *A Streetcar Named Desire*," *Coup de Théâtre* [Publication du Centre de Recher-

ches sur les Arts Dramatiques Anglo-Saxons Contemporains], no. 3
["Femmes"]:17–27) complete this year's short dramatic offering. In
her article Pitavy-Souques analyzes the passage from need to desire
in these plays by O'Neill and Tennessee Williams.

h. **20th Century: Poetry.** A mere handful of articles dealing with
modern poetry appeared this year: the editor's "E.E. Cummings, ou
la révolutionnaire conservateur" (in Roger Asselineau, ed., *Nouveaux
Fragments du Puzzle Américain* [Paris: Presses de l'Université de
Paris-Sorbonne], pp. 62–74) stresses an apparent contradiction in
Cummings's work; Monique Lojkine–Morelec's "Poétique et Religion
dans l'Oeuvre de T. S. Eliot" (*Poétiques*, pp. 211–26) endeavors to
demonstrate that, far from being merely a theme, religion informs the
poetics of T. S. Eliot and constitutes indeed a singular theorization
of the "poiein," that religion is not only a doctrinal ensemble but also
a particular mythic structure seized by the imagination to solve its
internal conflicts. Of the three pieces by Jacqueline Ollier, one traces
William Carlos Williams's fascination with the figure of the unicorn,
as often seen and questioned at The Cloisters in 1956–57 ("Une
Licorne du Nouveau-Monde," *Corps Ecrit*, no. 6:181–18); the second
deals with the overall "poetical dynamics" of the poet ("La dynami-
que poétique de William Carlos Williams," *EA*, 36,1:45–55); and the
third is a more general article dealing with the relation between
poetry and the visual arts over the last decade ("La Relation entre
poésie et peinture aux Etats-Unis, 1970–1980: analyse de quelques
exemples," *Poétiques*, pp. 373–94). In her study of H.D.'s *End to
Torment* ("End to torment: Etude de l'interrogation dans la mémoire
de H.D.," *All Men Are Created Equal*, pp. 147–56), Jeanne Blanche-
nay–Kerblat traces the various interrogative modes underlying H.D.'s
analysis under Eric Heydt, triggered by Norman Holmes Pearson
to help document the case of Ezra Pound then locked up at St.
Elizabeth's.

It should finally be mentioned that a recently deceased poet has
been honored with an article in the most important French encyclopaedia (Joel Shapiro, "Archibald McLeish," Universalia 83, *Encyclopaedia Universalis*).

i. **Early 20th-Century Fiction.** Jeanine Brun–Rovet's study, "L'Education de Henry Adams: une autobiographie" (*RFEA*, no. 16:23–30)

was omitted from last year's report and deserves mention here. The American naturalists received a triple token of attention. Roger Asselineau wrote "Jack London as a Crypto-Transcendentalist" (in Jacqueline Tavernier–Courbin, ed., *Critical Studies on Jack London*, Boston: G. K. Hall, pp. 260–65), while André Poncet analyzed "Antiracist strategies in Frank Norris's fiction" (*Les Américains et les Autres*, Université de Provence [1982]:55–63), on the one hand, and "Functional Jeffersonianism in the Naturalistic Novel" (*All Men Are Created Equal*, pp. 137–46) on the other.

Authors of the twenties also received some attention. Patricia Bleu reexplored the ideological information contained in Dos Passos's use of biographies ("Les Biographies de *42nd Parallel*: miroir(s) d'une idéologie," Grenoble: Publications du Centre de Recherches d'études anglophone); Christiane Johnson contributed "Freedom, Contingency, and Ethics in 'The Adjuster'" to *The Short Stories of F. Scott Fitzgerald: New Approaches in Criticism*, ed. Jackson R. Bryer (Wis. 1982), while Simone Vauthier published "Perspectives are Precipices: Points of View in John Peale Bishop's *Act of Darkness*" (*Ranam* 15:195–211).

In the latter journal, there appeared also three pieces on Gertrude Stein that had found no room available in the issue of the *Revue Française d'Etudes Américaines* given over to the general theme of autobiography two years ago.

Noelle Batt, in "Le cas particulier de *L'Autobiographie d'Alice B. Toklas*" (*Ranam*, 15:127–34) studies Stein's sentence structures and concludes hypothetically that the *Autobiography* allowed her to return to communication, to get away from mere "autography." Nancy Blake's "*Everybody's Autobiography*: Identity and Absence" (pp. 135–46) explores "sameness" and "otherness" as the poles between which identity must discover itself, positing time and space as obstacles to the discovery of identity. She concludes that identity is something that makes us, willy-nilly, copies of others and points to writing as "on the contrary, an activity like playing and loving: an evidence of the absence of identity." Christian Susini's long and admirably written "Lithographie, de Stein" (pp. 147–68) is a highly idiosyncratic and enormously informed theoretical speculation on the word "lithography," the first half of which is taken as "litho-stone-Stein," with the second half obviously referring to the activity of writing. Inscribing the self is, in this perspective, a phenomenon that invites redoubling, homonymy and bio- (rather than mono-) graphy while remaining impossibly linked with the iconic. No summary could possibly do justice to this utterly brilliant piece.

Joel Shapiro also wrote a "Djuna Barnes" article for "Universalia 83" (*Encyclopaedia Universalis*).

j. **Faulkner.** If 1982 was a Faulkner year, so is 1983, and I must open a new section here to cope with an overwhelming production! Roger Asselineau joined forces with the better-known specialists on the southerner by contributing an article to the special issue of *L'Arc* devoted to him ("L'Humour Noir" [on *As I Lay Dying*] *L'Arc*, nos. 84–85, pp. 157–62). The other contributors all have authored or edited one or several books on Faulkner over the last few years: André Bleikasten ("Figures de la Mort," pp. 109–22), Jean Rouberol ("Le Conteur de Sud," pp. 13–21), Michel Gresset ("La métaphore du sujet," pp. 123–35, and "Et maintenant, que faire?", an unpublished piece he translated and presents here, pp. 136–40), François Pitavy ("Le Héros, la Guerre et le Rêve: l'Idéalisme faulknérien revisité," pp. 93–108) and Monique Pruvot ("Le Bestiaire," pp. 144–56). This beautiful, lavishly illustrated volume also contains articles by critics better known for their work in other directions: Marc Saporta sums up "La vie et l'oeuvre" by way of introduction (pp. 3–12) and enriches our knowledge of bears in "L'Ours amoureux" (pp. 72–80), adding a chronological panorama as conclusion (175–82); Giliane Morrell, whose book on "The Dynamics of Faulkner's imagination" is in progress, studies "La force du désir" (pp. 38–58); Jacques Cabau concentrates on "The Snopes" (pp. 163–67), while Jeanne–Marie Santraud examines "scarlet women" in the works ("La Femme Ecarlate," pp. 59–71) and Aurélien Ferenczi, a specialist in the movies, explores Faulkner's stay in the "salt mines of Hollywood" ("Dans les Mines de Sel, à Hollywood," pp. 168–74).

Pretty much the some team—for obvious reasons—contributed to *Faulkner and Idealism*: Michel Gresset, ("Introduction," pp. 3–14; "The God of Faulkner's Fiction," pp. 51–70), André Bleikasten ("For/Against an ideological reading of Faulkner's novels," pp. 27–50—reproduced from the French version printed in *Sud*, nos. 48–49, pp. 237–60), Monique Pruvot, ("Faulkner and the Voices of Orphism," pp. 127–43), F. Pitavy ("Idiocy and Idealism: A Reflection on the Faulknerian Idiot," pp. 97–111).

The same goes for the special issue of *Sud* ("Faulkner," nos. 48–49) in which, besides the Bleikasten article already mentioned, one can read articles by Henri Justin ("Keats, Poe, Faulkner," pp. 189–200), Monique Pruvot ("La légende dorée de Faulkner," pp. 167–88), F. Pitavy ("L'Irrémédiable et les voies de la transcendance: le temps dans *Requiem pour une Nonne*," pp. 145–66) and M. Gresset ("Avant-Propos," pp. 3–8, and "La France de Faulkner," pp. 262–92). This thick issue includes a translation by Gresset of an unpublished short story entitled "As I Lay Dying" presented by Jacques Pothier, three enlightening comparisons (one with Melville—Phillippe Jaworski, "Faulkner/Melville?," pp. 201–5—one with Hawthorne—Jean Normand, "Hawthorne et Faulkner," pp. 206–16—and one with Sherwood Anderson—Marion Brugière, "Les Oeuvres Croisées de Sherwood Anderson et de William Faulkner," pp. 217–36).

To this rather awesome collection of works, André Bleikasten has added "'Cet Affreux Goût d'Encre': Emma Bovary's Ghost in *Sanctuary*" (*William Faulkner: materials, studies, and criticism* [Tokyo], Vol. 5, pp. 1–25). One regrets not being able to analyze at greater length the work of this exceptional team of Faulknerians whose reputation in the United States keeps growing with each prolongation of their collective and individual activities. It is only to be wished that *ALS* readers interested in William Faulkner will see to it that the special issues of the French journals mentioned above are made widely accessible to their libraries and added to their personal collections.

k. **Contemporary Fiction.** Marc Chénetier authored two general articles this year: "Le roman américain contemporain" ("Memento de l'Association des Professeurs de langue vivante de l'Enseignement Public," *Les Langues Modernes*, 76, nos. 4–5:591–96) and "Le Groupe René Tadlov de recherche sur la littérature américaine contemporaine" (*MSH Informations*, Fondation de la Maison des Sciences de l'Homme de Paris, no. 43:28–31) where the most important French research group on contemporary American fiction is introduced.

Caliban (20, "Aspects du picaresque en Angleterre et aux Etats-Unis") contains four articles dealing with American literature. Two (Pierre–Yves Pétillon's "Picaro en démocratie," pp. 61–68, and Didier Vidal's "Mythe du picaro et mythe picaresque, pp. 107–14) are general or theoretical statements on the status of the picaresque in American culture and literature and feed their argument by sweeping through several periods in a most convincing manner. One (Marc Chénetier's "Picaresque et Picarisme: aspects de la fiction américaine des années 1970," pp. 83–106) examines the variations undergone by the original European concept on the American literary continent and focuses on Thomas McGuane, Thomas Glynn, Carol Smith and Tom Robbins. A fourth deals with Saul Bellow (see below).

Staying with writings of a general import for a moment, one must turn to the volume (edited by Maurice Couturier on *Representation and Performance in postmodern fiction* (Montpellier: DeltaES); the collection gathers some of the papers given at an international conference in Nice in 1982. Besides papers by Tony Tanner, William Gass, Ihab Hassan, Thomas LeClair, and an extraordinary combination paper/text of fiction by Stanley Elkin, it includes texts by other European and American critics and four French contributions: Maurice Couturier's interview with Michel Butor (pp. 193–207), Régis Durand's "The Disposition of the Familiar" (pp. 73–84), which discusses Walter Abish's practice of the familiar in the light of Henry James, Couturier's own "Presentation of the topic" (pp. 3–8), and Claude Richard's paper on causality (see the first section of this report) taking his examples from John Barth's "Two Meditations."

Françoise Sammarcelli published her own piece on Barth ("L'Intertextualité dans l'Oeuvre de John Barth") in *Théorie-Littérature-Enseignement*, drawing particular attention to *Letters*.

Contemporary authors were covered very unevenly this year. A number of them were the object of only one article: Salinger (Raphaelle Costa de Beauregard's "Ecrivain et marginalité: le roman de Salinger, *The Catcher in the Rye*," *La Marginalité dans la Littérature et la Pensée Anglaises* [Actes du Centre Aixois de Recherches Anglaises]) Aix: Université de Provence), and William Styron (Elizabeth Boulot's, "*Les Confessions de Nat Turner* ou les ambiguités du je," *L'Autre dans la Sensibilité Anglo-Saxonne*, Reims: Presses Universitaires de Reims), both articles concerning books of mainstream repute; as far as more experimental writers are concerned, the short list includes Pynchon (C. Richard's "Oedipa Regina" in *Dires*), Joan Didion, seen as a "witness to the crisis of values in California" (Elizabeth Béranger's "Joan Didion, journaliste et romancière, témoin de la crise des valeurs en Californie" in "Civilisations et Littératures de l'Amérique du Nord," *Le Facteur Religieux en Amérique du Nord*, no. 4 and ["Religion et Engagement: Intellectuels et Militants au Canada et aux Etats-Unis," Bordeaux: Maison des Sciences de l'Homme d'Aquitaine], pp. 135–52), Walker Percy, through the interview he gave to Peggy Castex ("An Interview with Walker Percy") for *Nouveaux Fragments du Puzzle Américain*, and Hawkes (in M. Chénetier's essay: "The Pen & the Skin: Inscription and Cryptography in John Hawkes's *Second Skin*," *RCF*, 3,iii: 167–77).

Others received somewhat more intensive coverage. Saul Bellow, for example, was the object of two studies; one from the point of view of picaresque literature (Roger Decap, "Picaresque et Nouveau Roman: *The Adventures of Augie March*," *Caliban*, 20:69–82) and another from that of intellectual commitment (Elyette Andouard–Labarthe, "Intellectuels et Engagement dans *The Dean's December*," *Le Facteur Religieux en Amérique du Nord*, no. 4:107–34). Special issues of *DeltaES* on Bellow and on Ellison are in preparation. Danièle Pitavy–Souques, whose "thèse d'Etat" on Eudora Welty was defended in 1982, contributed two articles on her favorite authoress: "Watchers and Watching: Point of View in Welty's 'June Recital'" (*SoR*, 19,3:483–509); and "Optique, Erotique: 'A Memory', de Eudora Welty" in a new journal specializing in the short story (*Cahiers de la Nouvelle*, no. 2, Presses de l'Université d'Angers).

A special issue of *DeltaES*, edited by Maurice Couturier (no. 17, "Vladimir Nabokov") is dedicated to an author the French insist should be considered American in spite of the qualms of some critics in the United States. In it, along with articles by Americans, appear Valerie Burling's study of the tricks played on and with visual perception, "Nabokov et le trompe-l'-oeil" (pp. 11–22); a delightful essay on the games Nabokov plays with names in *Ada* (J.L. Chevalier, "Le Jeu de l'Oncle—Divertimento: à propos d'un personnage d'*Ada*, pp. 75–86) and two very sophisticated analyses of the same novel: Pierre Gault, indulging in fertile spoonerism and relying on stylistic and linguistic constructs in tracking down the syntactic structure of desire ("Ethos et nar(r)atos. Ada et ses cousines. Quête d'une syntaxe du désir," pp. 87–101) and editor Couturier's concluding essay that describes *Ada* as a "treatise on poetic exchange" ("*Ada*, traité de l'échange poétique," pp. 101–28).

In his book *Richard Brautigan* (Methuen) Marc Chénetier attempts to reshape the image of one eternally described and decried as a faddish writer for the hippie youth of the 60s and 70s, demonstrating in six brief chapters that Brautigan's technique is infinitely more sophisticated than has been so far granted. Straying far and wide from the thematic approaches that have so far held currency concerning this author, he insists on formal and stylistic features, calls on genre theory and draws attention to Brautigan's peculiar handling of time, space, surfaces and textures (see also chapter 15, 7b. above).

l. **Ethnic Literature.** *Le Facteur Ethnique aux Etats-Unis et au Canada,* jointly edited by Monique Lecomte and Claudine Thomas (Lille: Université de Lille III [Collection UL3]) combines a series of historical, sociological and cultural articles with a number of literary studies. French contributors include Marcienne Rocard ("Ambiguité ethnique du chicano: à la recherche d'un discours adéquat"), Claude Julien ("Deux aspects de l'ethnicité dans le roman: *Homebase* de Shawn Wong et *Soul Catcher* de Frank Herbert") and Daniel Royot ("Problématique de l'humour ethnique: quelques aspects"). The volume poses the question of knowing whether the "ethnic revival of the 70s may be just another stage in the process of self-definition which immigrant societies seem forever condemned to undergo" and whether the concept of "ethnicity" itself might not be "little more than an 'efficient fiction.'"

Jean Cazemajou and Jean–Pierre Martin's *La Crise du Melting-Pot: Ethnicité et Identité aux Etats-Unis de Kennedy à Reagan* (Paris: Aubier), even though predominantly animated by political and cultural concerns has a chapter (IV) on the bearing ethnicity and literature mutually have on each other: "Ethnicité et littérature: L'étranger *intra muros* vu par les siens" (pp. 99–122).

m. **Science Fiction and the Fantastic.** The "Actes du 1er colloque international sur la science-fiction de Nice" (April 21–23, 1983) will occupy a whole issue of *Métaphore* (nos. 9–10, March 1984) to which we shall return in due time. Suffice it for now to mention four of John Dean's articles on the subject: "'If This Be Magic, Let It Be an Art Lawful As Eating': Contemporary American Fiction of the Occult" (*Fantasy Commentator* 5,ii [New York]: Winter 1983–84), "Magic and Mystery in the Fiction of Ursula K. Le Guin," (*Social Sciences*

Information [Paris], 23,1), "Fresh Inspections of the Marvelous: Recent Works in Science Fiction and Fantasy Scholarship" (*Fantasy Commentator*, 5,iii: Summer 1983) and "The Use of Stars in the Literature of Science-Fiction and Fantasy" (*Métaphores* no. 8).

This section should be somewhat more substantial next year as a couple of books on the subject are being printed at the moment of writing.

Université d'Orléans

ii. German Contributions

Rolf Meyn

1983 was a year of collective endeavors. Four publications, which will be dealt with below, contain almost half of the articles written by German Americanists. Bi-or tri-national explorations of genres, motifs and themes remained in vogue, as well as book-length overviews embracing several decades of American literature. Interest in ethnic literature is still increasing, while colonial literature seems to have reached a nadir in German scholarship.

a. Literary Criticism and Theory: Comparative Studies. In 1983, comparative studies increased, while theoretical problems were mostly tackled within the framework of discussions of literary periods or specific works. Among comparative studies, *American-German Literary Interrelations in the Nineteenth Century*, edited by Christoph Wecker (München: Wilhelm Fink) clearly stands out. In this collection of essays by five well-known German scholars, a wide range of interrelations comes under close scrutiny. Martin Christadler in his "German and American Romanticism" (pp. 9–26) contradicts those American critics who are aware of the American Transcendentalists' indebtedness to German Idealism and Romanticism, but claim that Emerson and his contemporaries were looking to Germany only for corroboration of their faith. Goethe, Christadler holds, had a deep impact on Emerson, Thoreau, Fuller and Melville not only because his ideas were congenial, but because he provided "a challenge to their moral, aesthetic and metaphysical assumptions."

Hans–Joachim Lang in "Hawthorne, Melville, and the German Nineteenth Century" (pp. 27–51) agrees largely with Henry A. Poch-

man, who in his monumental study *German Culture in America* found
that the influence of German literature on Hawthorne was relatively
small. Yet there is one exception: Hawthorne was definitely influenced by the Faust legend, as his story "The Birthmark" proves.
Herman Melville is a different case. Lang takes over Pochman's
thesis that Kant "furnished Melville with the backbone upon which
to build his anatomy of despair." A much stronger influence, however, was exerted by Goethe. Both Goethe's exposition of the demonic
and his *bildungsroman Wilhelm Meister*, Lang speculates, may have
contributed to the genesis of *Moby-Dick*. As for Hawthorne's and
Melville's reception in Germany, Lang comes up with some cogent
observations. The author of *Typee* and *Omoo* was of some influence
on German writers, e.g., Friedrich Gerstäcker, his translator. In contrast to English and American audiences, Hawthorne's novels did not
impress a large German one, though some of them were translated
very soon after their publication. Lang attributes this to the fact that
the Germans expected everything else from America, but not "authors
of melancholy temper and intricate symbolism."

These qualities, argues Gerhard Hoffmann in his "Edgar Allan
Poe and German Literature" (pp. 52–104), by far the longest essay
in this collection, Poe found in German Romantic literature, though
he vehemently denied the influence of E. T. A. Hoffmann, Tieck,
Arnim and Schlegel on his writing. Hoffmann, however, is careful
with regard to pointing to specific sources. Literary influences rarely
amount to a shaping effect on a writer's weltanschauung. What happens more often is that a mere affinity between writers provides con-
firmation and sanction for the younger author. There can be no doubt
that German Romanticism had a lasting impact on Poe, yet at the
same time his literary borrowings from other writers, poets and
philosophers were eclectic and included English, French and other
sources. The German Romantic writers, especially E. T. A. Hoffmann,
played with "various kinds of mediation between the fantastic and
the 'real.'" This certainly stimulated Poe to do the same, but he preferred the special device of the first-person narrator who comes from
the outside and is drawn into the fantastic situation. In Europe, Poe
became the revered master for the French symbolists and the English
detective novel writers. In 19th-Century Germany, however, Poe's
influence remained scanty, though Friedrich Spielhagen, his first
translator, considered him the greatest American poet. This situation

changed dramatically at the turn of the century, when a shift towards the fantastic led to a revival of interest in E. T. A. Hoffmann and a rediscovery of Poe, whose complete works were translated after 1900. It comes as no surprise, then, that Hoffmann's essay extends far beyond the 19th century into present times, ranging from German expressionist writers like Meyrink and Kubin to Jünger, Kafka and even the postmodernist Arno Schmidt, in all of whom Hoffman senses, if not a direct influence, then at least an affinity.

In contrast to Hoffmann's emphasis on congeniality and affinity, Helmut Grandel in "Henry James and Germany" (pp. 105–23) sticks to blunt facts. James was not too impressed by the Germany he became acquainted with in his early years. He loved the countryside, but found middle-class Germans to be "ugly" and "tasteless." His animosity towards the young German "Reich" and its aggressive nationalism can clearly be detected in some character portraits of his earlier works. But there are also exceptions. Madame Blumenthal in his tale "Eugene Pickering" is a temptress and a charming woman, bearing a close similarity with his famous Madame de Vionnet. As for German literature, James was deeply interested in Goethe, whom he viewed with a mixture of admiration and reservation. Conversely, the Germans had an equally biased attitude toward James. Whereas Bret Harte was praised as a realistic writer whose compassion and optimism were regarded as truly American qualities, James was blamed for his expatriation that was criticized as a flight from American reality. James's stylistic brilliance was generally acclaimed, yet his treatment of European scenery was thought to be too narrowly restricted to the traditional route of the Grand Tour. The fact that most German critics showed some hostility towards James's female characters, Grandel attributes to the conventional and traditional society that had "no understanding for citizens of a freer society." James's reception only changed in the 1920s and 30s, when he was rediscovered by intellectual circles "who were united by their hostility toward modern mass society."

Two American poets who were virtually unknown in 19th-century Germany are dealt with in Hans Galinsky's essay "Northern and Southern Aspects of Nineteenth Century American-German Interrelations: Dickinson and Lanier" (pp. 124–65). According to Galinsky, Dickinson's contact with Germany began with a children's travel book, the traces of which he detects even in some of her later poetry.

Longfellow, Byron, the Brownings, and of course the Transcendentalists provided more book-mediated information about Germany.
Then, there were also her German lessons. Between 1850 and 1864
Dickinson discovered three German literary figures—Schiller, Thomas
à Kempis, and Heine. Goethe's *Faust* was also available in the family
library. In addition to this book-mediated knowledge of Germany,
Galinsky also mentions German music, science, mineralogy, astronomy and philosophy. How far these various contacts materialized in
Dickinson's poetry, he doesn't answer. Only two poems containing
Alpine and Rhine scenery are analyzed at some length. In regard to
Sidney Lanier, Galinsky is on far safer grounds. Carlyle was the
southern writer's mediator, but after 1870 he set out to discover more
German culture on his own. The music of Richard Wagner, the research of the physicist Helmholtz and the art of Novalis had definitely an effect on Lanier's only novel *Tiger-Lilies* (1867). While
Dickinson's reputation in Germany has steadily increased, Lanier's
star has risen much more slowly. This, for Galinsky is not only a
result of Dickinson's superior poetic qualities, but also of an unjusti-
fied neglect of the southerner's achievements, which only gradually
have been recognized by a few German scholars.

On the whole, *American-German Interrelations in the Nineteenth
Century*, with its fine balance between well-founded speculations
and painstaking research, should soon become indispensable for German and American scholars working in this field of comparative
literature. Here another little monograph ought to be mentioned.
Dietlinde Giloi's *Short Story und Kurzgeschichte. Ein Vergleich
Hemingways mit deutschen Autoren nach 1945* (Tübingen: Stauf-
fenburg) begins with a comparison of the German genre "Kurzgeschichte" with its American equivalent short story. In her next step,
Giloi discusses the possible influence of Hemingway on German
postwar authors such as Wolfgang Borchert, Wolfdietrich Schnurre
and Heinz Piontek. The author succeeds in evading the trap of over-
interpretation. Yet her study demonstrates how lasting and pervasive Hemingway's impact on the German postwar generation of
writers was.

Problems of genre are also approached in Hiltrud Gnügs comparative study *Der Utopische Roman* (München: Artemis). The book
covers the development of utopian literature from Plato and Morus
to the 20th-century dysotopias of Samyatin, Huxley and Orwell.

Written in a clear, condensed style, it offers an instructive overview of the main works in this genre. Edward Bellamy's *Looking Backward: 2000–1887* is treated, together with William Morris's *News From Nowhere* and H. G. Wells's *The Time Machine* and *When the Sleeper Wakes* in a chapter called "Utopias of Time in the Second Half of the Nineteenth Century." Gnüg sees in Bellamy the influence of French utopian writers like Mercier and Cabet at work, though Bellamy remains more abstract than the latter. All three authors idealize planning, order and centralization, they also share a love of the colossal. Bellamy, however, leaves more room for self-determination, in spite of his concept of an industrial army. Gnüg is impressed by Bellamy's view of the woman's position in a future America. She is economically independent, though her work is less hard and less time consuming. Mutual respect and love are now the sole basis for marriage.

Problems of genre and subgenre are also addressed in Gerhard Hoffmann's voluminous essay "Social Criticism and the Deformation of Man: Satire, the Grotesque and Comic Nihilism in the Modern and Postmodern American Novel" (*Amst* 28:141–203). Social Criticism, argues Hoffmann, "is not only content-oriented in the sense of criticizing partial deficiencies in social life, but it reflects comprehensive attitudes towards the world which can be systematized as meaning models." Satire, the grotesque and the comic are such models, designating both human attitudes and literary categories, all of them concerned with the relation between the individual and society and having a classifying principle in the form of an in-built opposition of harmony and disharmony. Hoffmann's real subject is the postmodern American novel, yet in order to explain its epistemological scepticism and ethnic insecurity, he goes far back into literary and social history. The wavering between realism and romanticism, between optimism and pessimism in view of a rapidly changing world led to a blending of the comic and the satiric in Mark Twain's later works. Yet it was Edith Wharton who established modern satire in the American novel, and Sinclair Lewis who radicalized it. Dos Passos, Faulkner and West turned satire into a grotesque by exposing the deformation of man without being able to set an ideal against it. After World War II, American novelists increasingly felt a loss of unity regarding social, economic and cultural spheres. Value standpoints, e.g., a clear-cut differentiation between saneness and mad-

ness, positive and negative values, disintegrated, so that the borderline between the real and the fantastic ceased to exist. For Hoffman,
satire, the grotesque and comic nihilism existed beside each other,
but also developed out of each other. Thus, McCarthy, Bellow, Mailer,
Ellison, Reed and Vonnegut provide a background against which
Barth, Barthelme, Brautigan, Hawkes, Heller, Kosinski, Pynchon
and West are discussed as writers who prefer the grotesque and its
final stage, comic nihilism.

Literary theory without connection to any specific work is the
theme of Winfried Fluck's essay "Literature as Symbolic Action
(*Amst* 28:361–71). Fluck finds Kenneth Burke's concept of literature as symbolic action extremely helpful "for a more precise understanding of some of the uses and functions of literary texts within
culture." Burke, he reminds us, used the term "situation" as a "pattern of experience" explaining our social structure. In this respect, the
social context of a literary text can be said to be a response to cul-
turally problematic situations. This, of course, does not answer the
question to what extent a literary text can serve as a source of cultural
and literary insight. The final evaluation has to rest on a critical but
balanced view of the symbolic materials of a culture.

b. **Literary History.**   Of the 1983 contributions in Germany, three
books deserve presentation. Franz Link's *Geschichte der Amerikanischen Erzählkunst 1900–1950* (Stuttgart: Kohlhammer) is a sequel
to his *Geschichte der Amerikanischen Erzählkunst im 19. Jahrhun-
dert* (1980). Link's selective literary history begins with a chapter
called "Regional Realism," devoted to the main novels of Edith
Wharton, Willa Cather and Ellen Glasgow. Then follows a treatment of such representative Naturalists as Jack London, Theodore
Dreiser and Upton Sinclair. The "critical realists" of the 1920s, Sherwood Anderson, Sinclair Lewis, John Dos Passos and F. Scott Fitzgerald follow suit. The "Social Realism" of the 1930s is assessed on
the basis of writers like James T. Farrell, Richard Wright, Erskine
Caldwell and John Steinbeck. Henry Miller and Nathanael West are
discussed under the heading of "Surrealism." Ernest Hemingway,
whose literary achievement Link considers, together with that of
Faulkner, as the highlight of the period between 1900 and 1950,
enjoys the privilege of a special chapter. It is followed by one on the
"symbolic realists" William Faulkner, Robert Penn Warren, Kather-

ine Ann Porter, Eudora Welty and Carson McCullers. Thomas Wolfe, analyzed under the heading "Idea and Reality" and Thornton Wilder, the "neo-humanist," conclude the book. It is, and this is by no means meant to be disparaging, a very conventional literary history, restricted to writers whose reception both in the United States and in Germany has always been without doubt. Each writer and his most important novels are approached from both a socio-cultural viewpoint and in terms of literary innovations. Thus, a clear line is drawn from the realism of a William Dean Howells to a point around 1930, when a "new art of consciousness" came into being. Ultimately, Link concludes, American fiction in the first half of the 20th century can be described as a collective attempt to capture the fleeting moment of experience in ever more precise terms.

A shorter time span is covered in Dieter Meindl's monograph *Der Amerikanische Roman zwischen Naturalismus und Postmoderne 1930–1960* (München: Wilhelm Fink). Meindl's aim is, as he puts it in his summary, "to transcend the customary division of the American novel into pre-and post-Second World War types, the former marked by alienation and protest, the latter by accomodation and private search." This is done by delineating three stages in the evolution of the American novel between 1930 and 1960: 1) the naturalistic phase of social criticism in the Great Depression (Dos Passos, Steinbeck, Farrell), 2) its gradual supersession by an existential or modernistic strain (Faulkner, Wolfe, Miller), which 3) after the war resulted in the rise of the novel of identity (Trilling, Warren, Bellow, Mailer, Kerouac). Since the major novels of the 1930s for the most part employ the third person, whereas after the war the first-person novel dominates, Meindl begins his study with constructing a model of narrative discourse and its modes, i.e., scene, report, metaphor and comment. Attention is also paid to the essential function of the third-person and first-person narrator, the first expressing authority, the second authenticity. The authors and their novels under consideration are throughout the study subjected to the test of Meindl's model. This procedure, in combination with a thorough illumination of the political, ideological and cultural background as the ultimately shaping forces makes this book a stimulating and highly original contribution to the many attempts at pointing out lines of development from modernism to postmodernism in America. The monograph ends with a brief, but substantial vista of postmodernism, with John

Barth as its first important representative. Meindl contradicts Jerry
Bryant's thesis in his *The Open Decision* that process philosophy and
modern physics instigated postmodernist writers to discard traditional concepts of objectivity. Literature, Meindl holds, is a mode of
knowledge in its own right.

A kind of literary history devoted to ethnic literature is *Amerikanische Gettoliteratur. Zur Literatur ethnischer, marginaler und
unterdrückter Gruppen in Amerika* (Darmstadt: Wissenchaftliche
Buchgesellschaft), edited by Berndt Ostendorf. The ten contributing
scholars understand ghetto literature, as Ostendorf emphasizes in his
introduction, "in the widest sense: as city literature . . ., but also as
literature of a cultural and political consciousness and symbolic
worlds like Yiddishkeit, Black Consciousness, Atzlán or Puertor-
riquenidad, which originated in America as reactions to the politics
of ghettoization." Thus, they are able to cover the first immigrant
generation's refusal of assimilation, the compromises of the second
and the "New Ethnicity" of the third that returns to the wounds of
the first, thereby questioning the process of acculturation. The three
essays on Jewish and Black ghetto literature—Kurt Dittmar's
"Jüdische Gettoliteratur: Die Lower East Side, 1890–1924," Günter
H. Lenz's "Gettoerfahrung, Gettokultur, Gettoliteratur: Zur afroamerikanischen Literatur zwischen den Weltkriegen (1914–1945),"
and Klaus Ensslen's "Das Getto in der afroamerikanischen Literatur
nach 1945" take more than half of the book. This is not surprising,
since the literary productivity of these two ethnic groups surpasses
that of other immigrant groups by far. Dittmar (pp. 50–112) traces
Jewish ghetto literature from its beginnings to that point where it
ends in a Jewish-American literature. Historical, cultural and social
conditions are amply commented on in order to illustrate the factors
contributing to the birth of an ethnic literature that from about 1930
on became part of the national literature. In contrast to Dittmar, Lenz
(pp. 149–233) has more difficulties in demonstrating a linear development in black literature before 1945. Though he starts out from
an examination of black Harlem and the South Side of Chicago as
"paradigmatic Black communities," he has to admit that black literature presents too complicated a picture in order to be judged from a
clear-cut ghetto perspective alone. The "double consciousness" of
black intellectual authors such as James Weldon Johnson, Jean
Toomer, Walter White, Nella Larsen and Countee Cullen gave birth

to themes like the search for an African heritage, the passing from black to white society and vice versa and the historical dimension of black experience rooted in the "folk culture" of the South. Writers like Sterling Brown, Claude McKay and Langston Hughes described black community life in the ghettoes, yet they often saw them as places of cultural self-assertion instead of exploitation. It needed the Great Depression to change this view, and it was Richard Wright who in *Native Son*, by depicting the violence born out of racism and capitalism and its impact on a black man's psyche, opened a new access to the socio-cultural dynamics of the ghetto community. Klaus Ensslen (pp. 234–92) also considers Wright a trailblazer whose motif of the therapeutic function of hate for a new self-awareness was taken up by many later writers, among them Ann Petry and Chester Himes. Autobiography, from Wright to Sandra Young one of the most fruitful genres after 1945, always deals with various forms of violence, exerted by the white society and threatening Black existence, a theme that found unique expression in Ralph Ellison's *Invisible Man* (1952). Ensslen holds that leaving the ghetto, whether by the writers themselves, as in the case of Wright, Himes and Baldwin, or by their fictional counterparts, rarely offers a real alternative. Many exiled protagonists discover new forms of racism in Europe and return to the American ghettoes, convinced that violent repression is part of a "white" strategy all over the world. The years from 1964 to 1969 constitute a turning point in black literature. The growing awareness that the ghetto will never be abolished, given the system of a "dominant" society, results in a new political radicalism that insists on black experience as something separate from mainstream culture in America. This is most obvious in Afro-American poetry, in which the ghetto's idiom forms "a center of gravitation."

Dieter Herms in his essay "Die Literatur des Chicano Movement: Identitätssuche, Kulturkonflikt und Protest" (pp. 293–322) comes to similar conclusions. He defines "Chicanismo" as "a new identity and a political program," which developed in the wake of civil rights movements and student rebellions in the 1960s among US citizens of Mexican origin. Ideological center is the mythic region of "Aztlán," the southwest of the United States, where supposedly the Aztecs lived. The core of radical identity is the "Mestizo," product of an interbreed between Indians and their Spanish conquerors. Herms sees a cultural nationalism at work, in the course of which mythic figures like Quetzalcoatl and La Virgen de Guadalupe were joined by folk heroes like Emiliano Zapata and Pancho Villa and, finally, by new charismatic leaders of various political activities, e.g., César Chavez and "Corky" Gonzales. All these divergent figures nevertheless illustrate the heterogeneity of this movement that includes the search for a mythic center, the adaptation of forms of popular culture rooted in Mexican folk culture and the experience of an exploited class of immigrants. For all of them, the term "ghetto" denotes either "city of destruction" or "barrio," an idealized place of security and aspiration like the mythic region "Aztlán." It is instructive to compare Herms's findings with those of Wolfgang Binder in his paper "Die Nordwanderung der Puertoricaner und ihre Literatur" (pp. 323–55). Puerto Rican literature, according to Binder, is still in its initial stage. Virtually all of its authors write in English. Spanish words and phrases, however, are interwoven in many texts. Autobiographies and autobiographical novels dominate. Poetry, plays and short stories, rare as they are, often deal with Puerto Rico as an idyll of a dreamy rural world of security, seen from the harsh reality of New York slums. Race relations in America are often experienced as a cruel shock to Puerto Rican newcomers to the "mainland," since many of them are henceforth Blacks. Piri Thomas's novel *Down These Mean Streets* (1967) serves as a case in point. Puerto Rican literature, Binder summarizes, has produced so far no work dealing positively with the American success myth.

The last essay aiming at a comprehensive view is Heinz Ickstadt's "Exploring the Abyss: Die Entdeckung des sozialen Untergrunds in der amerikanischen Fiktion des späten 19. Jahrhunderts" (pp. 27–49), which is concerned with the discovery of social injustice in American literature at the turn of the century. Ickstadt notices four different perspectives. The first is the "touristic-journalistic" one. The world of poverty is seen through the eyes of a sympathetic observer, as in Howells's *A Hazard of New Fortunes* or in London's *People of the Abyss*. The second is the picturesque as sentimentalizing transfiguration of a hard and simple life, as in Alice Hegan Rice's *Mrs. Wiggs of the Cabbage Patch*. This idealization of intact ghetto communities is turned around in a third perspective, in which slum conditions are part of a Darwinian struggle for survival. This naturalistic melodrama occasionally develops into a fourth perspective emphasizing human depravity and moral decay, as in Norris's *McTeague*.

All these four views contribute to the literature of the Progressive Era. As for the ghetto theme, Ickstadt observes in the novels of this period, notably in Upton Sinclair's *The Jungle*, the destruction of ethnic identity in order to demonstrate the need for assimilation.

The remaining three essays are much shorter and mainly devoted to case studies. Gudrun Birnbaum in her "Eine Stimme aus dem slowakischen Stahlarbeiter-Getto in Pennsylvanien: Thomas Bell" (pp. 123–48) tries to resurrect a writer who in the 1930s and 40s was labeled as "radical" or "proletarian." In her opinion, Bell is first and foremost an ethnic writer, the chronicler of three generations of Slovakian steel workers. W. Chojnacki in "Gettoliteratur der polnischen ethnischen Gruppe in den USA in den Jahren 1870–1939" (pp. 113–22) points out that Polish immigrants became more ardent readers than those who had stayed at home. Mass literature, e.g., prayer books, almanacs and sensational novels, prevented illiteracy and paved the way for the reception of "higher" literature, which until 1939 predominantly appeared in Polish translations. Karin Meissenburg in "Chinesisch amerikanische Literatur: Eine Fallstudie anhand zweier Autobiographien" (pp. 356–80) focuses on books by two Chinese-American woman writers, Jade Snow Wong's *Fifth Chinese Daughter* (1950) and Maxine Hong Kingston's *The Woman Warrior* (1976). In Meissenburg's view, Wong's autobiography is an attempt to contribute to an understanding of the Chinese way of life in Chinatown. Positive elements of "model minorities" are stressed, yet the social structures of the ghetto are touched upon only marginally. This is also the case in Kingston's *The Woman Warrior*, but in contrast to Wong Kingston sees herself "as avenger of the injustices and difficulties the Chinese group, especially the women, were subjected to."

c. Colonial and 19th-Century Literature. Colonial literature is, as has been mentioned before, hardly represented in recent German scholarship. An interesting contribution, combining the focus on the Colonial period with the current interest in the interplay of literature and history, is Hans Galinsky's *Amerikanisches Geschichtsbewußtsein im Dichtwerk. Kolonialzeit als fortwirkendes Thema in der amerikanischen Literatur des 20. Jahrhunderts* (Frankfurt: Diesterweg). The book provides models of interpretation for German students. Four genres of 20th-century writing, each dealing with a segment of early American history, are discussed. William Carlos Williams's essay "The Destruction of Tenochtitlan" (1925), Carl Sandburg's prose poem "Cool Tombs" (1916), Langston Hughes's "The Negro Speaks of Rivers" (1921), Arthur Miller's "The Crucible" (1953) and John Barth's *The Sot-Weed Factor* (1960) are interpreted as variants of an American consciousness of history. A special concern of Galinsky is to show overlapping themes in these different texts, e.g., hunger for gold and land, slavery, religion, sexuality and pastoral idylls.

19th-century literature has decidedly met with larger interest than in years before, partly due to an *Amerikastudien* collection of essays devoted to Transcendentalism and the literature of the Jacksonian era. Roland Hagenbüchle in his "Spontaneity and Form: Unresolved Tensions in American Transcendentalism" (*Amst* 28:11–22) points to the "uneasy status of form" that all transcendentalists were aware of. Hagenbüchle notices an opposition between immediate experience and its representation in language, between metaphor and metonymy in most of their writings. To overcome this juxtaposition, Emerson, Thoreau and Alcott resort to a strategy that combines organicism with elements of syncretism. This, however, leads to a collapse of categorical boundaries: Nature and Spirit, language and life, word and object become intertwined. The controlling metaphor of the OverSoul ultimately becomes a mask, because fragmentation dominates. This line of argument is carried further in Dieter Schulz's "Emerson's Visionary Moments: The Disintegration of the Sublime" (pp. 23–32), which posits the thesis that Emerson "reduces the status of the senses." The soul, thrown back upon itself, must supply the necessary power to generate the vision. Yet the revelatory vision is discontinuous with experience. Ultimately, Schulz claims, Emerson anticipated "the notion of empty transcendence," in other words, "he was on the verge of discovering the void."

Herwig Friedl in his paper "Mysticism and Thinking in Ralph Waldo Emerson" (pp. 33–46) deals with a contradiction Emerson calls "the double consciousness," i.e., "the mystically gained assurance of identity with Being and the seeming aimlessness in a world of shifting values." The task of the philosopher, of "Man Thinking," is to come to grips with the double consciousness. The moment of mystical enrapture is the starting point in the process of thinking, which is always open-ended. This view is somewhat contradicted by Ulrich Horstman's essay "The Whispering Sceptic: Metaphysical

Enclaves in American Transcendentalism" (pp. 47–57). Emerson's
subjugation of matter to mind, Horstman argues, supported the exploitation of nature by man and entered an alliance with 19th-century
scientific rationality. At the same time, he avoided brute facts of life
and was afraid of a meaningless universe. Thoreau is a different case.
He did not revert to the Transcendental OverSoul and moved away
from Emerson's anthropocentrism to nature, to the rediscovery of
plain facts, thereby becoming an early advocate of modern ecological consciousness. Horstmann's harsh attitude toward Emerson is
not shared by Olaf Hansen, whose "Truth-The Irresistible Metaphor: Emerson's Concepts of History, Nature and Language" (pp.
59–74) provides the necessary corrective to the picture of an Emerson who was hardly able to hide scepticism, fear of the void and his
awareness of the 19th-century spiritual crisis under the gusto of
declarative rhetoric. Emerson, Hansen holds, tried to answer the old
question of how "to conceive of secular history without giving up
the idea of the divine." Emerson's dilemma was rooted in a philosophy of history that tried to uphold the idea of the messianic in an
unfolding realm of the profane. As a philosopher, his refusal to be
forced either into a system of natural philosophy or into a philosophy
of identity and his conscious use of the metaphor as a medium of
cognition, made him the spiritual kin of Kierkegaard, Benjamin and
Nietzsche. Like Horstmann, Hansen discovers in Emerson's concept
of Nature "a kind of cosmic scepticism." Emerson accepted illusion,
so that meaning and truth became possible as metaphors. At the
same time, he demanded active involvement with the world of natural
phenomena. In this respect, Hansen concludes, Emerson's Transcendentalism was already close to Peirce's pragmatism.

While the essays introduced so far deal mainly with philosophical
implications, Manfred Pütz in his "Emerson and Andrew Jackson:
An Antagonism and Its Alleged Reasons" (pp. 75–83) discusses
Emerson as a political writer. Pütz's thesis is that Emerson's idealism
usually starts out from "positive abstract preconceptions to empirical
embodiments of such preconceptions, establishing a philosophical
hierarchy of decreasing perfection." Yet in Emerson's political thinking this is turned around. Negative abstractions are now applied to
actual politics, as his opinion on Andrew Jackson proves. For Pütz,
this gap between abstract preconceptions and the shortcomings of
reality is in Emerson's case not just the usual dilemma of the idealist,

but based on inbuilt contradictions. Emerson's political ideals were preinvested with a negativity the politics of his time could only verify. Politics and classic American writers is also the theme of Hans–Joachim Lang's essay "Classic American Writers and Jacksonian Democracy: Some Preliminary Remarks and Case Studies" (pp. 87–106). It encompasses a far wider scope than any of the essays mentioned before. Lang's intention is to call for a reinterpretation of the classic American literature. For him, the influential F. O. Matthiessen and, more recently, Larzer Ziff canonized Emerson, Thoreau, Hawthorne, Melville and Whitman, but condemned Poe and Stowe to the attic of literary achievement. After all, Poe influenced both Hawthorne and Melville. Lang's criterion applied to classic American literature is the notion of "centrality," i.e., the writer's ability to incorporate national themes in his works. According to Lang, even Poe's work contains more expositions of American aspects than most critics so far have observed. Melville's *The Confidence-Man* offers a picture gallery of contemporary Americans, from Emerson to Bayard Taylor, most of them satirical portrayals. The America of the Jacksonian era and the decades thereafter offered two different views, the P. T. Barnum show of rough-and-tumble party affairs and rowdy journalism, and the Whig culture of genteel learning. The first milieu with its fiery literary nationalism was inspirational enough, yet those writers who had been nourished by the second too often did not possess enough of Melville's scepticism to deal with it adequately.

Not a part of the papers on Transcendentalism but thematically related to them, is Herwig Friedl's "Making It Cohere: Walt Whitman's Idea of History" (pp. 295–307). Friedl examines three areas of historical coherence: 1) the conflicts between individuals and political institutions, 2) the interplay of macro-and micro-history and 3) Whitman's various attempts to symbolize universal history as a whole. Whitman's transcendentalist position forced him to endeavor the finally impossible task of harmonizing all historical events and at the same time emphasizing their uniqueness. Jacksonian politics is also at the core of Walter Grünzweig's essay " 'Where Millions of Happy People Might Live Peacefully': Jacksons Westen in Charles Sealfields *Tokeah; or, the White Rose*" (pp. 219–36). Grünzweig considers the Austrian-American's first novel heavily influenced by Cooper's early fiction, but also shows that Sealfield's Indians are created along an ideological line that is in deliberate contrast to

Cooper's way of presenting Indians. For Sealfield, the Indian has to make room for the white man and his civilization. The novel's white protagonist, the squatter Copeland, embodies both Ishmael Bush's relentless westward drive and Natty Bumppo's human qualities. Jackson himself appears in the novel as the spokesman of his age, threatening the Indians with extinction if they do not conform to the white man's life.

The 19th-century contributions end with Hans–Joachim Lang's "Looking Backward at the Second Revolution in Massachusetts: Edward Bellamy's *The Duke of Stockbridge* as Historical Romance" (pp. 309–22). Lang sees Bellamy as Hawthorne's successor in the way he used allegory and dealt with political institutions. Yet *The Duke of Stockbridge* is not only a historical novel concerned with Shay's Rebellion. Many of the horrors described in the book can also be applied to the United States of the 1870s. Lang praises Bellamy's descriptions of regional customs, but is even more taken by the novel's political implications that amount to the author's questioning "the long-range benefits of the American Revolution."

d. **20th-Century Literature.** German contributions should fittingly begin with Olaf Hansen's "Henry Adams: *Mont-Saint-Michel and Chartres*" (*Amst* 28:323–34). Hansen puts Adams into the spiritual vicinity of Nietzsche, because both "had come to realize that the only justification for the world's existence had to be an aesthetic one." *Mount-Saint-Michel* was one of Adams's numerous brief flights from a present tainted by general corruption and moral decay. But in Hansen's view it is also a search for images of unity manifested in the architecture and poetry of an era long gone, the essence of which can only be grasped by the re-creative faculties of man's intuitive power of reflection.

Volker Bischoff's *Amerikanische Lyrik zwischen 1912 und 1922* (Heidelberg: Carl Winter) is concerned with one of the most interesting decades in 20th-century American poetry. From Ezra Pound to the Chicago Renaissance the reader is provided with a painstaking account of all poetic achievements. Bischoff does not come up with radically new insights, but the value of this carefully structured study lies in the balanced compilation of the period's contributions that many American critics have dealt with, but rarely have viewed in such breadth. This decade is also touched upon in Lothar Hönninghausen's "The Role of Swinburne and Eliot in Faulkner's Literary Development" (*Amst* 28:467–83). Hönninghausen cogently proves how much the early Faulkner poems were influenced by Swinburne, comparing "Aubade" and "Sapphics" with the English poet's "Before Dawn" and his ventures in the classical Greek manner. As for Eliot's influence, Faulkner's "The Lilacs" is taken as an example of how the young poet, like Eliot, incorporated late romantic elements to give his verses a symbolistic dimension. Hönninghausen even suspects that the poetic quality of Faulkner's prose style owes something to the early excursions into poetry. Faulkner's short stories, too often neglected by many of his critics, are examined in Carin Freywald's dissertation *Untersuchungen zur Symbolik in den Kurzgeschichten Faulkners* (Frankfurt: Lang). Freywald's thesis is that all of Faulkner's stories share beneath their seemingly realistic surface a reference system of symbols, among which the symbol of the room is the most important one. In addition, animal and body symbolism is also analyzed. Of special interest for all Faulkner scholars should be her discussion of a "symbol of existential movement" that is seen in close connection to Faulkner's idea of "life is motion."

Dos Passos has always had his devoted proponents among German scholars. After Frank Fingerhuth's dissertation *John Steinbeck und John Dos Passos—"American Tradition" und gesellschaftliche Wirklichkeit: Untersuchung zum literarischen und gesellschaftlichen Entwicklungsdiagramm zweier Schriftsteller des 20. Jahrhunderts* (Hamburg: Hamburger Buchagentur 1981), Hartwig Isernhagen's *Ästhetische Innovation und Kulturkritik: Das Frühwerk von John Dos Passos 1916–1938* (München: Wilhelm Fink) followed suit in 1983. The author bases his study on his conviction that Dos Passos refused to subject his art to traditional concepts of genre. Instead, he employed different subgenres and modified them, e.g., the war novel in *Three Soldiers*, the city novel in *Manhattan Transfer* and the national epic in *U.S.A.* Furthermore, Isernhagen takes over the notion of an innate opposition between two concepts in Dos Passos's works, namely, the art novel and the collective novel, which Malcolm Cowley and Alfred Kazin had pointed out a long time ago. Dos Passos's aim to dissolve this dichotomy resulted in artisic innovations. They can only be evaluated, however, if one takes into account his cultural criticism. There is no doubt that Isernhagen's book provides new insights as far as Dos Passos's works of the 1920s are concerned.

Yet in comparison with the writer's "artistic negativity" of the modernist 1920s, his change in the 1930s is too briefly dealt with.

Among German publications on American literature after 1945, the collection *Essays on Contemporary Drama*, edited by Hedwig Bock and Albert Wertheim (München: Hueber), completes and enriches earlier studies in this field. Most of the contributors are Americans, but four essays by Germans deserve mention. Hedwig Bock in "Tennessee Williams, Southern Playwright" (pp. 5–18) evaluates the dramatist as a regional playwright who wrote about the forces that destroyed a South he loved, but who also became an artist to escape from madness. Jürgen Wolter in "Arthur Kopit: Dreams and Nightmares" (pp. 55–74) deals with a playwright whom he ranks among the best of the 1960s and 1970s. Wolter notices a common theme in all of Kopit's plays, that of "dreams and nightmares resulting from identity crises." The German interest in ethnic literature is again reflected in two contributions. Peter Bruck in "Ed Bullins: The Quest and Failure of an Ethnic Community Theater" (pp. 123–40) focuses on the pattern of "a cultural de-brainwashing," that can be found in almost all of Bullins's plays. Bruck disagrees with those critics who maintain that the plays lack a political or ideological content. The overt political message, he argues, is contained in the fact that Bullins time and again confronts his audience with the misery and violence of urban "lumpen Blacks," thereby trying to make the black community discover themselves in his characters. Bullins's failure to get a cathartic response from his audience Bruck diagnoses as a consequence of the playwright's political helplessness, since he never tells how to survive in a "whiteman's land." Dieter Herms's contribution "Luis Valdez, Chicano Dramatist: An Introduction and an Interview" (pp. 257–78) is, as the title implies, a concise introduction into the works and political goals of a Chicano artist who is trying to incorporate history and myth, social criticism and cultural self-consciousness, the demands of folk theater in the barrios and Broadway performances. Klaus Ensslen's study *The Autobiography of Malcolm X* (München: Wilhelm Fink) is part of a series of "model analyses" of modern English and American writers and their works. Ensslen begins with a detailed analysis of the reception both in America and in Germany. After briefly discussing its genesis, he interprets the autobiography as a "mirror of collective experience" with the stages of interdiction, "self-alienation by pseudo-integration, ghettoization and criminalization." The most important step, in Ensslen's opinion, is "the conversion as stocktaking and build-up of a new identity," that is, from victim to activist. This leads to the final stage, the belief in surmounting the ghetto by internationalization, that is, by seeking alliance with the world of Islam and Third World movements. For Ensslen, a didactic purpose in the autobiography is obvious.

Two essays discussing postmodern literature conclude this 1983 survey. Joseph C. Schöpp in "*Slaughterhouse-Five*: The Struggle with a Form that Fails" (*Amst.* 28:335–45) shows that "the failure of the conventional form became the novel's aesthetic achievement." Heinz Ickstadt in "History, Fiction and the Designs of Robert Coover" (*Amst* 28:347–60) focuses on *The Public Burning*, which for him is "the postmodern novel of politics par excellence." Although Ickstadt is aware of two narrative voices—the viewpoint of the auctorial narrator and the personal voice of Richard Nixon—he convincingly shows that the public voices of a vindictive and bigoted society dominate the novel, demonstrating that Coover's target was the collective mind as contained in official rhetoric, a perverted national mythology and popular culture.

Universität Hamburg

iii. Japanese Contributions

Keiko Beppu

Japanese scholarship on American literature, over the past decade, has been on a steady upward curve; our coverage in *ALS* has yearly increased to meet the productivity of both established and rising generations of our scholars. Japanese contributions for 1983 were as impressive as those registered for the previous year. Qualitatively, our scholarship for this year may be characterized by its international scope, which is best illustrated by the joint compilation of research, foreign and Japanese, on Herman Melville: *Kujira to Tekisuto: Melville no Sekai* [*The Whale and the Texts: The World of Herman Melville*] ed. Kenzaburo Ohashi (Kokusho Kankokai).

The publication of the book is symbolic of scholarly activities in this country in two ways. Since the time of Ohashi's report "Japanese

Scholarship on American Literature: Its Problems and Its Future"
(*ALS 1979*, p. 519), scholars in this country have become self-
conscious, à la Emerson, of our dependence on foreign scholarship,
and exceedingly needful of establishing and maintaining a Japanese
viewpoint on American literature. *The Whale and the Texts* is a fruition of such efforts made by our scholars. Secondly, this prodigious
achievement crowns the completion of Noboru Sakashita's translation of Melville's works: *The Collected Works of Herman Melville*
(11 volumes), a good indication of the correspondence between criticism and translation in the studies of foreign literatures in this country. A similar project on Henry James is in progress; *Selected Short
Stories, The Golden Bowl, The Wings of the Dove,* and *Selected
Literary Criticisms and Reviews* appeared in 1983. Other translations
of interest are John Irving's *The World According to Garp,* a sequel
to *Poems of Emily Dickinson,* and Willa Cather's *One of Ours.*

The Whale and the Texts exemplifies critical trends for 1983
in yet another respect. Japanese scholarship on American literature
this year is monopolized by research on 19th-century authors; this is
testified by the serialization of textual readings of major 19th-century
writers in *EigoS*: Herman Melville by Masayuki Sakamoto (129:
221–23, 289–91, 344–46, 378–80); Mark Twain by Toshio Watanabe
(129: 24–26, 77–79, 131–33, 180–82); Henry James by Tsuguo Aoki
(129: 440–42, 498–500, 552–54, to be concluded). Also *EigoS* featured articles on Tennessee Williams (129: 4) and on William Carlos
Williams (129: 6); the first in commemoration of the playwright's
death and the latter in celebration of the centennial of the poet's
birth. Individual achievements for 1983 are grouped for the present
review as follows: general and literary history; 19th-century fiction;
20th-century fiction; contemporary literature—fiction, poetry and
drama. Articles here examined are restricted to those published in
our major journals: *EigoS, SALit,* and *SELit.* Unless otherwise indicated books discussed were published in Tokyo.

Studies in American literature in general covering the whole or
certain phases of its history are prepared each year to meet various
demands of students in this country. Among such works produced in
1983 two deserve comment here: *America no Bungaku* [*American
Literature*] (Nan'un-do) coauthored by Toshio Yagi and Masao
Shimura; *America Bungaku no Shintenkai: Shosetsu* [*Post World*

War II Evolution of American Writers: Fiction] ed. by Toshihiko Ogata (Kyoto: Yamaguchi Shoten). *American Literature* consists of essays originally written for NHK's English Programs (the Japanese broadcasting company); the book presents quite an authentic picture—minus pedantry—of American literature as a whole from such Puritan writers as John Winthrop, William Bradford, and Jonathan Edwards to such modernist poets as T. S. Eliot and Ezra Pound, with chapters on science fiction and popular literature in the bargain. *Post World War II Evolution of American Writers: Fiction* is the fourth volume in *Studies in American Literature*; Ogata's introduction to the present volume makes a good survey of contemporary American literary scene, followed by discussions on some 27 major American authors who have created American fiction since 1945 (further comment below).

Significant achievements in 19th-century fiction are: the aforementioned *Whale and the Texts*; Nobuyuki Hayashi's *Hawthorne, Melville to Sono Shuhen* [*Hawthorne, Melville and Their Circle*] (Hokuseido); Satoshi Tatsumi's *Rappaccini no Musume: Hawthorne Sakuhin Kenkyu* [*Rappaccini's Daughter: Studies in Hawthorne's Short Fiction*] (Kyoto: Koyo Shobo); Koh Kasegawa's *America no Shizen Bungaku: Thoreau Eno Michi* [*Natural History Essays in American Literature: Thoreau and His Precursors*] (Nagata Shobo); Hisae Miwa's *Thoreau no Shiteki Katsubo* [*Thoreau's Microcosm at Walden*] (Ohshisha); Kazuo Ogawa's *Waga Edgar Poe* [*My Edgar Poe*] (Kochiku Shuppan); and *America Bungaku no Seikimatsu* [*The Fin de Siècle and American Writers*] (Nan'un-do) ed. Rikuo Taniguchi.

As has been noted earlier, *The Whale and the Texts* is a feat of scholarly enterprise, international in its scope. Contributors to the book include both American and Japanese Melville scholars, an anthropologist, one foreign and two Japanese novelists. With a detailed chronology and a thorough, up-to-date bibliography of Melville scholarship, the book runs in this country to over five hundred pages; the bibliography alone has its drama to tell—the evolution of reception of the artist over half the century (1927–83).

Hidekatsu Nojima's high-flown rhetoric in the opening chapter, "Melville and the Modern World," places the novelist in the context of Western civilization. Nojima argues that the fate of the novelist closely parallels that of the modern world in the West and concludes that like his protagonist who fell a victim to the irreconcilable forces inherent in the modern world, Melville was indeed the American Adam "in the Darbies" (pp. 3–41). In "Melville and Hawthorne" (pp. 68–107), Ginsaku Sugiura sounds the depths of their friendship and contends that Melville realized as early as in 1852 an overestimation he made of the deeply thinking mind of his friend. Toshio Yagi's "*Moby Dick* Mosaic" (pp. 108–74) is an exercise in the foremost mode of literary criticism rampant in academe here and abroad; yet Yagi's close reading of Melville's text is this critic's own original reshuffling of the mosaic pieces.

Placed in the center are foreign contributions as diverse as Charles Olson's mythological reading of *Moby Dick*, Carolyn L. Karcher's socio-political criticism, or Barbara Johnson's deconstructionist "execution" of Melville's novella, *Billy Budd*. Clive William Nicol's "A Heretical View of *Moby Dick*" (pp. 375–85) is still another different approach to the whale and the text; Toshio Yagi's annotations to the essay (pp. 386–97) serve as critical rejoinder that corrects the ecologist's "heretical view" of the masterpiece. Masao Yamaguchi's discussion, "*The Confidence Man*" (pp. 175–89), which locates Melville's confidence man in the genealogy of Hermes the trickster, is a valuable contribution to numerous studies on this controversial work. Masao Shimura's "Reading *After the Pleasure Party*" (pp. 341–73) is, as he claims, an exercise in explication of a poem. Even so, accompanied by his judicious translation of the poem, it is an excellent analysis of the least discussed of Melville's texts in this country, and as such deserves special attention. Besides, Shimura points out some textual misreadings hitherto committed by American scholars; however minor such misreadings may be, he judges them fatal for the comprehension of the poem's structure, which, Shimura suggests, closely resembles the mechanism of Hermaphrodite.

Kenzaburo Ohashi, the editor-writer, concludes *The Whale and the Texts* with his study of the reception of the American novelist in our country (pp. 426–54), happily placed after the marginalia contributed by two Japanese novelists: Nobuo Kojima and Meisei Goto. As in his Faulkner study, Ohashi's interest in Melville lies primarily in the impact the novelist might have made on Japanese literature. Ohashi demonstrates, with examples, how the reading of Melville affects the creative imagination of Japanese writers. Of special interest is his comparison of Koichiro Uno's prizewinning short story,

"Kujira Gami," with Melville's *Moby-Dick*; the comparison brings out a fundamental difference in the sensibilities of the two writers, American and Japanese. Overall, *The Whale and the Texts* presents a distinctly Japanese perspective on Melville's *opus magnum*, while embracing scholarship both foreign and Japanese. It is an ambitious scholarly venture to give bold relief to Melville scholarship East and West in our time.

Nobuyuki Hayashi's *Hawthorne, Melville and Their Circle* is a modest collection of a few original essays and some previously published in various journals. The book bifurcates into discussions on Hawthorne and Melville; other writers who may constitute "their circle" (with the exception of Mark Twain) are hardly touched. This is only natural, provided that the writer's objective is to discuss these "twin flowers of American literature." Yet, Hayashi's comparison of these 19th-century American authors fails in what it attempts to accomplish. The suggested equation—the Apollonian-Hawthorne and the Dionysian-Melville—if valid, is not pursued in the book. (Ginsaku Sugiura's brilliant discussion on the same topic in *The Whale and the Texts* comes to mind.) A redeeming feature of the book is Hayashi's endearing profile of Hawthorne in his late years (pp. 3–28, 261–71), and his comparison of Melville and Twain in their humor and in their "confidence games" (pp. 189–233).

Satoshi Tatsumi's *Rappaccini's Daughter: Studies in Hawthorne's Short Fiction* is a curious monograph: the first part consists of elaborate analyses of short stories—"Fancy's Show Box," "Roger Malvin's Burial," "My Kinsman, Major Molineux," "Dr. Heidegger's Experiment," and "Rappaccini's Daughter"; the second half comprises the writer's *free* translations of "Fancy's Show Box," "Dr. Heidegger's Experiment," and "Rappaccini's Daughter." These stories are chosen for examination, it seems, to illustrate the critic's theological stance derived from his readings in Hawthorne and in Kierkegaard in particular. Noteworthy here is Tatsumi's emphasis on the religio-ethical meaning of the Adamic myth in contrast to the generally accepted socio-cultural view of the myth (p. 22). So, this curious study on Hawthorne—without references to his romances (excepting one to *The Scarlet Letter*, p. 32)—sheds light into the recesses of Hawthorne's imaginative world.

Two book-length studies on Thoreau appeared in 1983, a long-awaited accomplishment in view of Thoreau's popularity in this

country. Koh Kasegawa's *Natural History Essays in American Literature: Thoreau and His Precursors* is a collection of essays previously
published in academic journals—a culmination of Kasegawa's re-
searches in Thoreau's writings, especially those of the titular genre.
The first chapter is a good survey of the natural history essays in
American literature, informative and well-supported by solid scholarship. Given the title of his book *The Natural History Essays in
American Literature*, however, the survey is much too brief and
leaves something to be desired. Also a greater emphasis should be
given to Thoreau as an expert surveyor and bona fide naturalist to
make more viable the relation between "Thoreau and His Precursors." All the same, Kasegawa's contribution, now in book form, is
the first of its kind here; it is a valuable addition to Thoreau scholarship, and a good stimulus for future studies of the writer and the
genre in American literature. It may also be mentioned that Kasegawa's observations on Thoreau's view of nature (p. 120, 141) are
shared by John Hildebidle in his recent book, *Thoreau: A Naturalist's
Liberty* (Harvard, 1983). Hisae Miwa's *Thoreau's Microcosm at
Walden* includes three brief chapters on Thoreau and his experiment
at Walden with annotated excerpts from "Where I Lived, and What
I Lived for," and "Solitude." Worthy of note here is Miwa's discussion of Thoreau and Emerson in their attitudes toward nature. Miwa's
judicious implementation of Holbrook Jackson's "Thoreau" in his
Dreamers of Dreams (1948) clarifies the difference between Thoreau
and Emerson on their view of nature (p. 50), a helpful footnote to
Kasegawa's discussion on the theme not sufficiently covered in *The
Natural History Essays in American Literature.*

Like Hayashi's or Kasegawa's book, examined above, Kazuo
Ogawa's *My Edgar Poe* is a collection of hitherto published essays by
our noted scholar of English romantic poets and of poetics. Ogawa's
appraisal of the American poet-critic is summed up by what he calls
the originality of Poe's "Philosophy of Composition": its detached
psychoanalysis of creative process. Such uniqueness is appreciated
by French symbolists, but not by Anglo-Saxon critics; hence, Eliot's
misunderstanding of Poe's (or Valéry's) poetic principle. The best
(and longest) discussion in the book is Ogawa's 1980 essay, "Poe's
Poetry, Poetics, and Prose Fiction" (pp. 109–75). It begins as a point-
by-point analysis of "The Raven" à la Poe, and turns out to be an
impassioned refutation of Eliot's "From Poe to Valéry" in *To Criti-*

cize the Critic. Our seasoned scholar even questions Eliot's critical insight given in this essay, arguing that Valéry's enthusiasm for the American poet-critic was based on misunderstanding because the French poet understood English "imperfectly." To be sure, self-vindication is not a legitimate literary criticism; nonetheless, Ogawa's self-vindication, for it is that, is successfully done in defense of Poe and Valéry, the two poets of his first love.

Another significant study is Ken Inoue's exploration of Poe's aesthetics in *The Fin de Siècle and American Writers,* ed. Rikuo Taniguchi. The book's title may sound strange to the readers who conventionally associate decadence and the 1890s with English and French writers and artists. The purpose of this collection is to answer such questions; the American writers selected for illustration of the theme are William Faulkner, Herman Melville, Stephen Crane, and Edgar Allan Poe. Of these four only Melville and Crane belong, chronologically, to "the fin de siècle," whose raison d'être for being used as the title of the book is not at all clarified in the discussions of the respective authors. Thus, expert as they are, the discussions cloud the purpose of this otherwise interesting project, only conceivable to Japanese scholars. But the other two essays on Faulkner and Poe more than sufficiently serve the purpose of the book.

Ken Inoue's "Poe and the Fin de Siècle Aesthetic" (pp. 157–206) shows his solid scholarship in both European and Japanese literature. Based on his close reading of "The Fall of the House of Usher" and on relevant Poe scholarship, Inoue delineates *his* "French Face of Poe": Poe's aesthetic, that still remains intact, well anticipated the French poets and artists of the 1890s. Then he establishes Poe's lineage, either direct or via Baudelaire, Valéry, Mallarmé, or Roudon, to such Japanese writers as Junichiro Tanizaki and Ryunosuke Akutagawa who extolled the "art for art's sake" manifesto in the practice of their writing. Thus, Inoue's essay is a valuable contribution to Poe scholarship and to comparative studies here and abroad. On the other hand, in his "The Fin de Siècle Writers and Faulkner" (pp. 11–60), Kenzaburo Ohashi explores a liaison between the American writer and English writers and artists. Using Thomas Beer (1926) and Larzer Ziff's classic decade study, *The American 1890's* (1966), Ohashi argues that the fin de siècle as literary phenomenon came to bloom in the United States 20 years later, in the 1920s, which corresponds to Faulkner's apprenticeship years. And he offers abundant proofs of Faulkner's indebtedness to Swinburne, Ansole, or to Beardsley, from his early poems, the scenario of "The Marionettes," and from his early drawings and playbills, which is of special interest to readers unfamiliar with Faulkner's early plays and drawings. It is also a model example of influence study.

The following three articles dealing with 19th-century writers deserve at least mention here: Hideo Masuda's "The 'Rescue' of Nanda in *The Awkward Age*" (*SALit* 19:51–63); Yoshitaka Aoyama's "Salvation Theme in *The Scarlet Letter*" (*SELit* 60,ii:245–60); and Hiroko Washizu's "Re-Building a House: An Approach to *The House of the Seven Gables*" (*SELit* 60,ii:293–309). The last mentioned needs comment here: Washizu's is a fairly successful implementation of the deconstructionist approach to solve the problem concerning the denouement of Hawthorne's romance. (Washizu's article is available in English; so is Hideo Masuda's essay on James's *The Awkward Age*.)

In contrast to the impressive list of books on 19th-century American writers above surveyed, Japanese scholarship on 20th-century American fiction was meager this year; there has been a sharp decline both in volume and variety. Only one book-length study in this category appeared; Kenji Nakajima's *Hemingway no Kangaekata to Ikikata* [*Ernest Hemingway: His Life and His Work*] (Yumi Shobo). As the title indicates, Nakajima's book is a critical biography of this American writer, who because of *The Old Man and the Sea*, is perhaps best-known among Japanese high school as well as college students. One notes the writer's wholehearted commitment to Hemingway's life style and to his work, which for the writer, is epitomized in a single story (!) of Hemingway's, "The Big Two-Hearted River." Despite such commitment of the critic-biographer, his book is an ordinary achievement and lacks the gusto of Shoichi Saeki's *Hemingway Biography* (See *ALS 1979*, p. 522). The writer might have greatly profited from Hemingway's spare, clear-cut prose style.

Articles on 20th-century writers selected for this review concentrate on William Faulkner: Ikuko Fujihira's "Truth in Uttering: The Speaking Voice in *The Sound and the Fury*" (*SALit* 19:33–50); and Haruka Haraguchi's "The Technique and Consciousness in the Writings of William Faulkner" (*EigoS* 129:158–62). In consideration of the scarcity of scholarly achievements in this group for 1983, two articles on Faulkner, in addition to Ohashi's chapter in *The Fin de Siècle and American Writers*, is an eloquent testimony of unflagging popularity this American novelist enjoys among scholars in this country. Here, Michiko Naka's article on Ellen Glasgow deserves to be underscored, because despite professed interest in and enthusiasm for American women writers and poets, they received little critical attention in 1983. Naka's "'Aging' and a Vision of Equilibrium" (*EigoS* 129:54–58) is a thoughtful study of Glasgow's trilogy—*The Romantic Comedians* (1926). *They Stooped to Folly* (1929), and *The Sheltered Life* (1932). And substantial studies on women writers, regardless of the periods, are yet to be written.

Contemporary American literature has always been the object of great critical concern among Japanese students, scholars and artists. Significant accomplishments in this group for 1983 are equally divided in fiction, poetry and drama: the aforementioned *Post World War II Evolution of American Writers: Fiction*; *J. D. Salinger Bungaku no Kenkyu* [*Studies in J. D. Salinger*] ed. Hisashi Shigeo and Ayako Sato (Tokyo Shirakawa Shoin); Yorifumi Yaguchi's *America Gendai Shi no Ichimen* [*Some Aspects of Contemporary American Poetry*] (Ohshisha); *Sengo America Engeki no Tenkai* [*American Drama since 1945*] ed. Kuniaki Suenaga and Koji Ishizuka (Buneido); and Haruma Okada's *Tennessee Williams: Sakuhin ni Miru Genso to Shinjitsu* [*Tennessee Williams: Illusion and Reality in His Works*] (Yashio Shuppan).

As stated at the outset of this review, the editor's introduction to *Post World War II Evolution of American Writers* presents a panoramic picture of contemporary literary scene in the States, a supplementary sequal to Ihab Hassan's *Contemporary American Literature 1945–1972*. Discussions of individual writers contributed by 22 scholars of American literature loosely conform to a format: a brief profile of the writer, followed by examination of his/her works in general, or elaboration of a particular theme in his/her works.

The list of writers includes what is expected of such an anthology of American literature: Norman Mailer, Truman Capote, William Styron, Richard Wright, Ralph Ellison, James Baldwin, Bernard Malamud, Saul Bellow, J. D. Salinger, Philip Roth, Isaac Bashevis Singer, John Updike, Henry Miller, John Barth, John Hawkes, Joseph Heller, Thomas Pynchon, Kurt Vonnegut, Jack Kerouac, and Vladimir Nabokov. The following variables are an indication of far-ranging interest of Japanese scholars in recent American writers: John O'Hara and Gore Vidal (by Toshihisa Koizumi); James Gould Cozzens

(Kazuto Ono); Ring Lardner, James Thurber and Dorothy Parker as humorists (Kunio Mori). Of this large group of contemporary American novelists, only two women writers are each given a chapter: Katherine Anne Porter (Yoshie Itabashi) and Toni Morrison (Keiko Beppu). With its bias and limitation (which is unavoidable), *Post World War II Evolution of American Writers: Fiction* is an all-round *encyclopaedia* of contemporary American fiction.

Studies in J. D. Salinger is a comprehensive collection of essays devoted to the novelist's *opus*, with special attention given to *Nine Stories* and the Glass Saga. Worthy of note here is Shigeo Hamano's discussion on the Jewishness in Salinger: Salinger's "diluted and discolored Jewishness" is that of the people in general today.

As for articles on contemporary American novelists, *EigoS* featured a special forum on "The City and Contemporary American Writers" (129:62–71): "Re-Examination of American Urbanism" (by Iwao Iwamoto); "Machine, Businessmen, Lawyers, Gangsters: Bellow's Chicago" (Yuzaburo Shibuya); "Meta-Fiction—The City in Barthelme and Pynchon" (Yoichiro Miyamoto); "Joan Didion's Mirage City in the Desert" (Konomi Ara); "Enclosing the City in Pastoral Romance: John Gardner" (Arimichi Makino). The discussions as a whole sample a prominent leitmotif in contemporary American literature, which becomes *the* theme (more properly, the cause) for some contemporary American poets in Yaguchi's *Some Aspects of Contemporary American Poetry*.

Yaguchi's book collects the poet-critic's personal notes and lectures on contemporary American poets (first published in local literary magazines in 1973–74, and 1978–79), and his self-conducted interviews (in 1976–77) with Richard Shelton, William Stafford, Denise Levertov, and Robert Creeley. The notes and lectures, and interviews constitute a charming introduction to contemporary American poets—Carl Solomon, John Hollander, Richard Shelton, Gary Snyder, William Stafford—and makes these very new (some here unheard of) American poets quite accessible to general readers. With very new American poets and novelists, often pleasurable personal introductions rather than mere facts yield a deeper understanding of their works.

The title essay in the book, "Some Aspects of Contemporary American Poetry" (pp. 285–327) is, as already pointed out, a discussion on one of the pressing issues of postindustrial American society. As in his notes and lectures, Yaguchi dispenses with academic exploration of the theme, and lets the poems (in his lyrical translations) speak for themselves. Such direct expressions of American poets' concern with ecology become a powerful indictment of urbanization, commercialism, and invasion of nature by high technological civilization. Interestingly, Yaguchi spares some space for Pound and his condemnation of commercialism in *The Cantos* (a truism today), but in the book's context, the reference brings a new historical perspective on the tradition of American poetry, and also on the impending problem of our time.

Among our scholarly work on contemporary American literature for 1983, *American Drama since 1945* is the most significant if only because drama, unlike fiction or poetry, receives little critical attention in this country. Tomoko Kusuhara's introductory essay is a succinct summary of dominant trends in American drama and stage since 1945; "Americanness of American Drama" defined in her essay is well substantiated by the discussions that follow on major American playwrights: O'Neill (by Kazuo Ichinose); Miller (Masunori Sata); Williams (Fumiyasu Ariga); and Albee (Koji Ishizuka). The choice of the playwrights is well made, representing the whole spectrum of American literature in general as well as contemporary American drama. Demonstrations of respective dramaturgy of these playwrights illuminate indeed the interactions among the dramatists and thereby the "Americanness of American Drama." *American Drama since 1945* is, however, more than an anthology of American drama on literary texts; larger part of the book is devoted to chapters on Broadway musicals, off-Broadway and off-off-Broadway theaters, black theaters, and the experimental theater. It is an important scholarship on contemporary American drama, and an excellent "Baedeker" to theatrical arts in the States.

The death of Tennessee Williams (February, 1983) occasioned a few tributes to the playwright in *EigoS* (referred to earlier); another tribute is Haruma Okada's *Tennessee Williams: Illusion and Reality in His Works*. In this collection of his previously published essays, Okada explores a familiar theme in Williams—illusion vs. reality—in his early plays but mostly in his short stories such as "Hard Candy," "Three Players of a Summer Game," and "Sabbatha and Solitude." Okada's appreciation of Williams's peculiar world of "solitary confinement inside [one's] skins" is unabashedly subjective; his *Tennes-*

see Williams is indeed *a* personal testimonial to one of the great contemporary American artists.

To conclude this review, a few remarks should be made on Masashi Kimura's *America no Chimei: Yurai to Shiteki Haikei* [*Place Names in America: Their Origins and Historical Meanings*] (Yumi Shobo). This study in toponymy is an anomaly among the books thus far surveyed; just the same, correct reading of place names is indispensable to studies in American culture and literature, which is characterized by its ethnicity and regionalism. (It was Hemingway who said: ". . . finally only names of places had dignity.") Kimura's linguistic expertise is shown in his assessments of documentation on names of states, cities, counties, villages, and streets in America; results of extended statistical research are given in the Appendix. With its companion piece by the same author, *English and American Names* (1980), *Place Names in America* is a valuable addition to Japanese scholarship on American literature.

Kobe College

iv. Scandinavian Contributions

Mona Pers

Within the field of American literary scholarship, 1984 was an active year in Scandinavia. Old favorites like William Faulkner and other southern writers, black and Jewish novelists, and T. S. Eliot still attract the Scandinavians, but a widening circle of modern poets as well as writers of popular fiction have now managed to arouse critical interest, too.

Is popular fiction really considered a "serious" enough subject for bona fide literary criticism nowadays? At least some of it ought to be, according to Mårten Nilsson's essay, "Marlowe och Hamlet" (*BLM* 1:25–31). Similarities to Hamlet in the character of Philip Marlowe have been spotted by critics before, but Nilsson carries the comparison a few steps further, at times a little too far. Chandler might in fact have been provoked to include him in the group of critics he irritably called "primping second-guessers."

Chandler's thrillers continue to be popular with the readers, and so do those of Ian Fleming, John le Carré and Len Deighton. In

"Literature in Figures: An Essay on the Popularity of Thrillers" (*OL* 38:93–107), Lars Ole Auerberg investigates the genre as a whole, concentrating on Fleming, Le Carré, and Deighton. Auerberg was able to confirm what many has suspected—that the thriller has "enjoyed an overall popularity which no other kind of fiction can show," although he acknowledges that it is "difficult to make reliable comparisons, as there are no uniform statistics available." The lack of standard investigation procedures and a shared genre terminology tend to make comparisons misleading. By submitting various statistical sources to critical scrutiny Auerberg has managed to outline the general tendencies in the area of literature "as a market commodity."

The object of his study on popular fiction, *A World Made Safe: Values in American Best Sellers, 1895–1920* (Uppsala: Almqvist & Wiksell International), Erik Löfroth says, was "to learn something of the attitudes and ideals of the writers and their readers from the 1895 to 1920 period and to discover how they used particular values in their work." The opening year for the investigation was more or less given, he maintains, because prior to 1895 no annual best-seller lists were available. After 1920 the world created up till then by a united corps of best-seller writers was suddenly abandoned. The currents of the previous 25 years had run their course, and 1920 thus proved a suitable closing year for Löfroth's investigation.

After an informative introduction, containing, among other things, a discussion on the use of best sellers to investigate popular values and an explanation of the procedures followed in the selection and exploration of primary sources, Chapter One offers a general survey of the worldview and the ideals that prevailed in the 25-year period covered by the study. The rest of the book is devoted to subperiods "in which particular values are affirmed with greater force than at other times": Chapter Two to the years around the turn of the century, Chapter Three to the 1905 to 1915 period, and Chapter Four to 1920. In each of the separate chapters Löfroth concentrates on one book that he considers to be typical of that particular subperiod: an adventure story, a mystery, and a Western, a varied selection that has prevented his presentation from growing repetitive.

Löfroth's book, in addition to making a substantial contribution to the study of popular fiction, is entertaining reading, in no small measure attributable to his attitude to the material. His style of writing is mildly humorous and at times playfully stand-offish, with not a trace of academic snobbery despite the fact that none of the books he deals with can be classified as "a great work of fiction."

A world in all respects the opposite of the old best-seller "world made safe" is depicted in most of the writings emanating from minority groups. A sense of alienation and loss suffuses the world created by ethnic writers. In his essay, "Jewish Nationalism: A Reading of Ludwig Lewisohn's *The Island Within*" (*AmerSS* 15:59–68), Helge Normann Nilsen demonstrates how the author in this "realistic novel with a clear message" is out to "teach by example." For Lewisohn, assimilation is an illusion, and in *The Island Within*, he sets out to demonstrate that Jews can never become integrated into the larger society, and at the same time he rejects orthodoxy, thus staking out a middle way that Nilsen traces in his analysis of the novel.

Although he was far from the only one, it is true that "Lewisohn was ahead of his time in his strong commitment to ethnic values," as Nilsen maintains. Sigmund Ro's " 'Desecrators' and 'Necromancers': Black American Writers and Critics in the Nineteen-Sixties and the Third World Perspective" (*AmerSS* 15:15–33) deals with one area where this type of strong commitment to ethnic values has spread and intensified in later decades. Ro sees a distinctive design in the new black writing of the sixties: "a metamorphosis of the traditional pattern of rage and celebration under the impact of a compelling desire to repudiate the aesthetic derived from 'the-Negro-as-America's-metaphor' by detaching the black man from the West and bringing him into the orbit of the post-Western humanism" of an Afro-centric Third World. Ro suggests that the writers of the 6os, by functioning both as "desecrators" and "necromancers," carried out "the historical task of de-Westernizing" their culture "in preparation for a new era of 'afterwhiteness color.' "

It is not only the "otherness" of ethnic writers that attracts critical attention. Much of the literary research on southern fiction invites the speculation that southern writers are of special interest mainly insofar as they deviate from what is nebulously taken to be mainstream USA. Maria Haar's book, *The Phenomenon of the Grotesque in Modern Southern Fiction* (Umeå: Almqvist & Wiksell International) is a case in point. Haar sees "the abundant use of the Grotesque" in southern fiction intimately "linked to the distinctiveness of that region as compared to the rest of the United States." Consequently, she sees no need to put the southern use of the Grotesque into an American perspective. Haar had originally planned her study to be "exhaustive in the field," i.e., trace the Grotesque in the works of all white southern writers. She eventually lowered her ambition, and her survey now covers approximately fifty years, from William Faulkner in the 20s through the 60s, concentrating on a handful of writers (besides Faulkner, Caldwell, O'Connor, McCullers, Welty, and to a lesser extent Capote and Goyen). The structure and the first two chapters of Haar's book seem to be remnants of her original plan. Chapter One is a detailed account of how other scholars have defined "Grotesque" over the years, and Chapter Two reports on Alan Spiegel's ideas about "Southern Grotesque." In the rest of her study, Haar makes little use of those definitions, however; they turned out to be both inadequate and insufficient for her revised purposes. Her own definition does not come until the end of the book, unfortunately, as a kind of summing up or empirical conclusion based on the examples cited in the previous chapters, entitled "The Macabre-Grotesque" (Three) "The Repulsive- and/or Frightening Grotesque" (Four), and "The Comic-Grotesque" (Five). Under each of these headings Haar furnishes an ample and varied selection of telling illustrations from works by some or all of her chosen writers, to which she offers critical comments. The overall impression is somewhat fragmented, however; a coherent pattern does not emerge until in the "Summary and Conclusion," to my mind the most stringent part of this study.

The elegant structuring of the material is one of the many strong points of Thomas Nordanberg's well-written and carefully researched study, *Cataclysm as Catalyst. The Theme of War in William Faulkner's Fiction*. (Uppsala: Almqvist & Wiksell International). Nordanberg's approach is largely chronological, his dissertation structured around what he has termed "the three phases" of Faulkner's use of the theme of war: World War I (works written between 1925 and 1932), The American Civil War (1930 to 1942), and World War II (1941 to 1959). The stated purpose of Nordanberg's study is to "demonstrate the changing function of the theme of war in Faulkner's fiction, and furthermore to show how three different wars serve not only as material for his fiction, but provoke three different veins of writing." Nordanberg's sensitive analysis of Faulkner's "war phases" discloses that the works of the first phase center on individual experiences of "lost generation" characters, the second phase "marks a widening of Faulkner's use of the war theme," evaluating the "Lost

Cause," and the third phase brings the author still a step further, into using "the theme of war to deal with existential questions." The observation that Faulkner's attitude in the last phase is "affirmative, reversing the disbelief of the earlier phases," prompts Nordanberg to speculate that the development of the war theme in Faulkner's fiction may well have "played an important part in the formation of the positive world-view that he embraced in the later part of his career," and may help to solve the "often discussed problem of reconciling the pessimism of his early works with the optimism expressed in the Nobel Prize address."

Another southerner also dealing with war is the object of Hans H. Skei's review essay, "Mary Chesnut's Civil War" (*AmerSS* 15:35–45). Skei makes a thorough and incisive evaluation not only of C. Vann Woodward's newly published edition of Chesnut's diary but also of the former two versions (1905 and 1944), which he argues "hardly deserve to be called 'diary' at all." The lasting value of *Mary Chesnut's Civil War*, according to Skei, "does not lie in the information it gives about the war—which is not reliable at all points; it is rather her depiction of how the war somehow affected every aspect of daily life in the South . . . that gives the account such unusual strength." Because "there is nothing quite like it anywhere," Skei is confident that it will "remain one of the basic books in Southern literature."

Lars Bäckström's "Eliot igen" (Eliot Again, *Café Existens* 21:2–12) is like Skei's a review-essay comparing a new, enlarged edition of an old work to the original version. In both cases, the new versions include significantly more of the authors' original material. Here the parallels end. Bäckström, well-known Swedish poet and critic, gives us an impressionistic evaluation and comparison of the two 'Waste Lands,' tracing his own responses to the poem all the way back to the first time he read it. It is obvious that Bäckström senses an affinity with T. S. Eliot, a feeling he shares with other Swedish writers in whose work he recognizes Eliot's ghost.

In "Sounding the Secular Depth of *Ash-Wednesday*: A Study of Eliot's Allusional Design and Purpose" (*SN* 55:167–79) Lois A. Cuddy's aim is to demonstrate how Eliot's allusional system "expresses subliminally the poet's ethical and emotional preoccupations" without confessional catharsis. Cuddy's point of departure is the assumption that "recognition of the contextual significance of Eliot's borrowed material should explain the reasons readers feel such agony in a poem

that presumably attests to religious affirmation." By meticulously
examining the relation of the poem and the poet's life to "sources
presented in the title and first stanza of Part I": Shakespeare's Sonnet
XXIX (a line-by-line examination), Dante Gabriel Rossetti's translation (poem XXIV) of a Cavalcanti poem, and Dante Alighieri's
Vita Nueva and, by extension, *Inferno*, Cuddy comes to the conclusion that *Ash-Wednesday* is "much more a confession of emotional, ethical, and physical weaknesses than a statement of spiritual
achievement."

There is clear evidence that Scandinavia is warming up to modern American poetry. Whether the recently published first volume
of a new anthology is the cause or effect of this heightened interest
is hard to tell. One book on Ezra Pound, two articles each on T. S.
Eliot and Wallace Stevens, and one on Emily Dickinson is a richer
crop than Scandinavia has yielded in quite some time. In "Den
manliga musan. Om Emily Dickinson och den kvinnliga poetens
dilemma" (The Male Muse. On E.D. and the Dilemma of the Woman
Poet, *BLM* 4:250–57), Ingrid Elam and Ingrid Holmquist use the
poem "My life had stood—a loaded gun" as a basis for their feminist
interpretation of the poet's art, life, and personality. They argue that
Dickinson, "a woman white," was the woman poet's dilemma incarnate: present and absent as creative subject in a patriarchal culture. Their reading of her poems and letters led Elam and Holmquist
to the conclusion that Dickinson never found a solution to her dilemma and ended up a split personality.

Richard Andersen's short essay, "Stevens' "The Emperor of Ice-
Cream" (*AmerSS* 15:79–82) brings to the fore another kind of dilemma: "Few short poems have suffered as much from the enthusiasm of
their explicators as Wallace Stevens's 'The Emperor of Ice-Cream,' "
Andersen declares in the opening statement of his essay. He has
observed that "more recent devotees, perhaps pressured to come up
with something new, have begun reading 'The Emperor of Ice-
Cream' in a way that Stevens once warned against, namely, as an
imaginative construct instead of the work of an imaginative man
describing a real world." After bestowing some telling samples of
this recent trend, Andersen intimates that this poem "may contain a
message to critics who feel like letting themselves go, something
Stevens said he did while writing" it. If we read it in this light, the
poem "may be interpreted as a plea to let the transforming power

of the imagination be still for a change. Let us yield to the discipline of reality for once and take things for what they are," is Andersen's advice to weary readers and overly zealous critics.

Kjell Espmark's long essay, "Stevens uppgörelse med Mallarmé. En läsning av 'Landscape with a boat.'" (Stevens' Dispute with Mallarmé. A Reading of 'Landscape with a boat,'" *TEL* 1:4–17) is in part also Espmark's dispute with other critics (including Stevens himself) concerning the nature of this influence. Although Espmark concedes that "Landscape" is a strictly ascetic poem he nevertheless maintains that in large parts it is also a hidden polemic against Mallarmé's ideas in general on the via negativa to the absolute and against "Igitur" in particular.

Espmark's close reading "in terms of intertexuality" (to use his own definition in the English summary) reveals that the poet's relation to the author of "Igitur" is "a mixture of refutation and acceptance: Stevens's retort contains a certain amount of approval." In his conscientious line-by-line analysis of the poem, Espmark clarifies how, in the protagonist of "Landscape," Stevens "created a role which allowed him to test the reductionist position important to him by following certain possibilities into the absurd."

Espmark's essay, thanks to its pedagogical approach, could be used to great advantage as an "explication de texte" instrument. This holds true also for John Driscoll's study, *The China Cantos of Ezra Pound* (Uppsala: Almquist & Wiksell International), at least for the two chapters (three and four) devoted to a close reading of Cantos 52 and 53, in my opinion the most rewarding part of this uneven thesis. The purpose of Driscoll's work was "to provide readers with perspectives based on a comparison of the China Cantos with their two main sources, Joseph de Mailla's translation of the *Tong-kien-mu, Histoire de la Chine* and Seraphim Couvreur's translation of the *Li-ki*." Because "the poetic features of the China Cantos emerge from the interaction of poet and source material" perhaps more than in any other group of cantos, Driscoll has deemed this area a profitable subject of discussion.

After the Introduction, Driscoll undertakes a detailed investigation of "The Role of Translation in the China Cantos," an aspect that should have been dealt with at a later stage in the study. The most interesting Chapters, Three and Four, offer sensitive and sound analyses and keen observations, as does most of Chapter Five, en-

titled "Canto 55 and the Reforms of Ouang-ngan-ché." Chapters Six
and Seven both trace Pound's deviations from his historical source,
"The Selection of Detail" and "Omissions from *Histoire*." Chapter
Eight investigates the prevalence of allusions, of which there turned
out to be comparatively few in the China Cantos. Chapter Nine,
"Coloquialisms and Slang," is overly defensive of Pound. Unfortunately, this tendancy of Driscoll's to minimize Pound's artistic
blunders and make light of his political follies surfaces here and
there in the book and culminates in the Conclusion, an unworthy
ending to a work in many respects a valuable contribution to Pound
scholarship.

University College at Västerås

22. General Reference Works

Warren French

A landmark event in the updating of basic reference works about American literature was the publication of the fifth edition of *The Oxford Companion to American Literature*, still edited solely by James D. Hart. Hart conceived the idea for this encyclopedic guide to American literature almost 50 years ago and had the first edition ready for publication in 1941. Subsequent editions appeared in 1948, 1956, and 1965, but this is the first in almost two decades that has seen enormous changes in the American literary scene. As is appropriate, the format has been completely redesigned and enlarged, and 590 entries have been extensively rewritten. Although there are also 240 new author entries and 115 new book summaries, Hart has managed to hold the text to 896 double-columned pages, generously spaced for easy reading. Little has been dropped except Canadian entries now assigned to another volume in the Oxford University Press series. Hart has not attempted to cover recent popular literature; Neil Simon and Frances Parkinson Keyes, for example, are omitted. Perhaps, however, reflecting a California viewpoint, the Beat Generation, including Charles Bukowski, is well represented. Certainly no one else has covered so much material with such discernment, conciseness, and authority. This new edition reasserts the supremacy of this landmark enterprise as the anchor volume in any American literature scholar's library.

For the first time, however, Hart's *Companion* has a rival, although only in a very limited sense. The new *Cambridge Guide to English Literature*, edited by Michael Stapleton, also contains entries on American literature, although, because of the scope of the material that must be covered in 992 pages, British material predominates and only the most important American authors and works are mentioned. The convenient format of this single volume at a quite reasonable price commends it for teachers' use, but those seeking information beyond the level demanded by introductory college courses will find the three-volume *Great Writers of the English Language*, edited by James Vinson (St. Martin's, 1979), still most satisfactory.

What J. Albert Robbins last year called "the ambitious Gale series," the *Dictionary of Literary Biography* continued to proliferate, adding even more and more varied volumes in 1983 than in 1982. Most of those new volumes following the original plan of dealing with writers of a particular period or genre concern British writing; but three others, *Twentieth-Century American Historians* (*DLB* 17), *American Writers for Children, 1900–1960* (*DLB* 22), and *American Newspaper Journalists, 1873–1900* (*DLB* 23), are of peripheral interest to users of this review. The last-named volume contains lengthy essays on Ambrose Bierce, Mark Twain, Richard Harding Davis, Harold Frederic, Henry George, Finley Peter Dunne, and Bill Nye, which examine their journalistic careers.

Of unique value among the series' projects to date is the formidable two-volume *The Beats: Literary Bohemians in Postwar America* (*DLB* 16), edited by Ann Charters, author of the first important biography of Jack Kerouac. This hefty study is commented upon at some length in both chapters 15 and 17 of this volume, so one only needs agree here with Lee Bartlett's observation that the profusely illustrated work is "the best single reference source on these writers, very likely to remain unsurpassed." Unquestionably, arguments will continue about inclusions and omissions, and the authority and objectivity of the long studies of key figures and short accounts of otherwise often unnoted writers varies greatly; but even at the forbidding price of $152, this basic guide to the most distinctive literary movement in this country since World War II should be in any library that wishes to offer adequate resources for the study of our culture.

Undoubtedly, updatings of the record of secondary works on the Beats will appear in subsequent volumes of the *DLB Yearbook*. Just as the 1981 edition of this new reference tool was a marked improvement over the inaugural volumes (see *ALS 1982*, p. 519), so the 1982 edition is also improved over its predecessor. The editors are rapidly turning this annual review into an episodic history of the literary year that we have not seen the like of before. The latest number includes not only 13 updated entries (on recently deceased authors like Nelson Algren, John Cheever, John Gardner, Archibald MacLeish, and Kenneth Rexroth, as well as on new works by our most active authors) and 28 new entries on writers like Anne Beattie, Cynthia Ozick, John Rechy, and Herman Wouk, but also it adds a detailed record of literary prizes, censorship and plagiarism cases, and conferences honoring writers like Scott Fitzgerald, Jack Kerouac, and James Joyce. It branches out also into long appraisals of classic authors, like Gay Wilson Allen's essay on Emerson, and into descriptions of the resources of libraries like the University of Texas Humanities Research Center. As is customary in the series, all of these entries are heavily illustrated.

Still another *DLB* project, the "Documentary Series," has gone into a third volume, which includes "illustrated chronicles" of the careers of Saul Bellow, Jack Kerouac, Norman Mailer, Vladimir Nabokov, John Updike, and Kurt Vonnegut. At the present price of $76 a volume, however, Gale's inventiveness is beginning to overtax libraries' resources; these new documentary volumes, which reproduce a treasure trove of materials, so far are not available at any library even in a city the size of Indianapolis.

Meanwhile, another Gale project, *Contemporary Literary Criticism*, continues to supplement the *DLB* volumes with lengthy quotations from reviews and critical books and articles. *CLC* 23 contains judgments on a diverse lot, including Donald Barthelme, Paddy Chayevsky, Howard Fast, Frank Herbert, John Irving, Vladimir Nabokov, Irwin Shaw, and John Updike. A new venture, *Nineteenth Century Literary Criticism*, provides in *NCLC* 3 long surveys ranging over more than a century of criticism. American authors among the 23 included are Eugene Field, William Gilmore Simms, Harriet Beecher Stowe, Royall Tyler, and Herman Melville, who by commanding 63 double-columned pages has the second largest entry after the 66 pages devoted to Dickens. While these compilations serve a useful purpose in making obscure and out-of-print sources available to libraries with small collections, the inclusion of recent material from easily available sources threatens to establish a canon of approved criticism that may prove a genuine disservice to teachers and students who make no effort to seek out original materials. Analyses of the biases in these volumes would be forbidding tasks; but more attention needs to be paid to just what is going into these collections to which students are likely to turn increasingly as libraries with limited funds turn more and more to compilations that seem to offer the most for the money.

Bringing some order into one of its long-standing projects that many users have recently found getting chaotically out of hand, Gale has also provided a *Cumulative Index* to volumes 1–108 of *Contemporary Authors*, which also includes references to all entries in *CA's* "New Revision Series" and "Permanent Series," as well as the *CLC* volumes mentioned above, "Something About the Author" (volumes 1–30) and "Authors in the News" (volumes 1–2). One can thus track down five sources on J. D. Salinger and even two on Warren French.

Despite the publication of three large reference works on Western literature in 1982, still another has followed—*Encyclopedia of Frontier and Western Fiction*, edited by Jon Tuska and Vicki Piekarski (McGraw-Hill). It includes alphabetical author entries from Edward Abbey to Owen Wister, as well as a number of articles on subjects like "Historical Personalities," "Native Americans," and "Women on the Frontier," spread over 365 generously spaced pages, and seems aimed principally not at scholars but at the apparently large body of affluent collectors of the genre.

Another ambitious work on a popular genre seems more nearly aimed at academics who have shown a growing interest in Gothic and occult fiction. Everett F. Bleicher's *The Guide to Supernatural Fiction* (Kent State), provides author, title, and motif indexes for 1,775 specimens of "ghost stories, weird fiction, stories of supernatural horror, fantasy Gothic novels, occult fiction and similar literature," published between 1750 and 1960. Bleicher's work is especially valuable for the motif index, which groups works under a wide variety of topics from "abductions, supernatural" to zombies and Zoroastrians that will prove very helpful in course planning. Bleicher also contributes an essay on "The Phenomenology of Contranatural Fiction," which argues that it is not inferior to mainstream fiction, "but a range of literature with an extensive collection of motifs of its own." Whereas mainstream fiction is "primarily societal and psychological," Bleicher is concerned with a genre that is "ultimately concerned with the impersonal individual and with universals of existence in story abstractions that are sometimes very primitive."

Turning to another body of literature that is attracting even greater attention today, one finds that the four-volume *American Women Writers: A Critical Reference Guide from Colonial Times to the Present* (Ungar, 1979–82) has already been supplemented by *American Women Writers: Bibliographical Essays* (Greenwood), edited by Maurice Duke, Jackson R. Bryer, and Thomas Inge. Modeled on Floyd Stovall's *Eight American Authors* and similar subsequent volumes of review-essays, the book seeks to provide "an authoritative guide to the work that has been published on some of the country's most important writers." Omitting writers like Willa Cather and Emily Dickinson, who have been included in earlier similar surveys, 9 of the 14 essays, more than half of them written by women, deal at length with studies of Kate Chopin, Edith Wharton, Gertrude Stein, Ellen Glasgow, Katherine Anne Porter, Eudora Welty, Flannery O'Connor, Carson McCullers, and Zora Neale Hurston. The other five essays concern groups of puritan women, local colorists, experimental writers, recent popular writers, and contemporary women poets (the selection for this last of Marianne Moore, Anne Sexton, and Sylvia Plath may make this the most controversial inclusion).

Finally, the year has been marked by the resumption of one of the most important and ambitious aids to American literary study that has been slowed ten years by the death of the founding editor. At last, however, the seventh volume of *Bibliography of American Literature* (Yale), compiled by the late Jacob Blanck, and edited and completed by Virginia L. Smyers and Michael Winship, has appeared. Since this volume deals alphabetically with writers from James Kirke Paulding to Frank Richard Stockton, the end is in sight for this project, the first volume of which appeared in 1955. Invaluable for its meticulously compiled accounts of minor but prolific 19th-century writers, the book is indispensable not just for scholars, but also librarians and antiquarians, who have long been concerned about its completion. Its resumption in the same year as the publication of the enriched edition of James Hart's *Oxford Companion* brightens the prospects for the study of the whole vast span of American literature to temper the overconcentration on the limited group of major figures that provide the continuing subject for an increasing number of brief research and bibliographical guides that seem to offer no advantage over already available volumes and that indeed, during a period of rapidly mounting expenses, many libraries have simply ceased buying.

Indiana University–Purdue University at Indianapolis

Author Index

Subject Index